The Liberal Heartland

The Liberal Heartland

A Political History of the Postwar American Midwest

EDITED BY
JON K. LAUCK AND CATHERINE MCNICOL STOCK

UNIVERSITY PRESS OF KANSAS

© 2025 by the University Press of Kansas
All rights reserved

Published by the University Press of Kansas (Lawrence, Kansas 66045), which was organized by the Kansas Board of Regents and is operated and funded by Emporia State University, Fort Hays State University, Kansas State University, Pittsburg State University, the University of Kansas, and Wichita State University.

Library of Congress Cataloging-in-Publication Data

Names: Lauck, Jon, 1971– editor. | Stock, Catherine McNicol, editor.
Title: The liberal heartland : a political history of the postwar American Midwest / edited by Jon K. Lauck and Catherine McNicol Stock.
Other titles: Political history of the postwar American Midwest
Description: Lawrence : University Press of Kansas, 2025. | Includes index.
Identifiers: LCCN 2024042504 (print) | LCCN 2024042505 (ebook)
ISBN 9780700638642 (cloth) ISBN 9780700638659 (paperback)
ISBN 9780700638666 (ebook)
Subjects: LCSH: Middle West—Politics and government—History—20th century. | Political culture—Middle West—History—20th century. | Democratic Party (US)—History—20th century. | Party affiliation—Middle West—History—20th century. | Liberalism—Middle West—History—20th century. | Progressivism (United States politics)—History—20th century. | BISAC: HISTORY / United States / State & Local / Midwest (IA, IL, IN, KS, MI, MN, MO, ND, NE, OH, SD, WI) | SOCIAL SCIENCE / Activism & Social Justice
Classification: LCC F354 .L534 2025 (print) | LCC F354 (ebook) | DDC 320.510977/0904—dc23/eng/20250206
LC record available at https://lccn.loc.gov/2024042504.
LC ebook record available at https://lccn.loc.gov/2024042505.

British Library Cataloguing-in-Publication Data is available.
Authorised Representative Details: Easy Access System Europe
Mustamäe tee 50, 10621 Tallinn, Estonia | gpsr.requests@easproject.com

For our fathers,

Dale W. Lauck, July 15, 1932 – December 15, 2022
Arthur J. Stock, April 22, 1931 – May 14, 2023

*whose dedication to the Midwest, conservative principles,
and the country never waivered*

Contents

❖ ❖ ❖ ❖ ❖ ❖ ❖

Preface: Finding the Democratic Tradition in the Midwest
Jon K. Lauck / xi

Introduction
Catherine McNicol Stock / 1

Part 1: In the Shadow of the New Deal

1. In the Shadow of FDR and Harry Truman
Missouri's Liberal Senatorial Turn, 1950–1987
Jon E. Taylor / 17

2. Red Power Turned Blue
The Eisenhower Presidency and Democratic Party Ascendancy on Indian Reservations in the Dakotas
Sean J. Flynn / 35

3. "No Back Seat Drivers"
Women and the Nonpartisan League in North Dakota from Lydia Cady Langer to Heidi Heitkamp
Charles McElwain Barber and Catherine McNicol Stock / 48

4. Green as a Shade of Blue
Political Rhetoric, the Democratic Party, and the Early Environmental Movement in the Upper Midwest
Camden Burd / 63

5. That Other Minority
The UAW, Midwestern Politics, and Pre-Stonewall Queer-Labor Solidarity
James McQuaid / 76

Contents

6. The Fall of the Last Democratic Political Machine
East Chicago, Indiana, and the Rise of Community Activism
Emiliano Aguilar / 94

Part 2. Expanding Citizenship in the Age of Liberation

7. Humphrey, McGovern, and Mansfield
National Liberals and American Indian Self-Determination
Dean J. Kotlowski / 113

8. "I Gave a Dam about a Dam"
Jim Jontz and the Fight for Big Pine Creek in Indiana
Ray E. Boomhower / 128

9. "Your Problem Is Our Problem"
Mary Jean Collins's Midwestern Feminism
Katherine Turk / 141

10. Creating a Blueprint for Black Power
Muigwithania, Mayor Hatcher, and the 1972 National Black Political Convention in Gary, Indiana
Nicole Poletika / 165

11. "Where Was the Social Justice?"
La Raza Activism at the University of Notre Dame
Leticia Rose Wiggins / 184

12. Gay Liberation and the Social Gospel
Religious Support for Gay Employment Rights in Wisconsin
Stephen Colbrook / 198

13. Paul Wellstone and the Reshaping of Minnesota's Populist-Progressive Tradition
Michael C. Steiner / 211

Part 3. Battling the New Right from Nixon to Trump

14. The Rise and Disappearance of Liberal South Dakota
Marc C. Johnson / 231

Contents

15. Wild About Harry
Walter Mondale, Ronald Reagan, and the Liberal Legacy of Harry Truman in the 1984 Midwest
Jeffrey Bloodworth / 249

16. "Why We Must Save the Family Farm"
Midwestern Liberalism and Progressive Farm Policy, 1985–1996
Cory Haala / 263

17. Capital Punishment in the Midwest
Liberal Struggles, Race, and Legacy
Emma Ricknell / 285

18. "Alone in the Fight"
Senator Louis Mahern and the Fight for Gay Rights in Indiana
Tiffany Costley / 298

19. Lambs That Strayed from the Democratic Flock
Catholic Voters in the Midwest
Chad Kinsella / 315

20. The Great Blue Hope
How Senator Sherrod Brown Won Reelection in Donald Trump's Ohio
Christopher J. Devine / 330

About the Contributors / 347
Index / 353

Preface: Finding the Democratic Tradition in the Midwest

JON K. LAUCK

❖ ❖ ❖ ❖ ❖ ❖ ❖

In 2012, after a long career in Midwestern politics and several decades in Washington, former Senator George McGovern died in his home state of South Dakota. His path to political power took him from a small prairie town to a South Dakota Methodist college to World War II to graduate school in Chicago to the US House and Senate and, finally, to service as the Democratic presidential nominee. His presidential campaign ended in spectacular defeat, which he witnessed early one night on the top floor of a newly built Holiday Inn in downtown Sioux Falls in November 1972.[1] A final humiliation came in 1980, when McGovern lost his Senate seat in the Reagan wave. McGovern's path through American politics is emblematic of broader political trends in the nation, especially the eclipse of Great Society liberalism and the coming of modern conservatism. But it also provides a window onto Midwestern political culture and key elements of a particular style of Midwestern liberalism and the traits of many of its standard-bearers: agrarian sympathies, calm and discerning bearings, intellectualism often fused and intermingled with Christian moralism, a main-street friendliness and decency, and a broad-based common-man populism.

McGovern was born in the small town of Avon, South Dakota (population 600), where his father was the local Methodist minister. In a preacher's home, books, history, and reading were mainstays, and McGovern absorbed the habit and considered the ministry himself. He was also a successful debater. After service in World War II, McGovern passed on the ministry and attended graduate school in history at Northwestern University in Chicago, writing his dissertation about the struggles of mine workers during the Wilson presidency (his advisor was the Wilson biographer Arthur Link). McGovern returned to South Dakota to teach at Dakota Wesleyan University in Mitchell and to settle down to a college professor's life (he was a finalist for a position at the University of Iowa, but he lost out to "a Harvard guy," as he said with a bit of anti-Eastern animus).[2] While painting his little house in Mitchell one night in 1952 McGovern listened to Adlai Stevenson on the radio and was inspired. His fellow Midwesterner, also intellectually inclined and sedate in his comportment, lured McGovern into politics.[3] The key to McGovern's success was harnessing a core Midwestern constituency: farmers. He exploited the unpopularity of Republican farm policies in the Midwest and captured a US House seat in 1956.[4]

In those early decades after World War II other Democrats in the Midwest similarly succeeded by focusing on bread-and-butter issues and pragmatic problem-solving. Harry Truman of Independence, Missouri, shocked the pollsters in 1948 by promoting a common-man populism in farm country and separating himself from the aristocrats, central planners, and radicals of FDR's New Deal. Truman remained grounded in the communal politics of Jackson County, Missouri, and skeptical of the "striped pants boys" from Harvard and the Hudson Valley, who orbited around FDR, a descendent of patrician New York who saw Truman as a naïve small-town Midwesterner.[5] Truman's old Missouri Senate seat was eventually won by the pragmatic and moderate Stuart Symington, who defeated a critic of Truman and held the seat from the early 1950s until the late 1970s. With a background in business, especially manufacturing, Symington focused much of his energy on building up the American armed forces, questioning those who pinched pennies on defense: "What the hell good is it to be the richest man in the graveyard?"[6] Other successful Midwestern Democrats similarly plotted a moderate course in the US Senate and focused on farm prices and good governance, including William Proxmire of Wisconsin, Jim Exon of Nebraska, Don Riegle of Michigan, Tim Johnson of South Dakota, and Harold Hughes of Iowa. Hughes recognized that Iowa was generally a conservative state, but whose citizens practiced a conservatism of "prudence, rather than fear and inertia." He drew on his experience in sports and trucking and his embrace of Methodism, which cured his alcoholism, and became a successful but moderate reformer as Iowa governor and then US senator.[7] Hughes belonged in a category with US Senator Alan Dixon of Illinois, a moderate from downstate known for restraint and civility.[8] If some of these leaders had an obvious agrarian and small-town grounding, others were more labor oriented, including Richard Gephardt of Missouri, Howard Metzenbaum of Ohio, and Paul Douglas of Illinois.

Altogether these political leaders shaped a particular kind of pragmatic postwar Midwestern liberalism that, alas, some prominent intellectuals now insist on ridiculing.⁹ These old-time heartland liberals often emerged out of small towns and embodied the tenets of a traditional Midwestern political culture—interest in sports, respect for military service, entrenchment in the joining culture of service clubs, main-street moderation, agrarian sympathies, and a Midwestern rootedness—and attended to the concerns of farmers and workers and basic constituent services while in office. It was a grounded style, one that blended into the mores of the region, far from countercultural, and willing, within reason, to promote social reforms and liberal causes. Think of Paul Simon, the son of a Lutheran minister who ran the newspaper in Troy, Illinois, and, after serving in the US Army, later expanded his journalism work and eventually owned fourteen weekly newspapers in central and downstate Illinois. Simon, with his bowtie and glasses, soberly and carefully promoted social reforms and rose through Illinois politics, winning a US Senate seat in 1984. In the Senate, Simon worked on sensible efforts to balance the federal budget. Iowans responded to Simon's Midwestern reformer spirit during the 1988 Iowa caucuses, and he surged ahead in the polls, but lost a close race to neighboring Missourian Richard Gephardt.[10] Simon and his Midwestern persona and pragmatism represented a version of the "vital center" politics once explained by Arthur Schlesinger Jr., a product of Xenia, Ohio, and Iowa City, Iowa.[11] In later years during his general-election appeals, Barack Obama of Illinois attempted to channel the soothing mainstream appeal of Simon and McGovern's hero, Adlai Stevenson.[12]

While this older version of Midwestern Democratic centrism may appeal to many in an age of what political scientists call "negative partisanship," there were other parts of Midwestern Democratic politics. These include urban machines in Chicago, Detroit, and Gary and the hard-boiled tactics of big labor in Midwestern industrial cities. It also included, especially in the 1960s and after, the growing power of Native American activists and voters on Midwestern Indian reservations, members of the women's rights movement, gay rights activists, supporters of the Black Power movement, environmentalists, left-leaning liberals in college towns, and more radical reformers and more outspoken liberals such as Senator Paul Wellstone of Minnesota. They are all covered here in *The Liberal Heartland*, a companion to *The Conservative Heartland* (2020), which chronicled the diminishment of the 1930s Democratic surge in the Midwest, especially during the 1960s and 1970s. We are in a new era now, one closer to the early twentieth century, when Democratic fortunes in the Midwest were ebbing. Once-purple toss-up states such as Iowa, Missouri, and Ohio are currently trending Republican, a development that caused national Democrats to terminate the once-crucial Iowa

Democratic presidential caucuses, symbolizing the end of one particular era of Midwestern politics that some persistent Iowa liberals did not appreciate.[13] Former Iowa Democratic congressman Dave Nagle argues that Democrats have abandoned the Midwest and act as if "rural America's gone."[14] Midwestern Democrats still in the US House, frustrated at their complete absence from House leadership and its coastal focus, started a new caucus to try to promote the interests of the remaining Midwestern Democrats in the House (Michigan congresswoman Debbie Dingell, in her failed leadership bid, showed her colleagues a map of where Democrat leaders came from: "The map shows clusters in California, the Northeast and mid-Atlantic regions; a smattering of stars in the Southeast and Pacific Northwest; and a total void in the middle of the country").[15] The Democrats' decision to focus on other regions, in part due to the shocking weakness of the one-time Midwestern "blue wall" in 2016 and 2024, should not blind us to the more distant past.[16] This book is a chance to look back to a previous era, which can only be understood by studying the fortunes of both parties in the Midwest over the past century, during which the region was often home to the key swing states of American politics.

NOTES

1. Daniel Max Gerling, "Fear and Loathing: McGovern '72," in Jon K. Lauck and Patrick Hicks, eds., *City of Hustle: A Sioux Falls Anthology* (Cleveland: Belt Publishing, 2022), 92–99.

2. The University of Iowa history department hired Samuel P. Hays. The chair of the department informed McGovern's advisor Ray Billington, "You might like to know that McGovern was the second on our list and that, if Hays had refused, we should have offered the job to him. The final decision was not an easy one." W. O. Aydelotte to Ray A. Billington, March 4, 1953. McGovern told Billington that "I can't help feeling on the basis of a remark dropped by Stow Persons to a friend of mine (we were all in the same coach returning from Washington to Chicago) that Iowa was at that time about ready to offer the job to a Harvard guy." McGovern to Billington, March 2, 1953. Hays earned his PhD from Harvard in 1953. Both letters are located in the Billington Papers at the Huntington Library.

3. McGovern's recollection: "I think that if there was one moment that I knew that I had to become a Democrat it was listening to Adlai's acceptance address at the 1952 national convention. We lived down the street here in a white house about four or five blocks from here, not the White house I tried to get to twenty years later [laughs]. I was painting the living room at one o'clock in the morning and on comes this marvelous voice. It was about the only thing you could get on the radio. There was no television then to speak of. I had the radio on and this guy started to speak. I had never heard a politician talk like that. It showed obvious intelligence and sensitivity and vision. I think that if there was any one moment, it was that night about one o'clock in the

morning. And I thought, this is for me." Interview of George McGovern by Jon K. Lauck and John E. Miller, in Mitchell, South Dakota, November 25, 2003, on file at South Dakota State Historical Society.

4. Jon K. Lauck, "George S. McGovern and the Farmer: South Dakota Politics, 1953–1962," *South Dakota History* 32, no. 4 (Winter 2002): 331–353.

5. See Jeffrey Frank, *The Trials of Harry S. Truman: The Extraordinary Presidency of an Ordinary Man, 1945–1953* (New York: Simon & Schuster, 2022).

6. Eric Pace, "Stuart Symington, 4-term Senator Who Ran for President, Dies at 87," *New York Times*, December 15, 1988.

7. Jerry Harrington, *Thunder from the Prairie: The Life of Harold E. Hughes* (Lawrence: University Press of Kansas, 2023).

8. Kim Geiger, "Former Sen. Alan Dixon Dead at 86; 'He Took Really Great Care of People,'" *Chicago Tribune*, July 7, 2014. See also Alan Dixon, *The Gentleman from Illinois: Stories from Forty Years of Elective Public Service* (Carbondale: Southern Illinois University Press, 2013).

9. Samuel Moyn, *Liberalism Against Itself: Cold War Intellectuals and the Making of Our Times* (New Haven, CT: Yale University Press, 2023).

10. Bill Peterson, "Simon Slips in Iowa," *Washington Post*, January 14, 1988.

11. Arthur Schlesinger Jr., *The Vital Center: The Politics of Freedom* (Boston: Houghton Mifflin, 1949).

12. Richard Babcock, "The Adlai Issue," *Chicago Magazine*, August 21, 2008.

13. Art Cullen, "Democrats to Iowa: Drop Dead," *Storm Lake Times Pilot*, December 7, 2022.

14. David Siders, "The DNC Thought It Killed the Iowa Caucuses. It's Not Dead Yet," *Politico*, February 15, 2023.

15. Justin Papp, "'Not Fly-Over Country': Dingell and Other Midwestern Democrats Start Heartland Caucus," *Roll Call*, January 25, 2023.

16. Jon K. Lauck, "Trump and the Midwest: The 2016 Presidential Election and the Avenues of Midwestern Historiography," *Studies in Midwestern History* 3, no. 1 (January 2017): 1–24.

Introduction

CATHERINE MCNICOL STOCK

❖ ❖ ❖ ❖ ❖ ❖ ❖

In the summer of 2020 Democrat Kirk Bangstad, owner of the Minocqua Brewing Company (MBC) in Wisconsin's rural Oneida County, did not think he could actually beat his opponent for state assembly, four-term incumbent Republican Rob Swearington.[1] But he did think that his "up north" neighbors could defeat Donald Trump. In 2016 Trump had won the state by only 22,742 votes when the Clinton campaign made a fatal miscalculation: they gave up on white voters in the rural Midwest. Hillary Clinton's advisers and most left-leaning pundits assumed Clinton would win the mythic "blue wall" of Midwestern states simply by running up the score in urban centers like Milwaukee. In Bangstad's tiny hometown, Minocqua, they had not even made campaign signs available.[2]

Bangstad had a different "idea" about Wisconsin politics.[3] He believed, first of all, that in a battleground state in a battleground region, every vote counted. This was true even when rural/urban polarization seemed as inexorable within an individual state as it was in the nation as a whole.[4] Moreover, he believed he would find more Democratic voters in his rural community if he stuck to issues that mattered at the local level, like the lives and jobs lost due to Trump's ineffective COVID policies.[5] He combined intensive "front-porch politics"—his team distributed over a thousand yard signs—with a near-ubiquitous and sometimes unapologetically combative social media presence.[6] Next he brewed "Progressive beers" and matched them with humorous and memorable slogans, like "Biden Beer—inoffensive, especially to women."[7] When the votes were counted and recounted, Bangstad had achieved his goal: he had lost, but Biden had won. Two thousand more votes were cast in Oneida County for Biden in 2020 than had been cast for Clinton in 2016. In other words, nearly 10 percent of the 22,000 votes by which Biden won the state came from "up north."[8]

Bangstad's multipurpose campaign reflects the complex, challenging, and evolving history of politics in the Democratic Party and on the left as a whole in the American Midwest since 1945.[9] After early decades of strength among unionized workers, Catholics, small farmers, and Black voters and subsequent efforts to expand the party to include female, LGBTQ, Latinx, and Native voters, cultural and racial conflict and economic decline fractured the Democratic coalition and gave rise to support for the small-government and law-and-order ideals of new conservatism, particularly among blue-collar and rural whites.[10] From the "Tuesday night massacre" of 1980 to the Tea Party triumph of 2010 and beyond, some of the region's most highly regarded Democratic leaders—George McGovern, Walter Mondale, Birch Bayh, John Culver, Tom Daschle, and Claire McCaskill—were vanquished by well organized, nationally funded attacks that pundits and campaign advisers underestimated again and again.[11] To some observers, Illinois native Hillary Rodham Clinton's defeat was merely the final blow.

Yet the continued momentum of Bangstad's hyper-local effort to bring progressivism back to rural Wisconsin after the 2020 election reveals the history of the Left in the Midwest to be far more than one of fracture and decline. In early 2021 Bangstad learned that even though every local storeowner in northern Wisconsin refused to carry his brands because he was "too progressive," he could sell even more beer without relying on what he called the "Old Boys Network of Minocqua (OBNOM)."[12] Whites did not have a monopoly on sovereignty in northern Wisconsin after all. His neighbors, the Lac Du Flambeau (LDF) band of the Lake Superior Chippewa (Ojibwe), offered to become MBC's sole distributor at its reservation's general store. Rather than fault lines, they saw a common cause based in a common political opponent. As LDF Country Market marketing and public relations coordinator Zach Allen explained, the Ojibwa had also faced opposition from white conservatives, most viciously during the "Walleye Wars" of the 1980s and 1990s.[13]

However unusual, this progressive beer-and-antiracism political coalition quickly grew. After the January 6, 2021, Capitol attack in Washington, DC, Bangstad created a political action committee (PAC) with the motto "dark money for good" and made it widely known that he would allocate 5 percent of all MBC beer sales to fighting against any Wisconsin politician who had objected to the certification of the 2020 presidential vote.[14] He leased billboards with messaging that accused Republican Senator Ron Johnson of treason; he posted photos of the murals local artists painted to cover the hate-filled graffiti on walls near the brewery.[15] In one episode of his "Up North" podcast, titled "Dear White People," Bangstad urged a local town committee to pass a diversity statement—after five years of trying.[16] MBC soon became the "least popular place in town."[17] Perhaps so, but Bangstad sold a lot of "progressive beer" and raised a lot of money. Soon retailers in Milwaukee and Madison carried the full assortment of MBC brands. Even stores in some of the small- and medium-sized cities that dotted the region did too: Ashland, Duluth, Eau Claire, and dozens more.[18] In the spring and summer of 2022, when state Republicans launched newly gerrymandered districts that would give Republicans an even more outsized voice in state government, a local priest even jumped on the Bangstad bandwagon, urging parishioners to "vote like your life depended on it."[19]

Like the Kansans who voted down abortion restrictions by large margins in the summer of 2022 and the South Dakotans who approved the expansion of Medicaid later that same year, Kirk Bangstad's movement demonstrated that, however outnumbered in state legislatures, left-leaning Midwesterners had not given up the fight.[20] Moreover, it suggested that pundits and historians who make political calculations based on an assumption of extreme rural/urban or white/nonwhite polarization miss the more nuanced aspects of Midwestern politics, where sometimes voters—even in the 2020s—are "less beholden to ideological labels" and more willing to "create their own flavor" of political culture.[21] As this volume will show, these twenty-first-century efforts have relied on the innovative, collaborative, multiracial, and ecumenical strategies that the Midwestern Left employed throughout the postwar era. Whatever the odds, they have strived, in Cory Haala's words, to make the heartland—even now—America's "progressive center."[22]

Like its companion volume, *The Conservative Heartland* (2020), this anthology examines the political history of the Midwest in the decades after 1945. Both books rest on a pair of foundational ideas: first that the postwar Midwest has been understudied for decades, however much the national media "discovers" it every four years.[23] Thus, many of the chapters that follow incorporate distinctive elements of the Midwestern experience: demographics, economics, and geography. But the tendency for academics to "fly-over" the Midwest has had an even more acute impact on the study of the Left in the region than it has had on the study of the Right. Beginning in the 1990s, American political history began an intensive "conservative turn," producing a large number of very significant works on conservatism in all regions, including the Midwest.[24] Of course, the Midwestern Left was not wholly forgotten, as evidenced by the rich literature cited by contributors to this volume.[25] Even so, gaps remain. One example is the study of the LGBTQ political history, which for decades was limited to studies of coastal cities, as if all gay people left the Midwest for New York or San Francisco.²⁶ New political histories—including four chapters in total between our two volumes—have challenged this coastal-centric narrative. Nevertheless, more work on Midwestern gay- and trans-political culture—particularly in the Black, Native, and immigrant communities—waits to be done.²⁷

Second, both *The Conservative Heartland* and *The Liberal Heartland* contend that the Midwest has been the only true regional battleground in American politics in the postwar era and deserves intensive study as such. As Daniel Birdsong and Christopher Devine have quantified, the Midwest stands out from other regions due to its large number of independent voters and its perennially close national elections.²⁸ Until recently, it was common for two senators representing the same state to be from different parties.²⁹ Ask any resident of the region: candidate visits and campaign ads are almost inescapable from before the primaries to Election Day.³⁰ We argue that this bright light has contributed to and magnified the vibrancy of local political culture and led to unique patterns and practices, such as high levels of ticket splitting, frequent use of initiative and referendum, and intense efforts at redistricting. Understanding these aspects of Midwestern political culture may become even more important as new states or subregional groups of states—Arizona, New Mexico, and Nevada, for example—join its ranks. The Midwest has had a head start, for better or worse, in managing deep intrastate polarization and the glare of the press for months and even years each presidential cycle. At the very least, its history should tell the newcomers that they had better buckle up.

Like the history of the Right in the Midwest since 1945, the history of the Left follows the broad trajectory of American political history. Thus, chapters in this volume are organized into familiar and largely chronological units. The chapters in the first section, "In the Shadow of the New Deal," detail the postwar histories of reforms introduced by the Franklin Roosevelt administration, including union and environmental activism; the ongoing influence of liberal politicians in states like the Dakotas and Missouri that would later turn hard to the right; and the impact of progressive women working in politics, some by their better-known husbands' sides. At the same time, these chapters reveal the forces like the civil rights movement and the war in Vietnam, that would eventually unravel the New Deal coalition and challenge its underlying, and inequitably applied, ideals about racial, gender, and economic equality.³¹ As Michael Kazin has written, FDR "had largely succeeded in keeping its internal tensions of class and race, region and ideology at bay. Then an unfinished battled for equal rights at home and a stymied war of counterinsurgency abroad shattered the prospect for even an anxious unity."[32] The Midwest was no stranger to these pressures; indeed, it was the fertile ground in which they grew.

The chapters in the second section—"Expanding Citizenship in the Age of Liberation"—explore a wide variety of race- and gender-based freedom movements in the Midwest that arose during the years during and after the Southern civil rights campaigns. While white Midwesterners like Harry Truman and Hubert Humphrey provided political leadership in pursuit of de jure racial equality, it fell to little-known activists on the ground in Midwestern cities and towns to demand that the promise of full citizenship become a reality.[33] Four chapters introduce forgotten local organizations in Illinois and Indiana. Along with two others, they suggest links between the strategies of Black Power, La Raza, women's liberation, and the American Indian Movement while also reminding us of their differences: Native groups, for example, sought self-determination and sovereignty rather than inclusion. Taken as a whole, the section reveals that many freedom movements worked outside the structures of the Democratic Party, and they did so because they had found the party's vision of reform inadequate to the problems they faced. Radical liberation movements are a critical legacy of the Left in the Midwest in our time.

The final section, "Battling the New Right from Nixon to Trump," examines the struggles faced by Americans on the left, those inside and outside the Democratic Party—during the rise of the new conservative movement. As in the story of Kirk Bangstad in Wisconsin, these chapters recount examples of innovative political planning and coalition-building in unexpected places. But the chapters also reveal that in the era of Ronald Reagan, the Bush presidencies, and Trump, these campaigns were hard-fought, and victories in some states were few and far between. Increased political pressure from the Christian Right amplified divisions on cultural issues like abortion, prayer in schools, gun control, and, as explored in this volume, LGBTQ rights and the abolition of the death penalty in communities where there had once been more common ground. Even so, the Midwest as a region, at the national if not always at the state level, continued to be up for grabs well into the twenty-first century.

This book's aim is not only to add stories from the Midwest to the usual narrative of liberal politics, however, but also to argue that many of those stories originated and played out first in the Midwest; that they can teach us things about American history as a whole that we did not know before and needed to learn. Together with *Conservative Heartland*, this volume puts the Midwest at the center of political history and provides evidence that the way American history itself played out was shaped or determined there, moving from the center out, rather than from the coasts inland. One chapter in this volume is particularly salient. In "'Your Problem Is Our Problem': Mary Jean Collins's Midwestern Feminism," Katherine Turk reveals that 75 percent of the original founders of the National Organization for Women (NOW) were from the Midwest, and one of the most active offices of NOW was in Chicago. She suggests that second-wave feminism benefited from their distance from the coasts, developing a "flexible, practical, and locally rooted" approach to change. At the same time, however, the greatest threats to one of NOW's most important goals, passage of the Equal Rights Amendment (ERA), also came from the Midwest: Phyllis Schlafly, the Eagle Forum, and the anti-ERA campaign. This is no mere coincidence of geography. The passions of postwar liberalism and conservatism—whether regarding the legacy of the New Deal, feminism, the Vietnam War, environmentalism, or a host of other important issues—became magnified in the Midwest even more than in other regions. After all, it was not just NOW that originated and shined brightly in the Midwest. So did Phyllis Schlafly's Eagle Forum, the antifeminist organization that successfully took on NOW's quintessential project, passage of the ERA. As two liberal residents of Fergus Fall, Minnesota, explained in 2018, the intensity of their local politics was predicated on the proximity with which liberals and conservatives lived, interacted, and even upon occasion "shared a meal."[34]

Other political developments in the nation as a whole find illumination, origin, explanation, or correction through the Midwestern experiences detailed in these pages. The rise of influential "populist" senators Paul Wellstone (Minnesota), Tom Harkin (Iowa), and Heidi Heitkamp (North Dakota), among others, reminds us, for example, of the essential third-party roots of the modern Democratic Party. Whether it was Populists, nonpartisan "Leaguers," Progressives, or Socialists—Sara Egge tells us the most radical of which were women—all these activists were devoted to "moral capitalism": an insistence, in Michael Kazin's words, "that the economy should benefit the ordinary working person, whether farmer or wage earner, and that governments should institute politics to make that possible—and to resist those that do not."[35] This legacy of this devotion to economic fairness endures in the Democratic Party even if many Americans do not know its origins in small towns, farms, mines, and factories of the Midwest. It likewise lives on in the Left's culture and practice of coalition-building. In fact, nearly every chapter in *The Liberal Heartland* provides an example of coalitions built in the modern era. As a young union activist in Kansas City told historian Heather McGhee, the conservative idea that if "they" get something, "we lose" was exactly what the Democrats did not believe. They believed instead, she said, that "If we are divided, we are conquered."[36]

These chapters also remind us that support and inspiration for the Left can come from unexpected—or misremembered—places and institutions. In particular, we are reminded that the Catholic Church has long been a source of inspiration and power for liberal as well as conservative movements. Chapters in this volume detail the Church's support for feminism, farm supports, the abolition of the death penalty, unions, and equal employment rights for LGBTQ residents. Furthermore, taken together, the chapters suggest that Midwestern Catholicism's unique culture—inspired by the collectivism of its Scandinavian and German immigrant populations and the growing power of Latino Catholics—may have influenced progressive Catholics across the county. How that came to be, how it came under pressure after 1980, and how its legacy has since been forgotten are important areas for future work.[37]

Fourth, the Midwest stands at the center of the story—indeed it *is* the story—of the transformation of the two most important sectors of the postwar American economy: manufacturing and agriculture. Both the corporatization of small farming and the abandonment and de-unionization of manufacturing have led to depopulation, increased poverty, and substance abuse across the Midwest.[38] Communities of all sizes have seen hospitals, schools, and even grocery stores close. As we learn in the chapters in this volume and in the *Conservative Heartland*, some white and Black Midwesterners saw these crises as linked and their futures as one; but others came to believe that the Democratic commitment to racial equality and legal immigration paralleled the abandonment of their industries. Political followed economic disruption. Catholic voters peeled away from the Democratic Party; whites in rural areas increasingly blamed their difficulties on nearby cities and their residents. To win, Ohio's Senator Sherrod Brown learned to hide the real nature of his liberal voting record in the Senate. Whether that will be enough for him to win reelection in 2024, we will have to see.

Intersecting all of the aforementioned issues, making a vast web of connection and disconnection in the postwar era, is the divide between elected political leaders, their white constituents, and the Black, Latino, and Native citizens of the region. And here again, understanding the Midwestern experience is central to understanding the American experience, both literally and metaphorically. The Midwest, we read again and again, is the "heartland" of America, known for, in Tamar Winfrey-Harris's words, "small towns, country music, conservatism, casseroles, and amber waves of grain. Whiteness."[39] It follows that if the Midwest is the heartland, then it captures the best and truest of American life. And, even on these pages, there is much of which to be proud: prominent Midwestern senators, nearly all white and male, who were strong proponents of racial equality when few others would stand up and say so. No less a leader than Senator Hubert Humphrey famously told his colleagues at the 1948 Democratic National Convention that "the time has arrived . . . to get out of the shadow of states' rights and walk forthrightly into the bright sunshine of human rights."[40] And yet even Humphrey, we learn here too, did not understand his Native constituents' desire for sovereignty and cultural integrity, could not escape the settler culture in which he was raised. And where were the progressive senators speaking against the war in Vietnam when activists of color gathered in other places we have visited here: in East Chicago, and in Gary and South Bend, Indiana? As Winfrey-Harris and others explain, the Midwest is a region whose definition depends on racial innocence. To be Black there, then, is to be invisible—by definition.[41]

As the strong backlash to the 1619 Project revealed, many white Americans, wherever they live, largely prefer a comfortable "10,000-foot" view of that "battle for the bright sunshine of human rights" to anything up-close and uncomfortable. The murder of George Floyd was shocking, horrifying, even nauseating. But for Blacks and other people of color in Minneapolis it was not surprising. They knew that the *US News and World Report* list that perennially placed Minneapolis near the top of the "best places to live in America" was not meant for them. They lived on a different list, a list invisible to whites, a list called "the worst places for Blacks to live in the United States," a list where Minneapolis ranked number four.[42] This divide is not geographic; it is a divide in knowledge, empathy, imagination, experience, understanding, and the conceptualization of freedom. And it puts the Midwest where it belongs: at the true center of American history and our collective quest for a more perfect union.

As with all anthologies, *The Liberal Heartland* opens more doors for new research than it can possibly close with its own contributions. Of particular importance and absent here is the study of newer immigrant groups: Central Americans, Asians, and Africans, including many Muslims, who populate both cities and towns across the region, and have strong pretenses in industrial, de-unionized workplaces like hotel and restaurant work and meatpacking. As Tara Rose writes of the "post-white" city of Dearborn, Michigan, the one thing that could bring together whites who "usually hated each other's guts" was their shared antipathy for their new Muslim neighbors.[43] Likewise, this anthology does not explore the impact of specific international events, despite their critical importance to the economy of the region. Third, the region is home to many important military bases, and the impact of those bases on the politics of their communities needs further exploration, as do the experiences of combat veterans from Vietnam, Iraq, and Afghanistan wars, which include many Native, Black, and Latino people as well as white men and women from small towns and cities. We particularly regret not being able to explore the protests against the Vietnam War in the many small and large college towns in the region, or the history of organizing against police violence and mass incarceration.[44]

Soon, new states will join those in the Midwest as perennial battlegrounds each election cycle. The history of grit and resilience, innovation, and activism told on these pages can act as a roadmap for those newly purple places and their leaders on the left. But those states and regions also have their own histories and traditions, own ethnic groups and stories, and will navigate their own paths through political hurricanes they encounter in the future. Meanwhile, Midwesterners on the left are likely to go forward together, as there is, and never has been, any other way. They may do well to remember that even a loss can be a win, for it brings into community like-minded citizens, ready for the next fight.[45]

NOTES

1. "Representative Rob Swearingen," https://docs.legis.wisconsin.gov/2019/legislators/assembly/1828. The state GOP had held that seat for more than a generation. Thanks to Katherine Turk, Charles Barber, Cory Haala, and Michael Lansing for their suggestions on earlier drafts of this chapter.

2. The Trump campaign won the election by a total of 77,744 votes in Wisconsin, Michigan, and Pennsylvania. As Martha Bayne notes, "That's less than the capacity of the University of Michigan's football stadium." Martha Bayne, ed., *Red State Blues: Stories from Midwestern Life on the Left* (Cleveland: Belt Publishing, 2018), 7. For the mistakes of the Clinton campaign and the fallacy of the "blue wall," see Jon K. Lauck and Catherine McNicol Stock, *The Conservative Heartland: A Political History of the American Midwest* (Lawrence: University of Kansas Press, 2020), 1–3; David Plouffe, "What I Got Wrong about the Election, *New York Times*, November 11, 2016, https://www.nytimes.com/2016/11/11/opinion/what-i-got-wrong-about-the-election.html; Nate Silver, "There Is No Blue Wall," FiveThirtyEight, May 12, 2015, https://fivethirtyeight.com/features/there-is-no-blue-wall/. For examples of the outpouring of academic work on the "reddening" of the rural Midwest, see Catherine McNicol Stock, *Nuclear Country: Origins of the Rural New Right* (Philadelphia: University of Pennsylvania Press, 2020); Katherine J. Cramer, *The Politics of Resentment: Rural Consciousness in Wisconsin and the Rise of Scott Walker* (Chicago: University of Chicago Press, 2016); Sarah Smarsh, *Heartland: A Memoir of Working Hard and Being Broke in the Richest Country on Earth* (New

York: Scribers, 2018); Ross Benes, *Rural Rebellion: How Nebraska Became a Republican Stronghold* (Lawrence: University of Kansas Press, 2021).

3. Robert Lafollette and the state's dedication to the "Wisconsin idea" virtually invented progressive politics. See Russel Nye, *Midwestern Progressive Politics: A Historical Study of Its Origins and Development, 1870–1950* (East Lansing: Michigan State College Press, 1951). See also the roundtable discussion of Nye's book at sixty years, in *Middle West Review* 8, no. 1: 133–169.

4. David A. Hopkins, *Red Fighting Blue: How Geography and Electoral Rules Polarize American Politics* (New York: Cambridge University Press, 2017), 202–212. See also Zachary Michael Jack, "Red Rogues Orbit Blue Stars: 'Astral Politics' in the Trump Era Midwest," in Lauck and Stock, *The Conservative Heartland*, 286–302. For a broad national view of the rural/urban split, see Astead W. Herndon and Shane Goldmacher, "Democrats Thought They Bottomed Out in Rural, White America. It Wasn't the Bottom," *New York Times*, November 6, 2022, https://www.nytimes.com/2021/11/06/us/rural-vote-democrats-virginia.html.

5. Reid J. Epstein, "How Virus Politics Divided a Conservative Town in Wisconsin's North," *New York Times*, October 29, 2020, https://www.nytimes.com/2020/10/29/us/politics/wisconsin-trump-biden-coronavirus.html.

6. Michael Stewart Foley, *Front Porch Politics: The Forgotten Heyday of American Activism in the 1970s and 1980s* (New York: Hill & Wang, 2014). Bangstad had pages on Facebook, Instagram, and YouTube, and beginning in 2021, a podcast dedicated to discussing issues impacting people in northern Wisconsin. See https://www.upnorthpodcast.com/. There are also a number of social media sites devoted to opposing Bangstad and his views.

7. To see all of MBC's brews and slogans, see https://minocquabrewingcompany.com/.

8. *Utica Observer-Dispatch*, November 3, 2020, https://www.uticaod.com/elections/results/race/2020-11-03-presidential-WI-0/. "Wisconsin Results Are In: Trump Wins," *New York Times*, August 1, 2017, https://www.nytimes.com/elections/2016/results/wisconsin-president-clinton-trump; Epstein, "How Virus Politics Divided a Conservative Town." Bangstad attacked Trump's lack of guidance on pandemic policy, which had forced him to shut down and lay off workers. For more on his campaign, see Kathy Flanigan, "Giant Biden Campaign Sign Ignites Controversy for Minocqua Brewing Company Owner," *Milwaukee Journal Sentinel*, October 7, 2020, https://www.jsonline.com/story/entertainment/beer/2020/10/07/minocqua-brewing-co-owner-vows-keep-giant-joe-biden-sign-up/3637173001/ and his campaign website, https://www.bangstadforwisconsin.com/. Bangstad was not the only politician or pundit who thought the Midwest—and thereby the election—might be in play for the Democrats. They sought to turn out more Black voters, win over a few more conservative suburban women, and tamp down the stream of non-college-educated white voters in rural and urban areas. See Tim Alberta, "Three Reasons Biden Won the Midwest," *Politico Magazine*, November 4, 2020, https://www.politico.com/news/magazine/2020/11/04/three-reasons-biden-flipped-the-midwest-434114.

9. Throughout this volume, we use the terms "liberalism," "progressivism," and "the Left" somewhat interchangeably, and in distinction at times from the Democratic Party. While populism and progressivism actually preceded liberalism as a term to describe the Left in the years before the New Deal, the word "liberal" became a kind

of slur in the Reagan era. In these pages, we try to use the term that candidates and movements themselves employed. Also, for this volume as in *Conservative Heartland*, we specify these twelve states as making up the Midwest: North and South Dakota, Nebraska, Minnesota, Iowa, Kansas, Missouri, Wisconsin, Michigan, Illinois, Indiana, and Ohio.

10. For the broad view of these changes in and beyond the Midwest, see Jefferson Cowie, *Stayin' Alive: The 1970s and the End of the Working Class* (New York: New Press, 2010); Thomas Sugrue, *The Origins of the Urban Crisis: Race and Inequality in Postwar Detroit* (Princeton, NJ: Princeton University Press, 2005); Gary Gerstle, "Race and the Myth of the Liberal Consensus," *Journal of American History* 82, no. 2 (September 1995): 582–583; Kevin M. Kruse and Julian E. Zelizer, *Fault Lines: A History of the United States since 1974* (New York: Norton, 2019).

11. Marc Johnson, *Tuesday Night Massacre: Four Senate Elections and the Radicalization of the Republican Party* (New York: Oxford University Press, 2021); Arnold A. Offner, *Hubert Humphrey: The Conscience of the Country* (New Haven, CT: Yale University Press, 2018); Thomas J. Knock, *The Rise of a Prairie Statesman: The Life and Times of George McGovern* (Princeton, NJ: Princeton University Press, 2017); Hilary Rodham Clinton, *What Happened* (New York: Simon & Schuster, 2017). In 2010 midterm elections, the GOP-organized "Red Map" project encouraged donors to give to state house races, resulting in the loss of more than seven hundred seats to the GOP nationwide, just in time for the results of the 2010 census to allow for partisan redistricting in Ohio, Wisconsin, and other "purple" Midwestern states. See Jane Mayer, "State Legislatures Are Torching Democracy," *New Yorker*, August 6, 2022, https://www.newyorker.com/magazine/2022/08/15/state-legislatures-are-torching-democracy.

12. Darren Thompson, "Stunned by Retailers, Lac du Flambeau Tribe Answers Call to Sell "Progressive" Beer, Nativenewsonline, February 8, 2021, https://nativenewsonline.net/business/shunned-by-retailers-lac-du-flambeau-tribe-answers-call-to-sell-local-brewery-s-progressive-beer.

13. In 1987 the US Court of Appeals in the Seventh District upheld Native treaty rights that promised that Ojibwe could practice traditional spear-fishing during walleye spawning season even in "ceded" territories. Furious that, in their view, Native people now had rights that local whites did not and that federal law was enforced over state policies, armed and angry mobs of whites surrounded the docks, threatening violence and using racial epithets. As Brooks Big John recalled in 2022, "It became about much more than the fish." "Ojibwe Fishing Rights and Wisconsin's Spear-Fishing Controversy," WORT 89.9FM, April 25, 2022, https://www.wortfm.org/ojibwe-spearfishing-wisconsin/. For more on this conflict, see Larry Nesper, *The Walleye War: The Struggle for Ojibwe Spearfishing and Treaty Rights* (Lincoln: University of Nebraska Press, 2002).

14. Pat Kreitlow, "Johnson, Tiffany Slammed in Billboards up North for Rhetoric Contributing to Riot," *Up North News*, January 15, 2021, https://upnorthnewswi.com/2021/01/15/tiffany-johnson-slammed-in-billboards/.

15. Facebook, Minocqua Brewing Company, October 1, 2021. See the comments of visitors who posted the photos they had taken in front of the new murals.

16. "Dear White People," *Up North* podcast, episode 10, May 22, 2021, https://www.upnorthpodcast.com/videos/ep-10-dear-white-people.

17. Bangstad adopted this slogan going forward. See Susan Lampert Smith, "Local Brewery Makes the Most out of Being 'the Least Popular Place in Town,'" *Up*

North News, August 1, 2022, https://upnorthnewswi.com/2022/08/01/local-brewery-makes-the-most-out-of-being-the-least-popular-place-in-town/.

18. "Retail Locations: Minocqua Brewing Company," https://minocquabrewingcompany.com/pages/locations?fbclid=IwAR0lH6Rnzui7ge6VK7K3eM4lxBLxD4jAfw1jLnFz4D2Ivq2uWBLPjSIsWSg.

19. Email to author from Charles Barber, July 13, 2022.

20. Katie Bernard and Lisa Gutierrez, "'No' Prevails: Kansans Vote to Protect Abortion Rights in State Constitution," *Kansas City Star*, August 5, 2022, https://www.kansascity.com/news/politics-government/election/article263832087.html; Dominik Dausch, "South Dakota Passes Amendment D to Expand Medicaid," *Sioux Falls Argus Leader*, November 9, 2022, https://www.argusleader.com/story/news/politics/2022/11/09/south-dakota-poised-to-expand-medicaid-as-election-day-continues/69614530007/.

21. Mitch Smith on *New York Times* podcast *The Daily*, "How to Understand the Kansas Abortion Vote,' August 4, 2022, 17:00; on the "different flavor," see Sabrina Tabernisi, ibid., 17:17. See also Ian Toller-Clark's review of Timothy L. J. Lombardo, *Blue-Collar Conservatism: Frank Rizzo's Philadelphia and Populist Politics*, in *Middle West Review* 8, no. 1 (Fall 2021): 183–185. Toller-Clark states that "rural-urban divide is far too simple" (184).

22. Cory Haala, "The Progressive Center: Midwestern Liberalism in the Age of Reagan, 1978–1992," (PhD diss., Marquette University, 2020). See also Cory Haala, *How Democrats Won the Heartland* (Champaign-Urbana: University of Illinois Press, forthcoming).

23. In two recently published major reconsiderations of the history of the Democratic Party, the Midwest is overlooked almost entirely. See Michael Kazin, *What It Took to Win: A History of the Democratic Party* (New York: Farrar, Straus & Giroux, 2022); Lily Geismer, *Left Behind: The Democrats' Failed Attempt to Solve Inequality* (New York: Public Affairs, 2022). On the movement to rejuvenate the field of Midwestern history, see Jon K. Lauck, *The Lost Region: Toward a Revival of Midwestern History* (Iowa City: University of Iowa Press, 2013); Kritika Agarwal, "Midwestern History Is on the Map," *Perspectives: The Newsmagazine of the American Historical Association*, December 3, 2018.

24. The intense interest in conservatism began with a call to action in Alan Brinkley, "The Problem of American Conservatism," *American Historical Review* 99 (April 1994): 409–429. See also Leo P. Ribuffo, "Why Is There So Much Conservatism in the United States and Why Do So Few Historians Know Anything about It?" *American Historical Review* 99 (April 1994): 438–444. By the 2010s, the study of conservatism risked being called "trendy." Kim Phillips-Fein, "Conservatism: A State of the Field," *Journal of American History* 98, no. 3 (December 2011): 723–743.

25. For a new anthology of the progressive Midwest, see Amanda L. Isso and Benjamin Looker, eds., *Left in the Midwest: St. Louis Progressive Activism in the 1960s* (Columbia: University of Missouri Press, 2023).

26. Martin Manalansan et al., eds., "Queering the Middle: Race, Region, and a Queer Midwest," *Journal of Lesbian and Gay Studies*, 20 (March 2014).

27. For examples of new work, located in both the urban and rural Midwest, see C. J. Janovy, *No Place Like Home: Lessons in Activism from LGBT Kansas* (Lawrence: Kansas University Press, 2018); Timothy Stewart-Winter, *Queer Clout: Chicago and the Rise of Gay Politics* (Philadelphia: University of Pennsylvania Press, 2017); Stewart Van Cleve,

Land of 10,000 Loves: A History of Queer Minnesota (Minneapolis: University of Minnesota Press, 2012); Kevin P. Murphy, Jennifer L. Pierce, and Larry Knopp, eds., *Queer Twin Cities* (Minneapolis: University of Minnesota Press, 2010); Will Fellows, eds., *Farm Boys: Lives of Gay Men from the Rural Midwest* (Madison: University of Wisconsin Press, 1998); Taylor Brorby, *Boys and Oil: Growing up Gay in a Fractured Land* (New York: Norton, 2022).

28. Hopkins, *Red Fighting Blue*; Daniel R. Birdsong and Christopher J. Devine, "Fly-To Country: The Midwest as Presidential Battleground, 1946–2016," in Lauck and Stock, eds., *Conservative Heartland*, 72–94.

29. Hopkins, *Red Fighting Blue*, 207. Examples include Senators Chuck Grassley (R) and Tom Harkin (D) of Iowa, who represented the state from 1985 to 2015.

30. Birdsong and Devine, "Fly-to Country."

31. The New Deal coalition—the New Deal itself in fact—was conditioned on the support of Southern segregationists, which doomed it and brought racial structures into its programs from the beginning. See Richard Rothstein, *The Color of Law: A Forgotten History of How Our Government Segregated America* (New York: Liveright, 2017). But attacks on the New Deal came from the Right outside the South as well. Conservative historians have returned to questions about the opposition to the New Deal and its impact on the making of the modern New Right some decades later. See Kimberly Phillips-Fein, *Invisible Hands: The Businessman's Crusade against the New Deal* (New York: Norton, 2010). For Jefferson Cowie and Nick Salvatore, the question is larger than that: they wonder if in fact the New Deal and Great Society years were but a "great exception" in the course of a largely conservative country. Cowie and Salvatore, "The Great Exception: Rethinking the New Deal in American History," *International Labor and Working-Class History* 74 (Fall 2008), 3–32.

32. Kazin, *What It Took to Win*, 244.

33. Jennifer Alice Denton, *Making Minnesota Liberal: Civil Rights and the Transformation of the Democratic Party* (Minneapolis: University of Minnesota Press, 2002).

34. Michelle Anderson and Jake Krohn, "*Der Spiegel* Journalist Messed with the Wrong Small Town," *Medium*, December 19, 2018, https://medium.com/@michele anderson/der-spiegel-journalist-messed-with-the-wrong-small-town-d92f3e0e01a7. The authors are responding to a German article that paints the town as racist and fully pro-Trump. For more on the article and the town's response, see Matt Furber and Mitch Smith, "Small Town Defamed by German Reporter Ready to Forgive, *New York Times*, December 27, 2018, https://www.nytimes.com/2018/12/27/us/der-spiegel-fergus-falls-minnesota.html?searchResultPosition=9.

35. Kazin, *What It Took to Win*, ix; Sara Egge, "Midwestern Progressives Were Radicals," *Middle West Review* 8, no. 1 (Fall 2021): 163–168.

36. Heather McGhee, *Slate Political Gabfest* (Slate Plus segment), "There's Nothing the Matter with Kansas," August 4, 2022, 55:00. See also Heather McGhee, *The Sum of Us: How Racism Costs Everyone and How We Can Prosper Together* (London: Oneworld, 2021).

37. See Felipe Hinojosa, Maggie Elmore, and Sergio M. Gonzalez, eds., *Faith and Power: Latino Religious Politics since 1945* (New York: New York University Press, 2022).

38. Cowie, *Staying Alive*; Sugrue, *The Origins of the Urban Crisis*.

39. Tamar Winfrey-Harris, "Stop Pretending the Black Midwest Doesn't Exist," in Terrion L. Williamson, *Black in the Middle: An Anthology of the Black Midwest* (Cleveland: Belt Publishing, 2020), 169–170.

40. As quoted in Denton, *Making Minnesota Liberal*, xi.

41. Today more Black people live in the Midwest than in either the Northeast or the Far West. Winfrey-Harris, "Stop Pretending the Black Midwest Doesn't Exist," 169–170. See also Britt E. Halvorson and Joshua O. Reno, *Imagining the Heartland: White Supremacy and the Making of the Midwest* (Berkeley: University of California Press, 2022). Important recent work on Black people in the modern history of the Midwest includes Ashley Howard, "The Burnings Began: Omaha's Urban Revolts and the Meanings of Political Violence," *Nebraska History* (Summer 2017), 83–97; Christy Clark-Pujara and Lisa-Anna Cox, "Many Tulsa Massacres: How the Myth of a Liberal North Erases a Long History of Violence," Museum of American History blog, August 25, 2022, https://americanhistory.si.edu/blog/many-tulsa-massacres; Austin McCoy, *The Quest for Democracy: Black Power, New Left, and Progressive Politics in the Post-Industrial Midwest* (Chapel Hill: University of North Carolina Press, forthcoming). See also Black Initiative project, https://www.theblackmidwest.cm/about.html.

42. Williamson, *Black in the Middle*, 14–15.

43. Tara Rose, "The Burgers at Millers," in Bayne, ed., *Red State Blues*, 47.

44. On this topic, see Michael Mertz, *Radicals in the Heartland: The 1960s Student Protest Movement at the University of Illinois* (Champaign-Urbana: University of Illinois Press, 2019).

45. Another example of a Democrat in a very red state who understood he could not even get close to Republican nominee Kristi Noem in 2018 was Billie Sutton. He built a coalition among liberals in Sioux Falls, Lakota and other Native people, and libertarian ranchers from "West River," where he was from. He was endorsed by both major newspapers in the state. After losing by only a few thousand votes and winning counties in each section of the state, he said, "We rise to the occasion together. No matter what the obstacles ahead, no matter what the challenges, we can work together to make South Dakota everything it can be." Since then, South Dakotans have approved recreational marijuana, expanded Medicare, and may overturn the state's abortion ban. Christopher Vondracek, "A Democratic Hopeful from Ranch Country," in Bayne, *Red State Blues*, 149–150.

PART ONE

In the Shadow of the New Deal

1

In the Shadow of FDR and Harry Truman

Missouri's Liberal Senatorial Turn, 1950–1987

JON E. TAYLOR

❖ ❖ ❖ ❖ ❖ ❖ ❖ ❖ ❖ ❖ ❖ ❖ ❖ ❖ ❖

In 1940 Harry S. Truman won a close Senate reelection primary by appealing to a broad coalition of Missouri constituents that had come to be part of President Franklin Roosevelt's New Deal coalition, which included rural, union, women, African American, and immigrant voters.[1] That November, Missouri voters went to the polls and supported Truman for the Senate and, surprisingly, Republican Forrest Donnell for governor. Donnell ran an anti-machine campaign against Democratic candidate Lawrence McDaniel and prevailed by a mere 3,613 votes, making Donnell the state's first Republican governor since 1933.[2] Four years later, in 1944, FDR tapped Harry Truman to serve as his running mate, and Donnell, who had finished his term as governor, won election to the US Senate. Truman went on to become president after Franklin Roosevelt died on April 12, 1945, and while Truman became the leader of the national Democratic Party, in Missouri he was anything but the Democratic leader. Missouri voters continued to toggle between the liberalism of the New Deal and candidates like Harry Truman, who embraced the New Deal, but who were still tainted by machine politics.[3]

Missouri served as an important proving ground as to whether the New Deal coalition that Franklin Roosevelt created, and which Harry Truman drew upon for his 1940 Senate primary and general election victories, could work in a border state. Democratic party leaders put Truman on the Democratic ticket in 1944 to appeal to labor and to African

American voters, but the question remained whether he could hold that coalition together in the post–World War II period and even expand the coalition during his presidency. The true test of this coalition occurred in the 1946 midterm elections.[4]

In 1946 Missouri voters went to the polls and elected Republican James P. Kem to the US Senate over the Democratic-endorsed and Truman-supported Frank P. Briggs. President Truman also suffered the loss of a Kansas City congressional seat, when Republican candidate Albert Reeves Jr.—son of federal judge Albert Reeves Sr., who had presided over a number of vote fraud cases that resulted in the destruction of the Pendergast machine in the 1930s—defeated Truman-supported candidate Enos Axtell.[5] Missouri political historian Thomas F. Soapes noted that Republicans won nine of thirteen Missouri congressional seats, including one in Kansas City and two in St. Louis, and expanded their control over the Missouri state legislature. Furthermore, he argued that Missouri Republicans had performed well because of low voter turnout and they had cut the Democratic margin of victory in the state's African American urban centers because African American voters had either stayed home or supported Republican candidates. Soapes also noted that labor was upset at Truman's proposal to draft all striking railroad workers into the armed forces and that Missouri's farmers had outright rejected Truman's farm policies. Soapes concluded, "The 1946 elections in Missouri were unanimously interpreted as a rejection of the national leadership and platform of the Democratic party."[6]

Nationally, the 1946 midterm elections returned Republican control to both houses of Congress for the first time since 1930.[7] Many of the same factors that were at work in Missouri were also at play nationally. Truman's decision to ask for the resignation of progressive Democrat Henry A. Wallace shortly before the midterm elections angered Democratic progressives and dampened Democratic enthusiasm. The reconversion from a wartime to a peacetime economy had brought economic challenges to Americans, and they rejected the Truman's administration poor handling of reconversion.[8]

After the 1946 midterm elections Harry Truman moved to the left, and he broadened the base of the Democratic Party specifically with the civil rights initiatives that he had taken with his appointment of the President's Committee on Civil Rights and with his decision to issue Executive Order 9980 in 1948, which ended a segregated military.[9] However, Truman's move to the left on civil rights was tempered by the fact that in March 1947 he issued Executive Order 9835 establishing a permanent loyalty program, which challenged American civil liberties within the context of the Cold War and forced a revision to New Deal liberalism to include a commitment to anticommunism, which threatened civil liberties in the Cold War. Truman embraced the loyalty program, which put him at odds with some liberals, but he completely rejected a more extreme loyalty program established by the McCarran Act of 1950 when he vetoed the law. The measure became law despite his veto, and subsequent presidents and congressional leaders continued to carry out an internal anticommunist security program into the 1970s.[10]

The Cold War also forced a reevaluation in America's role in the world. Truman, who had embraced internationalism in the Senate, supported internationalism while president when he advocated for America's entry into the United Nations and drafted and implemented the Cold War containment policy. Not all Missourians were immediately on board with this new role, as they had supported isolationist Republican US senators like Forrest Donnell and James Kem prior to 1950.[11]

This chapter explores how Senators Hennings, Symington, Long, and Eagleton embraced New Deal liberalism with their support of civil rights and voting rights measures during their respective terms in office, and how these senators supported and challenged the Cold War liberal consensus that developed under President Truman and his successors as they waged anticommunist campaigns at home and abroad.[12] Senators Hennings and Long, while supportive of some anticommunist measures, vociferously condemned elements of the domestic internal security program that threatened American civil liberties. The chapter concludes by examining how Senators Symington and Eagleton struggled to reconcile their support of Cold War liberalism with America's involvement in Vietnam.

Thomas Hennings Jr. served three terms in the US House, elected in 1934, 1936, and again in 1938; prior to that, he served as assistant circuit attorney for six years in St. Louis, where he prosecuted felony cases. As a member of Congress, he served on the Foreign Affairs Committee and on a House investigative committee that examined campaign expenditures. Hennings advocated for neutrality in the lead-up to World War II and successfully sponsored a bill that led to the suppression of the sale of marijuana. He cosponsored the anti-lynching law, which never passed but earned him the endorsement from the Black press in St. Louis. He also hired African Americans to work on his congressional staff.[13] The *St. Louis Globe-Democrat* concluded: "His record on major measures has been a progressive one, and he has voted with the [Roosevelt] administration on certain bills and against it on others."[14]

Hennings left politics in 1940 and successfully ran for circuit attorney of St. Louis but took a leave of absence in 1941 to serve in the US Navy.

He contracted influenza in 1943 and received a medical discharge. He returned to St. Louis and resumed work as circuit attorney, leaving that position in 1945 to enter private law practice. When Franklin Roosevelt asked Harry Truman to serve as his running mate in 1944, Hennings was the frontrunner for the appointment to replace him in the Senate, but the appointment went to Frank P. Briggs. In 1950 Hennings sought election to the US Senate, but Truman instead endorsed Emery Ellison. The president told confidant Harry Easley: "Tom Hennings was in the House for about six years when I first came here and he did not do much work. His war record will not bear the examination of a microscope and anyway I'd like very much to have at least one Senator here for two years who could be personally friendly to the first President from Missouri."[15] The press speculated that Truman favored Ellison because he thought he could capture the rural Missouri vote and Hennings could not. Another view speculated that Truman supported Ellison to pay a political debt he owed to James M. Pendergast, who attempted to rebuild his uncle's [Tom Pendergast] political machine against increasing pressure from Kansas City Democratic rival Charles Binaggio, who had endorsed Hennings.[16]

When Hennings ran for the US Senate in 1950, African Americans made up 7.5 percent of voters in Missouri and were an important constituency in the state. Hennings touted the primary endorsements from the predominately African American Eleventh and Nineteenth Wards of St. Louis, and President Truman did come around to support him in the general election, but the Republicans tried to make Truman's lack of support in the primary a campaign issue in the general election. On November 3, 1950, candidate Hennings told the Twenty-Fourth Ward Democratic Club: "I welcome the endorsement of the head [President Truman] of my party. I've had the indorsement since last August and as far as I'm concerned there never has been any question about it."[17] On November 4, 1950, President Truman came to St. Louis and spoke at a large Democratic gathering at the Keil Auditorium, where he told the crowd: "Here in Missouri we are going to elect Tom Hennings to the Senate; and we are going to send a Democratic delegation to the House of Representatives from Missouri."[18]

From 1951 until he died in 1960, Senator Hennings was the most influential and outspoken Missouri politician on civil liberties and civil rights. Prior to Hennings's election to the US Senate, in 1947 Truman issued Executive Order 9835, which created a loyalty program and established loyalty review boards for federal employees. When Hennings campaigned in 1950, he did not condemn the program. It was only after he got into office that he expressed misgivings. Despite Hennings's criticism of Truman's

Figure 1.1. Senator Thomas Hennings speaking at the Missouri Democratic Ham Breakfast at the Missouri State Fair in Sedalia, Missouri, August 18, 1951. Courtesy of Harry S. Truman Library and Museum, Accession #96-472-12.

policy, in 1952 Truman told a political confidant: "Tom has turned out to be an excellent Senator and has been very cooperative with me."[19]

In 1953 the Democratic Party leadership appointed Hennings to the Subcommittee on Civil Rights, which was part of the Judiciary Committee; however, the subcommittee was renamed the Subcommittee on Constitutional Rights after 1955. The loyalty program continued under President Dwight Eisenhower's administration when he issued Executive Orders 10450 and 10865, and it was through the Subcommittee on Constitutional Rights that Hennings challenged Eisenhower's executive orders. Senator Hennings argued that these internal security measures violated free speech and due process under the law because the enforcement of internal security created a new administrative criminal law apparatus, in violation of the Bill of Rights.[20]

Senator Hennings's Subcommittee on Constitutional Rights introduced four separate bills in 1956 and again in 1957 that would have strengthened voting rights protections in federal elections and primaries, created a Civil Rights Division in the Department of Justice, provided federal protection for members of the armed forces who were physically assaulted, and created a federal anti-lynching law.[21] He participated in the Civil Rights Caucus and served as the secretary of the Senate Democratic Policy Committee. As a member of the Civil Rights Caucus, he favored the elimination of Rule 22, which required a two-thirds majority vote for cloture on bills and which he saw as an impediment to the passage of civil rights legislation, and he cast his vote in favor of the Civil Rights Act of 1957 and the Civil Rights Act of 1960.[22]

Hennings took on Senator Joseph McCarthy as a member of the Senate Committee on Rules and Administration and served as a member of the Subcommittee on Privileges and Elections. As a member of that subcommittee, he investigated McCarthy's role in the Maryland senatorial election of 1950; when the committee released its report, Hennings was serving as chair of the committee. According to Donald J. Kemper, "the responsibility for McCarthy's decline rested with no single senator. . . . Nevertheless, it must be noted that Hennings made singular contributions to McCarthy's ultimate fall."[23]

After Hennings died on September 13, 1960, the Missouri State Democratic Convention named Edward V. Long as its choice for the US Senate. Governor James Blair accepted that decision and appointed Long to fill out Hennings's term, which began on September 23, 1960, and ended on November 8, 1960, when Missouri voters elected him to complete the remaining two years of Hennings's term. After serving the remaining two years, Long successfully ran for a full six-year term in 1962.[24]

Like Senator Hennings, Senator Long focused on civil rights and civil liberties. In February 1963, Long voted to change Senate Rule 22, but the attempt to reduce the number of senators required for cloture was defeated again. At the 1964 Democratic National Convention, Long supported reforms that would have made it possible for more Black participation in future Democratic Party conventions. Long cast his vote in favor of the Civil Right Acts of 1964 and 1968 and the Voting Rights Act of 1965. In 1966 Long published the book *The Intruders: The Invasion of Privacy by Government and Industry*, in which he argued that technological advances threatened individual privacy and that federal laws needed to be passed in order to prevent abuses of civil liberties. He even proposed a bill that would have made postal surveillance of mail a federal crime.[25]

Life magazine conducted an expose of his Senate record and accused him of trying to prevent the prosecution of Teamsters leader Jimmy Hoffa, who had been convicted on federal charges. The article also accused Long of using federal funds to pay his housekeeper and to pay rent on the law office he ran in Bowling Green, Missouri. A Senate committee investigated those charges and he was cleared of any wrongdoing, but the accusations tarnished his 1968 reelection bid and he lost to Democrat Thomas F. Eagleton in the Democratic primary; Eagleton went on to win in the November general election.[26]

The Senate careers of Hennings and Long overlapped with their colleague Stuart Symington. When Symington ran for the US Senate in 1952, Truman did not endorse him in the Democratic primary even though Symington had served with distinction in the Truman administration. Truman first met Symington when Truman was chair of the Senate Investigative Committee. Symington, then president of the St. Louis–based Emerson Electric Company, had led the effort to integrate its workforce and obtained war contracts to build rotating gun turrets that were used on military aircraft in World War II. When Truman became president in 1945, he asked Symington to become chair of the Surplus Property Administration, which oversaw the disposition of surplus property generated from World War II contracting. In 1946 President Truman appointed him assistant secretary of war for air, and he became a key advocate to establish the air force as a separate and independent branch of the military. Truman appointed Symington as the nation's first secretary of the air force on September 18, 1947, a position he held until he resigned on April 24, 1950, over differences he had with the president about the level of funding for the new branch of the armed services, but not before he had taken steps to comply with Truman's EO 9980, which required the military to integrate. Truman then appointed Symington chair of the National Security Resources Board, which he held for a short time before becoming chair of the Reconstruction Finance Corporation—the last position he held in the Truman administration prior to running for the US Senate in 1952.[27]

Symington wrote to President Truman on March 11, 1952, and informed him that he planned to file for election to the US Senate. Truman did not respond, but instead put his infamous "File it" notation on it. Truman later told one political confidant that he was concerned about Symington's lack of political experience and that Symington's chances for election might be diminished because like Symington, Senator Hennings was from St. Louis, and he doubted "if the State would be willing to have two Senators from Saint Louis at the same time." The president told another confidant: "I was a little slow in getting around to the Senatorial situation for I had at one time thought I might run for it myself but I changed my mind."[28]

Symington announced that he would run for election to the US Senate on March 20, 1952. His biographer, James Olson, noted that he faced an uphill battle to win the Democratic primary. He was not from Missouri, having only relocated from New York to St. Louis in 1938 to work at Emerson, and then quickly went to work in Washington, DC. He therefore had little interaction with outstate Missouri voters, which he would need to capture to win any political contest. However, Symington defeated his Democratic primary opponent, J. E. "Buck" Taylor, who Truman had endorsed, by a two-to-one margin in the primary and then faced off against Republican incumbent and prominent Kansas City attorney James P. Kem.[29] Kem had bitterly opposed the Truman administration and remained staunchly isolationist in his views opposing the nation's entry into NATO and the Marshall Plan. In contrast, Symington supported both.[30] Symington conducted a campaign that continued to focus on meeting as many Missourians as he possibly could, and in November 1952 he prevailed over his Republican challenger and won in a landslide by earning the votes of more than one million Missourians.[31]

Unlike Harry Truman, who had arrived in the US Senate in 1935 as the "Senator from Pendergast," Symington arrived with a national reputation. He had already well-established relationships with Senate minority leader Lyndon B. Johnson and with the incoming president, Dwight Eisenhower. Symington received Johnson's support to serve on the Armed Services Committee and an appointment on the Committee on Governmental Operations, where he engaged in combat, as had Senator Hennings, with the committee's chair, Senator Joseph McCarthy.[32] McCarthy had come to Missouri to campaign on behalf of Kem and had accused Symington of being a "Communist sympathizer."[33]

It was difficult to accuse Symington of being a communist sympathizer given Symington's role in the Truman administration as secretary of the air force, but when McCarthy began accusing the US State Department of harboring communists and when one of the counselors McCarthy hired claimed that Protestant clergy were the largest single group supporting communist organizations, Symington could no longer remain silent. All three Democratic members of the committee resigned in protest over McCarthy's remarks. Eventually the three senators returned to the committee, and when the Democrats won back majority control of the Senate in 1954, a Democrat replaced McCarthy as chair and Symington turned his energies to serving on the Armed Services Committee. Truman told Symington: "I think McCarthy's mind ought to be picked to the bottom, if there is any bottom to it. I don't think he ought to get away with smearing everybody else when he never told the truth in his life."[34]

As a member of the Armed Services Committee, Symington became an open critic of Eisenhower's decision to slash the defense budget and continued to advocate for a strong air force, but Congress implemented the cuts.[35] Symington's concerns gained some traction when the Democrats took back the majority in the Senate and a Democrat was installed as chair of the Senate Armed Services Committee. It was Symington who took charge of a subcommittee to determine where the United States stood with its nuclear missile development. He was concerned that the Soviets had overtaken the United States in its production of long-range nuclear weapons and wanted to explore this issue.[36]

Symington developed a national profile, and some supporters suggested he seek the Democratic nomination for the presidency in 1956. Harry Truman, however, endorsed Averell Harriman. It was a surprising endorsement because according to James C. Olson, "Harriman was even less popular in the South than [Adlai] Stevenson," the Democratic front-runner going into 1956. Olson wrote that of the Democratic candidates mentioned, "Symington seemed to be in the best position to consolidate the southern and northern big-city wings of the Democratic party." Senator Thomas Hennings nominated Symington at the convention, but Stevenson won on the first ballot.[37]

Harry Truman endorsed Averell Harriman, governor of New York, in a press conference held prior to the Democratic National Convention. Truman explained that he was concerned that the Democratic Party was "becoming a caretaker Party" and that Adlai Stevenson was becoming more moderate in his views. Truman continued:

> President Franklin Roosevelt was not a moderate—as some are now suggesting—in 1940 he was even prepared to decline the nomination when the convention threatened to abandon the progressive and liberal principles of government for which his Administration stood. . . . I am shocked that any liberal Democrat would advocate or encourage the abandonment of the New Deal and the Fair Deal as out of date when there are many millions of people who are in urgent need of creative, forward looking social purposes of the New Deal and Fair Deal. The destruction of this social philosophy is the aim of the conservatives and reactionaries of both parties.[38]

In 1956, Symington chaired the finance committee of the Senate Democratic Campaign Committee and campaigned on behalf of Senate Democrats across the United States. The Democrats captured a slight majority in the Senate, which allowed Lyndon Johnson to become Senate majority leader. Johnson told Symington, "I don't know of anyone who worked harder than Stu Symington or anyone who was more effective. It took days and nights of sustained effort, and you came through with a top-notch performance that meant the difference between victory and defeat in many states."[39]

Symington continued to attack the Eisenhower administration over its lack of funding for air power and for its farm policies. Symington's criticisms of Eisenhower's lack of funding for air power gained new life after the Soviets successfully launched Sputnik in 1957. As a member of the Senate Armed Services Committee, he supported President Eisenhower's decision to reorganize the Department of Defense, but he continued to criticize Eisenhower for not funding American defense; that underfunding collectively began to be referred to as a "missile gap" between the United States and the Soviet Union. Symington made the "missile gap" a campaign issue in his successful reelection campaign in 1958, and Missourians reelected him by the widest margin for any candidate that had ever run for statewide office.[40] His appeal for a strong national defense resonated with Missouri voters, and he also supported the Civil Rights Acts of 1957 and 1960. When Eisenhower wanted to dismantle the New Deal fixed price supports for agriculture, he criticized Eisenhower's farm policies and Ezra Taft Benson, Eisenhower's secretary of agriculture, who was tasked with carrying out those policies.[41]

Symington's national profile was on the rise, and in 1959 he began to explore a run for the presidency. Symington checked all the boxes for Harry Truman, much like Averell Harriman had in 1956, and Truman endorsed his candidacy. Symington announced that he would be a candidate on March 24, 1960, but his biographer noted, "his candidacy failed to generate much enthusiasm in liberal circles." Symington placed third in the delegate voting, behind frontrunner John F. Kennedy and second-place finisher Lyndon Johnson.[42]

Symington won reelection to a third Senate term in 1964 at the same time that the United States was beginning to get mired in Vietnam and President Johnson pushed his Great Society to the forefront, which included a commitment to expanding civil rights and health care. Symington supported all of Johnson's Great Society measures relating to civil rights, including the Civil Rights Acts of 1964 and 1968, the Voting Rights Act of 1965, and Medicare and Medicaid. Initially he supported the war in Vietnam by casting a vote in favor of the Gulf of Tonkin Resolution, but after taking a trip to Vietnam in September 1967, he drafted "A Proposal Looking toward Peace in Vietnam" that called for a cease-fire and a negotiated peace. His proposal resulted in a break with President Johnson and strained his relationship with his former boss, Harry Truman, who never made a strong outspoken statement against US involvement in Vietnam.[43]

In 1969 Senator J. William Fulbright, who chaired the Senate Foreign Relations Committee, appointed Symington to chair the Subcommittee on US Security Agreements and Commitments Abroad. The subcommittee did not examine America's role in Vietnam; however, it did explore

Figure 1.2. President Lyndon Johnson seated (on left) with former President Harry Truman, signing the Medicare Act into law at the Harry S. Truman Library, July 30, 1965. Standing, from left: Missouri Senator Edward Long, Missouri Senator Stuart Symington, Missouri Governor Warren Hearnes, Montana Senator Mike Mansfield, Lady Bird Johnson, Vice President Hubert Humphrey, and Bess Truman. Courtesy of Harry S. Truman Library and Museum, Accession #66-63.

Richard Nixon's direction of US military assets in neighboring Cambodia. Symington became acting chair of the Armed Forces Committee in 1970, and under his chairmanship the committee explored how the CIA had illegally surveilled Daniel Ellsberg, a Department of Defense employee who had been involved in releasing the Pentagon Papers to the press at the direction of the White House.[44]

Senator Symington sought reelection in 1970 and defeated Republican candidate Jack Danforth by a mere 43,000 votes, his smallest margin of victory. In his last Senate term he focused on reducing defense expenditures and international peace. His biographer observed: "During his first term he had been recognized as a superhawk; in his last he was a leading Senate dove."[45] But Symington was not the only Missouri senator who expressed concern about America's involvement in Vietnam.

In 1968 newly elected Thomas F. Eagleton joined Symington in the Senate. Like Hennings and Symington, Eagleton was from the St. Louis area; unlike them, he had served in two Missouri state offices: as attorney general from 1960 to 1964, and as lieutenant governor from 1965 to 1968. Eagleton announced that he would be a candidate for the US Senate on September 11, 1967, and a few days after the announcement he publicly stated that the United States should halt its bombing campaign of North Vietnam. A week later, Senator Symington gave Eagleton some cover when he too questioned the US role in Vietnam. Eagleton's Democratic primary challengers, incumbent Edward V. Long and True Davis, had been indifferent about America's role in Vietnam. In the fall he faced Republican challenger Thomas B. Curtis and defeated him by a narrow margin of 51 percent over Curtis's 49 percent. Nationally, Richard Nixon became president, and for the first time since 1928, except for the 1952 and 1956 Eisenhower victories in Missouri, a Republican won the state— by a mere 20,488 votes over Democratic presidential challenger Hubert Humphrey.[46]

Senator Eagleton arrived in Washington as a member of the Democratic Party's liberal wing. He served on the District of Columbia Committee and on the Public Works Committee, where he was vice-chair of the Environmental Subcommittee. His biographer, James Giglio, noted that he "played a key role in the implementation of the National Environmental Policy Act" and drafted the 1970 Clean Air Act amendments, which strengthened the 1967 Clean Air Act, followed by the Clean Water Act in 1972. In the area of civil rights, he opposed the Nixon administration's attempt to weaken the Voting Rights Act of 1965 and voted to approve a strengthened extension of the law. He supported labor and Missouri agriculture by advocating for federal subsidies for cotton producers.[47]

Like his senior colleague from Missouri, Stuart Symington, Eagleton focused much of his time on foreign policy and defense issues, which included opposition to the Vietnam War and Nixon's handling of that war. Eagleton's outspokenness caught the attention of many, and in 1972 he made the short list to become George McGovern's running mate, and McGovern selected him. Tom Eagleton's mental health became the subject of intense scrutiny, and he participated in a press conference where he revealed hospitalizations for exhaustion and depression and that he had participated in electric shock therapy. Then stories emerged in the press about numerous arrests for reckless and dangerous driving, which were never proven, but the damage was done. George McGovern asked Eagleton to resign from the ticket, and he did.[48]

Eagleton continued his work in the Senate, where he played an important role in supporting the War Powers Act of 1973, and he faced his first reelection campaign in 1974. Missouri voters were not concerned about the revelations about his mental health, and so the November election featured a rematch between Eagleton and his Republican challenger, Thomas Curtis, who he defeated by more than 354,000 votes. His biographer noted that in the next ten years he served, his Americans for Democratic Action (ADA) ranking from 1975 to 1979 "ranged from 72 percent to 50 percent," which indicated that the "country had become more conservative." In 1978, as chair of the Senate Subcommittee on Aging he wrote the Older Americans Act, which among other programs, resulted in the creation of the Meals on Wheels program. Despite this national and Missouri trend toward conservatism, Missourians reelected Eagleton again in 1980 in the Republican wave that brought Ronald Reagan to power and ushered in Republican control of the Senate for the first time since 1954.[49]

Not surprisingly, Harry Truman, who had died in December 1972, made a brief appearance in Eagleton's 1980 reelection campaign. Eagleton's Republican opponent, Gene McNary, asserted in the campaign that if Truman were alive today, he would be a Republican. Senator Eagleton asked Harry Truman's daughter, Margaret Truman Daniel, to answer McNary's charge. She told McNary: "Senator Eagleton, [sic] is the kind of peoples' Democrat that Harry Truman would have been eager to endorse. Thus, I am afraid that you cannot have the Truman endorsement for the Republican party in 1980."[50]

Eagleton spent his last Senate term opposing President Reagan's supply-side theory of economics, which created budget deficits and resulted in cuts to existing social welfare programs. His ADA voting record in his last term increased to 80 to 90 percent over his previous term of 50 to 72 percent. In 1982 he drafted the "Confession of an Unreconstructed Roosevelt New Dealer," in which he stated: "I am an unreconstructed Roosevelt New Dealer and proud of it."[51]

This chapter examined the senatorial careers of Thomas Hennings Jr., Edward V. Long, Stuart Symington, and Thomas Eagleton within the context of the New Deal liberalism of Franklin Roosevelt and Harry Truman and the transition to the Cold War liberalism that developed under Truman and subsequent presidents. These senators supported the Civil Rights Acts of 1957, 1960, 1964, and 1968 as well as the Voting Rights Act of 1965.[52] While Senators Hennings and Long were concerned about the threat to civil liberties posed by internal security programs, they were willing to tolerate some anticommunist measures. Senator Symington, who initially embraced US involvement in Vietnam as part of his Cold War liberalism, became disillusioned with Harry Truman's Cold War liberalism that included the containment policy, which led to US involvement in Vietnam. Senator Eagleton joined Senator Symington in this transition away from supporting Cold War liberalism when Eagleton clearly identified with the New Deal liberalism of Franklin Roosevelt and Harry Truman and not Harry Truman's Cold War liberalism when he ran for reelection in 1980.[53]

The election of Missouri senators Jack Danforth in 1976 and Kit Bond in 1986 signaled the end of a successive line of Democratic senators that followed in the shadow of Franklin Roosevelt and Harry Truman. Initially Harry Truman had a difficult time supporting Democratic Senate candidates like Hennings and Symington because they were essentially Democratic newcomers and they did not have a strong connection to Missouri's machine politics, but Missouri voters taught Truman a bitter lesson by rejecting the old machine-affiliated candidates when they supported Senators Hennings, Long, Symington, and Eagleton.

Missouri Republican Senators Danforth and Bond, who took the place of Symington and Eagleton respectively, were seen as moderates, as were Democratic Senators Mel and Jean Carnahan and Claire McCaskill, who came after them. What had changed in Missouri after Senator Eagleton left office in 1987? Missouri senatorial politics from 1950 to 1987 revolved around local politics, and Missouri voters supported candidates that worked for their urban and rural interests. Harry Truman's Senate campaigns of 1934 and especially 1940 reflected this, as Truman campaigned across the state in urban and rural areas—those folks mattered to him and he knew he was accountable to them. Even though Senator Symington was not a native Missourian, he worked hard to cultivate relationships with urban and rural Missourians, as had Eagleton. Local politics mattered to Missouri voters, but in the period after 1987 local politics became nationalized as the Republican Party made cultural and economic issues central to their campaigns, and the Democratic Party and the candidates who once dominated the state began to focus their campaigns more narrowly on specific issues and on specific areas and constituencies within the state. In the areas that Democrats ceded to Republicans, personal relationships were replaced with Missourians establishing relationships with national conservative media outlets like Fox News. Jeff Roe, Republican strategist, recently mentioned this trend, but 2022 Missouri state Democratic Senate candidate Ayanna Shivers noted that one of the antidotes to this is to focus on the importance of building relationships. She said: "Part of being in rural America is understanding that relationships really do matter."⁵⁴ Despite Shivers's call to build relationships, in November 2022 the urban-rural divide was on full display as conservative Republican Eric Schmitt defeated Democratic candidate Trudy Busch Valentine by 13 percentage points, and in Missouri counties with a population of under 50,000 people, Schmitt held Valentine to around 20 percent or under.⁵⁵

NOTES

1. For more on the New Deal and its legacy, see William E. Leuchtenburg, *The FDR Years: On Roosevelt and His Legacy* (New York: Columbia University Press, 1995).

2. Matthew C. Sherman, "'The Most Serious Senator': A Reconsideration of Forrest C. Donnell of Missouri and the North Atlantic Treaty," *Missouri Historical Review* 101, no. 2 (January 2007): 78–98.

3. For more on Truman's ties to the Pendergast machine, see Lyle Dorsett, *The Pendergast Machine* (New York: Oxford University Press, 1968); Robert H. Ferrell, *Truman and Pendergast* (Columbia: University of Missouri Press, 1999); Lawrence H. Larsen and Nancy J. Hulston, *Pendergast!* (Columbia: University of Missouri Press, 1997).

4. For Harry Truman and the 1940 Senate election and the presidential election of 1944, see Jon E. Taylor, *Freedom to Serve: Truman, Civil Rights, and Executive Order 9981* (New York: Routledge, 2013). For more on the Democratic expansion into the border states and the South, see William E. Leuchtenburg, *The White House Looks South: Franklin D. Roosevelt, Harry S. Truman, Lyndon B. Johnson* (Baton Rouge: Louisiana State University Press, 2005).

5. See Brian Burnes, "New Film Documents Legendary KC Ballot Theft Case," November 19, 2021, https://flatlandkc.org/arts-culture/new-film-documents-legendary-kc-ballot-theft-case/.

6. Thomas F. Soapes, "Republican Leadership and the New Deal Coalition: Missouri Republican Politics, 1937–1952" (PhD diss., University of Missouri, Columbia, 1973), 117–119.

7. Alonzo Hamby, *Man of the People: A Life of Harry S. Truman* (New York: Oxford University Press, 1995), 384; Lizabeth Cohen, *A Consumers' Republic: The Politics of Mass Consumption in Postwar America* (New York: Alfred A. Knopf, 2003), 105.

8. Alonzo Hamby, *Beyond the New Deal: Harry S. Truman and American Liberalism* (New York: Columbia University Press, 1973), 120–145.

9. For Truman's civil rights record and the integration of the military, see Taylor, *Freedom to Serve*; William C. Berman, *The Politics of Civil Rights in the Truman Administration* (Columbus: Ohio State University Press, 1970); Richard M. Dalfiume, *Desegregation of the U.S. Armed Forces: Fighting on Two Fronts, 1939–1953* (Columbia: University of Missouri Press, 1969); Raymond H. Geselbracht, ed., *The Civil Rights Legacy of Harry S. Truman* (Kirksville, MO: Truman State University Press, 2007); Michael R. Gardner, *Harry S. Truman and Civil Rights: Moral Courage and Political Risks* (Carbondale: Southern Illinois Press, 2002); Carol Anderson, *Eyes off the Prize: The United Nations and the African American Struggle for Human Rights, 1944–1955* (Cambridge: Cambridge University Press, 2003).

10. On the internal security program, see Eleanor Bontecou, *The Federal Loyalty-Security Program* (Ithaca, NY: Cornell University Press, 1953); Richard M. Fried, *Nightmare in Red: The McCarthy Era in Perspective* (New York: Oxford University Press, 1990); Jonathan Bell, *The Liberal State on Trial: The Cold War and American Politics in the Truman Years* (New York: Columbia University Press, 2004).

11. For Donnell's isolationism, see Sherman, "The Most Serious Senator." For Kem's isolationism, see James C. Olson, *Stuart Symington: A Life* (Columbia: University of Missouri Press, 2003), 232.

12. For more on Cold War civil rights, see Thomas Borstelmann, *The Cold War and the Color Line: American Race Relations in the Global Arena* (Cambridge, MA: Harvard University Press, 2009); Mary L. Dudziak, *Cold War Civil Rights: Race and the Image of American Democracy* (Princeton, NJ: Princeton University Press, 2011). For more on anticommunism and Cold War liberalism, see Arthur M. Schlesinger Jr., *The Vital Center* (Boston: Houghton Mifflin, 1949); Alonzo L. Hamby, *Liberalism and Its Challengers: From F.D.R. to Bush*, 2nd ed. (New York: Oxford University Press, 1992); H. W. Brands, *The Strange Death of American Liberalism* (New Haven, CT: Yale University Press, 2001); Jennifer A. Delton, *Rethinking the 1950s: How Anticommunism and the Cold War Made America Liberal* (New York: Cambridge University Press, 2013).

13. John Kyle Day, "Senator Thomas C. Hennings Jr. of Missouri: Political Champion of the Black Freedom Struggle," *Missouri Historical Review* 114, no. 3 (April 2020): 188–189.

14. "Records of Circuit Attorney," *St. Louis Globe-Democrat*, November 3, 1940.

15. For quote, see Harry S. Truman to Harry Easley, June 26, 1950, President's Secretary's Files, Missouri: Harry Easley Folder, Harry S. Truman Library.

16. See Donald J. Kemper, *Decade of Fear: Senator Hennings and Civil Liberties* (Columbia: University of Missouri Press, 1965) 11–19.

17. Quoted in "Hennings 'Welcomes' Truman's Indorsement," *St. Louis Globe-Democrat*, November 3, 1950.

18. Harry Truman, November 4, 1950, speech, https://www.presidency.ucsb.edu/documents/address-kiel-auditorium-st-louis.

19. For Truman's loyalty program, see Kemper, *Decade of Fear*, 78–79. Also see Eleanor Bontecou, *The Federal Loyalty-Security Program* (Ithaca: NY: Cornell University Press, 1953). For quote, see Harry S. Truman to Dr. W. L. Brandon, January 22, 1952, President's Secretary's Files, Dwight D. Eisenhower Folder, Harry S. Truman Library.

20. Kemper, *Decade of Fear*, 100.

21. See *Congressional Record*, Proceedings and Debates of the 85th Congress, First Session, Vol. 103, Part I, 347–349.

22. For biographical information, see "Hennings Is Dead; Missouri Senator," *New York Times*, September 14, 1960; on Hennings's participation in the Civil Rights Caucus and as a member of the Senate Democratic Policy Committee, see John Kyle Day, *Southern Manifesto: Massive Resistance and the Fight to Preserve Segregation* (Jackson: University Press of Mississippi, 2014), 38–41. Also see Kemper, *Decade of Fear*.

23. For quote, see Kemper, *Decade of Fear*, 72. For a different view of the impact of the Hennings report, see Thomas C. Reeves, *The Life and Times of Joe McCarthy: A Biography* (New York: Stein & Day, 1982), 411–416.

24. See Michael E. Meagher, "Edward V. Long," in Lawrence O. Christensen,

William E. Foley, Gary R. Kramer, and Kenneth H. Winn, eds. *Dictionary of Missouri Biography* (Columbia: University of Missouri Press, 1999), 498–500.

25. Meagher, "Edward V. Long," 499.

26. Meagher, "Edward V. Long," 499–500.

27. Olson, *Stuart Symington*, 194–231.

28. For the Symington letter and "File it," see Stuart Symington to Harry Truman, March 11, 1952, President's Secretary's Files, Stuart Symington Folder, Harry S. Truman Library. For the first quote, see Harry Truman to Dr. W. L. Brandon, February 11, 1952, and Harry Truman to Dr. W. L. Brandon, May 9, 1952, President's Secretary's Files, Truman Library.

29. Olson, *Stuart Symington*, 244–245.

30. Olson, *Stuart Symington*, 232.

31. Olson, *Stuart Symington*, 248.

32. Olson, *Stuart Symington*, 253–254.

33. Olson, *Stuart Symington*, 276.

34. Harry Truman to Symington, June 14, 1954, in Stuart Symington [1 of 4] Folder, Box 116, Post Presidential Papers, Harry S. Truman Library and Museum.

35. Olson, *Stuart Symington*, 297–304.

36. Olson, *Stuart Symington*, 309–310.

37. Olson, *Stuart Symington*, 323–324.

38. Handwritten speech by Harry S. Truman dated August 15, 1956, in Adlai E. Stevenson [1 of 2] Folder, President's Post Presidential Papers, Box 116, Harry S Truman Library.

39. Quoted in Olson, *Stuart Symington*, 318.

40. Olson, *Stuart Symington*, 326–337.

41. For defense, see Olson, *Stuart Symington*, 326–337; for civil rights votes, see https://www.govtrack.us/congress/votes/85-1957/s105; for agriculture, see Olson, *Stuart Symington*, 338–347.

42. Olson, *Stuart Symington*, 348–360. For quote, see 355.

43. Olson, *Stuart Symington*, 377–391.

44. Olson, *Stuart Symington*, 392–405.

45. Olson, *Stuart Symington*, 416.

46. See James N. Giglio, *Call Me Tom: The Life of Thomas F. Eagleton* (Columbia: University of Missouri Press, 2011) 62–82.

47. Giglio, *Call Me Tom*, 83–93.

48. Giglio, *Call Me Tom*, 105–133.

49. Giglio, *Call Me Tom*, 134–161.

50. Giglio, *Call Me Tom*, 173.

51. Giglio, *Call Me Tom*, 181.

52. For the data on the votes, see https://www.govtrack.us/congress/votes/.

53. For more on liberalism in the 1970s and beyond, see Bruce Schulman and Julian E. Zelizer, eds., *Rightward Bound: Making America Conservative in the 1970s* (Cambridge, MA: Harvard University Press, 2008); Amanda L. Izzo and Benjamin Looker, eds., *Left in the Midwest: St. Louis Progressive Activism in the 1960s and 1970s* (Columbia: University of Missouri Press, 2022); Nicholas F. Jacobs and Sidney M. Milkis, *What Happened to the Vital Center: Presidentialism, Populist Revolt, and the Fracturing of America* (New York: Oxford University Press, 2022).

54. "Democrats Once Controlled Northern Missouri Then Local Politics Went National," St. Louis Public Radio, October 27, 2022, https://news.stlpublicradio.org/government-politics-issues/2022-10-27/democrats-once-controlled-northeast-missouri-then-local-politics-went-national.

55. Jason Hancock, "Five Takeaways from Missouri Election Night 2022," *Missouri Independent*, November 9, 2022, https://missouriindependent.com/2022/11/09/five-takeaways-from-missouri-election-night-2022/; Jason Rosenbaum, Sarah Kellogg, and Rachel Lippmann, "9 Takeaways from Missouri's Election that Produced Wins for Both Parties," St. Louis Public Radio, November 9, 2022, https://news.stlpublicradio.org/government-politics-issues/2022-11-09/9-takeaways-from-missouris-election-that-produced-wins-for-both-parties.

2

Red Power Turned Blue

The Eisenhower Presidency and Democratic Party Ascendancy on Indian Reservations in the Dakotas

SEAN J. FLYNN

An analysis of the 2020 presidential election map reveals that in the Upper Midwest, American Indians remain the most stalwart of Democratic Party loyalists. In the conservative Dakotas, Indian reservations and counties with significant numbers of Indians regularly defy election trends, resulting in election maps that exhibit a few islands of blue surrounded by a sea of Republican red. In 2020, Donald Trump carried North Dakota and South Dakota with 65 percent and 62 percent of the vote, respectively. Yet Joe Biden won in counties where tribal members comprise the majority, and he overachieved in counties where Indians reside in significant numbers. Biden scored lopsided victories in South Dakota's Oglala Lakota County, Todd County (Rosebud Sioux Tribe), and Buffalo County (Crow Creek Sioux Tribe), and in North Dakota's Sioux County (Standing Rock Sioux Tribe) and Rolette County (Turtle Mountain Band of Chippewa). Though Fort Berthold Reservation encompasses parts of six North Dakota counties won by Trump, Biden performed well among voters of the Three Affiliated Tribes. Among all American Indians, Biden defeated Trump by a 60 to 35 percent margin, an outcome that underscores the party preference of most tribal voters.[1]

When they adopted the cause of civil rights in the 1960s, white liberals cemented the relationship between Democrats and American Indians that was evident in the 2020 vote. Yet the migration of American Indian voters to the Democratic Party began in the 1950s, the decade that witnessed the Eisenhower administration's implementation of a "termination" policy that authorized the transferring of services performed by the Bureau of Indian Affairs (BIA) and other federal agencies to states and localities. Reminiscent of pre–New Deal assimilationist measures that were unpopular with the nation's tribes, the termination policy irreparably damaged the Republican Party's reputation among Indian voters in the Upper Midwest. Resistance to the Eisenhower presidency was expressed at the ballot box, where more Indian voters endorsed Democratic candidates. The Kennedy and Johnson administrations secured their advantage by boosting funding for Indian education and health programs. Despite the Nixon administration's repudiation of termination, Republicans, having alienated tribes in the 1950s, watched their political opponents consolidate the Indian vote, an outcome that provides Democrats with advantages in closely contested congressional races in the Dakotas.

Ironically, the unpopular policies associated with Dwight Eisenhower surfaced during the administration of his Democratic predecessor, Harry Truman, a confirmation that termination was once a bipartisan strategy.[2] Convinced that American Indians were competent enough to manage their affairs, Truman officials adopted a "moderate form of termination" to encourage greater Indian involvement in state and local governments.[3] Upon becoming BIA commissioner in 1950, Dillon S. Myer advised that termination measures replace "Indian New Deal" programs that had revived tribal institutions and promoted tribal self-governance.[4] Myer's views dovetailed with those of Cold War nationalists who depicted reservations as breeding grounds for a form of "communism" that delayed Indians' absorption into American society.[5]

The momentum for termination, then, existed before Eisenhower assumed office in 1953. Nonetheless, Eisenhower officials and their allies in Congress instituted an extreme version of termination that replaced the more moderate approach of the Democrats. Measures like House Concurrent Resolution 108 and Public Law 280 came to symbolize, in the minds of American Indians, a callous GOP attitude toward tribes. Though receptive to the candidacy of an esteemed former general who commanded Allied forces in World War II, American Indians quickly discerned that Eisenhower the president did not represent their interests.

In a general sense, Indian affairs in the 1950s embodied "Eisenhowerism," a conservative philosophy rooted in the president's conviction that national harmony was attainable through cooperation between business, government, and interest groups. As applied to Indian affairs, Eisenhowerism envisioned an Indian middle class that valued individual initiative and social mobility.⁶ It found expression in a Republican-controlled Congress where notions of nationalism and limited government shaped policies to integrate tribal peoples into American society.⁷ Eisenhowerism was evident in the composition of the president's cabinet, which included strong-willed corporate leaders committed to enhancing bureaucratic efficiency.⁸ Yet as Eisenhower's biographers and others have documented, policy decisions were made by the president, who, though he might defend federal expenditures for construction projects, wished to minimize spending on reservations by transferring Indian programs to state authorities.⁹

The shift in policy was not welcome in Indian Country, where those who cast votes for Eisenhower regretted their choice. Tribal leaders had sought assurances from GOP lawmakers that an Eisenhower administration would consult with them before formulating Indian policy. Mindful that the Indian vote could be critical to his electoral prospects, candidate Eisenhower had promised to prioritize tribal programs and to "welcome the advice and counsel of Indian leaders in selecting the Indian Commissioner." His statements and his genuine admiration for Indian combat veterans won over Indian voters in the Upper Midwest.¹⁰ In North Dakota, counties with large American Indian populations—Mountrail, Rolette, and Sioux—voted overwhelmingly for Eisenhower.¹¹ A similar outcome occurred in South Dakota, where voters in Buffalo, Charles Mix, Roberts, Shannon, and Todd Counties chose Eisenhower over Adlai Stevenson.¹² Indians displayed confidence in Eisenhower, writes Donald L. Fixico, because they "did not anticipate any repercussions that might occur from his plan to free them of second-class citizenship."¹³

They soon discovered that Eisenhower's plan discouraged tribal sovereignty. Eisenhower's electoral coattails were long, and in their trail the Republicans gained control of Congress and fortified their grip on Indian affairs.¹⁴ GOP terminationists blamed the Indian New Deal for delaying Indian integration and called on states to assume jurisdiction on reservations, subject Indians to state taxes, and deliver K–12 education to Indian students. Persuaded that reservation-confined Indians would never assimilate while walled-off from American life, terminationists looked forward to a day when Indians' relationships to state and local governments would be equivalent to their white neighbors.¹⁵

Republican philosophy took form in House Concurrent Resolution (HCR) 108 and Public Law (PL) 280. HCR 108 targeted tribes in nine states, among them the Turtle Mountain Band of Chippewa in North Dakota, for removal from federal supervision.¹⁶ In the summer of 1953, the Turtle Mountain Chippewa, comprising nearly 40 percent of North Dakota's

Indian population, discovered that federal services to their reservation were to be "terminated" and reservation residents "freed of federal supervision as soon as possible."[17] Yet any hope the BIA had for a smooth Chippewa transition to "independence" was dashed when Turtle Mountain leaders organized opposition to HCR 108. In an overflowing Belcourt School Auditorium on October 19, 1953, BIA officials fielded complaints from dozens of Chippewas who registered their "unanimous objection" to termination. Objections to HCR 108 ranged from concerns about treaty obligations to fears about the loss of reservation health-care services. Several hundred individuals signed petitions protesting the suspension of federal services on the reservation.[18] As one woman pleaded, "We can't make it without the Federal Government, a few of us have made it maybe, but not whole tribes."[19]

In anticipation of congressional hearings on Turtle Mountain termination scheduled for March 1954, the *Minot Daily News* produced a six-part investigative series about the reservation that highlighted the effects of poverty, parental anxieties about education, the political inexperience of the Chippewas, and concerns among reservation residents that the state and Rolette County lacked the resources to address their condition. Underpinning these issues was the Chippewas' bitterness over the Eisenhower administration's failure to obtain their consent before implementing a policy that, from their perspective, threatened their survival.[20]

Events on the reservation reverberated across the state. Patrick Gourneau, chairman of the Turtle Mountain Advisory Committee, and Martin Cross, chairman of the Tribal Business Council of the Three Affiliated Tribes and vice president of the National Congress of American Indians (NCAI), proposed establishing a council of Indian leaders to address threats facing North Dakota tribes.[21] Their proposal was realized in May 1954 with the founding of the North Dakota Council of Indians, an anti-terminationist organization committed to improving conditions among the state's American Indians.[22] Republicans, moreover, misjudged the reaction of North Dakota officials to the assumption of tribal supervision by state and county authorities. Representatives of the Employment Service Office, Indian Affairs Commission, and Public Welfare Board and the commissioners of Rolette County criticized Washington officials for failing to appreciate the financial burden that Turtle Mountain termination would shift to the citizens of North Dakota.[23] Furthermore, the Chippewas benefited from pan-Indian condemnations of Republican policy, the NCAI alleging that termination without tribal consent violated treaty agreements between the United States and Indian tribes.[24]

Hearings on S. 2748, the bill to terminate the Turtle Mountain

Reservation, were held before the Joint Subcommittee on Indian Affairs on March 2–3, 1954. The entirety of the bill was rejected by the North Dakota witnesses who testified. Lamenting the rapid pace of change in federal policy, David P. DeLorme, a Turtle Mountain Band member and doctoral candidate at the University of Texas, cited tribal illiteracy rates, the reservation's dilapidated infrastructure, and the Chippewas' low median income as reasons for his opposition to termination.[25] Leveraging his title as vice president of the NCAI, Martin Cross called on Congress to fulfill its trustee responsibilities to the Chippewas, a people facing termination without their consent. John B. Hart of the North Dakota Indian Affairs Commission opposed terminating the Chippewas because the act was "discriminatory towards the Turtle Mountain band," the only North Dakota Indians selected for termination by federal officials. North Dakota Representative Orin L. Dunlop, calling attention to the inferior soils on the Turtle Mountain reservation, testified that if he were to pursue a profitable farming operation on said lands he would not begin "unless I had at least one-twelfth of the whole reservation."[26]

The testimony had its intended effect. Impressed by a long list of witnesses that included US Senator Milton Young, the subcommittee voted to remove the Turtle Mountain Reservation from the termination list, the witnesses having convinced lawmakers that, rather than eliminate support for the Chippewas, Washington should boost assistance to them.[27] Though racial acculturation was to be a by-product of Eisenhowerism, the selection of the Chippewas as a test case in termination clearly backfired.

The federal government's misjudgment had lasting consequences for North Dakota politics. Convinced that the GOP was insensitive to their welfare, North Dakota Indians switched their allegiance to the Democrats, a shift apparent in the results of the 1956 and 1960 elections. After having defeated Adlai Stevenson in Rolette County by more than 35 percentage points in 1952, Eisenhower lost the county to Stevenson in 1956. Four years later, Vice President Richard Nixon lost badly to John F. Kennedy in Rolette County. The 1956 and 1960 results in Mountrail County favored Stevenson and Kennedy, and in 1960, voters on the Standing Rock Reservation swung their votes to Kennedy and the Democrats.[28] As will be seen shortly, the electoral swing in North Dakota Indian Country that began during the presidency of Dwight Eisenhower became a permanent feature of the political landscape of a state that is otherwise one of the nation's most conservative.

A similar transformation occurred in South Dakota, where no tribes were designated for termination but where a separate feature of Eisenhower policy threatened the state's American Indian population. Signed into law by Eisenhower in 1953, HR 1063—known thereafter as PL 280—authorized state criminal jurisdiction over reservations in five states while providing additional states the option of assuming jurisdiction on tribal lands. The "optional" states included South Dakota, which, by amending its constitution, could expand its jurisdictional reach by dint of PL 280. Generally, PL 280 empowered state and county law enforcement to replace BIA police and substituted state trial courts for federal courts. As a result, write Duane Champagne and Carole Goldberg, "the reach of non-tribal law enforcement and criminal justice on reservations grew longer."[29]

Having not been consulted about PL 280, South Dakota Indians were stunned by its approval. Initially troubled by the absence of a consent provision, Eisenhower had urged Congress to amend the legislation. Nevertheless, he approved PL 280 without the provision. Considering that Congress overrode Eisenhower's vetoes on only two occasions, it is conceivable that had Eisenhower vetoed PL 280, it would have died.[30] But he signed the legislation, because, in his words, "its basic purpose represents still another step in granting equality to all Indians in our nation."[31] This led Oliver La Farge of the Association on American Indian Affairs to conclude that the termination movement did not originate in Congress but in the executive branch, wherein bureaucrats viewed tribal consent protocols as "contrary to the best interests of the Indians." Ironically, a bipartisan effort to honor Eisenhower's request to amend PL 280 failed, providing proof, writes Larry J. Haase, that "a consent amendment simply could not be achieved under the Republican administration."[32] Eisenhowerism, it appears, resisted the influence of Eisenhower himself.

If non-tribal law and order were to reach into Indian reservations, it would be due to the efforts of Congressman E. Y. Berry of South Dakota, chair of the House Indian Affairs Committee in 1953 and 1954 and an architect of Indian policy in the 1950s.[33] Having spent his adult life as an attorney and newspaper publisher on the Standing Rock Reservation, Berry regarded himself as an authority on federal Indian policy, which, he believed, should restore the assimilationist aims pursued in the decades before the 1930s. Furthermore, Berry represented what Steven C. Schulte describes as "a credo of Republican Party faith . . . that state government is a far more efficient governing mechanism than the more distant and less accountable federal bureaucracy." Berry, who desired the uniform application of South Dakota laws to "all citizens regardless of whether they are white or red," challenged state legislators to establish their authority over South Dakota Indian reservations.[34]

The legislature met Berry's challenge, and, in 1957, Governor Joe Foss signed House Bill (HB) 892, empowering South Dakota with "the assumption . . . of all civil and criminal causes of action arising" within Indian Country. Significantly, the bill's Section 5 stipulated that jurisdiction over a tribe would occur only when a majority of tribal voters, through the instrument of a referendum, approved jurisdiction. Hence, reservation voters possessed the power to reject HB 892 and resist Eisenhower's Indian policy. Not surprisingly, in 1958, the Rosebud Sioux, Cheyenne River Sioux, Pine Ridge Sioux, and Standing Rock Sioux registered their opposition to HB 892. The depth of opposition on the Pine Ridge Reservation was especially noteworthy: of the 1,249 votes cast by Oglala Lakota voters, only 154 voters favored state jurisdiction.[35]

Unvanquished, the proponents of PL 280 continued their fight to extend the state's reach into Indian Country. In 1963, Governor Archie Gubbrud signed HB 791, empowering South Dakota to assume criminal and civil jurisdiction on the state's reservations. In response, the tribes pooled their political clout and organized the United Sioux Tribes of South Dakota, which chose the state's referendum instrument to block execution of HB 791. Twenty thousand citizens signed the petition to place the bill before the voters, who, in 1964, rejected HB 791. The 79 percent of South Dakotans who voted against the bill were fearful of increased taxes and disturbed by the state's failure to seek the consent of affected tribes prior to assumption of jurisdiction.[36]

The failure of HB 791 ended GOP efforts to enforce PL 280 in South Dakota. Those efforts, combined with the assimilationist legacy of the Eisenhower presidency, sullied the Republican Party's image among reservation voters. Indian voter registration had been on the rise since the 1950s, and the Democrats, having decided they would not support termination without tribal consent, benefited from the trend.[37] South Dakota Republicans were increasingly confronted with anti-terminationist rhetoric. After attending the 1955 meeting of the NCAI and being exposed to an influential group of tribal officials, veterans, and intellectuals opposed to GOP policies, the Reverend Vine Deloria Sr., a Dakota Sioux and holder of national office in the Episcopal Church, began lobbying members of Congress and church leadership to discontinue termination.[38] In 1957, Helen L. Peterson, an Oglala Lakota and executive director of the NCAI, observed that an increase in Indian voter registration was an expression of Indians' "fuller awareness of their own best interests and the clear and forceful defense of them." Peterson cited high voter turnout on one South Dakota reservation and suggested that "in close races" in North Dakota, "the Indian vote could be—and in some cases has been—a decisive factor." She concluded that on once Republican-friendly reservations in South Dakota, Indians were expressing their disappointment with termination by voting for Democrats.[39] In 1960, Rosebud Sioux president Robert Burnette echoed Peterson's analysis, emphasizing that Indians in South Dakota "were going Democrat."[40]

Election results bolstered Peterson's and Burnette's assessments. In 1952, Eisenhower and Congressman Berry carried Shannon and Todd Counties in Republican-heavy West River South Dakota. In 1956 both men lost in both counties.[41] The Democratic trend continued in 1960, despite a plank in the Republican platform declaring the party's opposition to termination.[42] In South Dakota, Richard Nixon defeated John F. Kennedy by fifty thousand votes, but he lost or broke even in most of the counties in Indian Country. Though Democratic candidate Lyndon Johnson carried South Dakota with 55.6 percent of the vote in 1964, his popularity in Indian Country was far greater. Johnson defeated Barry Goldwater in Roberts County by almost thirty percentage points, in Shannon County by over fifty percentage points, and in Todd County by twenty-four percentage points. Four years later, Vice President Hubert Humphrey, the loser of the popular vote in South Dakota, defeated Nixon in the counties encompassing Indian Country.[43]

The Eisenhower presidency having soured American Indians on the GOP, the Kennedy and Johnson administrations took steps to cement Indian loyalties to the Democrats.[44] President Kennedy took little interest in Indian affairs, but Democratic-sponsored programs like the Public Housing Administration and the Area Redevelopment Administration targeted reservation communities.[45] President Johnson's Great Society and War on Poverty programs were even more popular with American Indians. Especially welcome was the Office of Economic Opportunity, an authority that, by encouraging local control of government funds, became the first federal program to advance the cause of tribal self-determination.[46]

Surprisingly, there was no stronger proponent of self-determination than President Nixon, who in his historic "Special Message to the Congress on Indian Affairs" of July 8, 1970, declared bluntly that "termination is wrong." Nixon urged Congress to "renounce, repudiate and repeal the termination policy" and replace it with appropriations to permit "Indian control of Indian programs."[47] Reflecting on the various examples of tribal self-determination evident from 1970 to 1975, Francis Paul Prucha wrote that "in many ways the years under Nixon and Gerald Ford produced more constructive legislation relating to Indians than any other period in the nation's history."[48]

Yet the reversal in Republican attitudes toward Indian affairs did not reverse the migration of American Indian voters to the Democratic Party.

In the Dakotas, tribes retained their loyalty to the Democrats, who invited Indian activists into their ranks in the 1960s and 1970s, when Indian affairs were transpiring in an emotional political environment characterized by cultural pluralism, minority consciousness, and a "Red Power" movement committed to land restorations and the revival of traditional languages, customs, and institutions.[49] Studies of voting patterns since the 1970s reveal that American Indians continue to lean Democrat. In the Dakotas in the 1980s and 1990s, Indian voters showed "a strong preference" for Democrats, who were remarkably effective in their outreach to reservation residents.[50] In 1992 the Democrats made history by establishing a separate organizing committee for Indians. At their 1996 national convention, the party held a reception for American Indians, and during that year's presidential campaign, the party hired its first outreach worker for reservation communities. A national registration drive in 2004 boosted reservation voter turnout, and four years later, 154 American Indian delegates attended the Democratic National Convention. Bill and Hillary Clinton enjoyed strong support among reservation voters, as did John Kerry and Barack Obama.[51]

The Indian vote has become a critical factor in congressional races in the Dakotas. In the US Senate contest in South Dakota in 2002, voters on the Pine Ridge Reservation provided Democratic incumbent Tim Johnson with the margin of victory over his Republican challenger, Congressman John Thune. In an election decided by 542 votes, it was Johnson's capturing of 92 percent of the Pine Ridge vote that determined the outcome. Two years later, Thune challenged Senator Tom Daschle, who counted on reservation voters to send him back to Washington. But Daschle's clear-cut advantage among the state's American Indian population was not enough to defeat Thune, whose strong showing in eastern South Dakota boosted him to a 4,508-vote victory.[52]

The Indian vote in South Dakota proved decisive in Democratic congressional candidate Stephanie Herseth's narrow special-election victory over Republican Larry Diedrich in June 2004. Herseth benefited from the phenomenal rise in Indian voter turnout in Buffalo, Dewey, Shannon, and Todd Counties, which increased 22.5 percent between 2000 and 2004.[53] Reflecting on the large Indian turnout propelled by a get-out-the-vote campaign, a South Dakota Republican leader concluded that Diedrich would have won the special election "if you take out the Indian reservation."[54] Eight years later, the Indian vote proved decisive in the US Senate race in North Dakota between Democrat Heidi Heitkamp and Rick Berg, the Republican candidate who was expected to win the election. The Democrat eked out a narrow win because of exceptionally high voter turnout in

Sioux County and Rolette County, where over 80 percent of Indian voters cast their ballots for Heitkamp, the candidate most attentive to reservation concerns.[55]

These recent examples of close elections in the Dakotas demonstrate American Indians' loyalty to the Democratic Party, a loyalty forged in the years of the Eisenhower presidency. For, as Stephen Cornell observes, the policy of termination, though auditioned in the rhetoric of Truman officials, "was made explicit in the 1950s" when Republicans "reinforced in most Indian communities a profound suspicion of federal motives."[56] Taking advantage of the realization among American Indians that the party of Big Business wanted out of the Indian Business, the Democrats strengthened their relationship with tribes—an accomplishment that had a significant impact in the Dakotas, where, in the 1950s, the Democratic Party ascended in popularity among Indian peoples. The GOP remains disadvantaged on North Dakota and South Dakota reservations, where, despite the conservative political culture of the two states, Indian voters are the decisive factor in elections involving formidable Democratic challengers.

NOTES

1. South Dakota Secretary of State, "Election History"; American Election Eve Poll 2020, electioneve2020.com/poll/#/en/demographics/native-american/; North Dakota Election Results 2020, politico.com/2020-election/results/north-dakota.

2. Charles F. Wilkinson and Eric R. Biggs, "The Evolution of the Termination Policy," in John R. Wunder, ed., *Constitutionalism and Native Americans, 1903–1968* (New York: Garland, 1996), 198.

3. Francis Paul Prucha, *The Great Father: The United States Government and the American Indians*, vol. 2 (Lincoln: University of Nebraska Press, 1984), 1013–1014, 1028–1029; Donald L. Fixico, *Termination and Relocation: Federal Indian Policy, 1945–1960* (Albuquerque: University of New Mexico Press, 1986), 48, 54–55.

4. Brian W. Dippie, *The Vanishing American: White Attitudes and U.S. Indian Policy* (Lawrence: University Press of Kansas, 1982), 336–337; Sean J. Flynn, *Without Reservation: Benjamin Reifel and American Indian Acculturation* (Pierre: South Dakota Historical Society Press, 2018), 115; Prucha, *The Great Father*, vol. 2, 1030, 1034–1035.

5. Daniel M. Cobb, "Indian Politics in Cold War America: Parallel and Contradiction," *Princeton University Library Chronicle* 67, no. 2 (Winter 2006): 394, 396; Joane Nagel, *American Indian Ethnic Renewal: Red Power and the Resurgence of Identity and Culture* (New York: Oxford University Press, 1996), 214; Larry W. Burt, "Roots of the Native American Urban Experience: Relocation Policy in the 1950s," *American Indian Quarterly* 10, no. 2 (Spring 1986): 86.

6. Kenneth R. Philp, "Stride toward Freedom: The Relocation of Indians to Cities, 1952–1960," *Western Historical Quarterly* 16 (April 1985): 179–180; Donald L. Fixico, *The*

Urban Indian Experience in America (Albuquerque: University of New Mexico Press, 2000), 166.

7. Larry W. Burt, *Tribalism in Crisis: Federal Indian Policy, 1953–1961* (Albuquerque: University of New Mexico Press, 1982), 19–20; Larry J. Hasse, "Termination and Assimilation: Federal Indian Policy, 1943 to 1961" (PhD diss., Washington State University, 1974), 211.

8. Stephen E. Ambrose, *Eisenhower*, vol. 2, *The President* (New York: Simon & Schuster, 1984), 19–20, 23–24, 33–34.

9. Ambrose, *Eisenhower*, vol. 2, 10, 159; Jean Edward Smith, *Eisenhower: In War and Peace* (New York: Random House, 2012), 569; Duane Champagne and Carole Goldberg, *Captured Justice: Native Nations and Public Law 280*, 2nd ed. (Durham, NC: Carolina Academic Press, 2020), 11.

10. Fixico, *Termination and Relocation*, 69–70; Oliver La Farge, "Helping Elect the Great White Father," *The Reporter*, October 28, 1952, 31–33; Burt, *Tribalism in Crisis*, 9–10.

11. North Dakota Secretary of State, "Archived Election Results."

12. South Dakota Secretary of State, "Election History."

13. Fixico, *Termination and Relocation*, 70.

14. Burt, "Roots of the Native American Urban Experience," 88.

15. Flynn, *Without Reservation*, 92–93; Paul C. Rosier, "'They Are Ancestral Homelands': Race, Place, and Politics in Cold War Native America, 1945–1961," *Journal of American History* 92 (March 2006): 1301; Peter d'Errico, "Native Americans in America: A Theoretical and Historical Overview," *Wicazo Sa Review* 14 (Spring 1999): 23; Wilkinson and Biggs, "The Evolution of the Termination Policy," 207–208; Hasse, "Termination and Assimilation," 209.

16. Fixico, *Termination and Relocation*, 97; Burt, *Tribalism in Crisis*, 23.

17. *Turtle Mountain Star* (Rolla, ND), July 23, 1953; "North Dakota Indian Affairs Commission Third Biennial Report," October 1, 1954, Folder 1, Box 1, Series 30605, Archives of the State Historical Society of North Dakota, Bismarck; "A Bill to Provide for the Termination of Federal Supervision over Property of the Turtle Mountain Band of Chippewa Indians" (copy), September 14, 1953, Folder 3, in ibid.

18. *Turtle Mountain Star*, October 15, 1953; October 22, 1953; and November 5, 1953.

19. Nagel, *American Indian Ethnic Renewal*, 216.

20. *Minot* (ND) *Daily News*, February 20, 1954; February 23, 1954; February 24, 1954; February 25, 1954; and February 26, 1954.

21. *Minot Daily News*, February 15,1954; *Turtle Mountain Star*, February 18, 1954.

22. Mary Jane Schneider, *North Dakota's Indian Heritage* (Grand Forks: University of North Dakota Press, 1990), 131; *Turtle Mountain Star*, May 20, 1954.

23. Minutes of the North Dakota Indian Affairs Commission, August 6, 1949, Folder 1, Box 1, Series 30852, Archives of the State Historical Society of North Dakota; Third Biennial Report of the North Dakota Indian Affairs Commission, 10; *Turtle Mountain Star*, February 11, 1954; *Minot Daily News*, February 13, 1954.

24. Hasse, "Termination and Assimilation," 240–241.

25. *Minot Daily News*, March 4, 1954; *Turtle Mountain Star*, December 31, 1953, and January 28, 1954; David P. DeLorme, "A Socio-Economic Study of the Turtle Mountain Band of Chippewa Indians and a Critical Evaluation of Proposals Designed to Terminate Their Federal Wardship Status" (PhD diss., University of Texas, 1955), 144–145, 159; Burt, *Tribalism in Crisis*, 40.

26. *Minot Daily News*, March 4, 1954.

27. *Turtle Mountain Star*, March 4, 1954; Burt, *Tribalism in Crisis*, 40.

28. North Dakota Secretary of State, "Archived Election Results"; Fixico, *Termination and Relocation*, 179.

29. Champagne and Goldberg, *Captured Justice*, 8; Valentina Dimitrova-Grajzl, Peter Grajzl, and A. Joseph Guse, "Jurisdiction, Crime, and Development: The Impact of Public Law 280 in Indian Country," *Law & Society Review* 48 (March 2014): 133; Carole E. Goldberg, "Public Law 280: The Limits of State Jurisdiction over Reservation Indians," in Wunder, *Constitutionalism and Native Americans*, 305.

30. Edward Charles Valandra, *Not Without Our Consent: Lakota Resistance to Termination, 1950–59* (Urbana: University of Illinois Press, 2006), 43.

31. Fixico, *Termination and Relocation*, 111–112.

32. Haase, "Termination and Assimilation," 210, 238, 242–243.

33. Fixico, *Termination and Relocation*, 100–101.

34. Steven C. Schulte, "Removing the Yoke of Government: E. Y. Berry and the Origins of Indian Termination Policy," *South Dakota History* 14 (Spring 1984): 49–55, 58, 64–65.

35. Valandra, *Not Without Our Consent*, 223–228.

36. Valandra, *Not Without Our Consent*, 223; Flynn, *Without Reservation*, 193–194.

37. Haase, "Termination and Assimilation," 244.

38. Philip J. Deloria, "Vine V. Deloria Sr., Dakota," in R. David Edmunds, ed., *The New Warriors: Native American Leaders since 1900* (Lincoln: University of Nebraska Press, 2001), 92–93.

39. Helen L. Peterson, "American Indian Political Participation," *Annals of the American Academy of Political and Social Science* 311 (May 1957): 123–125.

40. *Aberdeen (SD) American-News*, November 1, 1960.

41. South Dakota Secretary of State, "Election History."

42. Ben Reifel to Simeon Rozonowski (copy), October 27, 1960, Folder 5, Box 9, MA 9.6, Benjamin Reifel Papers, University Archives, South Dakota State University, Brookings.

43. South Dakota Secretary of State, "Election History."

44. Nagel, *American Indian Ethnic Renewal*, 216.

45. Thomas Clarkin, *Federal Indian Policy in the Kennedy and Johnson Administrations, 1961–1969* (Albuquerque: University of New Mexico Press, 2001), 77–79.

46. Clarkin, *Federal Indian Policy in the Kennedy and Johnson Administrations*, 106, 124–126, 280; George Pierce Castile, *To Show Heart: Native American Self-Determination and Federal Indian Policy, 1960–1975* (Tucson: University of Arizona Press, 1998), 35.

47. *Public Papers of the Presidents of the United States: Richard Nixon, 1969–1974*, 6 vols. (Washington, DC: Government Printing Office, 1971–1975), 2: 564–576.

48. Prucha, *The Great Father*, 2: 1111–1113.

49. Flynn, *Without Reservation*, 206–209.

50. Paula D. McClain and Joseph Stewart Jr., *"Can We All Get Along?": Racial and Ethnic Minorities in American Politics*, 6th ed. (Boulder, CO: Westview Press, 2014), 99–100; David E. Wilkins and Heidi Kiiwetinepinesiik Stark, *American Indian Politics and the American Political System*, 3rd ed. (Lanham, MD: Rowman & Littlefield, 2011), 179–180.

51. Laughlin McDonald, *American Indians and the Fight for Equal Voting Rights* (Norman: University of Oklahoma Press, 2010), 260–261; Daniel McCool, Susan M. Olson,

and Jennifer L. Robinson, *Native Vote: American Indians, the Voting Rights Act, and the Right to Vote* (New York: Cambridge University Press, 2007), 177–180; Eileen M. Luna, "Mobilizing the Unrepresented: Indian Voting Patterns and the Implications for Tribal Sovereignty," *Wicazo Sa Review* 15 (Spring 2000): 97, 100; McClain and Stewart, *"Can We All Get Along?"* 100; Wilkins and Stark, *American Indian Politics*, 179–180.

52. Jon K. Lauck, *Daschle vs. Thune: Anatomy of a High-Plains Senate Race* (Norman: University of Oklahoma Press, 2007), 31, 185–188; McCool, Olson, and Robinson, *Native Vote*, 179, 182.

53. McDonald, *American Indians and the Fight for Equal Voting Rights*, 258.

54. McCool, Olson, and Robinson, *Native Vote*, 177, 182.

55. McClain and Stewart, *"Can We All Get Along?"* 131.

56. Stephen Cornell, *The Return of the Native: American Indian Political Resurgence* (New York: Oxford University Press, 1988), 160–161.

3

"No Back Seat Drivers"

Women and the Nonpartisan League in North Dakota from Lydia Cady Langer to Heidi Heitkamp

CHARLES MCELWAIN BARBER AND
CATHERINE MCNICOL STOCK

❖ ❖ ❖ ❖ ❖ ❖ ❖ ❖ ❖ ❖ ❖ ❖ ❖ ❖ ❖

North Dakota Senator Heidi Heitkamp won her seat in 2012 by a very slim margin—three thousand votes. The chance that she would hold on to it in 2018 was slimmer still.[1] When she refused to vote to confirm Brett Kavanaugh, President Donald Trump's nominee to the Supreme Court who had been accused of sexual assault, it vanished entirely. Heitkamp knew it. She admitted, "If this were a political decision for me, I certainly would be deciding this the other way."[2] She recognized that many voters in the state either supported the president or held conservative views on gender issues—or both. Approaching the third decade of the twenty-first century, North Dakota stood in forty-second place among the fifty states in its proportion of women in the state house; it belonged to a rapidly shrinking minority of states where a woman had never served as governor; and in the preceding decade lawmakers had added significant restrictions to reproductive care and moved to rescind the 1975 ratification of the ERA.[3] In fact, when Heitkamp voted no on Kavanaugh, choosing to "stand up and fight" for the interests of "girls and young women," she lost the only elected office in the US Congress that a woman from her state had ever won.[4]

A loyal member of the Democratic-Nonpartisan League (D-NPL) in a red state, Heitkamp was by her own admission a political "unicorn."[5]

Yet a view of women on the left in North Dakota politics that peers only through a 2018 prism misses over a century of path-breaking activists whose achievements and frustrations shed light on what many women politicians in the heartland have experienced. North Dakota can rightfully claim the first woman in the United States to win statewide elected office (1893)—Laura Eisenhuth, superintendent of Public Instruction; the first woman in the United States to serve as Speaker of a state house (1933)—Minnie Craig; and the longest-serving member of any state house—Brynhild Haugland (1940 to 1990).[6] North Dakota women set state and national "firsts" after 1945 as well. In 1973 more women served as state legislators in North Dakota than in any other state.[7] Governor George Sinner's administration (1986 to 1992) boasted a trio of remarkable women activists: the nation's first commissioner of agriculture, Sarah Vogel, and the state's first female lieutenant governor, Ruth Meiers. Meiers joined forces with the state's first female tax commissioner—a young attorney just starting out in electoral politics, Heidi Heitkamp.[8]

The remarkable success of women on the left in twentieth-century North Dakota politics is explained by the ideals and commitments of the party they represented: the Nonpartisan League (NPL)—first an independent organization, then a faction of the Republican Party, and finally, in 1954, part of the Democratic-Nonpartisan League (D-NPL).[9] The NPL then as now was devoted to what Lizabeth Cohen and Michael Kazin have called moral capitalism: the insistence "that the economy should benefit the ordinary working person, whether farmer or wage earner, and that governments should institute policies to make that possible—and to resist those that do not."[10] The NPL championed the interests of small farmers against corporate power, creditors, railroads, and other "middle men." From 1915 through the 1930s, leaders founded and preserved a state-owned bank, elevator, and grain mill—all of which stand to this day. To supporters and detractors alike, the NPL program made North Dakota the most radical state in the nation.

Part of the NPL's radicalism lay in its leaders' belief that all members of the farm family—women included—were producers and thus deserved to benefit from their work and participate in public life.[11] As Barbara Handy-Marchello has written, "A woman married to a farmer is also a farmer whether she plants or harvests or not. . . . The instability of wheat farming made women's productive activities on the farm central to the family's survival and success, not peripheral." One early farm woman put it succinctly: the NPL knew that they were "farmers' wives not farmettes." She also reminded her peers that "'we the people' meant men AND WOMEN."[12]

The NPL saw women as essential political producers too. Historian Michael Lansing explains:

> Farm women... became especially crucial. As the backbone of rural communities, women already served as the primary connection across rural neighborhoods. But with the full extension of suffrage, they became direct players in electoral politics. The League's initial focus on agrarian manhood gave way [and] made women full members of the organization and supported the creation of women's NPL clubs [which] farm women... turned into vehicles for citizen education and action.[13]

"Leaguer-ism" was, in short, a "family affair" in pursuit of progressive values. Growing up in a family of nine children in the 1930s, Ruth Meiers recalled that "politics and public affairs were served like bread and butter at our supper table."[14] She credited both parents for her success.

Partnership did not mean the same thing as full equality in the farm home or the NPL, however. In the early decades, NPL leaders understood women to share the experience of their class position but rarely interrogated their experiences as *women* in particular.[15] Though far from a "terrible party," as Kazin characterized the nineteenth-century Democratic Party, the NPL, its voters, and opponents held fast to conventions of gender and patriarchy.[16] While married women were welcomed and put to work, for example, the party found little use for widows or single women.[17] Moreover, politically active women faced what Kim Nielsen calls a unique "paradox": the more they segregated themselves from men through clubs and auxiliaries to tamp down opponents' accusations of radicalism, the more they centered their discussions on women's issues and, in some cases, the more they were inspired to seek leadership positions in electoral politics—only confirming the accusations.[18] It would take the far more encompassing, albeit still controversial, social and cultural changes of second-wave feminism in the 1970s and 1980s—and the D-NPL's willingness to endorse them—for North Dakota women to be seen as individuals rather than as partners. The paradoxical struggle women faced to convince opponents of their commitment to farm and family, however, only increased with time.

Lydia Cady Langer's political career perfectly exemplified the opportunities and obstacles that the ideal of family partnership posed for women in the NPL.[19] Langer was not born and raised in North Dakota; a Washington, DC, reporter wrote in 1940 that she was "as much at home at *The Mayflower* and *Chevy Chase* as she would be at a honyocker hoedown dancing with heavy-footed farmers."[20] But her dedication to NPL ideals and to her husband William "Wild Bill" Langer was unassailable. Langer was among the most controversial politicians of his time. As governor in the early years of the Great Depression, he enacted an embargo on wheat, critiqued New Deal agricultural policy, and called on local people to resist farm foreclosures, saying, "Treat the banker like a chicken thief. Shoot him on sight."[21]

It was not easy to stand by a man who made enemies in his own party, across the aisle, and in the White House. Lydia Langer, four daughters in tow, joined Bill on the campaign trail even when it put them at risk. In 1935 she stood by as anti-League Republicans and the Democrats' US attorney, Powless "Peter" Lanier, charged Governor Langer with defrauding the federal government.[22] On March 6, 1935, O. E. Erickson, chairman of the NPL wing of the Republican Party, wrote to state committeemen to remind them of the threat that this latest assault posed to the Langers. The Democrats, he argued,

> would not have thrown William Langer out if, during his term, he had not fought for and obtained for North Dakota the first Old Age Pension Law we have ever had and also secured for us the moratorium, the embargo and fought for the poor man in general. . . . He is facing the penitentiary and disgrace—his children are mocked in school and his wife and four children are ostracized. Let us show that we know how to fight and that we will fight for a fighter who is fighting for us![23]

Through it all, Lydia Langer stayed calm, even "soft-spoken."[24] She later advised another woman in politics, "You must put on a veneer. Don't let them get under that veneer; don't let them touch you."[25]

Lydia Langer's political career moved from congenial, albeit stalwart, companion to candidate when Governor Langer appealed his conviction on the charges of fraud.[26] She was named the NPL-endorsed candidate for governor in his place. As Congressman Usher Burdick put it, "The candidacy of Mrs. Langer for the governorship meets with the enthusiastic approval of people everywhere. . . . There is no question but what the farm people, and a large percentage of the people in the cities and villages will support her."[27] Unwilling to run a campaign from her kitchen table, Lydia Langer traveled extensively, giving a dozen or more speeches per day. She was committed to continuing the policies of her husband—including the controversial embargo on wheat—but fought for her own priorities too.[28] And she moved quickly to quell rumors that she would be a mere figurehead: "There will be no back seat driving in my administration. . . . I'll take advice, but there'll be no one standing on the side telling me what to do. I promise you that." [29] Burdick suggested that Lydia might actually have more independence than her husband: "She can, and will make her own selection of advisers. . . . She clings tenaciously to the principles which . . . will best serve the greatest number of people in North Dakota during these hectic times."[30]

Given Bill Langer's numerous enemies and the fact that only fourteen years had passed since women had the vote, it is not surprising that Lydia lost the race for governor. Looking back years later, NPL leader Agnes Geelan, the first woman in the state to be elected mayor (Emerlin,1946) and the first woman elected to the state senate (1951), explained the loss and revealed what Lydia Langer had endured. "Considering the attitude at that time toward women in politics, the wonder of it was that Lydia Langer came within 17,000 votes of victory out of a total of 275,000 votes."[31]

When Bill Langer, finally exonerated, was elected to the US Senate in 1940, Lydia returned to her role as political partner—back in the passenger's rather than the driver's seat, but never, ever in the back. She remained unusually engaged in public life—sitting in on Senate floor debates; deflecting criticism and corrosive rumors that her husband was ill or even deceased; entertaining visitors from the state and dignities from abroad; attending ceremonial events with the senator; and campaigning in election cycles, along with her daughters.[32] (Mimi Langer Gokey remembers the 1952 campaign as "fun."[33]) Yet the legacy that Bill and Lydia Langer built together was his alone to enjoy in perpetuity. Upon his death, the Senate entered into the minutes more than 180 pages of eulogies and memorials. His partner in politics was mentioned only a handful of times. Nearly all eulogies referred to the couple's steadfast love, not to Lydia's real political work on his behalf. Only Usher Burdick used more than a single sentence to describe her: "Mrs. Langer was a delightful woman and a real fighter, being a descendant of the patriots of '76. She stood like the Rock of Gibraltar in all these trying experiences. Their daughters, too, were fighters and held their chins up in adversity. They can be proud of their parents, who were united in marriage, in life, and now in death."[34]

Other than Burdick's oblique and minimal mention of Lydia Langer's commitment to the political ideals of the NPL, public acknowledgment of her accomplishments remains rudimentary today.[35]

Some NPL women in the early and mid-twentieth century stepped outside the political partnership model exemplified by Lydia Cady Langer and held elected office in their own right. They encountered even more directly the paradox that politics on the left presented to women: while the ideals of the NPL, learned from members of their families and in women's clubs, had animated their ambitions and public lives, conservative ideas about women as leaders, held by both men and women and on both sides of the aisle, stood in the way of their full participation and diminished—even erased—their legacy.

Minnie Craig was raised on a Maine farm; the oldest surviving child of nine, she knew hard work. After meeting Edward Craig, a North Dakota man visiting the East Coast, she moved to Fargo, supported his work in banking, discovered the ideals of the NPL, and soon was elected as the first president of the NPL women's clubs statewide organization.[36] As a state representative, Minnie Craig dedicated her committee work to defending the Bank of North Dakota and introducing legislation to secure women's legal rights.[37] When her NPL colleagues nominated her to serve as Speaker of the House in 1933, a stunned national media followed the story. One local reporter assuaged them: "[It] was not such a radical step for [the NPL] as it might appear, for they have a tradition of fairness to women."[38] Years later, however, Craig was unconvinced that she had benefited from "fairness" at all. At every turn, she recalled, the "old boys club"—in both parties—made it difficult for a woman to wield power or influence.[39] Leading NPL representatives rarely consulted her on matters of strategy. One signed his name, not hers, on new pieces of legislation. Another rarely showed up to perform his duties at all.[40] In an unpublished autobiography, she concluded, "Male legislators [were] so accustomed to 'running things,' they didn't want my point of view. . . . After all, men don't like to follow a woman. They may appreciate her services, but they are much happier when those services are confined to a secretarial job, to routine work."[41] Craig got little help from press cartoonists depicting her wielding a rolling pin rather than a speaker's gavel, and whose reporters described her personal appearance, praised her cooking and housekeeping skills, and suggested that the secret to her success as Speaker was her "henpecking."[42]

It wasn't only men who looked askance at women in politics, whatever their ideals about partnership. Coming up through the ranks in Mountrail County, Ruth Meiers struggled to convince older farm women to vote for her. She knew how they wielded power in their homes—"one on one" with the men in their family, before or after public meetings, and without looking "pushy."[43] They were wondering, "How can this farm wife presume to think she can [be a legislator]?"[44] To succeed—and just barely—she won her first campaign by 75 votes—she created a strategy based on gender-conforming behaviors: what she called "the three I's—be interested, be informed, be involved."[45] She established her credibility in the most conventional women's role: as a mother of four. Talking about her children connected her with voters. It also reminded them that her children were grown; she knew that voters would have resoundingly rejected a woman candidate who had children at home.[46]

The final decades of the twentieth century brought a new generation of women on the left to power in North Dakota in one of the most important and transformative moments in history for the rural Midwest: the Farm Crisis. Facing the most desperate economic times since the 1930s, women from farms, towns, and cities worked to save family farms and to rejuvenate and reimplement NPL policies and ideals.[47] But this group also benefited from organizations, opportunities, and ideas derived from and embedded in second-wave feminism. Along with protections for farmers, they would sponsor a wave of legislation—more than thirty pieces in the 1970s alone—pinpointed to help women achieve equality in marriage, finance, education, child care, the courts, and health care. Most controversially, despite frequent bipartisan support, they advocated for reproductive choice and the Equal Rights Amendment.[48] Seeing that they could enhance their power by collaborating, legislators launched the D-NPL women's caucus in 1984 and actively promoted women candidates for election or appointment.[49] Even so, these leaders and activists could not avoid the obstacles that women on the left had encountered for decades. With an opportunistic twist, modern conservatives, cloaked in their own rhetorical populism, railed against government regulations, social welfare programs, and cultural change. Suddenly those who righteously purported to work on behalf of the small farmers, North Dakota families, and even North Dakota women increasingly sat across the aisle.

Even though she was born after World War II—graduating from the University of North Dakota in 1967—Sarah Vogel had the richest of political inheritances on the left. Her grandfather, Frank Vogel, had chaired the Bank of North Dakota and been a personal adviser to Bill Langer. She too had politics with her bread and butter over supper. For her, the most important lesson was that the government could do—was morally obligated to do—something to help farmers in crisis.

> As a young girl growing up in a League family, I absorbed the lessons of the 1930s.... I believed that during terrible economic times, foreclosures of farmers were unjust and unfair. I believed that the Farmers' Holiday Association, the masses of angry farmers, and the politicians who stuck up for them like my grandfather Frank Vogel, Langer, and Burdick were on the right side. I believed

that lenders who cracked down on farmers during tough times were on the wrong side.[50]

Sarah Vogel would make her own mark as a defender of small farmers in the 1980s as the lead attorney who brought a class-action lawsuit against the Farmers Home Administration (FmHA) on behalf of the "Dakota 9" in *Coleman v. Block* (1983). She argued that the FmHA did not provide all the information about alternative financing to farmers threatened with foreclosure. The decision in her favor, rendered by US District Court judge Bruce Van Sickle in Bismarck, brought a two-year halt to threatened foreclosures of sixteen thousand farms across the nation and increased rights for borrowers in both public and private lending systems.[51] This victory revealed the increased influence of women attorneys and the ongoing relevance of the values and strategies of the NPL that she had been raised to admire. Pathbreaking politician and Langer biographer Agnes Geelan wrote Vogel's parents, "Wouldn't Bill Langer be proud to know that the grand-daughter of his most trusted advisor and friend is carrying on his fight for people? My admiration for Sarah and my best wishes for you."[52]

Sarah Vogel was not done making history; in 1987 she was the first woman in US history to be elected state commissioner of agriculture. This role also guaranteed a seat on the all-important North Dakota Industrial Commission, where a woman also had never served. How she became a candidate in the first place reveals the transformative influence of the women's movement on her life. While she was interested in running for agriculture commissioner, she knew very little about the primary process, a crucial aspect of D-NPL politics. As months dragged on, other D-NPL candidates emerged: two men who were state senators and who had farming or ranching backgrounds. Just as she was about to quit, "a group of Democratic-NPL women with experience in running campaigns (led by the inestimable Carole Jean Larsen) came to my house one weekend. They said if I would run, they would tell me what to do and would help me."[53] They gave her a crash course in winning over delegates, the press, and the voters. Luci Calauti, a campaign worker in Kent Conrad's 1986 senate run, "gave her the best campaign advice" of all: to hold weekly press conferences to stress the importance of the family farm. When only a single reporter came to one in Fargo, he told her why: "Everyone already knew that I was for family farmers and my opponent was for big business." To the D-NPL candidate, there could be no higher praise.[54]

But Vogel, like so many other women before her, still had to explain how a woman could do the job of agriculture commissioner. She addressed the issue with humor and even a bit of self-deprecation. "I told them it was a desk job, no heavy lifting."⁵⁵ To counter the fact that she was not a farmer or rancher but a New York–educated attorney, she complimented rural voters by saying they "already knew how to farm" and reminded them that her skills as an attorney would help them—had already helped them—more than her ability to grow a crop. One issue, previously disqualifying, she simply tried to solve on her own. As a divorced woman with a young child, she had to find the energy and courage to campaign in the evenings and then drive home hundreds of miles to spend mornings with her son.⁵⁶

While Vogel fought for farmers—all farmers—and benefited from changing ideas about women's leadership and their emerging networks, Heidi Heitkamp increasingly worked directly to protect women's rights, health, and safety. Like so many others on the left, she carried with her a political legacy: her grandmother was a "strong and verbal New Dealer" who inspired Heidi's belief in activist government and her work on consumer protection, including negotiating the enormous settlement made by the states with the tobacco industry.⁵⁷ She provided her own legacy too, having first worked on behalf of the ERA, passed in North Dakota when she was twenty years old. In the new context of the women's liberation movement's tenet that the "personal is political," Heitkamp was also inspired to action by her mother's teenaged sexual assault—a trauma, she learned, that was all-too-common among North Dakota women of all backgrounds, Native women in particular.⁵⁸

In both her 2012 and 2018 senate campaigns, Heitkamp stressed the basics of D-NPL ideology: that rural America was under-resourced and under-valued; that an activist government and trade policies can help save family farms; that universal health care can save rural lives. She said proudly that "she was born in North Dakota, raised in North Dakota, and hope to die in North Dakota. This is the place I understand."⁵⁹ She also felt honored to serve in the body where Quentin Burdick, Kent Conrad, and Bill Langer had served.⁶⁰ Given the rise of conservatism in the state, however, she was also careful to tout her bipartisan work, including on behalf of the energy industry. She even acknowledged having an "important working relationship" with President Trump.⁶¹ Finally, Heitkamp ascribed her success reaching voters in words that echoed Minnie Craig's "three I's": "You try to be nice, to listen, and to respond."⁶²

Rick Berg and Kevin Cramer, however, like so many opponents of the D-NPL before them, painted Heitkamp as a "radical" whose views were not "the North Dakota way." Both tagged her views on women's rights as the most radical of all. In the lead-up to her vote against Kavanaugh, the focus of Cramer's attacks was her support for reproductive rights.[63] In an ad called "Respecting Life," Cramer used close-up shots of his pregnant daughter's belly to excoriate Heitkamp's vote against a twenty-week abortion ban. "Can you even imagine?" Cramer's daughter asked. Implying that a woman couldn't be trusted to protect women, she gave voters a clear alternative: "North Dakota can trust my dad to protect life."[64] Cramer also portrayed Heitkamp as "anti-woman" overall. In a controversy over his wife, Kris, being paid for her work on his campaign, Cramer not only called Heitkamp "anti-woman" but donned the mantle of the "political partnership," which had long been the hallmark of NPL women's public work. In an op-ed, Kris Cramer wrote, "Let me be clear: for Senator Heitkamp to attack my work as Kevin's campaign manager is an affront to all professional women, especially those working side-by-side with their spouses in the thousands of small businesses and family farms across our state."[65]

Heidi Heitkamp's victory in 2012 was a milestone for the D-NPL and for the women of North Dakota, reflecting generations of "firsts" by women activists scarcely remembered. Her slim margin of victory in 2012 and her defeat in 2018, however, revealed both the increasing precarity of the Left in the rural Midwest and the success of the modern conservative movement's attack on New Deal liberalism, activist government, and the cultural changes of second-wave feminism and other liberation movements.[66] Perhaps most unnerving has been the revisionist political history that conservatives have dished out in their attempts to rewrite what North Dakotans—North Dakota women in particular—experienced and achieved in the past. In attacking Heitkamp's vote against Kavanaugh, Cramer explained that North Dakota women like his wife and mother hadn't experienced sexual harassment or assault because "they are pioneers of the prairie. These are tough people whose grandparents were tough and great-grandparents were tough." Like so many others, Cramer has conveniently forgotten the tough women on the left whose lives and experiences—and the support they gained from the NPL—led the way for others, including conservative women, to rise to power—no matter what they had faced.[67]

"Ray and Doreen Heitkamp didn't raise me to vote a certain way so that I could win, they raised me to vote the right way," she said.[68] For her, North Dakota politics on the left were still a family affair.

NOTES

1. Josh Voorhees, "Heidi Heitkamp Never Really Had a Chance in North Dakota," *Slate*, November 6, 2018, https://slate.com/news-and-politics/2018/11/heidi-heitkamp-north-dakota-senate-race-midterm-elections.html.

2. Madison Pauly, "Heidi Heitkamp Just Lost Her North Dakota Senate Seat to Conservative Kevin Cramer," *Rolling Stone*, November 11, 2018, https://www.motherjones.com/politics/2018/11/democrat-heidi-heitkamp-just-lost-her-north-dakota-senate-seat-to-conservative-kevin-cramer/.

3. Heitkamp lost the 2000 gubernatorial race to John Hoeven, campaigning even after her diagnosis and treatment for breast cancer. For gender in state legislatures, see https://cawp.rutgers.edu/facts/state-state-information; for the abortion debate, see https://reproductiverights.org/maps/abortion-laws-by-state/?state=ND, and Faye Ginsberg, *Contested Lives: The Abortion Debate in an American Community* (Berkeley: University of California Press, 1998). On the final ERA vote, see Adam Willis, "North Dakota Passes Rollback of 1975 ERA Ratification," *Dickinson Press*, March 19, 2021, 1.

4. Elana Schor, "Heitkamp to Vote No on Kavanaugh," *Politico*, October 4, 2018, https://www.politico.com/story/2018/10/04/heitkamp-vote-no-kavanaugh-869443.

5. Alexi McCammond, "Republicans Worry about Trump-Heitkamp Alliance," *Axios*, May 30, 2018, https://www.axios.com/2018/05/30/heidi-heitkamps-relationship-with-trump-north-dakota.

6. Kjuersten Nelson, "Forward," in Susan E. Wefald, *Important Voices: North Dakota Women Elected State Officials Share Their Stories, 1893–2013* (Fargo, ND: Institute for Regional Studies, 2014), v.

7. Ann M. Rathke, *Lady, If You Go into Politics: North Dakota's Women Legislators, 1923–1989* (Bismarck, ND: Sweetgrass Communications, 1992), 81.

8. D-NPL women have also made important marks in the twenty-first century. The nation's youngest-ever state party chair, Kylie Oversen, was elected by the D-NPL in March 2015.

9. The first anti-League Republican elected in the state was Emma Bates, elected superintendent of public instruction in 1895. A higher percentage of women in North Dakota have represented parties or factions on the left than the right. This is particularly striking today. In the 2021 legislature, 64 percent of elected D-NPL representative were women (9 of 14) while 16 percent of elected GOP representatives were women (13 of 80). https://en.wikipedia.org/wiki/North_Dakota_House_of_Representatives#Members_of_the_67th_House.

10. Michael Kazin, *What It Took to Win: A History of the Democratic Party* (New York: Putnam, 2021), ix.

11. Barbara Handy-Marchello, *Women of the Northern Plains: Gender and Settlement on the Homestead Frontier, 1870–1930* (St. Paul: Minnesota Historical Society Press, 2005), 6–7. Jenny Barker Devine demonstrates that Iowa farm women followed a similar path toward activism and faced similar challenges as North Dakota farm women. The strength of the NPL in North Dakota, however, may have lifted some North Dakota women to public positions that Iowa women were denied. See Jenny Barker Devine, *On Behalf of the Family Farm: Iowa Farm Women's Activism since 1945* (Iowa City: University of Iowa Press, 2013), 2–14, 137–143.

12. As quoted in Maren Claus, "Minnie D. Craig: Gender and Politics in North Dakota," *North Dakota History* 62, nos. 2 and 3 (Fall 1996): 32–33.

13. Michael Lansing, *Insurgent Democracy: The Nonpartisan League in North American Politics* (Chicago: University of Chicago Press, 2015), 140.

14. Susan E. Wefald, "A Lively Interest in Politics: Ruth Lenore Meiers," in Wefald, *Important Voices*, 304.

15. Historians agree that to the leaders of labor and agrarian movements in the nineteenth and early twentieth centuries, class struggle was a more salient category of social analysis than gender or race. Lizabeth Cohen, *Making a New Deal: Industrial Workers in Chicago, 1919–1939* (New York: Cambridge University Press, 1990); Lansing, *Insurgent Democracy*. This diminution of gender analysis in leftist organizations continued into the 1970s. See Sara Evans, *Personal Politics: The Roots of Women's Liberation in the Civil Right Movement* (New York: Random House, 1979).

16. Kazin, *What It Took to Win*, x.

17. Kim E. Nielsen, "'We Are All Leaguers by Our House': Women, Suffrage, and Red-Baiting in the National Nonpartisan League," *Journal of Women's History* 6, no. 1 (Spring 1994): 32.

18. Nielsen, "'We Are All Leaguers by Our House.'"

19. Most reporters referred to Lydia Cady Langer as Mrs. Langer. Because this chapter aims to disrupt the ideal of partnership while avoiding confusion with Governor Langer, it refers to Mrs. Langer as Lydia. No disrespect is intended.

20. Louis H. Cook, "They Didn't Bury Him on the Lone Prai-ree," *Saturday Evening Post*, June 7, 1941, 29, 108. Honyocker was a pejorative expression used to describe immigrant farmers from Eastern Europe.

21. Catherine McNicol Stock, *Main Street in Crisis: The Old Middle Class on the Northern Plains in the Great Depression* (Chapel Hill: University of North Carolina Press, 1992), 139–142.

22. On Langer's three trials, see Robert Vogel, *Unequal Contest: Bill Langer and His Political Enemies* (Mandan, ND: Crain Grosinger, 2004), chaps. 2–6.

23. O. E. Erickson to State Committeemen, July 20, 1935, Box 1, John Mikklethun Papers, Minnesota Historical Society, St. Paul.

24. "Lydia Langer: The Unexpected Candidate Amid 1930s Political Scandal and Intrigue," *Writin' for the Brand: Tales of the Ranch*, October 27, 2016, https://writinforthebrand.com/lydia-langer-unexpected-candidate-amid-1930s-political-scandal-intrigue/.

25. Agnes Geelan, *The Dakota Maverick: The Political Life of William Langer Also Known as "Wild Bill" Langer* (Fargo, ND: Kaye's Printing Co., 1975), 70.

26. Vogel, *Unequal Contest*, 36.

27. *Farmer-Labor Defender and the Dunn County Journal* (Dunn Center, ND: Defense Council of the North Dakota Holiday Association, August 29, 1934).

28. Lydia Langer had a lifelong commitment, like many other NPL women, to creating equitable access to education for women. On early women legislators' record of activism, see Rathke, *Lady, If You Go into Politics*, chap. 1.

29. "Lydia Langer," *Writin' for the Brand*.

30. *Farmer-Labor Defender and the Dunn County Journal*, August 29, 1934, 4.

31. Geelan, *The Dakota Maverick*, 76.

32. In an undated handwritten letter from early 1941, Lydia Langer reassured Ethel

Mills, former private secretary to Governor Langer, that "Bill is perfectly well! I can't imagine how such a story ever got started! For he is in his seat in the Senate every day!" She also comments on how interesting she finds the debate over the Lend-Lease Act. Betty Mills Papers, Mandan, North Dakota. Possession of Barber. These papers also include a 1946 photograph of Senator and Mrs. Langer at the launching of the USS *Sampan Hitch* on July 12 in Superior, Wisconsin.

33. Personal conversation with Mimi Langer Gokey, Charles Barber, West Fargo, North Dakota, May 7 and June 25, 2017.

34. Usher Burdick, "Memorial Services in Eulogy of William Langer, Late a Senator from North Dakota," Eighty-Sixth Congress, Second Session (Washington, DC: Government Printing Office, 1960), 180.

35. Claus provides an insightful compilation of the erasure of Minnie Craig from the scholarly and public history records. In one example, a steamboat is mentioned as a "North Dakota woman," but Craig is not. Maren Claus, "Minnie Craig," 29n2. Even as basic a record as Lydia Cady Langer's obituary is difficult to find. A recent effort by author Barber to understand the Langers' political partnership is Charles Barber, "No Back Seat Driver," a musical produced and performed in Bismarck and West Fargo in summer 2017. "North Dakota History Comes to Life in New Musical," *High Plains Reader*, June 18, 2017, https://hpr1.com/index.php/arts-entertainment/theatre/north-dakota-history-comes-to-life-in-new-musical/. Jocelyn Burdick, who was appointed to her husband's US Senate seat, barely appears in Quentin Burdick's biography. Dan Rylance, *Quentin Burdick: The Gentle Warrior* (Fargo, ND: Institute for Regional Studies, 2007). On the larger phenomenon of women's work and legacies being subsumed into their husbands', see Ann Oakley, *Forgotten Wives; How Women Get Written out of History* (Bristol, UK: Bristol University Press, 2021).

36. The best—indeed the only—full scholarly treatment of Craig is Claus, "Minnie Craig."

37. Rathke, *Lady, If You Go into Politics*, 42, 46, 50.

38. Rathke, *Lady, If You Go into Politics*, 52.

39. Rathke, *Lady, If You Go into Politics*, 56.

40. Rathke, *Lady, If You Go into Politics*, 56.

41. Rathke, *Lady, If You Go into Politics*, 56.

42. Claus, "Minnie Craig," 34. On her "henpecking," see Merry Helm, "Minnie Craig," *Dakota Datebook*, April 25, 2022, Prairie Public Broadcasting, https://news.prairiepublic.org/show/dakota-datebook-archive/2022-04-25/minnie-craig.

43. Wefald, "A Lively Interest in Politics: Ruth Lenore Meiers," 307.

44. Wefald, "A Lively Interest in Politics: Ruth Lenore Meiers," 307.

45. Wefald, "A Lively Interest in Politics: Ruth Lenore Meiers," 307.

46. Claus, "Minnie Craig," 33.

47. On the activism of farm women in the 1980s, see Cory Haala's chapter in this volume.

48. Rathke, *Lady, If You Go into Politics*, 60–61.

49. "Electoral Success Encourages Efforts of Women's Caucus," *Bismarck Tribune*, November 27, 1984, 17. The success of the D-NPL women's caucus (said to be "charging fast and hard") prompted Republican women to start their own caucus four years later. Stan Stetler, "GOP Women Seek Even Greater Role," *Bismarck Tribune*, April 16, 1988, 4B.

50. Sarah Vogel, *The Farmer's Lawyer: The North Dakota Nine and the Fight to Save the Family Farm* (NY: Bloomsbury, 2021), 17. See also Wefald, *Important Voices*, 65, 88.

51. Curt Stofferahn, "Farm Advocate Elected Ag Commissioner," *North American Farmer*, December 1988, 4.

52. Vogel, *Farmer's Lawyer*, 301

53. Sarah Vogel, "Advocate for Agriculture," in Wefald, *Important Voices*, 68.

54. Vogel, "Advocate for Agriculture," 70–71.

55. Vogel, "Advocate for Agriculture," 69.

56. Vogel, "Advocate for Agriculture," 70–71.

57. Mary Kathryn "Heidi" Heitkamp, "Standing up for Every North Dakotan," in Wefald, *Important Voices*, 5.

58. This concept originally appeared in an essay by Carol Hanisch in 1969, available at https://webhome.cs.uvic.ca/~mserra/AttachedFiles/PersonalPolitical.pdf. On both Heitkamp's mother's impact and her experience in the attorney general's office, see Jonathan Martin, "#Metoo Is a Movement towards 'Victimization': GOP Candidate Says," *New York Times*, October 8, 2018, https://www.nytimes.com/2018/10/08/us/politics/heidi-heitkamp-kevin-cramer-metoo.html. The murder of Savanna Fontaine-Greywind inspired Heitkamp to sponsor an amendment to the Violence against Women Act. "Savanna's Act Passes US Senate," *High Plains Reader*, December 7, 2018, https://hpr1.com/index.php/feature/news/savannas-act-passes-us-senate.

59. Heidi Heitkamp, "Farewell Speech," December 28, 2018, https://twitter.com/SenatorHeitkamp; "Heidi: Human-to-Human Connections that Change the World," *High Plains Reader*, January 31, 2018, https://hpr1.com/index.php/feature/news/heidi-human-to-human-connections-that-change-the-world.

60. Heidi Heitkamp, podcast, *One Country: Hot Dish*, episode 17, "Chat with Former Senator Kent Conrad," December 14, 2018, 21:00, https://anchor.fm/thehotdish/episodes/Episode-17-Chat-with-Former-North-Dakota-Senator-Kent-Conrad-e2p2bb.

61. Trump called Heitkamp "a good person," creating anxiety in the Cramer camp. Alex Isenstadt and Burgess Everett, "GOP Sweats Trump's Heitkamp Flirtation," *Politico*, May 30, 2018, https://www.politico.com/story/2018/05/30/trump-heitkamp-democrats-midterms-dakota-611563.

62. Heitkamp, podcast, *One Country*, episode 17, 11:50. In 2012 she said she believed that "if someone is mad at me, I stand with them for 20 minutes, and they can't stay mad." Gail Collins, "Land of the Mega-Voter," *New York Times*, July 28, 2012, https://www.nytimes.com/2012/07/28/opinion/collins-land-of-the-mega-voters.html.

63. Heitkamp did not support public funding for abortion or the right to a third-trimester abortion. See "Heidi Heitkamp on Abortion," *On the Issues*, October 9, 2018, https://www.ontheissues.org/social/Heidi_Heitkamp_Abortion.htm.

64. "Respecting Life," https://vimeo.com/288068042. In 2012, Berg announced his support for criminal penalties for abortion providers and no exceptions for abortion except to save the life of the mother. Steve Benen, "Rick Berg Tackles Abortion, Rape Victims," *NBC News*, October 15, 2012, https://www.nbcnews.com/news/world/rick-berg-tackles-abortion-rape-victims-flna1c6475884.

65. Kris Cramer, "Heidi Heitkamp Has Hit a New Low," *Say Anything Blog*, October 2, 2018, https://www.sayanythingblog.com/entry/kris-cramer-heidi-heitkamp-has-hit-a-new-low/.

66. The reasons for the success of new conservatism in the rural Midwest are beyond the scope of this chapter. For an overview of the region's history of postwar conservatism, see Jon K. Lauck and Catherine McNicol Stock, *Conservative Heartland: Political Histories of the Postwar Middle West* (Lawrence: University of Kansas Press, 2020).

67. Martin, "#Metoo Is a Movement towards 'Victimization.'"

68. Martin, "#Metoo Is a Movement towards 'Victimization.'"

4

Green as a Shade of Blue

Political Rhetoric, the Democratic Party, and the Early Environmental Movement in the Upper Midwest

CAMDEN BURD

In 1963, Gaylord Nelson arrived in Washington, DC, with a goal to make environmental concerns a cornerstone of the Democratic Party. The young senator had made environmental legislation a key feature of his political career in Wisconsin and intended to turn his local successes into national ones. So when President John F. Kennedy prepared to embark on a nationwide conservation tour in 1963, Nelson urged him to emphasize the environmental issues that faced the nation. He believed the president needed to "make a nation-wide appeal for the preservation of our vital resources," because as Nelson saw it, this was "America's last chance." He urged Kennedy to stress the need to protect waterways, conserve resources, and legislate against hazardous pollutions that affected wildlife and human health. The Wisconsin senator considered these issues both incredibly important and politically popular. "Americans in all walks of life are interested in natural resources," he wrote to the president. "It cuts across political party lines, economic classes and geographical barriers." "This is a political issue to be settled at the political level." The Midwestern politician's message to the president was simple: it was time for the Democratic Party to embrace the modern environmental movement.[1]

Nelson's insistence to the president signaled the rising concern for environmental issues in the early 1960s. The modern environmental movement developed slowly during the 1940s and 1950s, a period of postwar industrialization and economic development that dramatically changed the American landscape. The effects of suburban sprawl and unprecedented material consumption inspired a wave of disparate communities to advocate for the creation of suburban and urban parks, the regulation of pollution, the preservation of particular landscapes, and increased conservation practices. The publication of Rachel Carson's *Silent Spring* in 1962 served as a catalyzing force for the movement as it brought attention to the harmful effects of pesticides, in particular dichlorodiphenyltrichloroethane (DDT), on larger ecological systems. Removing the veneer of scientific jargon from her text, Carson presented a clear moral argument against the indiscriminate use of DDT, which had boomed in post-WWII America. The book resonated with Americans, and onlookers began to question the use of a variety of chemicals—not just DDT. The threat appeared to be everywhere. Exhaust from cars and power plants, oil spills, laundry detergents, hazardous working environments—the hallmarks of industrial society—all represented a potential threat to human health and cherished landscapes. By the mid-1960s, environmental concerns began to shape national politics.[2]

Though environmentalism was a national movement, its presence was especially pronounced in the Upper Midwest—a region defined by large industrial centers, sprawling suburban communities, and vast agricultural landscapes. The visible and chemical evidence of the postwar economic boom were evident in the exhaustive iron mines of the Upper Midwest, the polluted waters of the St. Clair River near Detroit, the burning waters of the Cuyahoga River in 1969, the collapsing of the Great Lakes fisheries, agricultural pollution, algae blooms throughout the Great Lakes, and the toxic contamination of dairy cows with polybrominated biphenyls (PBB). In the decades after World War II residents of the Midwest witnessed or directly experienced some of the harshest realities of environmental pollution. Though concern for the environment was wide-ranging, citizens who took up environmental causes did so for a variety of reasons. The political energies that grew from the postwar era were diverse and loosely aligned. The environmental movement brought together a coalition of activists including housewives, conservationists, students, labor unions, civil rights advocates, and intellectuals. Politicians from both parties tried to respond to, and channel, those energies. Though the early environmental movement was largely bipartisan, the ways in which members of either party framed their environmental rhetoric varied. Across the region, Democrats framed their environmental agenda in familiar terms that often fit into preexisting political ideologies that grew from the New Deal era. As a result, Democrats in the Upper Midwest argued for environmental legislation in a language that demonstrated a distrust of industrial power, a concern for American workers, a strong commitment to the notion of a public commons, and the need for a strong government to ensure the movement's success.[3]

Though the modern environmental movement developed over the course of the 1960s, concerns about the natural world had been central to the Democratic Party since the New Deal. The massive economic program contained several components that explicitly focused on the environment, including the Civilian Conservation Corps, the Tennessee Valley Authority, and the Soil Conservation Service. New Dealers saw a direct connection between economic scarcity and environmental degradation. By building dams, planting forests, and restoring exhausted soil, New Deal Democrats harnessed the power of the government to raise incomes and conserve resources. Economic stability, social uplift, and environmental conservation were all connected under the banner of New Deal liberalism. So, when Democrats encountered 1960s environmentalism, they channeled a language and political vision that had been established during preceding decades.[4]

Conservation rhetoric was hardly new to Midwesterners when the New Dealers' political descendants began discussing the environmental harm of the postwar period. The region has long been home to prominent conservationists interested in exploring the connection between humans and the natural world. Writers such as Aldo Leopold and the lesser-known Paul Lester Herrington brought ecological writing and Midwest landscapes to mainstream audiences. Leopold's *Sand County Almanac* (1949), published shortly after his death, and Herrington's *Of Men and Marshes* (1957) challenged readers to question their own relationship with the natural world by arguing for a land ethic that placed humans within ecological settings.[5] Their writings spoke to a particular moment when audiences found themselves in a whirlwind of economic development, unprecedented consumption, and the resulting environmental change of those factors. Channeling those sentiments, regional politicians spoke a language that was cultivated from and directed toward the Midwest.

Take, for instance, the political rhetoric of Adlai E. Stevenson, who regularly spoke on industrial greed, corporate overreach, the destruction of the commons, and a concern for the health and financial security of American workers. In speeches while governor of Illinois, from 1949 to 1953, Stevenson supported the conservationist principles established during the New Deal, including a call "to cooperate with the Federal Government in control of floods and erosion" as a means to protect the livelihood of Illinois farmers. Such rhetoric is unsurprising for a politician whose career began working as a lawyer for the Agricultural Adjustment Administration during the early years of FDR's administration. As a New Dealer, Stevenson maintained a healthy skepticism toward industry's role in society, arguing that "the plain, hard fact is that the industrial age has created problems of health, housing, education, transportation and employment." As such, he believed it was the role of government to improve the material well-being of the nation's citizens, articulating a connection between economic and environmental health. This sentiment was clear in his 1956 presidential nomination speech. "With leadership, Democratic leadership, we can conserve our resources of land and forest and water. We can develop them for the benefit of all of our citizens."[6] The speeches, though not specifically focused on the environment, demonstrate a political ideology that could embrace a movement giving preference to workers' and farmers' economic and physical well-being.[7]

Stevenson's tone more closely aligned with that of the environmental movement in the later years of his political career. By 1960, while seeking a third bid for the Democratic Party's nomination for president, Stevenson again harnessed language that would later be echoed more forcefully by environmental advocates. He stressed the common good as well as public spaces and resources while criticizing the unprecedented consumerism that had come to define the postwar period. "This year we will be making a choice between two approaches," he argued in the early days of his campaign. "We shall have to decide whether to go on putting private consumption first or shift the priority to our public needs." Stevenson even targeted what would eventually be a key issue of the early environmental movement—phosphate-rich detergents. "We can no longer pretend that the challenge of the twentieth century can be met with better detergents and more toothpaste—with private opulence and public squalor. It can only be met with better education and more attention to our public needs." It is important not to overstate Stevenson's environmental agenda. During his brief 1960 campaign Stevenson did not articulate harsh regulations on pollution or strict environmental legislation. However, it is clear that he was familiar with the rising social and political tensions that would foment into a larger environmental movement just a few years later.[8]

In Michigan, Senator Philip Hart won his 1958 election with a platform that focused on a range of social and economic platforms: establishing a more active integration plan for desegregated schools, securing protections for organized labor, expanding social security to cover hospitalization, increasing federal medical aid, and providing greater assistance for lower-income and disabled Americans. It was not until he served on the Senate Select Committee on National Water Resources that he began to take a more proactive stance on environmental issues. In speeches and meetings Hart advocated for more efficient management of water resources and an increase in federal planning and conservation of resources. The senator saw these issues to be of particular importance "in Michigan, as in most of the Middle West," where "industrial waste and municipal sewage, resulting from our heavily populated and highly industrialized communities, have reached a stage where they are a real threat to our use of water." At a 1960 interstate conference on water resources held in Chicago, Hart argued that the "United States is shockingly in arrears in the prudent management of its water resources." He expressed concern about wasteful practices, lack of sewage treatment, industrial dumping, and a decline in recreational opportunities. For Hart, water touched all aspects of society. Proper water-resource management, he argued, "critically affects national security, public health, interstate commerce, and opportunities for full employment and economic prosperity."[9]

The Michigan senator made sure to note that water pollution was a local problem with national consequences. After all, lakes, rivers, and streams do not concern themselves with political boundaries. For this reason, Hart embraced a federal approach to water management. "Sewage poured into a stream travels down that stream and has no conscious awareness of where the township or city or state boundary begins or ends," he outlined to constituents as the Senate debated the Federal Water Pollution Control Act Amendments of 1961. "No township is an island unto itself in this matter of water pollution." The bill, eventually signed into law, provided the federal government more power to coordinate and oversee water treatment plant construction across the country.[10]

In addition to his early work on water pollution, Hart became a loud advocate for the protection of land for public use. In 1961 he proposed legislation to create two National Recreation Areas: spaces that would eventually become the Sleeping Bear Dunes National Lakeshore and the Pictured Rocks National Lakeshore. His arguments expressed a concern for a rapidly industrializing society as well as a need to preserve natural spaces for the larger public. "There is handwriting on the wall for all to see who will but open their eyes," he noted while introducing the bills. Due to foreseeable increases in the American population, Hart argued, "more people will have more leisure and more money to spend than has been available for previous generations." While Hart envisioned this future as sign of the economic progress of the region, it was still concerning. "Simultaneous with this greater demand will be—and indeed already there has been—a rapid and permanent destruction of our remaining outdoor recreation sites through private development and acquisition for industrial purposes." Hart argued for the preservation of these spaces so that every American had access to a "vanishing shoreline." In the face of privatization and industrialization, Hart's proposal stemmed from an ideological commitment to protecting a recreational and environmental commons for public use.[11]

Perhaps no Midwestern politician embodied the environmental movement quite like Wisconsin Democrat Gaylord Nelson. Prior to his arrival on the national political scene, he made conservation a central component of his governorship. In Wisconsin, market-oriented politicians hoped to end a program where state funds supported county governments that placed forests into a broader system of conservation management. Opponents of the program wanted county governments to manage their own forests and sell the land for private development. If successful, their proposal would have placed nearly two million acres of public land onto the marketplace. In 1961, Nelson vetoed the bill and spent the remaining two years of his term strengthening the original program by passing legislation making the county system permanent. Nelson learned that conservation and environmental legislation could be a winning political issue on the local level.[12]

Though many national Democrats were slow to adopt environmentalism as a political priority, Nelson continued to make it a cornerstone of his legislative agenda. In his very first year in the Senate, Nelson began to craft legislation that would require that detergents be made with biodegradable products after it was discovered that phosphate-rich detergents were contaminating water and causing algae blooms. He continued his fight against harmful chemicals by taking direct aim at DDT. In 1966 he introduced legislation that banned the sale of the chemical. After a long legal battle with manufacturers, Nelson's political movement proved successful when a federal appeals court finally banned the use of the chemical in 1973. He also supported the creation of the Apostle Islands National Lakeshore on the northern tip of Wisconsin, arguing that iconic landscapes belong to all Americans, especially those caught in the "cradle of problems called the industrial Midwest." In the midst of blight, pollution, and landscapes scarred by industrialization, Nelson saw the Apostle Islands National Lakeshore as public commons fit to meet the unique needs of the Midwesterner. "This area must be saved for them and their children and their children's children."[13]

In 1969, Nelson began to envision a broader grassroots movement around issues of environmentalism. Inspired by the 1969 oil spill near Santa Barbara, California, he hoped to combine the style of antiwar teach-ins with the political imperatives of environmentalism. By April

1970, Nelson had established an office, staff, and bipartisan collaboration to sponsor and support more than ten thousand Earth Day events across the country. During appearances at rallies, he spoke to audiences with a rhetoric that blended antiwar sentiments, Great Society promises, and a criticism of citizens and industries that openly polluted the commons. "Our goal is not just an environment of clean air and water and scenic beauty," he argued while giving a speech in Ann Arbor, Michigan. "Our goal is an environment of decency, quality, and mutual respect for all other human beings and all other living creatures—an environment without ugliness, without ghettoes, without discrimination, without hunger, poverty or war." The task was large and would require "a long, sustained, political, moral, ethical, and financial commitment far beyond any effort ever made." But he was optimistic. With such a large signal of support, Nelson hoped that the popularity of his environmental message might encourage deeper societal change.[14]

The rhetoric used by Midwestern Democrats was not lost on those voters who had traditionally supported the party. One example was the support that Hart and Nelson received from labor unions. Flyers and pamphlets produced by the United Auto Workers (UAW) regularly called for environmental action over the course of the 1960s and early 1970s. The UAW had been a proponent for environmental issues since the mid-1950s and even established a Department of Conservation and Resource Development in 1966. Organized and run by Olga Madar, the department rallied support around environmental issues that directly touched the lives and communities of industrial workers. One 1970 flyer blended a concern for the environment with a traditional pro-worker position. "The G.M. worker must be assured that the environment in which he works is as free of hazards to life and limb," it read. "Moreover, he has a right to expect—and insist—that the environment of the community is kept healthful and pleasant to the extent that the company he works for can help make it so." The pamphlet called for strict federal guidelines for water and air pollution, civilian action groups, and an active campaign of letter-writing to politicians. The pamphlet also made sure to celebrate the Midwestern politicians who championed this environmental ethic, including Nelson and Hart. As the UAW leadership saw it, environmental and labor concerns were two sides of the same coin.[15]

As the 1960s progressed, many Democrats attached environmental rhetoric to the larger Great Society programs. "I want to talk to you about the Great Society," Hubert Humphrey proclaimed in one 1965 speech. "You know here the pressing need of our cities and of the need for better mass transit. You know the problems of the elder citizen who needs housing, medical care, hospitals, and you know the problem that can least of all be postponed: the need for better educational facilities and better teaching." Included in a long list of legislative priorities, Humphrey emphasized "how important it is that we maintain our heritage of natural beauty." Environmental issues, Humphrey argued, were one component of a larger political project to improve the lives of all Americans—particularly those at the bottom of the economic spectrum.[16]

By 1970, after Humphrey failed to win the 1968 election, his environmental rhetoric had become more pointed. At a symposium in Cloquet, Minnesota, Humphrey laid out an ambitious agenda. He hoped to declare "the decade of the 1970's as the decade of people, environment and peace [PEP]," believing, "they're all tied together." This was to be the "PEP decade"—a period "set aside to concentrate on the battle of physical pollution and the environment . . . and dedicated to peace." At the international level, Humphrey called for the creation of a United Nations Board of Environmental Control "to establish enforceable standards for clean air and clean water . . . to prevent contamination of international rivers and oceans." Humphrey believed state and local communities could establish advisory boards where "industry, lay public, labor, young people and interested citizens" would monitor pollution, coordinate efforts to clean up the environment, and promote conservation and recreational activities. His proposal included national standards for all forms of pollution so states did not have to compete against one another. This was essential for the then Senate-candidate from Minnesota. He believed in strong federal oversight and pollution standards that "would prevent economic blackmail where a major employer could cast aside the public's interests and put a gun to the community's head by threatening to close a plant and put thousands of people of out of work." He was resolute that "no business has the right to say that to a community." Like many Midwestern Democrats, Humphrey maintained a tradition of skepticism toward industries that used economic threats to dissuade local dissent or regulation.[17]

Humphrey further combined his vision for economic justice and environmental restoration when he, along with Augustus Hawkins, crafted the Humphrey-Hawkins Act—a bill that sought to lower inflation, ease the economic concerns of the early 1970s, and provide well-paid jobs for out-of-work Americans. The Minnesota senator argued that every American had "the right to productive and gainful employment" as well as "the right to a clean and wholesome environment" and "the right to a clean and decent neighborhood." The authors of the bill sought to expand civil rights, building on the 1960s movement while addressing the new economic and environmental realities of the early 1970s.[18]

Though these political movements were ambitious, many Midwestern Democrats saw them stall as the 1970s progressed. As scholars have noted, early environmentalism was a bipartisan project. Both Democrats and Republicans supported a variety of legislation that sought to reform wasteful practices, protect human health, and regulate industrial activities. But as the 1960s closed, Republicans shifted their legislative priorities. Consider, for instance, a GOP pamphlet from 1970 that sought to remind voters about the difference between the two parties. The document was not inherently anti-environmental, acknowledging that "we have allowed a serious imbalance between man and nature." "Republicans believe that the most important element in renewal of our environment is people," it began. "There must be creative interplay between government at all levels, private industry, individual citizens. Acting together, we can gain control of our environment." The pamphlet was vague as to what a GOP environmental agenda might actually look like at the dawn of the 1970s. President Nixon established the Environmental Protection Agency (EPA) in 1970—a point of contention for many conservatives within the Republican Party who sought to limit the reach of federal agencies, not expand them. What was clearer, however, were the ways in which the Republican Party sought to critique the Democratic agenda. Its leadership condemned the growth of the federal agencies, the regulatory state, and the diminished power of local government—a criticism that held double meaning on the tail-end of the 1960s. Most significantly, the Republican Party pamphlet criticized how their political rivals conceived of the American population. "They assume that society is collectively responsible for each of its members"—a philosophy at odds with free enterprise and individualism. The pamphlet criticized how Democratic politicians framed many of its political priorities, including environmentalism. By 1970, Republicans had not fully embraced anti-environmentalism, just the rhetorical tools that Democrats had used to support environmental reforms.[19]

Conservative critiques of environmentalism became more pointed over the course of the decade. Advisers within Gerald R. Ford's presidential administration worked to fit an anti-environmental agenda into the political principles of New Federalism. They took aim at the Environmental Protection Agency, which, as they saw it, gave preference to environmental concerns over "energy, economic, or social goals." Believing that the EPA was too strict in its enforcement of the Clean Air Act and actions against other pollutants, advisers hoped to diminish the power of the agency that had been established by Ford's predecessor. Such issues, the advisers noted, should be left to the states and local governments—a political philosophy that prioritized ideology over ecological realities.[20]

As conservativism developed into a more realized anti-environmental political movement, the New Deal coalition that had enabled Midwestern Democrats to propose their ambitious plans for environmental reforms also began to fracture. A stagnant economy, inflation, rising unemployment rates, and energy crises, as well as political backlash against the Vietnam War, the civil rights movement, and the Watergate scandal, rocked the political landscape. In extractive communities in the Upper Midwest, environmentalism was soon seen as a burden that threatened the economic livelihood of miners—often union members. In Michigan's Upper Peninsula, for example, a coalition of miners, antigovernment voters, and Democratic political leaders led a secession movement throughout the 1970s in the hopes of combatting and repealing the environmental legislation of the 1960s. Supporters of the new "State of Superior" explicitly denounced the Clean Air Act, the National Wilderness Preservation System, and the anti-economic development rhetoric of the more radical wings of the environmental movement. In other parts of the region, a new public-interest movement embraced environmentalism but criticized the role of government. Believing the government was impeding environmental reforms, leftwing critics led by Ralph Nader undermined faith in public institutions. As the 1970s progressed, an increasing number of Americans lacked trust in the ability of the government to tackle pressing environmental problems. The fractured New Deal order would give rise to a neoliberal one in which free markets, free movement of people and goods, and cosmopolitan ideas could improve the material lives of American citizens. For many liberals and conservatives, there was no place for the pro-government environmentalism that politicians like Hart, Nelson, and Humphrey had promoted throughout the 1960s and early 1970s.[21]

Revisiting the rhetoric of these Midwestern Democrats provides a lens to understand the broader trajectory of the environmental movement since its arrival in the 1960s. Though the proposals and rhetoric that politicians like Hart, Humphrey, and Nelson brought forward throughout the 1960s ultimately faded through the 1970s and 1980s, their encompassing environmental vision seems remarkably relevant today. The most devastating effects of climate change have shifted the political dialogue regarding the role of government in solving the most pressing environmental issue in human history. For many, climate change cannot alone be solved with individual responsibility, corporate benevolence, or nonprofit advocacy. An example is the rhetoric and vision embodied in the Green New Deal. The proponents of the resolution call on the power of the federal government to enforce carbon emission standards while ensuring well-paying jobs, investing in infrastructure, addressing poverty, and guaranteeing clean and healthy environments—all while promoting justice and equity. The broad vision of the resolution, a point of controversy among conservatives and many centrist Democrats, would have been familiar rhetoric alongside the speeches and proposals of these Midwestern Democrats, who also believed that environmental legislation required a strong government to enforce rules, corral unchecked capitalism, protect workers, and advance economic equity.[22]

NOTES

1. Letter from Gaylord Nelson to John F. Kennedy, August 29, 1963, Box 231, Folder 16, Nelson Collection mss1020, Wisconsin Historical Society Archives, Madison.

2. Rachel Carson, *Silent Spring* (Boston: Houghton Mifflin, 1962).

3. For a sampling of the environmental changes in the post-WWII era, see Christopher W. Wells, *Car Country: An Environmental History* (Seattle: University of Washington Press, 2014); Adam Rome, *The Bulldozer in the Countryside: Suburban Sprawl and the Rise of American Environmentalism* (Cambridge: Cambridge University Press, 2001); Dan Egan, *The Death and Life of the Great Lakes* (New York: W. W. Norton, 2017); David Stradling and Richard Stradling, *Where the River Burned: Carl Stokes and the Struggle to Save Cleveland* (Ithaca, NY: Cornell University Press, 2015); Joseph S. Cialdella, *Motor City Green: A Century of Landscapes of Environmentalism in Detroit* (Pittsburgh: University of Pittsburgh Press, 2020); Jeffery T. Manuel, *Taconite Dreams: The Struggle to Sustain Mining on Minnesota's Iron Range, 1915–2000* (Minneapolis: University of Minnesota Press, 2015); Nancy Langston, *Sustaining Lake Superior: An Extraordinary Lake in a Changing World* (New Haven, CT: Yale University Press, 2019); Edward C. Lorenz, "Containing the Michigan PBB Crisis, 1973–1992: Testing the Environmental Policy Process," *Environmental History Review* 17, no. 2 (1993): 49–68; Adam Rome, *The Genius of Earth Day: How a 1970 Teach-In Unexpectedly Made the First Green Generation* (New York: Hill & Wang, 2013). For more on environmental politics, see Samuel P. Hays, *A History of Environmental Politics since 1945* (Pittsburgh: University of Pittsburg Press, 2000).

4. For environmental histories of the New Deal, see Sarah T. Phillips, *This Land, This Nation: Conservation, Rural America, and the New Deal* (Cambridge: Cambridge University Press, 2007); Neil M. Maher, *Nature's New Deal: The Civilian Conservation Corps and the Roots of the American Environmental Movement* (New York: Oxford University Press, 2008).

5. Aldo Leopold, *Sand County Almanac* (New York: Oxford University Press, 1949); Paul Lester Errington, *Of Men and Marshes* (Ames: Iowa State University Press, 1957).

6. Adlai Stevenson, "Address Accepting the Presidential Nomination at the Democratic National Convention in Chicago," American Presidency Project, https://www.presidency.ucsb.edu/node/275477, accessed November 10, 2022.

7. Adlai E. Stevenson, "Inaugural Address, January 10, 1949," in Walter Johnson and Carol Evans, eds., *The Papers of Adlai E. Stevenson, Volume III: Governor of Illinois, 1949–1953* (Boston: Little, Brown, 1977), 24; Adlai E. Stevenson, "Address to Inland Daily Press Association, October 19, 1949," in ibid., 170.

8. Adlai E. Stevenson, "Jefferson and Our National Leadership," *Virginia Quarterly Review* 36, no. 3 (1960): 348.

9. For more on Philip Hart, see Michael O'Brien, *Philip Hart: The Conscience of the Senate* (East Lansing: Michigan State University Press, 1995); "Senator Philip A. Hart's Report from Washington, for Release in Michigan Papers Beginning Monday, January 30, 1961," Box 97, Folder 61–9, Philip A. Hart Papers, Bentley Historical Library, University of Michigan, Ann Arbor (hereafter, Hart Papers); "Remarks by Senator Philip A. Hart (D-Mich) before the Inter-State Conference on Water Problems of Council of State Govts, Tuesday, December 6, 10:00am, Chicago, Ill.," Box 97, Folder 60–81, Hart Papers.

10. "Philip A. Hart Radio Blurb—Water Pollution (1:06min.)," Box 97, Folder 61–88, Hart Papers.

11. "Remarks of Senator Philip A. Hart (D-Mich) on Introducing Bills to Establish in Michigan the Pictured Rocks National Recreation Area and the Sleeping Bear Dunes National Recreation Area, June 27, 1961," Box 97, Folder 61–88, Hart Papers.

12. Bill Christofferson, *The Man from Clear Lake: Earth Day Founder Senator Gaylord Nelson* (Madison: University of Wisconsin Press, 2004), 156.

13. Christofferson, *The Man from Clear Lake*, 214–215, 273–279, 239–250, 302–312; "Revised Script for Apostle Islands Region TV film," Box 123, Folder 27, Nelson Collection mss1020, Wisconsin Historical Society Archives, Madison.

14. Christofferson, *The Man from Clear Lake*, 302–312; Rome, *The Genius of Earth Day*, ix–xi; "Nelson's Notes for a Speech in Ann Arbor on the First Earth Day, April 22, 1970," Box 231, Folder 57, Nelson Collection mss1020, Wisconsin Historical Society Archives, Madison.

15. "United Auto Workers Pamphlet about Environmental Activities of the Union," Box 47, Folder 26, Nelson Collection mss1020, Wisconsin Historical Society Archives, Madison; the relationship between the UAW and the environmental movement can be found in a variety of works. See Robert Gottlieb, *Forcing the Spring: The Transformation of the American Environmental Movement*, rev. and updated ed. (Washington, DC: Island Press, 2005); Andrew Hurley, *Environmental Inequalities: Class, Race, and Industrial Pollution in Gary, Indiana, 1945–1980* (Chapel Hill: University of North Carolina Press, 1995); Brandon M. Ward, *Living Detroit: Environmental Activism in an Age of Urban Crisis* (London: Routledge, 2022).

16. "Remarks by Vice President Hubert H. Humphrey, Senator Dodd Dinner, March 6, 1965," Speech Text Files, Hubert H. Humphrey Papers, Minnesota Historical Society, St. Paul.

17. "Excerpts from Speech by Hubert H. Humphrey, Environmental Symposium—April 6, 1970, Cloquet, Minnesota," Speech Text Files, Hubert H. Humphrey Papers, Minnesota Historical Society, St. Paul.

18. "Civil Rights Speech at LBJ School of Public Affairs Symposium, Austin, Texas, December 10–11, 1972," Speech Text Files, Hubert H. Humphrey Papers, Minnesota Historical Society, St. Paul; Arnold A. Offner, *Hubert Humphrey: The Conscience of the Country* (New Haven, CT: Yale University Press, 2018), 371–373.

19. Gregg Coodley and David Sarasohn, *The Green Years, 1964–1976: When Democrats and Republicans United to Repair the Earth* (Lawrence: University Press of Kansas, 2021); James Morton Turner and Andrew C. Isenberg, *The Republican Reversal: Conservatives and the Environment from Nixon to Trump* (Cambridge, MA: Harvard University Press, 2018); "There Is a Difference," MSS-076, Box 1, Folder 47, Charles H. Varnum Papers,

Central Upper Peninsula and Northern Michigan University Archives, Northern Michigan University, Marquette.

20. "Memo, Examples of EPA Activities and Actions that Reflect Philosophies Different from Those of the Administration, July 5, 1974," Folder: Environmental Protection Agency New Federalism Review, Box 7, Michael Raoul-Duval Files, Gerald R. Ford Library, Grand Rapids, Michigan.

21. "A New 'State of Superior': Political Fracture and Anti-environmentalism in the Upper Midwest," in Jon Lauck and Catherine McNicol Stock, eds., *The Conservative Heartland: A Political History of the Postwar American Midwest* (Lawrence: University Press of Kansas, 2020), 153–170; Paul Sabin, *Public Citizens: The Attack on Big Government and the Remaking of American Liberalism* (New York: W. W. Norton, 2021); Gary Gerstle, *The Rise and Fall of the Neoliberal Order: American and the World in the Free Market Era* (New York: Oxford University Press, 2022).

22. "H.Res.109—116th Congress (2019–2020): Recognizing the Duty of the Federal Government to Create a Green New Deal," February 7, 2019.

5

That Other Minority

The UAW, Midwestern Politics, and Pre-Stonewall Queer-Labor Solidarity

JAMES MCQUAID

❖ ❖ ❖ ❖ ❖ ❖ ❖ ❖ ❖ ❖ ❖ ❖ ❖ ❖ ❖ ❖

"I have just lost my husband from an overdose of sleeping capsules," a letter to the United Auto Workers' *Solidarity* magazine began. "All of the doctors knew he was, as you say, part of 'that other minority,' with personality problems." A mother of "four small children, [aged] 11 months to seven years," the author was responding to earlier articles about the UAW's new mental health-care program, introduced in 1966:

> He had attempted suicide before with poison but had been saved each time. At times he wanted help, and begged for it. At other times he plunged back into alcoholism to escape whatever it was that terrified him. [I] couldn't help thinking that he had been crying for help in his own twisted way. . . . But no help came for David.[1]

In reprinting the letter in *Solidarity*, editors removed personal information to protect the author from "undue embarrassment." Even if the author knew what "terrified" David, it may be impossible for us to identify the source of that fear today. Following World War II, tens—and perhaps hundreds—of thousands of American GIs returned home struggling with anxiety and post-traumatic stress, and often in unbearable isolation. At the same time, many postwar gay men and lesbian women were outed in increasingly common security investigations; they faced incarceration and deportation, and some even took their own lives.[2]

Following World War II and the emergence of Cold War rivalries, nationwide political, economic, and social anxieties contributed to a resurgence of traditional, conservative politics in opposition to earlier, pro-union New Deal liberalism. These politics were anti-union, anti-Left, and anti-queer. The UAW, like most postwar labor unions, took a hard line against communists and militants within the movement and embraced gendered respectability politics. These changes represented strategic shifts adopted by the union as part of a wider patriotic appeal to defend labor's wartime gains and maintain political alliances between unions and the Democratic Party. The UAW took little visible effort to force queer workers from the labor movement, however, and queer workers who did not substantially challenge the union's rightward turn could even advance into union leadership roles.[3] Far from the stereotypically heteronormative, masculine working environment many have come to understand it as, the auto industry shop floor served as a major site of queer transgression, identity articulation, and community building necessary for later queer political activism.[4]

UAW unionists recognized the emergence of nascent, postwar queer communities, encouraged tolerance of their difference, and represented working-class queer interests along discrete lines. Such hospitality was not unnoticed by labor's opponents, though the UAW's historical discretion still helped erase its pre-Stonewall legacy of queer-labor solidarity. Instead of forcing queer workers from the union, organizers effectively represented their interests on pre-identity driven lines. The union accomplished this by reframing the criminalization of queer intimacies, government surveillance programs, and police brutality as violations of constitutional rights. The union also countered the pathologizing of queer workers in the mental health field by creating its own mental health programs emphasizing tolerance and acceptance of queer transgressors and social "others." These early advances and discrete solidarities helped to lay the groundwork needed for an open, post-Stonewall movement tied not only to Democratic Party strongholds on the coasts, but across the Midwest as well.[5]

Although public acceptance and awareness of gay, lesbian, trans, and other queer identities improved after their politicization amid the Stonewall Uprising, before Stonewall, queer people nonetheless carved out spaces of belonging in accommodating environments.[6] Prior to the shift toward identity-focused politics and the solidification of the homo-hetero binary's dominance in postwar sexual politics, the labor movement often served as a haven for sexual and gender-transgressive workers. Such pre-Stonewall, queer-labor solidarities have been obfuscated in history, however, because of the discrete nature on which their success often depended.[7] While open, identity-affirming displays of queer-labor solidarity did occur prior to 1969, such instances were also scarce.[8] When more discrete, less visible acts of labor unity and advocacy are considered, historical sources show the UAW and other labor unions functioned as protective spaces, allowing workers to contest restrictive gender and sexual norms.[9]

Labor's discrete acceptance and advocacy of queer workers left an indelible mark on Midwestern sexual and gender politics. After World War II, American unions enjoyed widespread popularity for their role in elevating American working and living standards over the previous decade. The UAW and other unions effectively leveraged this popularity in the political realm by building alliances with the Left-leaning New Dealers in the Democratic Party, which allowed unionists and their allies to enshrine labor as a recognized institution, central to postwar American work and life.[10] In exchange for representation in the postwar order, labor's contributions to the Democratic labor-liberal alliance also promised to gradually elevate the standing of postwar queer constituencies. George McGovern, an early supporter of the rights of "homosexually-oriented individuals" and the Democratic presidential candidate in 1972, got his political start thanks to UAW funds.[11] McGovern struggled to finance his first campaign and raised only $5,000 in his bid to represent South Dakota in Congress as a Democrat. After achieving a narrow victory that some allies dismissed as impossible, it later emerged that $4,400 of McGovern's campaign funds had come directly from the UAW—88 percent of his total contributions.[12]

UAW contributions to allied, progressive candidates were not restricted along partisan lines, either. After the Stonewall Uprising and emergence of the gay liberation movement, discrete manifestations of queer-labor solidarity gave way to more open, public statements of affirmation and alliance.[13] In 1972, Nancy Weschsler and Jerry DeGrieck became the first two elected officials to come out as homosexual while in office. Weschsler and DeGrieck were elected to the city council of Ann Arbor, Michigan, on a staunch, pro-labor platform, winning them support from the UAW and the American Federation of State, County, and Municipal Employees (AFSCME). When the independent Human Rights Party nominated Kathy Kozachenko for Ann Arbor's city council in 1974, UAW support remained even though she was an open lesbian, and proved decisive in her 1974 victory. This made Kozachenko America's first elected, openly queer political representative.[14]

Although the UAW advocated for queer workers, the union's tendencies toward queer-labor solidarities were severely limited by the politically precarious position in which the labor movement found itself after World War II. Historical perceptions of the American labor movement as widely popular during the postwar era are not ill-informed; however, such approval must be qualified within its historical context. While a remarkably high percentage of the public "approved" of unions in the immediate postwar years, approval rates could fluctuate wildly, suggesting that the support unions enjoyed was far more precarious than historical narratives often portray.[15] To defend recently won bargaining rights and gains, the UAW and other industrial unions worked to retain public support, devoting significant research and effort to investigating the sources informing labor's popularity.

UAW organizers found that the majority of Americans criticized labor's reputation for militant politics and protest, believing that "unions are a good idea, but they ought to grow up. They have gained great power and the public interest requires that they be made responsible."[16] Postwar trends toward maturity and respectability politics led an increasingly bureaucratic International UAW to silence many of its most radical (and dedicated) shop-floor organizers.[17] Public desire for a more "grown up" labor movement, if gone unheeded, could pose a direct threat to the UAW and other industrial unions' goals for an expanded New Deal welfare state, which could hopefully be achieved through cooperation with Democratic allies in the postwar labor-liberal alliance.[18] Despite labor's repression of shop-floor militancy, progressive industrial unions—and the UAW-CIO (Congress of Industrial Organizations) in particular—continued to face widespread red-baiting in the media.[19] Vilification of the UAW's "labor reds" was often accompanied by open queer-baiting, tying unionization and social interdependence with effeminacy, queer transgression, and even the decline of "Western Civilization."[20]

The UAW's discursive association with gender and sexual transgression was afforded greater legitimacy by progressive sexologists like Alfred C. Kinsey. Kinsey achieved near-celebrity status after publishing *Sexual Behavior in the Human Male* in 1948, and in addition to confronting millions of Americans' postwar gender and sexual anxieties, his research helped recast the UAW within a milieu of sexual taboo and queer transgression.

In his research, for example, Kinsey noted that semi-skilled and skilled workers associated with auto manufacturing and like industries were up to eleven times more likely to self-report homosexual experiences than workers associated with other industries.[21]

Kinsey did not suggest that same-sex behavior was an outgrowth of a respondent's working or living environment, but rather that a worker's individual sexual history accorded more "with the pattern of the social group into which [they] ultimately move[d]." This distinction is significant because it invites historians to rethink how queer workers perceived of their working environment and, consequently, discrete union solidarity and advocacy. Kinsey contended that many queer workers entered unionized auto factories at higher rates than other fields specifically because tolerance at unionized workplaces "accord[ed] more with . . . the sexual mores of the individual" worker.[22] Kinsey's findings show how boundaries of historically "queer work" can apply to industries that while not overtly seen as sexually or gender-transgressive, can still operate as forms of "queer work" by providing transgressive workers with greater agency and protection through covert acts of solidarity.[23] His findings prompted public outrage and panic in national discourse as well as within the UAW and the rest of the labor movement, where his research could be weaponized to queer-bait union activists' factional opponents.[24] Such tactics could be effectively employed against union opponents on the political left, as well as within conservative circles on the right, making queer-baiting an especially pernicious threat to the UAW's internal unity and wider political efficacy.

Historians have shown that substantial red-baiting was directed at the UAW throughout the postwar years; however, scientific studies, contemporary editorials, and the union's own archival records show the UAW was also the target of substantial queer-baiting. Such anti-union queer-baiting occurred at a time when gender and sexual transgression was increasingly tied to sexual perversion and mental illness, international communism, and the downfall of the "West." While a sizeable cohort of UAW organizers and leaders engaged in acts of queer-baiting to their own (or factional) benefit, these practices appear largely abnormal, and at least partially run contrary to the union's postwar legacy of queer-labor solidarity. Anti-queer hostility directed at labor did not emerge out of a vacuum, moreover, but rather developed in response to the UAW's reputation of transgressive political advocacy, which included discrete—though otherwise unapologetic—working-class queer advocacy through union-led reform groups like the Americans for Democratic Action (ADA).

In order to defend labor's interests in an increasingly conservative postwar era, the UAW and other industrial unions sought to unite disparate progressive interests in a way that could effectively influence national politics. These efforts led to the creation of the first political action committee in American history, the CIO-PAC. Although initially intended as an independent committee to represent the entirety of labor's legislative goals, the UAW heavily influenced the CIO-PAC's postwar trajectory. The union put forward an idealistically progressive platform that included nationally enshrined gender-wage parity, "an adequate national health and housing program, organization of [all] unorganized [with] full support for the CIO southern organizing drive [and] annual wage" guaranteed by the federal government.[25]

As the CIO-PAC grew, ideological divisions began driving the organization apart, especially where disagreements emerged over political strategies. While one faction wanted to build up an independent third party, most of the CIO-PAC opposed this. A split was formalized in 1946 when third-party activists left to join Henry Wallace's Progressive Party, leaving the majority faction to reorganize as the Americans for Democratic Action in 1947. The UAW continued to provide "indispensable" political and financial support for the ADA's work against orders from the CIO.[26] Communications between the UAW and ADA show that both groups saw McCarthyism's political rise as an existential threat to liberal democracy and progress.[27]

By cooperating with the Democratic Party, UAW and ADA activists hoped to push President Harry Truman leftward on issues unionists saw as crucial to labor's success, such as the CIO's Southern organizing drive and federal support for civil rights.[28] The ADA also gave substantial pushback against legislation to allow wiretapping in cases outside of espionage.[29] Distancing themselves from Wallace's Progressive Party cleared neither the ADA nor UAW from suspicions of secret communist affiliation, however, especially as union support for postwar privacy rights grew more pronounced.[30] Despite such instigation, the UAW expanded its efforts to include policing reform, urging the Detroit, Michigan, Police Department to prioritize its "service to the community," and embrace reforms friendly to departmental transparency and public oversight in a 1950 report. UAW activists also called for greater punishments for officers breaking regulations protecting rights to privacy and due process while on duty.[31]

Reforms offered by the joint union-ADA Citizens Advisory Committee could have had a significant impact on the experiences gender and sexual minorities had with the criminal justice system, as gay, lesbian, and trans citizens suffered an inordinate share of incidents of police brutality and harassment.[32] By addressing one-sided power dynamics inherent in the existing officer-civilian relationship, activists hoped to reduce incidents of brutality, even if existing ordinances targeting gender and sex transgressors could not be overturned.[33] By calling for greater community oversight of the police and for the creation of a clear pathway to appeal unnecessarily restrictive arrests and detentions, reformers sought to provide discrete queer communities with added legal shielding against damaging convictions.[34] While most of Detroit's Police Department cooperated with the Citizen's Advisory Committee, the Vice Bureau's reluctance to participate in (and hostility to) reform dialogues is telling.[35]

Union efforts to defend due process and individual privacy rights extended beyond advisory committees and onto the automotive shop floor. Historically manifesting through a multitude of expressions, ranging from platonic, homosocial hazing to more overtly sexual intimacies, evidence shows a clear and continued presence of same-sex encounters on the shop floor, as well as tacit union approval of it.[36] Although UAW leaders sought to appear more "mature" and respectable to the public, this did not require the UAW to abandon the interests, discretion, and individual privacy of its queer members. The union provided strong resistance to efforts by management to introduce greater surveillance and other security systems onto the shop floor, which it argued violated time-study agreements and workers' privacy rights on the job. The union also contested actions taken when General Motors (GM) invited police onto company parking lots to search workers' cars, attempted to force employees to submit to polygraph tests in dispute resolutions cases, and tried to bring felony sabotage charges against employees at a Texas GM plant, despite lacking adequate evidence.[37]

Although the UAW was initially complicit in early postwar purges against communists in labor, the ADA served as a space where organizers began to push back against red-baiting and queer-baiting practices that they saw dividing their union. "We couldn't continue this line as a political tactic," UAW and ADA activist Paul Shrade recalled of labor movement complicity with political purges. "It was dividing the organization and we needed to find new ground."[38] The union's rejection of red-baiting and other discriminatory tactics proved to be an empowering force for progressive causes in the political realm. A more inclusive ADA, less apologetic for its political advocacy at the start of the 1960s, sought to build new political coalitions with marginalized communities like the homophile movement, leading the ADA to become one of the first organizations to openly endorse "decriminaliz[ing] private homosexual sex."[39]

The ADA made its first successful push to decriminalize same-sex intimacies when it introduced a reformed legal code to the Illinois legislature in 1961, which was approved by the state legislature and signed into law before its provisions decriminalizing consensual, same-sex behavior became widely known. The inclusion of these provisions was not the result of a lack of oversight, but instead demonstrated a clear commitment to the privacy rights of queer people nationwide. Despite substantial political pushback, the ADA submitted its reformed legal code to other state legislatures after its victory in Illinois. Idaho's state legislature similarly passed the ADA's updated legal code, but reversed course and repealed the new law once its decriminalization measures were discovered.[40]

Although the UAW and ADA's updated criminal code faced considerable opposition in local and state legislatures, outside the legal realm, public consensus was shifting in favor of Americans' right to privacy and the decriminalization of "private acts between consenting adults."[41] At the same time, the ADA emerged as a nexus for pre-Stonewall homophile activism at the start of the 1960s, providing a growing homophile movement with a platform through which they could present their views and goals to the public. This dialogue led several publications, such as the *Village Voice*, *Harpers*, and the *New York Times*, to publish a series of discussions on the homophile movement as a serious political issue, helping to increase the visibility of queer communities.[42] The UAW's history of queer-labor solidarity is also evident in the realm of mental health and patient rights, where the union's open advocacy for expanding employment rights to include workers with "emotional problems" laid the foundation for later, post-Stonewall, identity-centered nondiscrimination protections.

In 1966 the UAW's Social Security Department director, Melvin A. Glasser, lamented how "only a few business organizations have demonstrated [their] sophistication and knowledge" by providing mental health benefits to their employees. Glasser and other UAW unionists had hoped that by pressuring more companies to extend such benefits, they could also begin to destigmatize mental illness in society by normalizing the benefits of benign, community-focused psychiatric care. In addition to providing for a better quality of life for working families, unionists argued that normalizing mental health care could also lead to greater employment protections for workers pathologized by the medical and psychiatric communities, criminalized by the state, or both:

> The referral of an employee for psychiatric treatment should not end the company's responsibility toward him. Management must recognize that emotional illness . . . does not imply the individual will subsequently be incapable of carrying out his responsibilities. [A] worker who is sick because of an emotional problem requires essentially the same kind of job and benefit protection as a worker sick with a physical problem.[43]

Just two years earlier, only ten of 560 companies surveyed reported employing the services of a psychiatrist on an even part-time basis. As dire as this situation was, however, Glasser and his fellow unionists pledged that the situation was starting to change: "The UAW has produced the first nationwide, collectively bargained, in-and-out-of hospital mental health program in industry [which] provides coverage to some 2,750,000 UAW members and their dependents in 34 states and the District of Columbia."[44] The UAW's nationwide mental health program was groundbreaking. With the inclusion of dependents in mental health-care benefits, the UAW extended mental health care to approximately nine million working-class Americans—slightly more than 4.5 percent of the national population.[45]

In framing transgressive behaviors associated with "emotional problems" as disabilities in the context of community mental health warranting employment protections, the UAW was able to contribute to an alternative discourse of patients' and workers' rights for gender and sexual minorities pathologized by orthodox psychiatry. UAW literature made the details between these two movements clear: "Community mental health is [concerned] with an individual's growth, development, and functioning in his community, [while orthodox] programs are often designed without communication with the community they are to serve." As a result of these tactics, UAW leaders contended, existing approaches "fail to meet [a] community's real needs" and often prescribe treatments "which the community is unprepared or unwilling to accept."[46] In an era of pre-identity queer politics, the UAW's mental health program sought to articulate a system wherein queer autoworkers would see their employment rights defended, and their fears of forced institutionalization substantially eased.

Orthodox psychologists vigorously opposed such changes in thinking, however. While some professionals insisted that 90 percent of homosexuals could be cured of their afflictions, so long as they demonstrated a sincere desire to change, others chided their lax colleagues, instead asserting that reconversion therapy could be universally effective when utilizing the proper coercive measures.[47] Specific corrective measures employed could vary based on different conditions, but methodologies ranged from damaging, confrontational individual and group therapy and hypnosis to electroshock therapy and even lobotomization, or "psychosurgery."[48] Meanwhile, controversial figures like Walter Jackson Freeman asserted that costly and therapy-intensive institutionalization should be replaced with a procedure of his own invention, the trans-orbital lobotomy.[49]

Although Freeman was not a neurosurgeon and lacked basic training in that field, his lobotomy was met with widespread acclaim, and he was invited to demonstrate the new procedure at no less than fifty-five different hospitals across twenty-three states.[50] Freeman's techniques did not go unchallenged forever, and over time, both public and professional opposition to his methods began to build.[51] Additionally, mental health-care professionals and public figures grew increasingly concerned over lobotomy's potential to be used as a tool for social control.[52] Freeman repeatedly and publicly touted the lobotomy as "a new avenue of attack on sex crimes" and went so far as to publicly suggest Christine Jorgenson—a national advocate for trans rights—should have a lobotomy to cure her "abnormal behavior."[53] These and similar abuses informed many working-class Americans' hesitancy to interact with mental health-care professionals. If the union was to effectively advocate for comprehensive mental health coverage, it needed to first counteract the hesitancies of normative and queer workers alike.

Before the UAW could demand mental health benefits in its 1964 contract negotiations with automakers, the union also had to prove not only that running such a program was possible, but that it was needed by its members. To do this, the UAW first organized its mental health-care program as an independently financed and union-run endeavor. Starting out of UAW Local 259 in New York, the union's mental health-care initiative began when local president Sam Meyers reached out to progressive psychiatrists associated with the community mental health movement for help with drafting a plan. The initial program extended mental health-care coverage to the local's expansive membership of more than four thousand manufacturing and service technicians. As a leading member of the postwar labor-liberal coalition, the UAW's promotion of community mental health as an alternative to psychiatric institutionalization affected the entire discipline.[54]

The progressive, community-centric specialists the UAW recruited to build its program were based out of New York's William Alanson White Institute (WAWI) and served as a radical choice for Local 259's leadership. WAWI publicly broke from orthodox psychiatry in the 1940s when it began championing an altogether different, "interpersonal" approach to psychiatry that opposed "clinical inflexibility" and "paternalistic domination" of patients. Instead of seeking to eradicate transgressive behavior, WAWI and other community mental health advocates stressed self-acceptance for homosexuals and other queer patients.[55] UAW publications regarding its new program worked to assuage fears among its "emotionally disturbed" members that, in coming forward, they might only be dooming themselves to institutionalization or other potential retaliation. Although informational material from the union stressed the need to prevent ridicule of "emotionally disturbed" workers seeking help, these same publications did not offer unrealistic guarantees of uniform acceptance: "Patients who need and want help . . . sometimes have to ignore the prejudices of all those people [who] cannot accept psychiatry as [part of] medical care." In contrast with orthodox psychiatric treatments, however, UAW negotiated mental health benefits placed the decision to interact with the mental health professionals exclusively on the member.[56]

Contrary to fears some union leaders had regarding the merits of a union-run mental health program, and whether members would even be accepting of the new benefits, records show considerable interest in mental health care and corresponding employment protections. Following a short period of initial hesitancy on the part of some members, the UAW's mental health-care program saw widespread use following its national implementation. Most union members used their benefits to pay for outpatient talk therapy sessions, in contrast to prescriptive methods based on conversion therapy.[57]

As the UAW and other CIO unionists struggled to find a foothold for labor in postwar American life and society, they also navigated a complex and nuanced political environment. Although supportive of labor's Great Depression and wartime-era gains in principle, public anxieties over union radicalism and sexual and gender panic placed severe limitations on the possible scope of labor's postwar transgressive advocacy. At first seeking to placate an anticommunist turn in American politics at the start of the Cold War, the UAW distanced itself from militant activism, painting itself as a respectable vanguard of the noncommunist American Left. Despite such concessions, however, the UAW continued to be both red-baited and queer-baited by its political opponents.[58] The UAW's history of postwar activism shows that once unionists understood that differentiating between transgressive and nontransgressive solidarities would not help secure desired progressive reforms, the union instead sought to win "as much perhaps as was possible [from] a resistant and powerful corporate and political establishment" by bringing previously marginalized communities into the labor-liberal coalition, expanding progressive, pro-union influence into the postwar era in the process.[59]

The postwar UAW faced considerable queer-baiting in addition to political red-baiting that targeted its progressive postwar agenda. Even so, the UAW's postwar activism included queer-labor solidarities, albeit solidarities often eschewed by queer working cultures that prioritized discretion over identity-based political activism. Instead of forcing queer workers from the labor movement, the union effectively represented queer workers' interests in a still largely pre-identity-driven era in American gender and sexual politics. The union lent crucial support to electoral allies, opposed expansive surveillance efforts and police brutality, fought for the decriminalization of same-sex intimacies, and helped queer workers resist the pathologizing narratives targeting them from the mental health field. Through their efforts, UAW activists hoped to continue using the postwar labor-liberal alliance as a vehicle to bring about greater social democratic reforms and an economic shift toward industrial democracy. While many of the UAW's most ambitious political and organizing goals so far remain unachieved, the union's cooperation with the Democratic Party helped to further victories made by labor in postwar politics, as well as by pre-Stonewall queer workers and communities.

NOTES

1. George Ryder, "A Breakdown Won't Wait," *UAW Solidarity*, UAW Research Department Records, Part I, Box 56, Folder 12, Walter P. Reuther Library, Archives of Labor and Urban Affairs, Wayne State University, Detroit, Michigan.

2. David K. Johnson, *The Lavender Scare: The Cold War Persecution of Gays and Lesbians in the Federal Government* (Chicago: University of Chicago Press, 2004), 158; Margot Canaday, *The Straight State: Sexuality and Citizenship in Twentieth-Century America* (Princeton, NJ: Princeton University Press, 2009), 219. Provided in isolation, the evidence above should not lead us to definitively conclude that David was a homosexual, nor that his struggles with sexuality contributed in any way to his suicide. Rather, this chapter begins with David's story specifically because of the ambiguity surrounding his motivations and the way that ambiguity is illustrative of wider, systemic source challenges common to queer historical scholarship. For more on the use of ephemeral sources in queer history and alternative methods of oppositional, anti-hegemonic consciousness and organizing, respectively, see José Esteban Muñoz, "Ephemera as Evidence: Introductory Notes to Queer Acts," *Women & Performance: A Journal of Feminist Theory* 8, no. 2 (June 3, 2008), 5–7; Chela Sandoval, "U.S. Third World Feminism: Differential Social Movement I," in *Methodology of the Oppressed* (Minneapolis: University of Minnesota Press, 2000), 41–64.

3. Timothy Ford Retzloff, "City, Suburb, and the Changing Bounds of Lesbian and

Gay Life and Politics in Metropolitan Detroit, 1945–1985" (PhD diss., Yale University, 2014), 303.

4. Erik Loomis, *A History of America in Ten Strikes* (New York: New Press, 2018), 162–165.

5. Historical stereotypes that portray the American queer past as inherently urban and coastal have been increasingly challenged by studies mindful of queerness expressed differently along lines of race, sex, gender, and place. See John Howard, *Men Like That: A Southern Queer History* (Chicago: University of Chicago Press, 1999); Siobhan B. Somerville, *Queering the Color Line: Race and the Invention of Homosexuality in American Culture* (Durham, NC: Duke University Press, 2000); Brock Thompson, *The Un-Natural State: Arkansas and the Queer South* (Fayetteville: University of Arkansas Press, 2010).

6. Miriam Frank, *Out in the Union: A Labor History of Queer America* (Philadelphia: Temple University Press, 2014), 17; George Chauncey, *Gay New York: Gender, Urban Culture, and the Making of the Gay Male World 1890–1940* (New York: Basic Books, 1994), 31.

7. Select UAW contracts from the 1940s specify that employees "engaging in carnal acts" with the opposite sex will face immediate termination, though nothing is said of same-sex encounters outside of provisions regarding any "constant breach[es] of safety rules." See "Agreement between Ford Motor Co. and the UAW-CIO, 1942," John Cole Collection, Walter P. Reuther Library, Archives of Labor and Urban Affairs, Wayne State University; Stephen Meyer, *Manhood on the Line: Working-Class Masculinities in the American Heartland* (Urbana: University of Illinois Press, 2016), 124–125; Frank, *Out in the Union*, 1–4.

8. Allan Bérubé, *My Desire for History: Essays in Gay, Community, and Labor History* (Chapel Hill: University of North Carolina Press, 2011), 294.

9. Rochella Thorpe, "'A House Where Queers Go:' African-American Lesbian Nightlife in Detroit, 1940–1975," in Ellen Lewin, ed., *Inventing Lesbian Cultures in America* (Boston: Beacon Press, 1996), 40; "Rochella Thorpe Oral History Project Files, 1992–1995," Division of Rare and Manuscript Collections, Cornell University Library, Ithaca, New York.

10. Although initially decried as un-American by both business and leaders of the older AFL craft unions, the industrial organizing approach of the CIO played a key role in elevating working conditions and the purchasing power of unionized households, helping to ease economic and social stress during the Great Depression. The industrial unions also (largely) adhered to a wartime "no-strike" pledge, boosting their patriotic appeal. Kevin Boyle, *The UAW and the Heyday of American Liberalism, 1945–1968* (Ithaca, NY: Cornell University Press, 1995), 7; Nelson Lichtenstein, *Labor's War at Home: The CIO in World War II* (Philadelphia: Temple University Press, 2003), 6; John Barnard, *American Vanguard: The United Auto Workers during the Reuther Years, 1935–1970* (Detroit: Wayne State University Press, 2004), 461.

11. Stacey Flores Chandler, "A Pride Month: The LGBTQ Rights Movement and the 1972 Presidential Campaign," JFK Library Archives: An Inside Look (blog), John F. Kennedy Presidential Library and Museum, June 23, 2017, https://jfk.blogs.archives.gov/2017/06/23/pridemonth-the-lgbtq-rights-movement-and-the-1972-presidential-campaign/; "Gay Citizens for McGovern" (press release), Frank Mankiewicz Personal Papers, Box 19, Gays, John F. Kennedy Presidential Library and Museum, John F. Kennedy Library.

12. Christopher Lydon, "Mild-Spoken Nominee with a Strong Will to Fight: George Stanley McGovern," *New York Times*, July 13, 1972, 24; "McGovern, George S(tanley)," in Charles Moritz, ed., *Current Biography Yearbook, 1967* (New York: H. W. Wilson, 1968), 264; George S. McGovern, *Terry: My Daughter's Life-and-Death Struggle with Alcoholism* (New York: Villard Books, 1996), 51; Thomas J. Knock, *The Rise of a Prairie Statesman: The Life and Times of George McGovern* (Princeton, NJ: Princeton University Press, 2016), 204.

13. Frank, *Out in the Union*, 102.

14. "Human Rights Party Candidates for the Ann Arbor City Council," *Michigan Daily*, March 29, 1972; "Press Release Form: The Human Rights Party of Ann Arbor," HRP Campaigns, 1972: City Council Elections, Box 1, Human Rights Party (Ann Arbor, Mich.) Records, Bentley Historical Library, University of Michigan, Ann Arbor.

15. Megan Brenan, "Approval of Labor Unions at Highest Point since 1965," *Gallup*, September 2, 2021. For more on postwar employment stability and perceptions of union militancy in the auto industry, see Daniel J. Clark, *Disruption in Detroit: Autoworkers and the Elusive Postwar Boom* (Urbana: University of Illinois Press, 2018).

16. "The Postwar Role of Labor Unions," Public Opinion Index for Industry, August 1945, 4, UAW Region 1B Records, Box 104, Folder 9, Walter P. Reuther Library, Archives of Labor and Urban Affairs, Wayne State University.

17. Lyn Goldfarb, Judy Boddy, and Nancy Wiegersma, *Separated and Unequal: Discrimination against Women Workers after World War II; the UAW, 1944–1954* (Washington, DC: Women's Work Project, Women's Labor History Film Project, 1976), 35.

18. Elizabeth Faue, *Rethinking the American Labor Movement* (New York: Routledge, 2017), 104–106.

19. "Labor's Communists Come Under Fire," *Life* 22, no. 12 (1947): 31–35; Robert H. Zieger, *The CIO, 1935–1955* (Chapel Hill: The University of North Carolina Press, 1997), 38.

20. "The Family," *Life* 22, no. 12 (1947): 36; Malcolm W. Bingay, "Good Morning: Those Queer People," *Detroit Free Press*, May 6, 1950; Malcolm W. Bingay, "The Strike Nobody Won," *Detroit Free Press*, May 6, 1950.

21. Alfred C. Kinsey, Wardell B. Pomeroy, and Clyde E. Martin, *Sexual Behavior in the Human Male* (Philadelphia: W. B. Saunders, 1948), 75–82. While the categories Kinsey references should not be taken to serve as a stand-in representing UAW members only, many of Kinsey's respondents were unionized autoworkers, especially those living in the industrial Midwest, where Kinsey based much of his research. Stephen Meyer, emails with the author, November 11, 2019, through January 21, 2020.

22. Kinsey, *Sexual Behavior in the Human Male*, 419.

23. Bérubé, *My Desire for History*, 297–298; Chauncey, *Gay New York*, 31–127; Johnson, *The Lavender Scare*, 1–14.

24. Simon LeVay and Elisabeth Nonas, *City of Friends: A Portrait of the Gay and Lesbian Community in America* (Cambridge, MA: MIT Press, 1995), 51; Wardell B. Pomeroy, *Dr. Kinsey and the Institute for Sex Research* (New York: Harper & Row, 1972), 361–362; "The Truth About the Kinsey Report: A Short Digest for UAW-CIO Stewards and Committeemen," n.d., Clayton W. Fountain Collection, Box 2, Folder 13, Walter P. Reuther Library, Archives of Labor and Urban Affairs, Wayne State University.

25. Zieger, *The CIO*, 181–182; "A Program for Unity in the UAW-CIO," Louisville, KY, March 20, 1947, UAW Research Department Records, Part I, Box 4, Folder 8, Walter P. Reuther Library, Archives of Labor and Urban Affairs, Wayne State University.

26. "A Program for Unity"; "Rift in Liberal Forces Becomes More Marked," *New York Times*, January 5, 1947; "CIO to Quit Two Groups," *New York Times*, February 21, 1947; UAW-CIO Public Relations Department Press Release, February 22, 1948, UAW Research Department Records, Part I, Box 2, Folder 21, Walter P. Reuther Library, Archives of Labor and Urban Affairs, Wayne State University; "Unions Pay Third of ADA Expenses," *New York Tribune*, July 12, 1950; Letter to Walter Reuther, January 9, 1951, UAW Research Department Records, Part I, Box 2, Folder 19, Walter P. Reuther Library, Archives of Labor and Urban Affairs, Wayne State University.

27. Letters between Washington, DC, ADA and Frank Winn, 1950, UAW Research Department Records, Part I, Box 2, Folder 19, Walter P. Reuther Library, Archives of Labor and Urban Affairs, Wayne State University.

28. Although historians and union activists alike have shown the UAW's record on racial justice and equality to be far from perfect, the UAW's historical support for civil rights speaks to a legacy of activism many autoworkers take pride in, and racial solidarity between Black and white workers nevertheless played a crucial role in many of the union's first organizing success. See August Meier and Elliott Rudwick, *Black Detroit and the Rise of the UAW* (Ann Arbor: University of Michigan Press, 2007); Dan Georgakas and Marvin Surkin, *Detroit: I Do Mind Dying, A Study in Urban Revolution* (Chicago: Haymarket Books, 2012), xv–xx.

29. "Reuther Offers 6-Point Better-Living Program," *Cleveland Press*, January 28, 1949; "Democrats Woo ADA: Three Promise Civil Rights Support," *Detroit Free Press*, May 18, 1952; "ADA Condemns New Smith Act," *Daily Worker*, June 2, 1952; "Lehman Slaps McCarthyism," *Detroit Times*, May 23, 1953; "ADA Asks Ike to Slap McCarthy," *Detroit Free Press*, May 25, 1953; Mark L. Kleinman, "Americans for Democratic Action," in Paul S. Boyer, *The Oxford Companion to United States History* (New York: Oxford University Press, 2001), 34.

30. Letter to the Republican State Central Committee of Minnesota from Lewis L. Drill, UAW Research Department Records, Part I, Box 2, Folder 19, Walter P. Reuther Library, Archives of Labor and Urban Affairs, Wayne State University; Clayton Knowles, "ADA Calls Itself a 'Liberal Lobby,'" *New York Times*, July 12, 1950; "Smearing the ADA," *Detroit Times*, October 12, 1950; Fulton Lewis Jr., "Who Will ADA Back?" *Detroit Times*, June 5, 1952; "GOP Nominee Rips into ADA," *Detroit Times*, September 4, 1952; "Disgusted by Praise of ADA in Editorial," *Detroit Times*, September 5, 1952; "ADA Denies Leftist Links, Group Says Charges Are 'Preposterous,'" *Detroit News*, October 20, 1952; "As Others See It: Asserts ADA Perils Nation," *Detroit Free Press*, February 19, 1955.

31. Citizens' Advisory Committee Report on Police Procedures, April 4, 1950, 9–12, UAW Region 1B Records, Box 199, Folder 32, Walter P. Reuther Library, Archives of Labor and Urban Affairs, Wayne State University.

32. Queer activists who got their start by working in unionized factories attest to this fact in interviews and memoirs. See Leslie Feinberg, *Stone Butch Blues*, 20th anniversary ed.) (Self-published, 2014), 72.

33. John D'Emilio, *Sexual Politics, Sexual Communities: The Making of a Homosexual Minority in the United States, 1940–1970* (Chicago: University of Chicago Press, 1983), 50. These and other UAW-advocated reforms overlapped considerably with concerns articulated by postwar queer Americans regarding any potential encounters with law

enforcement. See Joey L. Mogul, et al., *Queer (In)Justice: The Criminalization of LGBT People in the United States* (Boston: Beacon Press, 2011), 45.

34. Arrests and detentions for gender and sex transgression targeted Black men and other men of color to the extent that sentencing disparities between Black and white offenders were visible even within individual court cases. In one 1950 incident in Flint, Michigan, a Black autoworker and white power company executive were both detained on "sexual psychopathy" charges after police found them having sex in a parked car. The Black autoworker was committed to Ionia State Hospital for nine years while the white executive was released and never brought up on felony charges. See Tim Retzloff, "Cars and Bars: Assembling Gay Men in Postwar Flint, Michigan," in Brett Beemyn, ed., *Creating a Place for Ourselves: Lesbian, Gay, and Bisexual Community Histories* (New York: Taylor & Francis, 1997), 227–229.

35. Detroit's Vice Bureau was responsible for targeting acts of gender and sex transgression. Unlike other bureaus, data provided by Vice was vague, and often contained only minimal, required information requested by the committee. The Detroit Police Department's continued legacy of anti-homosexual and other forms of anti-queer bias in its history of vice operations has been thoroughly documented. See Report of the Citizens' Advisory Committee on Police Procedures, 2; Rudy Serra, *"Bag a Fag:" Police Misconduct, Entrapment and Crimes against Gay Men in Michigan* (Detroit: Triangle Foundation, 2000), 3–5.

36. Jeremy Milloy, *Blood, Sweat, and Fear: Violence at Work in the North American Auto Industry, 1960–80* (Toronto: UBC Press, 2017), 73; Frank, *Out in the Union*, 67; Meyer, *Manhood on the Line*, 124–126; Gary Kapanowski, interviewed by the author, May 30, 2018; "Ed Liska Reports," Ed Liska Papers, Box 2, Folder 10, Walter P. Reuther Library, Archives of Labor and Urban Affairs, Wayne State University.

37. "Report of the Arbitrator, Arbitration Case No. CK-12," October 27, 1966; "Letter from Hubert Gillespie on Theft Detecting Devices," February 27, 1969; "Letter to John Fillion on Invasion of Privacy at Arlington GMAD," June 6, 1969; "Polygraph Tests," March 5, 1970, all in UAW Vice-President's Office: Donald Ephlin Records, Box 2, Folder 43, Walter P. Reuther Library, Archives of Labor and Urban Affairs, Wayne State University.

38. Paul Schrade, interviewed by William Chafe, March 16, 1989, "Reminiscences of Paul and Monica Schrade," Columbia University Libraries, Digital Collections.

39. D'Emilio, *Sexual Politics, Sexual Communities*, 159; Engel, *The Unfinished Revolution: Social Movement Theory and the Gay and Lesbian Movement* (New York: Cambridge University Press, 2001), 37; Stephen Engel, "Making a Minority: Understanding the Formation of the Gay and Lesbian Movement in the United States," in Diane Richardson and Steven Seidman, eds., *Handbook of Lesbian and Gay Studies* (Thousand Oaks, CA: Sage Publications, 2002), 384.

40. D'Emilio, *Sexual Politics, Sexual Communities*, 211.

41. Engel, *The Unfinished Revolution*, 37; Engel, "Making a Minority," 384.

42. Jack Gould, "Radio: Taboo Is Broken: 'Live and Let Live' on WBAI Presents Homosexuals Discussing Problems," *New York Times*, July 16, 1962; Milton Bracker, "Homosexuals Air Their Views Here: Radio Station Lets Eight Appear in Panel Discussion," *New York Times*, July 16, 1962; Ramom de Souza Torrecilha, "The Mobilization of the Gay Liberation Movement" (MA thesis, Portland State University, 1986), 125–126.

43. "Crosscurrents of Opinion," *Medical Tribune*, December 17–18, 1966 (Weekend Edition), UAW Research Department Records, Part I, Box 56, Folder 12, Walter P. Reuther Library, Archives of Labor and Urban Affairs, Wayne State University.

44. "Crosscurrents of Opinion," *Medical Tribune*.

45. This figure assumes that each of the 2.75 million union members Glasser references is one member of a 3.3-person household, the average number of people per household in 1966. When this amount is divided against a national population in 1966 of 196.6 million, it can be estimated that the UAW's mental health program provided coverage to 4.62 percent of the US population. See "Table HH-4. Households by Size: 1960 to Present," United States Census Bureau: Historical Households Tables, December 2020; "Population, Total—United States," World Bank.

46. Ryder, "A Breakdown Won't Wait" and "What Is Community Mental Health Anyway?" in *Oakland County Community Mental Health Services Board: Annual Report, 1968*, UAW Region 1B Records, Box 159, Folder 43, Walter P. Reuther Library, Archives of Labor and Urban Affairs, Wayne State University.

47. Kenneth Lewes, *The Psychoanalytic Theory of Male Homosexuality* (New York: Simon & Shuster, 1988), 15; Edmund Bergler, "Curable Disease?," *Time*, December 10, 1956; Irving Bieber, *Homosexuality: A Psychoanalytic Study of Male Homosexuals* (New York: Basic Books, 1962), 319.

48. Ronald Bayer, *Homosexuality and American Psychiatry: The Politics of Diagnosis* (Princeton, NJ: Princeton University Press, 1987), 15; Jennifer Terry, *An American Obsession: Science, Medicine and the Place of Homosexuality in Modern Society* (Chicago: Chicago University Press, 1999), 308; Sarah Baughey-Gill, "When Gay Was Not Okay with the APA: A Historical Overview of Homosexuality and Its Status as Mental Disorder," *Occam's Razor* 1, no. 2 (2011): 9.

49. Jeffrey C. Wood, *Therapy 101: A Brief Look at Modern Psychotherapy Techniques and How They Can Help* (Oakland, CA: New Harbinger Publications, 2008), 151–154; Ann Jane Tierney, "Egas Moniz and the Origins of Psychosurgery: A Review Commemorating the 50th Anniversary of Moniz's Nobel Prize," *Journal of the History of the Neurosciences* 9, no. 1 (2000): 29.

50. Jack El-Hai, *The Lobotomist: A Maverick Medical Genius and His Tragic Quest to Rid the World of Mental Illness* (Hoboken, NJ: Jack Wiley & Sons, 2005), 213; Jack El-Hai, "The Lobotomist," *Washington Post*, February 4, 2001; Jenell Johnson, *American Lobotomy: A Rhetorical History* (Ann Arbor: University of Michigan Press, 2014), 50–51; Michele Norris, "'My Lobotomy': Howard Dully's Journey," National Public Radio, November 16, 2005; Brief Case Histories of 20 Patients, Walter Freeman Papers, 1918–1972, Walter Freeman and James Watts Collection, Box 16, Folder 37, University Archives, George Washington University, Washington, DC.

51. In addition to a series of high-profile botched operations, Freeman's procedure was disproportionately used against women, queer people, and people of color. Of the five thousand prefrontal lobotomies Freeman conducted, 60 percent of patients were women, with considerable overlap with 40 percent of homosexual patients. Initially championed by skewed success rates at above 60 percent, the procedure's actual rates were later recalculated to rest as low as 18 percent, with a 10 percent fatality rate (potentially five hundred victims/deaths attributable to Freeman alone). See Gene Stone, "The Tiger Cure," *New York Magazine*, September 20, 2013; Johnson, *American Lobotomy*, 50; Bill Lipsky, "Vacaville 1956: California's First Gay Rights Protest," *San Francisco Bay*

Times, January 11, 2018; James P. Caruso and Jason P. Sheehan, "Psychosurgery, Ethics, and Media: A History of Walter Freeman and the Lobotomy," *Neurosurgical Focus* 43, no. 3 (September 2017), 4; Larry O. Gostin, "Ethical Considerations of Psychosurgery: The Unhappy Legacy of the Pre-Frontal Lobotomy," *Journal of Medical Ethics* 6, no. 3 (1980): 149.

52. Elliot S. Valenstein, "The History of Lobotomy: A Cautionary Tale," *Michigan Quarterly Review* 27, no. 3 (1988), 431.

53. Jenell Johnson, "Echoes of the Soul: A Rhetorical History of Lobotomy" (PhD diss., Pennsylvania State University, 2008), 106–107; Johnson, *American Lobotomy*, 43–44.

54. E. Fuller Torey, *American Psychosis: How the Federal Government Destroyed the Mental Illness Treatment System* (New York: Oxford University Press, 2014), ix–x; Ryder, "A Breakdown Won't Wait;" Scott Tyrrel, phone conversation with the author, September 29, 2021.

55. Frank X. Acosta et al., *Effective Psychotherapy for Low-Income and Minority Patients* (New York: Plenum Press, 1982), 37–38; Mary Julian White, "Sullivan and Treatment," *Contemporary Psychoanalysis* 13, no. 3 (1977), 342–343; Jay S. Kwawer, "Origins, Theory, and Practice: 1943-Present," William Alanson White Institute of Psychiatry, Psychoanalysis and Psychology (website), December 11, 2009; "That Other Minority: Mental Healthcare for Workers," 2, UAW Research Department Records, Part I, Box 56, Folder 12, Walter P. Reuther Library, Archives of Labor and Urban Affairs, Wayne State University.

56. Ryder, "That Other Minority;" Ryder, "A Breakdown Won't Wait;" "'Communication to All Local Union Presidents, Chairmen of Bargaining Committees, Education Committees, and Community Service Committees from Carroll M. Hutton,' June 16, 1966"; "Local Union Membership Meeting Education Program: Mental Health Care for Workers"; "Discussion Leader's Guide: The Issue—'Mental Health Care for Workers'"; and "Educating on the UAW's Mental Health Program: Seminar Schedule," all in UAW Research Department Records, Part I, Box 56, Folder 12, Walter P. Reuther Library, Archives of Labor and Urban Affairs, Wayne State University.

57. UAW members' utilization of full-session therapy, half-session therapy, and group therapy accounted for 71.7 percent, 19.5 percent, and 5.7 percent of the program's expenses respectively. Electroshock therapy, which the report indicates was used exclusively as a treatment option for severe instances of depression, accounted for 3.1 percent of utilized services. So far as reports indicated, no funds were ever used to pay for a prefrontal or transorbital lobotomy. See "Prepaid Psychiatric Care Experience with UAW Members," 7, UAW Region 1B Records, Box 159, Folder 43, Walter P. Reuther Library, Archives of Labor and Urban Affairs, Wayne State University.

58. Nelson Lichtenstein, *The Most Dangerous Man in Detroit: Walter Reuther and the Fate of American Labor* (New York: Basic Books, 1995), 431–433.

59. Barnard, *American Vanguard*, 461.

6

The Fall of the Last Democratic Political Machine

East Chicago, Indiana, and the Rise of Community Activism

EMILIANO AGUILAR

❖ ❖ ❖ ❖ ❖ ❖ ❖ ❖ ❖ ❖ ❖ ❖ ❖ ❖ ❖ ❖

In 1999 a group of East Chicago, Indiana, residents and municipal employees organized door-to-door canvassing ahead of the Democratic primary. The primary became a contentious race between Robert Pastrick, the community's mayor since 1972; and his former chief of police and current Lake County Democratic Party chair, Stephen R. Stiglich. While filming a documentary about Pastrick, documentarian Chris Sautter captured some of the municipal employees in action. Anthony Copeland, a firefighter and community activist with Citizens in Action, arrived with colleagues at a resident's door. Copeland stated, his peers nodding in agreement, "It is like you never get through with the problems. They just pile things one on another to another. You can move from the toxic dump to the city budget. It does not matter what we talk about[,] it comes down to accountability."[1] While the documentary didn't state who the firefighter was campaigning for, it clarified that Copeland and his peers opposed Pastrick and stressed the need for a transparent and accountable government. Copeland, a part of the well-oiled political machine Pastrick crafted to ensure his longevity in office, recognized the moment as an opportunity for change in the city's trajectory.

What exactly was that trajectory? The official history of East Chicago,

Indiana, claimed that the city was "born of railroad and steel" when industrialists and investors from Chicago helped incorporate the town in 1893, the same year as the famed Columbian Exhibition.² In his preface for the Indiana Writers' Program's *The Calumet Region Historical Guide*, Gordon F. Briggs proclaimed that "this region, within a few miles of the eastern city limits of Chicago, lay dormant during the nineteenth century waiting for electricity and the machine age to give it life."³ These industries arrived in a flurry of land purchases and groundbreakings in the region in the early twentieth century. At East Chicago's industrial sector's height, nearly fifty companies produced more than four hundred products shipped worldwide.⁴ However, the steel industry's decline exacerbated the city's financial situation in the 1970s and 1980s. While Inland Steel did not shutter, unlike neighboring steel mills such as US Steel South Works (1992) or Acme Steel (2001), it no longer served as the giant employer for East Chicagoans that it did in the early twentieth century. The dwindling tax base, which relied heavily on the various sectors, now saw factories permanently shut down or severely scaled back, which impacted the city's ability to distribute patronage appointments in municipal employment. In the 1990s, East Chicago turned to casino gaming.⁵

These economic changes fueled massive divestment as downtown stores shuttered, and the city's population dwindled to approximately 30,000 from its 58,000 height.⁶ In 2000, of the city's 32,414 residents, 36 percent were African American, 36.5 percent white, 23.9 percent "other," and 2.6 percent multiracial. Hispanic of any race proved the largest category, comprising 50.9 percent of the population, with the white population that was not Hispanic only accounting for 12.1 percent of the community.⁷ Despite the complications in tracking Latinas and Latinos in the US Census, this information shows that the deindustrialized East Chicago had become increasingly nonwhite.

Citizens in Action recognized the problematic situation in East Chicago firsthand. As representatives of that community organization, Copeland and his colleagues engaged in the democratic practices often popularized and celebrated as traditions of our government. The organization's mission was threefold. Citizens in Action intended to inform East Chicagoans about issues within the city, address possible solutions, and make the government accountable for its residents.⁸ Many of these goals echoed earlier efforts by grassroots organizations and their engagement with liberalism during the War on Poverty. However, as Annelise Orleck, Lisa Gayle Hazirjian, and their fellow contributors in *The War on Poverty: A New Grassroots History* detailed, this period instigated an upsurge of organizing and democratic activism and the political engagement of impoverished and working-class communities across the United States.⁹ Primarily, federal initiatives brought considerable funding into urban and rural communities across the United States. As scholars within this edited volume show, accountability and the direction of funds into meaningful programming became vocal points of conflict between bureaucratic forces and residents.

Participating and engaging in these democratic practices in 1999, Citizens in Action was actively involved in a pivotal moment for the Democratic Party and liberalism. Lily Geismer's *Left Behind: The Democrats' Failed Attempt to Solve Inequality* describes this crucial moment of the rise of "New Democrats" in the waning decades of the twentieth century. According to Geismer, this new group of Democratic politicians and their form of liberalism advocated for "fusing government reform and economic growth with opportunity and equality."¹⁰ However, as Geismer noted, the public-private partnerships and faith in capitalism did not solve inequality, instead enshrining market-based solutions as a core of the Democratic Party policy.¹¹ Interestingly, this reinvention of liberalism had detractors among Democrats, such as Jesse Jackson, who believed that the party's future rested on incorporating those often marginalized and excluded: women, Black, and Latina/o communities.¹² As Geismer's work highlights, the late twentieth century proved a moment of considerable internal tension within the Democratic ranks. In comparison, Geismer focused on the turmoil at the national level, and the activism of Citizens in Action grants insight into how Democratic officials and voters strived for the character of their local party. While many voters might not have been familiar with the policy changes discussed at national conventions, residents did encounter Democratic power in their day-to-day experiences.

This chapter discusses how a multiracial coalition of predominantly Black and Latina/o residents engaged with liberalism at this crucial crossroads. In particular, the scholarship concerning Latinas and Latinos and liberalism is relatively scant. While Latinas and Latinos tend to vote or lean toward the Democratic Party and its political philosophy of liberalism, histories of their political engagement and relationship with it have left a plethora of recent and provocative work. Eduardo Contreras has argued that the inclination toward the Democratic Party "did not translate into a wholesale embrace of Democratic policies or candidates."¹³ While the political machine did incorporate Latinas and Latinos, these residents did not wholly embrace its structure in their community. I echo Contreras's claim that determining why most Latinas and Latinos align closely with liberalism and challenging the concept will expose the malleability of the ideology.¹⁴ Understanding how activists within Citizens in Action critiqued their elected officials, this chapter presents frustration with the status quo in a postindustrial community. Additionally, Latinas and Latinos found themselves essential members of the waning machine and some of its supporters. Understanding these critiques of liberalism offers an opportunity to understand the non-monolithic group, which serves numerous benefits depending on location, such as trending toward the GOP.[15]

In East Chicago, these residents confronted liberalism through the presence of a vibrant political machine. As previous scholarship argued, machine politics and New Deal Liberalism were at odds with the ascent of Franklin D. Roosevelt despite his close relationship with Tammany Hall politician Al Smith. New Deal reforms targeted urban machines by shifting government spending from the local and state levels to the federal level, an element that weakened the power of patronage. Those machines that survived through the Progressive Era were the antagonists of social and civil rights movements of the 1960s and 1980s; East Chicago's machine endured into the waning months of the twentieth century. In 1989, *U.S. News & World Report* proclaimed that East Chicago represented "the last political machine" in the United States.[16] While many politicians might find the idea of running a machine a deride on their integrity, longtime mayor of East Chicago, Robert Pastrick, embraced the city's designation. In 1999, Pastrick proclaimed, "East Chicago has always been a very political community since Day One, as long as I've lived here."[17] An article in the *Indiana Business Magazine* noted, "When taxes go up, residents generally don't holler because the industry is footing most of the bill for what remains one of the most expensive city governments and school systems in the state."[18] Despite decades of reform and the dwindling of political machines elsewhere in the nation, such as in nearby Chicago and the Richard J. Daley apparatus, Pastrick endured. The engagement of Citizens in Action against the Pastrick machine complements the narrative of progressive forces from marginalized demographics while noting how Latina/o and Black residents perpetrated the unequal playing field of hardball politics. Exacerbated by deindustrialization, activists targeted the lack of transparency, excessive spending, and a spoils system relating to public works.

This chapter argues that Citizens in Action navigated their roles as residents and municipal employees to challenge the entrenched political machine in East Chicago, Indiana. At a time when nationally, New Democrats are finding a merger between public good and private enterprise, Mayor Pastrick retained his hold over the city as the head of one of the final political machines in the United States. Exacerbated by the economic difficulties of a postindustrialized city, East Chicagoans banded under the

Citizens in Action banner to articulate their disdain for the status quo and call for accountability and transparency. Particularly, Citizens in Action protested multimillion-dollar bonds deemed to be utilized for municipal improvements and served as a vital rebuke against the "last political machine." Their activism highlights a critical moment of renegotiating liberalism in a very blue portion of a deeply red state. The decline of the political machine apparatus contributes to the narrative of decline in once staunchly liberal portions of the Midwest.

The organization of everyday citizens against structural powers, like political machines, was not new in East Chicago, the region, or the country. A plethora of scholarship details the Progressive challenge to political machines in urban environments.[19] These challengers decried the outright bribery, election tampering, and patronage that they felt corrupted democracy and advocated for various reforms in their cities, states, and the nation. However, government accountability and transparency issues continued beyond ward bosses' days. As Guian McKee noted with the War on Poverty, residents who advocated for community action during this moment stressed "community empowerment, grassroots participation and democratization, and attainment of rights and resources for identifiable groups marginalized by this racialized welfare state."[20] Earlier groups in East Chicago protested the practices of patronage and the political machine, as well as their deliberate exclusion of Black and Latina/o residents. In particular, the Concerned Latins Organization, a coalition of neighborhood groups affiliated with the Industrial Areas Foundation established by organizer Saul Alinsky, worked for an affirmative action ordinance in the city. At the same time, other members joined Black firefighters to protest hiring and promotion practices in the city's fire department.[21] Activists hoped that an affirmative action ordinance would allow them to circumvent the political machine's patronage powers.

Political machines arguably represent one of the most critical elements of US political history. These institutions evoke various names and places to scholars and the public: Richard J. Daley, Boss Tweed, and Tammany Hall, for example. How do these political machines operate? And more important, how do they endure? The political scientist duo Edward C. Banfield and James Q. Wilson defined a political machine as "a party organization that depends crucially upon inducements that are both specific and material."[22] For decades, political scientists and historians grappled with the machinations of political bosses and the extent of their corruption. Central to their inner workings is the idea of an exchange. To win elections and retain power, political machines exchanged or traded voters in their community and offered various items to secure their votes. While machines differed between cities and regions, Bernard Ross and Myron Levine outlined several general characteristics in *Urban Politics: Power in Metropolitan America*. First, political machines often operated under a hierarchical structure with centralized control; however, in-fighting did occur. Second, officials relied on material incentives to gain favor with potential voters. Third, a successful machine often focused on a singular objective: winning elections to retain power, which often saw the machine forgo ideological stances. Last, the hierarchical structure relied on machine agents to develop personal relationships with voters in their blocks and neighborhoods.[23]

East Chicago and its Democratic political machine possessed many of these characteristics. However, central to developing a political machine in the region, masses of immigrants arrived to work in the heavily industrialized region's manufacturing economy. These groups helped the city's longtime political leader, Robert Pastrick, develop a well-oiled machine that fueled his longevity in office. Like the rise of a Democratic machine in Chicago and its inventor, the Bohemian immigrant Anton Cermak, Pastrick sought to establish his own "house for all peoples."[24] Whereas Cermak incorporated German, Polish, Czech, and Jewish communities into leadership positions within the machine that was once exclusively Irish-dominated, Pastrick had to account for the growing presence of ethnic Mexicans, Puerto Ricans, and Black residents and the decline of the city's ethnic Eastern European contingent. During Cermak's time, these groups represented smaller percentages of Chicago's residents or communities that residential segregation could marginalize. However, as future Chicago mayors and other political bosses, like Pastrick, discovered, these new demographics forced them to reconceptualize their understanding of an ethnic European political machine that served as a "house for all peoples."

Citizens in Action emphasized grassroots power held by individual citizens. As a multiracial coalition, Citizens in Action attempted to organize in a structure that resisted decades of manipulation by the political machine. In a column for *The Times*, a regional newspaper that covered East Chicago and Northwest Indiana, Citizens in Action vice president Copeland exclaimed,

> The commoners of East Chicago have boiled everything down to colors. Look, the Mexicans are taking over. The blacks, they got everything. There's another illegal alien taking my job. Who are those peoples? The blacks, they think they

can say anything they want, while the whites who are left in this city feel like a sandwich cookie. One day, East Chicago, you will wake up and see that it's not about colors, it's about power.[25]

Whereas political machines previously relied on ethnic and racial divisions to mobilize voters and maintain access to patronage, Copeland acutely noted the regressive impact this held on the community. However, he was not the only one to do so. Rich James, a reporter for the *Gary Post-Tribune*, claimed, "Politics in East Chicago is kind of one of the last bastions of the old bosses and the old machines. And Pastrick's technique over the last couple of years was divide and conquer. He divided the whites, he divided the Hispanics, he divided the Blacks."[26] For decades, Pastrick made his career by dividing the residents of East Chicago; Citizens in Action recognized this and banded together, across racial and ethnic lines, to protest for a change. The formation of a multiracial coalition sought to undo the work of machines to divide a common cause.

A central component of their activism included communicating with residents and the broader region. Members frequently relied on canvassing door-to-door, as seen in the documentary *The King of Steeltown*. Additionally, members worked to televise their meetings, such as their discussion with State Senator Lonnie Randolph concerning changing East Chicago's school board from a mayoral-appointed board to an elected board.[27] Additionally, local public access television stations granted another avenue to discuss issues: candidate forums and accountability concerning the cost of a new police station.[28] Writing pieces against Mayor Pastrick and his administration, as Anthony Copeland did numerous times, also offered a public venue for dissent.

However, communication also referred to the perceived lack of transparency from the municipal administration. In 1996, Citizens in Action sued the City of East Chicago for violating the Indiana Open Door Law. Members of the organization requested notification about city council meetings about the municipal budget. Despite persistent calling by Citizens in Action activists and the media, no group received notice of the hearings until July 1998. The voicemail claimed that the council's finance committee had met behind closed doors already, surprising Citizens in Action member Colleen Aguirre. The organization hired legal counsel, who argued, "What happens especially in smaller cities or smaller towns is people who have been in office for a long time tend to develop a sense of ownership and tend to forget that they are servants of the people."[29] By arguing for transparency, Citizens in Action hoped to make their elected officials responsive to their demands.

Members of the Pastrick administration frequently battled with Citizens in Action members publicly. When member Gilda Orange asked Myrna Maldonado why neither the administration's East Chicago TV News program nor the public relations department employed Black residents, according to accounts, Maldonado, "peppering her speech with profanities," began a screaming match against Orange. Expressing regret over the incident to *The Times*, Maldonado blamed the internal divisions in the city's political hierarchy after the 1999 election. She claimed, "The political agendas are still strong and so are the affiliations. I'm dealing with political issues here, not issues relating to government." Describing the atmosphere for the reporter, Maldonado proclaimed, "I thought, God, I'm in a zoo."[30] The official meeting minutes noted twice that a "vocal argument took place" during this conversation about municipal employment.[31]

Another notable incident occurred between Latino residents Dr. Jorge Benavente and Edward Egipciaco and Puerto Rican councilman George Pabey. Egipciaco stated, "I was almost fired for fighting for the little guys. I even went to Federal Court. It took me five years but we beat the City. I don't care who the Councilman is, I am going to tell it like it is. When you [Pabey] ran for Councilman, you said now is the time to stand up for the little guys, but it seems to me that you have become a greedy politician."[32]

As the city prepared to enter the twenty-first century, the Citizens in Action targeted exorbitant expenses and how the council anticipated funding new construction. The proposed $30 million police station and municipal services building was one vital problem. An editorial in *The Times* phrased the issue succinctly: "Without a police presence, there would be anarchy in the streets. Without a citizen's voice, there would be a dictatorship holed up in an urban fortress." While acknowledging the importance of law enforcement for the community, the paper noted that proposals concerning them should not be taken at face value. Notably, as Citizens in Action reported, the value proved too high for the city.

Central to this work became organizing against the financing for a $30 million municipal service building, which would house the East Chicago Police Department, the city's clerk's office, the East Chicago Municipal Court, emergency radio dispatchers, and the paramedic service.[33] The current police department opened in 1961, and the city remodeled and expanded the structure in 1975.[34] In June 1998, the East Chicago City Council joined with representatives from the architecture firm Bittner and Detella, Inc., to present the plan for a new police station. The public hearing about the construction of the multimillion-dollar station welcomed feedback from the audience.[35]

The bond issue for a new building raised competing stances from the municipality and community. Initially, city officials labeled this attempt as anti-police and -law in the face of rising crime. An East Chicago police sergeant claimed, "Our lives are on the line every day. The people who are against the police station don't work at the police station."[36] While one neighborhood in the community, Roxana, previously attempted to hire a private security company to patrol its blocks, officials in Roxana Crime Watch criticized the city officials. They claimed officials should have come to the city's residents with multiple options.[37] According to coverage of the incident, the city believed that the idea of security guards for a neighborhood proved "unnecessary and insulting to police officers" and raised concerns about detaining suspects.[38] Inland Steel's counsel believed that the city should fund the project with revenue financed from the casino industry and not property taxes.[39] Citizens in Action member Colleen Aguirre claimed that Citizens in Action's protest originated as an accountability issue. During the meeting, Aguirre claimed, "We always wanted better pay for the Police. I think $25,000,000 is a lot of money. Maybe we should get a bid on the building."[40] Observing transparency, Lake County councilman and East Chicago resident John Aguilera argued, "They [the council] are putting one group against another. There are a lot of questions to be answered. Where are the riverboat monies? Fourteen million from riverboat that we don't have a record for? We need itemized documents about the money you have used and what do we have left."[41] The lack of transparency by the administration fostered doubt in the residents, and their demands for accountability highlighted the need for a change to the city's governing.

Citizens in Action turned to draft a petition for the city's proposed development. The community group delivered to the county auditor 518 signatures collected in the town, hoping to initiate a remonstrance-petition process among homeowners.[42] Previously, the organizers had an iteration of this petition to the city council on June 11, 1998. The petition claimed, "We the tax payers] of East Chicago, In. are objecting to the East Chicago City Council passing any legislation pertaining to a new Police Station until all information about said projects is made available to the taxpayers. This includes copies of all bids, plans and all information pertaining to bonds and/or financing."[43]

The petition lists forty-five names. Sixteen petitioners lived within seven unique addresses, showcasing the immediate family's role in organizing.

Additionally, twenty-two of the petitioners lived in the Roxana neighborhood, with the rest residing in the Harbor or South Side neighborhoods.[44] This initial petition was by no means representative of the entire city. Previously, a petition from the Lake County Democratic chairman, Stephen Stiglich, had opposed the bond issue. He was joined by Augusto Flores, a Puerto Rican city resident; both were former chiefs of police of the city of East Chicago.[45] Stiglich and Flores expressed their status as former police officers and chiefs of police for the department, as well as property owners and taxpayers, as their credentials for protesting what they deemed an "exorbitant" expense for the municipality.[46] Their inclusion as a protest against the bond issue diluted the firm law-and-order stance that some administration members stressed.

The work by Citizens in Action forced city officials to respond. At the end of July, during a public hearing, officials highlighted a series of revisions. The revised plan included reducing the size of the new police station by roughly seven thousand square feet, the cost to $20.9 million (from $27.5 million), and utilizing casino revenue for communication equipment updates. These changes reduced the bond required for the building from $37 million to $25.3 million.[47] At this revised hearing, city officials from the East Chicago Police Department and city controller's office presented video evidence of the dilapidated conditions in the current building and then explained the budget breakdown of the new municipal services building. The city controller's presentation claimed, "We're not trying to hide anything." Additionally, the city council doubled its stance as pro-law enforcement and passed an ordinance to provide police and fire department personnel with a 10 percent raise.[48]

Bonds remained a vital issue for Citizens in Action. In 1999 the organization and its activists protested the second round of $15 million for miscellaneous repairs, specifically sidewalk work throughout the city. During a public hearing, residents overwhelmingly voiced disagreement with the bond issue. The few residents who stated agreement with the bond indicated that in the first bond, the city and contractors did no work near their property and, in some cases, even their entire block. Other residents claimed that the contractors removed their fence and even a carport without fixing them. Two Citizens in Action members, Colleen Aguirre and Gilda Orange, expressed dual concerns about the work done with the previous bond. Aguirre claimed, "I want to put on a complete investigation. I want to know the contractors and who was responsible in authorizing the sidewalks. Homes have complete sidewalks around them." Orange concurred with the accountability issue, stating, "I am against it. We could use tax money to do private patios, private driveways and so forth? How much did this cost? You do not have an exact amount. Somebody okayed this?"[49]

The sidewalk repairs became a focal point during the campaign season of the 1999 Democratic primary for mayor of East Chicago. In 1999 a fierce Democratic primary between long-time incumbent Robert Pastrick and his former chief of police, Stephen "Stig" Stiglich, led to one of the most extensive corruption cases in Indiana's history. According to the US Attorney's Office, Pastrick's administration transformed an estimated $20 million in public funds into concrete and landscaping work for votes in the primary.

However, the extent of corruption was only partially known during the 1999 primary. The probe revealed a startling conclusion of concrete votes in East Chicago. The investigation, a combined effort of the federal and state governments, began in 2002. Initial work investigated the contractors hired to provide the aesthetic work throughout the city. Before the end of the year, a federal jury indicted an East Chicago business for wire, tax, and bankruptcy fraud. The federal attorneys accused the owner of overbilling the city of East Chicago for $302,388 for nonexistent trees. This same firm allegedly poured half a million dollars of concrete to curry favor for Mayor Pastrick in the 1999 primary.[50] The scheme, labeled sidewalks-for-votes, entailed public funds utilized to pay for concrete work on private property. The result was not limited to sidewalks but included driveways, patios, basketball courts, pools, basements, and landscaping work. Six of the administration's highest-ranked officials, nicknamed the Sidewalk Six, were involved. The resulting lawsuit, *State of Indiana v. Pastrick et al.*, named twenty-six defendants, including special advisers to the Pastrick administration and a few companies engaged in the work. Mayor Pastrick continuously stressed that he had "no knowledge" of the affair.

In a full page of coverage after Indiana attorney general Steve Carter announced the civil lawsuit against Pastrick and his administration, *The Times* noted the varied responses by those involved and everyday citizens. A resident, Luis Santiago, received a driveway in 1999 despite claiming that he did not want it; by 2004 it was crumbling. He proclaimed that "the concrete's no (expletive) good." His neighbor Frank Lumbreras contended that the lawsuit was just an extension of the Republican state battling the Democratic city government; an unnamed resident pessimistically proclaimed, "It doesn't seem like there's going to be much change.

But I wish something would change."[51] State Senator Earline Rogers, a Black woman and a representative from nearby Gary, Indiana, expressed concerns over how Hammond, Gary, and East Chicago spent their city's casino money. She claimed, "I've been disturbed about how the money has been spent . . . and think that when more people are involved in the decision-making that better decisions get made."[52]

Pastrick and members of the Democratic Party responded to the charges as an extension of the upcoming political campaign season. In his comments to *The Times*, Joe De La Cruz, a councilman in the city, said, "To me, it's all politically motivated to keep the Lake County Democrats down. Being a Republican, it's good ink for him downstate."[53] City councilman Joe Valdez's attorney questioned why the lawsuit was not filed in neighboring Hammond instead of South Bend. However, many of the twenty-six defendants listed and political officials not listed did not want to comment as they had not seen the lawsuit. The newspaper noted that their responses were typical for everyone reached in the two days since the announcement.[54]

However, Pastrick and his surrogates began an early defense against these charges. Before the state filed the charges, the city worked to set up a legal defense for its civil servants. In 2002, months before Pastrick formally announced his intention to run for reelection, the city council passed an ordinance requiring the city to defend public servants in civil and criminal cases where officials "believed they were acting legally and in the best interests of the city."[55] Activist Colleen Aguirre surmised it best when she questioned, "What are they doing, getting ready for indictments. Only in East Chicago. Not only do they break the law, but our tax dollars have to pay for their defense."[56]

As members of his administration faced indictment and charges, Pastrick issued a pledge for fair and ethical practices across all levels of government. In an editorial by *The Times* entitled "East Chicago Enters Its Ethical Phase," the newspaper proclaimed, "In his waning years as mayor of East Chicago, Robert Pastrick has finally found the religion of ethics."[57] The editorial noted Pastrick's call for a new position of an independent inspector general and the irony of the pledge, stating, "So now, late in the game, Pastrick is calling for ethics in his city. Better late than never."[58] The columns within the paper even extended to biting commentary against the Sidewalk Six and the citizens of East Chicago. Columnist Mark Kiesling proclaimed simply that "Pastrick won at the expense of the city treasury." When discussing city engineer Pedro Porras serving as a witness against some of his colleagues, Kiesling noted that the former's name is "Porras (pronounced "pour us," as in "pour us a driveway, please)." However, perhaps the most damning line of the column was Kiesling's conclusion that "many of the people who were having their driveways, patios and the rest poured at city expense knew exactly what was happening, and winked at it. The trial of the Sidewalk Six sends this message to them—your councilmen keep getting indicted because you keep taking their illegal largesse."[59] While some residents, such as Citizens in Action, worked to rebuke the machine, the antics continued because the administration incorporated the new demographics and worked to incentivize support from them. In 2004, Pastrick lost to his former chief of police, Puerto Rican George Pabey, in a special election. Pabey ran against Pastrick in 2003 but lost and mounted a legal defense, alleging widespread voter fraud as the absentee ballots skewed toward the political boss.[60]

Citizens in Action represented a crucial moment of community activism and direct public participation in democratic practices. From their demands for accountability and transparency to their more proactive steps toward a new political regime, Citizens in Action organized at a moment of increasing frustration with the status quo. Deindustrialization and its economic woes exacerbated tensions between the decaying machine and residents. Some residents turned to the stressed administration for support, from jobs to public works projects, and advertently supported the political machine. Other residents, like the Citizens in Action, demanded transparency from their officials and open communication for residents. In doing so, Citizens in Action advocated for a transparent process, responsive to informed residents, that did not have to be beholden to the political machine. Their frustration culminated in a scandal concerning the very bond issues that the activists protested, showing the very tangible impact of complacency. When a combined state and federal probe exposed that the Pastrick campaign utilized funds for municipal improvements to curry favor with residents across the municipality, the damage was already done. However, the growing discontent with Pastrick eventually paved the way for more dissenters and the election of some Citizens in Action members to office, such as Anthony Copeland, in 2003. Others, such as Colleen Aguirre, continued a career of activism, even when it placed her opposed to former Citizens in Action members who then served as elected officials.[61] These tensions highlighted the continued internal challenges in negotiating liberalism, even within a Democratic stronghold like East Chicago.

NOTES

1. *The King of Steeltown: Hardball Politics in the Heartland* (Sautter Communications, 2001).
2. "A Brief History of East Chicago," http://www.eastchicago.com/page80/page101/index.html, accessed December 2, 2022.
3. Indiana Writers' Program, *The Calumet Region Historical Guide: Containing the Early History of the Region as Well as the Contemporary Scene within the Cities of Gary, Hammond, East Chicago (including Indiana Harbor), and Whiting* (Gary, IN: Garman Printing Co., 1939), ix.
4. Indiana Writers' Program, *The Calumet Region Historical Guide*, 219.
5. "Riverboat Bill Floats through Ind. House," *Post-Tribune*, January 28, 1992; "UCO, Showboat Officials Pleased with Initial Talks," *The Times*, January 13, 1994; "E.C. Bids for Casino 'Still Open,'" *The Times*, January 31, 1994; "East Chicago Casino Hearings to Resume," *Indianapolis Star*, October 19, 1995.
6. 1950 Population Census Report, vol. III, chapter 10 (Washington, DC: Government Printing Office, 1952); "East Chicago, Indiana," *United States Census Quick Facts*, accessed December 2, 2022.
7. 2000 Population Census Report (Washington, DC: Government Printing Office, 2001); "East Chicago, Indiana," *United States Census Quick Facts*.
8. "Anthony Copeland," City of East Chicago, Indiana Directory, https://www.eastchicago.com/directory.aspx?EID=34, accessed June 20, 2022.
9. Annelise Orleck and Lisa Gayle Hazirjian, *The War on Poverty: A New Grassroots History, 1964–1990* (Athens: University of Georgia Press, 2011), 4.
10. Lily Geismer, *Left Behind: The Democrats' Failed Attempt to Solve Inequality* (New York: PublicAffairs, 2022), 19.
11. Geismer, *Left Behind*, 6–7.
12. Geismer, *Left Behind*, 111–112.
13. Eduardo Contreras, *Latinos and the Liberal City: Politics and Protest in San Francisco* (Philadelphia: University of Pennsylvania Press, 2019), 4.
14. Contreras, *Latinos and the Liberal City*, 5.
15. On the Latina/o vote as a nonmonolith, see Jasmine Aguilera, "Why It's a Mistake to Simplify the 'Latino Vote,'" *Time*, November 5, 2020. On Latina/os in the GOP, see Geraldo Cadava, *The Hispanic Republican: The Shaping of an American Political Identity, from Nixon to Trump* (New York: Ecco Press, 2020).
16. Paul Glastris, "The Last City Machine in America," *U.S. News & World Report* 107, no. 8 (1989): 29.
17. "Last City Machine in America," *Indiana Business Magazine*, March 1999; Mayor Robert Pastrick Folder, East Chicago Public Library (hereafter, ECPL), Main Branch, East Chicago History Room.
18. "Last City Machine in America," *Indiana Business Magazine*, March 1999, 10; Mayor Robert Pastrick Folder, ECPL.
19. Although not exhaustive, works include James Q. Wilson, *The Amateur Democrat: Club Politics in Three Cities* (Chicago: University of Chicago Press, 1962); Terry Golway, *Machine Made: Tammany Hall and the Creation of Modern American Politics* (New York: Liveright, 2014); Tyler Anbinder, *Five Points: The 19th Century New York City*

Neighborhood that Invented Tap Dance, Stole Elections, and Became the World's Most Notorious Slum (New York: Free Press, 2010); Steven P. Erie, *Rainbow's End: Irish-Americans and the Dilemmas of Urban Machine Politics, 1840–1985* (Berkeley: University of California Press, 1990); Richard Schneirov, *Labor and Urban Politics: Class Conflict and the Origins of Modern Liberalism in Chicago, 1864–97* (Urbana: University of Illinois Press, 1998); Mark Wahlgren Summers, *The Era of Good Stealings* (New York: Oxford University Press, 1993); James J. Connolly, *An Elusive Unity: Urban Democracy and Machine Politics in Industrializing America* (Ithaca, NY: Cornell University Press, 2010).

20. Guian A. McKee, "This Government Is with Us': Lyndon Johnson and the Grassroots War on Poverty," in Annelise Orleck and Lisa Gayle Hazirjian, eds., *The War on Poverty: A New Grassroots History* (Athens: University of Georgia Press, 2011), 34.

21. For more, see Emiliano Aguilar, "The Ratio of Inclusion in East Chicago, Indiana," in Theresa Delgadillo, Ramón H. Rivera-Servera, Geraldo L. Cadava, and Claire F. Fox, eds., *Building Sustainable Worlds: Latinx Placemaking in the Midwest* (Urbana: University of Illinois Press, 2022), 204–223.

22. Edward C. Banfield and James Q. Wilson, *City Politics* (New York: E. P. Dutton, 1963), 27.

23. For a conversation about these characteristics, see Bernard H. Ross and Myron A. Levine, *Urban Politics: Power in Metropolitan America*, 5th ed. (Itasca, IL: F. E. Peacock, 1996), 145–150.

24. See "A House for All Peoples," in Adam Cohen and Elizabeth Taylor, *American Pharoah: Mayor Richard J. Daley, His Battle for Chicago and the Nation* (Boston: Back Bay Books; reprint ed., 2001), 50–91; John Allswang, *A House for All Peoples: Ethnic Politics in Chicago, 1890–1936* (Lexington: University Press of Kentucky, 1971); Roger Biles, *Richard J. Daley: Politics, Race, and the Governing of Chicago* (DeKalb: Northern Illinois University Press, 1995); Steven P. Erie, *Rainbow's End: Irish-Americans and the Dilemmas of Urban Machine Politics, 1840–1985* (Berkeley: University of California Press, 1990).

25. "Superintendent Situation Is About Money, Power and Ignorance," *The Times*, January 1, 1997.

26. *The King of Steeltown: Hardball Politics in the Heartland*.

27. "Meeting Hits the Airwaves," *The Times*, January 26, 1997.

28. "Primary Candidates Appearing on Program," *The Times*, April 30, 1998; "Club Corner: East Chicago- Citizens in Action," *The Times*, June 25, 1998.

29. "A battle to Be Heard—and Informed," *The Times*, February 28, 1998.

30. "Councilman," *The Times*, March 15, 2000.

31. East Chicago Common Council Meeting, Regular Session, March 13, 2000.

32. East Chicago Common Council Meeting, Regular Session. March 13, 2000.

33. "Petition Derby Likely on Project," *The Times*, July 9, 1998; "Public Hearing on the Construction of a New Police Station Project," De La Garza Ivy Tech State College, Monday, June 8, 1998, East Chicago City Clerk's Office (hereafter, ECCC).

34. "East Chicago Police Department Folder," ECPL.

35. "Public Hearing on the Construction of a New Police Station Project," ECCC.

36. "Plan," *The Times*, July 28, 1998.

37. "Security Guard Plan on Hold," *The Times*, July 16, 1998.

38. "Security Guard Plan on Hold," *The Times*, July 16, 1998.

39. "Plan," *The Times*, July 28, 1998; "Public Hearing on the Construction of a New Police Station Project," ECCC.

40. Public Hearing on the Construction of a New Police Station Project," ECCC.
41. Public Hearing on the Construction of a New Police Station Project," ECCC.
42. "Petition Derby Likely on Project," *The Times*, July 9, 1998.
43. "Petition for Public Information," June 11, 1998, ECCC.
44. "Petition for Public Information," ECCC.
45. "Public Hearing on the Construction of a New Police Station Project," ECCC.
46. "Written Remonstrance in Opposition to Proposed Bond Issue for Construction of East Chicago Police Station," ECCC.
47. "E.C. Police Station Plans Revised," *The Times*, July 28, 1998.
48. "Regular Meeting, East Chicago Common Council," De La Garza Ivy Tech State College, Monday, July 27, 1998, ECCC.
49. "Public Hearing of the East Chicago Common Council," De La Garza Ivy Tech State College, Monday, July 12, 1999, ECCC.
50. "Contractor Indicted in East Chicago Scandal," *The Times*, December 10, 2002.
51. "Charges Don't Faze City Residents: Some Say Political Gain at Heart of State's Action," *The Times*, August 4, 2004.
52. "Senator Questions Use of Casino Cash," *The Times*, July 16, 2002.
53. "E.C. Mayor Says State's Lawsuit Is a Political Ploy: Other Defendants Agree, Question Lawsuit's Timing So Close to the Fall Election," *The Times*, August 4, 2004.
54. "E.C. Mayor Says State's Lawsuit Is Political Ploy," *The Times*, August 4, 2004.
55. "Town Looks to Protect Officials in Ordinance," *The Times*, June 26, 2002; East Chicago Ordinance 02-0011, "An Ordinance Prescribing Indemnification of City Employees and Elected Officials," ECCC; East Chicago Common Council, Regular Session, June 24, 2002, ECCC.
56. "Officials," *The Times*, June 26, 2002.
57. "East Chicago Enters Its Ethical Phase," *The Times*, March 19, 2004.
58. "East Chicago Enters Its Ethical Phase," *The Times*, March 19, 2004; East Chicago Common Council, Regular Session, March 8, 2004, ECCC.
59. "You Get What You're Bribed For," *The Times*, October 8, 2004.
60. *Pabey v. Pastrick*, 816 N.E.2d 1138 (Ind. 2004).
61. "East Chicago Residents Fear for Their Health," WBEZ Chicago, October 17. 2016.

PART TWO

Expending Citizenship in the
Age of Liberation

7

Humphrey, McGovern, and Mansfield

National Liberals and American Indian Self-Determination

DEAN J. KOTLOWSKI

During the 1960s, liberal politicians were out of step with American Indian self-determination. Liberal ideology, which promoted racial equality and economic opportunity for all Americans, often overlooked the unique aspirations of Indigenous peoples. Liberals also assumed that Indians sought the same rights as African Americans: to vote, get an education, find a job, and share the material comforts of an ever more prosperous America. In 1966, Senator Fred R. Harris, Democrat of Oklahoma, espoused "helping the American Indian become a full-fledged citizen, able to move with ease into the mainstream."[1] Yet the rise of the Indian rights movement in the late 1960s made such thinking passé. In 1972, Vine Deloria Jr. (Standing Rock Sioux), the former executive director of the National Congress of American Indians (NCAI), dismissed the presidential campaign of Senator Edmund S. Muskie, Democrat of Maine, as a "backward step" for Indians. "His recent mailing to Indians stressed his votes of the past on civil rights," Deloria complained. Muskie "looks like a liberal who wants to integrate Indians."[2]

Indians increasingly sought self-determination rather than equal rights or integration. Self-determination, a reporter for the American Indian Press Association explained, involved "giving federally recognized tribes greater control over their existence without ending the federal trust responsibility."[3] The National Congress of American Indians, the leading pan-Indian organization, advocated Indian control over federal programs, consultation on legislation that affected Indians, and curtailment of termination, the postwar policy that sought to end the trust relationship between tribes and the US government. In 1966 the NCAI asserted that many Indians did not "want to swim in the mainstream they largely regarded as polluted."[4] Instead, the celebration of Indigenous cultures received renewed emphasis. By 1968 young Indian activists spoke of "red power," that is, the "right not to demand anything from the white man's culture—and not to be dominated by it."[5] Great Society liberals evinced little understanding of such thinking. To be sure, federal funding to develop reservations, along with some War on Poverty initiatives, boosted tribal authority and Indian empowerment. Yet repudiation of termination did not happen until 1970, in a statement by Richard Nixon.

One might have thought heartland liberals were more attuned to American Indian self-determination, but Hubert H. Humphrey, George S. McGovern, and Mike Mansfield showed that this was not necessarily the case. Although all three men became national leaders, they emerged from modest circumstances in the northern reaches of the Great Plains. After earning postgraduate degrees, they gained entrance into what Humphrey called "the councils of the great and powerful."[6] In the US Senate, they represented states—Minnesota, South Dakota, and Montana—known for having conservative and progressive traditions as well as significant Indian populations. None of them became passionately identified with Indian causes. Partially this was because their ambitions and interests extended beyond the heartland. Humphrey became US vice president (1965 to 1969) and the Democratic nominee for president in 1968, as was McGovern in 1972. Mansfield served as majority whip (1957 to 1961) and majority leader (1961 to 1977) before becoming US ambassador to Japan (1977 to 1988). Their careers intersected with the Cold War and America's war in Vietnam, which Humphrey reluctantly supported and McGovern and Mansfield opposed. At home, expanding opportunity for all Americans animated all three men. They thus saw Indians not as distinctive cultural groups, having a unique relationship with the US government, but as isolated, destitute people who deserved a better life. In 1964, Humphrey averred: "The American Indian is in miserable shape and needs all the help we can give him."[7] The trio found themselves balancing the ingrained, settler-colonial outlook of their region's non-Indian majority, of which they were a part, against the demands of a vocal Indian minority.

The fact that Humphrey, McGovern, and Mansfield had to consider the concerns of American Indians underscores the degree to which Minnesota, Montana, and the Dakotas differed from states in the East, which had few federally recognized tribes. All three leaders could count on the support of Native Americans, who largely voted Democratic. Such loyalty owed much to Franklin D. Roosevelt's Indian New Deal, which had strengthened tribal authority, and efforts by liberal Democrats to moderate and slow the push for termination during the 1950s.[8] Tribes were also grateful for the funds they received from Great Society programs. Yet, political support from Indians may have led Humphrey, McGovern, and Mansfield to believe that they were more in sync with Native aspirations than they were.[9] The liberals' failure to repudiate termination gave Nixon an opening, which he seized. Nixon had an easier time endorsing Indian self-determination in part because his political roots lay beyond the Midwest and Great Plains, where Indians and non-Indians had long competed for land and resources.

Mansfield, Humphrey, and McGovern made uneven contributions to American Indian self-determination. Mansfield proved a passive figure who allowed fellow Montana Democrats, such as Senator James E. Murray, to handle Indian issues. Humphrey remained in lockstep with LBJ and the Great Society, touting economic assistance to impoverished Indians while exhibiting limited understanding of self-determination. Although McGovern exuded Eurocentric and integrationist biases, he went the farthest in asserting that Indians preferred an existence separate from mainstream American society. McGovern pushed ideas that best anticipated the Indian policy put into place by President Nixon, who defeated the South Dakota senator in the election of 1972. United by liberal values while possessing distinct leadership styles, personalities, and political sensibilities, Mansfield, Humphrey, and McGovern failed to press strongly or consistently for Indian self-determination.

Mansfield's ascent to Senate leadership and preoccupation with foreign affairs left him little time for American Indians. Born in New York, orphaned, and then raised in Montana, he worked in coal mines and earned a BA and MA from the University of Montana, where he taught Asian history. Elected to the House in 1942 and the Senate a decade later, Mansfield became known for his taciturn personality, assistance to constituents, and familiarity with China and Indochina, where he supported (and later opposed) US efforts to build a noncommunist state in South Vietnam. He backed New Deal–style public power projects and the unionization of Montana's workers. Yet this self-described "conservative-liberal" possessed a "cautious political view" that eased his ascent to Senate majority whip in 1957 and majority leader in 1961, when he succeeded Lyndon

Johnson.[10] Humphrey remembered Mansfield as "a quiet, contemplative leader, never forcing his own deeply held convictions on others."[11] On race, he remained middle-of-the-road, voting for LBJ's weak Civil Rights Act of 1957 and jettisoning a voting rights bill in 1962 after Southern Democrats threatened a filibuster. Mansfield did not fight hard for Indian rights. In 1954 he was unaware of a vote to terminate federal responsibility for the Ute Indians because he was in a meeting of the Senate Foreign Relations Committee, where he occupied a seat throughout his career in the Senate (1953 to 1977).[12]

Mansfield was more follower than leader in opposing assimilationist policies, particularly termination. Sanctioned by House Concurrent Resolution 108 (1953), termination sought to end the ways of life that kept Indians distinct from other Americans. Under the policy, tribes were to lose all privileges under treaties with the US government, Indians were to become subject to the same state laws as non-Indians, and tribal lands formerly held in trust by the federal government could be opened to sale. The NCAI fought termination during the 1950s and 1960s, as did Montana's tribes. The Confederated Salish and Kootenai Tribes of the Flathead Reservation deemed termination a threat to their culture and property. Agreeing, Representative Lee Metcalf, Democrat of Montana, argued that tribes had to be prepared for termination and that would take time.[13] Mansfield eventually adopted Metcalf's position. In 1954 he had pushed the idea that Indians needed to help themselves.[14] Such thinking was common among the "cowboy-settler constituency," that is, non-Indians who knew that ending federal supervision over tribes would ease the sale of Indian lands.[15] Nevertheless, 4 percent of Montana's population lived on Indian reservations, and the state's Blackfeet Nation also resisted assimilation.[16] By 1959, Mansfield had decided that termination "is fine" if Indians were "prepared for it" and "the majority of those living on the reservation favor termination."[17] This gradualist approach already had gained traction among Senate liberals, led by Montana's James Murray, who buried a bill to terminate the Flathead.[18] In 1960, Metcalf succeeded Murray in the Senate, where he reiterated that termination was acceptable only if a majority of a tribe wanted it.[19] A de facto division of labor ensued: Metcalf focused on Indian issues, becoming chair of the Senate Subcommittee on Indian Affairs in 1965, while Mansfield concentrated on national and international affairs.

Like many liberals, Mansfield backed economic assistance to American Indians. Yet, he sensed opposition from Dwight D. Eisenhower's White House, known for its fiscal conservatism, and from members of the Senate Interior Committee, principally Westerners attuned to the interests and votes of non-Indians.[20] Mansfield could not afford to ignore non-Indian voices—nor those of Montana's Indians. The squalor on Hill 57, a community of homeless Indians in Great Falls, led him to question the effectiveness of an administration program to relocate Indians from reservations to urban areas. Mansfield's answer was more social services for Indians in cities rather than halting this assimilationist project.[21] He cosponsored a resolution, pushed by Murray and later shelved by the Senate, that required tribes to reach economic parity with non-Indians before the government considered terminating them. Supporting this resolution did not signal deepening interest in Indians: Mansfield mistakenly referred to House Concurrent Resolution 108, the cornerstone of the termination policy, as "Senate Concurrent Resolution 108."[22]

Mansfield's approach to Indian issues remained reactive and unimaginative, even as federal policy shifted. By backing the War on Poverty, Mansfield strove to help needy people in general as well as tribes. He also cosponsored early versions of the Indian Self-Determination and Education Assistance Act, proposed by Nixon and signed by President Gerald R. Ford in 1975, which allowed federal agencies to contract out services to tribes.[23] Yet he continued to support termination, if approved by tribes, even after Nixon officially renounced the policy in 1970.[24] Mansfield saw no role for the Senate Foreign Relations Committee in ending the seventy-one-day armed occupation of Wounded Knee, South Dakota, by members of the American Indian Movement (AIM). In 1973 AIM took over Wounded Knee, on the Pine Ridge Indian Reservation, partially to displace the elected Oglala Sioux government. Another demand, to revise the Oglala Sioux's 105-year-old treaty with the US government, left Mansfield unmoved: "Evidently, the Foreign Relations Committee was not consulted, nor did it pass on the treaties when they were originally entered into." Rather than reviewing treaties, he urged enactment of "appropriate legislation" to assist Indians, whom he called "troubled and unhappy citizens."[25] Overall, Mansfield saw "Indian sovereignty" not as a means to empower tribes, but as a "very difficult" problem that Indians and non-Indians had to work out together.[26] The Montanan's stance reflected his cautious demeanor as much as the political demographics of his state.

Humphrey's engagement with Indian issues surpassed Mansfield's, even if their outlooks differed little. One percent of Minnesota's population was Indigenous, a figure that has remained constant since 1860. Federally recognized tribes included the Sioux, Ojibwe, and Chippewa. Many Indians had migrated to cities, where activism flourished—AIM was organized in Minneapolis in 1968. Earlier, as mayor of Minneapolis (1945 to 1948), Humphrey had appointed the first Indians to the city's

Human Rights Commission. He crowed about that and about being adopted as "Chief Leading Feather" into the Red Lake Band of Chippewa, whose chair, Roger Jourdain, was a political ally. Such boasts came during an address before the NCAI—in 1969, as demands for self-determination gathered momentum.[27] Before that, as a senator (1949 to 1964), Humphrey, along with Murray and Mansfield, espoused gradual, "constructive termination" and programs "to raise the Indian standard of living."[28] In 1964 he bemoaned deficiencies in Indian health care, education, employment, and housing, which he called "a mirror" of the country's wider poverty crisis. One culprit, according to Humphrey, was tribal ways: "Indians have special cultural problems which make it more difficult to integrate them into the economic life of a modern society with its rapid technological developments." Such "isolation" made Indian poverty uniquely difficult, and strong government action was necessary. Humphrey asserted that "Indians and their reservations must be prime targets in the war on poverty that President Johnson has asked us to undertake."[29]

Humphrey's thoughts derived from several sources. His belief in equality of opportunity reflected his own rise—and optimism. Humphrey's attachment to his native region exceeded that of Mansfield. He extolled his early life in South Dakota, which had grown dramatically, he noted, after "Indian lands" became "available to settlers." Humphrey revered his father, a pharmacist, whose veneration of the Great Plains sounded like a paean to settler colonialism: "We are in the middle of this great big continent, here in South Dakota, with the land stretching out for hundreds of miles, with people who can vote and govern their own lives, with riches enough for all if we take care to do justice."[30] After earning a BA from the University of Minnesota and MA in political science from Louisiana State University, Humphrey entered politics and strove to advance justice and opportunity. He reminded a group of Indians that he had "come a long way" from his birthplace in Wallace, South Dakota. In the same address, he applauded "our fellow citizens of Indian ancestry."[31] The terminology was predictable. Equal rights and opportunities for all citizens had long been a goal of Humphrey's, from his stirring speech before the Democratic National Convention in 1948 to his success, as Senate majority whip—under Mansfield—in winning passage of the Civil Rights Act of 1964. In Minneapolis, he had seen "rampant prejudice" toward Blacks and American Indians and resolved to stamp it out.[32] Such priorities matched those of Minnesota's Democratic-Farmer-Labor Party, in which Humphrey became a key figure. Partially to counter his image as "an unpolished Midwesterner," Humphrey built "a national constituency" that included workers, farmers, minority groups, and people in need.[33] In 1954 he simultaneously helped farmers, attacked global poverty, and laid the foundation for the Food for Peace program when he coauthored legislation to sell surplus US agricultural goods overseas.[34]

In 1964, Humphrey raged against poverty's "destructive toll on the human spirit" without recognizing his own biases. He saw no difference between the aspirations of Blacks and American Indians. He disparaged Native cultures for stressing "a limited agriculture" and "mystical" ties to the land that discouraged Indians from thinking "in economic terms."[35] Determined to "make Rural America modern"—reservations as well as non-Indian areas—Humphrey praised the Economic Development Administration, which funneled federal dollars to hard-up communities, and the Office of Economic Opportunity (OEO), which waged the War on Poverty.[36] Yet the OEO's Community Action Program empowered local people and governments, including tribes, to design and administer antipoverty projects. It thus encouraged liberals, including Humphrey, to envision tribes as participants in, rather than as obstacles to, economic advancement. In 1967, Vice President Humphrey endorsed a "true partnership" that would tether "federal technical and financial assistance" to "active tribal participation" in solving "local problems."[37] In so stating, he began to acknowledge some form of Indian self-determination.

As the vice president's political ambition grew, his views on Indian rights evolved, at least to a point. Sensing rising American Indian activism, LBJ in 1968 endorsed Indian "self-help, self-development, self-determination."[38] Johnson's statement suggested sympathy toward Native peoples and agency without abandoning ethnocentric rhetoric about the benefits of economic modernization and racial integration. Nevertheless, Humphrey hailed the message as a "charter of new freedom and new opportunity." He also predicted that the National Council on Indian Opportunity (NCIO), established by Johnson and chaired by the vice president, would marshal federal programs to unleash the "great potential" of Indian Country.[39] To appeal to American Indian voters during the 1968 campaign, Humphrey trumpeted his role in the council, which included government officials and established Indian leaders such as Roger Jourdain. At the NCIO's first meeting, Humphrey welcomed "greater Indian participation" in federal programs and the council's Indians as "not only as equals, but in many respects as the senior members."[40] Yet since the vice president lost the election to Nixon and left office in 1969, his involvement with the NCIO lasted only a few months. In 1972, Vine Deloria vented that Humphrey "has done little actual work for Indians." He had been "long on talk, short on performance for tribes outside of Minnesota."[41] AIM leader Clyde Bellecourt (Ojibwe) agreed: "Every time he (Humphrey) ran for office he made a tour of the reservations, and was made an honorary chief here, a warrior there, etc. And he didn't do a damn thing."[42]

After returning to the Senate (1971 to 1978), Humphrey helped a Wisconsin tribe when he endorsed restoring the Menominee, terminated in 1961, to federally recognized status. The Menominee Restoration Act (1973), pushed by Menominee activists such as Ada Deer, won enactment following Wounded Knee, when Indian issues had gained the public's attention. The law reinforced Nixon's earlier repudiation of termination. It was, the Native American Rights Fund averred, "a symbol for all Native Americans" that the US government "can be used as a tool to preserve Indian culture."[43] Yet Humphrey's denunciation of the Menominee's termination came after prodding by Ada Deer, and he asserted that restoration was in order because a "united" tribe demanded it.[44] Most important, Humphrey's support came during the Democratic presidential primaries in 1972, after rivals Muskie and McGovern had championed the Menominee's cause.[45]

George McGovern went further than either Mansfield or Humphrey in endorsing Indian self-determination. Although McGovern's causes included relief to farmers, alleviation of global hunger, and world peace—which he tied together as director of the Food for Peace program (1961 to 1962)—he was attuned to the needs of South Dakota's 35,000 Indians. In 1958, McGovern explained, as few US officials had, that integration had little appeal in Indian Country. Indians, he noted, disparaged non-Indian culture as "materialistic and grasping." They sought "to perpetuate their tribal identification and tradition" and resented being "thrown into the American melting-pot."[46] Eight years later, he told Senate colleagues that "self-determination" had to be "the foremost characteristic" of Indian policy. McGovern rejected "arbitrary" termination, relocation programs, and chatter about "the attributes of 'mainstream' society.'" He proposed expanding OEO programs and allowing the government to contract out federal services to tribes—a foretaste of Nixon's policy.[47] "I am impressed by what the Senator says and how he says it," declared the Chicago-based activist Robert K. Thomas (Cherokee). "Maybe, we have a new day dawning on the Indian scene!"[48] McGovern put his thoughts into a resolution, which Deloria hailed for quelling fears of "premature termination."[49] The Senate approved the resolution in 1967, but the House never passed it.

McGovern's actions reflected various influences. The son of a minister and grandson of a miner, McGovern grew up in a state that stressed individualism, welcomed government relief during the Great Depression, and was grounded in settler colonialism—as a boy, McGovern devoured books about "the American frontier, Indian scouts, hunters, [and] trappers."[50] After receiving the Distinguished Flying Cross in World War II, he earned a PhD in history from Northwestern University and taught at Dakota Wesleyan University, where he displayed unease with America's containment-centered foreign policy and sympathy for "social revolutions" against "economic distress."[51] As a member of the US House (1957 to 1961) and Senate (1963 to 1981), he was less of a Cold Warrior than Humphrey, a mentor, or Mansfield, with whom he shared an interest in Asia. In addition to drawing connections between foreign and domestic policy, especially in fighting global hunger, he promoted "a very inclusive liberalism" encompassing farmers, workers, young people, and minority groups such as American Indians.[52] Yet inclusion often meant integration. Like other liberals, McGovern favored foreign-aid-style assistance to tribes, arguing that the method "has been applied successfully in underdeveloped areas of the world" and could enable "Indian communities" to achieve the same standard of living as non-Indian areas.[53] As Indian issues gained national attention in the late 1960s, McGovern's interest grew. Between 1967 and 1972, he chaired the Senate's Subcommittee on Indian affairs.

McGovern's tenure as chair of the Indian Affairs subcommittee proved frustrating. In 1970, Nixon seized the limelight when he renounced termination and signed legislation to return the area around Blue Lake, in New Mexico, to the Taos Pueblo. The pathbreaking settlement of the Blue Lake dispute—in land rather than in cash—had been pushed earlier by McGovern.[54] Further Indian reforms languished, however, as conservatives remained entrenched on the House and Senate Interior committees. Facing such obstructionists, and increasingly focused on the Vietnam War and presidential politics, McGovern threatened to resign as chair of the Indian Affairs subcommittee.[55] In 1973 fellow Democrat (and South Dakotan) James G. Abourezk succeeded him. A non-Indian born on the Rosebud Indian Reservation, Abourezk focused intently on a range of Indian issues. He coauthored the Indian Self-Determination Act (1975), co-sponsored (with Humphrey and McGovern) the Indian Child Welfare Act (1978), and helped to establish the American Indian Policy Review Commission.[56] Such breakthroughs came after termination proponents Clinton P. Anderson, Democrat of New Mexico, and Gordon Allott, Republican of Colorado, had departed the Senate in 1972. The Wounded Knee occupation also provided a boost, causing Americans to ask Congress: "What are you going to do for the poor Indians?"[57]

McGovern showed little leadership during Wounded Knee. Non-Indians in South Dakota opposed AIM's takeover of the area. Caught between "hostile constituent sentiment" and his past "liberalism on Indian causes," McGovern walked "a tightrope," according to one journalist.⁵⁸ He assailed Nixon's "containment policy"—negotiations that ultimately ended the standoff—while urging forcible removal of the occupiers: "We cannot have one law for a handful of publicity-seeking militants and another law for the ordinary citizens."⁵⁹ Nixon might have said the same about the antiwar protesters whom McGovern had embraced. In response to Wounded Knee, McGovern did little beyond advocating a review of federal Indian programs and voicing solidarity with elected tribal leaders.⁶⁰ Although he and Abourezk negotiated the release of eleven hostages held by AIM, the initiative originated with Abourezk.⁶¹ After Wounded Knee, Abourezk became the face of Indian policy in Congress, while McGovern concentrated on other matters, including foreign policy and the liberal organization Americans for Democratic Action, where he served as president.⁶² The division of duties resembled the one between Mansfield and Metcalf in Montana.

In 1972, Vine Deloria, scholar as well as activist, graded the Indian records of leading presidential candidates. Mansfield escaped notice, for his leadership ambitions had been fixed on the Senate rather than the White House. Humphrey received harsh criticism: the Minnesotan needed to "get to work on Indian rights" if he wanted "to get the Indian vote." McGovern was a better choice for Indians, but he seemed "preoccupied on the Vietnam issue" and had been blocked by Senate conservatives "from doing much" with the Indian Affairs subcommittee. The sitting president's repudiation of termination impressed Deloria, who concluded: "Nixon has the best record of anyone."⁶³ (The comment was more an observation than a political endorsement.) There were many reasons why Nixon backed Indian rights. Doing so enabled him to appeal to younger, liberal-minded Americans as well as to the wider public. Red Power protest put Indian self-determination on the president's agenda. His moderate Republican ideology kept it there. Bolstering tribes meshed with Nixon's effort to devolve federal programs to states, cities, and local governments. Nixon's antipathy to forced integration between Blacks and whites led him to see value in supporting minority-run institutions, including Indian tribes.⁶⁴ President Ford continued Nixon's policy when he signed the Indian Self-Determination Act, dubbing it "a milestone" designed "to strengthen tribal governments."⁶⁵

Humphrey, McGovern, and Mansfield lagged behind Nixon and Ford in pushing for self-determination. National and international events, and ambitions, distracted each Democrat from American Indian matters. Representing states with overwhelmingly non-Indian populations, they treaded cautiously as tribes sought greater authority. Humphrey, McGovern, and Mansfield eventually supported the Indian Self-Determination Act. Until the 1970s, however, aspects of their liberal ideology proved unhospitable to Indian concerns. Ideals of equal rights and racial integration, when pressed, signaled something harmful to Indians: the end of their unique rights, privileges, and institutions and renewed efforts to assimilate them into non-Indian society. Indians instead preferred to celebrate their cultures, empower tribes, maintain the federal trust relationship, and, as Annie Wauneka (Navajo) put it, be recognized "as a special people" with "our own special rights and dignity."[66] "We're talking about human rights, not civil rights," Clyde Bellecourt insisted. "We're not talking about equality. . . . We're talking about rights that were taken away from us."[67] For much of their careers, Humphrey, McGovern, and Mansfield emphasized fighting poverty and bringing Indians into the mainstream. It was a characteristically liberal appeal to the desires of Americans generally rather than those of Indians specifically.

NOTES

The author presented an early version of this chapter at Central Region Humanities Center Speakers' Series, Ohio University, Athens, in 2023. He thanks Katherine Jellison for arranging the lecture and for her helpful comments. Further comments and guidance were provided by Dean J. Fafoutis, Jon K. Lauck, Catherine McNicol Stock, and the anonymous reviewers of this volume.

1. Fred R. Harris, "American Indians—A New Destiny," *U.S. Congressional Record*, April 21, 1966, 8312, Folder 10, Box 42, Fred R. Harris Collection, Carl Albert Congressional Research and Studies Center (hereafter, CAC), University of Oklahoma, Norman.

2. American Indian Press Association (AIPA) news release, "Politics 1972—A Preliminary Glance," undated, AIPA—News Releases—Newspaper Clippings Folder, Box 145, Series 5: Indian Rights Organizations, National Congress of American Indians Papers (NCAI) Papers, National Anthropological Archives, Smithsonian Institution, Suitland, Maryland.

3. AIPA news release, August 9, 1974, A.I.P.A. Folder, Box 9, Bradley H. Patterson Jr. Files, Staff Member and Office Files, Richard M. Nixon Presidential Papers (hereafter, NPP), Richard Nixon Library, Yorba Linda, California.

4. Daniel M. Cobb, "Philosophy of an Indian War: Indian Community Action in the Johnson Administration's War on Indian Poverty, 1964–1968," *American Indian Culture and Research Journal* 22, no. 2 (1998): 74.

5. Kimmis Hendrick, "U.S. Indians Ask Voice in Land-Policy Decisions," *Christian Science Monitor*, April 25, 1968, Indian Message Responses Folder, Box 368, Frederick Panzer Files, Lyndon B. Johnson Library (hereafter, LBJL), Austin, Texas.

6. Hubert H. Humphrey, *The Education of a Public Man: My Life and Politics* (Minneapolis: University of Minnesota Press, 1991), 7.

7. Hubert H. Humphrey press release, May 9, 1964, Washington, DC: American Indian Capitol Conference Folder (press release and text), May 8, 9, 1964, Box 13, Speech Text File, Hubert H. Humphrey Papers, Minnesota Historical Society, St. Paul (hereafter, MHS).

8. For the role of Eisenhower-era termination policy in turning Dakota Indians against the Republican Party, see Sean Flynn's chapter in this collection. Although the Indian New Deal contained assimilationist impulses and not all tribes embraced FDR's policy, it became a positive reference point for later advocates of self-determination. A journalist for the American Indian Press Association asserted in 1974: "The Nixon administration, beginning January 20, 1970, has been in the eyes of even the most critical observers one of the most active in Indian affairs since that of the so-called 'Indian New Deal' under Democratic President Franklin D. Roosevelt in the 1930s and 1940s." AIPA news release, August 9, 1974, A.I.P.A. Folder, Box 9, Patterson Jr. Files, NPP.

9. Encouragement by leaders such as Roger A. Jourdain, chair of the Red Lake Band of Chippewa Indians, reinforced such sentiments. Jourdain was a force in Minnesota politics and a long-time supporter of Humphrey and Walter F. Mondale. In 1976, Jourdain reminded Vice President-Elect Mondale: "Tribal leaders in Minnesota eagerly and publicly supported the Carter-Mondale ticket." Roger A. Jourdain to Walter F. Mondale, December 9, 1976, 1977, In Jan.-March Folder, Location #149.J.12.10, Vice Presidential Papers, Walter F. Mondale Papers, MHS.

10. Don Oberdorfer, *Senator Mansfield: The Extraordinary Life of a Great American Statesman* (Washington, DC: Smithsonian Books, 2003), 59.

11. Humphrey, *Education of a Public Man*, 181.

12. Mike Mansfield to Cornelius Byrne, May 14, 1954, Leg Interior Indian Aff. S. 2670 Utah Withdrawal Bill Folder, Box 9, Series 9, Mike Mansfield Papers, University of Montana, Missoula (hereafter, UM).

13. Typescript notes for a radio address, undated [1954], Folder 1, Box 225, Lee Metcalf Papers, Montana Historical Society, Helena.

14. Mike Mansfield, "Failure of the Indian Bureau," *U.S. Congressional Record—Appendix*, February 3, 1954, A868, Termination and Federal Control of Indians 1954–1955 Folder, Box 46, Series 10, Mansfield Papers.

15. Philleo Nash Oral History, June 5, 1967, 680, Harry S. Truman Library, Independence, Missouri.

16. Typescript statement, "No China Policy for the Indians of the United States," [1950s], Folder 1, Box 352, Series 1, James E. Murray Papers, UM.

17. Mansfield to Madeline Skinner Colliflower, July 14, 1959, Folder 3, Box 58, Series 9, Mansfield Papers.

18. James E. Murray to Raymond W. Gray, March 2, 1954, Folder 2, Box 276, Series 1, Murray Papers.

19. Lee Metcalf to Indian Tribal Officials, August 6, 1966, Folder 5, Box 227, Metcalf Papers.

20. Mansfield to John Woodenlegs, June 23, 1958, and Mansfield to Margaret Curran, August 5, 1958, Folder 11, Box 39, Series 9, Mansfield Papers.

21. Mansfield, "Federal Indian Policy," *U.S. Congressional Record—Senate*, April 9, 1956, 5280–5283, Folder 3, Box 47, Series 10, Mansfield Papers.

22. Mansfield, "Federal Responsibility towards Indians," *U.S. Congressional Record—Senate*, March 5, 1959, 2954, Folder 3, Box 58, Series 9, Mansfield Papers.

23. S. 3157, February 9, 1972, Folder 26, box 67, and S. 1017, February 26, 1973, Folder 4, Box 83, both in Series 8, Mansfield Papers.

24. Mansfield to Charles Kennedy, March 9, 1971,Indians—Flathead Re: Proposed Termination of Reservation Folder, Box 444, Series 10, Mansfield Papers.

25. Mansfield statement, March 6, 1973, Folder 2, Box 31, Series 22, Mansfield Papers.

26. Mansfield to R. W. Gustafson, November 13, 1975, Folder 1, Box 488, Series 10, Mansfield Papers.

27. Humphrey remarks, April 9, 1969, National Congress of American Indians, Chicago, Illinois, April 9, 1969, Folder, Box 40, Speech Text File, Humphrey Papers.

28. Indian Rights Association News Notes, August 12, 1955, Folder 33, Box 6, William Zimmerman Jr. Papers, Center for Southwest Research and Special Collections, Zimmerman Library, University of New Mexico, Albuquerque.

29. Humphrey speech, May 9, 1964, Washington, DC: American Indian Capitol Conference Folder (press release and text), May 8, 9, 1964, Box 13, Speech Text File, Humphrey Papers.

30. Humphrey, *Education of a Public Man*, 7, 6.

31. Undated speech draft, Indians Folder, Box 1332, Vice Presidential Speech and Miscellaneous Files, Humphrey Papers.

32. Humphrey, *Education of a Public Man*, 67.

33. Humphrey, *Education of a Public Man*, 112, 105.

34. Arnold A. Offner, *Hubert Humphrey: The Conscience of the Country* (New Haven, CT: Yale University Press, 2018), 104.

35. Humphrey speech, May 9, 1964, Washington, DC: American Indian Capitol Conference Folder (press release and text), May 8, 9, 1964, Box 13, Speech Text File, Humphrey Papers.

36. Humphrey handwritten comment on Humphrey remarks, April 9, 1969, National Congress of American Indians Folder, Chicago, Illinois, April 9, 1969, Box 40, Speech Text File, Humphrey Papers.

37. Robert W. Fenwick, "Humphrey Pledges Victory Over Poverty," *Denver Post*, September 10, 1967, Newspaper Clippings by Date—Sept. 1–29, 1967, Folder, Box 1348, Vice Presidential Trip Files, Humphrey Papers.

38. White House press release, the President's Message to Congress on "The Forgotten American," March 6, 1968, Indian Message—1968 Folder, Box 18, Fred Bohen Files, LBJL.

39. Thomas A. Britten, *The National Council of Indian Opportunity: Quiet Champion of Self-Determination* (Albuquerque: University of New Mexico Press, 2014), 46.

40. Humphrey press release, Indian Opportunity Council Folder, July 16, 1968, Box 34, Speech Text File, Humphrey Papers.

41. AIPA news release, "Politics 1972," undated, AIPA—News Releases—Newspaper Clippings Folder, Box 145, Series 5, NCAI Papers.

42. Anna Pearse, "Minneapolis: Emergence of Indian Power" [ca. 1970], 165, Location #153.L.10.13B, Senate Papers, Mondale Papers.

43. *Native American Rights Fund Announcements*, October–December 1973, 9, http://narf.org/nill/documents/nlr/nlr2-3.pdf, accessed March 13, 2022.

44. Humphrey statement in response to a request by Ada Deer [1972], Statement

on Menominee Indians, March 31, 1972, Folder, Box 46, Speech Text File, Humphrey Papers.

45. "Dan S." to Joe Cerrell, March 31 1972, Statement on Menominee Indians, March 31, 1972, Folder, Box 46, Speech Text File, Humphrey Papers.

46. McGovern speech, "The Inconvenient Indian" [late 1958], Folder 14, Box 134, Association on American Indian Affairs (AAIA) Papers, Seeley G. Mudd Manuscript Library, Princeton University, Princeton, New Jersey (hereafter, PU).

47. George S. McGovern, "Indian Policy—1966," *U.S. Congressional Record*, October 13, 1966, S. Con. Res. 114—McGovern Folder, Box 598, George S. McGovern Papers, PU.

48. *Indian Voices*, October 1966, 20, Indian Voices Folder, Box 8, Minnesota Department of Human Services Library Collection, Social Welfare History Archives, University of Minnesota Library Special Collections and Archives, Minneapolis.

49. Vine Deloria Jr. to George S. McGovern, October 17, 1966, S. Con. Res. 114—McGovern Folder, Box 598, McGovern Papers.

50. George S. McGovern, *Grassroots: The Autobiography of George McGovern* (New York: Random House, 1977), 14.

51. Thomas J. Knock, *The Rise of a Prairie Statesman: The Life and Times of George McGovern* (Princeton, NJ: Princeton University Press, 2016), 138.

52. Knock, *The Rise of a Prairie Statesman*, 99.

53. AAIA, "A Legislative Program for 1959," February 1959, Folder 33, Box 33, Departmental Series, Carl Albert Collection, CAC.

54. Dean J. Kotlowski, *Nixon's Civil Rights: Politics, Principle, and Policy* (Cambridge, MA: Harvard University Press, 2001), 202–203.

55. McGovern to Henry M. Jackson, January 26, 1971, Indian Affairs 6–1 Folder, Box 278, McGovern Papers.

56. "Legislation Sponsored or Cosponsored by James Abourezk,"congress.gov website, https://www.congress.gov/member/james-abourezk/A000017?r=66&q=%7B%22house-committee%22%3A%22Natural+Resources%22%2C%22bill-status%22%3A%22passed-both%22%7D, accessed March 15, 2022.

57. William Greider, "New Spirit in Congress Brightens Outlook for Indian Legislation," *Washington Post*, July 8, 1973, G1.

58. William Claiborne, "Wounded Knee Is McGovern's Achilles Heel," *Washington Post*, April 12, 1973, A4.

59. United Press International, "McGovern Urges U.S. Oust Indians," *Washington Post*, April 22, 1973, A5.

60. John Kifner, "Federal Offer Is Spurned by Indians as Talks Go On," *New York Times*, March 6, 1973, 30; William Chapman, "'Main Line' Indians Resent Militant Role," *Washington Post*, March 29, 1973, A3.

61. Associated Press, "11 Hostages Freed at Sioux Village," *Baltimore Sun*, March 2, 1973, A1; James G. Abourezk, *Advise and Dissent: Memoirs of South Dakota and the U.S. Senate* (Chicago: Lawrence Hill Books, 1989), 207–209.

62. Jon K. Lauck, "The Decline of South Dakota Democrats and the Fall of George McGovern," in Jon K. Lauck and Catherine McNicol Stock, eds., *The Conservative Heartland: A Political History of the Postwar American Midwest* (Lawrence: University Press of Kansas, 2020), 255–256.

63. AIPA news release, "Politics 1972," undated, AIPA—News Releases—Newspaper Clippings Folder, Box 145, Series 5, NCAI Papers.

64. Kotlowski, *Nixon's Civil Rights*, 192–195.

65. White House press release, January 4, 1975, 1975/01/04 S1017 Indian Self-Determination and Educational Assistance Act Folder, Box 21, Legislation Case Files, Gerald R. Ford Library, Ann Arbor, Michigan.

66. Annie Wauneka to Walter J. Hickel, September 25, 1969, Folder 9, Box 155, 91st Congress, Congressional Papers, Barry Goldwater Papers, Arizona State University Library, Tempe.

67. Pearse, "Minneapolis: Emergence of Indian Power," 163, Location #153.L.10.13B, Senate Papers, Mondale Papers.

8

"I Gave a Dam about a Dam"

Jim Jontz and the Fight for Big Pine Creek in Indiana

RAY E. BOOMHOWER

❖ ❖ ❖ ❖ ❖ ❖ ❖ ❖ ❖ ❖ ❖ ❖ ❖ ❖ ❖ ❖

For those struggling to survive during the height of the Great Depression in the 1930s, dams—great earthen or concrete structures that controlled rampaging rivers or created cheap hydroelectric power—were viewed with pride as marks of progress and prosperity. In the 1940s and 1950s, the US government sought to control flooding on the Wabash River basin in both Indiana and Illinois. The US Army Corps of Engineers drew up plans to build thirteen dams on tributaries of the Wabash and more than a hundred other projects to meet the needs of the 33,000-square-mile watershed until the year 2020. One of the proposed dams and resulting reservoir and lake was to be constructed on Big Pine Creek, which flowed from southwestern White County in Indiana and south through Benton and Warren Counties before entering the Wabash River near Attica.

Along its route Big Pine Creek ran through scenic sandstone cliffs and Fall Creek Gorge, noteworthy for the large potholes carved into the floor of the steep-sided canyon. The canyon walls are covered with ferns, mosses, and liverworts, while red-tailed hawks swoop overheard scanning the tops of white pine trees on the sandstone bluffs for unwary squirrels and the ground below for cottontail rabbits. In October 1965 the US Congress, in its Flood Control Act, had authorized the Corps of Engineers to build an earth-and-rockfill dam on Big Pine Creek at an estimated cost of $28 million. Once the engineers had finished building the dam, the resulting reservoir and lake it created would cover more than a thousand acres northeast of Williamsport, Indiana. This new recreational area would join the other reservoirs already built by the Corps in the state over the years: Cagles Mill (1953), Cecil M. Harden (1960), Monroe (1965), Salamonie (1966), Mississinewa (1967), and Huntington (1968). William J. Watt, administrative assistant during Indiana governor Otis R. Bowen's two terms in office, noted that state legislatures were glad to endorse such projects "because of their recreational benefits and the perceived economic growth brought to surrounding areas in the form of enterprises to serve tourists and the increased value of residential land."[1]

The dam, which received support from Republican congressman John T. Myers, who represented the Seventh Congressional District, as well as the powerful Wabash Valley Association that represented business and political interests in the region, drew protests from state environmental groups, which viewed such projects as a blight on the land. "If all the dams, channelization, and stream 'improvements' are built," noted Thomas E. Dustin, Indiana executive secretary of the Izaak Walton League, "by 1985 Indiana will have said good-bye forever to its best remaining scenic streams." In their place, Dustin added, would be "silent muddy waters, stagnating behind huge rolled earth or concrete structures." Environmentalists and the Corps of Engineers had often battled over such projects. Many of those who worked on behalf of the environment believed, as Indiana University professor Lynton Caldwell noted, that government agencies such as the Corps had emerged "more often than not as a partner, promoter, or protector of activities that diminished the quality of the environment."[2]

The approximately nine thousand residents of Warren County saw the planned Big Pine dam as a dagger aimed at the heart of their way of life. A poll conducted by a county newspaper, the *Williamsport Review-Republican*, indicated a ten-to-one margin against the project, with most viewing it as "another dam senseless squandering of the taxpayers' money." Local groups opposing the dam, including the Committee on Big Pine Creek and the Friends of the Big Pine Creek, charged that if it were to be constructed it would engulf sixty homes, ten commercial properties, 2,347 acres of cropland, 2,200 acres of pastureland, and 1,995 acres of woodlands. The project also threatened such uncommon plants as the walking fern and snow trillium and threatened to destroy habitat for the bigeye chub and blue-breast darter, as well as badgers—all species considered rare or endangered in Indiana and throughout the Midwest. "The Corps of Engineers wants to build the Big Pine dam because it would make more work for them," said Bill Parmenter, president of the Committee on Big Pine Creek. "A lot of government agencies think that way. They won't lose any land, their neighbors won't have to move away, they don't pay taxes in Warren County, and they could care less about the beauty of Pine Creek."[3]

Hoping to protect a portion of the area from destruction, the Nature Conservancy in the late spring of 1973, with the help of a $20,000 loan from a Purdue University janitor, bought a forty-three-acre site in Warren County—property that included the Fall Creek Gorge. "This is a place that needs to be preserved because there is not another place like it in this whole area of Northwestern Indiana," said Helmut Kohnke, vice chairman of the Indiana chapter of the Nature Conservancy. "This is why we are so fussy about this, because it is unique. Not unique, period, but unique for this area."[4]

To help protect and promote what the area had to offer, the Nature Conservancy turned to Jim Jontz, a young environmentalist from Indianapolis who had spoken out against the Corps of Engineers' reservoir projects while a student at Indiana University (IU) during his time as president of the Indiana Eco-Coalition. While working for the Indiana Conservation Council (ICC) as its conservation director after graduating from IU, Jontz was picked by the Nature Conservancy to serve as an unpaid caretaker and program director for the Fall Creek Gorge beginning in the fall of 1973. In a November 21, 1973, letter addressed to his friends, Jontz wrote he had moved to the Fall Creek Gorge property to serve as its "resident caretaker," and reminded them to become ICC members, as that was where "my salary comes from." He lived in a small handmade house in Liberty Township next to the preserve. Joining him there were his new wife, Elaine, two dogs (Brother and Sister), and two cats (Vance and Birch, named for Indiana's two US senators at that time, Vance Hartke and Birch Bayh, both Democrats). In his letter, Jontz invited his friends to "come by some time, visit the Gorge, and enjoy Big Pine Creek. Opportunities exist here for some of the finest camping, hiking, canoeing, fishing, and nature study in the Midwest. Give me a call ahead and/or stop in at the Gorge (I'll send you a map) and I'll do what I can to make your visit enjoyable."[5]

Elaine remembered that she and her husband each had a desk in one tiny room of the house and there were two compact bedrooms, a kitchen, and a bathroom. Jontz later decorated the walls with posters stating "We Care About Endangered Wildlife," "Save Our Wetlands," and "Ecology: A Wild Idea." A stuffed owl peered down from a shelf high on a wall on bookcases with volumes on Indiana's natural resources, covered bridges in the Midwest, and classic works by writers such as Homer and Sophocles. In the winter months, Elaine had to walk down to Fall Creek to haul water back to the house so they could flush the toilet. Her father, Lynton

Caldwell, sometimes visited, working to get rid of poison ivy and helping to pull trash out of the creek.[6]

Jontz organized crews to help maintain the trails, ran summer events to introduce visitors to the beauties of Fall Creek Gorge, and hosted board meetings for the Nature Conservancy. "There was always something going on," said Elaine. Jontz helped make ends meet by taking a job filling gumball machines at stores in the nearby rural communities he reached by driving his AMC Gremlin (an automobile *Time* magazine listed as one of the fifty worst cars of all time). Although raised in a big city, Indianapolis, he soon came to appreciate what Warren County had to offer. "It's close-knit," he said of the area. "Many are opposed to change. They like the quiet lifestyle and there's a backwoodsy atmosphere in parts of the county."[7]

Often dressed in his trademark blue-jean bib overalls, Jontz quickly became one of the leaders in the fight against the Big Pine dam, which his wife called "a total boondoggle." Parmenter, who knew Jontz from earlier state environmental gatherings, said that he had the ability to "make people do things—more than they thought they would be able to do." While there were plenty of people involved in trying to stop the dam, Jontz served as the "sparkplug" for the effort. "We were so young then," Parmenter remembered, "with so much confidence in our rightness. Well, we *were* right, and the Corps of Engineers, the Congress, and the Indiana legislature, to say nothing of the Wabash Valley Association, were wrong." Laura Ann Arnold, a student at Purdue University at that time and one of the leaders of Purdue Environmental Action, a student chapter of the Izaak Walton League, remembered Parmenter and his wife, Penny, bringing Jontz to one of the group's meetings. Arnold quickly became impressed by the young environmentalist's enthusiasm and commitment to the cause. "Jim was one of those people whose leadership style was to roll up his sleeves and to be involved right along with the troops," said Arnold. "He wasn't just somebody who barked out orders and expected everybody else to do the dirty work. He was there working beside you—usually working twice as hard as anybody else."[8]

Using his IU degree in geology, Jontz, with the assistance of another ICC staff member, David Dreyer, prepared a thick report outlining the arguments against building the dam on Big Pine Creek. Dreyer, who went to high school in Richmond, Indiana, had been with the Peace Corps before returning to Indiana. Because he had worked with state government on a tax package that had been passed by the legislature during the administration of Governor Bowen, Dreyer concentrated on the economic side of the dam proposal, while Jontz worked on the conclusion. "Cowriting with

Jim was difficult," Dreyer recalled. "I tended to be a little more poetic, and he just wanted the facts somehow to be poetic in themselves. He rewrote a lot of what I wrote."[9]

Issued in March 1974, the report blasted the plans of the Corps of Engineers and predicted that the dam on Big Pine would have "disastrous environmental consequences" for the area. These included replacing "excellent sport fishing, whitewater canoeing, and other rare outdoor recreational opportunities with poor quality fishing and extremely limited boating in an aesthetically undesirable reservoir which does not meet the real recreational needs of the region." Jontz and Dreyer said the project was a waste of taxpayers' money and, in the end, would destroy people's lives and their rural lifestyle forever. Instead, they advocated including the Big Pine Creek in a state or national scenic river system, asked Warren County government officials to institute proper zoning and land-use policies, and sought for environmental groups such as the Nature Conservancy to purchase additional land in the area for protection. The report also included part of an editorial by Henry Cripe of the *Williamsport Review-Republican* that noted: "We should keep trying to improve our community and meet the challenges of changing times. But, we shouldn't make drastic changes in the name of progress unless we're really sure we're going to like it afterward. No one is going to restore Warren County to its present state once the reservoir is built, even if it all proves to be a big mistake."[10]

The powerful political figures in the area, including Congressman Myers and Indiana State Representative Jack Guy, who represented the Twentieth District (Benton, Newton, Warren, and White Counties), lined up to support the dam. Jontz attempted to find someone to run for the state legislature against incumbent Guy, a Monticello attorney, in the rural district. Jontz believed that having someone who opposed the project in the legislature was essential because the Indiana General Assembly could halt the project in its tracks by refusing to appropriate funding for the state's share of the federally built dam's costs. "Without state approval, the Corps of Engineers simply couldn't build he dam," he noted. "It would be dead—just as dead as if it were deauthorized at the federal level. I think we need a State Representative who will stand up against the schemes of the federal bureaucrats and work to cut wasteful federal spending, not promote it."[11]

Unable to find someone to run as a candidate for the Democratic Party nomination, Jontz approached party leaders in the area and told them he wanted to run for the state representative post (he had thought about running for state senator but was not yet old enough to do so). In spite of his young age (twenty-two), Jontz said that party leaders "were tickled to death that someone wanted to do it." He ran unopposed in the Democratic primary and prepared to tackle Guy, the majority leader of the Republican-controlled Indiana House, in the general election that fall. Few, if any, political pundits believed the rookie candidate could pull off the upset against such a powerful figure as Guy. Announcing his candidacy, Jontz said his campaign would be based on "the disappointment which my neighbors sense about what is going on in Indianapolis. People aren't upset about their taxes if they know their money is being spent wisely. They aren't upset about granting powers to their government if they feel those powers are being used responsibly. Yet, people are upset, and there is good reason."[12]

With help from his wife and a few friends, Jontz began a shoe-leather, door-to-door campaign, visiting every house in such small communities in the district as Boswell, Brook, Brookston, Chalmers, Fowler, Goodland, Kentland, Monon, Morocco, Otterbein, Oxford, Reynolds, West Lebanon, Wolcott, and many others. An advertisement for the Jontz campaign that ran in local newspapers under the title "I'll Be at Your Door Soon" included a photograph of a grinning Jontz, his tie loosened and displaying the sole of one of his shoes battered and full of holes from his door-to-door effort to introduce himself to voters. "I realize people are busy and my purpose is not to inconvenience anyone," he said. "If someone has a question for me or wants to tell me something, I will be pleased to stay as long as necessary. Otherwise, I will simply leave a piece of literature with my phone number and address, so I can be contacted in the future." Jontz also spread the word about his candidacy by attending every community fish fry he could find and going to three straight weeks of county fairs, shaking hands with countless potential voters. "I campaigned on the personal attention idea," Jontz said. "Issues are important to people, but more important to them is feeling that government is responsive."[13]

By his side throughout the campaign was Jontz's wife, Elaine, who acted as his unofficial campaign manager. She remembered sending out letters and press releases, placing leaflets on car windows, organizing meetings, and rounding up farmers and their wives to go to Washington, DC, to testify against the Big Pine dam. "We always tried to keep the level of awareness up," she noted. They did everything they could to fight the dam, including raising money for the cause by raffling off canoes at county fairs and even having one of the farm wives give belly dancing lessons. "I really believed in what he was doing," Elaine said, remembering life with her husband as "a constant campaign." The expense of fighting the dam and running for the legislature meant that the young couple was often broke. Elaine remembered trips to the grocery store where she wandered up and down the aisles wondering what she could prepare for meals with the five dollars she had for buying groceries. Luckily, Jontz's favorite food was Senate bean soup with white beans and ham, which she could make very cheaply.[14]

In the literature he handed out to voters, Jontz emphasized that he was not a lawyer or an experienced politician (both of which Guy were). "I don't have anything against lawyers," he noted, "but I do think we need more different kinds of people in the General Assembly." If elected to the legislature, Jontz said he "would bring a fresh perspective, some youthful energy, and a few new ideas to Indianapolis." To connect with the mostly conservative voters that inhabited the district, he called for reducing "excess government expenditures," recommended cutting down on unwise public work projects, and said he knew the problems of "trying to pay upper-class prices and upper-class taxes with a middle-class income and middle-class values."[15]

Guy, who had started his career in the legislature in 1971, touted his experience as his biggest asset and downplayed Jontz's calls for a debate. In interviews and advertisements, the Guy campaign said that while it was "commendable" that Jontz had traveled throughout the district to meet voters, there was "more to being a representative of the people than knocking on doors, saying hello, and then vanishing into the political night leaving vague promises of change." But Kathy Altman, a longtime Democratic Party worker in White County along with her husband, Jerry, remembered Guy as being overconfident, believing he could cruise to an easy victory over his rookie opponent. Altman witnessed firsthand how hard Jontz worked to connect with voters. After campaigning for the day in Monticello, an exhausted Jontz would stagger to the Altmans' home "and eat like he was ravenous—just a huge appetite after he had been out door to door all day and had not stopped to do anything but talk to people."[16]

The issue that dominated Jontz's campaign was his opposition to the Big Pine dam. At a July 1974 meeting in the Williamsport school's gymnasium, staff from the Corps of Engineers' Louisville district were greeted by nearly two thousand residents, out of which only four spoke in favor of the project. Jontz quickly energized the audience by asking for those attending to stand up if they were for or against the dam. "He basically ran the show, much to the chagrin of the Corps," Elaine remembered. The crowd reacted with suspicion to anything the Corps of Engineers presented. When one Corps official pointed to the recreational activity at a lake project in Ohio, estimating that forty thousand to fifty thousand people visited over a weekend, an audience member reminded him that the reservoir planned for Big Pine would sometimes have its water level seventy-five feet below its banks. "What are you going to do," asked the local resident, "build steps, or let people slide down to the water?" (Those in the audience might have been even more upset if they had known that officials in the Indiana Department of Natural Resources (DNR) had already estimated that the reservoir's lake would be too small for its visitors to use motorboats.) Also at the meeting, Dreyer rose to state that the Corps of Engineers' claims of a flood control benefit "is actually a subsidy to a select group of downstream landowners which helps them increase their profits at the expense of others." It would be cheaper for taxpayers, Dreyer continued, to make direct cash payments to farmers affected by flood damage than to spend the millions of dollars for building the Big Pine dam.[17]

Even before the meeting with the Corps of Engineers, dam opponents had taken direct action against those who supported the project. For a number of years the Warren County Republicans had held a golf outing to raise funds for Congressman Myers. The fifth annual event, held at the Big Pine Golf Course, had some unexpected visitors as between two hundred and three hundred Warren County residents showed up to protest Myers's support for the dam. Late in the afternoon a caravan of approximately a hundred vehicles descended on the course full of farmers and their wives and children bearing signs proclaiming "Save Our Land, Stop the Dam," "Farmers Produce More than Motorboats," and "Dam the Corps." A plane flew overhead towing a banner reading: "Please John [Myers] No Dam." The protesters handed out a letter asking Myers and Governor Bowen, who attended the golf event, to halt their support of the dam, and a group gathered to discuss the issue with Myers. "We weren't there to disrupt Golf Day or debate the merits of the dam, but simply let our Congressman know we are upset about it," said Jontz, who appeared at the rally dressed in his usual bib overalls. As one county resident added, "We'd just like to have someone listen to us for a change." The demonstration failed to change Myers's position. He told a reporter that the mail he received consistently ran two to one in favor of the Big Pine dam and he intended to continue his support of the project. His only intention on supporting the project, the congressman later said, was a "sincere desire to do what we can to stop the senseless flooding of the farmland and to provide an adequate water supply for future generations."[18]

The controversy about the Big Pine dam in 1974 had drawn the attention of officials in the Bowen administration in Indianapolis. Natural resources advisers to the governor were worried that controversies about reservoirs would only worsen as time passed. According to Watt, "it was necessary to devise workable philosophies to assess the value of individual projects." He noted that he met with Joseph Cloud, DNR director, and John Hillenbrand II, longtime DNR commission chairman, to research the matter, and they had agreed that the project on Big Pine Creek "should be scuttled." Although they urged Bowen to drop state support for the dam, he turned down their recommendation. "The timing was not yet right," Watt said of the governor's decision. "He was reluctant to trigger what surely would be a nasty confrontation with Myers over a project in the congressman's home district."[19]

National events that summer may also have given a boost to Jontz's first-time efforts for public office, as well as the campaigns of other Democrats across the country. On August 8, 1974, President Richard Nixon announced his resignation. Two years earlier, on June 18, 1972, a team of burglars organized and funded by Nixon's presidential reelection campaign had been caught and arrested inside the offices of the Democratic National Committee in the Watergate office complex in Washington, DC. What a White House spokesman called "a third rate burglary" mushroomed into a huge political scandal and cover-up that saw a number of senior presidential officials go to jail for their crimes and led to Nixon's leaving office in favor of Vice President Gerald Ford, who declared upon assuming the presidency, "our long national nightmare is over." (On September 8, 1974, Ford announced a "full, free and absolute" pardon for Nixon for any offenses he "has committed or may have committed.")

The momentous events in Washington trickled down to Jontz during his door-to-door campaign for state representative in Indiana's Twentieth District. So many voters asked him what he thought about the Watergate scandal and Nixon's resignation that he issued a press release on the matter. Instead of debating past misdeeds by both political parties, Jontz said voters should resolve to make sure such abuses did not happen in the future. Although he pledged never to lie to voters as a candidate or as an elected official, Jontz said that what was more important than any candidate's pledge "are the responsibilities of all of us as citizens. There is, indeed, only one way I know of and one way I can recommend as a means of stopping abuses of power. This is for all of us to do a more conscientious job as citizens."[20]

The fallout from Watergate and voters' ire about the GOP-controlled legislature's doubling of the state sales tax the year before resulted in a huge win for Democrats in Indiana in the 1974 election. Five incumbent Republican congressmen—Earl Landgrebe, William Bray, David Dennis,

Roger Zion, and William Hudnut—lost their reelection contests (Myers survived the debacle), and Indianapolis mayor Richard Lugar fell to incumbent Bayh in the race for the US Senate. Democrats captured such statewide offices as secretary of state, state treasurer, and state auditor, and also took control of the hundred-member Indiana House of Representatives, the first time they had enjoyed such an advantage since 1965. One of the closest races that year involved Guy and Jontz. In spite of all their hard work, in the end Elaine did not think her husband would win. Late in the evening of Election Day, November 6, it appeared as though Jontz had failed in his attempt to unseat the Republican incumbent. Elaine remembered returning to their small home then and she could tell that Jontz was thinking what his next move might be if he lost.[21]

Jontz went to bed believing he had gone down to defeat after hearing a report from the final precinct in Warren County indicating he was behind by only two votes. "It was a total shock when we heard the news the next morning," Elaine recalled. There had been an error, and Jontz had won by the same slim margin. "One more vote than I needed to win!" he exclaimed. His razor-thin victory earned Jontz the nickname "Landslide Jim" from his wife. Jontz credited his victory to his opposition to the Big Pine dam. "Guy refused to oppose the dam and that hurt him," he said. Jontz noted that although Democrats were a minority in the district "and often don't think it's worth their time to go out and vote, this time they were encouraged. And the independents were more inclined to look favorably on the Democrats." He added that Democrat challenger Floyd Fithian's defeat of incumbent GOP congressman Earl Landgrebe in the Second Congressional District also helped, as Benton, White, and Newton Counties were part of that district.[22]

A weary Guy, who in 1977 returned to the legislature as a state senator, expressed deep disappointment about his loss to Jontz. "I quite frankly thought that what I had done for the people in the 20th House District deserved better support than I received," he told a reporter. Especially upsetting to Guy was seeing the four-thousand-vote margin he enjoyed in the election two years earlier in White County (his home county) fall to less than eight hundred votes in 1974. The unexpected result stunned election officials, with one deputy clerk in Warren County marveling, "I never before realized just how important that one vote can be." Later, when he was asked what it was that had drawn him to a career in politics, Jontz could provide a simple answer: "I gave a damn about a dam." For years he also used this victory of average citizens against a politically powerful foe as an important lesson to young and old alike "who see injustice and want to believe that you can make a difference—you *can* make a difference."[23]

Keeping his campaign promise to stop the Big Pine dam became one of the first legislative tasks Jontz undertook during his first two-year term of office. With his cosponsor, Republican William L. Long of Lafayette, Jontz introduced House Bill 1478. The measure would have repealed an act passed by the 1967 Indiana General Assembly that directed the state Department of Nature Resources to cooperate with the Corps of Engineers to construct the dam. On February 20, 1975, the House voted by an 83 to 8 margin to pass the bill. For the measure to become law, however, it still needed to pass the Republican-controlled Indiana Senate and be signed by GOP governor Bowen. Unfortunately for dam opponents, Jontz's bill never made it out of an Indiana Senate environmental subcommittee and died for that session.

Dam opponents received a boost just under a year later when the Army Corps of Engineers' Louisville district recommended that the Big Pine project be abandoned. The decision came thanks to a process initiated by Jontz's father-in-law, Caldwell, who had been responsible in the late 1960s for helping write legislation requiring environmental impact statements for all federal projects. The Corps found that the Big Pine dam would significantly harm the wildlife and natural features in the area where it was to be built and that its economic benefits did not justify its costs. "The Corps' credibility is at stake all over," said Colonel James N. Ellis, district engineer. "We are going to continue to take a hard look at all of our projects."[24]

In spite of the Corps' recommendation, the fight over the Big Pine dam continued to drag on for years, as its supporters continued to seek funding for the project in Washington, DC. The end finally came on January 12, 1990, when the Corps of Engineers formally deauthorized the project, as well as a dam on Wildcat Creek near Lafayette, as Congress had allocated no funds to construct either one. "This deauthorization is the result of the efforts of many committed conservationists and area residents over the years," said Jontz. "People who make their homes in these areas will finally have the peace of mind of knowing that these projects are no longer on the books."[25]

When Jontz won election to the US House of Representatives in 1986, representing the Fifth Congressional District, he took his passion for environmental and other social justice causes with him to Washington, DC, and became a hero to conservationists for attempting to protect old-growth forests in the Pacific Northwest from logging companies. "I looked around and saw a lot of people were very close to the timber industry," Jontz said. "That's OK: they need some support: but why should they have it all? There are other voices, too. People don't want those other voices to be heard." The zeal in which he pursued protecting nature frustrated and sometimes infuriated congressmen from other states, who saw him as meddling in matters that were outside the district he represented. Jontz's sponsorship of the Ancient Forest Protection Act, which would have forbid cutting stands of ancient timber in three Western states, caused one Oregon congressman to call him "a rank opportunist," while another member of the Oregon delegation became so mad at Jontz during a meeting that he kicked him out of his office.[26]

To the end of his life Jontz, who died on April 14, 2007, remained optimistic that coalitions could be formed to work together to save forests and other wild areas from destruction. For years he had been inspired in his efforts on the environment's behalf by Doctor Seuss's book *The Lorax*. The book is a powerful comment on the destruction of nature, telling how a greedy character named the Once-ler fails to heed the warnings of the Lorax and ravages Truffula trees to service his factories until the air is polluted and the animals have fled. The sad Lorax floats away through the smog, leaving behind a pile of rocks on which are etched the word: "UNLESS." Suess's book offered some hope, as the now despondent Once-ler hands a young boy he has been telling his story to the last remaining Truffula seed. Throughout his life, Jontz symbolized that same sense of hope. According to fellow environmentalist Brock Evans, Jontz's most enduring legacy is his constant reminder that "even seemingly hopeless causes can be won. All we need is the right kind of leader, a person of high spirit and sunny optimism, and, above all, a large and courageous heart."[27]

NOTES

1. William Watt, *Bowen: The Years as Governor* (Indianapolis: Bierce Associates, 1981), 111–112; Leland R. Johnson, *The Falls City Engineers: A History of the Louisville District, Corps of Engineers, United States Army, 1970–1983* (Louisville, KY: US Army Engineer District, 1984), 101.

2. George Neavoll, "Saving Scenic Streams," *Christian Science Monitor*, February 11, 1974.

3. "Big Pine Economic Benefits Wishful Thinking: Parmenter," *Attica Daily Ledger Tribune*, July 17, 1974; "Ballots Rolling in on Big Pine Question," *Williamsport Review-Republican*, July 18, 1974.

4. Norman Bess, "Fall Creek Gorge 'Protected,'" *Indianapolis News*, June 12, 1973.

5. Jim Jontz, "Dear Friends" letter, November 21, 1973, Jontz Papers, Calumet Regional Archives, Indiana University Northwest, Gary, Indiana.

6. Author interview with Elaine Caldwell Emmi, May 13, 2010 (hereafter, Emmi interview).

7. Emmi interview; Patrick Siddons, "'Unbelievable:' Jim Jontz, Possibly Youngest Member of House, Recalls His Close Victory," *Louisville Courier-Journal*, January 12, 1975.

8. Emmi interview; author interview with Bill Parmenter, April 26, 2010; author interview with Laura Ann Arnold, May 10, 2010.

9. Author interview with David Dreyer, November 1, 2010.

10. Jim Jontz and David Dreyer, *Big Pine Creek: A Report on Big Pine Creek, Warren County, Indiana, and Its Future* (Attica, IN: Committee on Big Pine Creek, 1974).

11. "'General Assembly Can Stop Big Pine Dam,' Says Candidate Jontz," *Williamsport Review-Republican*, October 10, 1974.

12. "Jim Jontz, Possibly Youngest Member of House, Recalls His Close Victory" and "Running for District 20 Representative in Primary Election," *Monticello Daily Herald-Journal*, March 18, 1974.

13. "Jim Jontz Plans Door-to-Door Effort," *Williamsport Review-Republican*, September 5, 1974; Grace Witwer, "This Boy-Next-Door Legislator Gives a 'Dam about Dams,'" *Indiana Daily Student*, March 15, 1975.

14. Emmi interview.

15. Jim Jontz, "Why I'm a Candidate for State Representative" flyer, Jontz Papers.

16. "Young Democrat Hopes for Upset," *Monticello Daily Herald-Journal*, November 4, 1974; author interview with Kathy Altman, May 12, 2010.

17. "Public Big Pine Meeting Confirms 10–1 Sentiment Against Dam," *Williamsport Review-Republican*, August 1, 1974; Emmi interview.

18. "Warren County Farmers Protest Dam," *Williamsport Review-Republican*, August 8, 1974.

19. Watt, *Bowen*, 113.

20. "Jontz Makes Statement of Views," *Williamsport Review-Republican*, August 15, 1974.

21. Emmi interview.

22. Witwer, "This Boy-Next-Door Legislator Gives a 'Dam about Dams'"; Emmi interview.

23. Jeff Fisher, "Jontz Tops Guy by Two Votes," *Daily Herald-Journal*, November 6, 1974; Witwer, "This Boy-Next-Door Legislator Gives a 'Dam about Dams'"; Americans for Democratic Action Conference, June 13, 1998, C-Span Video Library, http://www.c-spanvideo.org/program/Americansfor.

24. Johnson, *Falls City Engineers*, 107.

25. "Big Pine Project Finally Deauthorized," *Williamsport Review-Republican*, January 12, 1990.

26. George Stuteville, "Movin' On: Defeated Jontz Knew He Was Living on Borrowed Time," *Indianapolis Star*, December 16, 1992; Mike Thoele, "Hoosier Fights for Northwest Forests," *Eugene Register-Guard*, June 3, 1990; and Doug McDaniel, "Forest Bill Puts Jontz in Middle of Controversy," *Indianapolis Star*, June 24, 1990.

27. Brock Evans, "Remembering Jim Jontz," June 2007, in "Soul of a Hero: A People's Tribute to Jim Jontz," prepared by Brian Vincent, unpublished collection of tributes to Jontz, copy in author's collection.

9

"Your Problem Is Our Problem"

Mary Jean Collins's Midwestern Feminism

KATHERINE TURK

❖ ❖ ❖ ❖ ❖ ❖ ❖ ❖ ❖ ❖ ❖ ❖ ❖ ❖ ❖

"Worry Your Pretty Head—Strike August 26." Members of the National Organization for Women (NOW) taped these eye-catching flyers to lamp poles all over Chicago in the summer of 1970 to mobilize for their Women's Strike for Equality.[1] This forty-city protest, timed to mark the fiftieth anniversary of the Nineteenth Amendment's passage, outlined three goals: equal rights at work and school, accessible abortion, and round-the-clock childcare centers. NOW's national leaders expected the march down Fifth Avenue in Manhattan to attract the most people and media attention.[2]

But feminists in Chicago took a broader approach in their planning for the event. August 26 would be a "do-your-own-thing day for women," Chicago NOW president Mary Jean Collins told a reporter. Some would rally downtown, ditching jobs and housework; others would attend to those regular tasks, but they would start new dialogues with coworkers, bosses, and husbands about "changes that need to be made."[3] Privately, Collins and her allies doubted that their open-ended protest would succeed. The local press advertised their plans in terms that toggled between curiosity and scorn. "We were so worried," Collins recalled, that "fourteen people [would] show up, and then what [were] we going to say?"[4]

In 1970 Collins was thirty-one years old and a seasoned activist. She had forged her feminism by coming of age amid liberal Midwestern institutions: a modernizing Catholic Church, a Democratic Party attentive to Irish Catholics like her, a forward-looking women's college, a robust

NAACP chapter, and a labor movement that women helped to steer.[5] From the 1960s until the 1990s, Collins moved in and out of porous groups in Wisconsin, Illinois, and Washington, DC, sharpening her skills and perspective and imprinting those organizations along the way.

Collins does not fit easily into existing narratives of "second-wave feminism," the push for gender equality and social justice born in the late 1960s.[6] Scholars have examined that uprising from various angles: by offering detailed accounts of many participants; analyzing national groups and local cells; tracing key campaigns, collaborations, and divisions; and following its roots back and its branches forward in time.[7] Still, this sprawling literature tends to focus on coastal cities—framing the Midwest as a region that received rather than generated feminist ideas—and emphasize the borders within the movement, especially those related to perspective and identity.[8] Centering Midwesterners like Collins brings feminism and liberalism into new conversation while shedding fresh light on both. Far from the epicenters of national political, cultural, and media power, Midwestern liberals built pragmatic alliances and pushed for tangible change. Sometimes they worked inside local institutions; at other times they applied external pressure. Midwestern feminism was spontaneous, collective, and above all, practical.

Collins swelled with pride on August 26, 1970, when up to fifteen thousand people amassed for NOW's lunchtime program in Chicago's downtown Civic Plaza.[9] The enormous crowd listened to speeches by Black, white, and lesbian women from the labor and student movements, local politics, and the city's four largest feminist groups.[10] Toward the end of the rally, a woman stepped up to the stage. She had just been fired from her job at a nearby meat company, she explained, for bringing her child to work that day.[11] "We were exhausted by then," Collins said later, and "just wanted to go and have a beer." But soon several thousand protestors began "trotting down the street" to the meat company's headquarters.[12] They demanded to meet with its leaders in support of the fired mother. Those officials "were totally freaked out," said Collins, and they "took her [the fired woman] back in a minute."[13] This improvised and communal solution would come to define Midwestern feminists' style. "Every time somebody showed up," Collins said, "we would add her." Their motto: "Your problem is our problem."[14]

Mary Jean Collins was born in 1939 in Superior, a tiny town in northwestern Wisconsin. Women across that state were advancing the New Deal's democratic values—values that were personified on the national scene by Franklin D. and Eleanor Roosevelt, and which the members of the Collins family also embraced in their own lives. When the Collins family moved south to Milwaukee in 1946, their Irish heritage, Catholic faith, and working-class ties all helped them assimilate to the industrial city checkered with white ethnic enclaves.[15] Collins and her older sister Patricia dutifully attended Mass and handed out Democratic Party literature alongside their parents, who held that "the Democrats were on your side and the Republicans were on the side of the rich," Collins explained. "That was fundamental."[16]

The Collinses were a tight-knit family. Still, "growing up what I saw," Collins later reflected, "was not a life I wanted to have."[17] Her mother had little control over her own circumstances, and as her father's alcoholism worsened, the family lost their home. Collins's babysitting money and her mother's low-wage secretarial work kept them solvent.[18] Although she resented the obedience demanded by Catholic church and school, Collins entered Alverno College, a local Catholic women's school, in 1959, soon after her sister joined a convent.[19]

At Alverno, Collins met strong liberal nuns including Sister Joel Read, her European History professor. Read and the other sisters who taught the approximately eight hundred working- and lower-middle-class Catholic women students also ran the place.[20] "There were male professors but women were in charge," said Read.[21] "A women's college *is* a feminist institution."[22] Read and her colleagues stretched their students' horizons, encouraging them to study abroad and to pursue careers.[23] Their efforts coincided with Vatican II, a broader campaign inside the Catholic Church to modernize by liberalizing its rituals and policies.[24] For class of 1963 graduate Mary Jean Collins, professors like Read led her "not to become an atheist but to hold on to the underlying principles of what Christianity should be."[25] Read would become Collins's lifelong mentor and, in three years' time, a co-founder of NOW.

After graduating from Alverno, Collins began a frustrating quest for rewarding work in Milwaukee's sex-segmented job market. She found an outlet for her democratic values in the burgeoning civil rights movement. Members of the city's expanding Black population were organizing against racial segregation in local schools, workplaces, and neighborhoods. Collins "never went to the South," but she had been "reading about" the Milwaukee movement, she said. "When it came to my town I had to be involved." Although her father worried for her safety, he supported her participation in the open-housing marches that plunged through working-class white neighborhoods for two hundred consecutive nights, often facing violent resistance.[26] Milwaukee's civil rights movement was deeply inflected by

Figure 9.1. Mary Jean Collins was featured in the *Alverno Campus News* alongside fellow members of the class of 1963. Courtesy of the Alverno College Archives.

liberal Christianity. Its leaders included Father James Groppi, a white Catholic priest, and Edith Finlayson, a Black surgical nurse and a stalwart in civil rights and uplift organizations including the Milwaukee Urban League and the NAACP. In 1963 Finlayson founded and directed the E. B. Phillips Day Care Center, whose namesake was the pastor of her Greater Galilee Baptist Church; three years later she co-founded NOW along with Read.[27]

Finlayson was present for NOW's founding in 1966 because she had been one of three women of color appointed to the inaugural Wisconsin

Governor's Commission on the Status of Women in 1963—the year of Collins's college graduation.[28] In addition to Finlayson, the commission's accomplished middle-aged members included its chair, political science professor Kathryn "Kay" Clarenbach. She ran the University of Wisconsin Extension School, a continuing education program for women that fostered a strong statewide network of women and nurtured their local activism.[29] With Clarenbach in charge, Wisconsin's women's commission worked on issues of pay equity, domestic violence, and more, and it convinced the state Industrial Commission to advocate for new labor protections including minimum-wage legislation.[30] The commission was "truly representative" and "one of the best in the country," declared member and NOW co-founder Catherine Conroy, a prominent labor leader in the state who became a key mentor to Collins.[31]

Conroy, Finlayson, Clarenbach, and others from the Wisconsin commission traveled to Washington, DC, in June 1966 to attend the third annual gathering of State Commissions on the Status of Women. Forty-four state commissions were represented there.[32] Finlayson chaired the workshop on daycare; Clarenbach led a session on "Creating Positive Attitudes."[33] On the conference's second night, a cluster of East Coast feminists proposed forming a new kind of women's organization that would pressure, not just collaborate with, government agencies. Their vantage point in the nation's capital had convinced them that federal officials were neglecting the ban on workplace sex discrimination included in Title VII of the Civil Rights Act of 1964.[34]

The Wisconsin women initially resisted this proposal, reflecting their pragmatic approach. They pointed out that they had collaborated productively with state lawmakers through their commission. But those Midwesterners also believed in taking action, and they changed their minds the next morning when the conference organizers refused even to allow a debate about the issues raised the previous evening. Over lunch a group of conference-goers founded NOW, which would become the largest and most expansive feminist organization of its era. Clarenbach agreed to be temporary chair, and Conroy drew from her union experience when she placed $5 dues on the table and urged others to do the same.[35] Of the twenty-eight women who created NOW on June 30, 1966, nineteen were from the Midwest.[36] The fact that two-thirds of these founders hailed from the middle of the country suggested a deeply rooted feminism there that remained largely unknown to the rest of the nation.

Back in Milwaukee, Collins discovered NOW when Read returned from the group's first official conference that October. Read set up a Milwaukee chapter and tapped Collins as its treasurer.[37] "You didn't have to recruit in

Figure 9.2. Mary Jean Collins returned home to Milwaukee in 1978 to help the city's NOW chapter honor her mentor Catherine Conroy as Woman of the Year. From left: Conroy, Kathryn "Kay" Clarenbach, Collins, and Gene Boyer. Credit: ©Rick Greenawalt—USA TODAY NETWORK.

those days," Read said later of NOW's first few months in Milwaukee.[38] Word spread quickly through women's networks as the chapter held events around the city. In one such protest, members targeted a Catholic church that had expelled a woman who had gone hatless to Mass—a rule that did not apply to men. NOW members attended on Easter Sunday and piled hats onto the Communion rail. The priest admonished them, "No, not there, on your head," Collins recalled, as if "we were completely stupid."[39] Months later, Collins accompanied Conroy to Washington for

NOW's second national conference in late 1967. The group's membership had multiplied fourfold to 1200.[40] "I had never been in a room with women like that," Collins said of the government and corporate officials, activists, attorneys, educators, and labor leaders who debated "amazing argument[s]" in "a pure discussion of, who are we and what are we for?"[41] Her own nascent feminism was about to flourish.

Collins moved to Chicago in 1968 with her new husband, Jim Robson, whom she had met at a Milwaukee civil rights march. The couple, who made the then-unusual choice to hyphenate their surnames during their short marriage, arrived in time to take part in the protests at the Democratic National Convention. They settled in Hyde Park, a racially diverse hamlet on the city's South Side.[42] There, the pair "tried to really live out our principles, in terms of what we believed should happen in the late sixties—the interracial nature of society that should come," Collins said later.[43] Chicago was diverse but deeply segregated. Mayor Richard J. Daley worked his Democratic Party machine with an iron fist.[44] The city was a stronghold of organized labor as the longtime home of the United Packinghouse Workers of America (UPWA).[45] Saul Alinsky's Industrial Areas Foundation had also organized many working-class communities there. These and other storied institutions in the city offered "organization to go up against" in the late 1960s, explained feminist journalist and activist Karen Fishman.[46] Working women's advocate and Milwaukee native Anne Ladky agreed. "There were just little pockets of things" around town, where people understood that "you had to have a strong voice to change anything in Chicago."[47]

As Collins settled in the city, she found that Catherine Conroy had also recently moved there on an assignment from her union. She hosted Chicago NOW's organizing meeting downtown one evening, hoping to attract working women and helping to set the chapter's focus on labor issues.[48] Collins was there, as was her Alverno College classmate Mary-Ann Lupa, who lived in the Chicago suburbs. "I didn't come for consciousness raising," Lupa said later. "I came to get my anger out using something that wasn't illegal."[49] Ladky soon signed up, too. The recent college graduate especially valued the chapter's action-oriented approach: "'what are we going to organize around?,' not 'what are we going to research, what are we going to study,'" she described it.[50]

The trio framed a feminism that addressed women's immediate problems and met them where they were. They built Chicago NOW, which staged massive protests like the Women's Strike for Equality and targeted local employers, such as retailer Sears, Roebuck, and Company, for maintaining sex- and race-segregated labor forces. Collins was chapter president from 1968 until 1970, when national leaders appointed her NOW's Midwest regional director. They assigned her $100 and thirteen states. When anyone from her region "called the national office and said they wanted to form a chapter, we would get into our car and go there," Collins said. "We'd say, get a room and get a crowd."[51] Her husband opened a printing business that handled national NOW's clerical work, and Collins quit her job at an electronics company to volunteer full-time for the organization.

Most Chicago NOW members were white liberals, but through the group Collins tapped into a loose yet thriving network of women who were expanding democracy through grassroots organizations across the city. Reverend Addie Wyatt was a leader of the civil rights, labor, and religious movements as well as a longtime supporter of Chicago NOW who often attended and addressed its gatherings.[52] Wyatt's family had moved from Mississippi to Chicago four decades earlier as part of the Great Migration of millions of African Americans from the Jim Crow South to the industrial North.[53] A trailblazer in her union, the Amalgamated Meat Cutters (formerly UPWA), Wyatt pushed the women's movement to attend to the concerns of women of color and working women while urging those women to join organized feminism. Wyatt's capacious activism also addressed police brutality, housing segregation, and racial health disparities.[54] Along with Catherine Conroy, Wyatt cofounded the Coalition of Labor Union Women in Chicago in 1974.[55]

Through Chicago NOW, Collins also locked arms with New Left women like Heather Booth. Booth had attended the Mississippi Freedom Summer Project in 1964 as an undergraduate at the University of Chicago, and the following year she founded Jane, an abortion counseling service and provider that would perform more than eleven thousand underground abortions in the city by mid-1973.[56] Booth also helped build a socialist-feminist movement in Chicago, organizing women around accessible childcare and cofounding the Chicago Women's Liberation Union (CWLU).[57] The CWLU, which sought to end economic and sexual oppression and was the earliest and most productive such union nationwide, linked up with many different groups of women around the city.[58] In 1973 Booth formed the Midwest Academy, a training school for community organizers and leaders, whose first class was composed of working women's advocates.[59] Collins attended along with others in Chicago NOW.

The feminist scene in Chicago was unique for its emphasis on finding women's commonalities. Although the CWLU was "the socialist feminists" and "NOW was the reform feminists," explained CWLU member Chris Riddiough, "it also was pretty clear as we worked on different issues that there was a lot of overlap in terms of thinking and membership."[60] She and other CWLU members focused on the practical over the theoretical. "We're talking about the things all women need," Booth told a group of women who were meeting in Chicago for the National Women's Agenda Day in 1975. "All women are concerned with physical safety. All women with children need better child-care supports."[61]

Collins found that she could advance her pragmatic feminism not only through creative collaborations but also through a range of institutions. Booth helped her run for NOW's national presidency in 1974 and 1975. After losing both times in faction fights among the national membership, Collins came out as lesbian and ended her marriage, so she needed both full-time work and some distance from NOW. Through her Chicago activism, Collins had met Anne Zimmerman, the director of the Illinois Nurses Association (INA).[62] The INA was a constituent of the American Nurses Association and, according to a reporter, "the official voice of nursing in Illinois."[63] Public workers in Illinois including these nurses had been organizing for decades, but they gained enforceable bargaining rights in 1973 when Democratic Governor Daniel Walker granted formal union protections to state employees. This provision sparked a major organizing drive.[64] The INA established a collective bargaining arm for the state employee nurses, and it won a new contract.[65]

Her NOW leadership, Collins discovered, had sharpened and shown off her capabilities. Although the INA typically hired nurses in its staff jobs, Zimmerman tapped Collins to be the group's collective bargaining representative.[66] Collins found that she had "the skills required" because of the "crossover" with her NOW work. As a regional director, she had traveled to "all these little places all over the Midwest and organized people. That's exactly what I was doing" in meeting with and representing nurses who worked for public health facilities, prisons, and the city of Chicago—about a thousand nurses statewide.[67]

Collins set out to "apply" her "feminist principles" to the nurses' problems of low pay and disrespect in Illinois.[68] "Nurses have had to struggle because doctors have viewed them as handmaidens, rather than people with an independent profession and role," Collins told a reporter in 1978.[69] The INA expressed this perspective when it backed a nurse who had filed a complaint with the state Fair Employment Practices Commission after she was fired for refusing to wear the annoying cap that was part of women nurses' uniforms (but not men's). "Hospital administrators and patients alike should be more concerned with a nurse's competence than

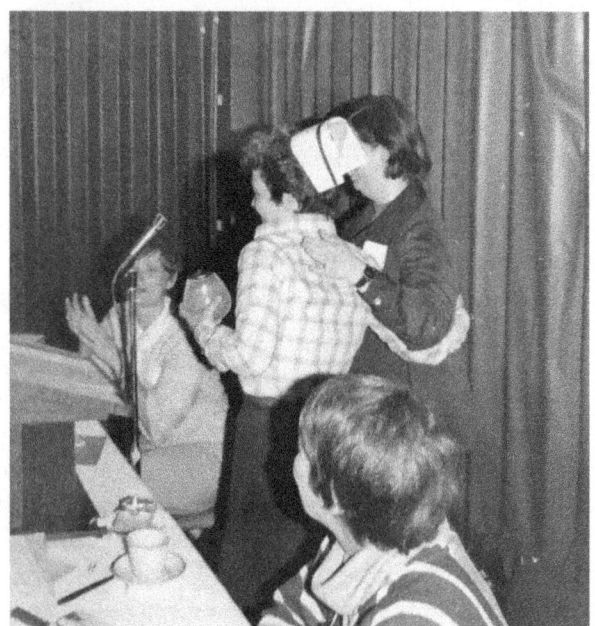

Figure 9.3. The Illinois Nurses Association capped Mary Jean Collins as an "honorary nurse" at a 1977 meeting. Marna Seibert is on Collins's left, and Marie Flosi stands beside her. Courtesy of Mary Jean Collins.

with whether she clings to an outmoded form of dress," claimed Zimmerman.[70] INA nurses in two Chicago-area hospitals staged a thirty-eight-day walkout over proposed cuts to their sick pay in 1976, where they walked a picket line in subzero temperatures until they won many of their demands.[71]

Collins reveled in her role helping these workers pursue a shared agenda. "Nurses are as tough as it gets," she said. "They love their profession, they care for their patients, and they fight like hell."[72] Collins also appreciated that while nurses across the state held diverse politics, they valued her efforts. "These women from small towns" were "probably more conservative than I was," she said, but they were also "proud to have a women's rights leader connected to them."[73] Collins's mentors, clients, and fellow activists had convinced her that "woman" was a broad and meaningful identity that could unite its bearers across their differences.

❖ ❖ ❖

Mary Jean Collins had also come to believe that many kinds of changes could improve women's lives. After five years with the INA, and unable to rise in its ranks without a nursing degree, Collins returned her attention to NOW in the late 1970s.[74] She ran and won the race for Chicago chapter president, which was by then a salaried position. In that role, she helped drive national NOW's campaign to ratify the Equal Rights Amendment (ERA).[75]

The ERA, which would enshrine equal rights for women in the US Constitution, had been a longtime goal for some feminists. NOW had endorsed the provision in 1967, and it easily cleared both houses of Congress five years later.[76] The proposed amendment needed approval from thirty-eight state legislatures in order to take effect. Twenty-two states ratified the ERA in 1972, then eight states the following year, and then just three states in 1974. With five states to go, the progress stalled. Illinois and Missouri were the only Midwestern states among the fifteen still unratified in 1977.[77] ERA coalitions began germinating across Illinois, and national NOW began to concentrate its resources there. "Illinois is the largest state and Chicago is the largest city" where the ERA had not been ratified, explained NOW president Eleanor Smeal in announcing NOW's major campaign in the state in 1979.[78]

Collins was back at the Midwestern center of organized feminism. "The ERA wasn't my favorite issue," she said later, but "if you wanted to be involved in the women's movement, this was where it was." She also saw the amendment's value as "a political objective that did empower women."[79] Collins became codirector of NOW's Illinois ERA countdown campaign alongside Illinois NOW president Linda Miller. The pair supervised a fifty-person staff and recruited local hosts for dozens of out-of-town volunteers.[80] Collins placed teams in each of the state's fifty-nine legislative districts, oversaw "massive phone banks in Chicago," and sent volunteers to lobby and protest at the capital in Springfield, a quiet town about three hours southwest of Chicago, for several days per week when the legislature was in session.[81] Among the bus riders from Chicago was CWLU member Chris Riddiough.[82] Her socialist-feminist group's approach was always "fairly pragmatic," she said, and she believed that the "ERA would be one step on the road to more radical change."[83] Addie Wyatt backed the ERA and worked with NOW toward ratification in Illinois. Centrist women's groups like the League of Women Voters were also "a massive help," Collins said, since they were more influential in conservative parts of the state.[84]

Also vying for Illinois women's attention was antifeminist Phyllis Schlafly, who proffered a different stereotype of the Midwestern woman: the plucky, pious, and wholesome housewife opposed to social change.[85] The conservative Roman Catholic activist and author lived in Alton, Illinois, an industrial city of thirty-five thousand people across the Mississippi River from St. Louis.[86] Schlafly was already famous as an anticommunist hawk, but as she watched the ERA's gathered momentum, she set out to rebrand the provision as a grave threat to American life. Schlafly formed STOP ERA, a group that defeated ratifications in several key states by 1974. Like NOW, STOP ERA placed a coordinator in each of the state's fifty-nine legislative districts.[87] STOP ERA's supporters were part of a grassroots movement that sought to push the Republican Party rightward by emphasizing cultural issues, race-baiting, and weaponizing conservative Christianity.[88] "In my scale of values, home, family and husband come first, and I think that's the way most people feel," Schlafly said. She defined feminism as "an antifamily movement" because it backed the ERA and abortion rights.[89] Schlafly allied with the Illinois Federation for Right to Life and the National Council of Catholic Women.[90] Other anti-ERA groups in the state included the John Birch Society, Happiness of Womanhood, and Right to Be a Woman.[91]

To Collins, Schlafly was confounding. "My experience with the nurses was that they loved having me" and "seemed to identify with feminism."[92] By contrast, Schlafly rejected equality outright, and her movement was gaining momentum in Springfield. Her supporters "didn't show up in massive numbers every week, like we did," Collins said, "but they showed up strategically when they needed to."[93] While ERA backers traveled from across the country by the thousands to attend massive rallies in Springfield, anti-ERA women trickled in consistently, one carload at a time, to lobby targeted lawmakers.[94] "They brought food," said Collins, and "they said to these men, you have wives who take care of you and that's what we're trying to preserve."[95] Such tactics were well-matched to the older white men who largely populated the state legislature. After a major pro-ERA demonstration in Springfield in 1975, state senator and ERA supporter Dawn Clark Netsch said she doubted the protest would yield results. "Because Phyllis Schlafly has her people here so often the proponents [are] kind of nervous."[96]

Netsch and other lawmakers in Illinois, which became the most embattled state in the ERA fight, debated the amendment each year until it expired.[97] The Democrats held a majority in the General Assembly, but their widening divisions put the more united Republicans in a strong position.[98] And while the provision frequently had majority backing in both chambers, a recent rules change required constitutional amendments to secure a three-fifths majority.[99] In the House, the ERA became fodder for power struggles between Chicago's Black lawmakers and Mayor Daley's Cook County machine.[100] Both the mayor and the Cook County Democratic chairman said they backed the ERA but did not deliver it. "We're getting lip service," said Chicago NOW executive director Nancy Scheir. "When the Chicago Democrats want something, they can get it."[101]

Governor James R. Thompson was also a flaky ally. He claimed to back the ERA but rallied none of his fellow Republicans to it.[102] State lawmakers observed that many of their pro-ERA letters and calls came from outside of their districts and thus did not reflect their constituents' perspectives. Even ERA backers in the legislature tired of the repeated votes on the provision and wanted to turn to other issues.[103] Some switched their votes at the last minute or abruptly left the floor before voting.[104] Others voted "yes" only once they knew it would fail in order to preserve their support in liberal districts.[105]

ERA advocates buckled down. Collins called Illinois "the crucial state for 1980" and appealed to feminists to "break through the inertia of the last several years."[106] Chicago NOW raised more than $30,000 in 1979 toward the ERA and grew by 40 percent.[107] Chapter members studied up on local politics and phone banked, lobbied, and canvassed.[108] National NOW poured $35,000 into the ERA fight in Illinois each month.[109] More than 90,000 ERA supporters from around the country marched in Chicago in 1980, representing more than three hundred delegations and organizations.[110] The protest was a dramatic show of force, as was a twenty-one day fast by seven women at the state capitol and seventeen protestors who chained themselves to the Senate chamber. Governor Thompson wrung his hands. "The chains haven't helped, the fasters haven't helped, the marchers haven't helped, the picketers haven't helped." Thompson's running mate for reelection, the conservative Speaker of the House George Ryan, scorned the spectacle: "Why should I want to watch those idiots?" Anti-ERA women added to the show by eating candy bars in front of the fasters.[111]

Although 60 percent of Illinoisans favored the ERA, the measure failed in the state legislature in 1980 for an eighth time.[112] "We are up against a solid opposition," Collins wrote to Chicago NOW with "intense anger and frustration."[113] Still, these advocates of women's equality did not want to be accused of surrendering. "It was a very good campaign but we didn't win," Collins later explained. "If it didn't pass in '80 it wasn't going to pass. But we just had to drag ourselves along for two more years."[114] The ERA expired in June 1982, three states short of ratification.

After the ERA defeat, Collins decided to bring her Midwestern-style feminism to a different context. She was elected NOW's vice president for action in late 1982, which was a salaried job in the new national office in Washington; her fellow Wisconsinite and longtime friend Judy Goldsmith won the national presidency. As Collins experienced in Illinois and rediscovered in the capital, the nation's political and social landscape was shifting away from liberalism. The New Right, which Schlafly had stoked and shaped, had won increasing clout inside the Republican Party.[115] Illinois native Ronald Reagan carried that strand of conservatism to the White House in 1980 by linking anti-statism to hierarchical family values.[116] He and his allies slashed taxes and social programs, thrusting millions of women into poverty.[117] As Reagan ousted liberals from federal agencies, replacing them with antifeminists and opponents of affirmative action, Republicans in Congress began to limit gay and lesbian rights and curtail reproductive freedoms.[118] Feminists worried that all of their recent victories would slip away.

Collins had run for the vice presidency as a "grassroots activist for NOW." Arriving in Washington, she discovered that many advocacy organizations were newly focused on the capital, where they pursued fundraising, lobbying, and research more than local membership.[119] The clannish scene was "a whole other ballgame," Collins said. "Coming from outside of Washington and trying to break into the Washington power structure among the groups is a fucking nightmare."[120] The other women's rights groups, which generally dismissed NOW as "too radical," would bring "in their people once a year for an annual lobby day and that was the grassroots plan."[121] Collins took a different tack, re-expanding NOW's agenda after the focused ERA struggle and engaging local chapters on a range of issues by launching new programs on lesbian rights and racial and economic justice.

She also believed that NOW should respond directly to the practical problems women faced in their lives. "We looked around," she said, and asked, "What's the thing that's crying for intervention that's an extreme bad thing?"[122] It was the abortion opponents who had begun bombing abortion clinics in 1982 and increased their attacks fourfold in less than three years.[123] Collins devised a new strategy for NOW members nationwide to sit in at clinics.[124] Starting on the weekend of January 18 to 21, 1985, on the eve of the anniversary of the *Roe v. Wade* opinion, NOW asked members nationwide to take part in a "Vigil for Women's Lives" through a round-the-clock sit-in at their local abortion clinics.[125] "It was an act of defiance," Collins said, to "dare them to come and get us."[126] Other pro-choice groups declared the tactic to be "as irresponsible as it can be."[127] But NOW members and supporters occupied at least thirty clinics in eighteen states over that weekend.[128] No one was harmed, and the press coverage the vigil commanded "was the size of the New York telephone book," Collins boasted.[129] It also gave NOW leaders a specific issue for hammering President Reagan, whose anti-abortion stance Goldsmith denounced for "giving comfort to the attackers of the clinics."[130]

But feminists found little traction in the broader political landscape. While Reagan condemned the clinic violence after months of pressure, NOW determined that uprooting him from office was the only path to progress on feminist issues. Conservatives kept gaining ground in cutting state programs and stocking courts and agencies with their allies.[131] As the 1984 elections approached, NOW tightened its focus on electing the Democratic candidate, former vice president and Minnesota Senator Walter Mondale and his running mate Geraldine Ferraro, a congresswoman from New York, who was the first woman on a major party presidential ticket.[132] As in the ERA campaign, NOW engaged its members primarily as canvassers, phone bankers, and donors. Reagan triumphed in a landslide, the Democrats lost ground in the House of Representatives, and Republicans held the Senate.[133] Collins lost her reelection bid in a tight race in 1985. She left NOW to focus on engaging the grassroots from another angle.[134]

Deciding to foreground her identity as a progressive Catholic, Collins became field director of Catholics for a Free Choice (CFFC) in 1985. Three Catholic members of NOW from New York had created that organization in the wake of the 1973 *Roe v. Wade* opinion to try to crack Church leaders' opposition to legal abortion from inside the Catholic community. CFFC presented Catholics "with arguments about how the Catholic Church had regarded abortion in the past," Collins said, in order to "point out the contradictions to get people to see that they could exercise their own conscience." The group lobbied on the Hill, and Collins organized the field.[135] CFFC's studies revealed that Catholics used birth control and pursued abortion care at the same rates as their Protestant counterparts. The group did not have a formal membership, but ten thousand people subscribed to its bimonthly newsletter *Conscience* in 1987.[136] "My sister was a nun," Collins said, and while Collins "didn't push" the abortion issue with her or with the Alverno College nuns who were her lifelong mentors, they all knew of her work for CFFC. Catholic faith was "part of my heritage," Collins said, "and I'm not giving it to anybody." [137]

After seven years at CFFC, Collins ended her career as the field director of People for the American Way (PFAW). Collins's job at that liberal First Amendment advocacy group was to "take all my organizing skills and figure out how to do something with the field."[138] She spearheaded programs around liberal religion and public education, connecting white Northerners to Southern Black ministers. While Collins found the ministers to be "quite conservative" on some issues, she encouraged others in PFAW not to "just run away from" others whom they believed did not "have the right idea right now."[139]

Mary Jean Collins has remained in Washington, DC, since retiring in 2008. "I appreciate living here and working here," she said.[140] Still, Midwesterners like her "never leave our midwestness behind," Collins said. "We understand that power needs to come out of those places that have power"—local communities and state governments—"and we ignore that to our peril."[141] Channeling that power required developing "the ability to talk to people who don't agree with you in everything."[142] It meant embracing practical goals and flexible tactics, connecting people across their differences, and taking a clear-eyed approach to institutions.

Located far from the government, media, and cultural capitals on the nation's coasts, Collins and other Midwestern "second-wave" feminists found space to build and improvise. Less stymied by the divisions that scholars tend to apply to the movement on the whole, Midwesterners pressured and worked through existing structures—political, religious, educational, and labor movement organizations—to attack the rigid hierarchies that shaped American life. Feminists were thus at the heart of efforts to fortify liberalism in the Midwest. There, they pursued personal autonomy, economic security, and meaningful equality protected by democratic institutions that worked for everyone. Their local efforts rippled outward and galvanized a backlash that continues to shape our politics.

A national spotlight was once again on Midwestern communities and their democratic demands in January 2017. As many as 100,000 people gathered at Wisconsin's state capitol in Madison, Collins's home state. They were part of the two million people who took part in women's marches nationwide to protest the inauguration of Republican president Donald J. Trump. "I thought a few hundred would gather at the Capitol. Look at us now!" claimed organizer Ophelia Bailly. Her statement echoed Collins's amazement at the massive participation in Chicago's Strike for Women's Equality half a century earlier. The Madison protest stretched longer than half a mile, connecting the capitol building to the campus of the state's flagship public university.[143]

The demonstrators included women and men, the elderly, and children in strollers. Chanting and carrying signs that read "We've Got Mad Girl Power" and "Another World Is Possible," they declared their support for policies ranging from affordable health care to well-supported public schools and the rights of women as well as immigrants and people of color. UW–Milwaukee student Chelsea Miller had authored the Facebook post that had helped to spark this protest. "I think a lot of people will leave here with sustained activism," she declared.[144]

NOTES

1. "Women's Lib Strikes Again, 'Strike for Women' Is Set," *Chicago Daily Defender*, August 22, 1970, 20; "Media Women Will Air 'Lib' Views Here," *Chicago Daily Defender*, November 16, 1970, 17; Mary-Ann Lupa interviewed by Katherine Turk, December 10, 2015, 10, 11.

2. Carol Kleiman, "American Women, Today Is Your Day!," *Chicago Tribune*, August 26, 1970, B1; Judy Klemesrud, "A Herstory Making Event," *New York Times*, August 23, 1970, SM4.

3. "Women's Lib Strikes Again, 'Strike for Women' Is Set," *Chicago Daily Defender*, August 22, 1970, 20.

4. Mary Jean Collins interviewed by Noreen Connell, 21, Tully-Crenshaw Feminist Oral History Project, Folder 6, Box 8, Schlesinger Library, Harvard Radcliffe Institute.

5. Mary Jean Collins interviewed by Katherine Turk, October 30–31, 2015, 1.

6. Scholars have rightly criticized the "second wave" label, which participants adopted for themselves as a link to the "first wave" push for suffrage, from valuable perspectives. See the essays in Nancy A. Hewitt, ed., *No Permanent Waves: Recasting Histories of U.S. Feminism* (New Brunswick, NJ: Rutgers University Press, 2010). As Hewitt writes, the "second wave" moniker dates at least to 1968, but "the concept of waves surging and receding cannot fully capture these multiple and overlapping movements, chronologies, issues, and sites." Nancy A. Hewitt, "Introduction," *No Permanent Waves*, 1, 2. Overviews of the movement include Dorothy Sue Cobble, Linda Gordon, and Astrid Henry, *Feminism Unfinished: A Short, Surprising History of Women's Movements* (New York: Liveright, 2014); Sara M. Evans, *Tidal Wave: How Women Changed America at Century's End* (New York: Free Press, 2004); Estelle B. Freedman, *No Turning Back: The History of Feminism and the Future of Women* (New York: Ballantine Books, 2003); Annelise Orleck, *Rethinking American Women's Activism* (New York: Routledge, 2015); and Christine Stansell, *The Feminist Promise, 1792 to the Present* (New York: Modern Library, 2010).

7. On participants, see, for example, Daniel Horowitz, *Betty Friedan and the Making of "The Feminine Mystique": The American Left, the Cold War, and Modern Feminism* (Amherst: University of Massachusetts Press, 2000); Rachel Shteir, *Betty Friedan: Magnificent Disrupter* (New Haven, CT: Yale University Press, 2023); Kimberly Springer, *Living for the Revolution: Black Feminist Organizations, 1968–1980* (Durham, NC: Duke University Press, 2005); Sherie M. Randolph, *Florynce "Flo" Kennedy: The Life of a Black Feminist Radical* (Chapel Hill: University of North Carolina Press, 2015); Rosalind Rosenberg, *Jane Crow: The Life of Pauli Murray* (Oxford: Oxford University Press, 2017); and Jennifer Scanlon, *Until There Is Justice: The Life of Anna Arnold Hedgeman* (Oxford: Oxford University Press, 2016). On local and national organizations, see, for example, Maryann Barakso, *Governing NOW: Grassroots Activism in the National Organization for Women* (Ithaca, NY: Cornell University Press, 2004); Melissa Estes Blair, *Revolutionizing Expectations: Women's Organizations, Feminism, and American Politics, 1965–1980*

(Athens: University of Georgia Press, 2014); Tamar Carroll, *Mobilizing New York: AIDS, Antipoverty, and Feminist Activism* (Chapel Hill: University of North Carolina Press, 2015); Stephanie Gilmore, *Groundswell: Grassroots Feminist Activism in Postwar America* (New York: Routledge, 2013); and Anne M. Valk, *Radical Sisters: Second-Wave Feminism and Black Liberation in Washington, D.C.* (Champaign: University of Illinois Press, 2010). On campaigns, see, for example, Winifred Breines, *The Trouble between Us: An Uneasy History of White and Black Women in the Feminist Movement* (Oxford: Oxford University Press, 2007); Marisa Chappell, "Rethinking Women's Politics in the 1970s: The League of Women Voters and the National Organization for Women Confront Poverty," *Journal of Women's History* 13, no. 4 (January 2002): 115–179; Stephanie Gilmore, ed., *Feminist Coalitions: Historical Perspectives on Second-Wave Feminism in the United States* (Champaign: University of Illinois Press, 2008); Venus Green, "Flawed Remedies: EEOC, ATT and Sears Outcomes Reconsidered," *Black Women, Gender + Families* (Spring 2012): 44–70; Deborah Dinner, "The Universal Childcare Debate: Rights Mobilization, Social Policy, and the Dynamics of Feminist Activism, 1966–1974," *Law and History Review* 28 (August 2010): 577–628; Lisa Levenstein, "'Don't Agonize, Organize!' The Displaced Homemakers Campaign and the Contested Goals of 1970s Feminism," *Journal of American History* 100 (March 2014): 144–168; Traci Parker, "Sears Discriminated against Me Because of My Sex and Race': African American Women Workers, Title VII, and the Sears Sex Discrimination Case," *Journal of Women's History* 33 (Spring 2021): 12–36; Benita Roth, *Separate Roads to Feminism: Black, Chicana, and White Feminist Movements during the 1960s and 1970s* (Cambridge: Cambridge University Press, 2003); and Kirsten Swinth, *Feminism's Forgotten Fight: The Unfinished Struggle for Work and Family* (Cambridge, MA: Harvard University Press, 2018).

8. Stephanie Gilmore, "The Dynamics of Second-Wave Feminist Activism in Memphis, 1971–1982: Rethinking the Liberal/Radical Divide," *NWSA Journal* 15, no. 1 (Spring 2003). Existing accounts of feminism in sites across the Midwest include Stephanie Gilmore and Elizabeth Kaminski, "A Part and Apart: Lesbian and Straight Feminist Activists Negotiate Identity in a Second-Wave Organization," *Journal of the History of Sexuality* 16, no. 1 (January 2007): 95–113; Finn Enke, *Finding the Movement: Sexuality, Contested Space, and Feminist Activism* (Durham, NC: Duke University Press, 2007); Judith Ezekiel, *Feminism in the Heartland* (Columbus: Ohio State University Press, 2002); Erin M. Kempker, *Big Sister: Feminism, Conservatism, and Conspiracy in the Heartland* (Champaign: University of Illinois Press, 2018); and Katherine Turk, "Out of the Revolution, into the Mainstream: Employment Activism in the NOW Sears Campaign and the Growing Pains of Liberal Feminism," *Journal of American History* 97 (September 2010): 399–423. Pioneering women's historian Gerda Lerner spearheaded a project at the University of Wisconsin–Madison, "Documenting the Midwestern Origins of the Twentieth-Century Women's Movement, 1987–1992," which consists of interviews of twenty-two Midwestern feminists. The collection is held at the Wisconsin Historical Society.

9. "Women's Lib Strikes Again, 'Strike for Women' Is Set," *Chicago Daily Defender*, August 22, 1970, 20; Bonne J. Nesbitt, "No Bra Burning in Rally," *Chicago Daily Defender*, August 27, 1970, 3, 32. Crowd size estimates varied widely; this source says five thousand; Collins estimated fifteen thousand.

10. "Women's Lib Strikes Again, 'Strike for Women' Is Set"; Collins interviewed by Connell, 21.

11. The *Chicago Tribune* had suggested this action previous day. Carol Kleiman, "American Women, Today Is Your Day!," *Chicago Tribune*, August 26, 1970, B1.

12. Collins interviewed by Connell, 21–22.

13. Collins interviewed by Connell, 21–22.

14. Collins interviewed by Turk, October 30–31, 2015, 6–7.

15. Patrick D. Jones, *The Selma of the North: Civil Rights Insurgency in Milwaukee* (Cambridge, MA: Harvard University Press, 2009), 15–7.

16. Collins interviewed by Turk, October 30–1, 2015, 1.

17. Collins interviewed by Connell, 3.

18. Collins interviewed by Turk, October 30–31, 2015, 1.

19. Collins interviewed by Connell, 15; Collins interviewed by Turk, October 30–31, 2015, 1.

20. Peggy House, "Fulltime Students Total 844," *Alverno Campus News*, October 18, 1960, 4.

21. Joel Read and Mary Jean Collins interviewed by Turk, September 3, 2016, 11.

22. Read and Collins interviewed by Katherine Turk, September 3, 2016, 7; Joel Read, "Letter from Alverno College," *Women's Studies Newsletter* 1, no. 5 (Fall 1973): 3. See also Anne Braude, "Faith, Feminism, and History," in Catherine A. Brekus, ed., *The Religious History of American Women: Reimagining the Past* (Chapel Hill: University of North Carolina Press, 2007).

23. "What Alverno Offers You," Alverno College Student Handbook, 1962, 4–6, Alverno College Archives; "Alumnae Act as Cooperating Teachers," *Alverno Campus News*, October 18, 1961, 3.

24. Robert C. Doty, "Pope Paul Closes Vatican Council Amid Pageantry," *New York Times*, December 9, 1965, 1.

25. Collins interviewed by Connell, 3; Collins interviewed by Turk, October 30–31, 2015, 2.

26. Jones, *The Selma of the North*, 2, 93–94, 179–200; Collins interviewed by Turk, October 31, 2019, 1.

27. "Finlayson, Edith N., 1925–2001," Civil Rights Digital Library, http://crdl.usg.edu/people/f/finlayson_edith_n_1925_2001/?Welcome; E. B. Phillips Daycare Center, Inc., https://opencorporates.com/companies/us_wi/6P05976; Jones, *The Selma of the North*, 38. This source dates the founding of the E. B. Phillips Daycare Center to 1962: "Congregation Beth Israel Synagogue, Milwaukee, Milwaukee County, Wisconsin," National Register of Historic Places Registration Form, United States Department of the Interior, February 1987, 7, https://npgallery.nps.gov/GetAsset/321d81a4–1d3c-4f8e-8462–544005f624d0.

28. Ronald H. Snyder, "Chief for Life: Harold Breier and His Era" (PhD diss., University of Wisconsin-Milwaukee, 2002), 109–110; "Edith Norman Finlayson," in Barbara J. Love, ed., *Feminists Who Changed America, 1963–1975* (Champaign: University of Illinois Press, 2006), 149; Sarah Slavin, ed., *U.S. Women's Interest Groups: Institutional Profiles* (Westport, CT: Greenwood, 1995), 592–593.

29. Genevieve G. McBride, ed., *Women's Wisconsin: From Native Matriarchies to the New Millennium* (Madison: Wisconsin Historical Society Press, 2005), 433–435. Kathryn Clarenbach's son, David Clarenbach, would become a state lawmaker who prominently advocated for gay rights protections in the Wisconsin Assembly. See Stephen Colbrook's chapter in this volume.

30. JAMAKAYA, *Like Our Sisters Before Us: Women of Wisconsin Labor* (Milwaukee: Wisconsin Labor History Society, 1998), 30; McBride, *Women's Wisconsin*, 437; *Targets for Action: The Report of the Third Annual National Conference of Commissions on the Status of Women* (Washington, DC: US Women's Bureau, 1966), 9.

31. JAMAKAYA, *Like Our Sisters Before Us*, 30; Mary Jean Collins email to Katherine Turk, July 28, 2016. On Midwestern pragmatism in South Dakota's women's commission, see Matthew Pehl, "Gender Politics on the Prairie: The South Dakota Commission on the Status of Women in the 1970s," in Jon Lauck, John Miller, and Paula Nelson, eds., *The Plains Political Tradition*, vol. 3 (Pierre: South Dakota Historical Society Press, 2018).

32. Cynthia Harrison, *On Account of Sex: The Politics of Women's Issues, 1945–1968* (Berkeley: University of California Press, 1988), 160–161; *Targets for Action*, 4–10.

33. *Targets for Action*, 29, 40–41.

34. Katherine Turk, *The Women of NOW: How Feminists Built an Organization that Transformed America* (New York: Farrar, Straus & Giroux, 2023), 19.

35. Susan Oliver, *Betty Friedan: The Personal Is Political* (New York: Pearson, 2007), 92; "Founders' Reception," September 4, 1971, *Now Acts* 4 (September 1971): 7.

36. This figure is drawn from the author's research into NOW's twenty-eight first founders, whose names are listed in "Honoring Our Founders & Pioneers," ca. 2011, http://now.org/wp-content/uploads/2014/02/Honoring-Our-Founders.pdf, accessed March 30, 2022.

37. Read and Collins interviewed by Turk, 1, 5.

38. Read and Collins interviewed by Turk, 5.

39. Collins interviewed by Connell, 7.

40. "NOW Origins Workshop Souvenir Journal," 1, Folder 1, Box 7, Tully-Crenshaw Feminist Oral History Project.

41. Collins interviewed by Connell, 17; Collins interviewed by Turk, October 30–31, 2015, 3.

42. Collins interviewed by Turk, October 30–31, 2015, 4.

43. Collins interviewed by Connell, 9.

44. On Mayor Richard J. Daley, see Mike Royko, *Boss: Richard J. Daley of Chicago* (New York: E. P. Dutton, 1971).

45. Emily Zuckerman, "The Cooperative Origins of EEOC v. Sears," in Stephanie Gilmore, ed., *Feminist Coalitions: Historical Perspectives on Second-Wave Feminism in the United States* (Urbana: University of Illinois Press, 2008), 227.

46. Anne Ladky and Karen Fishman interviewed by Katherine Turk, February 26, 2018, 4.

47. Ladky and Fishman interviewed by Turk, 4.

48. Collins interviewed by Connell, 7.

49. Lupa interviewed by Turk, 10.

50. Ladky and Fishman interviewed by Turk, 5.

51. Collins interviewed by Turk, October 30–31, 2015, 10.

52. Marcia Walker-McWilliams, *Reverend Addie Wyatt: Faith and the Fight for Labor, Gender, and Racial Equality* (Urbana: University of Illinois Press, 2016), 2, 113.

53. Walker-McWilliams, *Reverend Addie Wyatt*, 22–23.

54. Walker-McWilliams, *Reverend Addie Wyatt*, 4.

55. Walker-McWilliams, *Reverend Addie Wyatt*, 139–141.

56. Amy Kesselman with Heather Booth, Vivian Rothstein, and Naomi Weisstein,

"Our Gang of Four," in Rachel Blau DuPlessis and Ann Snitow, eds., *The Feminist Memoir Project: Voices from Women's Liberation* (New Brunswick, NJ: Rutgers University Press, 2007), 27.

57. Day Creamer and Heather Booth, "Action Committee for Decent Childcare: Organizing for Power," 2–3, "Women-Action Committee for Decent Childcare 1972" Folder, Box 48, Midwest Academy Records, Chicago History Museum; Zuckerman, "The Cooperative Origins of EEOC v. Sears," 229.

58. Kesselman et al., "Our Gang of Four," 46.

59. Carol Kleiman, "Learn to Organize," *Chicago Tribune*, October 6, 1974, D4.

60. Chris Riddiough interviewed by Katherine Turk, March 5, 2019, 1.

61. Donna Joy Newman, "Women: Time to Work Together for Equality," *Chicago Tribune*, December 4, 1975, B3.

62. Mary Jean Collins interviewed by Katherine Turk, May 2, 2022, 1.

63. Mike LaVelle, "Nurses Search for 'Cure' in Court," *Chicago Tribune*, April 1, 1975, A3; "Nurses in Confab," *Chicago Daily Defender*, November 5, 1973, 18.

64. "AFSCME Council 31—History & Today," *AFSCME Council 31*, https://www.afscme31.org/about/afscme-council-31-organizational-history, accessed May 10, 2022.

65. Collins interviewed by Turk, October 30–31, 2015, 25.

66. Collins interviewed by Turk, February 22, 2019, 2–3.

67. Collins interviewed by Turk, May 2, 2022, 1, 2.

68. Mary Jean Collins interview, Documenting the Midwestern Origins of the Twentieth-Century Women's Movement, 1987–1992, Tape 128, Side B, Wisconsin Historical Society.

69. Carol Kleiman, "'Nurses Are Getting Out of the Woodwork,'" *Chicago Tribune*, November 26, 1978, M5.

70. Jon Van, "Nurses Here Protest Dress Code," *Chicago Tribune*, April 20, 1974, C14.

71. Carole A. Carmichael, "Nurses Weigh 2-Year Pact: Outcome of Voting Uncertain," *Chicago Tribune*, December 11, 1976, W1.

72. Collins interviewed by Turk, May 2, 2022, 2.

73. Collins interviewed by Turk, May 2, 2022, 2.

74. Collins interviewed by Turk, May 2, 2022, 2–3.

75. Collins interviewed by Turk, February 22, 2019, 2.

76. On the Equal Rights Amendment, see Mary Frances Berry, *Why ERA Failed: Politics, Women's Rights, and the Amending Process of the Constitution* (Bloomington: Indiana University Press, 1988); Rebecca DeWolf, *Gendered Citizenship: The Original Conflict over the Equal Rights Amendment, 1920–1963* (Lincoln: University of Nebraska Press, 2021); Jane Mansbridge, *Why We Lost the ERA* (Chicago: University of Chicago Press, 1986); and Marjorie J. Spruill, *Divided We Stand: The Battle over Women's Rights and Family Values that Polarized American Politics* (New York: Bloomsbury, 2017).

77. NOW Legislative Office, "NOW ERA Timeline," undated, ca. 1975, 1, Folder 62, Box 54, NOW Records.

78. "Illinois ERA Blitz Planned," *Chicago Tribune*, August 28, 1979, 3.

79. Collins interviewed by Turk, February 22, 2019, 2, 3.

80. Collins interviewed by Turk, February 22, 2019, 2–3.

81. "Illinois ERA Blitz Planned," 3; Collins interviewed by Turk, February 22, 2019, 3.

82. Riddiough interviewed by Turk, 2.

83. Riddiough interviewed by Turk, 1.

84. Walker-McWilliams, *Addie Wyatt*, 168; Collins interviewed by Turk, May 2, 2022, 3.

85. Spruill, *Divided We Stand*, 76.

86. Donald T. Critchlow, *Phyllis Schlafly and Grassroots Conservatism: A Woman's Crusade* (Princeton, NJ: Princeton University Press, 2005), 31–3.

87. Critchlow, *Phyllis Schlafly and Grassroots Conservatism*, 235.

88. Evans, *Tidal Wave*, 112–113.

89. Judy Klemesrud, "Opponent of ERA Confident of Its Defeat," *New York Times*, December 15, 1975, 44.

90. Critchlow, *Phyllis Schlafly and Grassroots Conservatism*, 236.

91. Berry, *Why ERA Failed*, 67–68.

92. Collins interviewed by Turk, May 2, 2022, 4.

93. Collins interviewed by Turk, May 2, 2022, 4.

94. William E. Farrell, "Women from 30 States Carry E.R.A. Fight to Land of Lincoln," *New York Times*, May 17, 1976, 1.

95. Collins interviewed by Turk, May 2, 2022, 4.

96. Critchlow, *Phyllis Schlafly and Grassroots Conservatism*, 224, 236.

97. Critchlow, *Phyllis Schlafly and Grassroots Conservatism*, 235.

98. John Elmer and Neil Mehler, "The Disassembly in Springfield," *Chicago Tribune*, June 22, 1975, A1, A2.

99. Douglas E. Kneeland, "Backers of Equality Amendment Making Illinois a Prime Target," *New York Times*, May 30, 1978, B6.

100. Berry, *Why ERA Failed*, 67.

101. Kneeland, "Backers of Equality Amendment Making Illinois a Prime Target," A1, B6.

102. Kneeland, "Backers of Equality Amendment Making Illinois a Prime Target," B6.

103. Janet K. Boles, *The Politics of the Equal Rights Amendment: Conflict and the Decision Process* (New York: Longman, 1979), 130, 134.

104. Kneeland, "Backers of Equality Amendment Making Illinois a Prime Target," B6.

105. Critchlow, *Phyllis Schlafly and Grassroots Conservatism*, 237.

106. Mary Jean Collins, "From the President," *Act NOW* [Chicago NOW Newsletter], April 1980, 1, NOW Chapter Newsletter Collection, Schlesinger Library.

107. Chicago ERA Ratification Project Fund Raising Campaigns, undated, ca. 1979, Folder 34, Box 194, NOW Records.

108. Mary Jean Collins interviewed by Marie Scatena, June 14, 2019, University of Illinois at Chicago, in Mary Jean Collins's possession.

109. Eleanor Smeal to NOW Member, March 1980, Folder 421, Boston NOW Records, Schlesinger Library, Harvard Radcliffe Institute.

110. Sandy Roth, "Over 90,000 March in Chicago," *National NOW Times*, June 1980, 1.

111. Mary Frances Berry, *Why ERA Failed*, 81.

112. Mary Frances Berry, *Why ERA Failed*, 68, 74; Critchlow, *Phyllis Schlafly and Grassroots Conservatism*, 235.

113. Jean Collins, "From the President," *Act NOW* [Chicago NOW Newsletter], July 1980, 1, 2, NOW Chapter Newsletter Collection, Schlesinger Library.

114. Collins interviewed by Turk, October 30–31, 2015, 17.

115. Kevin Kruse and Julian Zelizer, *Fault Lines: A History of the United States since 1974* (New York: W. W. Norton, 2019), 123.

116. Robert Self, *All in the Family: The Realignment of American Democracy since the 1970s* (New York: Hill & Wang, 2013), 367.

117. Doug Rossinow, *The Reagan Era: A History of the 1980s* (New York: Columbia University Press, 2015), 59–63; Susan Faludi, *Backlash: The Undeclared War against American Women* (New York: Crown, 1991), xvii.

118. Evans, *Tidal Wave*, 177; Lynn Hecht Schafran, "Reagan vs. Women," *New York Times*, October 13, 1981, 23.

119. "Mary Jean Collins for Action-Vice President," undated, ca. September 1982, Folder 1, Box 25, Mary Jean Collins NOW Officer Records; Kenneth Cmiel, "The Emergence of Human Rights Politics in the United States," *Journal of American History* 86 (December 1999): 1244–1245; Theda Skocpol, *Diminished Democracy: From Membership to Management in American Civic Life* (Norman: University of Oklahoma Press, 2004), 127, 142–144.

120. Collins interviewed by Turk, February 22, 2019, 5.

121. Collins interviewed by Turk, May 2, 2022, 4.

122. Collins interviewed by Turk, October 30–31, 2015, 29.

123. "The 30 Abortion Clinic Arson and Bombing Attacks between May 29, 1982 and Jan. 3, 1985," January 4, 1985, UPI Archives, https://www.upi.com/Archives/1985/01/04/The-30-abortion-clinic-arson-and-bombing-attacks-between/6555473662800/, accessed February 13, 2022; Joe Pichirallo and Ruth Marchs, "No Conspiracy Seen in Clinic Attacks," *Washington Post*, January 6, 1985, A16; Lloyd Grove, "Abortion Clinics: Inside & on the Picket Line, the Resolve to Carry On," *Washington Post*, January 11, 1985, B1. On anti-abortion violence, see also Karissa Haugeberg, *Women against Abortion: Inside the Largest Moral Reform Movement of the Twentieth Century* (Urbana: University of Illinois Press, 2017), 75–90.

124. Mary Jean Collins to NOW National Board, re: Abortion, May 4, 1984, Folder 50, Box 5, NOW Records; NOW National Conference Resolutions, 1984, Folder 40, Box 25, NOW Records.

125. Collins interviewed by Turk, May 2, 2022, 4.

126. Collins interviewed by Turk, February 22, 2019, 6.

127. Margaret Engel, "NOW's Controversial 'Vigil,'" *Washington Post*, January 11, 1985, B4.

128. Barbara Vobejda, "Prochoice Volunteers Stage an Antiviolence Sit-in," *Washington Post*, January 22, 1985, D1; "Rights Activists Plan Abortion Clinic Vigils," *Boston Globe*, January 19, 1985, 6.

129. Collins interviewed by Turk, May 2, 2022, 4–5.

130. Barbara Vobejda, "Women Demand U.S. Action to Stem Clinic Attacks," *Washington Post*, March 16, 1984, C2.

131. Kruse and Zelizer, *Fault Lines*, 112, 120–122.

132. Steven M. Gillon, *The Democrats' Dilemma: Walter F. Mondale and the Liberal Legacy* (New York: Columbia University Press, 1992); News Release, "NOW PACs Raise More than $1 Million," November 3, 1984, Folder 31, Box 200, NOW Records; News Release, "NOW Members Register a Quarter of a Million New Voters," October 18, 1984, Folder 31, Box 200, NOW Records.

133. "Reagan and Bush Are Re-Elected in a Landside, 525 Votes to 13," *New York Times*, January 8, 1985, 14.

134. Marilyn Gardner, "Eleanor Smeal Elected NOW President After 'Intense' Campaign," *Christian Science Monitor*, July 22, 1985, 3.

135. Collins interviewed by Turk, May 2, 2022, 5.

136. Kelsey Kretschmer, "Contested Loyalties: Dissident Identity Organizations, Institutions, and Social Movements," *Sociological Perspectives* 52 (Winter 2009): 439–440; Ruth A. Wallace, "Catholic Women and the Creation of a New Social Reality," *Gender and Society* 2 (March 1988): 34; Boyce Rensberger, "Vatican 'Out of Step' on Birth Control, Group Finds," *Washington Post*, July 20, 1994, A12.

137. Collins interviewed by Turk, May 2, 2022, 5.

138. Collins interviewed by Turk, May 2, 2022, 5–6.

139. Collins interviewed by Turk, May 2, 2022, 6.

140. Collins interviewed by Turk, October 30–31, 2015, 29.

141. Collins interviewed by Turk, May 2, 2022, 6.

142. Collins interviewed by Turk, May 2, 2022, 7.

143. Bill Glauber, "'Look at Us Now!,' Women March against Trump," *Milwaukee Journal Sentinel*, January 21, 2017, https://www.jsonline.com/story/news/politics/2017/01/21/thousands-gather-madison-womens-march/96882846/, accessed April 28, 2022.

144. Glauber, "'Look at Us Now!,' Women March Against Trump."

10

Creating a Blueprint for Black Power

Muigwithania, Mayor Hatcher, and the 1972 National Black Political Convention in Gary, Indiana

NICOLE POLETIKA

The influence of the Jim Crow South and populous northern cities on Black liberalism has been well-established by historians. Frequently overlooked, however, are the contributions of Midwestern leaders, like those of Gary, Indiana, who created a new framework for obtaining Black political power. The Calumet region is fertile ground for study, as the tandem forces of the Great Migration and white flight created a populace primed for self-determination. Beginning in the early 1960s, Black professionals restructured politics from the bottom-up through coalition-building. By employing innovative campaign tactics, pooling resources, and forging a network of volunteers from all walks of life, a group called "Muigwithania" circumvented Gary's political machines and placed into power candidates committed to the needs of Black constituents. With their successful campaigns, Muigwithania created an organizational blueprint and cultivated an energized citizenry that helped make the 1972 National Black Political Convention (NBPC) possible in Gary. The city's significance to the struggle for liberation was cemented at the convention when Rev. Jesse Jackson anointed Gary—not New York City or Los Angeles—home to the "scattered tribes around the nation."[1]

From March 10 to 12, approximately ten thousand Black Americans convened at Gary's West Side High School, where they strategized about how to increase political power. Despite some disagreement about resolutions, the convention produced a formal Black Political Agenda, galvanized local activists, and helped increase the number of Black elected officials in the ensuing years. It can be argued that the convention was essentially an extension of Muigwithania, whose members had uniquely positioned Gary to bring together activists, citizens, and elected officials across the political spectrum.

An examination of Gary's founding is essential in understanding the disenfranchisement of its Black residents and the conditions that inspired Muigwithania's formation. In 1906, US Steel officials flattened sand dunes along the southern lip of Lake Michigan to make room for towering steel mills, effectively founding the city of Gary. Until around 1930, European immigrants, Black Southerners, Mexicans, and white migrants flocked to Gary seeking work in the steel industry.[2] US Steel scrambled to accommodate the influx of residents—and due to poor town planning, as historian James B. Lane contended, "two strikingly different Gary's emerged: one neat and scenic, the other chaotic and squalid."[3] North of the Wabash Railroad tracks, the families of upper-level managers and businessmen settled in quaint neighborhoods erected by the Gary Land Company. Poorly compensated immigrants and Black residents had little choice but to settle on the south side, which had been neglected by the Gary Land Company.[4] Many resided in tents, tarpaper shacks, barracks, and unventilated houses in a marshy region dubbed "the Patch," where overcrowding led to outbreaks of tuberculosis and malaria. Lacking access to the opportunities and amenities of their northern neighbors, residents were assailed with rampant crime and vice as "laborers entered the omnipresent bars armed . . . ready to squeeze a few hours of action into their grim lives."[5]

In the 1920s a few Black individuals began to consider politics as a possible vehicle for the social uplift of their community.[6] Voters elected to city council Black leaders A. B. Whitlock, Bill Burrus, and Dr. S. R. Blackwell, each of whom made history by "forcing through an open housing ordinance which mandated Blacks to live in any district of the city. This caused a great exodus of whites to suburbia making it possible to elect a Black as mayor of Gary [in 1967]." During the Great Depression, Gary's Black population undertook one of its first organized attempts to overcome economic disenfranchisement by employing the principle of self-governance. According to the *Gary Crusader*, the "spirit of buying black led to a cooperative movement in 1932 with a consumer organization. . . . Study convinced the group that cooperation would 'lift a race out of poverty and put it on the straight road to independence and prosperity.'"[7] This group formed a cooperative that met weekly to discuss business methods, and in 1934 members pooled their resources to open a thriving grocery store and the Co-Operative Credit Union.⁸ One observer marveled that these efforts "exemplified the Negro's growing sense of racial solidarity, his realization of the effectiveness of group-effort, and the awakening of a spirit of self-sufficiency."⁹

The demands of World War II likely disrupted socioeconomic and political organization. However, Black businessman Henry Coleman, who had gotten involved in precinct politics in the late 1930s, reinvigorated efforts.¹⁰ In 1956, Coleman applied his organizational expertise as manager of James T. Harris Jr.'s campaign for city councilman. According to *Gary Info*, despite a formidable fight, Harris was defeated, prompting Coleman to investigate why Black candidates consistently lost political races. He repeatedly searched "records and tally sheets in the dungeons of the County [Clerk's Office] building," where he uncovered various methods that had been used to steal votes. These insights enabled him to successfully manage the campaigns and safeguard the electoral victories of many trailblazing Black candidates in Gary, including Mayor Richard Hatcher.¹¹

The progress made by organizers like Coleman was bolstered by the 1960 formation of Black newspaper the *Gary Crusader*, which sought to be "the weapon of a disenfranchised and mistreated citizenry."¹² The paper exposed instances of injustice, which publications like the *Gary Post-Tribune* kept buried in filing cabinets. While working as a prosecutor in Lake County's Crown Point during the early 1960s, Hatcher provided the *Crusader* with legal documents. This enabled the paper to provide inclusive coverage of events in Gary, particularly those effecting minorities. The *Gary Crusader* not only documented historical events but also strove to make them, founding a "Black-White group" in 1962 to monitor local elections.¹³ The group examined voting machines for broken seals, reported tampering to the FBI, and monitored the polls on Election Day. Despite these efforts, fraud occurred in spades, as the *Crusader* noted: "Machines were broken into, votes pre-recorded on machines, [and there were] ghost voters and rampant phantom participants," all resulting in an ill-gotten political victory. The newspaper noted that those who protested the corrupt activities were jailed. Although the election confirmed the entrenched power of political machines, the *Crusader*'s efforts further galvanized Black individuals.

Like other American cities in the 1950s and 1960s, white residents fled Gary for the suburbs as the Black population increased.¹⁴ Anxious residents relocated to nearby Merrillville, depleting Gary's core of a significant tax base. But with this divestment came opportunities for Black residents to assume more control of their own community. Although crusading individuals and institutions had attempted to bolster Black power, it was not until around 1960 that a collective movement emerged. Young Black professionals like Houston Coleman, Dozier Allen, attorney Jackie Shropshire, and attorney Richard Hatcher formed a social club with the initial goal to increase welfare benefits for struggling residents. Realizing that their efforts were futile unless they could influence legislation, the club focused on obtaining political power.[15] According to journalist Alex Poinsett's 1970 *Black Power Gary Style: The Making of Mayor Richard Gordon Hatcher*, the idea for the social-political group originated from Lawshe's interest in "emerging Africa."[16] He believed that "blacks desperately needed something to hold onto in the midst of their American ordeal" and that Mother Africa could provide this "spiritual sustenance."[17] Lawshe named the group Muigwithania—meaning "we are together" in Kikuyu.

Muigwithania's founders sought to forge a path to "self-rule" by breaking the Democratic Party's stranglehold over disenfranchised Black voters in Gary. These voters had historically cast their ballots for Democratic candidates, knowing they would be thanked with favors, like a ten-dollar bill or a carton of eggs. Handpicked by the party, both Black and white candidates typically had little motive to respond to the needs of these constituents.[18] Hatcher recalled that Muigwithania's founders "were pretty much fed up with corrupt practices in Gary and the fact there was no room in the Democratic party for a young Negro if he was not blessed by the machine."[19]

These members circumvented the traditional path to political power, reflecting the separatist ideals of Black Nationalists, which would be vaunted at the 1972 convention. Founders of Muigwithania quietly recruited members, who paid $100 dues in monthly installments.[20] Growing in size, but still lacking operating funds, the young Turks successfully tapped the community and raised money from public events such as dances. Largely ignorant about the inner-workings of political campaigns, Muigwithania members volunteered with Democratic campaigns, learning the nuts and bolts of neighborhood canvassing and mobilizing voters to the polls. In 1962 six members challenged old-line party members for seats at the Democratic State Convention. Scholars Dr. William E. Nelson Jr. and Philip J. Meranto noted that, knocking on doors for support, they "found to their surprise that people were responsive to the idea of having one of the neighborhood boys represent them at the state convention."[21] All six Muigwithanians defeated their opponents and in June joined delegates at the State Fairgrounds Coliseum in Indianapolis, where they received an intense lesson in in electoral politics.[22]

Finally imbued with organizational experience, but unbeholden to the Lake County political machine, they ran their own candidates, who were truly committed to the needs of the Black community.[23] One such candidate would be Richard Hatcher, who had fought de facto segregation in Gary's public school system as an NAACP lawyer and represented victims of police brutality at Police Service Commission hearings.[24] Born in 1933 in Michigan City, Indiana, Hatcher was the twelfth of thirteen children. His family resided in the city's "Patch," and his father molded railroad cars at Pullman Standard. With few resources, higher education was all but off the table for young Richard, until his two older sisters scrimped to put him through college. He supplemented their contributions by waiting tables and securing an athletic scholarship, allowing him to earn his BS in government economics at Indiana University. Hatcher then obtained his law degree at Valparaiso University in 1959, putting it to use in Crown Point. He moved his law practice to Gary and entered the 1963 race for city council as an independent, ultimately earning more votes in the primaries than any other candidate for councilman-at-large in Gary's history. With his election to the council that fall through the backing of Muigwithania, Hatcher laid one of the first of many bricks on the road to Black political empowerment in Gary.

According to a 1965 *Muhammad Speaks* article, Hatcher's grassroots campaign for city council spurred the "community to new militancy."[25] Unlike many other Black council members, Councilman Hatcher prioritized his commitment to his Black constituency over retaining political power. He convinced the council to pass a strong open occupancy bill in 1965 and helped integrate hospitals and fire stations. His refusal to bend to the majority resulted in contentious meetings but earned him a loyal following of citizens, who showed their support by coming to the meetings.[26] Hatcher's 1963 election, made possible by the small but resourceful group, started to erode political complacency among disenfranchised Black residents, generating momentum for greater Black influence in the city.

Three years after Hatcher's election, Muigwithania cofounder Dozier Allen ran for Calumet Township assessor, coming within hundreds of votes of being elected.[27] A Munster, Indiana, *Times* article contended that with the showing of Allen, a "relative unknown," many believe "the Negro finally has realized his voting strength in the Steel City."[28] Capitalizing on this momentum, Muigwithania convened about the possibility of running one of their members for mayor. Although some favored Allen, they ultimately backed Hatcher, who, if successful, would become the first Black mayor of a large American city. The battle would be herculean, but Hatcher's participation in civil rights and labor protests, as well as his reputation as a councilman "for the people," had garnered a loyal following in the majority-Black city.²⁹ In a 1967 *Indianapolis Recorder* article about his candidacy, Hatcher noted that the club's members had been instrumental in campaigning, stating they "have been a great deal of inspiration to me. . . . They represent a kind of a new breed—young fellows who want a better community."³⁰

Muigwithania demonstrated that Black political power was not only possible but could foster a better life, catalyzing citizen support for Hatcher's campaign. Like the social-political group, many volunteers for Hatcher's mayoral run had no previous experience with political activism or campaigning but were inspired to get involved because of Hatcher's conviction and legislative accomplishments. This support would be crucial, as Hatcher's own Democratic Party refused to support him and actively opposed him—partly because of his race and partly due to his refusal to adhere to the patronage system.³¹ Lacking party support and resources, Hatcher relied on an army of energized and loyal volunteers, many of whom dedicated hours of their time without pay. Some Hatcher volunteers believed so ardently in his team that they took leave from work for months to campaign, and at least one took out a second mortgage to provide the campaign with funds.

Following Muigwithania precedent, Hatcher's volunteers were audacious in their tactics and stalwart in their disregard of Democratic machine hostility. Nelson and Meranto noted that because these were amateur campaigners, they "experimented with new as well as old techniques" in getting the word out about their candidate.³² They supplemented Muigwithania's voter registration drives, going door-to-door in Black neighborhoods, and visiting bars, churches, and theaters to register new voters.³³ Innovative campaign tactics included putting campaign literature under milk deliveries, which would stick to the bottom of the bottles from condensation. Once brought to the breakfast table, the pamphlet would fall off and, one volunteer recalled, "there's a picture of your candidate with his name on it. . . . The children are there and they pass the card around, let me see, let me see Mr. Hatcher."³⁴

Volunteers focused on overcoming residents' apprehension about not voting for traditional Democratic candidates for fear they would be found out. Nelson and Meranto noted that one volunteer encouraged residents to accept the grocery certificates given to them by Hatcher's opposition, but to vote for Hatcher, recalling, "I said take them. Feed your family. Deceive that bastard like he's been deceiving you. . . . He's been deceiving us since 1619. Deceive him—play his same game. Take everything he has to give you. Then go behind the machine and vote him out of there. They did it—and it was beautiful."³⁵ Such tactics, one volunteer said, let Hatcher's opponents know "this was a new black movement—that we were black and that we were not going to be cheated. They knew that we were going to resort to anything. . . . I think the message was received."[36]

In *Black Power Gary Style*, Poinsett noted that this volunteer network was responsible for Hatcher's "near-miraculous primary victory."[37] Poinsett especially credited a group of "semi-professional" women, organized by Muigwithanian Chuck Deggans, for this initial victory. Members of the group, dubbed the "Shock Troops," spoke at Black churches and sent literature to thousands of Gary mailboxes. Although their rallies never attracted the numbers that traditional Democratic campaigns did, they "struck a nerve. Black people seemed to have a need for what they were saying. Children took up the case for Hatcher. His picture went up in poolrooms."[38]

Hatcher's team had witnessed voter fraud in their primary campaign work, and they were determined not to let this undermine their intense campaign efforts at the polls on Election Day. That spring, Democratic Party leaders registered thousands of nonexistent white voters for the 1967 election, preferring a Republican victory over Hatcher's.[39] On November 7, vanguards of democracy like Muigwithanian L. T. Allison watched the polls vigilantly, as Hatcher and his Republican opponent, businessman Joseph Radigan, battled it out for leadership of Gary.[40] According to *Electing Black Mayors*, poll-watchers engineered a two-way communication system, contacting lawyers at central headquarters at the first sign of an issue when casting one's vote.[41] Their efforts were bolstered by students from across the country, who returned to their native Gary to monitor fraud and help voters get to the polls.

Both campaigns waited anxiously as results poured in late into the night. When at last it was announced that Hatcher clinched the election, Black residents flooded the streets, jubilantly chanting his name.[42] Children instantly regarded Mayor Hatcher as a celebrity, pleading for his autograph. Of the impact of his momentous victory, Hatcher noted, "There is no measuring the inspirational factor in the fact that people got the job done and they did it themselves. They can go on to more difficult tasks with confidence."[43] His statement highlighted the importance of Muigwithania, whose members' vision, ambition, and self-assurance helped transform Gary into the national seat of Black power. Not only did Muigwithania help elect more Black officials—including members Fred Work and Dozier Allen—but it helped dismantle Black citizens' internalized inferiority, transforming deference and apathy into a sense of empowerment.[44]

It was clear from the beginning of his mayoral term that Hatcher's administration intended to follow through on his commitment to make government an instrument of the people, establishing programs like Operation Showcase and the Mayor's Actions Program. Through these forums, citizens could share their individual struggles and their ideas for improving the city.[45] Under his direction, more minorities were appointed to administrative positions and government contracts increased for Black businessmen. In order to combat unemployment, housing insecurity, and crime, his administration excelled at earning federal grants, obtaining $106 million by the end of 1970.[46] Hatcher allocated part of this funding to his controversial Soul, Inc. program, which aimed to channel the energies of young gang members and formerly incarcerated individuals into constructive activities by providing recreational facilities.[47]

Such efforts reflected a new model of governance and endeared to him widespread community support, reflected by a conflict at a city council meeting. Poinsett noted that the council, notoriously hostile to Hatcher, attempted to pass a bill that would limit his ability to appoint officials to the Human Relations Commission.[48] Concerned with the potential dilution of the mayor's power, a "cross-section of the black community" arrived at the deciding council meeting. Among them were "Ph.D.'s and noD's, precinct officials and members of the League of Voters, NAACPers, and more than two hundred members of Gary's young gangs who probably had never before attended a City Council session."[49]

During the proceedings, the president of the Sin City Disciples motorcycle club, Kenneth "Sunny" McGee, informed the council that anytime the mayor needed them, "he only had to 'pull our leash and we bark and we bark hard.'" The warning elicited cheers and the lifting of fists into Black Power salutes.[50] Such pressure proved effective in keeping councilmembers accountable to all constituents, and the bill was defeated. Hatcher noted the incident proved that Black people could no longer be man-handled. The unique ability of Hatcher and Muigwithania colleagues to forge coalitions out of such disparate groups would prove essential in mediating the diverse interests of groups at the NBPC, or what historian Peniel Joseph called "the most important political, cultural, and intellectual gathering of the Black Power era."[51]

Former NAACP executive director Dr. Benjamin Chavis recalled that by 1972, Black Americans had "gotten tired of going to funerals. . . . So much of the Movement had been tragic."[52] Events in the 1960s, including the assassinations of Malcolm X and Martin Luther King Jr., had galvanized mass protests. And the Black Power movement inspired unprecedented cultural pride and artistic expression. However, transforming revolution into reform proved a challenge. While these movements induced some policy reform, Black Americans continued to experience political marginalization, socioeconomic disadvantages, and disproportionally high rates of police brutality and incarceration. Leaders therefore focused increasingly on assuming political power.[53]

This proved difficult because King's death created a leadership void, in which differences grew between the two major ideological factions: integrationists and Nationalists.[54] Nationalists, led by poet and founder of the Congress of African Peoples Amiri Baraka, sought to uplift the community through a self-sufficient Black "nation" and third political party. Integrationists, however, thought Black needs could be met by increasing representation within the existing two-party system. While the community diverged on strategies to overcome disenfranchisement, activists hoped to channel collective outrage into a cohesive political strategy.

With the impending 1972 congressional and presidential elections, Baraka and members of the Congressional Black Caucus (CBC) realized they needed to reconcile their differing ideologies in the name of Black Power, and undertook a series of strategy sessions beginning in 1971.[55] Leonard Moore described these as an "all-male affair with only token and symbolic participation by Black women," and the NBPC would be no exception.[56] Indeed, Moore contended that the Black Power movement afforded little opportunity for women to "step up and be visible, let alone lead. Much of the rhetoric coming from the black nationalist community . . . was centered around the idea of black men reclaiming their masculinity."

Nonetheless, the sessions culminated in the call for a national Black political convention, which would be co-chaired by Baraka, Congressman Charles Diggs, and Mayor Hatcher. CBC members decided on January 30 that Gary would host the unprecedented convention, despite the city having no major airport or convention center, and only one adequate hotel.[57] The unlikely city was chosen because it symbolized Black political power, predicated on the organizational abilities of Muigwithania, which *Current Biography* noted in 1972 "is still the main base of his [Hatcher's] political strength."[58] Muigwithania's legacy of self-determination, grassroots organization, and pooled resources reflected the ideals of Black Power and Nationalism and provided local conference planners with an organizational template. Not only did members set this precedent, but many helped organize and coordinate the NBPC.[59]

With only weeks to prepare, the National Black Political Convention would be another exercise in "getting ourselves together," as Hatcher and his supporters would say. Planners like Muigwithania member L. T. Allison were able to get residents to buy into the convention's vision, and what they lacked in time and resources they once again made up for in innovation, vision, and a commitment to Black empowerment.[60] The *Gary Post-Tribune* reported on a "massive cleanup campaign," organized by trailblazing campaign manager Henry Coleman, in preparation for the NBPC.[61] The paper noted, "Steel City dignitaries showed up at the city barns in casual dress today to direct a massive clean-up of Gary in preparation. . . . City street and sanitation crews combined with military outfits and the Boy Scouts to lift the face of the city."

In addition to beautifying the city, local planners were tasked with the formidable job of housing thousands of attendees.[62] Hatcher's administration and supporters did what they did best—mobilize forces for a shared cause. Residents throughout the city opened their homes to strangers for the weekend, forming lifelong friendships and helping to forge a national network of individuals committed to Black political power.[63] Rev. Dena Holland-Neal, seventeen years old at the time of the convention, contended that delegates staying with residents "brought people closer and enlightened people. It made it very personal."[64] In addition to private residences, organizers secured space at Indiana University Northwest dorms and public schools.[65]

Former State Representative Charlie Brown recalled that when it was announced that Gary would host the convention, "People thought Hatcher was crazy. We needed thousands of beds!"[66] But, Brown told interviewer Amy Clere, "we found some people who knew a lot of people and we created a network of contact for each one." He hosted his friend, journalist Ed Bradley, who repeatedly marveled that Gary was able to quickly accommodate so many and described these efforts in his report for CBS. When Bradley asked how they pulled it off, Brown replied, "That's how we are in Gary."[67]

Black Americans began arriving on the evening of March 10, admiring the city's congenial atmosphere and welcoming police force.[68] North Carolina delegate Benjamin Chavis recalled:

> When we first saw the sign saying "Welcome to Gary" and we got [to] downtown Gary, I mean, we thought we were in a different country. . . . To see a city in the United States, given the backdrop now of all this Nixon repression going on, all this sense of disillusionment in some quarters of the nation, to drive into Gary, Indiana, and see streamers, red, black and green [was empowering].[69]

On Saturday morning, volunteers, city employees, and parks department officials transported state delegates and attendees to the school in vehicles donated by local daycare centers, auto dealerships, and Muigwithanian and city council president Cleo Wesson.[70] Efforts were bolstered by members of the West Side Community Council and Citizens Good Neighborhood Patrol, who donated two-way radios and helped coordinate transportation logistics.[71]

The impending convention would be unprecedented not only because of the sheer number of delegates and attendees—estimated at ten thousand—but also because of the variety of backgrounds and political ideologies they represented. Marxists, Republicans, gang members, Black Panthers, feminists, professors, labor leaders, Democrats, capitalists, and Nation of Islam members were invited to help create a "Black Magna Carta."[72] While civil rights titans like Coretta Scott King and Betty Shabazz lined West Side's stage, it would be state delegates who helped craft resolutions for a formalized Black Political Agenda.[73] The agenda would represent the priorities of Black Americans, and those political candidates who pledged to support its resolutions would gain the voting bloc's support.

Waiting for convention activities to start on Saturday, delegates and attendees milled about West Side High School's hallways, "filled with vendors, half pushing wares and half pushing ideologies."[74] They purchased cosmetics and comic books with titles like "Integration Is a Bitch," chatted with volunteers about local watering holes, and read flyers distributed by the Gary Committee to Free Angela Davis.[75] At last, Mayor Hatcher stepped up to the podium and delivered the first convention address, which political observers called "one of the most important speeches of modern times."[76] Asserting that "the '70s will be the decade of an independent black political thrust,'" Hatcher bellowed, "We shall no longer bargain away your support for petty jobs or symbolic offices."[77] He asked, "Will we act like free black men or timid shivering chattels?" and concluded, "History will be our judge."

Reverend Jackson delivered the second keynote address, calling for Black Americans to unlearn white superiority and to create a third party in order to represent their own interests. This required ego, which he argued they lacked after enduring decades of abuse and oppression. He sought to empower the audience through a call-and-response based on Nationalist rhetoric, asking, "Brothers and Sisters, what time is it?"[78]

To which they responded, fists raised, "Nationtime!"

He followed up with questions like, "For 7.5 million registered Black voters and 6 million unregistered black voters, what time is it?"

To each, the crowd cried, "Nationtime!"[79]

With his electrifying speech, Jackson stepped into the leadership void left by King. In the words of attendee Byron Lewis, Jackson "was born in that convention." To fellow preacher Chavis, Black Power "came to be fulfilled in that moment, of crying that it's Nation-time, not next year, not next century, but now. In 1972. In Gary, Indiana."[80] To him, "Nationtime" meant unity of purpose. This would be needed when the delegates, energized by the speeches, debated potential resolutions for the Black Political Agenda. Cloistered in classrooms, delegates proposed fines for employers guilty of discrimination, employment priority for Black veterans, a prisoners' bill of rights, and an end to the Vietnam War.[81] Discussion and, at times, tense debate centered around topics like forced busing. In fact, the previous night, Yvonne Day, chair of the Gary Commission on the Status of Women, ignited arguments during a committee meeting when she proposed access to safe abortion.[82] Aggrieved male delegates alleged this would only perpetuate "'genocide' against the black race."

While debates endured into the night, some delegates took a break to attend a fundraiser at Roosevelt High School.[83] They took in performances by *Shaft* actor Richard Roundtree, soul musician Isaac Hayes, and singer Harry Belafonte.[84] Black Panther cofounder Bobby Seale stunned the audience with a surprise appearance, telling them, "If you are participating in changing the system in any way, you are a revolutionary, too. Use your vote like a shot in the forest."[85]

On Sunday, delegates returned to the school for the final day of the convention, where they had participated in workshops about political liberation, education, and technology.[86] Proceedings nearly fell apart after Baraka introduced a draft of the Black Political Agenda with delegates' proposed resolutions. To many, the agenda disproportionately represented Nationalist objectives, like opposition to forced busing.[87] Some delegates alleged that the agenda failed to offer strategies for implementing resolutions. Michigan delegation leader Coleman Young vocalized these concerns, as well as his discomfort about ratifying the agenda before giving local activists an opportunity to provide feedback. After reading a hastily composed statement opposing ratification to the crowd, the Michigan delegation filed out of the gymnasium.[88] With Illinois's delegation on the verge of following suit, Baraka pleaded with them not to leave, fearful that this would entirely derail the convention.

On the precipice of disbanding, the anxious crowd was ecstatic to realize that part of Michigan's delegation had indeed remained. Shouts of "Nationtime!" soon resounded as tenuous compromise was reached. By day's end, a draft of the Black Political Agenda had been adopted. The final version consisted of eight categories, to which political candidates would be held to account: Political Empowerment, Economic Empowerment, Human Development, International Policy, Communications, Rural Development, Environmental Protection, and Self-Determination for the District of Columbia. Numerous resolutions were included within each category, such as proportional representation in Congress, an end to gerrymandering, abolishment of "no-knock" police searches, and an end to government surveillance of Black communities.[89] Conveners also founded the National Black Political Assembly, which planned to meet regularly to follow through on the plans made at the convention.[90] With elections approaching, the agenda—released on May 19, Malcolm X's birthday—would be taken to the Democratic Party convention, and ideally the candidate who prioritized its resolutions would gain the support of Black voters.

Despite some expected logistical issues and disagreement about the agenda, most who attended felt the convention was a watershed moment for Black Americans.[91] *Pittsburgh Courier* writer Louis Martin praised "the massive response of blacks all across the nation who by their very presence in Gary gave proof of their interest in the political process and political action. This is a new day."[92] Journalist Ethel L. Payne concluded that the NBPC was meaningful in that attendees "now know what it means to be a part of the elective process," although she felt not enough women were involved in the convention's planning.[93] Indeed, looking back at convention footage, *Crusader* writer and NBPC attendee Wayne A. Young was "struck by how openly misogynistic and inaudibly homophobic our Black 'liberators' were.... Ms. King rises from her seat only to wave at her loyal subjects, and Ms. Shabazz is cast as the hallowed widow whose job is but to introduce the young Civil Rights prince Jesse Louis Jackson."[94] The NAACP also had qualms with the convention, particularly its Nationalist bent. However, executive director Roy Wilkins concluded that "America gains by this political awareness for it always gains when various blocs of voters come together.... Splinter voices got a hearing. Whatever the future may hold, the convention just by holding together for a scheduled time, was an event of significance."[95]

The immediate future was bright. Although the National Black Political Assembly fractured over the years, the convention helped increase voter participation, and Black elected officials grew from 1,469 in 1970 to 4,890 by 1980.[96] In Gary, the *Crusader* proclaimed in April 1972, "Historic Number of Blacks File for May Primary."[97] Columnist Conrad Strader noted that many candidates "have jumped on the band wagon because they feel this is a 'Black year' in politics."[98] Indeed, it was a "Black year" for Lake County, as candidates overwhelming won local elections and Rudy Clay became Lake County's first Black candidate elected state senator.[99] It was also a "Black year" for Marion County, with the election of State Representatives Bill Crawford and Julia Carson, who reportedly announced their intention to run at the NBPC.¹⁰⁰ Karen Freeman-Wilson, whose family hosted delegates, noted that the experience helped inspire her to run for office, and in 2011 she became the city's first female mayor. ¹⁰¹ Although they did not seek elected office, citizens like Rev. Dena Holland-Neal became activists because of the convention and continue to discuss its impact. She wrote in *The Gary Anthology* that the event "helped her self-esteem and inspired her own community activism."¹⁰²

Activists continue to draw inspiration from the National Black Political Convention as they grapple with transforming collective outrage into reform.¹⁰³ Certainly, the NBPC offers insights about organizational pitfalls and strategies for bringing together various segments of the community. Examining how the intrepid members of Muigwithania and their allies forged an unprecedented path to power could prove equally valuable, particularly in a time of heightened political polarization and racial injustice. Their sincerity of purpose, fervent organizing, and cultivation of meaningful relationships reflect a Midwestern ethos, not unlike that of Chicagoan Barack Obama's presidential campaign. Leaders should study Muigwithanians' techniques for making politics relevant, building upon incremental victories, removing barriers to voting, and penetrating the armor of political machines without many resources. The young Turks' legacy could perhaps provide inspiration at a time when, as Lawshe said, "blacks desperately needed something to hold onto in the midst of their American ordeal."

NOTES

1. Leonard N. Moore, *The Defeat of Black Power: Civil Rights and the National Black Political Convention of 1972* (Baton Rouge: Louisiana State University Press, 2018), 106; DVD, *Nationtime: A Film by William Greaves* (Kino Lorber, reissued 2020). Black filmmaker William Greaves was commissioned by organizers to document the convention. The footage, shelved for years because it was considered too controversial for television, was released as a documentary in 2020. *Nationtime* provides an invaluable window into the profound emotional impact the speeches of Hatcher, Jackson, and Seale had on convention attendees.

2. City Church, State Historical Marker notes, Indiana Historical Bureau, https://www.in.gov/history/state-historical-markers/find-a-marker/find-historical-markers-by-county/indiana-historical-markers-by-county/city-church/, accessed July 1, 2022.

3. James B. Lane, *"City of the Century:" A History of Gary, Indiana* (Bloomington: Indiana University Press, 1978), 34.

4. Nicole Poletika, "City Church: Spirituality and Segregation in Gary," Indiana History Blog, May 2019, https://blog.history.in.gov/city-church-spirituality-and-segregation-in-gary/.

5. Lane, "City of the Century," 36.
6. "Resume of Blacks in Gary Politics," *Gary Info*, March 9, 1972, 7.
7. "Early Gary Blacks Were Self-Sufficient," *Gary Crusader*, October 2, 1976, 32.
8. "Five Year Plan Adopted by Co-op Group in Gary," *Gary American*, January 12, 1934, 1.
9. "Early Gary Blacks," 32.
10. "Resume of Blacks in Gary Politics," *Gary Info*, March 9, 1972, 7.
11. "Black Political Power in Action," *Gary Info*, March 9, 1972, 16.
12. *Gary Crusader* (Gary, Ind.) 1960–current, Directory of US Newspapers in American Libraries, Library of Congress, https://chroniclingamerica.loc.gov/lccn/sn83025624/; quotation in 25th Anniversary—Special Edition, "Early Crusader Political Milestones," *Gary Crusader*, November 15, 1986, n.p.
13. 25th Anniversary—Special Edition, "Early Crusader Political Milestones," *Gary Crusader*, November 15, 1986, n.p.
14. Poletika, "City Church: Spirituality and Segregation."
15. William E. Nelson Jr. and Philip J. Meranto, *Electing Black Mayors: Political Action in the Black Community* (Columbus: Ohio State University Press, 1977), 196; "Who Is the Township Trustee?," *Gary Crusader*, October 12, 1974, 12; "Coleman Named to Probation Post," *Gary American*, March 10, 1961, 1.
16. Alex Poinsett, *Black Power Gary Style: The Making of Mayor Richard Gordon Hatcher* (Chicago: Johnson, 1970), 64–65.
17. Poinsett, *Black Power Gary Style*, 64–65.
18. Nelson and Meranto, *Electing Black Mayors*, 184–185; Gus Rose, "Katz Regains Some Lost Prestige," *The Times* (Munster, Indiana), November 28, 1966, 9.
19. Charles Sterling, "Dick Hatcher: Man on the Spot," *The Times*, June 18, 1967, 13.
20. Poinsett, *Black Power Gary Style*, 65; Jon C. Teaford, "'King Richard' Hatcher: Mayor of Gary," *Journal of Negro History* 77, no. 3 (Summer 1992): 127, Indiana State Library (ISL) Clippings File, Biography—Hatcher, Richard G.
21. Nelson and Meranto, *Electing Black Mayors*, 197.
22. Nelson and Meranto, *Electing Black Mayors*, 197; Robert P. Mooney, "Boswell Tally Clerks Reported Shoved Aside," *Indianapolis Star*, June 22, 1962, 1.
23. "Hatcher: Lofty Perch after Lowly Start?," *Indianapolis Recorder*, May 13, 1967; "New Breed Black Politician: Steel City's Courageous Councilman," *Muhammad Speaks* 4, no. 15 (March 5, 1965): 19; Poinsett, *Black Power Gary Style*, 66–68; Teaford, "'King Richard,'" 127–129.
24. Sterling, "Dick Hatcher: Man on the Spot," *The Times*; "Hatcher: Lofty Perch after Lowly Start?," *Indianapolis Recorder*; Poinsett, *Black Power Gary Style*, 68–69; Franklin Dunlap, "Hoosier in Profile: Mayor Richard G. Hatcher," *Indianapolis Star Magazine*, February 21, 1971, 14, ISL Clippings File, Biography—Hatcher, Richard G.
25. "New Breed Black Politician: Steel City's Courageous Councilman," *Muhammad Speaks* 4, no. 15 (March 5, 1965): 19.
26. Nelson and Meranto, *Electing Black Mayors*, 200.
27. Editorial, "Not All Cut and Dried," *The Times*, May 6, 1966, 14; Poinsett, *Black Power Gary Style*, 70.
28. Gus Rose, "Katz Regains Some Lost Prestige," *The Times*, November 28, 1966, 9.
29. At that time, approximately 55 percent of the city's population was African American, according to Nelson and Meranto's *Electing Black Mayors*, 177. The authors

drew upon Wes Scharlach, *Population Characteristics and Trends in the Gary-Hammond-East Chicago Standard Metropolitan Statistical Area* (Lake County Development Committee, 1968), 66.

30. "Hatcher: Lofty Perch after Lowly Start?," *Indianapolis Recorder*, May 13, 1967.

31. "Let's Get Ourselves Together," "Negro Voters Being Robbed," "Thinking It Over," *Gary Citizen* 1, no. 2 (October 29, 1967): 1–6, Richard G. Hatcher Collection, CRA086, Calumet Regional Archives, Indiana University Northwest Library; "Votes Put Negro in New Light," *Indianapolis News*, November 9, 1967, 53, ISL Clippings File; "Gary Vote Fraud Reports Probed," *Indianapolis News*, November 9, 1967, 8, ISL Clippings File, Indiana Politics; Poinsett, *Black Power Gary Style*, 88; Franklin Dunlap, "Hoosier in Profile: Mayor Richard G. Hatcher," *Indianapolis Star Magazine*, February 21, 1971, 12–14, 16, ISL Clippings File, Biography—Hatcher, Richard G.

32. Nelson and Meranto, *Electing Black Mayors*, 234.

33. Nelson and Meranto, *Electing Black Mayors*, 240.

34. Nelson and Meranto, *Electing Black Mayors*, 234.

35. Nelson and Meranto, *Electing Black Mayors*, 236–237.

36. Nelson and Meranto, *Electing Black Mayors*, 243.

37. Poinsett, *Black Power Gary Style*, 78–79.

38. Poinsett, *Black Power Gary Style*, 78–79.

39. *Gary's Citizen*, October 1967, 1–6; "Votes Put Negro in New Light," 53; "Gary Vote Fraud Reports Probed," 8; Poinsett, *Black Power Gary Style*, 85–88; Dunlap, "Hoosier in Profile," *Indianapolis Star Magazine*, 12–14, 16; Teaford, "'King Richard,'" 129.

40. Nelson and Meranto, *Electing Black Mayors*, 260.

41. Nelson and Meranto, *Electing Black Mayors*, 312–315.

42. Poinsett, *Black Power Gary Style*, 93–97; "Hatcher Victory Is Assailed as Fraud," *Anderson Daily Bulletin*, November 8, 1967; "Hatcher Vote Dooms Gary Machine Rule," "Unrepentant Krupa Blames Government 'Interference,'" *Indianapolis Recorder*, November 11, 1967, 1; with the 1967 election, Cleveland legislator Carl Stokes shared the title of the first Black mayor of a major city with Hatcher. However, Stokes served only one term, and his election victory depended much more on white support than Hatcher, who served as Gary mayor for nearly twenty years.

43. Poinsett, *Black Power Gary Style*, 96–97.

44. "Fence Plea by Jaycees," *The Times*, May 29, 1968, 19; *Gary Crusader*, May 22, 1972, 4.

45. Quotation in Poinsett, *Black Power Gary Style*, 121; Teaford, "'King Richard,'" 131.

46. Teaford, "'King Richard,'" 130.

47. "$250,000 Project for Gary Teens Is Running Smoothly," *Muhammad Speaks* 7, no. 43 (July 12, 1968): 2; Poinsett, *Black Power Gary Style*, 119–120.

48. Poinsett, *Black Power Gary Style*, 129, 138.

49. Poinsett, *Black Power Gary Style*, 138.

50. Poinsett, *Black Power Gary Style*, 138.

51. Moore, *The Defeat of Black Power: Civil Rights*, 2.

52. Benjamin Chavis, April 18, 1989, Washington University Libraries, Film and Media Archive, Henry Hampton Collection.

53. Louis Martin, "Racist Snakes Coming Out the Grass," *Pittsburgh Courier*, March 4, 1972, 3; Raheem Abdul Ali, "Black Youth: A New Direction," *Pittsburgh Courier*, March 25, 1972, 7.

54. Oral History Interview, Benjamin Chavis; Robert C. Smith, *We Have No Leaders: African Americans in the Post-Civil Rights Era* (Albany: State University of New York Press, 1996), 32–34.

55. Moore, *The Defeat of Black Power*, chap. 2.

56. Moore, *The Defeat of Black Power*, 10, 54, 60–62, 142; "The Gary Convention, 1972: Unity without Conformity," in Henry Hampton and Steve Fayer, eds., *Voices of Freedom: An Oral History of the Civil Rights Movement from the 1950s through the 1980s* (New York: Bantam, 1990), 565–586.

57. Moore, *The Defeat of Black Power*, 63–65.

58. "Hatcher, Richard G(ordon)," *Current Biography* (1972), 205, Richard G. Hatcher Collection, CRA086.

59. "Precedes Gary Convention: Indiana Blacks to Caucus," *Gary Post-Tribune*, February 15, 1972, B-1; "Blacks Dominate Gary Council," *Gary Post-Tribune*, March 9, 1972, 4.

60. John Smith, "Can You Dig It?," *Gary Post-Tribune*, March 18, 1972, 6; *Gary Post-Tribune*, March 11, 1972, A-1; "See 6,000 at Convention, No Problem with Lodging," *Gary Post-Tribune*, February 9, 1972, D-1.

61. "Private Citizens, Groups Solicited," *Gary Post-Tribune*, March 4, 1972, A-1.

62. Omar Clayton, "Omar's Black Bag," *Gary Crusader*, March 4, 1972, 8.

63. Jacqueline Brown, "Delegates Lodged in City Homes," *Gary Post-Tribune*, March 11, 1972, A-1; Amy Clere, "The Influence of the National Black Political Convention of 1972 on Indiana Politics: Views from and of a High School Gym in Gary, Indiana—Then and Now" (MA thesis, Indiana University Southeast, 2021), 14, https://scholarworks.iu.edu/dspace/bitstream/handle/2022/27714/CLERE_INFLUENCE OFTHENATIONALBLACK_2021.pdf?sequence=1&isAllowed=y; Ernie Hernandez, "Parley Settles Down to Action," *Gary Post-Tribune*, March 11, 1972, B-1; Rev. Jesse L. Jackson Sr., "A Tribute to Mayor Hatcher: An Urban Change Agent," *The Crusader*, December 14, 2019, https://chicagocrusader.com/90690-2/.

64. Dena Holland-Neal, "Can Any Good Come Out of Gary? Absolutely Yes!," in Samuel Love, ed., *The Gary Anthology* (Cleveland: Belt Publishing, 2020), 19.

65. Moore, *The Defeat of Black Power*, 78; Clere, "The Influence of the National Black Political Convention," 14.

66. Clere, "The Influence of the National Black Political Convention," 13.

67. Clere, "The Influence of the National Black Political Convention," 13.

68. Gwendolyn S. Cherry, "Cherry Notes from Florida," *Pittsburgh Courier*, March 25, 1972, 2.

69. Oral History Interview, Chavis.

70. Brown, "Delegates Lodged in City Homes," A-1; "Hatcher Acknowledge Transportation Committee," *Gary Info*, March 16, 1972, 17; "Hatcher," *Gary Post-Tribune*, March 4, 1972, A-2.

71. "Hatcher Acknowledge Transportation Committee," *Gary Info*, March 16, 1972, 14.

72. Oral History Interview, Chavis; Moore, *The Defeat of Black Power*, 2, 123; *Nationtime: A Film by William Greaves*; Hernandez, "Parley Settles Down to Action," B-1; Cherry, "Cherry Notes from Florida," 2; Editorial, "Convention Views Hit," *Pittsburgh Courier*, April 8, 1972, 6; "NBPC an 'Unexpected' but Predicted Success," *Gary Info*, March 16–March 22,1972, 1; "Republican Not So Lonely," *Gary Post-Tribune*, March 13, 1972, A-4.

73. "Agenda," *Gary Post-Tribune*, March 12, 1972, A-8; Richard Busse, "Woes Vanish at Gala," *The Times*, March 3, 1972, 1, 12; *Nationtime: A Film by William Greaves*.

74. Jacqueline Brown, "Carnival Atmosphere Greets Convention," *Gary Post-Tribune*, March 10, 1972, B-1; Virginia Thrower, "Crowd of 7,000 Tops Parley Expectations," *Gary Post-Tribune*, March 12, 1972, B-3.

75. "Black 1972 Convention Odds and Ends," *Gary Post-Tribune*, March 12, 1972, B-2; Brown, "Carnival Atmosphere Greets Convention," B-1.

76. " . . . We Must Pave the Way So That Others May Follow," *Pittsburgh Courier*, March 25, 1972, 10.

77. "Mayor," *Gary Info*, March 16, 1972, 17; " . . . We Must Pave the Way," 10.

78. Moore, *The Defeat of Black Power*, 106–108.

79. Moore, *The Defeat of Black Power*, 106.

80. Oral History Interview, Chavis.

81. "Black Convention at Showdown States," *Vidette-Messenger* (Valparaiso, IN), March 11, 1972, 1.

82. Mickey Thrower, "Rep. Chisholm, Busing Are Hot Black Issues," *Gary Post-Tribune*, March 11, 1972, A-1.

83. Moore, *The Defeat of Black Power,* 109–111; Cherry, "Cherry Notes from Florida," *Pittsburgh Courier*, 2.

84. "Chuck Deggans' Den," *Gary Post-Tribune*, March 14, 1972, C-8; "Convention Committee Reveals Program," *Gary Info*, March 9–15, 1972, 1; *Nationtime: A Film by William Greaves*.

85. Busse, "Woes Vanish at Gala," 1, 12; Moore, *The Defeat of Black Power*, 112.

86. "Black 1972 Convention Odds and Ends," *Gary Post-Tribune*, March 12, 1972, B-2; Smith, *We Have No Leaders*, 36.

87. "Black Caucus Split over Political Agenda," *Chicago Tribune*, May 20, 1972, 14.

88. Cherry, "Cherry Notes from Florida," 2.

89. "Segments of the Black Agenda: The Gary Declaration," p. 3, Folder 3, National Black Political Convention Collection, 1972–1973, SC 2643, Indiana Historical Society, Indianapolis; *The National Black Political Agenda*, Ratified May 6, 1972, Greensboro, North Carolina, reproduced by the Collective PAC, https://collectivepac.org/wp-content/uploads/2020/05/The-National-Black-Agenda-1972.pdf.

90. "Creation of 'The National Black Assembly' Concludes Black Political Convention," *Kokomo Tribune* (Kokomo, Indiana), March 13, 1972, 1.

91. Virginia Thrower, "Observers Criticize Planning," *Gary Post-Tribune*, March 12, 1972, A-1.

92. Louis Martin, "Challenges Laid Down in Gary," *Pittsburgh Courier*, March 25, 1972, 3.

93. Ethel L. Payne, "After Gary, What?," *Pittsburgh Courier*, March 25, 1972, 5.

94. Wayne A. Young, "A Gary Native Reflects on What 'Nationtime' Means Today," originally published in the *Chicago Crusader*, n.d..

95. "Black Convention Split over Separatism," *Terre Haute Tribune*, March 11, 1972, 1; quotation in Roy Wilkins, "Loud Clear Message from Gary," *Gary Crusader*, April 1, 1972, 1.

96. "Table 413. Black Elected Officials by Office, 1970 to 2002, and State, 2002," US Census Bureau, Statistical Abstract of the United States, 2011, https://www2.census.gov/library/publications/2010/compendia/statab/130ed/tables/11s0413.pdf.

97. "Historic Number of Blacks File for May Primary," *Gary Crusader*, April 1, 1972, 1.

98. Conrad Strader, "Common Sense Speaks," *Gary Crusader*, April 29, 1972, 8.

99. "Blacks Victorious in Lake County Election," *Gary Crusader*, November 11, 1972, 1.

100. Clere, "The Influence of the National Black Political Convention," 20, 29, 35; United Press International, "Legislature Leans to GOP," *Muncie Star*, November 8, 1972, 13.

101. Karen Freeman-Wilson, interview with Nicole Poletika, March 3, 2021, Giving Voice, Talking Hoosier History Podcast, https://podcast.history.in.gov/karen-freeman-wilson-national-black-political-convention/.

102. Erica C. Harrington, "Panel Boosts Black Activism," *The Times*, September 28, 1997, 17; Byron Lewis, Rev. Dena Holland-Neal, and Jacqueline Elena Featherston, interview with Wayne A. Young, Port of Harlem Talk Radio, November 12, 2020, https://anchor.fm/port-of-harlem-talk-radio/episodes/Nov-12—2020-Byron-Lewis-and-Rev—Dena-Holland-Neal—and-Jacqueline-Elena-Featherston-emdquf; Dena Holland-Neal, "Can Any Good Come Out of Gary? Absolutely Yes!," in Samuel Love, ed., *The Gary Anthology* (Cleveland: Belt Publishing, 2020), 18–19.

103. Victoria Moorwood, "First Black National Convention in Nearly 50 Years to Follow Washington, D.C. March," *Revolt*, August 28, 2020, https://www.revolt.tv/article/2020-08-28/71341/first-black-national-convention-in-nearly-50-years-to-follow-washington-d-c-march/; Jesus A. Rodriguez, "BLM Organizers See the 1972 National Black Political Convention as a Model. What Can They Learn from It?," *Politico*, August 28, 2020, https://www.politico.com/news/magazine/2020/08/28/1972-national-black-political-convention-black-lives-matter-blm-401706.

11

"Where Was the Social Justice?"*

La Raza Activism at the University of Notre Dame

LETICIA ROSE WIGGINS

❖ ❖ ❖ ❖ ❖ ❖ ❖ ❖ ❖ ❖ ❖ ❖ ❖ ❖ ❖

"NOTRE DAME JUSTICE SHOULD BEGIN HERE ON ND CAMPUS" read one of the signs brandished by students, faculty, and community members congregating outside the University of Notre Dame's administration building. These protestors gathered on a sunny day in the autumn of 1977 to oppose the university's sudden firing of twenty-one groundskeepers. Terminating the men's livelihoods directly challenged the image the University of Notre Dame sought to present; that of a preeminent Catholic institution and educational beacon of morality and social justice. The university's decision appeared especially suspect when considering the events leading up to the groundskeepers' abrupt dismissal.

A month prior, on October 4, the Notre Dame groundskeepers petitioned for the right to unionize with Teamsters Local 364 of South Bend, Indiana.[1] Few groundskeepers, many who were Latino, could support their families on the $75 they took home each week. Joining with the Teamsters meant the potential for better pay.[2] The day following their attempt to unionize, Notre Dame released an "Employer's Motion for Dismissal of Petition" eliminating the groundskeepers' positions effective November 1, 1977.[3]

---

* The quote in the chapter's title is taken from Olga Villa's reflections on the groundskeeper strike at Notre Dame. *La Raza* as this chapter and its actors use the term refers to a multiethnic Spanish-speaking population.

The mid-1970s marked the end of the postwar economic boom and a culmination of record-breaking strikes and union organization. These years also marked the beginning of "layoffs, plant closures, and union decertification drives," as scholar Jefferson Cowie writes.[4] Like many institutions, Notre Dame would "contract out" the groundskeepers' work to external companies in what was seen by many as a direct move to prevent unionization on campus.[5] Even more incriminating, the university hired a law firm with a history of labor union busting practice to handle any backlash.[6] An overwhelming response from the student body and local community on behalf of the groundskeepers ensued after the university's decision.

One of the groundskeepers' most vocal advocates, Ricardo Parra, director of the Midwest Council of La Raza (MWCLR), rallied support on campus and in the South Bend Latino community for the workers. The MWCLR promoted the well-being of the termed "Spanish-speaking" population, referred to as *La Raza* in South Bend and throughout the Midwestern United States.* Notre Dame supported the MWCLR with office space on its campus, thus affiliating the council with university. From within the university, Parra denounced the union-busting as a direct affront to the Catholic Church's preaching of social justice. He and nineteen other students, faculty, staff, and administration wrote in a letter to the editor for Notre Dame student paper *The Observer*, "What is the meaning of the 'Notre Dame Family' when it fails to care about its members (who also have families) and gets rid of them by simply firing them, laying them off or 'contracting out?' What about human rights for the grounds crews?"[7] The letter pointed again to the disconnect between Notre Dame's expressed policy of inclusivity and the actual treatment of its workers.

From 1970 to 1978, the MWCLR used the language of the Catholic Church to advocate for the economic and social well-being of La Raza and hold the University of Notre Dame to its promise of social justice. This chapter identifies moments of resistance from the MWCLR and other Chicano organizations on Notre Dame's campus to incorporate Catholicism into the historical narrative surrounding the struggle for civil rights on behalf of Latinos in the 1970s.

In the 1960s and 1970s, Notre Dame was the preeminent Catholic university in the country. Led by president Father Theodore Hesburgh, who declared the denial of civil rights a moral issue—the university operated on a new tenet of civil rights and justice.[8] The MWCLR and La Raza used this new, liberal version of Catholicism in their activism. Their activism took on a unique form in the Midwest, challenging our understanding of the Chicano movement as being largely focused on Southwest and Western actors.

As the University of Notre Dame rose to prominence, the Catholic Church also expanded from a traditional charity organization to an arbiter of social justice—with ideations from Gustavo Gutiérrez's "liberation theology" and Vatican II's teachings, as well as the general consideration of social justice. Spanish speakers within the Church were aware of this shifting focus and pragmatically used the rhetoric of the Catholic Church to advocate for social justice and advance their rights.

The relationship between the Catholic Church and Latinos is longstanding, especially for Mexican Americans.[9] The Spanish conquest of what is now Mexico in the 1500s violently brought the Catholic religion to the region. Through often brutal conversion techniques Mexico became Catholic—a syncretic Catholicism influenced by indigenous beliefs and customs.[10] In the early 1920s, the Mexican migrant community coming to the United States encountered Catholic churches predominantly in urban settings.[11] Many Mexicans sought to maintain ties to the Mexican Catholic Church, as these places allowed them to "feel at home and be Mexican."[12]

Churches are historically important institutions for the integration of immigrants into US society as they provided outlets for immigrants to meet and form cultural communities.[13] Mexican and Latino immigrant populations in the Southwest, facing marginalization from Anglo-American people and institutions, found the Catholic Church a familiar and mostly welcoming entity.[14] In the Midwest, railroad connections with northern Mexico made the region an important site of settlement for Mexicans.[15] The sort of Midwest Catholicism that developed did so without "the symbolic artifacts of Spanish missions or a legacy of colonial Catholicism."[16] The Catholic response to Mexicans in the Midwest mimicked more closely the Church's treatment of the earliest European immigrants.

After World War II, Puerto Ricans also became an important part of the Midwest's Spanish-speaking population, settling around Chicago, Illinois; Milwaukee, Wisconsin; and Detroit, Michigan.[17] East Chicago, Indiana, a little over an hour's drive west of South Bend, by the mid-1960s would lay claim to about 6,500 Mexican migrants and 3,000 Puerto Ricans.[18] These new Spanish speakers comprised one-third of East Chicago's St. Patrick's parish, a historically Irish and Italian church.[19] Despite the population growth, Latinos had very little representation in the church. In fact, Anglo priests headed the office of the Bishops' Committee for Hispanics until 1967.[20] The church's early indoctrination efforts to make Latinos "American" birthed a complicated relationship between the Catholic Church and Chicanos during the Chicano movement—when Mexican Americans sought to reclaim their cultural practices.

By the mid-1960s, the Chicano movement criticized the Catholic Church's primary function as a charity home for Hispanics, rather than an institution that embraced the culture. *El Plan Espiritual de Aztlán*, written in 1969 by leaders at the Chicano Youth Liberation Conference, declared that "institutions in our community which do not serve the people have no place in the community. The institutions belong to the people."[21] This sentiment contributed to demonstrations against the Catholic Church in 1969, when one hundred Mexican Americans in Mission, Texas, painted the statue of the Virgin Mary brown; and in 1974, when the Brown Berets took over a parish in Brighton, Colorado, and refused to let anyone enter until the pastor agreed to offer a Spanish-language Mass each week.[22]

Hispanic clergy felt just as slighted as the parishioners. There were few Spanish Masses and no inclusion of Spanish-language training for clergy.[23] In the 1960s, only 8 percent of Spanish-speaking brothers were in full-time ministry, and only 25 out of 961 Hispanic sisters served other Hispanics.[24] Women also discussed the role of the Catholic Church and patriarchy in defining womanhood and the Chicano movement. While many recognized the "revolutionary potential of Chicanos organizing within the church," others stood in opposition to institutionalized religion.[25]

These cries for cultural recognition and change within the church also resounded in the Midwest. MWCLR's director Ricardo Parra, influenced by new socially conscious teachings, demanded that his religious institution, the University of Notre Dame, support La Raza's need for "self-determination, human development, and social and institutional change."[26] In the MWCLR newsletter, *Los Desarraigados* [The Uprooted Ones], Parra discussed theories like liberation theology, Vatican II, and *Conscientización*. In 1974 he quoted Peruvian priest Gustavo Gutiérrez's concept of "liberation theology" and observed that Latinos were in the church's "system without being of the system."[27] Liberation theology as defined by Gutiérrez sought to "reflect on the experience and meaning of the faith based on the commitment to abolish injustice and to build a new society; this theology must be verified by the practice of that commitment, by active, effective participation in the struggle which the exploited social classes have undertaken against their oppressors."[28]

Gutiérrez named faith as a tool to eradicate injustice and create a new society in his seminal 1971 work *A Theology of Liberation: History, Politics, Salvation*.[29] He detailed three important aspects of "liberation." First, a focus on political and social liberation—or the eradication of the causes of poverty and injustice. Second, he called to free the poor from oppressive circumstances and give them a right to live with dignity. Finally, Gutiérrez's liberation meant freedom from sin and a final reconnection with God and others.[30]

Liberation theology was inspired by the Catholic Church's Second Vatican Council, known as Vatican II. From 1962 to 1965, thousands of bishops, sisters, laypersons, and auditors met to reconsider what the Catholic Church meant in the larger world, where cultural values were changing following the second World War.[31] The resulting conversations pushed for the Church to focus less on growing its constituency and to act in a more missionary-like capacity.[32] The Catholic Church changed its politics to embrace basic notions of liberal democracy, particularly through *Dignitatis Humanae*, the "Declaration on Religious Freedom."[33] This change also meant that the Church became less exclusive, recognizing that Roman Catholicism was not the only way to connect with a higher power. The Catholic Church began accepting Judaism, Protestantism, and other religions as acceptable ways to reach God.[34] Of a more ecumenical or global mind, the Catholic Church also turned to address the poverty and conflict-ridden climate of Latin America.

Dignitatis Humanae further influenced Gutiérrez's push to remember and live by the model of Christ liberating the poor.[35] Though much of this chapter focuses on the relationship between Mexican Americans and the Church, Gutiérrez called the Catholic Church to be responsible for those in need in Latin America. To him, liberation theology then also resonated as "social justice"—the idea that Christian duty involved helping the less fortunate. Social justice, Vatican II, and liberation theology provided new standards for institutions like Notre Dame's commitment to its community and the larger world.[36]

Ricardo Parra was just twenty-five years old when he was appointed director of the MWCLR in July 1971.[37] Though young, Parra had great experience community organizing and activism—both had been passions since his high school days. He was fond of theories and saw change within institutions as possible. Among his theoretical tools were liberation theology as well as *Concientización*, a word coined by Brazilian philosopher Paulo Freire in his 1968 work, *The Pedagogy of the Oppressed*.[38] *Concientización* in this context referred to "learning to perceive social, political, and economic contradictions and to take action against the oppressive elements of reality."[39] Maintaining consciousness meant being aware of how to navigate the surrounding systems and one's place within the larger church, political system, and society—using these institutions to one's advantage when possible.

During the 1970s, Parra was not alone in calling for the university to serve La Raza. Some of the most vocal Latinos to push against Notre Dame were its students, many of whom were deeply involved with the MWCLR and sought to be cultural ambassadors. The Notre Dame chapter of the national Chicano group Movimiento Estudiantil Chicana/o de Aztlán (MEChA) sponsored the first La Raza Art Festival, at Notre Dame from April 21 to 24, 1971. The festival was a goodwill gesture intended to acquaint the university with the culture and customs of its Chicano students so that "ND might better understand and appreciate their Mexican heritage."[40] However, the effort lacked support from Notre Dame as the university refused financial support for the show, causing MEChA to expend its few resources.[41]

Before the final day, which featured a dance and ceremony, a professor from the art department disassembled the entire art exhibit and locked it away where no one could access it. He did not consult organizers, so festival goers that afternoon were shocked to find an empty building.[42] As MEChA had installed the exhibit in a rented university field house used for storage during the spring and summer, there was no reason to remove the display so hastily.

On May 15, 1971, Jose G. Gonzalez, a graduate student in the art department whose work was shown at the festival, delivered a speech at the university's Grotto of Our Lady of Lourdes.[43] Gonzalez saw the lack of attendance and support for the exhibit as representative of Notre Dame faculty's prejudice against Latino students:

> "When it comes to education, we are classed as second-rate citizens. We are good enough to carry rifles into combat, fighting foreign wars, but we are not good enough to carry books into our own universities in trying to further our education.
>
> Is this social justice? Is this what you label as equal opportunity? We think not! And because of this, we will continue to cry out until we are finally heard."[44]

A year prior, MEChA members sent a seven-page resolution to Notre Dame's director of admissions writing against the university's prejudice and historical exclusion of their culture. They argued that Notre Dame as a Catholic institution had a cultural obligation to Chicanos. "We have no alternative but to insist that Notre Dame and the Catholic Church give the same respect to the Chicano community as we have historically and spiritually given to the Church," they wrote.[45]

In 1973, MEChA also pushed for greater efforts to retain Chicano students.[46] With the exception of Julian Samora, a professor in the Department of Sociology from 1959 to 1985, Notre Dame Latino students had very few faculty representing their culture. They also lacked counseling services and scholarships. Socially, the primarily white institution also proved difficult to navigate, as questions like "How come you're white if you're Chicano?" and "If you're Chicano how come you don't speak Spanish?" were the norm.[47]

Despite cultural differences, MEChA met success in rallying Notre Dame students to act in solidarity with the United Farm Workers (UFW) from summer 1972 to spring 1973. The *South Bend Tribune* reported that Notre Dame's dining hall refused to serve grapes and lettuce, which were part of a national boycott. The university purchased only non-union lettuce when UFW lettuce was unavailable, a decision that cost the university an extra $100 each week.[48] In April 1973, the university polled the student body on whether to boycott the non-UFW lettuce.[49] MEChA urged Notre Dame students to support the "cause of the politically powerless, impoverished American workers by endorsing the boycott."[50]

On Monday, April 4, 1973, students at the University of Notre Dame voted to support the boycott—with an overwhelming 1,895 students in favor and only 523 against.[51] Students wrote that Notre Dame's role as the "leading Catholic university organization in the country" meant the boycott should continue for the sake of supporting the migrant workers.[52] This decision meant that when UFW lettuce was unavailable, there would be no salad in the dining halls. The vote especially moved Rev. William Toohey, the director of campus ministry at Notre Dame, who wrote, "Notre Dame students are willing to make sacrifices in the cause of social justice."[53]

A third group calling Notre Dame to address Chicano rights was the Centro de Estudios Chicanos e Investigaciones (Center for Chicano Studies and Research), a graduate-student-founded center that attempted to examine the Latina/o population of the Midwest. The Centro hosted one of the most successful events to discuss issues with the Catholic Church: its Human Rights and Social Justice and the Church Conference, April 19 to 20, 1975, at Notre Dame brought together three bishops of Mexican American heritage to discuss grievances with the Church.[54]

Gilberto Cardenas, a graduate student and part of the Centro, along with powerhouse Olga Villa, the secretary of the MWCLR, worked tirelessly to organize this conference, inviting well-known Chicano religious leaders to present: Bishop Patricio Flores from San Antonio, Texas; Bishop Gilbert Chavez from San Diego, California; and Archbishop Robert Sanchez from Santa Fe, New Mexico.[55] Securing these three esteemed men as speakers was quite a coup for conference organizers.[56]

These three bishops spoke together for the first time at this conference to address the inability of the Church to respond to the needs of the Chicano population in the Midwest and the nearly twelve million Spanish-speaking members nationwide.[57] The conference detailed the national concerns of educating Latino clergymen, sisters, and brothers while allowing them to retain their culture so they would not "return to their communities as foreigners."[58] Furthermore, rather than training Chicano bishops to serve, the Church often imported foreign Spanish-speaking missionaries to work in those neighborhoods, though they were less familiar with Chicano culture.

Bishop Flores mentioned that unlike European immigrants, Mexican migrants could not bring their priests with them; Chicanos came to the United States without any clergy to represent their cause.[59] Bishop Chavez argued that the Spanish-speaking population needed to increase its visibility, especially with the projection of twenty-five million Latinos existing in the United States by the year 2000, at which point "La Raza will comprise 30 percent of the Catholic Church members in this country."[60] Most importantly, Archbishop Sanchez emphasized that the Spanish-speaking population should not consider themselves a nuisance to the Church: "We are not a problem! We know that! The Church should think in terms of opportunity to serve."[61]

Flores, Chavez, and Sanchez also argued for the rights of undocumented citizens coming to the United States. The conference ended with a request by those attending for the bishops to use their esteemed positions to write a telegram interrogating the decision to airlift South Vietnamese to the United States while "Mexicanos" were being deported at the same time. This telegram called for amnesty for all undocumented immigrants.[62]

The conference addressed national issues as well as local ones. Father Robert Peña, then national president of PADRES, criticized Notre Dame for refusing scholarships to Midwest Chicano students while giving them solely to Southwest Chicanos. This practice perpetuated Notre Dame's tendency to ignore the Chicano population in its own backyard.

Notre Dame faculty and clergy's poor treatment of the visiting bishops came under fire during the conference when conference organizer and graduate student Lydia Espinosa, in a closed meeting with Father Theodore Hesburgh and the bishops, decried the administration's refusal to meet with the honored guests during their stay. She explained to the bishops that though Notre Dame was a Catholic school, "Not one member of the administration was there to welcome you and only one member of the faculty attended your presentation. I apologize to you on behalf of the Chicanos at Notre Dame. Maybe this is an indication of why so many of us have left the Catholic Church."[63]

The lack of recognition from any white clergy at the university presented a deep lack of respect for the bishops and their work, as did the fact that Notre Dame offered no resources other than a meeting space.[64] A press release noted that while Espinosa apologized to the bishops for Notre Dame's actions, Father Hesburgh sat silent.[65]

Of these moments of tension, Notre Dame's 1977 decision to fire the groundskeepers provoked what Parra says was his most "radical" response.[66] He was joined in his protest by the National Labor Relations Board, Notre Dame's student government, and members of the student body. Tom Soma, vice president of the student government, organized a meeting of more than two hundred students and faculty to discuss protest tactics to support the groundskeepers.[67] They decided to collect petitions outside of Mass on November 1 and in the dining hall to "keep the heat on."[68] Parra additionally worked with Soma to circulate the petition beyond the university to the surrounding community, rallying members from the Latino community of South Bend to sign on behalf of the groundskeepers.

Photos and oral histories portray a large and diverse group that gathered outside of Notre Dame's administration building, armed with signs, and calling to "reinstate the 21."[69] The MWCLR along with Notre Dame's student government worked in solidarity for the groundskeepers. Supporters also decided to raise awareness of the workers' plight during one of Notre Dame's most important football games. Mike Lawrence of the National Labor Relations Board rented a plane to fly persistently above the game towing a sign reading "Support the Groundskeepers" (much to the consternation of the Notre Dame board of trustees and alumni).[70]

In the students' opinion column for the campus newspaper, *The Observer*, Charles Anhut, a junior at Notre Dame, questioned the university's values:

> Fr. Hesburgh, Mr. Human Rights himself, as the president of the University, apparently sanctions this action. Last year he agreed that "values" were to be thrown at seniors in what appeared to be a post-Watergate attempt to add moral undertones to the "Notre Dame Mystique." Now he is beginning to define exactly what he calls "values," not attempting in the least to hide his hypocrisy. Personally, I will resist to the fullest any attempt to put me in a class where putting people in unemployment lines is valued over having them work.[71]

By making its new "Values Seminar" compulsory, Notre Dame defined acceptable moral principles. Anhut questioned if the university itself was held to these values. Furthermore, Father Hesburgh's status as one of the most committed religious leaders to civil rights (as Anhut declared, "Mr. Human Rights himself) made his union-busting particularly hypocritical. That President Hesburgh had marched for civil rights with Martin Luther King Jr. in 1964 and sided with students protesting the Vietnam War but would not concede to pay groundskeepers a fair wage did not escape the students' or community members' attention.[72]

Olga Villa, the MWCLR secretary who was closely involved with the organizing, reflected on the groundskeepers' dispute over thirty years later in a retrospective, "We were shocked and surprised when the university so aggressively opposed improving the workers' lot. Where was the social justice?"[73] Ricardo Parra remembered feeling incensed with Father Hesburgh—with whom he'd had a cordial relationship until that point. Parra grew more aggressive in his condemnation of Notre Dame and its practices during the groundskeepers' dismissal.[74] Reflecting on the incident in 2015, he wondered even then if Hesburgh had moved past the ill will resulting from the groundskeepers' strike.[75]

After the Teamsters Local 364 filed three unfair labor practice charges against the university for their firing of the groundskeepers, the University of Notre Dame accepted a settlement from the National Labor Relations Board. Part of the settlement agreement required the university to

1) Not threaten to contract out for the purpose of discouraging workers from unionizing,

2) not announce wage boost and benefits to discourage unionization, [and]

3) not layoff or threaten to lay off or discriminate in order to discourage union activities.[76]

Organizers for the groundskeepers saw this settlement as a win, a moment where social-justice language effectively advocated for the Latino workers. The university re-employed the groundskeepers and was banned from discouraging their unionization with the Teamsters.

In the MWCLR newsletter, *Los Desarraigados*, one quote from Camilo Torres Restrepo, a Colombian socialist Roman Catholic priest, sums up the promise of Catholicism to Latinos: *Ser todo Catolico es hacer la revolucion* [To be Catholic is to make the revolution]. ("Catolico" in this sense means universality rather than colonization.)[77] The notion of Catholicism as "universality rather than colonization" reclaimed religion to serve the impoverished rather than contribute to their oppression.[78] The MWCLR possessed a unique relationship with a Catholic institution that had expressed a commitment to address the injustices that the Latino population experienced. Latino students and MWCLR staff made sure to hold the university accountable to that commitment.

NOTES

1. *Los Desarraigados*, Fall/Winter 1977, MS 2009.8, Binder Section 6, Julian Samora Library, University of Notre Dame, Notre Dame, Indiana; "Union Hearing for N.D. Workers," *South Bend Tribune*, October 4, 1977; "Union Meeting Postponed," *The Observer*, October 12, 1977, University Notre Dame Archives online. http://www.archives.nd.edu/observer/1977–10–12_v12_032.pdf, p. 3.

2. *Los Desarraigados*, Fall/Winter 1977, MS 2009.8, Binder Section 6, Julian Samora Library, University of Notre Dame; "Workers Set to Fight Lay-Off," *The Observer*, October 11, 1977.

3. Alberto López Pulido, Barbara Driscoll de Alvarado, and Carmen Samora, eds., *Moving Beyond Borders: Julian Samora and the Establishment of Latino Studies*. (Urbana: University of Illinois Press, 2009), 85.

4. Jefferson R. Cowie, *Stayin' Alive: The 1970s and the Last Days of the Working Class* (New York: New Press. 2011), xxv.

5. Cowie, *Stayin' Alive*, xxv.

6. *Los Desarraigados*, Fall/Winter 1977, MS 2009.8, Binder Section 6, Julian Samora Library, University of Notre Dame, 4.

7. Ricardo Parra, "Caring About Members," *The Observer*, October 12, 1977, University Notre Dame Archives online, http://www.archives.nd.edu/observer/1977–10–12_v12_032.pdf, 6.

8. Paul T. Murray, "'To Change the Face of America': Father Theodore M. Hesburgh and the Civil Rights Commission," *Indiana Magazine of History* (June 2015): 111–154, 122.

9. Jay P. Dolan and Gilberto M. Hinojosa, ed., *Mexican Americans and the Catholic Church, 1900–1965* (Notre Dame, IN: University of Notre Dame Press, 1994), 1.

10. Dolan and Hinojosa, *Mexican Americans and the Catholic Church*, 242.

11. Dolan and Hinojosa, *Mexican Americans and the Catholic Church*, 240. Another wonderful resource for this early twentieth-century history is Anne M. Martínez, *Catholic Borderlands: Mapping Catholicism onto American Empire, 1905–1935* (Lincoln: University of Nebraska Press, 2014).

12. Dolan and Hinojosa, *Mexican Americans and the Catholic Church*, 241.

13. Lizabeth Cohen, *Making a New Deal: Industrial Workers in Chicago, 1919–1939* (New York: Cambridge University Press, 1990), 91.

14. Mario. T. García, "The Chicano Southwest: Catholicism and Its Meaning," *U.S. Catholic Historian* 18, no. 4 (fall, 2000): 1–24.

15. Dolan and Hinojosa , *Mexican Americans and the Catholic Church*, 237.

16. Dolan and Hinojosa, *Mexican Americans and the Catholic Church*, 308.

17. Dolan and Hinojosa, *Mexican Americans and the Catholic Church*, 290.

18. Dolan and Hinojosa, *Mexican Americans and the Catholic Church*, 291.

19. Dolan and Hinojosa, *Mexican Americans and the Catholic Church*, 291. In *Brown in the Windy City* (Chicago: University of Chicago Press, 2012) and *Making the MexiRican City* (Urbana: University of Illinois Press, 2023), historians Lilia Fernandez and Delia Fernandez, respectively, study this cultural coalescence between Latinos in the Midwest in detail.

20. Moises Sandoval, *On the Move: A History of the Hispanic Church in the United States*, (Maryknoll, NY: Orbis Books, 1990), 77.

21. *El Plan Espiritual de Aztlán*, 1969, University of Michigan's student project site, http://www.umich.edu/~ac213/student_projects05/ip/plandeaztlan1.html.

22. Sandoval, *On the Move*, 81.

23. Sandoval, *On the Move*, 81.

24. Sandoval, *On the Move*, 81.

25. Maylei Blackwell, *Chicana Power: Contested Histories of Feminism in the Chicano Movement* (Austin: University of Texas Press, 2011), 178.

26. *Los Desarraigados* I, no. 4, November 1973, MS 2009.8, Binder Section 2, Julian Samora Library, University of Notre Dame.

27. *Los Desarraigados* II, no. III, June 1974, MS 2009.8, Binder Section 2, Julian Samora Library, University of Notre Dame.

28. *Los Desarraigados* I, no. 4, November 1973.

29. Gustavo Gutiérrez, *A Theology of Liberation: History, Politics, and Salvation* (Maryknoll, NY: Orbis Books, 1971).

30. Gutiérrez, *A Theology of Liberation*.

31. Peter Huff, *The Voice of Vatican II: Words for Our Church Today.* (Barnhart, MO: Liguori, 2012).

32. Huff, *The Voice of Vatican II*.

33. Norman Tanner, *Vatican II: The Essential Texts* (New York: Image Books, 2012), 23.

34. Tanner, *Vatican II*, 23.

35. John Dear, "Gustavo Gutierrez and the Preferential Option for the Poor," *National Catholic Reporter*, November 8, 2011, http://liberationtheology.org/library/National_Catholic_Reporter_-_Gustavo_Gutierrez_and_the_preferential_option_for_the_poor_-_2011-11-09.pdf.

36. Gustavo Gutiérrez is now an endowed professor—the John Cardinal O'Hara Professor of Theology at the University of Notre Dame; another connection between the university and his doctrine of liberation theology.

37. Leo Rivera, "Executive Director Report for 1970 Year Ending April 30, 1971," CMCL 1/26: Miscellaneous Memoranda and Correspondence (1974), University of Notre Dame Archives.

38. Ricardo Parra, "Concientizacion and Organization," November 17, 1973, MS 2009.8, Ricardo Parra Writings, Ricardo and Olga Villa Para Papers, Julian Samora Library, University of Notre Dame Archives.

39. Paulo Freire, *Pedagogy of the Oppressed* (New York: Continuum, 1986), 19.

40. Mela Olivo, "Was It Discrimination at Notre Dame?," *Latin Times*, May 29, 1971, in Barbara Driscoll, "Newspaper Account of South Bend, Indiana Latino Population," Olga Villa and Ricardo Parra Papers, Julian Samora Library, University of Notre Dame, 259.

41. Olivo, "Was It Discrimination at Notre Dame?," 259.

42. "Notre Dame, Indiana," *El Grito del Norte*, August 20, 1971, in Driscoll, "Newspaper Account of South Bend, Indiana Latino Population," 259.

43. Driscoll, "Newspaper Account of South Bend, Indiana Latino Population," 260.

44. Driscoll, "Newspaper Account of South Bend, Indiana Latino Population," 260.

45. Letter to Dr. Peter P. Grande from Armando Alonzo, Director of Admissions. November 20, 1970, 6, Gilberto Cárdenas Papers, Julian Samora Library, University of Notre Dame.

46. "MECHA's Message: Chicanos Are American," March 27, 1973, untitled newspaper; in Driscoll, "Newspaper Account of South Bend, Indiana Latino Population," 312.

47. Driscoll, "Newspaper Account of South Bend, Indiana Latino Population," 312.

48. John Rumbach, "Lettuce Boycott Referendum Set," *South Bend Tribune*, April 12, 1973, in Driscoll, "Newspaper Account of South Bend, Indiana Latino Population," 315.

49. Rumbach, "Lettuce Boycott Referendum Set."

50. "MECHA Pres. Endorses Lettuce Boycott," *South Bend Tribune*, April 16, 1973, in Driscoll, "Newspaper Account of South Bend, Indiana Latino Population," 320.

51. "N.D. Students to Eat Only Union Lettuce," source unknown, April 17, 1973, in; Driscoll, "Newspaper Account of South Bend, Indiana Latino Population," 321.

52. "Boycott Lettuce," source unknown, 1973, in Driscoll, "Newspaper Account of South Bend, Indiana Latino Population," 316.

53. "Boycott Lettuce."

54. Gilbert Cardenas, *Press Release: Bishops Conference*, Box 1, Folder 15, Julian Samora Papers, 00173, Michigan State University Archives & Historical Collections, East Lansing, Michigan, 1.

55. Cardenas, *Press Release: Bishops Conference*.

56. Bishop Flores, originally from Jackson County, Texas, served as the diocesan director of the Bishops' Committee for the Spanish Speaking in Texas and as a national chairman for PADRES (the National Chicano Priest Movement). *Time* magazine named him one of the most outstanding young leaders in the nation. Bishop Chavez, from Ontario, California, and a member of PADRES, worked as executive director of the Mexican-American Commission and vicar general of the San Diego Diocese. Archbishop Sanchez, from Santa Fe, New Mexico, served as the Southwest representative to the National Federation of Priests' Councils and as president of the Archdiocesan Priests Senate.

57. Cardenas, *Press Release: Bishops Conference*, 2.

58. Cardenas, *Press Release: Bishops Conference*, 3.

59. Cardenas, *Press Release: Bishops Conference*, 4.

60. Cardenas, *Press Release: Bishops Conference*, 5.

61. Cardenas, *Press Release: Bishops Conference*, 6.

62. Cardenas, *Press Release: Bishops Conference*, 6.

63. Cardenas, *Press Release: Bishops Conference*, 6. Women in the Chicano movement often provided the main organizational support. More can be read on La Raza women at Notre Dame in Leticia Rose Wiggins, "Women Need to Find Their Voice": Latinas Speak Out in the Midwest, 1972," in Dionne Espinoza, María Eugenia Cotera, and Maylei Blackwell, eds., *Chicana Movidas: New Narratives of Activism and Feminism in the Movement Era* (Austin: University of Texas Press, 2018), 76–90.

64. Conference Pamphlet, "A Symposium on Human Rights and Social Justice and

the Church," Box 1, Folder 15, Julian Samora Papers, 00173, Michigan State University Archives & Historical Collections.

65. Conference Pamphlet, "A Symposium on Human Rights and Social Justice and the Church."

66. Ricardo Parra Oral History conducted by Leticia Wiggins, South Bend, Indiana, January 14, 2015.

67. Michael Ridenour, "200 Protest Groundskeeper Lay-offs," *The Observer*, October 12, 1977, University of Notre Dame online student paper archives, http://www.archives.nd.edu/observer/1977-10-12_v12_032.pdf.

68. Ridenour, "200 Protest Groundskeeper Lay-offs."

69. Ricardo Parra Oral History.

70. Ricardo Parra Oral History.

71. Charles Anhut, "Opinion: Are These Values?," *The Observer*, October 12, 1977, University of Notre Dame online student paper archives, http://www.archives.nd.edu/observer/1977-10-12_v12_032.pdf.

72. Richard Conklin, "The Picture of Purpose," *Notre Dame Magazine* (Winter 2007–2008), https://magazine.nd.edu/stories/the-picture-of-purpose/.

73. Alberto López Pulido, Barbara Driscoll de Alvarado, and Carmen Samora, eds., *Moving beyond Borders: Julian Samora and the Establishment of Latino Studies* (Urbana: University of Illinois Press. 2009), 85.

74. Ricardo Parra Oral History.

75. Ricardo Parra Oral History.

76. *Los Desarraigados* V, no. 1, Spring 1978, MS 2009.8, Binder Section 2, Julian Samora Library, University of Notre Dame, 1.

77. *Los Desarraigados* III, no. 3, Winter 1976, MS 2009.8, Binder Section 2, Julian Samora Library, University of Notre Dame, 5.

78. *Los Desarraigados* III, no. 3, Winter 1976.

12

Gay Liberation and the Social Gospel

Religious Support for Gay Employment Rights in Wisconsin

STEPHEN COLBROOK

❖ ❖ ❖ ❖ ❖ ❖ ❖ ❖ ❖ ❖ ❖ ❖ ❖ ❖ ❖ ❖

Close to fifty people gathered in the committee room in the Wisconsin state capitol building on May 12, 1981. They were there for the first public hearing on Assembly Bill (AB) 70, which promised to furnish gay men and lesbians with legal protections against employment and housing discrimination. Seated in the audience were gay activists, elected officials, and a battery of religious leaders from across the state, including representatives from the Wisconsin Baptist State Convention, the Unitarian Universalist Church, the Lutheran Church, and the Catholic Archdiocese of Milwaukee. After the bill's sponsor, Assemblyman David Clarenbach, opened proceedings, these ministers rose one by one to urge lawmakers to protect gay people from job discrimination. Only one witness, Rev. Richard E. Pritchard, a stalwart Congregationalist conservative and culture warrior, expressed opposition to the measure.[1] After this initial hearing, AB 70 continued to attract broad-based support as it made it ways through the Wisconsin legislature. Hundreds of ministers from across denominational and theological lines united in defence of the measure, writing letters of endorsement, testifying during critical committee hearings, and meeting directly with lawmakers.[2] Thanks in large part to these lobbying efforts, AB 70 passed both chambers of the legislature and became law on February 25, 1982, making Wisconsin the first state in the nation to enact a statute protecting gay men and lesbians from job discrimination.

The faith-based support for AB 70 refutes the common notion that religion has served as an exclusively reactionary force in the history of the modern gay movement. Historians of LGBTQ politics have tended to minimize or ignore religion, analyzing it only when it acts as a barrier to gay rights and sexual liberation. Religious actors seldom make anything more than fleeting appearances in major accounts of the gay movement, except insofar as they serve as agents of conservatism and repression, intransigently opposed to the political gains made by sexual minorities. The ascendancy of the Religious Right in the 1970s and 1980s is largely responsible for the persistent assumption that religious institutions and the gay movement have been perpetually at odds. Conservative Christians were typically the loudest oppositional voices during political controversies over gay rights in the late twentieth century, leading to the impression that they spoke for all faith groups. In the 2010s, a steady stream of scholarship began to complicate and challenge this presumed antagonism between religious actors and sexual minorities. The work of Heather White, Gillian Frank, Whitney Strub, and Bethany Moreton, among others, has persuasively demonstrated the centrality of faith and religious institutions to the rise of the gay movement.[3] These histories have mapped out the beliefs, practices, and politics of people whose religious identities led them to support gay rights, revealing that the relationship between sexuality and religion is far more fluid and complex than a singular focus on the Religious Right can convey. Expanding on this new wave of scholarship, this chapter examines the crucial religious and theological underpinnings of support for AB 70—a statute that carried national significance as the first state-level law furnishing gay men and lesbians with legal protections based on their sexual orientation.

The story of AB 70 highlights the complex interactions between Catholicism and the gay movement during the 1970s and 1980s. In Wisconsin, Catholics numbered approximately one-third of the total population, more than any other faith group.[4] While Catholic priests, nuns, and laypeople served as a bulwark against gay rights in many cities and states, they played a critical role in the campaign for AB 70. Historians of sexuality have frequently portrayed Catholicism as a solely reactionary force characterized by its sexual conservatism, hard-line opposition to the gay movement, and emphasis on hierarchy and tradition.[5] In fact, Catholics took a wide range of positions on gay rights legislation in the 1970s and early 1980s. A sizeable section of liberal Catholics tried to bridge the chasm between the Catholic Church's traditional moral teachings on sex and the gay movement's push for legal protections grounded in sexual identity. To these liberals, the Second Vatican Council (1962 to 1965), which ushered in a new understanding of the relationship between contemporary society and the Church, appeared to sanction a more activist spirit that was extended to gay civil rights. Against this theological backdrop, Catholicism figured prominently in debates over gay employment rights. In Wisconsin's deeply Catholic political culture, members of the clergy, working powerfully behind the scenes, proved decisive in persuading legislators to enact AB 70 in 1982. The most prominent supporter of the bill was Milwaukee's archbishop Rembert Weakland, who leveraged his position and authority to argue that the measure conformed to Catholic social teaching. The history of AB 70 thus reveals that Catholicism has not always had a straightforward or oppositional relationship to the gay movement.

The study of LGBTQ politics in the Midwest has been an increasingly robust field of inquiry in recent years, as scholars have produced conceptually rich work on topics as diverse as gay electoral politics in Chicago, the battle over gay marriage in Iowa, and the role of the automobile in gay life in Michigan.[6] This chapter complements this growing body of literature by arguing that religious institutions and beliefs have been central to the region's gay rights movement. It makes this case by showing that a distinctive Catholic culture developed in Wisconsin that creatively adapted the Church's social teachings to issues surrounding gay civil rights. Despite the Church's claim to universalism, American Catholicism differs substantially from region to region, state to state, and diocese to diocese. The Catholic experience in Wisconsin, which involved a long history of activism centered on social justice, made the state fertile ground for the active involvement of the clergy in the battle for gay rights. The Catholic Church's instrumental role in the passage of AB 70 set Wisconsin apart from many other states, especially in the densely Catholic Northeast, where priests and laypeople often expressed opposition to employment protections for gay men and lesbians. Eschewing a simplistic binary that pits religion against sexuality, this chapter emphasizes the diverse, heterogeneous character of Catholic interactions with the gay rights movement, which varied significantly across different dioceses.[7]

Meeting for four sessions in Rome between October 1962 and December 1965, the Second Vatican Council inaugurated a new epoch in the history of the Catholic Church. Attended by thousands of delegates from across the globe, these historic talks ushered in several momentous alterations to Church practice: the vernacular replaced Latin in the liturgy, and priests began facing the congregation during Mass. The council also issued a series of major statements on ecumenism, religious freedom, and non-Christian religions. Most significantly, Vatican II encouraged the laity to reconceptualize their relationship with the Church hierarchy. It gave birth to the notion that the Church was a common community of laypeople and clergy rather than a hierarchical, static institution. Many ordinary churchgoers believed the council authorized them to exercise greater theological and ethical autonomy, even if that meant disregarding traditional Catholic teachings. Dissenting voices on issues like birth control, clerical celibacy, and divorce grew louder in the years after Vatican II.[8]

The council's deliberations transformed debates about gay rights within the Church. Although Vatican II made only fleeting references to sexuality, some reform-minded Catholics seized on its promotion of openness, dialogue, and lay leadership to argue for a broader liberalization of official teaching on sexual morality. To these liberals and reformers, the council's emphasis on individual conscience and ethical autonomy gave them permission to question traditional Catholic doctrine on sexuality and remain loyal to the Church.[9] Emboldened by Vatican II's emphasis on lay participation, gay churchgoers founded a plethora of new organizations in the 1960s and 1970s to develop gay-affirming pastoral care and theology. Foremost among these was Dignity/USA, a lay-led ministry established in 1969 that held support groups and prayer services for gay Catholics and aimed to facilitate greater dialogue between sexual minorities and the Church hierarchy. In direct defiance of traditional Catholic teaching, which only permitted procreative sex within heterosexual marriage, the organization's founding constitution stressed that homosexuality was "a natural variation on the use of sex."[10] Over the next decade, Dignity chapters sprouted up in eighty-seven towns and cities across the country, in places as diverse as New York City; Birmingham, Alabama; and Sioux City, Iowa.[11]

As the theological debate over homosexuality intensified, the relationship between sexual minorities and the Church hierarchy varied substantially across different dioceses. In New York City, Los Angeles, Chicago, and elsewhere, conservative bishops and priests vehemently opposed the gay movement.[12] By contrast, Milwaukee's archdiocese forged a close relationship with gay Catholic organizations and activists. Liberal Catholicism had long thrived in the city, where the clergy had a strong record of advocating for social justice and civil rights.[13] Galvanized by Vatican II's emphasis on openness, dialogue, and individual conscience, several priests reevaluated their attitudes toward sexuality during the 1970s. Of the gay-affirming members of the clergy in Milwaukee, none was more influential than Rembert Weakland, who became archbishop of the city in 1977. A fundamental commitment to the reforms inaugurated by Vatican II motivated Weakland's support for gay rights. The council inspired him to reassess the relationship between the Church and the world, promote a more active role for the laity, and develop a more positive theology of sexuality.[14] He would later reflect that he emerged from the experience of Vatican II with an affirmative view about "human sexuality and its beauty."[15]

During Weakland's tenure as archbishop, the Milwaukee archdiocese developed closer ties with gay and lesbian Catholics. Unlike many bishops, Weakland permitted the local chapter of Dignity to meet on Church property throughout the late 1970s and 1980s.[16] He also frequently called on Catholics to take an active stand against discrimination based on sexual orientation. In July 1980 he wrote a column for the *Catholic Herald*, the archdiocese's weekly newspaper, urging churchgoers to defend the "rights" of gay men and lesbians "so that no one is treated as a second-class citizen."[17] That same year, the archdiocese played a pivotal role in the campaign for a gay rights ordinance in Milwaukee, which added sexual orientation to the list of protected categories under the city's employment laws. Leon Rouse, a practicing Catholic and local gay activist, laid the groundwork for the measure's passage. In 1979 he established the Committee for Fundamental Judeo-Christian Human Rights (CFJCHR) to coordinate the advocacy and lobbying efforts of gay-affirming religious leaders in Milwaukee. The organization's members represented a diverse range of Christian denominations, including Catholics, Presbyterians, Methodists, Episcopalians, and Lutherans.[18] This nascent lobbying network came into its own during the push for an employment rights ordinance in 1980. As the Milwaukee city council debated the measure in June and July, ministers and priests affiliated with Rouse and the CFJCHR campaigned hard for its passage, providing crucial testimony during public hearings that gave the issue moral and political weight. One of the most prominent supporters of the bill was Father Jack Murtagh, who headed the archdiocese's social outreach office. After a floor debate dominated by religious language and rhetoric, the council adopted the ordinance by a 10 to 6 margin on July 8, demonstrating the success of local gay activists in mobilizing support for their movement among members of the clergy.[19]

On the heels of this victory, Rouse drew on the political connections and networks he had forged with religious leaders in Milwaukee to advocate for employment rights legislation at the state level. In consultation with the state's legislative drafting agency, he wrote the first version of what would become AB 70 in 1980. After several months of stalling, Assemblyman David Clarenbach agreed to sponsor the measure during the 1981 legislative session.[20] Elected to a safe Democratic seat in the liberal stronghold of Madison in 1974, Clarenbach quickly earned a reputation as the legislature's most visible advocate for gay rights, supporting measures including a repeal of the state sodomy statute and employment protections for sexual minorities. He would later come out publicly as gay, but only after his electoral career ended in the 1990s.[21]

At first blush, the Wisconsin legislature appeared an unlikely site for the passage of the first statewide gay employment law. While the state was home to a robust progressive tradition and the solidly liberal cities of Milwaukee and Madison, its politics swerved from left to right in the 1970s and 1980s, entering a protracted era of two-party competition.[22] The Democratic Party maintained slim majorities in both chambers of the legislature during most of this period, but Republicans frequently won statewide elections, including the race for the governorship in 1978, when Lee Sherman Dreyfus came to power on a platform promising to cut taxes and reduce government expenditure.[23] In the realm of sexual politics, progressive lawmakers like Clarenbach attempted to pass gay rights bills in nearly every legislative session during the 1970s, but to no avail.[24] Even as states across the country repealed their sodomy laws in the 1960s and 1970s, Wisconsin retained its statute until 1983, attaching the stigma of criminality to gay men.[25]

To overcome these obstacles, Rouse once again enlisted the support of religious leaders to give his campaign greater moral and political legitimacy. As AB 70 wound its way through the legislature in 1981 and early 1982, he tapped into the CFJCHR's network of ministers and priests to launch an extensive lobbying blitz that included letter writing, phone calls, and personal visits to the offices of state legislators. Leveraging their moral authority, religious groups across the denominational spectrum barraged lawmakers with letters in support of the bill, including the Episcopal Diocese of Milwaukee, the Presbytery of Milwaukee, the Wisconsin Conference of the United Church of Christ, the United Methodist Church of Wisconsin, and the Wisconsin Baptist State Convention.[26] Such correspondence aimed to reassure legislators that the measure enjoyed a groundswell of support beyond the local gay community and aligned with the religious convictions of ministers. All spring and summer long, Rouse also identified specific lawmakers whom he wished to persuade and asked local members of the clergy to bombard them with phone calls and letters endorsing the bill.[27] This sophisticated and targeted lobbying effort reflected Rouse's supreme skill at rallying religious leaders in favor of gay rights legislation.

Like the debate over Milwaukee's gay rights ordinance, the Catholic Church proved crucial to the passage of AB 70. In March 1981, Weakland came out in support of the measure after meeting with Rouse, drafting a letter of endorsement that proponents later circulated to lawmakers. To stay within the confines of official Catholic teaching on homosexuality, Weakland stressed that "homosexual activity" remained morally wrong but expressed support for protecting the "basic human rights" of gay people. With this argument, he emphasized the Church's distinction between sexual orientation and "homosexual" behaviour—the former being a morally neutral state for which individuals bore no culpability, the latter being unequivocally sinful. He insisted that AB 70 conformed with the Church's teachings because it did not grant recognition or approval of "homosexual activity" and merely protected people against unjust discrimination based on their sexual orientation.[28] The dichotomy between sexual acts and identity allowed Weakland to reconcile his support for the bill with the Church's condemnation of gay relationships and sex. Several other Catholic priests and organizations followed Weakland's lead in endorsing AB 70. A sizeable group of nuns, priests, and laypeople rallied in support of the bill. Endorsements came from organizations such as the Wisconsin Catholic Conference, the Milwaukee Archdiocesan Sisters Council, and the Justice and Peace Committee of the Diocese of Madison, as well as dozens of individual priests.[29]

After months of lobbying by the CFJCHR, AB 70 came up for a floor vote in the Wisconsin Assembly on October 23, 1981. Spectators packed the galleries in the legislature, including Rouse and a large contingent of supportive priests, nuns, and laypeople.[30] The floor debate primarily focused on the significance of religious support for the measure. Clarenbach spoke first, citing Weakland's letter and the range of endorsements from other faith groups. "The religious leaders of this state affirm the right to human rights for all minority groups, and oppose discrimination of all sorts," he proclaimed. Following Clarenbach's remarks, Representative John Shabaz, a Republican from southeastern Wisconsin and minority Assembly leader, rose in opposition to AB 70. He desperately tried to downplay the religious support for the bill, urging lawmakers to not vote "blindly in favor of it because you received a letter from your local minister or bishop."[31] As the debate continued over the next few hours, members of the CFJCHR attempted to persuade religiously minded lawmakers to vote for AB 70. Most notably, a representative from the Archdiocese of Milwaukee personally met with several Catholic lawmakers to remind them that Weakland favored the bill.[32] In the final vote count, this pressure from religious leaders convinced lawmakers to pass AB 70 by the narrow margin of 49 to 45. Despite Shabaz's opposition, the bill received a modicum of bipartisan support: six Republicans joined forty-three Democrats in voting for it.³³

As AB 70 moved to the state Senate, members of the Religious Right belatedly organized in opposition to it. Claiming to represent the interests of three hundred conservative churches, the Wisconsin chapter of the Moral Majority mounted an extensive campaign against the bill in early 1982.³⁴ At the Senate's first hearing on the measure in late January, the organization's president, Max Andrews, lambasted AB 70. In testimony that attempted to stoke fear and demonize sexual minorities, he repeated many homophobic tropes, including the claim that gay men "actively recruit others to be part of their sickness."³⁵ After the Senate passed the bill just over two weeks later, the Moral Majority's attention turned to GOP Governor Lee Sherman Dreyfus, who had not indicated whether he would sign the measure. The organization saturated the airwaves of Christian radio stations in Milwaukee, Madison, and Racine, running announcements multiple times a day that urged listeners to contact Dreyfus's office to demand he veto the bill.³⁶ Just one day after the legislature sent the bill to the governor, conservative Christians jammed the phone lines of the executive branch with 370 calls.³⁷ In the end, Dreyfus refused to bow to this pressure. Although a fiscal conservative, he was relatively liberal on cultural issues and had an ambivalent relationship with the Religious Right.³⁸ Flanked by Clarenbach and Rouse, he signed AB 70 into law at a press event on February 25, 1982.³⁹ In an explanatory note accompanying his signature of the bill, the governor acknowledged "the support of a wide-ranging group of religious leadership, including leadership of the Roman Catholic Church, several Lutheran synods, and the Jewish community."⁴⁰

After the passage of AB 70, the American Catholic Church veered forcefully in an antigay direction. In the culture wars moment of the 1980s and 1990s, as a growing number of Catholics entered the Republican fold, a large section of the clergy stressed that sexual immorality and abortion were the most pressing issues facing the Church. More than ever, conservative bishops deployed heated rhetoric against sexual minorities and framed their opposition to gay rights in morally charged terms as a deeply felt religious duty. In New York City, Cardinal John O'Connor emerged as the nation's leading spokesperson for traditionalist Catholics, positioning himself as a defender of the Church's orthodox teachings on sexuality against the hostile forces of theological liberalism and the gay movement. He repeatedly clashed with gay activists over a wide range of social issues, including job discrimination, the AIDS epidemic, and sex education.[41] In early 1986 he vociferously condemned the passage of a gay rights ordinance in the city, taking frequent swipes against the bill in newspaper editorials and press conferences.[42] The contrast with Bishop Weakland in Milwaukee, who continued to enjoy an amicable relationship with the local gay community in the 1980s and 1990s, could not have been more pronounced.[43]

While O'Connor garnered the most national attention, other priests and bishops took an equally hard-line stance against the gay movement. In the late 1980s and 1990s, statehouses across the country passed a wave of bills protecting sexual minorities from job discrimination, raising the ire of many traditionalist Catholics. When Massachusetts became the second state after Wisconsin to enact such a law in 1989, the Church hierarchy relentlessly attacked the measure in a series of letters and public statements.[44] The Massachusetts Catholic Conference, which lobbied on behalf of the state's four archdioceses, circulated a letter to lawmakers condemning the proposal and arguing it would serve "as a step toward legal approval of the homosexual lifestyle."[45] Elsewhere, in states as diverse as Florida, Louisiana, New Jersey, New York, and Oregon, conservative bishops mounted campaigns against employment rights legislation during the late 1980s and 1990s.[46]

Even as traditionalists and the Christian Right enjoyed greater visibility in battles over gay rights, a significant minority of progressive priests and bishops continued to endorse employment protection laws, offering a counterweight to the rightward direction of the Church. Echoing the passage of AB 70, an array of religious leaders supported a gay employment bill in Hawaii in 1991, including representatives from the Catholic Diocese of Honolulu. Utilizing tactics that he first used in Wisconsin, Rouse, who had recently moved to Hawaii, coordinated the lobbying activities of these ministers and priests. Clergy from across the state inundated lawmakers with letters of support and provided testimony in favor of the bill, which sailed through both chambers of the legislature and became law in March 1991.[47] Just two years later, a wide range of Catholic organizations backed a similar measure in the Illinois legislature. For two days in early April 1993, priests descended on the state capitol building in Springfield to lobby for the bill, meeting directly with Catholic lawmakers from across the political aisle to plead their case.[48] "The strong support of Catholics in this effort should put to rest the fallacy that Catholics oppose gay and lesbian civil rights legislation," proclaimed Rick Garcia, the chief lobbyist for the measure.[49] Despite these efforts, the bill stalled in the Illinois

Senate in May 1993, and it took the state twelve more years to enact a law protecting gay men and lesbians from job discrimination.[50] Outside of the Church hierarchy, lay disagreement with hard-line Catholic teachings on sexuality grew more pronounced in the 1990s. In June 1992, Gallup asked roughly eight hundred Catholics whether they supported equal employment opportunities for gay men and lesbians. Seventy-eight percent of respondents said they did, a 20 percent increase from a similar poll conducted two decades earlier.[51]

As the culture wars raged in the 1980s and 1990s, not every Catholic went in a conservative direction on gay rights. A sizeable number of priests and laypeople continued to fuse the Church's teachings on social justice with the political aims of the gay movement. If the ascendancy of the Religious Right has created a caricature of Catholicism as a monolithic bloc uniformly opposed to gay rights, the history of AB 70 and other employment laws points to the fluidity and complexity of Catholic attitudes toward homosexuality, challenging the conventional narrative that religious actors and sexual minorities are inherently at odds.

NOTES

1. Details of this hearing come from Steve Burkholder, "Bill to Ban Sex Bias Gains Strong Support," *Milwaukee Journal*, May 13, 1981, 25; "Assembly Committee on Health and Human Services Record of Action on Assembly Bill 70," Box 5, Folder 7, David Clarenbach Papers, Wisconsin Historical Society, Madison, Wisconsin.

2. Stephen Kulieke, "On, Wisconsin: How Gay Rights Won," *Chicago Gay Life*, March 5, 1982, 6.

3. Heather R. White, *Reforming Sodom: Protestants and the Rise of Gay Rights* (Chapel Hill: University of North Carolina Press, 2015); Gillian A. Frank, Bethany Moreton, and Heather R. White, eds., *Devotions and Desires: Histories of Sexuality and Religion in the Twentieth-Century United States* (Chapel Hill: University of North Carolina Press, 2018); Gillian Frank, Rachel Kranson, and Jonathan Krasner, "Introduction: Sexuality in American Jewish History," *American Jewish History* 104, no. 4 (2020): 487–491; Whitney Strub, "The Homophile Is a Sexual Being: Wallace de Ortega Maxey's Pulp Theology and Gay Activism," *Journal of the History of Sexuality* 25, no.2 (May 2016): 323–353. A related branch of literature has begun to decenter the cultural wars and the rise of the Christian Right in histories of religion and politics in the late twentieth century. For an excellent example of scholarship in this vein, see Darren Dochuk, ed., *Religion and Politics beyond the Culture Wars: New Directions in a Divided America* (Notre Dame, IN: Notre Dame University Press, 2021).

4. R. Richard Wagner, *Coming Out, Moving Forward: Wisconsin's Recent Gay History* (Madison: Wisconsin Historical Society Press, 2020), 237.

5. Noteworthy works that challenge this conception of Catholicism as an exclusively negative force in the history of sexuality and LGBTQ politics include James P. McCartin, "Sex Is Holy and Mysterious: The Vision of Early Twentieth-Century Catholic

Sex Education Reformers," in Frank, Moreton, and White, *Devotions and Desires*, 71–89; James P. McCartin, "The Church and Gay Liberation: The Case of John McNeill," *U.S. Catholic Historian* 34, no. 1 (Winter 2016): 125–141; Jason Steidl, "DignityUSA: LGBTQ Ministry, Catholic Morality, and the Limits of Institutional Reform," *U.S. Catholic Historian* 40, no. 1 (Winter 2022): 53–80. For more on the absence of Catholics in histories of sexuality, see R. Marie Griffith, "Crossing the Catholic Divide: Gender, Sexuality, and Historiography," in R. Scott Appleby and Kathleen Sprows Cummings, eds., *Catholics in the American Century: Recasting Narratives of U.S. History* (Ithaca, NY: Cornell University Press, 2012), 81–107.

6. Timothy Stewart-Winter, *Queer Clout: Chicago and the Rise of Gay Politics* (Philadelphia: University of Pennsylvania Press, 2016); Tom Witosky and Marc Hansen, *Equal before the Law: How Iowa led Americans to Marriage Equality* (Iowa City: University of Iowa Press, 2015); Timothy Retzloff, "Cars and Bars: Assembling Gay Men in Postwar Flint, Michigan," in Genny Beemyn, ed., *Creating a Place for Ourselves: Lesbian, Gay, and Bisexual Community Histories*(New York: Routledge, 1997), 227–252. For an excellent historiographical overview of recent work in the field of Midwestern LGBTQ history, see Matthew Pehl, "Midwestern History Is Out of the Closet," *Middle West Review* 6, no.1–2 (Fall 2019-Spring 2020): 190–196.

7. On the importance of region to the history of American Catholicism, see Michael J. Pfeifer, *The Making of American Catholicism: Regional Culture and the Catholic Experience* (New York: New York University Press, 2021).

8. For more lengthy explorations of the reforms inaugurated by the Second Vatican Council, see Leslie Woodcock Tentler, *American Catholics: A History* (New Haven, CT: Yale University Press, 2020), 297–326; Leslie Woodcock Tentler, *Catholics and Contraception: An American History* (Ithaca, NY: Cornell University Press, 2004), 204–263.

9. On the history of the Second Vatican Council and sexuality, see Jeffrey M. Burns, "Sexuality after the Council: Gay Catholics, Married Clergy, Rights, and Change in San Francisco, 1962–1987," in Kathleen Sprows Cummings, Timothy Matovina, and Robert A. Orsi, eds., *Catholics in the Vatican II Era: Local Histories of a Global Event* (Cambridge: Cambridge University Press, 2017), 3–27.

10. Quoted in Steidl, "DignityUSA," 55.

11. John D'Emilio, *Queer Legacies: Stories from Chicago's LGBTQ Archives* (Chicago: University of Chicago Press, 2020), 57.

12. Steidl, "DignityUSA," 56, 65; Stewart-Winter, *Queer Clout*, 167–172.

13. Patrick D. Jones, *The Selma of the North: Civil Rights Insurgency in Milwaukee* (Cambridge, MA: Harvard University Press, 2009).

14. Rembert G. Weakland, *A Pilgrim in a Pilgrim's Church: Memoirs of a Catholic Archbishop* (Grand Rapids, MI: Eerdmans, 2009), 91–110.

15. Weakland, *A Pilgrim in a Pilgrim's Church*, 109. Weakland's support for gay rights also likely stemmed from his own sexuality. Although he would only publicly come out as gay years later, he broke his vow of celibacy in the early 1980s to pursue a brief relationship with a man.

16. "Dignity/Milwaukee Celebrates Twenty Years of Giving, Love and Faith," *Wisconsin Light*, March 16–29, 1995, 5.

17. Rembert Weakland, "Who Is Our Neighbor?," *Catholic Herald*, July 19, 1980, clipping, Box 5, Folder 11, David Clarenbach Papers.

18. "Milwaukee Rights Law?," *GPU News*, June 1980, 6; Kulieke, "On, Wisconsin," 6.

19. Charles J. Sykes, "Gay Rights Measure Still Alive, Officials Say," *Milwaukee Journal*, June 21, 1980, 9; "City Council Passes Gay Rights Ordinance," *Milwaukee Journal*, July 8, 1980, 1; "Milwaukee Rights Law?"

20. Andrea Rottmann, "God Loves Them as They Are: How Religion Helped Pass Gay Rights in Wisconsin," *Wisconsin Magazine of History* 99, no.2 (Winter 2015-2016), 8.

21. Wagner, *Coming Out, Moving Forward*, 209–213.

22. On the progressive tradition in Wisconsin politics, see Leon Fink, *The Long Gilded Age: American Capitalism and the Lessons of a New World Order* (Philadelphia: University of Pennsylvania Press, 2015), 63–89; Romain D. Huret, *The Experts' War on Poverty: Social Research and the Welfare Agenda in Postwar America*, translated by John Angell (Ithaca, NY: Cornell University Press, 2018), 56–76.

23. Robert Booth Fowler, *Wisconsin Votes: An Electoral History* (Madison: University of Wisconsin Press, 2008), 186–195.

24. Wagner, *Coming Out, Moving Forward*, 213–220.

25. On the history of sodomy statutes during the 1970s and 1980s, see Wesley G. Phelps, *Before Lawrence v. Texas: The Making of a Queer Social Movement* (Austin: University of Texas Press, 2023).

26. William L. Wells (Executive Minister, Wisconsin Baptist State Convention) to Members of the Wisconsin State Legislature, April 10, 1981; Marjorie S. Matthews (The United Methodist Church, Wisconsin) to Members of the Wisconsin State Legislature, April 3, 1981; Ralph P. Ley (President) to Members of the Wisconsin State Legislature, April 1981; Carl R. Simon (Executive Presbyter, The Presbytery of Milwaukee) to Members of the Wisconsin State Legislature, March 20, 1981; Charles T. Gaskell (Episcopal Bishop of Milwaukee) to Members of the Wisconsin State Legislature, February 12, 1981, all in Box 5, Folder 11, David Clarenbach Papers.

27. Ron Gieman, "AB 70: A Look behind the Scenes," *Wisconsin's Escape Magazine*, March 26, 1982, 22.

28. Most Reverend Rembert G. Weakland to John Murtaugh, March 2, 1981, Box 5, Folder 11, David Clarenbach Papers.

29. Reverend Steven J. Scherer (St. Jude's Church, Green Bay, Wisconsin) to Jerome Van Sistine, February 2, 1982, Box 5, Folder 11, David Clarenbach Papers; Wagner, *Coming Out, Moving Forward*, 237.

30. Gieman, "AB 70: A Look behind the Scenes," 22.

31. "Debate on AB 70 Transcript," October 23, 1981, Box 5, Folder 11, David Clarenbach Papers.

32. Rottmann, "God Loves Them as They Are," 11.

33. Journal of the Assembly of the State of Wisconsin, 85th Regular Session, October 23, 1981, Box 5, Folder 20, David Clarenbach Papers.

34. "Moral Majority Attacks AB 70," *Our Horizons*, February 5, 1982, 1.

35. Quoted in "Moral Majority Attacks AB 70."

36. Kulieke, "On, Wisconsin," 8; Dan Allegretti, "Callers, Radio Stations Sparring over Bill for Homosexual Rights," *Capital Times*, February 23, 1982, 25.

37. "Dreyfus' Office Fielded 370 Telephone Calls," *Milwaukee Sentinel*, February 20, 1982, 7.

38. Wagner, *Coming Out, Moving Forward*, 241.

39. Stephen Kulieke, "Wisconsin Governor Signs Gay Rights Bill," *Chicago Gay Life*, March 5, 1982, 1.

40. Lee Sherman Dreyfus, "Statement upon Signing AB 70," n.d., Box 5, Folder 16, David Clarenbach Papers.

41. For more on the rightward direction of the Church in the 1980s and 1990s and O'Connor's clashes with the New York City gay community, see Anthony Petro, *After the Wrath of God: AIDS, Sexuality, and American Religion* (New York: Oxford University Press, 2015), 91–136.

42. Petro, *After the Wrath of God*, 100–108.

43. Kevin Richard-Quader, letter to the editor, *Dignity/USA Newsletter* 21, no. 4 (Summer 1989): 2; "Dignity/Milwaukee Celebrates Twenty Years of Giving, Love and Faith."

44. Christopher B. Daly, "Gay-Rights Bill Passes Massachusetts Legislature: Vote Seen Boosting Chances of National Law," *Washington Post*, November 7, 1989, A16.

45. Quoted in Peter M. Cicchino et al., "Sex, Lies and Civil Rights: A Critical History of the Massachusetts Gay Civil Rights Bill," *Harvard Civil Rights-Civil Liberties Law Review* 26, no. 2 (Summer 1991): 594.

46. Keith Clark, "New Jersey Approves State Gay Rights Law," *Bravo! Newsmagazine*, January 16, 1992, 1; Rex Wockner, "Gay Rights for New Orleans," *Outlines*, January 1992, 18; Betsy Brown, "Pro-Gay Activists Clash with Right Wing at Salem Hearing," *Women's Press*, March-April 1987, 4; Chris Nealon, "Gay Rights Measure Defeated in Florida," *Gay Community News*, September 9–15, 1990, 1; Jane Gottlieb, "Assembly Votes for Gay Rights," in unidentified newspaper, Series II: Subject Files, Box 1, Folder 2, Empire State Pride Agenda Records, Division of Rare and Manuscript Collections, Cornell University Library, Ithaca, New York.

47. "Gay Rights Bill is Law in Hawaii: Governor Signs Bill First Day He Received It," *Hawaii: The Gay Community News*, May 1991, 1.

48. "Catholics Lobby for Gay Rights in Illinois House," *Second Stone*, July/August 1993, 6.

49. Quoted in "Catholics Lobby for Gay Rights in Illinois House."

50. David Brown, "Senate Committee Blocks Gay Rights Bill," *State Journal Register*, May 6, 1993, 1.

51. David O'Connor, "Vatican Out of Sync with Most Catholics," *Bay Area Reporter*, July 23, 1992, 1; "Vatican Out of Touch with Followers," *American Gay and Lesbian Atheist*, September 1992, 5; Laura Sessions Step, "Vatican Supports Bias against Gays: Church Says Government Must Protect Traditional Family," *Washington Post*, July 17, 1992, A1.

13

Paul Wellstone and the Reshaping of Minnesota's Populist-Progressive Tradition

MICHAEL C. STEINER

❖ ❖ ❖ ❖ ❖ ❖ ❖ ❖ ❖ ❖ ❖ ❖ ❖ ❖ ❖ ❖

On November 6, 1990, a largely unknown forty-six-year-old professor and community organizer, Paul Wellstone, won an upset Senate victory over an established sixty-year-old Republican incumbent and businessman, Rudy Boschwitz. The unconventional political scientist from Carleton College and underdog champion of Minnesota's Democratic-Farmer-Labor Party (DFL) soon received a flood of messages from ecstatic DFL supporters. Their letters, postcards, and notes reveal a distinctive strain of Left-leaning politics that had characterized Minnesota since the 1930s. They also indicate how a feisty professor, politician, and transplant from the South known for his humor and for proclaiming "I'm short, I'm Jewish, and I'm liberal" deeply influenced a northern state's democratic ethos, giving it a more inclusive embrace.[1] During his thirty-three years in Minnesota, from his arrival from North Carolina in 1969 till his tragic death in a plane crash along with his wife Sheila, daughter Marcia, and five others on October 25, 2002, eleven days before his almost certain third term reelection to the Senate, Wellstone invigorated Democratic politics, created grassroots movements, and brought new life to Minnesota's progressive-populist tradition.[2]

The newly elected senator received praise from union members in the Mesabi Iron Range and farm activists on the prairie, from college- and non-college-educated voters, from radical activists and the Catholic hierarchy. Several congratulations captured the distinctive spirit and transformative message of his campaign. Twin Cities banker and philanthropist George H. Dixon praised Wellstone for being "spunky, extremely energetic and very assertive" and added, "In my home is a bedsheet and on it are painted these words, 'First Bank screws Carleton students, Minnesota farmers, Hormel workers, South African Blacks!' I believe you had something to do with its creation. Now, whatever its original intent, it has become a memento of my affection for Carleton." Liberal talk show host D. J. Leary wrote, "Your commitment to caring about things that have stirred my passions over the years—young people, Indian peoples, the disenfranchised and the disabled—has aroused in me a new sense of hope that I haven't known since Senator Humphrey died." Stressing that Wellstone had "picked up the dimming torch for common people," Leary concluded: "You are, quite honestly, one of the most decent people I have ever found in American politics."[3]

The most sweeping tribute highlighting Wellstone's distinctive contribution to Midwestern populist politics came from leftist civil rights attorney Kenneth E. Tilsen, the son-in-law of Minnesota radical Meridel Le Sueur. "You have an opportunity singularly unique in American history—totally unprecedented," he wrote. "Most of the great populist senators of the Midwest were racist or indifferent to the crucial problems of race in America. Some were isolationists—others severely limited in their vision. You have changed politics in Minnesota forever and have an opportunity to influence political change in the country."[4]

This chapter traces how a transplanted political scientist with a distinctive East Coast–Southern–Jewish background profoundly influenced the political culture of Minnesota, the Midwest, and the nation. After providing an overview of Paul Wellstone's accomplishments in the last twelve years of his life, it explores the sources of his progressive-populist vision, before and after his arrival in Minnesota in 1969.

AN UPSTART PROFESSOR AND GRASSROOTS POLITICIAN

Wellstone was not the first Minnesotan to address race and isolationism and transform the state's politics. Harold Stassen, a progressive Republican governor from 1939 to 1942, helped establish the United Nations in 1945 and was instrumental, in historian Hy Berman's words, "in moving the State from a frightened porcupine in foreign affairs to embracing its internationalist role." Hubert Humphrey, who helped create the DFL in 1944 and played a central role in expanding the nation's sense of racial justice, memorably declared at the Democratic National Convention in 1948: "My friends, to those who say that we are rushing this issue of civil

Figure 13.1. Paul and Sheila Wellstone campaigning in October 1996. Image provided and permission granted by photographer Terry Gydesen.

rights, I say to them we are 172 years late. . . . The time has arrived in America for the Democratic Party to get out of the shadow of states' rights and to walk forthrightly into the bright sunshine of human rights."[5]

Wellstone arrived in Minnesota in 1969, and his decades as an activist professor, community organizer, and political protestor brought new life to Humphrey's ideals. Like Humphrey, Wellstone was a joyful campaigner, vowing to serve "always, with a twinkle in my eye . . . the Democratic wing of the Democratic Party."[6] In contrast to his stern friend and fellow populist Bernie Sanders, he was admired for his disarming humor. "Some people are here to fight for the Rockefellers," Wellstone declared. "I'm here to fight for the little fellars."[7] His close friend and Minnesota Senator Al Franken described him as "a tireless, passionate champion. Paul made us all feel better."[8] Opposed to fake populists who cater to the masses while serving the super-rich, he was a populist with a multiracial vision who lived among the working- and middle-class constituents he championed. "I don't represent the big oil companies, I don't represent the big pharmaceutical companies, I don't represent the Enrons of this world," he declared. "They already have great representation in Washington. It's the rest of the people that need it."[9]

Wellstone represented "the rest of the people" by advancing universal health care, public education, and civil rights, while fighting against isolationism, racism, and militarism. In the process, he expanded the traditional Midwestern populist-progressive base. "Instead of relying solely on an agrarian, trade union base of supporters," Bill Lofy stressed, Wellstone "forged impressive coalitions with environmentalists, laborers, immigrants, gays, and lesbians, and people of color."[10] Arguing that "politics is not about left, right, or center. It is about speaking to the concerns and circumstances of people's lives,"[11] he helped raise the minimum wage and pushed for free early childhood education, fought to protect pension funds from corporate raiders and expanded health care to cover mental illness, led efforts to combat violence against women, and initiated legislation to aid homeless veterans.[12]

In 1997, as the only senator who had worked directly with welfare recipients, Wellstone began a seven-month national "poverty tour" to raise public awareness. He listened to the concerns of disadvantaged people in impoverished schools in Chicago, Los Angeles, and Baltimore, as well as Harlan County, Kentucky, and northern Minnesota, and in archaic mental health facilities in the South, and brought their concerns to the Senate floor.[13] Radical activist Ralph Nader emphasized that "Paul and Sheila Wellstone were always there for the poor, the homeless, the sick, and the defenseless.... Senator Wellstone always wanted to see situations for himself—in Bosnia, Thailand, Columbia, American prisons."[14] In one of his first Senate actions in January 1991, Wellstone courageously voted against the American-led Gulf War; in his last vote, only a few days before his death in 2002, he opposed the second invasion of Iraq. He was the antithesis of the pseudo populism of rancor and resentment often promoted by the Right, both during and after his lifetime.

"Paul Wellstone identified passionately with people at the bottom, people in trouble, people in the rough," Garrison Keillor wrote. "He was an old-fashioned Democrat who felt more at home with the rank and file than with the rich and famous. Paul walked the walk. He was a wonder."[15] Wellstone's close friend and campaign manager, Jeff Blodgett, described his "passion for people—he loved to listen to their stories and hear about their lives" and combined this with "a populist, progressive agenda based on what he called 'kitchen table issues': decent jobs, health care, good education, and security in retirement."[16] Stressing the need for universal health care, he would often cite activist Fannie Lou Hamer's straightforward complaint, "I'm sick and tired of being sick and tired." Journalist Joe Conason emphasized how "other politicians exude the common touch, real or counterfeit, and then betray the waitresses and busboys by voting against the minimum wage. With Wellstone, there was neither doubt nor contradiction."[17]

Wellstone was gifted with the ability to transform peoples' blind angst into constructive action. During his first Senate term he described being "confronted everywhere with the deep-seated anger of countless ordinary Americans" feeling ignored by politicians. Speaking as "an outsider on the inside," he stressed, "We won't accept our exclusion from the political process.... We deeply believe in the system of representative democracy and in the power of citizens to change what should be changed." "The politics of anger could lead to the assertion of citizen involvement and control of this government," he concluded, "or it could lead to erosion of our fundamental belief in representative democracy."[18] The "populist part," he stressed, "can't just be anger. St. Augustine said hope has two lovely daughters, anger and courage. Anger at the way things are and courage to see that they can be better. There's got to be a belief that we can be better," he concluded. "We made a theme of that, and I think it resonated with people."[19]

Wellstone achieved his distinctive strain of constructive populism through experiences both inside and outside the state. A study of the sources of his politics suggests its renewed significance for the nation in the second decade of the twenty-first century.

A JEWISH, EAST COAST, SOUTHERN BACKGROUND, AND SHEILA, 1944–1969

Paul David Wellstone was born in Washington, DC, on July 21, 1944, the second son of Minnie and Leon Wellstone, and grew up in a lower-middle-class neighborhood in Arlington, Virginia. His father had immigrated from Russia in 1914 as a seventeen-year-old on scholarship to study mathematics, and he remained in the United States after his family disappeared in 1917 as a casualty of the Bolshevik Revolution. Leon, who changed his last name from Wexelstein to Wellstone to blunt anti-Semitism, was fluent in ten languages and a prolific yet unpublished fiction writer. He corresponded with a number of prominent intellectuals, including Felix Frankfurter and Edward R. Murrow, and pursued a series of low-level careers as a journalist, an economist, and finally as a Russian translator for the US Information Agency in Washington, DC. Paul's mother, Minnie, was born on New York's Lower East Side to Russian immigrant parents, and she grew up steeped in Jewish socialist politics and devotion to the working class.[20]

Paul was deeply influenced by his father's intellectual zest and his mother's emotional commitment to fighting injustice. As an adolescent, he would sit with his father and discuss Abraham Heschel, Martin Buber, and other activist philosophers over hot tea and sponge cake and listen to Leon "talk about the world—about books, ideas, writing, knowledge, education . . . about persecution . . . and human rights" and the need "to love the First Amendment, and to love our country." Describing his father as "the wisest person I've ever known" who inspired his thirst for truth, Paul concluded it was not surprising that "I became a college teacher" and "an internationalist, interested in the world." Combining his father's love of learning "with my mother's passion for workers and fighting for the underdog," he realized, "you pretty much have the making of a life and a philosophy!"[21]

Paul's brother Stephen was seven years older, and his sudden plunge into mental illness when he was nineteen, and the financial and emotional suffering it brought to the Wellstone family, deeply affected Paul. The experience of his brother being "unjustly shunned, treated as an outcast" and his family being stigmatized and impoverished stuck with him. Visiting his brother at the only facility they could afford, twelve-year-old Paul was shocked. "It was a snake pit," he recalled. "I have the image of it in my mind right now. It will never leave me." Stephen's tragedy exhausted his family's resources, ending their hopes to achieve middle-class stability, and this stark injustice shaped Paul's passion to provide universal health care.[22] After a troubled early adolescence, partially caused by shame over his family's near-poverty, Paul followed his parents' devotion to learning and hard work, becoming an honors student and wrestling champion and earning an academic scholarship to the University of North Carolina in 1962.

His early life was also shaped by his future wife and life partner, Sheila Ison, who came from a radically contrasting background. She had moved to northern Virginia from Appalachia with her upwardly mobile Southern Baptist family that traced its roots back to the Kentucky coal-mining town of Kingdom Come. She and Paul met in 1960 when they were sixteen in Ocean City, Maryland—he was "this cute guy on the beach with muscles" she recalled.[23] They fell in love and were married in July 1963, a week after they turned nineteen, and forged a mutually creative lifelong relationship. "I was taken by her freckles. I came to love her in a hurry," Paul remembered. "Everyone who ever met him," Garrison Keillor recalled, "knew that he lived a whole life and that he and Sheila were crazy about each other. To be in love with one person for 38 years is nothing you can fake: Even the casual passerby can see it."[24]

Others testified to their vital relationship. Senator Patrick Leahy stressed that "it is impossible to talk about our colleague, Paul Wellstone, without mentioning Sheila Wellstone. They were inseparable," and Senator Christopher Dodd paid tribute to her role in passing the Violence Against Women Act in 1994, emphasizing, "If there are women today who are suffering less because of domestic violence, you can thank Sheila Wellstone who arrived here a decade ago and wanted to make this a matter of business of the U.S. Senate." Hillary Clinton recalled of Sheila that "she was made of steel" and that her persistence in "looking for ways to help and to shed the spotlight . . . into the darkest corners of human misery set her apart."[25]

Sheila Wellstone's legislative achievements began in the early 1990s soon after Paul's upset Senate victory, when, according to Kay Harvey, "those who noticed her . . . dubbed the couple co-senators." Senator Joe Biden, who worked closely with Sheila on domestic violence legislation, thanked Minnesota "for sending us two for one." One of Sheila's co-workers who helped her establish halfway houses nationwide for battered women testified that "her work saved the lives of countless numbers of women from danger and even death."[26] Looking back at her influence, journalist John Nichols concluded that "Paul Wellstone came to the Senate as an economic populist with a penchant for peace and social justice causes. Shelia Wellstone helped him to recognize that passing legislation to protect abused women was central to achieving justice."[27]

For the first decades of their marriage, Sheila focused on her growing family, working as a librarian to support Paul through his undergraduate and graduate school years at Chapel Hill, and raising their children, David, Marcia, and Mark. She was a moderating influence on her impetuous partner. "She tells me if she thinks I'm making a mistake," Paul acknowledged. "The difference between the two of us is that I tend to be emotional and instinctual. I make decisions very quickly. . . . Sheila is a person who steps back and says before you do this, you should wait, you should think about it."[28] Their close friend Jeff Blodgett stressed that "they did everything together" and that "Sheila was a steady rock for Paul" who "allowed him to blow off steam." Their oldest son described his mother's relationship with his impulsive father, stressing, "She loved his passion, but worried sometimes about his judgment," and concluded that "in her own way she was every bit as much a fighter as my father. . . . My mom was everything to us. My dad wasn't who he was without my mom."[29]

As newlyweds in North Carolina in the early 1960s, the Wellstones were soon drawn into local civil rights and student protest movements They were shocked by a 1964 confrontation in Chapel Hill in which angry whites beat up civil rights workers, and witnessed a Ku Klux Klan rally and cross burning where Grand Dragon Robert Shelton, under the protection of state police, urged violence against Blacks and "Christ-killing Zionist Jews." Deeply affected by such experiences, Paul entered the PhD program in political science in 1966 determined to become a teacher-activist and "began a long career of provoking authorities" by marching for open housing, advocating for Black cafeteria workers on strike, bringing students to political demonstrations, and refusing to teach orthodox text books that led to his banishment as a departmental instructor.[30]

His doctoral dissertation, "Black Militants in the Ghetto: Why they Believe in Violence," was based on oral histories done with 175 inner-city residents in Durham, North Carolina, during the summer of 1968. Researched and written after the assassinations of Martin Luther King Jr. and Robert Kennedy in April and June of that year, his study is filled with quotations from James Baldwin, Ralph Ellison, Eldridge Cleaver, Richard Wright, and other Black writers. It documents deep "anger with politicians" and "a high degree of militancy" in an "explosive city" where nearly 50 percent of Black residents "favor rioting as a way to make whites listen to their demands."[31]

Wellstone urged local officials to not only hear but also meet the needs of aroused ghetto residents to transform justified anger into constructive reform. "We live in a real world with real problems," he argued, and professors must move "toward making policy recommendations" with "the satisfaction of knowing that we have tried to influence the course of events." "Hopefully," he concluded, "we have something to contribute toward the improvement and even solution of serious social problems."[32] Wellstone's engaged scholarship along with his experience fighting for racial and economic justice in the South laid the groundwork for decades of academic activism and community organizing awaiting him in the Midwest.

TEACHING, ORGANIZING, AND ACHIEVING A MORE INCLUSIVE MIDWESTERN POPULISM, 1969–1990

Within months of completing his PhD, in spring 1969, twenty-five-year-old Wellstone accepted a tenure-track position in the Government Department at Carleton College in Northfield, Minnesota. He and Sheila were reluctant to move to this small college in a far-off region famous for brutal winters and taciturn folk. "We would have liked to have stayed in the South," Paul admitted, but they soon embraced the college and its students, the state, and its people. He formed lasting friendships with other activist professors, including physicist Barry "Mike" Casper, political scientist Norman Vig, and mathematician Sy Schuster, and embraced the culture surrounding the college. "I fell in love with the land," he recalled in a 1990 interview. "I loved the back roads of Rice County. Got to know a lot of farmers. It just penetrated my heart and soul."[33]

He was impressed with the civic sensibility of the Minnesotans he and Sheila met and their connection to the state's Democratic Farmer-Labor tradition. "More people than I'd known before paid attention to issues and wanted an honest politics," he noted. "Their deep respect for working people" reflected "a state with a sense of sympathy for people who are struggling." He learned much from his friendships with nearby hard-pressed farmers, especially Terese and Phil Van Zuilen, who "became my teachers about agriculture." "In a lot of ways," he concluded, "my politics has been rooted in the working people I've met over the years in Minnesota."[34]

He was drawn to what political theorists describe as the state's strong "moralistic political culture" and "communitarian spirit" shaped by early Yankee and Scandinavian settlers who forged a vigorous labor movement and focused on higher education and social equality.[35] The example of Minnesota's immensely popular left-wing governor from the 1930s, Floyd B. Olson, who despite strong currents of anti-Semitism in the state, forged a coalition between Scandinavian and Jewish constituents and declared in 1934, "I am frank to say I am what I want to be. I am a radical," had a vivid impact on Wellstone.[36] He was also influenced by the legacy of Hubert Humphrey, whose public stand as mayor of Minneapolis against the city's rampant racism and anti-Semitism in the mid-1940s and rousing 1948 convention speech were embedded in public memory. Humphrey's fight, in the words of a recent biographer, against "the Northern brand of Jim Crow" and his awareness of "how racial discrimination ran parallel to anti-Semitism, one form of hatred reinforcing the other," influenced the young professor.[37]

At the same time, Wellstone brought a wider ethnic and racial sensibility to his new state. His colleague Mike Casper, also newly arrived from the East Coast, recalled: "There was something about growing up in the Washington area, where local news is always national news, and maybe because from Jewish traditions, that made us similar." "Our politics were not quite the same as Midwestern populism," he continued, "but still we both grew up with the idea of struggling against the rich and the powerful and we both were ... ready to join in the populist tradition in the Midwest when we arrived at Carleton."[38]

As Wellstone began teaching, he assigned classroom readings from Minnesota activists and politicians he admired. His students recalled charged discussions on readings by Floyd B. Olson, Meridel Le Sueur, Hubert Humphrey, and Eugene McCarthy.[39] As a close friend and historian at neighboring St. Olaf College recalled, "Paul managed to soak up and place himself squarely in the Midwestern farmer-labor tradition, while also bringing to it the inspiration of the Southern Civil Rights movement and the pragmatism of the community organizing tradition."[40] With this potent combination of ideologies and his fiery personality, the young professor quickly became a popular figure on campus. "A lot of students . . . would take a Wellstone course to have had the Wellstone experience," one colleague recalled. "It was sort of like a Tilt-a-Whirl ride. It was something to experience."[41]

By his second semester, Wellstone was teaching action-oriented classes that merged an appreciation of Midwestern radical populism with Southern grassroots activism and that inspired students to tackle injustice. In a brief article, published a year after starting at Carleton, he brashly declared that "effecting rapid political and social change . . . is what I desperately want. The war is not over, people in our country are still poor and starving, and our environmental problems are getting worse."[42] Following famed activist Ella Baker's adage, "Give people light and they will find a way," he stressed listening to people at the grass roots and allowing them to forge their own solutions. His course "Social Movements and Grass Roots Organizing" drew an overflow of students and attracted radical guest speakers, including community activists Myles Horton from Appalachia and Saul Alinsky from Chicago, grass-roots advocate Francis Fox Piven from New York, and folksinger Si Kahn from North Carolina.[43]

By the mid-1970s, he directed Carleton's urban studies program in Chicago, helping students begin community organizing a decade before twenty-six-year-old Barack Obama began his political career there also as an Alinsky-inspired organizer. Describing Paul's pragmatic, action-oriented approach, his friend, political scientist Norman Vig, stressed, "He never got involved in any elaborate political philosophy, never really got into Marxist theory, but always adhered to simple populist principles. It wasn't really a philosophy; it was an outlook. How can you get the poor and powerless to get power and social notice, better living standards and material benefits?"[44]

Another close friend, Sy Schuster, recalled, "Paul's view of political science was that it was an instrument to help people improve their lives" and noted that by the beginning of his second year, he made waves in his department by signing up thirty students in an independent study to do fieldwork armed with Alinsky's manifesto, *Rules for Radicals*, to interview local residents about their experience of poverty. Describing this

Figure 13.2. Paul Wellstone teaching Summer Session, Carleton College, 1970. Permission of the Carleton College Archives.

mobilization project as "activism par excellence," Schuster stressed that it "didn't sit well with Paul's senior colleagues."[45] Although it led to the creation of a significant grassroots antipoverty movement, Organization for a Better Rice County (OBRC) in the early 1970s, and would result in the publication of Wellstone's first book, *How the Rural Poor Got Power: Narrative of a Grass-Roots Organizer*, in 1978, his unorthodox methods raised the hackles of many senior colleagues who saw him as an unruly firebrand with little respect for traditional scholarship.[46]

Wellstone raised alarms when he led a student strike that shut down classes in protest of the invasion of Cambodia in early 1970, and he distressed administrators after being arrested twice: at an antiwar protest on the steps of the Federal Building in Minneapolis in May 1970, and a few years later while protesting farm foreclosures at a local bank. Beginning in 1973, he helped organize the anti-powerline campaign among frustrated farmers in west-central Minnesota that included civil disobedience and sabotage and led to his second book, coauthored with Barry M. Casper, *Powerline: The First Battle of America's Energy War*, in 1981.[47] In addition to rural activism, he helped organize striking meat-packers in southern Minnesota, supported miners' grievances on the Mesabi Iron Range, and walked picket lines with striking cafeteria workers in Northfield.[48]

Throughout his early years at Carleton, Wellstone performed a perilous balancing act, juggling academic expectations and community activism. He was more consumed with organizing than publishing, and this raised questions about his survival as a college professor. "You have to act on your courage," Wellstone recognized in a 1990 interview, "to combine teaching with changing the world to become a better place." As his mentor and close friend Myles Horton noted after visiting Carleton, "Paul is one in a million. Few, if any, can do what he does in working-class communities and still hang on at a college like this."[49]

In fall 1973 his department chair, Hartley Clark, asked him to submit an evaluation to renew his contract, a sudden request made a year earlier than required by normal protocol. In January 1974 he was shocked to learn that his department, along with Carleton's president and board of trustees, had decided, based on what they deemed inadequate scholarship and questionable teaching, to terminate his position with one year's notice. As Robert Tisdale, then associate dean, recalled, "The political science department wanted to keep its hands clean of advocacy, even if it was only support for democratic organizing and pressure on the System for greater equity and responsiveness to human needs.... Paul's activities to encourage voting offended their idea of whatever passes for objectivity in political science."[50]

News of Wellstone's firing ignited a student rebellion in which more than half of Carleton's 1,600 students signed a petition demanding the decision be reversed. After months of mounting protests and negative publicity, the college agreed to submit Wellstone's case to an outside review, during which two highly respected political scholars—Peter Bachrach from Temple University and Ira Katznelson from Columbia University—visited campus, examined documents, and issued forcefully positive recommendations, praising Wellstone's teaching and maverick scholarship. By fall 1974, after being informed by the reviewers that administrators "had violated so many rules of proper tenure procedure" that Carleton could be nationally sanctioned,[51] the college reversed itself and granted Wellstone early tenure, several years ahead of schedule. Recalling this emotional rollercoaster twenty-six years later, he noted: "In one year, I went from being fired to being the youngest (age twenty-seven) tenured professor in the history of Carleton."[52]

During the next sixteen years Wellstone redoubled his role as an activist professor while being drawn into electoral politics. He continued to teach fiery classes and promote community organizing in the Myles Horton–Saul Alinsky tradition, believing at the time that "organizing people for power and direct action . . . was the only way to succeed" and that "running for office was a waste of time." He recalled how in 1981 a student, Jeff Blodgett, challenged this position in class by vigorously arguing for "electoral politics as a way to effect social change." "Over the years, I came around to Jeff's point of view," Wellstone acknowledged, "and nine years later he became the manager of my 1990 campaign. He again managed my 1996 campaign. It is a strange feeling to have your political life depend on former students!"[53] Sy Schuster put it more strongly, recalling that Wellstone "despised electoral politics and said so in class" until Blodgett, who became Paul's close friend and adviser, spoke out in class. "Jeff said you should not write off electoral politics. And so Paul eventually joined the DFL and became an electoral politician," beginning by running for Minnesota state auditor in 1982, then serving as Jesse Jackson's statewide presidential campaign manager in 1988, and culminating in his come-from-behind victory for the US Senate in 1990.[54]

Wellstone's subsequent political career was not flawless. Passionate and impetuous, he was often hindered by quick decisions and inconsiderate words. "My father was not only wickedly smart and generous with his understanding and insight," his oldest son recalled, "but he was incapable of sugarcoating anything or mincing words."[55] Despite Sheila's moderating influence, he was capable of reckless blunders sometimes salvaged by self-deprecating candor and humor. Within a few weeks of taking office in January 1990, for example, he held an impassioned antiwar press conference in front of the Vietnam Veterans' Memorial, an act that infuriated veteran groups. Although he quickly apologized and became a passionate advocate for veterans' health care, his habit of speaking before thinking was a liability as well as an asset to his reputation and political legacy.[56]

From his arrival at Carleton College in 1969 until his death thirty-three years later on the verge of winning his third term in the US Senate in 2002, Paul Wellstone exerted an increasingly significant influence on the populist-progressive politics of Minnesota and the Midwest. After growing up on the East Coast as the son of Jewish parents with deep sympathies for the working class and being educated in North Carolina during a significant phase of the civil rights movement, Paul, along with Sheila and their young family, moved to a dramatically different region where they would develop a distinctive form of activist grassroots populism that gave new life to the progressive traditions of their adopted state and the nation as a whole. Through his efforts as an inspiring teacher, open-minded community organizer, and jubilant campaigner promoting kitchen-table issues, Wellstone forged an expansive populism of hope and generosity that was the antithesis of the narrow populism of rancor and resentment promoted by right-wing demagogues during his lifetime and with increasing malice in the present.

Twenty years after Paul and Sheila Wellstone's deaths, the need for a resurgence of their generous, joyful populism is more urgent than ever, and one can hope that a newer generation of Midwestern populists, including Sherrod Brown, Amy Klobuchar, Pete Buttigieg, Gretchen Whitmer, Michelle Obama, and Minnesota governor and vice presidential candidate Tim Walz, who trained in the Wellstone tradition, can make use of their remarkable legacy.[57] In doing so, they and others might take a lesson from Wellstone's exuberant approach to fighting injustice and making the world a better place. They might listen closely to a fiery passage that he often quoted. He would remind audiences of the great abolitionist Wendell Phillips, who throughout the 1840s and 1850s bravely beseeched crowds to know that "slavery is a moral outrage, it should be abolished." "Wendell Phillips wouldn't give an inch," Wellstone continued. "And after he finished speaking and a friend came up to him and said 'Wendell, why are you so on fire?' Wendell said to his friend, 'Brother May, I'm on fire because I have mountains of ice before me to melt.'"[58] Like other great American radicals, Paul Wellstone persistently reminded us that we have mountains of ice to melt and that if we work together it can be done and lead to a truly equitable society.

NOTES

I am indebted to Carleton College archivists Nat Wilson, Tom Lamb, and Eric Hilleman; to Paul Wellstone's colleagues Jeff Blodgett, Bill Lofy, Robert Tisdale, and Al Franken who generously agreed to be interviewed; and to my friends George Brosi, Mark Cowett, Paul Felder, and especially Leila Zenderland for editorial advice.

1. See Robert L. Borosage, "Remembering Paul Wellstone: The Dreamer's Realist," *HuffPost*, December 28, 2012, for a discussion of this line from Wellstone's stump speech.

2. For a thoughtful personal account of the plane crash in northern Minnesota, see Paul David Wellstone Jr., *Becoming Wellstone: Healing from Tragedy and Carrying on My Father's Legacy* (Center City, MN: Hazeldon Foundation, 2012), xi–xvi. The most detailed narrative of the 1990 campaign is Dennis J. McGrath and Dane Smith, *Professor*

Wellstone Goes to Washington: The Inside Story of a Grassroots U.S. Senate Campaign (Minneapolis: University of Minnesota Press, 1995). See also Terry Gydesen, with Jeff Blodgett, *Twelve Years and Thirteen Days: Remembering Paul and Sheila Wellstone* (Minneapolis: University of Minnesota Press, 2003); *Paul Wellstone: Late a Senator of Minnesota: Memorial Addresses and Other Tributes* (Washington, DC: US Government Printing Office, 2003); Bill Lofy, *Paul Wellstone: The Life of a Passionate Progressive* (Ann Arbor: University of Michigan Press, 2005); and Bill Lofy, ed., *Politics the Wellstone Way: How to Elect Progressive Candidates and Win on Issues*, (Minneapolis: University of Minnesota Press, 2005).

3. George H. Dixon to Paul Wellstone, November 8, 1990, and D. J. Leary to Paul Wellstone, November 12, 1990, both in Box 1, Paul D. Wellstone Papers, Carleton College Archives, Northfield, Minnesota; John R. Roach, Catholic Archbishop of Saint Paul and Minneapolis, to Wellstone, November 9, 1990, Box 1, Wellstone Papers,

4. Kenneth E. Tilsen to Paul Wellstone, November 13, 1990, Box 1, Wellstone Papers.

5. Hy Berman, with Jay Weiner, *Professor Berman: The Last Lectures of Minnesota's Greatest Public Historian* (Minneapolis: University of Minnesota Press, 2019), 124; Hubert Humphrey, 1948 Civil Rights Speech, Democratic National Convention, in "Hubert H. Humphrey: An Inventory of his Speech Texts," Minnesota Historical Society, Manuscript Collection. Published versions include "Hubert Humphrey's Speech at the Democratic National Convention," *BlackPast* (December 14, 2010). See also Samuel G. Freedman's detailed account of Humphrey's rousing 1948 address and its aftermath in Samuel G. Freedman, *Into the Bright Sunshine: Young Hubert Humphrey and the Fight for Civil Rights* (New York: Oxford University Press, 2023), 221–226.

6. Paul D. Wellstone, *The Conscience of a Liberal: Reclaiming the Compassionate Agenda* (Minneapolis: University of Minnesota Press, 2002), 216.

7. Paul Wellstone, 1990 campaign speech, in Gydesen, *Twelve Years and Thirteen Days*, 9. Interviews with Wellstone's close friends contrasted Wellstone's humor to Sanders's dour sensibility. Michael Steiner, interviews with Al Franken, Bill Lofy, and Jeff Blodgett, December 11, 2021, January 11, 2022, February 13, 2022, respectively.

8. Franken, interview with Michael Steiner, December 11, 2021.

9. Wellstone, cited by Jeff Blodgett, "Portraits of a Passionate Man," in Gydesen, *Twelve Years and Thirteen Days*, 3.

10. Lofy, *Paul Wellstone*, 130.

11. Wellstone, *Conscience of a Liberal*, 29.

12. For a succinct list of his legislative battles and Senate achievements, see "Biography," in *Paul Wellstone: Late a Senator from Minnesota*, v–vi. Jeff Blodgett in his interview, February 13, 2021, emphasized the breadth of Wellstone's pragmatic populism.

13. See Wellstone, "A Trip to Tallulah," in *Conscience of a Liberal*, 58–63, and Lofy, "Going National," in *Paul Wellstone*, 104–105, for descriptions of this tour.

14. Ralph Nader, "A Tribute to Paul Wellstone," *CounterPunch*, November 16, 2002.

15. Garrison Keillor, "Minnesota's Shame," *Salon*, November 13, 2002.

16. Jeff Blodgett, "Portraits of a Passionate Man," in Gydesen, *Twelve Years and Thirteen Days*, 1, 3.

17. Joe Conason, "Paul Wellstone," *The Nation*, July 21, 2003. Wellstone cites Hamer's memorable phrase at the beginning of his chapter "If We Are Not for Our Children, Who Are We For?" in *Conscience of a Liberal*, 73.

18. Paul D. Wellstone, "The Politics of Anger: Reflections of an Outsider on the

Inside." I am indebted to Jeff Blodgett, Wellstone's campaign manager, for a copy of this unpublished speech, given in 1991 or 1992.

19. Paul Wellstone, interviewed by Barry M. Casper, February 1992, Box 1, Wellstone Papers. In a speech before the United Auto Workers in 1998, Wellstone reiterated the need for hopeful courage rather than angry resentment, describing how rural folk "who had no empowering explanation as to why they were losing their farms . . . became fertile ground (no pun intended) for politics of hatred: Posse Comitatus and some of the precursors to the armed militia, anti-Semitics, racists and all the rest." Excerpts cited by Jonathan Tasini, "I Cast My Vote for President: Paul Wellstone," *Working Life*, October 25, 2012.

20. For Leon and Minnie Wellstone's lives, see McGrath and Smith, "Russian Roots," in *Professor Wellstone Goes to Washington*, 21–28, and Lofy, *Paul Wellstone*, 11–19. Leon Wellstone's extensive correspondence, fiction, and other unpublished writings are in Box 3 of the Wellstone Papers.

21. Wellstone, *The Conscience of a Liberal*, 30–31. Wellstone's description of his father is contained in a 1990 campaign interview video, Wellstone Papers. In a 1992 interview, he said of his father, "I think about him literally every day. This determination to succeed as a senator in a way that would make him proud, that's very important." Wellstone interviewed by Barry Casper, February 1992, Wellstone Papers.

22. Paul Wellstone, cited by McGrath and Smith, *Professor Wellstone Goes to Washington*, 24; Bill Lofy, interview with Michael Steiner, January 11, 2022. Also see Wellstone, "A Radicalizing Experience," in his *Conscience of a Liberal*, 55–57, for a fuller account of the impact of his brother's misfortune.

23. Sheila Wellstone, cited by John Nichols, "Sheila Wellstone's Career," *The Nation*, October 22, 2022.

24. Paul Wellstone, rough cut of 1990 campaign video, Wellstone Papers; Garrison Keillor, "Minnesota's Shame."

25. Tributes by Senators Leahy, Dodd, and Clinton in *Paul Wellstone, Late a Senator from Minnesota*, 10, 11, 680.

26. Kay Harvey, "Sheila Wellstone: Driven by Principle and Passion on Domestic Abuse Issue," *MinnPost*, October 25, 2012.

27. John Nichols, "Sheila Wellstone's Career," *The Nation*, October 22, 2002.

28. Paul Wellstone, interviewed by Barry M. Casper, Wellstone Papers.

29. Jeff Blodgett, "Paul Wellstone: Minnesota Populist," Minnesota Public Television, April 27, 2021; Paul David Wellstone Jr., *Becoming Wellstone*, 9, 41.

30. McGrath and Smith, *Professor Wellstone Goes to Washington*, 28–30, quotations, 29; Lofy, *Paul Wellstone*, 23–28.

31. Paul David Wellstone, "Black Militants in the Ghetto: Why They Believe in Violence" (PhD diss., University of North Carolina at Chapel Hill, 1969), 30, 40. His study was considered so controversial that, according to Paul's son, "The FBI sent in agents to seize the dissertation. He eventually got it back, but it took some work—and he was rattled," Paul David Wellstone Jr., *Becoming Wellstone*, 2.

32. Wellstone, "Black Militants in the Ghetto," 83, 84.

33. Paul Wellstone 1990 campaign interview, rough cut, Wellstone Papers.

34. Wellstone, campaign interview.

35. Daniel J. Elazar, "Minnesota—the Epitome of the Moralistic Political Culture," in Daniel J. Elazar, Virginia Gray, and Wyman Spano, eds., *Minnesota Government and*

Politics (Lincoln: University of Nebraska Press, 1999). Also see Klas Bergman, *Scandinavians in the State House: How Nordic Immigrants Shaped Minnesota Politics* (St. Paul: Minnesota Historical Society Press, 2017), 195–220.

36. Floyd B. Olson, Farmer-Labor Convention Address, St. Paul Minnesota, March 27, 1934, in George H. Mayer, *The Political Career of Floyd B. Olson* (Minneapolis: University of Minnesota Press, 1951), 171. "I am a radical in the sense that I want a definite change in the system," Olson continued. "I am not satisfied with tinkering, I am not satisfied with patching, I am not satisfied with hanging a laurel wreath upon burglars and thieves and pirates and calling them code authorities or something else." Full passage cited in *Minneapolis Journal*, March 28, 1934. On Olson's interethnic coalition, see Hyman Berman, "Political Antisemitism in Minnesota during the Great Depression," *Jewish Social Studies* 38 (Summer-Autumn 1976): 247–264; and Berman, *Professor Berman*, 70–74. Also see Carey McWilliams's widely read expose of Minneapolis as a breeding ground of anti-Semitism, "Minneapolis: The Curious Twin," *Common Ground* 15 (Autumn 1946): 61–65; as well as Laura Weber, "Minneapolis: The Curious Twin: A Reexamination," *Middle West Review*, 8 (Spring 2022): 59–75.

37. Freedman, *Into the Bright Sunshine*, 367. See Freedman's vivid discussion of anti-Semitism in Minneapolis, McWilliams's 1946 article, and Humphrey's vigorous response as mayor, 221–226, 265–269.

38. Mike Casper, quoted in McGrath and Smith, *Professor Wellstone Goes to Washington*, 41.

39. Jeff Blodgett interview with Michael Steiner, January 11, 2022. See also Rhonda R. Gillman, *Stand Up! The Story of Minnesota's Protest Tradition* (St. Paul: Minnesota Historical Society Press, 2012); Annette Atkins, "The House that Hubert Built," in Atkins, *Creating Minnesota: A History from the Inside Out* (St. Paul: Minnesota Historical Society Press, 2016), 219–235; and Annette Atkins, "The State I'm In: Hubert Humphrey, Jesse Ventura, Bob Dylan, Garrison Keillor, and Me," *Western Historical Quarterly* 38 (Winter 2007): 501–507.

40. Eric Fure-Slocum cited in Lofy, *Paul Wellstone*, 130.

41. Stephen Schier cited in McGrath and Smith, *Professor Wellstone Goes to Washington*, 32.

42. Paul Wellstone, "Computers and Me," *Carleton: The Voice of the Alumni* 36 (Fall 1970): 43.

43. Wellstone interview with Barry Casper, February 1992. See Wellstone's foreword to Si Kahn's *How People Get Power*, rev. ed. (Washington, DC: National Association of Social Workers Press, 1994); and his tribute to Kahn in Paul D. Wellstone, *How the Rural Poor Got Power* (Amherst: University of Massachusetts Press, 1978), 206.

44. Norman Vig cited in McGrath and Smith, *Professor Wellstone Goes to Washington*, 48.

45. Sy Schuster, "Wellstone Oral History Project Interview with Sy Schuster," February 11, 2003, Wellstone Papers.

46. Wellstone, *How the Rural Poor Got Power*; Schuster interview,

47. Wellstone and Casper, *Powerline: The First Battle of America's Energy War* (Amherst: University of Massachusetts Press, 1981).

48. See Lofy, "Organizing Instead of Publishing," and "Wellstone Discovers Alinsky," in *Paul Wellstone*, 29–33; and Peter Dreier, "Paul Wellstone's Ordinary Life and Extraordinary Legacy," *HuffPost*, October 25, 2015.

49. Wellstone, rough cut of 1990 campaign video, Wellstone Papers; Myles Horton cited in Stephen Preskill, *Education in Back and White: Myles Horton and the Highlander Center's Vision for Social Justice* (Berkeley: University of California Press, 2021), 4.

50. Robert Tisdale to Michael Steiner, June 28, 2022, personal interview, June 30, 2022.

51. Tisdale interview.

52. Wellstone, *Conscience of a Liberal*, 4–7, quotation on 7. See also Lofy, *Paul Wellstone*, 36–38;, and Schuster interview.

53. Wellstone, *Conscience of a Liberal*, 7.

54. Schuster interview.

55. Paul David Wellstone Jr., *Becoming Wellstone*, 40.

56. For a detailed account of several early blunders, including Wellstone's regrettable decision to vote for the 1996 Defense of Marriage Act, see Lofy's chapter "Falling and Recovering" in his *Paul Wellstone*, 65–89. Wellstone discusses this vote this as a personal failure in his *Conscience of a Liberal*, 133–134.

57. See Robert Kuttner, "Our Progressive Populism: Populism Comes in Two Varieties—Progressive and Reactionary," *American Prospect*, August 31, 2010; and Jeff Blodgett, "Paul Wellstone: Minnesota Populist," Minnesota Public Television, April 27, 2021. Also see Ross Barkan, "If You Like Walz's Earthy Politics, You Should Know about Paul Wellstone," *New York Times*, September 15, 2024.

58. Paul Wellstone, Speech before the UAW in 1998, excerpted in Jonathan Tasini, "I Cast My Vote for President: Paul Wellstone." Wellstone used versions of this story throughout his political career. For a succinct example, see the final sentences of *The Conscience of a Liberal*, 216.

PART THREE

Battling the New Right from Nixon to Trump

14

The Rise and Disappearance of Liberal South Dakota

MARC C. JOHNSON

❖ ❖ ❖ ❖ ❖ ❖ ❖ ❖ ❖ ❖ ❖ ❖ ❖ ❖ ❖ ❖

It was hardly a conventional career move for a thirty-one-year-old history professor with a PhD and a young family, and to a person friends advised against it. The job of reviving the South Dakota Democrat Party in the Eisenhower era, a time when Democrats in the state legislature could have caucused on two stools in the Pierre coffee shop, seemed a hopeless task.[1] Yet long before he became a three-term United States senator, a champion of eradicating hunger and ending the Vietnam War, and before his ill-fated presidential campaign in 1972, George McGovern built a competitive Democratic Party in South Dakota. Yet, almost as quickly as a party that could win elections emerged in the 1950s, it collapsed in the twenty-first century. The reasons for the disintegration are many, including the concept of "negative partisanship" at every political level. This phenomenon, as political scientists Alan Abramowitz and Steven Webster describe it, is "like a bitter sports rivalry, in which the parties hang together mainly out of sheer hatred of the other team," resulting in intense "party loyalty, straight-ticket voting, and the increased nationalization of sub-presidential elections."[2] Additionally, in South Dakota and elsewhere, social issues that often energize conservatives—abortion, LGBTQ rights, same-sex marriage—tend to overwhelm state-level concerns, leaving red-state Democrats to either repudiate the national party or embrace unpopular policy.[3] The virtual disappearance of political "moderates" is a problem for both parties, but it is particularly acute for Democrats in a conservative state.[4] Disappeared as well, perhaps, is the urgent tenacity and political vision that a young professor once brought to South Dakota politics. "Liberalism suffered a slow death by a thousand cuts throughout the 1970s and 1980s," as historian Jeffrey Bloodworth put it, a slow death that perfectly coincides with the long slide down of South Dakota Democrats.[5]

The South Dakota Works Progress Administration guide, published in 1938, christened it "The Prairie State," and made clear that visitors expecting to encounter "near-naked Indians, gun toting cowboys, and Calamity Janes" would be disappointed. Instead, South Dakota offered, its substantial Native American population notwithstanding, the "spirit of the pioneer," fashioned from often-unforgiving soil by immigrants, "Germans, Swedes, Norwegians—strongly built and strong of will," and predictively conservative, too, at least most of the time.[6]

South Dakota embraced briefly, like most of the country, Franklin Roosevelt's Democratic Party in the 1930s. Roosevelt won the state's electoral votes and lost only one county in 1932, only the second Democratic presidential candidate ever to win in South Dakota. FDR prevailed again in 1936, but support for Democrats disappeared in 1940, as South Dakota reverted to its conservative instincts. Republican Wendell Willkie won only ten states that year. His largest margin came in South Dakota.[7]

Before McGovern's party building in the 1950s, South Dakota voters had not elected a Democratic governor since Roosevelt's first term. No Democrat had represented the state in the Senate since the early 1940s, and the last congressional win came in 1936. Since South Dakota achieved statehood in 1889, only seven Democrats have represented the state in the Senate, yet for most of the decade of the 1970s, a state with a conservative political tradition as pronounced as any in the nation was represented by the most liberal Senate delegation in the country. In the same period, Democrats occupied the governor's office. In the 1990s, South Dakota again sent two Democrats to the Senate. More recently, no Democrat has won statewide since 2008, and with the relatively recent emergence of a strong correlation between a state's presidential vote and its Senate preferences, the prospect of a modern-day McGovern seems decidedly remote.

This chapter explores how Democrats became competitive in South Dakota and why the party now faces not merely electoral challenges, but as political scientists Robert Saldin and B. Kal Munis have written, "something approaching an existential crisis."[8]

With almost nothing to work with—one newspaperman remarked that George McGovern, with the title of executive secretary, took over the Democratic Party "at a time when you couldn't call it a party"—McGovern relied on old-style, grind it out organizing.[9] He created a finance system—$10 monthly from willing payers—to cover his salary and gas money. He drove his own automobile, crisscrossing South Dakota to meet voters, learn their concerns, and accumulate contacts that were catalogued on forty thousand three-by-five index cards. The cards, containing contact and personal information, were arranged in a shoebox that McGovern organized by county. "Besides a teacher's facility for name recall," as McGovern biographer Thomas Knock has written, and thanks to the card file, "he could also ask how many merit badges Joey still needed to become an Eagle Scout or whether Sophie had finally gotten over those measles."[10] These personal connections blossomed into a statewide organization, but nothing about rebuilding a moribund party was easy or fast. One editor observed that McGovern displayed remarkable patience, "hewing to the old saw, 'Rome wasn't built in a day.'"[11] The challenges were evident when McGovern reportedly walked into a general store in one rural community and said he was told the proprietor was the Democratic county chairman. "Shhh," the man said. "I'd be out of business if my customers knew."[12]

By 1954, McGovern's organizational persistence produced results. Democrats won two dozen seats in the state legislature, while many reelected Republicans saw victory margins decline. Grassroots organizing was critical to creating a competitive party, but farm politics were just as essential. Republican Dwight Eisenhower enjoyed immense personal popularity—South Dakota voters gave Ike more than 69 percent of the vote in 1952—but Eisenhower farm policy, articulated by a doctrinaire, free-market agriculture secretary, Ezra Taft Benson, was deeply unpopular across the Midwest, and in no place more unpopular than in South Dakota. The administration's objective, Benson said, was to "reverse the 20-year trend toward socialism in agriculture." Midwestern farmers were surely repelled by the thought of socialism, but they also heard in Benson's rhetoric a threat—destruction of a New Deal legacy, farm price supports. Senator Karl Mundt, South Dakota's most influential Republican, bluntly told the White House, "Members of Congress on both sides of the Capitol are disgusted and mad at the apparent lack of political savvy on the part of the Secretary of Agriculture."[13]

Benson's unpopularity offered McGovern and Democrats a potent issue and a political opening, as well as a connection to South Dakota's populist tradition. Republican Governor and later Senator Peter Norbeck was among the state's first politicians to successfully navigate issues that impacted an agrarian economy, while also managing farm-state suspicions of big business and Eastern bankers. When, for example, the blossoming Nonpartisan League (NPL) movement, powered by agrarian social reformers—including socialists—attempted to gain a foothold in South Dakota in the 1920s, Norbeck appropriated many of the NPL's populist reforms, but rejected its "radicalism." Norbeck knew winning farmers' loyalty and honing the ability "to sense their desires," as his biographer wrote, were key to electoral success.[14] He developed a state-owned cement plant, grain elevators, and insurance programs, a popular, populist approach to government that would later include broad support for massive publicly funded water projects and even state ownership of rail lines.[15] Historian McGovern certainly understood this activist agrarian legacy and began reminding his audiences: "Vote Democratic, the farm you save may be your own."[16]

By 1956 the organizational work, combined with McGovern's energy and commitment, had revitalized his party. Every county had a party chair, and better candidates were emerging. "They all say that George McGovern rebuilt the Democratic party in South Dakota," one party official grumbled. "Horseshit. George rebuilt the party all right, but it wasn't the Democratic party, it was the McGovern party." McGovern agreed. "If there was to be any possibility for me as a candidate, I had to have Republicans and Independents for me. So, really, I was building two organizations: the party's and my own." McGovern's moment came in 1956. He challenged a lackluster four-term incumbent, Harold Lovre, and won a seat in Congress representing what was then the First Congressional District, the area east of the Missouri River.[17]

McGovern, sensing anger among farmers, pragmatically downplayed his partisan background and tied Lovre to the Eisenhower administration's unpopular programs. Lovre, realizing he was in a fight for political survival, accused McGovern, a decorated World War II veteran, of being soft on Communist China, even as the incumbent was accused of dodging the World War II draft. Eisenhower again carried South Dakota against Democrat Adlai Stevenson, but the president's margin shrunk by ten percentage points from 1952. Republican incumbents won Senate and congressional elections and kept the governor's office, but McGovern broke a barrier. Two years earlier, Lovre won thirty-eight of the forty-four counties in his district, but McGovern flipped the script, winning by nearly eleven thousand votes, running particularly well in rural east river counties and attracting significant Republican and independent support.

The willingness of voters to split their ticket, voting for Eisenhower for president and McGovern for Congress, was widespread and, given today's partisan polarization, remarkable. Eisenhower, for example, carried Beadle County (Huron) by nearly the same margin McGovern did. The pattern repeated in Brown (Aberdeen) and Davison (Mitchell) counties. Voters split tickets, handing winning margins to both Eisenhower and McGovern in twenty-two of the district's counties.[18] McGovern did not win on issues alone, a campaign aide insisted, although the administration's controversial agriculture policy provided a significant opening, but "because they had met him, shaken hands with him, and the second time he remembered their name." McGovern's calm, reassuring, articulate style, a particular Midwestern persona, matched the state's voters. McGovern told one mentor that he enjoyed his "political apprenticeship thoroughly," particularly the "opportunity to know and try to understand people of every possible type."[19] A Democratic template had been created—an in-depth, populist-oriented engagement on the state's vital agricultural issues and a "go everywhere" approach to campaigning. This approach had particular resonance in the Midwest and would serve as a template over many election cycles for, among others, the political careers of farm-state liberals like Birch Bayh of Indiana and Dick Clark of Iowa, fiscally conservative Democrats like Nebraska's James Exon and Wisconsin's William Proxmire, and even former Nonpartisan Leaguers like Quentin Burdick of North Dakota.

Through eighteen years in the Senate, for example, Bayh continued to manage the family corn and soybean farm and relentlessly championed the development of ethanol. Clark garnered national attention in his 1972 Senate campaign when he walked thirteen hundred miles across Iowa, often concentrating his political efforts on rural communities. Like McGovern, Exon chaired the state Democratic Party before running for office. As governor he repeatedly vetoed legislation he thought too profligate, and after moving to the Senate, Exon, comfortable as a conservative, frequently supported Republican budget priorities. Proxmire, often labeled a "maverick," regularly awarded a "Golden Fleece Award" to federal agencies for what he considered wasteful spending. Burdick, a veteran of NPL organizing efforts who earned the title "king of pork" for his dogged advocacy of federal spending, particularly on agricultural projects, was remembered by Senate Republican leader Robert Dole of Kansas as "a tireless fighter for rural America." These successful and long-tenured Midwestern Democrats often charted an independent course from the national Democratic Party and maintained a clear connection to state and regional issues, particularly agricultural issues, a stance that kept them popular—and regularly reelected—even as the national party moved to the political left.[20]

McGovern's rise in South Dakota—and the simultaneous resurrection of his party—did not escape the notice of the state's most influential Republican. Karl Mundt, a political force since going to Congress in 1938—like McGovern, Mundt had been a college professor—was a Midwestern conservative in the mold of Everett Dirksen of Illinois or Nebraska's Roman Hruska. Effective on the stump and a tough partisan, Mundt began his career as a foreign policy isolationist before embracing intense anticommunism. Mundt enthusiastically supported Wisconsin Senator Joseph McCarthy's communist witch hunting and skillfully, if not as crudely, used McCarthy tactics against his opponents. Mundt correctly saw McGovern, the smart, well-spoken college professor, as a threat and plotted to remove the threat, pushing a powerful attack line: essentially contending McGovern was not one with South Dakota—a strategy used repeatedly and ultimately in 1980 successfully against McGovern.[21]

A Mundt associate, Glenn Martz—Martz published a farm newsletter ironically entitled "The Low Down"—asserted in the summer of 1957 that McGovern supported "a communist-front known as the American Peace Crusade." It was a reckless, untrue accusation, and McGovern sued Martz for libel, saying, "I am sick and tired of being forced to prove that I am a loyal American every time an election comes around."[22] When McGovern subsequently linked Mundt to the smear, the allegations unraveled. "As we see it," Bob Lusk, the publisher of the Huron *Plainsman* wrote, "given a dime's worth of evidence, Martz can produce a thousand dollars worth of Communists with the twist of a tongue or the click of a typewriter key."[23] The allegation that McGovern was a closet radical—he had supported Henry Wallace's Progressive Party presidential candidacy in 1948 over Democrat Harry Truman, and never repudiated Wallace's Communist Party backing—surfaced again and again during his career.[24]

Mundt pressed on, recruiting two-term Governor Joe Foss, a legitimate war hero who downed twenty-six Japanese aircraft during World War II, as McGovern's challenger. Foss appeared the ideal opponent: outgoing, ruggedly handsome, a well-known cigar-chomping back slapper who, even at age forty-three, was known as "Old Joe."[25] However, the governor's image was better than his campaign and debate performance against the polished McGovern, who wisely stressed his bipartisan appeal. Playing defense over the still unpopular farm policy and amid a lingering recession, Foss attempted to make McGovern's substantial organized labor support a major issue, while McGovern countered with effective and reassuring performances during a number of joint appearances where Foss appeared stiff and ill-prepared. "What really worries them," McGovern said of Republican leaders, "is that thousands of members of their own party voted for me in 1956."[26]

Eisenhower endorsed Foss, and Richard Nixon campaigned with him in Sioux Falls, but Foss's prediction that Democrats had peaked and were "on the way down" was wildly off the mark.[27] With support from Republican farmers, McGovern won by fourteen thousand votes, carrying Foss's home county and thirty-one of forty-four counties in the district. Ralph Herseth became the first Democratic governor since 1934, and Democrats won elections for lieutenant governor, attorney general, secretary of state, and state auditor, as well as control of the state senate. One banner headline declared the election the greatest Democratic victory since the New Deal.[28] McGovern was entitled to gloat, at least a little. "Most people recognize there are now two strong, evenly balanced political organizations in South Dakota," he said. A McGovern friend wrote to thank him "for having rebuilt the Democratic Party."[29]

As Thomas Knock has noted, McGovern "was becoming especially adroit at integrating agriculture into his own nascent program and plying its intrinsic connection to both the New Deal and his concerns about American foreign policy."[30] With a seat on the House Agriculture Committee, McGovern became recognized, as historian Jon Lauck wrote, "as one of the foremost congressional advocates of the farmer."[31] Still, the carefully calibrated Democratic approach to largely conservative voters had limits, as McGovern discovered when he challenged the biggest force in South Dakota politics in 1960. In a brutal campaign rife with anticommunist and anti-organized-labor sentiment, the young congressman was outclassed and out politicked by Mundt, who utilized his Washington seniority to full advantage—a tactic that would later fail McGovern.[32]

McGovern's first Senate campaign became, as Robert Sam Anson wrote, "an ideological crusade, an epochal confrontation of left and right, or as it was so often cast . . . good and evil." The candidates, each intensely competitive and fiercely ambitious, harbored a genuine dislike for one another. "I don't know how he felt about me," McGovern said later, "but I knew I hated his guts," an attitude he attributed to Mundt's virulent anticommunism and support for McCarthy.[33] McGovern labeled Republican red-baiting "Mundtism," and while the senator carefully avoided open antagonism toward McGovern, he did not shy from delivering a political punch. Mundt's campaign manager told a friend he relished "the enjoyable project of trying to eliminate from the political scene of South Dakota one George McGovern."[34]

Mundt's campaign, with the assistance of helpful editors, tied McGovern and his organized labor support to controversial Teamster's president Jimmy Hoffa, a target Mundt investigated as a member of the Senate Rackets Committee, a panel probing labor union criminal activity. Helpfully, FBI director J. Edgar Hoover effectively endorsed Mundt's reelection. A photo of the senator chatting amiably with Hoover—with Mundt "a stalwart defender against all subversive elements," the director said of him—received generous pre-election play in South Dakota newspapers.[35] The barely veiled insinuation was that McGovern was soft on racketeers and dismissive of communists. It did not help the Democrat's campaign that Hoffa endorsed McGovern, support McGovern had to repudiate.[36]

In a state with a tradition of anti-Catholic sentiment, Mundt also benefited from the manufactured mythology that McGovern, son of a Methodist minister, was a secret Catholic. The smear amplified McGovern's connections to Catholic John Kennedy, the Democratic presidential candidate who would lose South Dakota by a wide margin in 1960. After a well-attended joint appearance with McGovern at the Corn Palace in Mitchell—Kennedy outlined his six-point farm program—the candidate reportedly told his campaign manager and brother, "Bobby, I think we just cost that man a seat in the Senate."[37]

McGovern's loss to Mundt stung the thirty-eight-year-old politician and seemed to signal a return to Republican domination, with Democratic Governor Herseth also losing. Yet a closer look at the results indicates a remarkable willingness by voters to ticket split even in a presidential election year. Richard Nixon won South Dakota in 1960 with 58 percent of the vote, yet Mundt ran six percentage points behind Nixon, while McGovern ran well ahead of Kennedy. For example, in Minnehaha County, the state's largest county, Nixon polled 3,200 more votes than Mundt. In rural Douglas County, Mundt ran five hundred votes behind Nixon. Still, bitter as the loss was, as historians Gretchen Hefner and Catherine McNicol Stock have noted, McGovern "learned one of the most important lessons of South Dakota's agrarian political culture, one echoed in the Populist and New Deal eras as well: to be successful on an anti-Republican platform nearly always requires building on agrarian discontent."[38]

McGovern's loss may have been a blessing. Shortly after the election, Kennedy appointed him to head the Food for Peace program, deepening McGovern's connection to issues of food production and hunger, a career-long passion, while elevating his national profile. From that position McGovern honed what became an important message: food was an economic and foreign policy tool for the United States.[39] By 1962, McGovern was ready for another Senate run, this time against incumbent

Republican Francis Case, a respected sixty-six-year-old legislative workhorse first sent to Congress in 1936. But before the campaign truly commenced, Case died of a heart attack. South Dakota Republicans feuded over a replacement before settling on Joseph Bottum, a frequent candidate who became lieutenant governor in 1960 and was, in the view of one McGovern partisan, "the worst guy they could have picked."[40]

Republican Governor Archie Gubbrud immediately appointed Bottum to fill the Senate vacancy, and the new senator/candidate went on the attack against the Kennedy administration and McGovern. Even as Kennedy's legislative agenda floundered, Bottum charged that the president was behaving like a dictator, while "Democrats try to hide their liberal, often socialistic views, their desire to control everything."[41]

McGovern was portrayed as a tool of the Kennedy White House, "dispatched," as one newspaper suggested, "back to the state to seek the senate seat." Furthermore, Bottum was "a conservative Republican," McGovern "a liberal Democrat," presumably making the choice an easy one for conservative South Dakota voters.[42] McGovern ran a much better campaign than he had against Mundt and still barely won, by 597 votes, and only then after a recount. A switch of five votes per county would have reversed the outcome. Turnout was lower than the presidential election year of 1960, but still the second-highest midterm turnout in state history. McGovern substantially narrowed Mundt's margin of two years earlier in South Dakota's largest counties, and once again voters divided their partisan loyalty, at least in the Senate race. Governor Gubbrud was reelected easily, as were the state's two GOP congressmen, and Republicans won every statewide office.[43]

McGovern was not content to settle into back-bench Senate obscurity, but was determined to become a national figure, a liberal leader from the prairie. His first Senate speech was not, as his constituents might have anticipated, on farm policy, but on Latin America, with McGovern warning "of a dangerous Castro fixation" driving US policy in the region.[44] Less than a year into his first term, McGovern, elected "to work for the land he was born too," as a slick campaign television ad declared, was delivering quixotic if heartfelt Senate speeches advocating diplomatic recognition of "Red China" and deep cuts to defense spending.[45]

Conservative syndicated columnist Fulton Lewis Jr. seized on the new senator's positions to connect McGovern to "a pacifist lobby" and to communist sympathizers, including highlighting McGovern's support for Wallace in 1948.[46] In February 1965, McGovern, one of the first senators to do so, offered a detailed critique of US policy in Vietnam. While not advocating a US military withdrawal, McGovern did endorse negotiations to end the war. It was a sharp break with President Lyndon Johnson, who won a landslide election victory the previous November, capturing forty-four states, including piling up a 55 percent margin in South Dakota. McGovern's critique of Vietnam policy—"early, severely, and persistently" as historian Ahrar Ahmad describes it—put him squarely at odds with Mundt, a Vietnam hardliner.[47] Mundt told an oral history interviewer in 1968 that on matters of foreign policy he, a conservative Republican, was more supportive of a Democratic president than McGovern, who, Mundt said, was guilty of "stabbing" Lyndon Johnson in the back.[48]

McGovern's eventual emergence as the face of American liberalism in the 1970s returned few political dividends at home, while reinforcing the charge that he was too liberal for South Dakota. In time McGovern began to suffer what long-time political reporter Chuck Raasch has described as the phenomenon of a South Dakota politician appearing to become "too big for his britches."[49] Nevertheless, voters at least initially tolerated McGovern's liberalism on national issues so long as he stayed engaged with South Dakota issues, working, for example, to advance irrigation projects or protect family farms. McGovern's work on the Senate Agriculture Committee attracted considerable support. A Sioux Falls businessman, a self-described Republican, for example, purchased a newspaper ad touting McGovern's 1968 reelection, mentioning how fortunate the state was to also have Mundt in the Senate.[50]

George McGovern eventually served three terms in the Senate, flirted with a presidential campaign in 1968, and captured the Democratic nomination in 1972 only to lose the presidency in a landslide, including the embarrassing loss of South Dakota. Yet, even as McGovern was losing badly at home to Richard Nixon, the state's voters again split their tickets, electing an unabashed liberal, James Abourezk, to replace Mundt, who had suffered a debilitating stroke that ended his political career, a loss that left South Dakota Republicans temporarily deficient in star power. Abourezk served one term in the House, only the second Democrat elected in the Second District, and for six years—Abourezk did not seek a second term—South Dakota had the most liberal Senate delegation in the country, a reality that concerned McGovern, who worried that voters might tolerate one South Dakota liberal in the Senate but would baulk at two.[51] As McGovern's appeal eroded after his presidential campaign—he won barely 53 percent of the vote in his 1974 Senate race against a decorated Vietnam veteran who criticized the senator's position on the war and his liberalism in general—he was increasingly seen in South Dakota as less the effective prairie populist and more the embodiment of his party's leftward tilt. McGovern's much publicized Cuba visit in 1975, his chairmanship of the liberal Americans for Democratic Action in 1976, and his consistent advocacy for defense spending cuts solidified the image.[52] Ironically, and at the same time, South Dakota Democrats enjoyed a decade of electoral success even as the seeds of party collapse were sprouting.[53]

Richard Kneip, an energetic, outgoing thirty-seven-year-old state legislator focused on rural development and tax policy, became governor in 1970 and held that office until 1978, still the longest Democratic gubernatorial tenure in state history. For a short period, Democrats commanded a slim majority in the state senate and matched Republican numbers in the state house of representatives.[54] Democrat Frank Denholm captured McGovern's old congressional seat in 1970 and held it for two terms; and in 1978, Tom Daschle, at age thirty-one, began his political rise by barely winning a House seat. Daschle eventually won three Senate terms and developed a national profile to rival McGovern's, serving as both Senate minority and majority leader. Tim Johnson, a veteran state legislator, replaced Daschle in the House and then pulled an upset in 1996, defeating three-term incumbent Larry Pressler, the only Senate Republican defeated that year. Johnson won three Senate terms of his own—three terms having become something of a South Dakota tradition—and survived both an extremely close 2002 race with John Thune—a 524-vote cliffhanger rivaling McGovern's margin in 1962—and a disabling brain hemorrhage that Johnson overcame to win a final term. For eight years, Daschle and Johnson, Democrats from conservative South Dakota, served together in the Senate. With Johnson's retirement in 2014, Democratic South Dakota largely ceased to exist.

The last campaigns of McGovern, Daschle, and Johnson are instructive in understanding the apparent end of liberal South Dakota. McGovern lost his bid for a fourth term in 1980 in the Reagan landslide accompanied by a hard push from the rising "New Right." The campaign was rife with a sense that McGovern's liberalism—"acid, amnesty, and abortion" as critics cast it—had finally and fatally put him at odds with South Dakota.[55] One ad questioning McGovern's values and positions on school prayer and sex education said the senator needed prayers, not votes.[56] The *Washington Post* noted that McGovern became the "biggest trophy yet for the ultra-conservative political movement that is using independent, largely negative campaigns to try to rid the Senate of its most liberal members." The Republican takeover of the Senate in 1980, the first GOP majority in a quarter century, heralded the nationalization of Senate campaigns that has since become a fixture of American politics.[57] McGovern's last campaign was hardly a masterpiece of the grassroots engagement he once championed. His staff literally begged the accomplished retail campaigner to spend more time connecting with voters. McGovern's fate was almost certainly sealed when an unknown primary opponent won 38 percent of the vote with a singular focus on McGovern's often distorted abortion position. The claim that McGovern was out of touch, even estranged from his state, was perfectly illustrated by a pheasant hunting trip late in the campaign that assumed statewide significance when the candidate could not produce the South Dakota driver's license needed to prove his residence.[58]

Daschle witnessed the end of the McGovern era firsthand and seemed committed to avoiding entanglements in national Democratic politics in ways that would alienate voters. Daschle's 1986 Senate campaign against Jim Abdnor, the New Right recruit who defeated McGovern, focused on Reagan's unpopular farm policies, an echo of McGovern's early approach. Daschle styled himself "a moderate," and few candidates worked harder to meet voters where they live. Early in his career, Daschle supported a balanced budget amendment and emphasized that his Catholic faith led him to oppose abortion, positions he later shaded or shed. Ultimately, Daschle's leadership of Senate Democrats, particularly during the George W. Bush presidency when he successfully resisted much of the Republican agenda, including military intervention in Iraq, played as poorly in South Dakota as McGovern's visits with Castro and calls for defense reductions had three decades earlier. And like George McGovern a generation earlier, Daschle, at least in the eyes of a majority of his constituents, embraced a kind of strident national liberalism that held little appeal for South Dakota's many rural, religious, and right-of-center voters. As Jon Lauck observed in his history of Daschle's last race, "his political success first came when he abandoned the politics of Peter, Paul and Mary; his defeat came when he embraced it again."[59] Republican John Thune's defeat of Daschle in 2004 marked the first time in fifty-two years a majority leader lost reelection, and again highlighted, as McGovern's loss had in 1980, the perils of a prairie liberal who becomes a national figure and ends up, or appears to end up, out of step with voters in a fundamentally conservative state.

Johnson's last campaign in 2008 had a decidedly different outcome. Despite being frequently confined to a wheelchair and able to speak only in a halting cadence due to his stroke, Johnson ran a small-town campaign and won easily against an underfunded opponent. Johnson largely avoided national liberal causes, focusing instead on local water projects, Native American concerns, and his position on the Banking Committee, critical to South Dakota's significant financial services industry. One South Dakota banking official said of Johnson's last reelection, while praising his attention to state issues, "historically he hasn't delivered mixed messages . . . he's pretty easy to understand."[60]

Steve Erpenbach, a long-time Democratic Party and Daschle staffer, contends the state party finds itself today essentially where it was in the 1950s—unappealing to conservative voters on many issues and struggling organizationally. As in McGovern's organizing days, Erpenbach said, "From a pure business sense it's hard to be a Democrat. Many keep it under the radar."[61]

Voter registration numbers tell some of the story. With Tim Johnson as the face of South Dakota Democrats in 2009, party registration peaked at 206,000, compared to 243,000 Republicans, and 86,000 independents. By June 2022, Republican registration had grown to 283,000, Democratic numbers declined to 151,000, and independents stood at 141,000. Democratic fortunes in the state legislature were better in 2022 than they were in 1952, but not by much, while the Democratic lockout of the governor's office is now in its fourth decade, twice as long as the drought that existed for Democrats in the days before McGovern's party building commenced.[62]

If there is a road ahead for Democrats in conservative, rural South Dakota it will almost certainly involve a return to the origins of the party's only real, sustained success when populist engagement on agrarian issues held the opportunity to appeal to independents and moderate Republicans. Given the reality of the country's profound partisan polarization, this is no simple task, and South Dakota and Midwestern Democrats continue to struggle to define themselves as distinct from a liberal national party finding increasingly little favor in the heartland. Yet, as historian Cory M. Haala has argued, a period of Democratic success in South Dakota, including the Senate years of Daschle and Johnson, illustrates "the undercurrent of grassroot, liberal populism" that has emerged when Democrats emphasize their opposition to outside forces, including the federal government, that threaten the state's agrarian independence and individualism.[63] That type of pragmatic focus on policy, coupled with reimagining a twenty-first-century equivalent of the tireless grassroots organizer with a shoebox stuffed with three-by-five cards, might constitute a road map out of the wilderness.

NOTES

1. *Rapid City Journal*, May 29, 1953. When McGovern became the Democratic Party's executive director, the party had two members among the 110 South Dakota state legislators.

2. Alan Abramowitz and Steven Webster, "Negative Partisan Explains Everything," *Politico Magazine*, September/October 2017, https://www.politico.com/magazine/story/2017/09/05/negative-partisanship-explains-everything-215534/; Alan I. Abramowitz, *The Great Realignment: Race, Party Transformation, and the Rise of Donald Trump* (New Haven, CT: Yale University Press, 2018), xi.

3. Pew Research Center Religious Landscape Survey, 2014, https://www.pewresearch.org/religion/religious-landscape-study/. The Pew survey found South Dakotans to be more ideologically conservative than voters in other conservative Midwestern states, including North Dakota, Iowa, Nebraska, Kansas, Missouri, and Indiana. A particularly good state-level assessment of the challenges faced by Democrats in a conservative state can be found in Ross Benes, *Rural Rebellion: How Nebraska Became a Republican Stronghold* (Lawrence: University Press of Kansas, 2021).

4. Steve M. Teles and Robert P. Saldin, "The Future Is Faction," *National Affairs*, Fall 2020, https://www.nationalaffairs.com/publications/detail/the-future-is-faction. See also *New York Times*, "The Vanishing Moderate Democrat," June 29, 2022.

5. Jeffrey Bloodworth, *Losing the Center: The Decline of American Liberalism, 1968–1992* (Lexington: University Press of Kentucky), 10.

6. Federal Writers' Project, *A South Dakota Guide* (Works Progress Administration and State of South Dakota, 1938), 1–3.

7. Philip A. Grant Jr. "Establishing a Two-Party System: The 1932 Presidential Election in South Dakota," *Presidential Studies Quarterly* (Winter 1980): 73–79; "Official Election Returns for South Dakota—General Election, November 7, 1940," South Dakota Secretary of State, https://sdsos.gov/elections-voting/assets/historicalelectiondata/1940G.pdf.

8. Robert Saldin and L. Kai Munis, "Go Local, Young Democrat," *Democracy: A Journal of Ideas*, Spring 2022, https://democracyjournal.org/magazine/64/go-local-young-democrat/.

9. Valerie R. O'Regan and Stephen J. Stambough, "From the Grassroots: Building the South Dakota Democratic Party," in Robert P. Watson, ed., *George McGovern: A Political Life, a Political Legacy* (Pierre: South Dakota Historical Society Press, 2004), 40.

10. Thomas J. Knock, *The Life and Times of George McGovern: The Rise of A Prairie Statesman*, (Princeton, NJ: Princeton University Press, 2016), 155.

11. *Rapid City Journal*, November 8, 1953. The *Journal* reprinted a column by Alex Johnson, the editor of the Watertown *Public Opinion*.

12. Robert Sam Anson, *McGovern: A Biography* (New York: Holt, Rinehart & Winston, 1972), 72–73.

13. Edward L. Schapsmeier and Frederick H. Schapsmeier, "Eisenhower and Ezra Taft Benson: Farm Policy in the 1950's," *Agricultural History* 44, no. 4 (October 1970): 369–378. See also Stephen E. Ambrose, *Eisenhower: The President* (New York: Simon & Schuster, 1984), 159–160.

14. Gilbert Courtland Fite, *Peter Norbeck: Prairie Statesman* (Columbia: University of Missouri, 1948), 60–69; 206. Historian Robert L. Morlan writes that Norbeck attacked

the Nonpartisan League as "Socialist agitators" even as the league proposed "much the same things as he recommended." And in his study of the NPL, historian Michael J. Lansing writes that "Norbeck carefully avoided alienating agrarian voters," while hammering the league's leaders and insisting that South Dakota's "farmers are not socialists." See Robert L. Morlan, *Political Prairie Fire: The Nonpartisan League, 1915–1922* (Minneapolis: University of Minnesota Press, 1955), 212; and Michael J. Lansing, *Insurgent Democracy: The Nonpartisan League in North American Politics* (Chicago: University of Chicago Press, 2015), 110.

15. *Los Angeles Times*, March 24, 1986; C. E. Lamberton, "Restructuring a Rail System: South Dakota's Experience from 1976–81," 1983, *Bulletins*, Paper 693, http://openprairie.sdstate.edu/agexperimentsta_bulletins/693.

16. Knock, *The Life and Times*, 159.

17. Anson, *McGovern*, 74–75.

18. "Official Election Returns of South Dakota, November 6, 1956," as compiled by the Secretary of State, https://sdsos.gov/elections-voting/assets/historicalelectiondata/1956G.pdf.

19. Knock, *The Life and Times*, 173, 160.

20. See Robert Blaemire, *Birch Bayh: Making a Difference* (Bloomington: Indiana University Press, 2019); Jerry Harrington, "Dick Clark's Walk across Iowa Earned Him a U.S. Senate Seat 50 Years Ago," *Iowa History Journal* 14, no. 5 (September/October 2022); "Former Senator J. James Exon, 83, Dies," *New York Times*, June 13, 2005; Jay G. Sykes, *Proxmire* (Washington, DC: Robert B. Luce, 1972); "Remembering Quentin Burdick," Robert J. Dole Archive and Special Collections, University of Kansas, Lawrence.

21. For Mundt's anticommunism and support for McCarthy, see R. Alton Lee, "'New Dealers, Fair Dealers, Misdealers, and Hiss Dealers': Karl Mundt and the Internal Security Act of 1950," *South Dakota History* 10 (Fall 1980):, 277–290; Sean J. Flynn, "The Eastern Establishment on Trial: Congressman Karl Mundt, 'Inland' Republicanism, and the Hiss Case," in Jon K. Lauck and Paula M. Nelson, eds., *The Plains Political Tradition: Essays on South Dakota Political Culture*, vol. 4 (Pierre: South Dakota Historical Society Press, 2022), 126–147; "Binding Assumptions: Karl E. Mundt and the Vietnam War, 1963–1969," *Mid-America: An Historical Review* 86, no. 3 (Fall 1994): 279–309; and John E. Miller, "McCarthyism before McCarthy: The 1938 Election in South Dakota," *Heritage of the Great Plains* 15 (Summer 1982): 1–21.

22. Knock, *The Life and Times*, 204–205; Adam J. Berinsky and Gabriel S. Lenz, "Red Scare? Revisiting Joe McCarthy's Influence on 1950s Elections," *Public Opinion Quarterly* 78, no. 2 (Summer 2014): 369–391.

23. *Daily Plainsman* (Huron, SD), December 29, 1957.

24. Knock, *The Life and Times*, 415; Sioux Falls *Argus Leader*, July 25, 2015; Bruce Miroff, *The Liberals' Moment: The McGovern Insurgency and the Identity Crisis of the Democratic Party* (Lawrence: University Press of Kansas, 2007), 122–123. The FBI accumulated a 1,400-page file on McGovern, including confirmation that he had fathered a child before his marriage in 1943.

25. *Daily Plainsman*, October 19, 1958.

26. Knock, *The Life and Times*, 205.

27. *Argus Leader* (Sioux Falls, SD), October 26, 1958; *Daily Plainsman*, October 22, 1958.

28. *Argus Leader*, November 5, 1958; *Pioneer-Times* (Deadwood, SD), November 5, 1958.

29. Knock, *The Life and Times*, 211.
30. Knock, *The Life and Times*, 214.
31. Jon K. Lauck, "George S. McGovern and the Farmer: South Dakota Politics, 1953–1962," *South Dakota History* 32, no. 4 (2002): 343–344.
32. Anson, *McGovern*, 92–93; Knock, *The Life and Times*, 254; Scott Heidepreim, *A Fair Chance for a Free People: a Biography of Karl E. Mundt, United States Senator* (Madison, SD: Leader Printing Co., 1988), 230–231; *Rapid City Journal*, October 17, 1960.
33. Anson, *McGovern*, 92.
34. Heidepreim, *A Fair Chance for a Free People*, 229.
35. Gretchen Hefner and Catherine McNicol Stock, "Missiles and Militarization: How the Cold War Shaped South Dakota Political Culture," in Jon K. Lauck, John E. Miller, and Donald E. Simmons Jr., eds., *The Plains Political Tradition: Essays on South Dakota Political Culture* vol, 3 (Pierre: South Dakota Historical Society Press, 2018), 220–221; *Pioneer-Times*, November 4, 1960.
36. Heidepreim, *A Fair Chance for a Free People*, 230–231; *Rapid City Journal*, October 17, 1960.
37. *Mitchell Daily Republic*, September 23, 1960; Knock, *The Life and Times*, 247. For the deeper tradition of anti-Catholic sentiment in South Dakota, see Jon Lauck, "'You Can't Mix Wheat and Potatoes in the Same Bin': Anti-Catholicism in Early Dakota History," *South Dakota History* 38, no. 1 (Spring 2008): 1–46.
38. "Official Election Returns of South Dakota, November 8, 1960," compiled by the Secretary of State, https://sdsos.gov/elections-voting/assets/historicalelectiondata/1960general0001.pdf; Hefner and Stock, "Missiles and Militarization," 222.
39. George McGovern, *The Essential America: Our Founders and the Liberal Tradition* (New York: Simon & Schuster, 2004), 111.
40. Knock, *The Life and Times*, 275.
41. Knock, *The Life and Times*, 278.
42. *Daily Plainsman*, October 14, 1962.
43. Knock, *The Life and Times*, 279–285; "Official Election Returns of South Dakota, November 6, 1962," compiled by the Secretary of State, https://sdsos.gov/elections-voting/assets/historicalelectiondata/1962generalpdf.pdf.
44. *Argus-Leader* (Sioux Falls, SD), March 15, 1963; Anson, *McGovern: A Biography*, 128–129.
45. Knock, *The Life and Times*, 279. The twenty-five-minute television ad—*A Dakota Story*—was produced by award-winning documentary filmmaker Charles Guggenheim, who had worked for Adlai Stevenson and would later work for Senators Robert and Edward Kennedy.
46. Fulton Lewis column in the *Standard-Speaker* (Hazelton, PA), November 11, 1963.
47. Ahrar Ahmad, "War and Peace in South Dakota," in Jon K. Lauck, John E. Miller, and Donald C. Simmons Jr., eds., *The Plains Political Tradition: Essays on South Dakota Political Culture*, vol. 2 (Pierre: South Dakota Historical Society Press, 2014), 198–202. Mundt won reelection in 1966 against a little-known state legislator by capturing 66 percent of the vote. Two years later, in a higher-turnout presidential election, McGovern won reelection against former Governor Gubbrud with 57 percent of the vote.
48. Robert Mann, *A Grand Delusion: America's Descent into Vietnam* (New York: Basic Books, 2001), 408–409; Karl E. Mundt Oral History, September 21, 1968, Lyndon B. Johnson Presidential Library, 18. Coincidentally, or perhaps not, McGovern's Vietnam

speech came on the same day as a Senate address by Frank Church of Idaho, another liberal from a conservative state. See LeRoy Ashby and Rod Gramer, *Fighting the Odds: The Life of Senator Frank Church* (Pullman: Washington State University Press, 1994), 192–193.

49. Author interview with Chuck Raasch, January 8, 2019.

50. Sam "Bud" Fantle, "A Republican Speaks About George McGovern," *Argus-Leader*, September 20, 1968.

51. Ross K. Baker, *Friend and Foe in the U.S. Senate* (New York: Free Press, 1980), 74. Abourezk, of Lebanese descent, was the first Arab American elected to the Senate. See James G. Abourezk, *Advise and Dissent: Memoirs of South Dakota and the U.S. Senate* (Chicago: Lawrence Hill Books, 1989). In his 1972 Senate race, Abourezk lost only eight counties and won with a nearly 44,000 vote margin over Robert W. Hirsch, a former legislator. In the presidential race, McGovern won just nineteen counties and lost the state by nearly nine points. Abourezk won Minnehaha County, for example, by nearly six thousand votes, while McGovern lost the same county by sixty-one votes.

52. McGovern's Cuba trip received extensive coverage in South Dakota; see *Rapid City Journal*, May 7, 1975, and *Argus-Leader*, May 8, 1975. The Americans for Democratic Action, the organization McGovern chaired in 1976–1977, was routinely referred to by the *Journal* as an "ultra-liberal group." See *Rapid City Journal*, February 7, 1976, and August 4, 1976. See also Catherine McNicol Stock, *Nuclear Country: The Origins of the Rural New Right* (Philadelphia: University of Pennsylvania Press, 2020).

53. Jon Lauck, "'It Disappeared as Quickly as It Came': The Democratic Surge and the Republican Comeback in South Dakota Politics, 1970–1980," *South Dakota History* 46, no. 2 (June 2016); and Lauck, "The Decline of South Dakota Democrats and the Fall of George McGovern, 1974–1980," in Jon K. Lauck and Catherine McNicol Stock, eds., *The Conservative Heartland: A Political History of the Postwar American Midwest* (Lawrence: University Press of Kansas, 2020), 247–257.

54. Tonnis H. Venhuizen, "Leaders in the Land of Infinite Variety: A Collective Portrait of South Dakota Governors," in Lauck, Miller, and Simmons, *The Plains Political Tradition: Essays on South Dakota Political Culture*, vol. 2, 260–261.

55. Roland Evans and Robert Novak, "McGovern on the Defensive," *Washington Post*, May 28, 1972. The "acid, amnesty, and abortion" label, ironically. was made by McGovern's first vice presidential pick in 1972, Missouri Senator Tom Eagleton. Eagleton, who McGovern later dumped from the ticket after revelations that Eagleton had received electric shock therapy for "nervous exhaustion," coined the phrase in a not-for-attribution interview with columnist Robert Novak, who disclosed his source in a 2007 memoir. See Robert D. Novak, *The Prince of Darkness: 50 Years Reporting in Washington* (New York: Three Rivers Press), 226.

56. *Rapid City Journal*, October 31, 1980.

57. In the 2020–2021 election cycle, of thirty-five Senate races, only one—Susan Collins in Maine—was won by a candidate of a party different than carried the state in the 2020 presidential election. See Pew Research Center, "Once again, nearly all Senate elections reflect states' presidential votes," January 8, 2021, https://www.pewresearch.org/fact-tank/2021/01/08/once-again-nearly-all-senate-elections-reflect-states-presidential-votes/.

58. *Washington Post*, July 8, 1980. See also the chapters on McGovern's 1980 Senate election in Marc C. Johnson, *Tuesday Night Massacre: Four Senate Races and the Radicalization of the Republican Party* (Norman: University of Oklahoma Press, 2021).

59. *New York Times*, September 20, 2004; Jon K. Lauck, *Daschle vs. Thune: Anatomy of a High Plains Senate Race* (Norman: University of Oklahoma Press, 2007), 251.

60. *New York Times*, October 22, 2008; *Argus-Leader*, November 7, 2008.

61. Author interview with Steve Erpenbach, May 9, 2022.

62. Voter Registration Tracking, South Dakota Secretary of State, https://sdsos.gov/elections-voting/upcoming-elections/voter-registration-totals/voter-registration-comparison-table.aspx.

63. Cory M. Haala, "Replanting the Grassroots: Remaking the South Dakota Democratic Party from McGovern to Daschle, 1980–1986, in Lauck, Miller, and Simmons, *The Plains Political Tradition: Essays on South Dakota Political Culture*, vol. 3, 182–202.

15

Wild About Harry

Walter Mondale, Ronald Reagan, and the Liberal Legacy of Harry Truman in 1984 Midwest

JEFFREY BLOODWORTH

❖ ❖ ❖ ❖ ❖ ❖ ❖ ❖ ❖ ❖ ❖ ❖ ❖ ❖ ❖ ❖

Harry Truman was not on the ballot in 1984. But a casual observer could have easily been confused. Ronald Reagan had not only refurbished Truman's train car, U.S. Car No. 1, but also adorned it with photos of the former president's 1948 campaign and used it to retrace portions of his iconic whistle-stop campaign.[1] Apoplectic at this, Walter Mondale, who had ridden portions of the whistle-stop train with Truman, inveighed against "grave robbing Republicans." His campaign peppered Reagan's whistle-stop events with handbills reading, "Ronald Reagan is no Harry Truman."[2] In 1984 two Midwestern-born candidates vied over the legacy of the nation's last previously elected Midwestern president[3] in the battleground states of the Middle West. At stake was the presidency and whether Truman's liberalism still resonated with Midwestern voters.

Harry Truman's 1948 campaign remains *the* mythic event of postwar American politics. Two years removed from a cataclysmic midterm defeat, the plainspoken incumbent headed a splintered party against a formidable GOP challenger. Left for political dead, Truman's 31,000-mile whistle-stop tour across middle America is credited with catalyzing his victory. The ultimate David-slays-Goliath fable, the election also established the basic political contours of postwar America. The Democrat's path to victory came through the Republican Middle West. Born in the Midwest, the GOP had "enjoyed a near stranglehold of voting at nearly every level" between the Civil War and Great Depression.[4] This reality held until FDR and the Great Depression made Democrats regionally competitive. After Roosevelt's death, Republicans had hoped their regional grip would return. Truman's 1948 victory showed this was not to be. Stunning almost every observer, he took the region, 50 to 48, winning Minnesota, Wisconsin, Iowa, Missouri, Illinois, and Ohio. Thereafter, the region became a political battleground.[5]

The Democratic path to relevance in the postwar Midwest began with Truman. More than a product of FDR's coattails, the Missourian crafted a liberalism fit for the postwar era and Midwestern voters. Born on a Missouri farm, Truman later moved to the city, where he failed in business before moving into politics.[6] The "gut" liberal from a small-town, Protestant Midwest milieu embodied the trials and tribulations of his fellow Midwesterners. Implicitly understanding the pulse of Middle America, his sense that postwar liberalism was aimed at protecting "every man or woman who works with hand or brain for a living" helped propel the Democrats to political parity in the region.[7] In the ensuing decades, many Midwestern laborers and farmers came to see liberalism as a force that buttressed their economic and social fortunes. But in 1984, Ronald Reagan attempted to make conservatism the political creed of the region's "plain people."

CAMPAIGN OPPORTUNITY

Reagan was a formidable incumbent aided by history and high poll ratings.[8] Historically, incumbent presidents rarely lose, especially when they were as popular as Reagan, whose approval rating in 1984 averaged 56 percent. Despite this reality, Wayne Cryts and Robert Vasquez gave Mondale hope, identifying a Midwestern route that could deliver the White House to the Minnesotan: farmers and labor.

In 1981, Cryts, a sixth-generation Puxico, Missouri, farmer, made national headlines for seizing his soybeans from a granary that went bankrupt.[9] Ignoring federal agents who guarded the silos, he, along with five hundred other area farmers, took their soybeans back.[10] A national folk hero, Cryts had touched a nerve. Farmers might have voted Reagan 2 to 1 in 1980, but sluggish commodity prices and high interest rates made the Middle Western farm belt his weakest region.[11] In the months before the election, Reagan's campaign manager, Ed Rollins, grudgingly admitted, "We've got some farm problems."[12] Farms were not Reagan's only political problem.

No city better symbolized the hard times the industrial heartland endured than Robert Vasquez's residence, Youngstown, Ohio. Starting in the late 1970s, the city began shuttering its mammoth auto and steel plants, throwing fifty thousand people out of work, including Vasquez, who headed the 3,100-member Steelworker Local 1330.[13] Across the industrial Midwest a "regional depression" pushed unemployment well into the double digits. Paul Laxalt, the Nevada senator who chaired Reagan's reelection campaign, confessed such circumstances meant, "In the industrial states, we've got a lot of work to do."[14]

With organized labor and farmers in the muck, Mondale had a theoretical opportunity to revive Truman's time-worn Midwestern coalition. To win the Midwest, however, Mondale needed to reconstitute the farmer-labor alliance that defined his political roots.

MONDALE'S LIBERAL MIDWESTERN ROOTS

Born in 1928, Walter F. Mondale came of age in Depression-era Minnesota defined by a populist Farmer-Labor coalition.[15] In 1944 his mentor, Hubert Humphrey, brought the moribund Democratic Party into the newly formed Democratic-Farmer-Labor Party (DFL). Humphrey and Mondale's DFL was founded upon programmatic liberalism, which held that voters were moved by national issues and particular programs, not ethnic loyalties or populist sensibilities.[16]

The "programmatics" represented a quintessential Midwestern liberal style. The region's highly informed and engaged citizenry enabled liberals to appeal to Midwestern voters via specific policy proposals rather than partisan identities or ethnic loyalties.[17] Exceptionally high degrees of social capital rendered Minnesotans especially suited for programmatic politics. If the Gopher State was fit for programmatic politics, then Mondale was similarly suited for Humphrey's DFL. Reared in the tiny hamlet of Elmore, Minnesota, young "Fritz" was the son of a pious, hard-luck Methodist minister whose struggles inspired a devotion to social justice.[18] Steeped in this milieu, Mondale, as a collegian, coordinated the state's Second Congressional District for Humphrey's 1948 Senate campaign. From this vantage point, he witnessed Truman and Humphrey craft a liberalism fit for Midwestern voters and a campaign style suited to hold a diverse coalition together.

Truman and Humphrey updated Democratic philosophy for a new liberal era. Rather than emphasize agrarian fundamentalism and small government, an activist liberal state buttressed the "common man," who they defined as farmers, labor, small enterprisers, and mid-rank professionals.[19] Always a threat to splinter, Truman and Humphrey incessantly rallied their diverse coalition. In 1948, Humphrey visited every one of Minnesota's eighty-seven counties twice in September and October. Meanwhile, Truman's whistle-stop train tour traveled thirty-one thousand miles. Postwar liberals, more so than conservatives, had to persistently woo and cajole their party's diffuse interest groups. This was the seminal politics of Mondale's young adulthood.[20]

As senator, Mondale called this "family politics." Through near-constant interaction with constituents, Mondale established a "relationship" and "reservoir of trust" with voters. Focusing on "tangible benefits" to particular interest groups, he believed he could balance competing interest groups' demands and bring them together.[21] Midwestern to his political and personal core, in 1984 Mondale battled a Hollywood actor turned California politician for the region's votes.

RONALD REAGAN: MIDWESTERNER

Ronald Wilson Reagan was an authentic son of the Midwest. Reared in north-central Illinois, at age twenty-six he left the region for Hollywood, where he acted in fifty-two movies and hosted television's *General Electric Theatre*. In these roles, Reagan usually played a version of himself—a handsome yet earnest everyman marked by emotional restraint who exuded virtue. This inner core was, according to his biographer Lou Cannon, the key to his political success.[22] Reagan's reprise of the Truman whistle-stop tour was designed to demonstrate this central personal narrative.

Tip O'Neill famously grumbled, "I never forgot where I came from. He [Reagan] kind of forgot"; but Reagan made his Midwestern roots a political touchstone.[23] In 1965, Reagan described his "Huck Finn–Tom Sawyer" childhood as one "that has shaped my body and mind for all the years to come after."[24] In this recount, Reagan did "forget" his roots. Far from tranquil, Reagan's childhood was marked by uncertainty, deprivation, and, above all, his father's alcoholism.[25] But Reagan's persistent optimism and emotional distance from nearly all who surrounded him bear the hallmarks of a child reared by an alcoholic parent.[26] When sober, Jack Reagan was a master salesman. Reagan's mother, Nelle, so thrived in her role as a lay evangelist and dramatic readings that he later said of her, "Performing, I think, was her first love."[27] Reagan surely absorbed his parent's performative talents.

A natural actor, Reagan parlayed connections from an Iowa radio job into a Hollywood screen test. Ironically, his departure for California also represented a quintessential Midwestern move. Due to the double shocks of the Depression and Dust Bowl, millions fled the region. In Iowa, where Reagan worked as a radio announcer, nearly one-third of those born in the state departed. Like Reagan, many went to Los Angeles. During the Depression, approximately one-sixth of the city were Midwestern born.[28] In a certain sense, Reagan was never as Midwestern as when he left for California.

Reagan's political philosophy, however, was scarcely tied to the Midwest.[29] A liberal Democrat by dint of family and the Depression, Reagan's turn to the right sprang from the postwar Sunbelt. The 1948 election taught many Republicans to accept New Deal and Cold War basics. Sunbelt conservatives believed that communism abroad and collectivism at home represented mortal threats, which necessitated an uncompromising stance.[30] More than this, they altered the definition of "conservative" from a "curse word" into "a roaring challenge to the established power."[31] When the events of the 1960s and 1970s soured the electorate on liberalism, Sunbelt conservatives, and Reagan, were well-positioned with a prescription—small government—and villain—liberals.

Prior to Reagan, conservatives usually lost. Filled with dire warnings of future catastrophe, conservatives struggled to woo voters. Lacking a snide edge, Reagan instilled Sunbelt conservatism with his "ebullient character."[32] His life trajectory convinced him that the American Dream was available to all who took chances and worked hard. Reagan's ability to explain his rise through a Midwestern "conversational narrative style" helped him translate Sunbelt conservatism to Midwestern voters. In personal stories about one's life, this motif stresses "good luck, good behavior, and particular personal skills" as the cause of one's achievements.[33] In his 1984 campaign kick-off speech at the Dixon, Illinois, High School gymnasium, Reagan demonstrated his mastery of the motif. Hailing Dixon for its "unchanged" values and traditions that "made America great," he extolled the Midwest as the source of American greatness and, in the process, credited Dixon with his own ascent.[34]

By 1984, Truman's plain people liberalism had, in the eyes of many voters, at least, become an elite philosophy so focused on the nation's faults that it lost sight of its virtues. In a 1984 speech to Ohio voters, Reagan termed liberals "the blame America first crowd." Reminding the crowd that he had been a Democrat "for a good share of my life," he extolled Truman and past liberals for recognizing the difference between "freedom and tyranny." With liberalism taken hostage, he invited Midwestern Democrats to join him on a "new path of hope and opportunity."[35]

DUELING BANJOS

Walter Mondale likely lost the 1984 race well before the fall campaign commenced. Strategists surmised that Mondale's best, and maybe only, route to victory was to nab the nomination early, and pivot to Reagan.[36] Once Gary Hart ruined that tactic, Mondale's only route to victory entailed taking the Northeast, a select Southern state or two, and sweeping much of the Midwest's 137 electoral votes.[37]

Likable, optimistic, and gracious, Reagan was a Rubik's Cube of an opponent, especially for Mondale. Weaned on Humphrey's prairie populism, Mondale's fiery frontal assaults on the incumbent backfired.[38] Before television became popular, campaigns provided mass entertainment to constituents who were neatly organized into unions, cooperatives, and fraternal organizations. By the 1980s, voters watched staged mass rallies on television pitched to the broad middle rather than a discrete interest group. Attuned to Sunbelt politics and television, Reagan understood that the medium was perfectly fitted for voters in the burgeoning suburbs of Atlanta, Dallas, Phoenix, and Los Angeles, and it prized even temperaments and canned, practiced lines.

Geraldine Ferraro's historic candidacy boosted the Democratic Party from a nineteen-point deficit to a two-point July lead.[39] At the Republican National Convention in Dallas, Reagan's soaring rhetoric, buoyed by a resurgent economy and triumphant Summer Olympics, enabled him to retake whatever ground the Democrats had gained.[40] Mondale looked to the October 7 debate as a final opportunity to turn the contest into a race.

At the debate, Reagan opened the door. In front of seventy million viewers, Reagan's early stumbles steadily worsened over the course of the ninety-minute event. At one point, Mondale feared the seventy-three-year-old incumbent would faint from exhaustion. A complete fiasco for Reagan, Mondale finally had an issue, "Reagan's capacity to govern," and a hope that he could flip the campaign script once and for all.[41] Within days, Reagan's lead fell from nineteen points to twelve, and his lead with younger voters collapsed by twenty-five points. For Mondale, his crowd size and their collective enthusiasm soared. As the contest became an actual race, it was the Midwest that became the immediate battleground. And it was in that region where Reagan was, according to his internal polls, weakest.[42]

In 1980, Reagan was weakest in the South and the six industrial states of the Middle West: Illinois, Michigan, Minnesota, Missouri, Ohio, and Wisconsin, plus Iowa.[43] By 1982, Reagan's position was further weakened by a recession that hit an economy dependent upon agricultural exports and an aging industrial base the hardest of any region.[44] In 1982 the seven Midwestern states with significant industry—Illinois, Indiana, Michigan, Minnesota, Missouri, Ohio, and Wisconsin—averaged 11 percent unemployment.[45]

The region's farmers were faring even worse than labor. In the years prior to the recession, farmers were economically pressed by commodity gluts, inflation, and debt. Median incomes for farmers fell in 1979 by 21.7 percent and by 11.8 percent in 1981.[46] After years of loans to expand production, a collapse in global demand put millions of farmers on the brink. Burdened by debt and inflation, farmers produced even more, resulting in massive surpluses that drove prices even further downward.[47] The 1981–1982 recession hit reeling farmers with the force of a knock-out blow.[48]

In 1982 the "economically stricken" Midwest represented the Democrat's "most important battleground" and a chance to build momentum for 1984.[49] With unemployment at 10.4 percent on election day, the midterms became a Democratic rout.[50] From 1946 to 1982, in first-term presidential midterms the ruling party lost an average of ten House seats. Blowing well past that marker, Democrats took out twenty-six GOP incumbents. Losing only one House seat to the GOP in the Midwest, Democrats flipped eight Midwestern seats and nabbed five Midwestern governor's mansions.[51] Buoyed by the strongest midterm turnout since 1962, House Democrats won men 53 to 43 percent, women 56 to 40 percent, and the farm vote.[52] For partisans looking to dismiss Reagan's victory as a flash in the pan, the 1982 returns provided succor.

In 1984, Ronald Reagan was *the* issue. His bold conservative agenda set the contours of the debate. But his appeal also transcended policy particulars. His sunny optimism appealed to an electorate fumbling in the wake of foreign policy cataclysms, economic judders, and social tumult. A telegenic media savant, Reagan communicated his Sunbelt conservatism in a plainspoken yet smooth Midwestern parlance, which had rendered him, according to one aide, into "our de Gaulle—a man who seemed in his very plainness to embody the character and dreams of the people."[53] But this august position also contained an Achilles heel. If Reagan's leadership and command were his paramount strength, then any event that proved fallibility could give Mondale real opportunity.

Reagan's devastatingly bad October 7 debate performance was just such an occasion. Reagan's own team of advisers privately acknowledged the disaster. Mondale himself thought the president seemed "confused," "out of touch," and even "senile." Recalling the performance, the vice president said, "It was scary. He just *left*."[54] By stumbling and bumbling over facts and appearing to be every bit the oldest man to run for the presidency, he had delivered a historically dismal performance in front of seventy million viewers.

Advisers and Reagan himself knew he had performed poorly. But it was Nancy Reagan who sounded the alarm bells. "Goddam angry" at advisers for over-coaching her husband, she and Laxalt took control.[55] For Laxalt, the only way to recover political momentum and soothe a candidate's psyche was to "let Reagan be Reagan."[56] A tired political maxim, in this case it was also smart tonic. "Reagan being Reagan" entailed tightly controlled settings filled with canned, practiced lines that were made for televised sound bites. As fate would have it, the Reagan campaign had planned to reprise portions of the Truman whistle-stop train tour five days after the first debate.

Scheduled for western Ohio, Reagan's train tour provided the perfect venue for media-friendly images and sound bites aimed at key constituencies. For Reagan to win and oversee a political realignment, he had to woo significant chunks of the electorate's twenty-two million blue-collar workers.[57] To draw these Democrats, the president constantly invoked Democratic heroes of the past and wrapped his former Democratic self into their political cloaks.[58] Though the president invoked JFK and FDR, Truman—the last Democratic presidential nominee Reagan had voted for—belonged in a special category to him and the campaign. Reagan was presenting himself as the heir to a "common man" incumbent who rallied the Midwest's plain people for an upset victory.[59]

Nancy Reagan understood that confidence was the key to her husband's rebound. Top aides were bypassed in favor of an Ohio-born political consultant, Roger Ailes, who was charged with restoring Reagan's buoyancy. Boosting Reagan with praise, Ailes prepared the president for what became the key campaign swing of the election.[60] In what aides billed as the "most expensive campaign trip ever," strategists had refurbished Truman's presidential railcar. Decorated with photos of FDR and Truman campaigning, the thirteen-car "Heartland Special" was slated to wind 150 miles from Dayton northward to the Toledo suburb of Perrysburg, making stops in Dayton, Sidney, Lima, Ottawa, Deschler, and Perrysburg.[61]

For the Heartland Special, campaign manager James Baker instructed speechwriters to invoke Truman's plain-spoken style. Following this tact, Reagan promised Truman-esque "very blunt truths" for his October 12 events. From the start, he did not disappoint. As the train left the station to begin the tour, Reagan said of a "Mondale's the Man" sign outside his car, "The hell he is."[62] Uttered into a hot microphone channeled into the train's press room, the episode demonstrated Reagan's "straight talk."[63] In another practiced line, Reagan told crowds he had stopped himself from warning Mondale at the debate that he was *"taxing* my patience." With a twinkle in his eye and sharp edge in his voice, Reagan claimed, "I caught myself. Why should I give him another [tax] idea?"[64]

Great for the candidate's ego and psyche, Reagan's homage to Truman was pitch perfect for a national television audience.[65] On the nightly news and in the newspapers, viewers and readers saw images of a vigorous president giving old-fashioned campaign speeches at small-town stops ringed with marching bands, Boy Scouts, and adoring throngs.[66] In Lima, five thousand supporters and eight high school marching bands greeted the president with cheers and martial music.[67] An estimated 120,000 attended the six main stops, which featured quick ten-minute speeches. Along the route, cars parked on overpasses, and crowds lined the entire route for, in the words of one voter, "the fun of seeing the president."[68] At every stop, Democrats passed handbills asserting, "Ronald Reagan is no Harry Truman"; journalists noted that these materials were left "unread" and "littered the ground."[69]

At the penultimate stop in Perrysburg, Reagan tore into Mondale, saying of his opponent's worldview, "If it's income, tax it. If it's revenue, spend it. If it's a budget, break it. If it's a promise, make it." After the speech, a fireworks display marked the Republican's renaissance. One week later, on October 21, Reagan entered the second debate invigorated.[70] Even Mondale understood that "when I walked off that platform after the second debate . . . the election was over."[71]

Reconciled to defeat, Mondale returned to his roots. Forced to reply to Reagan's Heartland Special, his campaign hastily organized a 117-mile bus tour into Illinois, Missouri, and Iowa farm country. Scheduled for October 25 and titled the "Mississippi Valley Harvest Tour," it was a Humphrey-style barnstorming excursion featuring the old-time liberal religion. Starting at a family farm in Quincy, Illinois, the tour traveled to Canton, Missouri, and ended in Burlington, Iowa. In Quincy, Mondale's sunrise speech reached an emotional crescendo when he recounted his experience on "the Truman train." With his voice "nearly cracking," he recalled how "they wrote Harry Truman off" and pleaded for a reprise of that comeback victory.[72]

On paper, Mondale had much campaign fodder. In Iowa alone, 28 percent of all family farmers were at risk of foreclosure.[73] Speaking at another family farm, in Canton, the one-time pea lice inspector inveighed that farm prices and debt were a result of electing "the most uninformed president in modern history."[74] But Mondale's farm appeals were muted by an increasingly urban-oriented party and his association with Jimmy Carter's Soviet grain embargo.[75] Despite enthusiastic crowds on the tour, farmers, according to polls, blamed Democrats for their economic ills almost as much as they did Reagan. To the Democrats' chagrin, the farm issue was not rural Midwesterners' overriding concern in the presidential race.

In the final week of the campaign, the rural Midwest's crowds were repeated in Boston, New York, Cleveland, and Youngstown, where tens of thousands turned out. Mondale believed the race was moving, as did veteran journalist Tom Wicker, who wrote, "Is there something wrong with all those polls so unanimously predicting disastrous defeat for Mr. Mondale?"[76] But 1984 was not 1948. Mondale's large enthusiastic crowds were Faulkner's sound and fury signifying nothing. Before noon on election day, advisers informed the vice president of his defeat. As afternoon moved into evening, the staggering nature of Reagan's victory became apparent. Winning 98 percent of the electoral college (525 to 13), Reagan took 59 percent of the popular vote. Broad and deep, Reagan took more than 60 percent of the vote in thirty-two states and garnered over 53 percent in eleven states.[77]

In 1984 the Midwest performed to type. Midwesterners voted in the highest proportion of any region, 65.7 percent, by a wide margin.[78] But in 1984, turnout was the extent of the Midwest's civic exceptionalism. Reagan won 59.8 percent of the Midwestern vote, which almost exactly mirrored his national share, 58.8 percent, and was smack dab in the middle between the Southern, 63 percent, and Western, 59 percent, Reagan vote. Though Mondale fared better in the Upper Midwest, Iowa, Minnesota, and Wisconsin, he was clobbered in the low-population agricultural states of Kansas and Nebraska, as well as in the high-population industrial ones, Ohio and Michigan. Along racial lines, African Americans in the Midwest mirrored the Black vote in every other region. As for the gender gap, it failed to materialize. Midwestern women voted for Reagan in the same basic proportion of other regions—59 percent. For farmers, it was much the same story. Taking Wayne Cryts' Stoddard, Missouri, county in a walk, Reagan also won 65 percent of the overall farm vote.[79] Winning the union vote by a narrow margin, 53 to 45, Mondale did capture Bob Vasquez's Mahoning County, but it was only one of six counties he won in a state saddled with 9.1 percent unemployment.[80]

Reagan's total victory signaled the death of Truman's "plain people" liberalism in the Midwest. Left-liberal populists did enjoy scattered success in challenging Reaganism in the Midwest during the 1980s and beyond. But the 1984 election proved the death of Truman-style liberalism in the region. The Gipper's victory demonstrated that a vast majority of Midwesterners no longer believed liberalism buttressed their interests.

Scarcely Sunbelt conservative ideologues, Midwestern voters had, nevertheless, unhitched their political wagon from the New Deal coalition. Moreover, by equating Midwestern values with conservatism, Reagan rendered his creed familiar and less threatening to voters. In this way, Reagan's deft use of the "Midwest" helped mainstream conservativism nationally.

NOTES

1. "Reagan Steps Up Mondale Attack during Whistle-Stop Tour of Ohio," *Akron-Beacon Journal*, October 13, 1984, 5; William Hershey, "Campaign Trains Rolls in Ohio," *Akron-Beacon Journal*, October 13, 1984, 1.

2. Maureen Brown, "Mondale Derides President's Tour," *Dayton Daily News*, October 12, 1984, 39; Hershey, "Campaign Trains Rolls in Ohio," 1.

3. Though Dwight Eisenhower was born in Texas and reared in Kansas, his military career and political base lay well beyond the Midwest. His political base was the East Coast wing of the Republican Party, not the Midwestern wing. Michigan-born Gerald Ford was appointed vice president and elevated into the presidency upon Richard Nixon's resignation.

4. Brown, "Mondale Derides President's Tour," 1.

5. Michael Barone, "The Surprising New Battleground," in Jon K. Lauck and Catherine McNicol Stock, eds., *The Conservative Heartland: A Political History of the Postwar American Midwest* (Lawrence: Kansas University Press, 2020), 45.

6. Alonzo Hamby, *Man of the People: A Life of Harry S Truman* (Oxford: Oxford University Press, 1995), 92–97.

7. Hamby, *Man of the People*, 217.

8. Frank Newport, "Ronald Reagan: From the People's Perspective," Gallup, October 29, 2021, https://news.gallup.com/poll/11887/ronald-reagan-from-peoples-perspective-gallup-poll-review.aspx.

9. Dan Ruck, "Farmers Want 'Deposit' Protection," *Kansas City Times*, February 24, 1981, 33.

10. Jeff Bloodworth, *Losing the Center: A History of American Liberalism, 1968–1992* (Lexington: Kentucky University Press, 2013), 57.

11. John Herbers, "Family Farms Reeling from Recession Blows," *New York Times*, October 16, 1982, 1A.

12. Hedrick Smith, "GOP to Attack Mondale's Turf," *New York Times*, August 21, 1984, 1A.

13. Derek Thompson, "A World without Work," *Atlantic*, July/August 2015, https://www.theatlantic.com/magazine/archive/2015/07/world-without-work/395294/.

14. Steven Weisman, "Reagan's Campaign Advisers Say He Would Face Tough Race in '84," *New York Times*, September 18, 1983, 1A.

15. Jennifer Delton, *Making Minnesota Liberal: Civil Rights and the Transformation of the Democratic Party* (Minneapolis: University of Minnesota Press, 2002), 2–9.

16. Delton, *Making Minnesota Liberal*, xvi, 18–23.

17. Peverill Squire, "Politics: Overview," in Andrew Cayton, Richard Sisson, and

Chris Zacher, eds., *The American Midwest: An Interpretive Encyclopedia* (Bloomington: Indiana University Press, 2006), 1616–1617; John Fenton, *Midwest Politics* (New York: Holt, 1966), 102–103; Daniel Elazar, *Minnesota Politics and Government* (Lincoln: University of Nebraska–Lincoln Press, 1999), 19.

18. Steve Gillon, *The Democrats' Dilemma: Walter F. Mondale and the Liberal Legacy* (New York: Columbia University Press, 1992), 23–26.

19. Hamby, *Man of the People*, 216–217.

20. Gillon, *The Democrats' Dilemma*, 28.

21. Gillon, *The Democrats' Dilemma*, 28–29.

22. France Fitzgerald, *Way Out There in the Blue: Ronald Reagan, Star Wars, and the End of the Cold War* (New York: Simon & Schuster, 2001), 28.

23. Shaun O'Connell, "Tip O'Neill: Irish-American Representative Man," *New England Journal of Public Policy* 18, no. 2 (2003): Article 5, 2.

24. Ronald Reagan, *Where's the Rest of Me? The Autobiography of Ronald Reagan* (New York: Karz , 1981), 17; Leon Litwack, "The Ronald Reagan Story; Or, Tom Sawyer Enters Politics," *New York Times*, November 14, 1965, 46.

25. Fitzgerald, *Way Out There in the Blue*, 42.

26. John H. Miller, "Midwestern Echoes in the Formation of Ronald Reagan's Personal and Political Identities," Ronald Reagan and the Midwest: A Conference, January 14, 2011, https://www.c-span.org/video/?297514-4/ronald-reagans-midwest-roots.

27. Fitzgerald, *Way Out There in the Blue*, 43.

28. Andrew Cayton, "Origins of Vision and Voice," Ronald Reagan and the Midwest: A Conference, January 14, 2011, https://www.c-span.org/video/?297514-4/ronald-reagans-midwest-roots.

29. Jon Peterson, "The Midwest and Reagan's Anti-Communism," Ronald Reagan and the Midwest: A Conference, January 14, 2011, https://www.c-span.org/video/?297514-4/ronald-reagans-midwest-roots.

30. David Farber, *The Rise and Fall of Modern American Conservatism: A Short History* (Princeton, NJ: Princeton University Press, 2010), 78, 80; Nancy Beck Young, *Two Sons of the Southwest* (Lawrence: Kansas University Press, 2019), 200.

31. Farber, *The Rise and Fall of Modern American Conservatism*, 79.

32. Farber, *The Rise and Fall of Modern American Conservatism*, 163–164.

33. Cayton, "Origins of Vision and Voice."

34. Ronald Reagan, "Remarks during Homecoming and Birthday Celebration in Dixon, Illinois," February 6, 1984, https://www.reaganlibrary.gov/archives/speech/remarks-during-homecoming-and-birthday-celebration-dixon-illinois.

35. Ronald Reagan, "Remarks at a Reagan-Bush Rally," Columbus, Ohio, October 28, 1984, https:/www.reaganlibrary.gov/archives/speech/remarks-reagan-bush-rally-columbus-ohio.

36. Peter Goldman and Tony Fuller, *The Quest for the Presidency 1984* (New York: Bantam Books, 1985), 271.

37. Goldman and Fuller, *The Quest for the Presidency*, 270–275.

38. Gillon, *The Democrats' Dilemma*, 28.

39. Gillon, *The Democrats' Dilemma*, 363.

40. Gillon, *The Democrats' Dilemma*, 370.

41. Gillon, *The Democrats' Dilemma*, 382–383.

42. Hedrick Smith, "GOP to Attack Mondale's Turf," *New York Times*, August 21, 1984, 1A.

43. Gary Orren, "The Struggle for Control of the Republican Party," *New York Times*, August 17, 1976, 31.

44. Andrew Malcolm, "Democrats and Republicans Focus on Contests in the Midwest," *New York Times*, October 29, 1982, 22.

45. "Most States Report Decline in Unemployment from '82," *New York Times*, August 17, 1983, 10A.

46. John Herbers, "Family Farms Reeling from Recession Blows," *New York Times*, October 16, 1982, 1A.

47. Gregory Jaynes, "U.S. Farmers Said to Face Worst Year since 1930s," *New York Times*, March 28, 1982, 1A.

48. Seth King, "Democrats Asking Help for Farmers," *New York Times*, March 21, 1982, 35.

49. Andrew Malcolm, "Democrats and Republicans Focus on Contests in the Midwest," *New York Times*, October 29, 1982, 22; "The Midwest," *New York Times*, September 5, 1982, 53.

50. Seth King, "Rate of Joblessness to 10.4% of Labor Force," *New York Times*, November 6, 1982, 1A.

51. Hedrick Smith, "Reagan Reduced," *New York Times*, November 7, 1982, 1A; Steven Roberts, "Democrats Regain Control in House," *New York Times*, November 4, 1982, 19A.

52. Adam Clymer, "Doubt on Reagan Plan Spurred Voters, Polls Show," *New York Times*, November 8, 1982, 11B.

53. Hedrick Smith, "One Campaign Issue Dominates: The Leadership of Ronald Reagan," *New York Times*, January 30, 1984, 1A; Goldman and Fuller, *The Quest for the Presidency*, 245.

54. Goldman and Fuller, *The Quest for the Presidency*, 320.

55. Goldman and Fuller, *The Quest for the Presidency*, 321–323.

56. Goldman and Fuller, *The Quest for the Presidency*, 323.

57. Smith, "One Campaign Issue Dominates: The Leadership of Ronald Reagan," 1A.

58. Goldman and Fuller, *The Quest for the Presidency*, 323.

59. Hershey, "Campaign Trains Rolls in Ohio," 1.

60. Lou Cannon, *President Reagan: The Role of a Lifetime* (New York: Public Affairs, 2000), 483–485.

61. "Reagan Steps Up Mondale Attack during Whistle-Stop Tour of Ohio," *Akron-Beacon Journal*, October 13, 1984, 5; Hershey, "Campaign Trains Rolls in Ohio," 1.

62. Tim Graham, "Blunt Reagan Rides the Rails," *Journal Herald* (Dayton, OH), October 13, 1984, 5.

63. Cannon, *President Reagan: The Role of a Lifetime*, 484.

64. Graham, "Blunt Reagan Rides the Rails," 1; Cannon, *President Reagan: The Role of a Lifetime*, 484.

65. Graham, "Blunt Reagan Rides the Rails," 1.

66. Marie Dillon and Mark Fisher, "Troy Satisfied for Just a Glimpse," *Journal Herald* (Dayton, OH), October 13, 1984, 1; "Reagan's Train Trip Popular," *Akron Beacon Journal*, October 13, 1984, 5.

67. Hershey, "Campaign Trains Rolls in Ohio," 1.
68. "Reagan's Train Trip Popular," 5.
69. Hershey, "Campaign Trains Rolls in Ohio," 1.
70. Cannon, *President Reagan: The Role of a Lifetime*, 481.
71. Gillon, *The Democrats' Dilemma*, 385–386.
72. "Mondale Bus Trip in Farming States Marked by Emotion," *News and Observer* (Raleigh, NC), October 25, 1984, 12; Gillon, *The Democrats' Dilemma*, 389.
73. Lee Sigelman, "Economic Pressures and the Farm Vote: The Case of 1984," *Rural Sociology* 52, no. 2 (1987): 151.
74. Bob Adams, "Reagan Farm Policy, a Real 'Stinkeroo,' Mondale Charges," *St. Louis Post Dispatch*, October 25, 1984, 10.
75. Adams, "Reagan Farm Policy," 10.
76. Adams, "Reagan Farm Policy," 10; Gillon, *The Democrats' Dilemma*, 388.
77. Gillon, *The Democrats' Dilemma*, 389.
78. *Voting and Registration in the Election of 1984*, Series P-20, No. 397 (Washington, DC: US Department of Commerce, 1985), https://www.census.gov/history/pdf/1984presidential_election-32018.pdf.
79. Sigelman, "Economic Pressures and the Farm Vote," 153.
80. "Portrait of an Electorate," *New York Times*, November 8, 1984, 19A.

16

"Why We Must Save the Family Farm"

Midwestern Liberalism and Progressive Farm Policy, 1985–1996

CORY HAALA

❖ ❖ ❖ ❖ ❖ ❖ ❖ ❖ ❖ ❖ ❖ ❖ ❖ ❖ ❖ ❖

"Midwesterners are turning on Republicans with a vengeance." This, argued League of Rural Voters founders Mark Ritchie and Kevin Ristau in January 1986, could only be attributed "to the farm situation. It is only recently that the plight of the farmers has been so well publicized."[1]

It has been decades since rural Midwesterners turned *against* Republicans, since Democrats were perceived to champion the causes of rural America. Today Midwestern Democrats complain the party "has not offered rural voters a clear vision that speaks to their lived experiences" as narratives of decline abound. Iowa lost its first-in-the-nation caucus status.[2] Culture wars, militarization, urban resentment, and low-wage labor turned rural America red.[3] In 1997 Democrats held eight of the Upper Midwest's ten Senate seats—today, they hold three. Few, though, highlight how Midwestern liberals built majorities by leading on farm policy and opposing Ronald Reagan's conservatism and Bill Clinton's neoliberalism.

Democrats thrived in the Midwest throughout the 1990s. Yet in new histories of the Democratic Party, post-1974 America, and even congressional politics in the Reagan era, the 1980s Farm Crisis receives no mention, obscuring the progressive base and economic populism of the rural Midwest. When farmers or farm policy enters Democratic narratives, they are fleeting allies in Jesse Jackson's quixotic presidential campaign or "special interest liberalism" from which conservative Democrats believed the party was "liberated" when it lost Congress in 1994.[4] But Midwestern liberals like advisers to Iowa Senator Tom Harkin had warned fellow Democrats: "Democratic members need a farm bill demonstrating that they can translate . . . rhetoric into action. We cannot surrender the high ground of standing for a substantially better deal for farm families and rural America than the Republicans are willing to support."[5]

Farm families were desperate. In the 1980s Farm Crisis, farm exports fell 50 percent. About 300,000 left farming. Bankruptcies reached tens of thousands. Land prices dropped 29 percent nationally and 50 percent in Nebraska from 1980 to 1984. By 1985 nearly one-third of all Iowa farmers had debt-to-asset ratios over 40 percent, compared to 19 percent nationally. The resulting psychological, civic, and economic stress—farmers killing their banker and then themselves or committing domestic violence—led to a raft of payments and attention to rural America, from tractorcades to FarmAid concerts and cross-bearing rallies.[6] Without long-term economic help, the family farm—and the people who owned and operated them—faced failure.

Amid both crisis and conservative revolution, Midwestern Democrats won behind a left-wing farm movement that transcended familiar gendered and racial boundaries. Far from populism as "fashion statement," these protests swelled into broad progressive activism rejecting neoliberalism for multiracial farm-labor activism.[7] Feminist advocates led the way: Minnesotan activist Anne Kanten became deputy commissioner of agriculture in Minnesota, while Denise O'Brien of Atlantic, Iowa, led PrairieFire's Rural Women's Leadership Development Program and Carol Hodne served as North American Farm Alliance (NAFA) executive director until 1989. Farm activism launched the political careers of Midwestern women like Iowa Democrat Jo Ann Zimmerman, elected lieutenant governor after targeting community and women's organizations impacted by the Farm Crisis, while North Dakotan Sarah Vogel won a 1983 class-action lawsuit against the US Department of Agriculture (USDA) and later became North Dakota's agriculture commissioner, serving alongside tax commissioner Heidi Heitkamp.[8]

Their efforts revealed how farm-labor organizers called on the progressive heritage of the Midwest—though often limited by demography and racial biases—to build broader, national coalitions across racial lines. At one 1985 summit, the Wisconsin Farm Unity Alliance (WFUA) paired Black farm loss with discriminatory lending and the shadow of sharecropping, while Dan Levitas of PrairieFire led training that pushed "containment and counteraction" to isolate racism, fascism, and anti-Semitism by using clergy, union members, and farm leaders to discuss economic and social justice. Iowa farm activist Brad Wilson and journalist Tracy Watson have detailed how the 1980s farm movement was bound, in Iowa, by an ecumenical commitment not to the destructive tendencies of right-wing radicals like Posse Comitatus, but constructive, interracial solidarity-building.[9] Their efforts yielded political fruit: the Midwestern-led Congressional Populist Caucus (CPC) benefited from two Black members, Charles Hayes of Chicago and Alan Wheat of Kansas City, who tightened the relationship between rural and urban interests along shared economic struggles. And the "rebellious lawyering" of Vogel and activists spurred victories for Black, Native, and Hispanic farmers against discriminatory farm lending and mediation.[10]

That Midwestern liberalism, often dubbed "prairie populism," supported federal intervention in the farm economy to protect small-scale producers and laborers from big business and free trade. Alongside the National Farmers Union (NFU) and organized labor but unlike previous movements that relied on boycotts or legal status as cooperatives, Midwestern liberalism relied on grassroots coalitions and direct action to win direct legislative reform. Groups like Minnesota's League of Rural Voters (LRV), Iowa PrairieFire, WFUA, NAFA, and others rebuilt a distinctive Midwestern liberalism around "progressive populism."[11] Redefining the Farm Crisis as everyone's issue, irrespective of race or gender, these activists launched the statewide political careers of those Midwestern senators and a new generation of female leaders, and offered an enduring vision for the Democratic Party.

It swelled into an effective regional movement capable of winning elections. While Reagan romped in 1984, Paul Simon of Illinois and Tom Harkin in Iowa defeated incumbent Republican senators. Farm-state Democrats Kent Conrad and Tom Daschle in North Dakota and South Dakota, respectively, won in 1986, joined by Minnesota's Paul Wellstone in 1990, Wisconsin's Russ Feingold in 1992, and South Dakota's Tim Johnson in 1996, all defeating Republican senators. North Dakotans elevated populist congressman Byron Dorgan to the Senate in 1992, and the Upper Midwest sent 161 of 208 total electoral votes to the Democrats from 1988 to 2008. Those senators—after 1996, eight of the region's ten—fought neoliberalism from the "market-oriented" farm policies of Reagan Republicans to Clinton-era Democrats' turn to privatization and the free market.

Midwestern liberals fought this, particularly, in the 1985, 1990, and 1995 farm bills, demanding increased federal supply management and price support for small family farmers, mortgage moratoria, "fair trade," the curtailing of corporate agricultural power, and more. But they lost repeatedly, as neoliberal Democrats allied with the Democratic Leadership

Council (DLC) and Clinton worked with Republicans to pass the North American Free Trade Agreement (NAFTA) and the 1996 Freedom to Farm Act, gutting protections for small family farmers. In those policy defeats, though, Midwestern liberals won their own electoral victories in hostile political climates, revealing how farm-state Democrats and their grassroots activist allies struggled for a future of progressive, economic populism that helped all people.

1985 FARM BILLS AND AFTERMATH

Since the Great Depression, farm bills had set minimum crop prices, with federal payments making up any shortfalls farmers experienced, while enforcing supply limitations to boost prices—a process of logrolling and interest-group placating. But Reagan had promised to slash government spending, including in the farm sector behind Secretary of Agriculture John Block. Ahead of the 1985 farm bill, Reagan joked that America should "keep the grain and export the farmers."[12]

As Congress debated the 1985 farm bill, Midwestern liberals plotted a farm policy turning from free-market conservatism toward economically populist alternatives. Crediting activists in the Iowa Farm Unity Coalition for his 1984 victory over conservative incumbent Roger Jepsen, Harkin proposed "a farm-labor populist alliance that can write a farm bill out here on the prairie . . . rather than having Washington tell you what a new farm program will contain." Midwestern farmers were receptive to reform: many abandoned the conservative American Farm Bureau, even booing its Iowan president at the 1985 National Crisis Action Rally in Ames, Iowa. South Dakota representative Tom Daschle sponsored a $1.8 billion Farm Emergency Credit Bill to help restructure farm debts. But Secretary Block and Office of Management and Budget director David Stockman advised Reagan to veto the Daschle bill in a highly publicized press conference, calling it "a massive new bailout that would add billions to the deficit."[13]

The veto handed farm-state progressives an opportunity. First-term Senate Republicans including Jim Abdnor of South Dakota, Bob Kasten of Wisconsin, and Chuck Grassley of Iowa wrote to Reagan, begging for farm credit assistance. One poll found 68 percent of Americans supported "substantial assistance for agriculture," and American Agriculture Movement activists planted 250 white crosses on the National Mall as Reagan vetoed the bill, one for every farm they claimed went out of business each day. Harkin and farm-state allies promised "a populist alternative—that would hold the line on government spending while strengthening, rather than bankrupting, the American family farmer." Progressives saw the veto as an organizing opportunity: PrairieFire hoped "rural and urban people can, *and must*, work together to confront and resolve our common economic and social problems through our common political actions."[14]

Progressives rallied to Harkin's Farm Policy Reform Act (S. 1083) building coalitions of farmers and labor. The 1985 Harkin bill called for a referendum on supply management among producers, mandated conservation practices, and set a price floor at the cost of production—$3.71 per bushel of corn, a dollar above contemporary prices—that eliminated direct subsidies and would save the government, proponents estimated, $12.5 billion. Part of their "broader visions of political economy," progressive farm groups called the Harkin bill "grassroots democracy in action": the Iowa Farm Unity Coalition (IFUC) and WFUA endorsed it, and the Iowa UAW and Wisconsin AFL-CIO circulated slideshows in support. In a March 1985 meeting in St. Louis, farm and labor groups including the NFU, National Farmers Organization (NFO), UAW, and Teamsters, endorsed the Harkin bill, while Harkin thanked activists in Chicago's Midwest Academy for their support: "Tonight and every night this year, Citizen Action canvassers get out a progressive, populist message to 80,000 Americans."[15]

As Congress wrestled over 1985 farm legislation, state-level activism demanding intervention in the farm economy won political victories. Minnesota Groundswell occupied the office of Democratic-Farmer-Labor (DFL) governor Rudy Perpich after the state's Republican-led House killed a farm foreclosure moratorium bill backed by Minnesota Citizens Organized Acting Together (COACT), NFO, and the Farmers Union. They alleged that "bank and grain company lobbyists worked against the farmer," a complaint echoed by the Dakota Survival League, decrying the defeat of a $50 million interest buy-down bill in North Dakota "to help bank failures." Republican Governor Terry Branstad created a crisis hotline for Iowa farmers over complaints that IFUC had run a hotline in Des Moines for two years before state action, but IFUC and PrairieFire won a foreclosure moratorium in October 1985 and a 1987 bill expanding rights of foreclosed-on farmers to regain their homesteads up to a year later.[16] While farm groups felt their gains were incomplete, they created momentum for larger-scale reform; passing the Farm Policy Reform Act at the federal level was next.

Thwarted by Republican opposition on the 1985 farm bill, which added conservation laws but froze target prices and slashed price supports, Harkin and farm-state allies gained political momentum to win new Senate seats and push the Democratic Party left in 1986 and beyond. The 1985 farm bill was a millstone around the necks of Abdnor and North Dakota Senator Mark Andrews, whose ties to Reagan left them exposed to the attacks of, respectively, Daschle and North Dakota tax commissioner Kent Conrad. Conrad recalled that Andrews's erroneous claim that the price of wheat had gone up doomed him.[17]

Rural Midwestern liberals hoped these victories would convince national Democrats to move left on economic policy. Countering party attempts to co-opt the resurgent Left and the conservative DLC by forming the Democratic Policy Council and canceling the party's midterm convention, strategist John Marttila believed, "National Democrats may unwittingly be helping to politicize" farm activists' ideas. With an electorate, one January 1987 poll showed, "increasingly concerned about their economic future and questioning the administration's agenda," economic populism would vault a progressive Democrat to the forefront in the 1988 presidential primaries.[18]

HARKIN, GEPHARDT, AND JACKSON: 1987–1988

Economically populist legislation and state-level organizing gave Midwestern liberals that opportunity, helping the Midwestern Left build alliances across racial and gendered lines to challenge the Democratic Party's emerging neoliberal consensus. As presidential hopefuls jockeyed in the 1988 primaries, farm issues led to a broader push for economic populism in the Democratic Party.

In 1987 Harkin and Missouri representative Richard Gephardt reintroduced Harkin's Farm Policy Reform Act as the "Save the Family Farm Act" ("Harkin-Gephardt"), pushing populist reforms for American farming. "We must save the family farm," Harkin intoned in 1988, because farmers, laborers, and consumers alike had been "dragged down by this administration's blind faith in free market ideology." Northeastern economists panned the bill, arguing that it favored Midwestern farmers, and the Farm Bureau funded studies claiming supply management would harm farm exports. Organizer labor, though, backed the bill: one Chicago UAW director submitted congressional testimony asserting that "hardship and economic dislocation on the farms cause great problems for many industrial workers as well."[19] Sustaining activism proved challenging, though, as markets stabilized and media declared the Farm Crisis "over."[20] The Senate, with conservative Democrats and farm-state Republicans eager to sign a reform bill, passed the Agricultural Credit Act of 1987, introducing competition into the Farm Credit System and providing $4 billion in long-term funding for farmers. While progressive lobbyists in the National Save the Family Farm Coalition (NSFFC) conceded it was "a step towards comprehensive Farm Credit legislation that addresses necessary reforms to ensure favorable treatment of financially distressed farmers," they criticized it as lukewarm, not structural, reform.[21]

But grassroots support for Harkin-Gephardt galvanized Midwestern liberals in the 1988 presidential primaries, particularly after progressive candidate Jesse Jackson endorsed the bill, calling it "the most humane piece of legislation in our time." The civil rights leader, driving a tractor and wearing a hat emblazoned "I'm Proud to be a Farmer" in a Chillicothe, Missouri, parade, took farm policy advice from NAFA leader Merle Hansen. Endorsing the 1985 Harkin bill, Jackson gave Midwestern farm activists a national mouthpiece. "There is a powerful strain of prairie populism" in Jackson's message, the *Des Moines Register* noted in March 1987, as Jackson announced his candidacy at the Greenfield, Iowa, farm of IFUC leader Dixon Terry. While Terry declared neutrality—though he joked "Dukakis Discovers Farm Crisis" after the Massachusetts governor and candidate proposed Iowa farmers grow blueberries or Belgian endive—he noted that "Jackson's introduction to rural Iowa seems of great benefit in our effort to elevate" progressive farm policy in the Democratic Party.[22]

Farm-labor protectionism characterized those Midwestern liberals' positions. Gephardt promised trade quotas for countries with "excessive" surpluses, similar to what was being done with Japanese, German, and Korean automotive manufacturing. While he drew criticism for those tactics, historian Jeffrey Bloodworth argued, the former chairman of the DLC abandoning its free-market centrism represented the power of the progressive populist coalition. "Conversion experiences" of Democrats on Harkin-Gephardt during the Iowa caucuses and economic justice planks in Jackson's 1988 Democratic National Convention proposals revealed that progressive farm policy had entered national conversations. As the League of Rural Voters observed, Democratic candidates "started identifying unbridled corporate power as the source of America's economic problems.... Economic justice is a powerful idea in 1988."[23]

But Democrats chose Massachusetts Governor Michael Dukakis, and the nation rejected the East Coast technocrat after he abandoned economic populism to defend against George H. W. Bush's race-baiting campaign. While Jackson and populist Texas agriculture commissioner Jim Hightower gave high-profile DNC speeches lauding progressive causes, the Dukakis team fended off populist planks for higher taxes on the wealthy.

Dukakis proclaimed 1988 was "not about ideology, it's about competence."[24] But Midwestern campaign director Ted Mondale admitted Dukakis needed regional appeal: "If rural voters are talking about the 1990 farm bill and who's going to bring them change, we win.... If they're talking about the pledge of allegiance and gun control, we lose." With a 58 to 29 lead in Iowa, Harkin advisers believed, "Prairiefire, AAM, Farmers Union, Save the Family Farm Coalition—I think we've educated [Dukakis]," who endorsed a Harkin-backed "Midwest plan" to "focus more sharply on rural issues" in October. Dukakis carried Minnesota, Iowa, and Wisconsin, but lost the presidency handily.[25]

Some in the Democratic Party establishment, convinced that activists had taken the party too far left, blamed the farm-labor movement. Democratic analyst Ted Van Dyk blamed Gephardt and Jackson for "tilting against a straw man 'establishment,' populated ... by the national media, big business, bankers, and Japanese automakers." Others complained that "something called the 'Save the Family Farm Act'" was the worst idea for solving the Farm Crisis.[26] Midwestern liberals failed to win a substantive national victory.

1990 FARM BILL

The 1990 farm bill—the Food, Agriculture, Conservation, and Trade (FACT) Act—became a flashpoint for renewed grassroots progressive farm action along class-based lines. WFUA, COACT, and South Dakota–based Dakota Rural Action sponsored press conferences in February 1990 "to promote our farmer-written plan for a 1990 Farm Bill," aimed at "overcoming attempts to divide dairy farmers by region." Opposing free trade and deregulation in the Democratic Party, one NAFA member hoped the farm movement would join "anti-corporate campaigns" demanding "economic and social justice for ALL."[27] One organization lobbied for a two-tier program of higher subsidies for family farmers with smaller herds and lower rates for corporate farms with larger herds, and Dakota Rural Action convinced Tim Johnson of South Dakota to introduce their amendment to the House Agriculture Committee.[28]

Building alliances among congressional Democrats, though, challenged Midwestern senators. Harkin and Conrad, Daschle, and Bob Kerrey and Jim Exon of Nebraska backed a permanent disaster fund, higher target prices, loan rate increases for Midwestern commodities, preservation of crop insurance funds, and ethanol subsidies on environmental and economic grounds. Harkin and Conrad also worked on relief for farmers forced to count debt forgiveness as a capital gain.²⁹ But during markup on the 1990 bill, Harkin's advisers conveyed concerns over a proposal by Vermont Senator Patrick Leahy, the ranking member on the Senate Agriculture Committee, that included no increases in target prices, a lower soybean rate, and increased loan rates only if farmers took on more debt: "This Leahy proposal puts 6 or 7 Senate seats in the Midwest in jeopardy. I cannot understand what Leahy and his people are up to. It is politically dumb," complained Harkin adviser Mark Halverson. Harkin tried to convince his party: "Democratic control of the Senate was accomplished largely through victories in 1984 and 1986 in states with a large farm and rural vote. . . . Those members have continued to criticize existing farm policy and to call for better protection of farm income. [They] need a farm bill demonstrating that they can translate that rhetoric into action." Instead, his advisers complained, "Southern Democrats appear willing to abandon the party."³⁰

Opposition from Democrats like Leahy and conservative Southern Democrats thwarted Midwestern liberals. Progressive farm lobbyists complained that Southern Democrats who opposed the two-tier dairy program were "committed to Dairymen Inc . . . advocating continued cuts," while Wisconsin Republican Steve Gunderson claimed, "$14.00 milk price was the norm in the Midwest and the 1985 bill was succeeding." Faced with a bill freezing price supports for wheat and dairy, Midwestern liberals looked ungrateful, struggling to explain opposition to a Harry Reid amendment to deny payments to any farmer grossing over $500,000, with Max Baucus of Montana claiming it would "turn the farm program into a welfare program." *Congressional Quarterly* observed, "Prairie-populist Democrats, insisting that the package is not generous enough, remain poised to leap off the edge and take the whole package down." Daschle complained that the bill "sacrifice[d] family farmers on an altar of imagined free trade," but party leadership chose "accommodating Republicans [and] disappointing the prairie-state Democrats" under "the cover of a compromise." The FACT Act paid farmers on only 85 percent of their land, claiming it gave flexibility to plant anything on the other 15 percent, and provided concessions on "swampbuster" legislation against the drainage of wetlands that appeased Democratic environmentalists.³¹

It left a bitter taste in progressives' mouths, as many concluded that lobbying had failed to win reform. One Wisconsin Farmers Union member complained, "Dairy prices were high and the politicians in Washington were sure a 'market oriented' farm policy would work. But now we're feeling the painful effects of that 1990 farm bill. . . . We knew it would bring lower prices!"³² Rural organizations attacked big business—Groundswell noted that Iowa Beef Packers, ConAgra, and Cargill controlled half the beef slaughter and 40 percent of the hog market by 1988. NAFA member Al Krebs blamed *"corporate agribusiness. . . .* Just as the 19th century agrarian populists declared, you cannot have genuine political democracy unless you have economic democracy," as PrairieFire lobbied in Iowa to challenge corporate farming and restrict big packers' ability to contract feed. But failure to alter the FACT Act convinced others they "should de-emphasize the Washington-legislative aspect of our struggle and turn back to grassroots, community organization." National Family Farm Coalition (NFFC) director Susan Denzer resigned in 1991, and others worried "funding is becoming increasingly tight."[33]

Others found reasons for hope. NAFA and COACT cheered Minnesota Senator-elect Paul Wellstone as "a bright hope for raising the visibility on these issues." PrairieFire's David Ostendorf hoped "we will by the mid-1990s be able to talk seriously and openly about the possibility of a land reform bill at the congressional level."[34] But as Democratic leadership proved willing to compromise, Midwestern liberals struggled to advance progressive farm policy reform within the party.

FREE TRADE

Midwestern liberals' criticisms of free trade, which they alleged helped corporations rather than family farmers, reinforced their belief that neoliberal Democrats abandoned small producers and laborers. But as George H. W. Bush signed the 1990 farm bill and free trade agreements including the Uruguay Round of the General Agreements on Trade and Tariffs (GATT) and NAFTA, Midwestern liberals found themselves isolated by neoliberals within the Democratic Party.

Progressive farm interests sought protection from free trade in the late 1980s. The NFFC Dairy Committee complained, "Farmers are being hit by the farm bill . . . the budget, and GATT," and PrairieFire listed GATT as the culprit in "the continuing plight of farm and rural people." Former League of Rural Voters chairman Mark Ritchie—who the *Wall Street Journal* called the "Paul Revere" of anti-free trade as head of the Institute for Agriculture and Trade Policy (IATP)—provided both groups with material criticizing GATT. Along with the AFL-CIO, farm, labor, and environmental activists fought NAFTA.[35]

They found allies in Midwestern Democrats. "The real goal of Bush in the GATT talks," one Harkin aide alleged, was "to destroy U.S. farm programs, rather than open up market opportunities for American farmers.... It is wrong to think U.S. agriculture will prosper by trying to export ever larger volumes of basic commodities at cheap prices." Wisconsin State Senator Russ Feingold cited a Farmers Union study of the risks GATT posed farmers, and North Dakota secretary of agriculture Sarah Vogel led opposition to GATT and NAFTA as "unfair to small farmers" as North Dakota tax commissioner Heidi Heitkamp reminded a Farmers Union meeting that Bush's concern was "bond holders, not the farmers.... Without fairness there is no free trade—it is just a fiction." Accused of being "protectionist," Wellstone shot back that Bush's trade policy was "dominated by elite special interests ... 42 top executives from large corporations and just two labor representatives."[36] Conrad, with Republicans John Heinz and Ernest Hollings, introduced a resolution to restrict Bush's "fast track" authority to only call for a Senate vote on the final NAFTA text. But neoliberals and the DLC endorsed fast-track, leaving Midwestern liberals isolated again.[37]

While Harkin hoped the 1992 election of Bill Clinton meant the United States would approach free trade "with a higher level of concern for U.S. farmers," other Midwestern liberals attacked. Running for Senate in 1992, Feingold battered incumbent Bob Kasten over his support of NAFTA and the two farm bills. Declaring "This is war," second-term Minnesota representative Collin Peterson organized an anti-NAFTA caucus with industrial Midwest congresspeople like Marcy Kaptur and Sherrod Brown of Ohio and David Bonior of Michigan. Peterson accused Clinton of allowing pro-NAFTA forces to lobby Congress, while in 1994 Sarah Vogel marched with North Dakota wheat farmers on the Canadian border, accusing Canadians of illegally subsidizing wheat production, driving down American prices.[38]

Harkin voted for NAFTA—under pressure, he noted in the Senate, from Iowans who, "36 percent in favor, 36 percent opposed, and 28 percent undecided," required markets for farm products. It made little difference: NAFTA passed overwhelmingly. Harkin was the only Upper Midwestern Democratic senator to support NAFTA. In the House, only two of thirteen Midwestern Democrats voted yes.[39]

FREEDOM TO FAIL

Democrat-supported free trade and deregulation led to Midwestern liberals' greatest defeat: "Freedom to Farm." Signed by President Clinton in April 1996, the FAIR Act followed an acrimonious year in Congress, as the Newt Gingrich–led revolution in 1994 gave budget-cutting conservatives control of Congress. It forced Clinton to "triangulate" with conservative Republicans and the free-market Democratic Leadership Council, signing a welfare-to-work bill in the summer of 1996.[40]

This neoliberal turn extended to farm policy: as conservatives used budget-cutting to force concessions from Clinton, Democrats conceded the heartland. Part of $894 billion in federal spending cuts over seven years, the budget that passed in June 1995 slashed $13 billion from farm spending. One adviser to Secretary of Agriculture Dan Glickman complained that "the Republican, suburban-oriented Congress is abandoning the farm sector" and rural communities. Agriculturally dependent farm counties, one USDA publication noted, included a nearly unbroken swath from the North Dakota–Canada border to north Texas, including large portions of Iowa and Minnesota. Farm advocates like the Nebraska-based Center for Rural Affairs, too, warned that inconsistent support for beginning farmers threatened the future of family farming. "For too many farm families," Harkin agreed, it was "freedom to go broke."[41]

Democratic unity, in early 1995, held budget-cutters at bay. When Indiana Republican Senator Richard Lugar proposed $15 billion in cuts and replacing food stamps with state block grants, Leahy quipped, "A decent farm bill would not tell millions of children, 'You have been block-granted. Have a hungry day!'" Kent Conrad snapped at conservative think-tank testimony that only Joseph Stalin's farm policy was worse than America's, calling it "as far off-base as any testimony I've heard." The House ignored this, passing Republican House Agriculture Committee chair Pat Roberts's bill to eliminate all acreage reduction policies and replace target prices with declining annual payments independent of price or production cost. Because that bill, though, was part of the 1995 budget reconciliation, Clinton sought a showdown with Gingrich and vetoed the bill. The 1995 farm bill became standalone legislation in 1996.[42]

While Clinton won his standoff with Gingrich over the 1995 to 1996 federal shutdown, Midwestern liberals were isolated in negotiations over the 1996 farm bill. The 1995 Roberts bill, called "Freedom to Farm," removed any links between federal support and farm prices: farmers could plant any crop on contracted acres. Requirements to purchase crop insurance were dropped. The market would dictate their choices.[43] These ramifications were acutely felt by the Midwest. USDA analysis of the FAIR Act noted, "In the short term . . . FAIR vs. FACT makes little difference," but warned that the Northern Great Plains would face "decapitalization." Kathleen Merrigan, then at the Wallace Institute of Alternative Agriculture and later deputy secretary of agriculture under Barack Obama, warned Glickman in March that Freedom to Farm meant "more money for the big guys" and no environmental laws or herd size limits, "perverting a national program into a benefits package for the largest livestock confinement operations." Harkin's staff painted a similarly grim picture: "Iowa's farm families and rural communities could not have recovered" in the 1980s "if that much assistance had been denied."[44]

Midwestern farm liberals concurred. Wisconsin Farmers Union demanded a veto; South Dakota Farmers Union reminded readers of "millions of American farmers who entrusted their future to 'market forces' between 1919 and 1933." The Environmental Working Group was less subtle. Hailing the "FREEDOM TO FARM $WEEPSTAKE$," it congratulated absentee landowners as "Agriwelfare Winners," arguing that a "sensible reform bill would retain a safety net for bona fide, working family farmers" and create affordable housing, small business aid, and environmental protections for rural America.[45]

But their Midwestern allies in Congress were cut out of the proceedings. Roberts won Southern Democrats over with price supports for cotton and rice and convinced Republicans of further budget-cutting. But to clear a Senate filibuster, Freedom to Farm needed Democratic votes. Daschle, now Senate minority leader, sought a deal with Republican Bob Dole of Kansas to extend the 1990 farm bill, buying time to work on a comprehensive farm bill. But Leahy made a deal protecting a New England dairy compact, school lunch funding, and conservation programs. Freedom to Farm had its Democratic votes.[46]

Midwestern liberals raged: Harkin said Freedom to Farm "sets [farmers] up for a big fall" and noted they would "suffer damage to their public image" from payments that came when prices were high. After his amendment to protect farmers against low prices and yields failed, Kent Conrad called Freedom to Farm "the beginning of the end of a farm program. . . . There is not the safety net that adjusts for falling prices." Wellstone called the Northeast Interstate Dairy Compact "outrageous." Clinton threatened a veto at Glickman's recommendation, but with farmers concerned about loans for planting in 1996 and Clinton facing reelection, time was not on their side.[47] Sold out by their Democratic allies, Midwestern liberals watched as Freedom to Farm became law.

CONCLUSIONS

The system implemented by Freedom to Farm collapsed almost immediately. The 1997 financial crisis, poor growing seasons, and a lack of price supports contributed to a collapse of the American farm economy that led Congress to appropriate billions in "market loss assistance payments" between 1998 and 2000. From just $7 billion in government aid in 1996, farmers took $28 billion in 2000 alone. Glickman called Freedom to Farm a failure, but the pleas of Daschle, Johnson, and Harkin to relitigate the bill went unheeded.[48]

Fights over US farm policy from the Reagan era through Freedom to Farm illustrated the declining influence of Midwestern liberals at the grass roots and in Congress. "Farmers are being steered toward getting bigger," lamented PrairieFire's Patricia Eddy at a July 1996 meeting of farm advocates. "We should have learned in the 1970s this does not work." Historian William Pratt concluded that year that "the 1980s may have witnessed the last significant progressive rural insurgency in American history."[49]

Small-producer populism waned, and with it, the fortunes of Midwestern Democrats. By 2001, rural sociologists observed that "most major farm organizations represent the interests of large producers" and "most farmers are disengaged from political action." Agricultural economist Bruce Gardner noted that by 1996, "many farmers no longer share[d] the populist anger at their economic situation that has served so well in the political arena."[50] Save the fifty-state focus of Howard Dean's 2004 presidential bid, the Democratic Party drifted from the authentic economic populism of Midwestern liberalism that sought to bridge racial gaps and work for the working class.

The economy of the rural Midwest shifted, too, from family farming to corporate agribusiness, emboldening small-town conservatism against the Democratic Party. As meatpacking and implement manufacturing, hostile to organized labor, held rural towns captive, others fought for scraps like prison-building. Market concentration in meatpacking meant that by 2018, the four largest poultry processors controlled 54 percent of the market, up from 35 percent in 1986. For hogs, that number rose from 33 percent in 1976 to 70 percent in 2018. Beef spiked from 25 percent in 1977 to 85 percent. The number of farms in America dropped as rural communities became dominated by what writer Patrick Wyman, in 2021, called the "American Gentry" of car dealerships and construction companies.[51] As racial resentment stoked by influxes of immigrant labor joined anti-interest group conservatism, neither subsidizing the rural economy nor harvesting a shrinking voter population was cost-effective for Democrats. It provided an opening for Republicans to appeal to the rural Midwest using deregulation, racialized issues like the border and urban welfare, and reinvented "family values"—despite ecumenical and interracial influences on 1980s farm protests—to drive identity-based wedges in the farm-labor alliance.

Harkin and rural Democrats—and allies like Texas agriculture commissioner-turned-populist organizer Jim Hightower—continued the fight for agricultural reform but were undercut permanently by Freedom to Farm. After the crisis of 1998 to 2002, farmers enjoyed government-funded "freedom to choose" as Congress sent billions in emergency aid. Long-term reform was no longer needed. Even Harkin, farm activist Brad Wilson alleged, "stopped advocating for price floors and supported a greened up version of the 1996 Farm Bill" after becoming Senate Agriculture Committee chair in 2002.[52]

But the compromise had been made a decade prior. "Clinton was too clever . . . to turn away from those positions dearest to his party's progressive base," Michael Kazin concluded in his history of the Democratic Party.[53] Except in the Midwest. To be sure, Clinton's signature on Freedom to Farm was the final blow dealt Midwestern liberals by members of their own party: after pushing aside Harkin's 1985 and 1987 reform bills, co-opting Jackson's progressive coalition, siding with Southern Democrats in 1990, and pushing free trade over farm-labor activists, allowing Freedom to Farm as long as northeastern Democrats got what they wanted made sense.

The rural Midwest drifted from its progressive populist heritage. Confident a check would come in crisis, socially conservative ruralites left the Democratic Party as their economies drifted from family farming. The promise of deregulation and absence of financial consequences created by budget-slashing conservatives and neoliberals undermined progressive Democrats' appeal to rural America. Defeats followed: Daschle in 2004, Feingold in 2010. Republicans took seats held by Wellstone, Conrad, Dorgan, Harkin, and Johnson after they died or retired. But for over a decade, fighting for the agricultural Midwest bolstered Democratic majorities in Congress and offered a legacy of economic populism that should characterize future understandings of Midwestern liberalism.

NOTES

1. "Political History of U.S. Farm Policy," Mark Ritchie and Kevin Ristau, League of Rural Voters, Minneapolis, Minnesota, January 1986, 24, Box 24, Farm Crisis Collection, 1980s, University of Northern Iowa, Cedar Falls (hereafter, Farm Crisis Collection).

2. Bill Hogseth, "Why Democrats Keep Losing Rural Counties Like Mine," *Politico Magazine* (online), December 1, 2020, https://www.politico.com/news/magazine/2020/12/01/democrats-rural-vote-wisconsin-441458; David Siders, "The DNC Thought It Killed the Iowa Caucus. It's Not Dead Yet," *Politico Magazine* (online), February 15, 2023, https://www.politico.com/news/magazine/2023/02/15/iowa-caucuses-democratic-national-committee-00082177.

3. Thomas Frank, *What's the Matter with Kansas? How Conservatives Won the Heart of America* (New York: Macmillan, 2007), 64–66; Ross Benes, *Rural Rebellion: How Nebraska Became a Republican Stronghold* (Lawrence: University Press of Kansas, 2021); Catherine McNicol Stock, *Nuclear Country: The Origins of the Rural New Right* (Philadelphia: University of Pennsylvania Press, 2020); Kathy Cramer, *The Politics of Resentment: Rural Consciousness in Wisconsin and the Rise of Scott Walker* (Chicago: University of Chicago Press, 2016); Amy Goldstein, *Janesville: An American Story* (New York: Simon & Schuster, 2017); Dan Kaufman, *The Fall of Wisconsin: The Conservative Conquest of a Progressive Bastion and the Future of American Politics* (New York: W. W. Norton, 2018).

4. Michael Kazin, *What It Took to Win: A History of the Democratic Party* (New York: Farrar, Strauss & Giroux, 2022), 278–289; Lily Geismer, *Left Behind: The Democrats' Failed Attempt to Solve Inequality* (New York: PublicAffairs, 2022); Kevin Kruse and Julian Zelizer, *Fault Lines: A History of the United States since 1974* (New York: W. W. Norton, 2019); Kenneth Baer, *Reinventing Democrats: The Politics of Liberalism from Reagan to Clinton* (Lawrence: University Press of Kansas, 2000), 230–231; Jeffrey Bloodworth, *Losing the Center: The Decline of American Liberalism* (Lexington: University Press of Kentucky, 2013); Patrick Andelic, *Donkey Work: Congressional Democrats in Conservative America, 1974–1994* (Lawrence: University Press of Kansas, 2019).

5. Mark Halverson to Tom Harkin, "Talking Points for Members Meeting May 10," May 9, 1990, 1, Legislative Working Files Series, Subseries 1: Agriculture, 1978–1995, Box 2, Folder 9, Thomas R. Harkin Collection, Drake University Archives, Des Moines, Iowa (hereafter, Harkin Papers).

6. Paul K. Conkin, *A Revolution down on the Farm: The Transformation of American Agriculture since 1929* (Lexington: University Press of Kentucky, 2008), 132–134; "Banking and the Agricultural Problems of the 1980s," in *An Examination of the Banking Crises of the 1980s and Early 1990s* (Washington, DC: FDIC Division of Research and Statistics, 1997), 259–290; Jonathan Coppess, *The Fault Lines of Farm Policy: A Legislative and Political History of the Farm Bill* (Lincoln: University of Nebraska Press, 2018), 163–165; Pamela Riney-Kehrberg, *When a Dream Dies: Agriculture, Iowa, and the Farm Crisis of the 1980s* (Lawrence: University Press of Kansas, 2022).

7. Michael Kazin, *The Populist Persuasion: An American History* (Ithaca, NY: Cornell University Press, 2018), 271. For accounts of progressive activism, see Michael Stewart Foley, *Front Porch Politics: The Forgotten Heyday of American Activism in the 1970s and 1980s* (New York: Hill & Wang, 2013); Ryan Grim, *We've Got People: From Jesse Jackson to Alexandria Ocasio-Cortez, the End of Big Money and the Rise of a Movement* (Washington, DC: Strong Arm Press, 2019); Mary Summers, "From the Heartland to Seattle: The Family Farm Movement of the 1980s and the Legacy of Agrarian State Building," in Catherine McNicol Stock and Robert D. Johnston, *The Countryside in the Age of the Modern State: Political Histories of Rural America* (Ithaca, NY: Cornell University Press, 2001).

8. Mary Turck, "Farm Activist Lou Anne Kling: From Pastures to Protests," *Minnesota Women's Press*, August 1, 2016, https://www.womenspress.com/farm-activist-lou-anne-kling-from-pastures-to-protests/; Tom Parker, "The Power of One: The Perspective of a Long-Time Activist," *Rural Papers* (Kansas Rural Center, 2018), 10, 17, https://static1.squarespace.com/static/5ff64612c539886ec4f1b21f/t/60b6a728147351 47fa4aa0dd/1622583090138/Rural-Papers-Winter-2018-FINAL.pdf; Foley, *Front Porch Politics*, 228–229; "Holding Our Ground: Farm Women Fight Back," Carol Hodne, ed., 1988, Carol Hodne Papers, Iowa Women's Archives, Iowa City; Jenny Barker-Devine,

On Behalf of the Family Farm: Iowa Women's Farm Activism since 1945 (Iowa City: University of Iowa Press, 2013), 137–143; Mark Friedberger, "Women Advocates in the Iowa Farm Crisis of the 1980s," *Agricultural History* 67, no. 2 (1993): 224–234; Sarah Vogel, *The Farmer's Lawyer: The North Dakota Nine and the Fight to Save the Family Farm* (New York: Bloomsbury, 2021).

9. Doug Harsh, "Black Farmers Are in Dire Need of Assistance, Too," *The Country Today*, September 18, 1985, 10; Charles Thompson Jr., *Going Over Home: A Search for Rural Justice in an Unsettled Land* (Hartford, VT: Chelsea Green Publishing, 2019), 138–139; Dan Levitas to Merle Hansen et al., "Proposed Training Sessions for Fall 1985," June 17, 1985, Box 3, Folder 35, Merle Hansen Papers (MS 595), Manuscripts Collection, Iowa State University Archives and Special Collections, Ames (hereafter, Hansen Papers); Dan Levitas, "Inroads & Influence of Far-Right Individuals and Organizations," May 8, 1986, 2, Box 7, Folder 9, Farm Crisis Committee Records (MS 482), Iowa State University Special Collections Department, Ames (hereafter, NSFFC Records); Tracy Watson and Brad Wilson, "Two Hidden Histories of Rural Racial Solidarity Movements," *Journal of Rural Studies* 82 (February 2021): 606–613. See Rebecca Shimoni Stoil, "Tied to Their Country: Agrarian Mobilization, Rural Discourses and the Farm Crises of 1977–1987" (PhD diss., Johns Hopkins University, 2018).

10. "Evaluation of Activities of the North American Farm Alliance, March 1985 through September 1986," 3, Hansen Papers, Box 6, Folder 39; Stephen Carpenter, "Family Farm Advocacy and Rebellious Lawyering," *Clinical Law Review* 24, no. 1 (Fall 2017): 79–134. Those cases were the *Pigford* case (Black farmers), *Keepseagle* (Native), *Love* (women), and *Garcia* (Latinx). Janie Simms Hipp and Toni Stranger-McLaughlin, "Sowing an Updated Dispute Resolution System," *Dispute Resolution* 27, no. 1 (2021): 22–26.

11. Jon Lauck, *American Agriculture and the Problem of Monopoly: The Political Economy of Grain Belt Farming, 1953–1980* (Lincoln: University of Nebraska Press, 2000), 93–94, 153.

12. Bruce L. Gardner, "The Federal Government in Farm Commodity Markets: Recent Reform Efforts in a Long-Term Context," *Agricultural History* 70, no. 2 (Spring 1996): 177–195; Coppess, *The Fault Lines of Farm Policy*, 7–8.

13. "Remarks of Sen. Tom Harkin," January 11, 1985, 2–3, 14, and address by Senator Tom Harkin, April 20, 1985, 11, both in Box 5, Folder 10, Harkin Papers; press release, "Daschle Says Farm Emergency Credit Bill Could Reach Reagan Tuesday," March 1, 1985, Thomas Daschle Papers, Series DA 1, Box 71, Folder 52, Thomas Daschle Papers, South Dakota State University Archives and Special Collections, Hilton M. Briggs Library, Brookings, South Dakota; George de Lama and Lea Donosky, "Reagan Kills Farm Bill," *Chicago Tribune*, March 7, 1985, https://www.chicagotribune.com/news/ct-xpm-1985-03-07-8501130185-story.html; Bernard Weinraub, "President Vetoes Bill on Farm Aid, Citing the Deficit," *New York Times*, March 7, 1985, A1.

14. Milton Coleman, "Reagan Farm Policy Makes Political Fodder in the Midwest," *Washington Post*, April 12, 1985; Louis Harris, "Overwhelming Support for Assistance to Farmers," *Harris Survey*, March 7, 1985, 1, Series II, Subseries A, Box 21, Folder 9, Tip O'Neill Congressional Papers, John J. Burns Library, Boston College; David L. Ostendorf, "Making Real the Vision: Building the Links between Rural and Urban America," PrairieFire, March 23, 1985, 6, Box 10, Folder 12, PrairieFire Rural Action Records (MS 313), Iowa State University Special Collections Department, Ames (hereafter, PrairieFire

Records); "Farmers Rally in Washington," *New York Times*, March 5, 1985, B5; "Senator Tom Harkin Reports on Agriculture," April 1985, 1, Box 5, Folder 10, Harkin Papers.

15. *Iowa Farm Unity News* 1, no. 1 (May 1985): 3, North American Farm Alliance Records, Box 2, Folder 27, Iowa State University Special Collections Department, Ames (hereafter, NAFA Records); Summers, "From the Heartland to Seattle," 304–306; Harry C. Boyte, Heather Booth, and Steve Max, *Citizen Action and the New American Populism* (Philadelphia: Temple University Press, 1986), 142–143; "Campaign Update," Farm Policy Reform Act of 1985, April 10, 1985, 1–2; "New Farm-Labor Alliance Adopts Position on 1985 Farm Bill," c. April 1985, both in Box 9, Folder 58, Harkin Papers; "Nuts & Bolts Tips for Organizing the 1985 Farm Bill Campaign," January 1985, 1, Box 1, Folder 1, WFUC Papers; Text of speech, Tom Harkin, "Address to Midwest Academy," Chicago, August 3, 1985, 1, Box L31, Harkin Papers; Ritchie and Ristau, "U.S. Farm Policy," *World Policy Journal* 4, no. 1 (Winter 1986/1987): 113–134. For text of the bill, see https://www.congress.gov/bill/99th-congress/senate-bill/1083?s=1&r=24.

16. Press release, "Governor Signs Farm Mortgage Bill," July 5, 1985, 1, Box 1, Groundswell, Inc. of Minnesota Records, Minnesota Historical Society, St. Paul (hereafter, Groundswell Records); Bill McAllister, "On the Farm," *Saint Cloud Times*, November 14, 1985, 1C; Lori Sturdevant, "Move to Halt Farm Foreclosures Urged," *Minneapolis Star Tribune*, October 31, 1985, 1B; "Some Fear Farm Act Won't Help," *Bismarck Tribune*, February 1, 1985, 2C; Dave Ostendorf to Coalition Executive Committee, "Hotline and Meeting Plans," January 2, 1984, 1–2, Box 1, Folder 19, PrairieFire (IA) Papers; "Farmers to Take Protest to Branstad," *Sioux City Journal*, September 6, 1985; Daniel Levitas, "Action Alert!," c. May 1987, 2, Box 7, Folder 1, NSFFC Records.

17. Lewrene K. Glaser, "Provisions of the Food Security Act of 1985," USDA Economic Research Service bulletin no. 498 (April 1986); Coppess, *The Fault Lines of Farm Policy*, 166; Fenno, "Interview with Kent Conrad," May 10, 1990, 5–6, https://rbscp.lib.rochester.edu/sites/default/files/atoms/files/D359-Box2-Folder3-Mark-Andrews-Kent-Conrad-May-10–1990.pdf.

18. John Marttila, "Preliminary Reaction to Monday Night's Meeting," July 19, 1985, 2, Box L31, Harkin Papers; Hamilton and Staff, "A Study of American Voters: Post-Election 1986," January 1987, 2. Box 660, Quentin Burdick Papers, Orin G. Libby Manuscript Collection, University of North Dakota, Grand Forks; William Schneider, "The Democrats in '88," *Atlantic Monthly*, April 1987, 37–59.

19. Harkin, "Why We Must Save the Family Farm," in Robert E. Levin, ed., *Democratic Blueprints: 40 National Leaders Chart America's Future* (New York: Hippocrene Books, 1988), 228–229; League of Rural Voters, "Projected Impacts of: The Family Farm Act of 1987 (The Harkin/Gephardt Bill)," February 26, 1987, Box 6, Folder 6, NSFFC Records; "Statement of Bill Stewart, Director, Region 4 International Union, United Automobile, Aerospace & Agricultural Implement Workers of America, UAW, before the Subcommittee on Wheat, Soybeans and Feed Grains, Committee on Agriculture, U.S. House of Representatives," March 31, 1987, 1, Box 8, Folder 11 Harkin Papers; "Consequences of S. 2869, 'Save the Family Farm Act,'" Office of Economics, U.S. Department of Agriculture, enclosed in David S. Christensen to State Farm Bureau Coordinators of National Affairs, November 13, 1986, Box 5, Folder 10, Harkin Papers; Harry M. Kaiser, Edward H. Heslop, and Robert A. Milligan, "Potential Income Effects of the Harkin-Gephardt Proposal on New York Dairy Farms," *Northeastern Journal of Agricultural and Resource Economics* (October 1987): 73–83.

20. Merle Hansen, "A Strategic Response to Assertation That 'The Farm Crisis Is Over,'" August 1987, Box 3, Folder 2, Farm Crisis Collection; James Gannon, "It May Be Heresy to Say This, but the Farm Crisis Has Ended," *Des Moines Register*, May 3, 1987, 1C; Foley, *Front Porch Politics*, 231–232.

21. Farrell E. Jensen, "The Farm Credit System as a Government-Sponsored Enterprise," *Review of Agricultural Economics* 22, no. 2 (Autumn-Winter 2000): 326–335; National Save the Family Farm Coalition, "Report from the Credit Committee," December 6, 1987, 1; Katherine Ozer to Jim R. Billington, February 28, 1988, Box 7, Folder 2, NSFFC Records.

22. James Gannon, "Jesse Jackson Plants His Flag in Rural Iowa," *Des Moines Register*, March 22, 1987; Dixon Terry, "Presidential Race Report," February 2, 1987, 2–3, and Terry, "Presidential Race Report #2," March 13, 1987, 3, both in Box 1, Folder 11, Jesse Jackson '88 Iowa Campaign Headquarters, State Historical Society of Iowa, Des Moines.

23. Bloodworth, *Losing the Center*, 228–229; Fred Barnes, "Charade on Main Street," *New Republic*, June 15, 1987, 15–17; Iowa League of Rural Voters, "The Iowa Caucuses: Farm Policy and the Populist Message," February 1988, 2, Box 6, Folder 6, NSFFC Records; Randall Mikkelsen, "Iowa Caucus Quashes Anti-farm Subsidy Views," *AgWeek*, February 15, 1988, 5.

24. Paul Taylor, "Jackson Salutes Dukakis, Promises Unity in Party," *Washington Post*, July 29, 1988; E. J. Dionne Jr., "Democrats Acclaim Dukakis and Assert Unity," *New York Times*, July 21, 1988; Baer, *Reinventing Democrats*, 115; Bloodworth, *Losing the Center*, 228.

25. Dennis Farney, "America's Political Minefield," *Wisconsin State Journal*, October 9, 1988, D1–D2; Rod Benson to Tom Harkin, "PrairieFire Fundraiser," June 15, 1988, 1, Box 10, Folder 7, Harkin Papers; John J. Pitney, *After Reagan: Bush, Dukakis, and the 1988 Election* (Lawrence: University Press of Kansas, 2019), 155; Bloodworth, *Losing the Center*, 8–9, 236.

26. Hobart Rowen, "Gephardt's Protectionist Campaign," *Washington Post*, February 11, 1988; Editorial, "The Democrats' Worst New Idea," *Washington Post*, November 6, 1986.

27. "American Unity Tour kickoff Is Scheduled," *The Country Today*, February 21, 1990, B7; Steve Hollis to Ed Marks, October 27, 1990, 6, Box 6, Folder 37, Hansen Papers; Marks to Hollis, November 4, 1990, 4, Box 6, Folder 38, Hansen Papers; Hollis, "An Open Letter to Members and Supporters of the National Family Farm Coalition: On the Future Direction of the NFFC, with a Focus on Farmers Home Administration Issues," c. 1990, Box 14, Folder 51, Hansen Papers.

28. Benny Bunting, "Credit Committee Report to the Board—1990," c. December 1990, 3; Curt Rohland and Tom Trantham, "1990 Dairy Committee Report to the Board," c. 1990, 1–2; both in Box 14, Folder 52, Hansen Papers.

29. Halverson to Harkin, "Farm Issues for South Dakota and Iowa," November 21, 1991, 3–4, Box 7, Folder 13, Harkin Papers; "Senate Gets Slightly Modified Farm Bill," *Bismarck Tribune*, June 22, 1990, 1A, 10A; Peyman Pejman, "Farm Bill Might Help on Deficiency Payments," *Bismarck Tribune*, July 31, 1990, 1A; "Kent Conrad's First-Term Record: Accomplishments for North Dakota," October 1992, 3–4, Box 1, North Dakota Elections Collection; Memo to Tom Harkin, "Farm Tax Issues," March 16, 1989, 1, Box 9, Folder 9, Harkin Papers; Laurie Erdman and C. Ford Runge, "American Agricultural

Policy and the 1990 Farm Bill," *Review of Marketing and Agricultural Economics* 58, no. 2–3 (August–December 1990): 109–126.

30. Halverson to Harkin, "Farm Bill Markup; Leahy Markup Draft," June 12, 1990, 1; Halverson to Harkin, "Talking Points for Members Meeting May 10," May 9, 1990, 1, both in Box 2, Folder 9, Harkin Papers; Larry Ballard, "Senate Democrats Unleash Their Own Version of Farm Bill," *Waterloo Courier*, April 4, 1990, A7; Harkin, Speech to Cedar Rapids Rotary Club, March 18, 1991, 1, Box L3, Folder 17, Harkin Papers.

31. Curt Rohland and Tom Trantham, "1990 Dairy Committee Report to the Board," c. 1990, 2, Box 14, Folder 52, Hansen Papers; Jane Norman, "Nagle to Push Farm Bill Package Today in Ag Panel," *Des Moines Register*, May 23, 1990, 2A; David S. Cloud, "Senate 'Prairie Populists' Lose as Panel Approves Farm Bill," *Congressional Quarterly*, June 23, 1990, 1953–1954; Coppess, *The Fault Lines of Farm Policy*, 177, 180–181; "House Says No to Balancing Bill," *Waterloo Courier*, July 22, 1990, A6.

32. Dennis Rosen, "Dairy Policy: A Fight We Can't Afford to Lose!," May 30, 1991, 1, Box 1, Folder 1, Wisconsin Citizen Action Records, Wisconsin Historical Society, Madison.

33. Groundswell, "Newsletter #45," December 1988, 4, Box 1, Groundswell Papers; Al Krebs to Helen Waller et al., "National Family Farm Coalition Policy," November 23, 1989, 2, Box 3, Folder 30, Hansen Papers; David L. Ostendorf to Linden Olson, September 15, 1989, 1, Box 1, Folder 2, PrairieFire Papers,; Hansen to NAFA Board, November 19, 1990, 2, Box 6, Folder 37, Hansen Papers.

34. Ed Marks to NAFA Board, October 12, 1990, 4, Box 6, Folder 37, Hansen Papers; David L. Ostendorf, "American Land Reform: Recent History and Future Prospects," *Community Economics* 17 (Spring 1989): 1–2, in Box 1, Folder 2, PrairieFire Papers.

35. Curt Rohland and Tom Trantham, "1990 Dairy Committee Report to the Board," c. 1990, 2, Box 14, Folder 52, Hansen Papers; David L. Ostendorf to Sue Hartung, April 14, 1989, 1–2, Box 1, Folder 4, PrairieFire Papers; Robert M. McGlotten, "Legislative Alert!," September 25, 1990, Box 3, Folder 35, Hansen Papers; Summers, "From the Heartland to Seattle," 324–325; Mark Ritchie, "Free Trade versus Sustainable Agriculture," September 9, 1992, https://www.iatp.org/documents/free-trade-versus-sustainable-agriculture.

36. Halverson to Harkin, "Farm Issues for South Dakota and Iowa," November 21, 1991, 6–7, Box 7, Folder 13, Harkin Papers; Russ Feingold, "GATT Talks Affect Wisconsin farmers," *Portage Daily Register*, December 7, 1990, 4; Vivenne Levy, "Groups Unite in Tariff Push," *Wisconsin State Journal*, October 25, 1990, 5B; Reed Karaim, "The Farmers' Firebrand," *Rural Electrification*, March 1995, 22, North Dakota Democratic-NPL Party Records (MSS 11078), Box 3, Folder 18, State Historical Society of North Dakota, Bismarck; Heidi Heitkamp, "Farmers Union Address," December 6, 1985, 2, Box 1, Tax Department Commissioner, State Archives, State Historical Society of North Dakota, Bismarck; editorial by Paul Wellstone, *Star Tribune*, May 13, 1991, 14A.

37. Susan A. Aaronson, *Taking Trade to the Streets: The Lost History of Public Efforts to Shape Globalization* (Ann Arbor: University of Michigan Press, 2011), 142–149, 226n42; Jeff Faux, "The NAFTA Illusion," *Challenge* 36, no. 4 (July/August 1993): 4–8; Baer, *Reinventing Democrats*, 179–180; William Avery, "Domestic Interests in NAFTA Bargaining," *Political Science Quarterly* 113, 2 (Summer 1998): 281–305.

38. Halverson to Harkin, "Interview with Gene Lucht of Iowa Farmer Today," January 20, 1993, 1, Box 7, Folder 11, Harkin Papers; Jeff Mayers, "Kasten, Feingold Tangle

over Taxing Issues," *Wisconsin State Journal*, September 12, 1992, 1D; "Kent Conrad's First-Term Record: Accomplishments for North Dakota," October 1992, 11, North Dakota Elections Collection, Box 1, Orin G. Libby Manuscript Collection, University of North Dakota, Grand Forks; Chet Lunner, "Peterson Forms Group to Oppose Trade Pact," *St. Cloud* (MN) *Times*, May 14, 1993, 2A; Jack Anderson and Michael Binstein, "Clouds over NAFTA," *Washington Post*, August 1, 1993; Reed Karaim, "The Farmers' Firebrand," 22; AP wire, "Two Rallies to Protest Canadian Grain Imports," *Bismarck Tribune*, January 29, 1994, 10A.

39. Tom Harkin, Congressional Record—Senate, S16618, November 20, 1993, Box 9, Folder 35, Harkin Papers. Tim Penny of Minnesota and Neal Smith of Iowa voted for NAFTA. Votes accessed at https://www.govtrack.us/congress/votes/103-1993/h575; https://www.senate.gov/legislative/LIS/roll_call_votes/vote1031/vote_103_1_00395.htm#state.

40. Geismer, *Left Behind*, 176–181; Kazin, *Populist Persuasion*, 289–290; Julian Zelizer, *Burning Down the House: Newt Gingrich, the Fall of a Speaker, and the Rise of the New Republican Party* (New York: Penguin Books, 2020); Nicole Hemmer, *Partisans: The Conservative Revolutionaries Who Remade American Politics in the 1990s* (New York: Basic Books, 2022).

41. Coppess, *The Fault Lines of Farm Policy*, 182–184; Nancy L. Thompson, Brian Foster, D. Kirk Darnell, Joy Johnson, and Annette M. Higby, "Financing Beginning Farmers: An Evaluation of Farm Service Agency Credit Programs," Center for Rural Affairs (Walthill, NE), November 1995, 27–29, Box L3, Folder 1, Harkin Papers; Karl Stauber and Barbara Meister, "USDA Interdepartmental Initiative to Assist Farmers in Managing the Budget Cuts to Commodity Programs," Decision Memorandum for the Secretary of Agriculture, c. 1995, 2–3, 5, Box 21, Folder 10, Papers of US Secretary of Agriculture Dan Glickman, Wichita State University Libraries Special Collections and University Archives, Wichita, Kansas (hereafter, Glickman Papers); "Points for Opening Remarks on Commodity Titles Hearing," June 13, 1995, 1, Box L3, Folder 4, Harkin Papers.

42. AP wire, "Farm Hearing Opens with Harsh Criticism," *Des Moines Register*, March 10, 1995, 5A; Coppess, *The Fault Lines of Farm Policy*, 187–188; Karl Limvere and Mark Halverson to Greg Frazier, fax dated July 25, 1995, 1, Box 21, Folder 15, Glickman Papers; Zelizer, *Burning Down the House*, 299–300.

43. Coppess, *The Fault Lines of Farm Policy*, 184; Economic Research Service/USDA, "1996 FAIR Act Frames Farm Policy for 7 Years," *Agricultural Outlook Supplement* (April 1996): 1–21, https://www.ers.usda.gov/media/v2hlwvsk/provisions-of-the-1996-farm-bill.pdf; "Statement of Senator Tom Harkin, Farm Bill Conference Report," March 27, 1996, 8, Box L3, Folder 5B, Harkin Papers.

44. "Implications of Passage of FAIR for the Agricultural Sector and USDA Policy and Programs," Economic Research Service, USDA, April 12, 1996, 4–5, Box 21, Folder 8, Glickman Papers; "1996 FAIR Act Frames Farm Policy for 7 Years," Economic Research Service, USDA (April 1996), https://www.ers.usda.gov/media/v2hlwvsk/provisions-of-the-1996-farm-bill.pdf; Kathleen Merrigan, "Letter to Secretary Glickman on Farm Bill Conference," March 5, 1996, 1, Box 22, Folder 6, Glickman Papers; Halverson to Harkin, "Economic Analysis of Republican Farm Bill," February 9, 1996, 4–5, Box L3, Folder 5B, Harkin Papers.

45. Arnie Hoffman, "Farm Leaders Disappointed, Upset over Farm Bill Changes,"

The Country Today, March 6, 1996, A3; Lynwood E. Oyos, *The Family Farmers' Advocate: South Dakota Farmers Union, 1914–2000* (Sioux Falls, SD: Center for Western Studies, Augustana College, 2000), 308–312; Kenneth A. Cook, "Foreword," in "'Freedom to Farm': An Analysis of Payments to Large Agribusiness Operations, Big City Residents and the USDA Bureaucracy, FY 1996 to FY 2002," *EWG Report No. 4* (February 27, 1996), i–iii, Box 7, Folder 43, Harkin Papers.

46. Dick Rebbeck, "Daschle Says Farm Bill Impasse Nearing End," *Rapid City Journal*, January 30, 1996, A8; Coppess, *The Fault Lines of Farm Policy*, 190.

47. "Statement of Senator Tom Harkin, Farm Bill Conference Report," March 27, 1996, 8, Box L3, Folder 5B, Harkin Papers; Don Davis, "N.D. Delegation Unhappy with Farm Measure," *Bismarck Tribune*, March 22, 1996, 9A; wire report, "Congress Passes Subsidy-Cutting Farm Bill," *St. Cloud Times*, March 29, 1996, 8C; "Clinton Holds Nose on Farm Bill," *Chicago Tribune*, February 9, 1996.

48. Coppess, *The Fault Lines of Farm Policy*, 194, 196; editorial, "Freedom to Farm Grows Subsidies," *Chicago Tribune*, October 12, 2000, 18.

49. "Speakers: Farm Bill Causing Stress on Family Farms," *The Country Today*, July 17, 1996, A3; William Pratt, "Using History to Make History? Progressive Farm Organizing during the Farm Revolt of the 1980s," *Annals of Iowa* 55, no. 1 (1996): 45n55.

50. Linda Lobao and Katherine Meyer, "The Great Agricultural Transition: Crisis, Change, and Social Consequences of Twentieth Century US Farming," *Annual Review of Sociology* 27 (2001): 112, http://www.jstor.org/stable/2678616; Gardner, "The Federal Government in Farm Commodity Markets," 182.

51. Claire Kelloway and Sarah Miller, "Food and Power: Addressing Monopolization in America's Food System," Open Markets Institute, September 2021, https://static1.squarespace.com/static/5e449c8c3ef68d752f3e70dc/t/614a2ebebf7d510debfd53f3/1632251583273/200921_MonopolyFoodReport_endnote_v3.pdf; Ian Toller-Clark, "From Breweries to the Super-Max: The Making of Carceral Populism in Metropolitan Milwaukee," in Jon K. Lauck and Catherine McNicol Stock, eds., *The Conservative Heartland: A Political History of the Postwar American Midwest* (Lawrence: Kansas University Press, 2020), 227–246; Patrick Wyman, "American Gentry," *Atlantic*, September 23, 2021, https://www.theatlantic.com/ideas/archive/2021/09/trump-american-gentry-wyman-elites/620151/.

52. Coppess, *The Fault Lines of Farm Policy*, 198; Brad Wilson, "The Harkin Compromise," *Family Farm Justice*, May 30, 2019, https://familyfarmjustice.me/2019/05/30/the-harkin-compromise/.

53. Kazin, *What It Took to Win*, 290.

17

Capital Punishment in the Midwest

Liberal Struggles, Race, and Legacy

EMMA RICKNELL

❖ ❖ ❖ ❖ ❖ ❖ ❖ ❖ ❖ ❖ ❖ ❖ ❖ ❖ ❖

In 2015, legislators in Michigan introduced a resolution that would allow for the reintroduction of the death penalty, in effect abandoning the state's almost 170-year-long ban. Michigan Catholic Conference president and CEO Paul Long was among the many vocal opponents to the resolution; he stated that "a government with the power to kill is a government with too much power."[1] Long's choice of words provides a bridge to those of the 1844 legislative committee that set the stage for the state's historic abolition of the death penalty, seeing as the committee viewed the death penalty as "an usurped power of government."[2] The resolution, much like previous attempts to resurrect the death penalty in Michigan, eventually failed and illustrates the power of a remarkably consistent liberal opposition in the state.

Michigan is, however, not alone in its opposition to the ultimate punishment, but is part of a long, pioneering movement toward abolition in the Midwest that has only gained national foothold in the past two decades as public support declines and executions become more and more rare.[3] As this chapter will show, this movement has involved local leadership from a variety of religious, political, professional, and immigrant communities. At the same time, the Midwest is home to a wide range of responses to handling particularly heinous criminal offenders, featuring everything from historic decisions to reject the death penalty altogether to maintenance of still active death penalty statutes. Indeed, the Midwest illustrates the "hodgepodge of state laws" that characterizes the death penalty in the United States, the result of a form of "place-specific cultural rootedness."[4] This chapter provides a contrasting analysis between the historically abolitionist states and still active death penalty states in the Midwest. It begins with an overview of two factors highlighted in the research on the death penalty in the United States, namely ideological patterns and the role of race.

While the argument does not necessarily hold over time, nor in all states, the research nevertheless points toward a general ideological division between proponents and opponents of capital punishment. Conservative politicians have been associated with support for the death penalty, and their liberal counterparts with anti–death penalty sentiments.[5] As David Garland points out, a historic look at classical liberalism and its thinkers reveals why liberals have traditionally been opposed to the death penalty—that is, because of a view of social order that values the freedom and autonomy of individuals as well as a limited governmental power order.[6]

The modern era of the death penalty exhibits multiple examples of ideological division, with some inconsistencies. The era is commonly described as beginning in the year 1972, when the US Supreme Court declared the death penalty unconstitutional in *Furman v. Georgia*[7] as it was applied under then-existing laws.[8] The decision in *Furman* triggered a push back, which resulted in an incremental acceleration of the death penalty that did not reach its peak until almost three decades later. It was primarily driven by conservatives, in stark contrast to the enthusiastic liberal response to *Furman*.[9] Garland describes the backlash as part of a much wider reaction that included opposition against the civil rights movement, Great Society liberalism, and the overall perceived disorder of the 1960s. This reaction resulted in the death penalty being seen as an issue of law and order, symbolic of the importance of states' rights, and a response to the new "war on crime," as well as a culture war issue.[10]

For many liberal politicians, promoting death penalty laws that did not adhere to the punitive turn was a losing battle in the era of a revived death penalty. Then came along a Democratic president, Bill Clinton, whose administration dismantled the partisan division on capital punishment by embracing the policy, enhancing it at the federal level and making it part of Democratic politics.[11] In 1999 the death penalty reached an all-time high in terms of executions, with ninety-eight performed in the United States that year.[12] This approach has since changed, yet the Democratic Party platform did not call for the abolition of the death penalty until 2016.[13]

While the modern era of the death penalty points to a general ideological cleavage, considerable academic attention has also been paid to the aspect of race. As an example, noted death penalty scholars Carol and Jordan Steiker describe America's retention of the death penalty as being "tied in part to its distinctive history of racial subordination and injustice."[14] The fact that since colonial times, execution rates of African Americans have been higher compared to those of whites most explicitly illustrates this distinctive history, but can also be extended to racial disparities—for example, when it comes to gruesomeness of execution methods and the number of death penalty–eligible crimes.[15] Research furthermore shows that contemporary levels of racial hostility result in more death sentences, particularly for African American offenders, and is overall strongly correlated with support for the continued use of the death penalty.[16] With the aspects of ideology and race in mind, this chapter will continue with an account of the Midwestern experience of the death penalty, beginning with the historically abolitionist states.

Michigan's decision to abolish the death penalty in 1846, followed by Wisconsin's in 1853, broke new ground. Death penalty abolition occurred in only two other states during the 1800s (Rhode Island in 1852 and Maine in 1887). From a global perspective, the events in these two pioneering Midwestern states were at the forefront of the world's abolitionist movement.[17] After Michigan and Wisconsin, the death penalty abolitionist section of the Midwest later expanded to Minnesota (1911), Iowa (1965), and North Dakota (1973). Following are accounts of the factors highlighted as instrumental in the process to abolish the death penalty in those states.

In Michigan, opposition to the death penalty had been established well before statehood. Out of a number of factors that likely influenced the decision, local leadership was a prominent one.[18] In fact, many of the vocal death penalty opponents had likely held such sentiments for some time before the decision to abolish was made, as they had immigrated to Michigan from New York or New England, where liberal anti–capital punishment and antislavery movements had been active for decades. The legislature in the 1840s to a significant extent consisted of individuals with such backgrounds, and embedded in these anti–death penalty sentiments were likely deep-seated convictions that were suspicious of state authority and the kind of power that should be imposed upon individuals.[19]

Uniquely to Michigan, opposition among leading figures has since not only been remarkably consistent but present in multiple realms of society via local leaders and political, economic, religious, and professional organizations.[20] In more modern times, bipartisan cooperation has contributed to the creation of a stable foundation for continued anti–death penalty work. For example, when the words "No law shall be enacting providing for the penalty of death" were entered in the 1963 Michigan Constitution, thereby making the return of the death penalty a matter requiring a constitutional amendment, efforts by Republican attorney Eugene Wanger, with the strong support of Democratic attorney Tom Downs, have been credited as essential.[21] By the 1970s, the same two attorneys would co-chair the influential abolitionist organization the Michigan Committee Against Capital Punishment.[22]

Similarly to Michigan, Wisconsin's decision to abolish was facilitated by the state's relatively small population, which allowed for groups calling for abolition to have influence.[23] The state's handling of capital punishment from a longer time perspective has furthermore been attributed to its cultural traditions of progressive liberalism, exemplified by Governor Robert La Follette, founder of the 1924 Progressive Party.[24] Recent scholarship, however, challenges the idea of Wisconsin becoming abolitionist as a consequence of a larger anti–death penalty movement sweeping in from the Northeast. In an effort to uncover how the decision to abolish actually came about, Daniel Belczak argues that abolition did not occur thanks to a convinced anti–death penalty legislature, but was rather influenced by a number of events that took place in proximity to the vote, such as the rare event of an execution in the state and the process toward building the state's first penitentiary.[25] Arguments presented in support of the abolition bill nevertheless had liberal undertones, conveying the idea that the death penalty had no place in a modern society, that it devalued human life, and that executions only served to punish instead of reforming offenders. Importantly, religious sentiments also played a role, and it was legislators from more liberal denominations that were able to significantly influence the final vote.[26]

The groundbreaking record when it comes to death penalty abolition in the Midwest also includes the state of Minnesota. The state became abolitionist during a significant wave of legal reform during the Progressive Era (1900 to 1918) that resulted in abolition in ten states, of which five were Midwestern (Minnesota, North Dakota, Kansas, South Dakota, and Missouri), even though only Minnesota and North Dakota remained abolitionist in the post-Progressive period.[27] Abolition efforts had been underway for decades before 1911, but the final push has been attributed to events following a botched hanging carried out in 1906, during which the convicted man took fifteen minutes to die from strangulation.[28] In reaction, Minnesota's Governor Adolph O. Eberhart threatened to resign if he had to oversee another execution, and stated that "I believe the interests of justice and humanity demand the repeal of the law."[29] Legislators who had previously supported abolition bills aided the process toward abolition a few years later.[30] Governor Eberhart was a Swedish Republican and part of a group of Scandinavian immigrants that had great influence on politics in Minnesota, often drawn to the Republican Party and its aims to end slavery and liquor reform.[31]

While Iowa and North Dakota abolished the death penalty much later compared to the aforementioned states, both nevertheless had a long abolitionist tradition. Iowa abolished the death penalty in 1872 but reinstated it in 1878 after a number of well-publicized lynchings and a perceived national crime wave. Iowa did not, however, ramp up its moderate use of executions after this point, and by the 1950s executions had become very rare.[32] The second abolition, in 1965, took place in a very different time period compared to the aforementioned states, one in which the influence of partisan politics was comparatively more explicit. Among the most significant factors influencing the successful abolition efforts in the 1960s are Democratic Governor Harold E. Hughes's strong convictions and charismatic leadership, the advocacy of Des Moines newspaper the *Register*, and campaigning efforts by church groups and other organizations, as well as the fact that Democrats were in control of both houses of the legislature. Furthermore, the repeal bill has been argued to have been a reaction to the brutality of the Southern response to the ongoing civil rights movement, emphasizing respect for all human life via abolition.[33]

Finally, the North Dakotan experience of the death penalty is in essence similar to that of Michigan and Wisconsin. The last execution carried out in the state occurred in 1905 and was the eighth on the state's record. North Dakota retained the option of being able to sentence to death prisoners convicted of murdering a prison guard while serving a life sentence when the state legislature voted to abolish in 1915, but this option was never utilized. A new criminal code finally removed all death penalty–eligible crimes in 1973.[34] Similarly to the earliest abolitionist states, immigrants who had settled in the state have been highlighted as a significant influence in the development of long-lasting anti–death penalty sentiments, bolstered by liberal ideas that fueled distrust toward state power over life and death.[35]

The preceding brief description of an in many respects groundbreaking response to capital punishment in five Midwestern states is not intended to be seen as a cohesive series of events. From a general perspective, it calls attention to a long abolitionist tradition in the Midwest involving strong leadership and local campaigning efforts by a variety of influential actors campaigning together, with clear ties to liberal thoughts on criminality and the role of government. Successful abolitionist efforts in the upper Midwest have indeed been argued as being partly a result of a true "culture of liberalism."[36]

Regarding the issue of race, the limited experience of practicing the death penalty among these Midwestern states could lead one to assume that racial bias never developed into a serious factor. In fact, strong anti-Southern sentiments, including express criticism against reprehensive racially motivated acts of violence among the five contiguous states, can aid our understanding why abolition occurred in the first place.[37] Such an assumption, however, disregards a number of facts, such as the existence of different manifestations of white supremacy in the region, for example, in antebellum, overwhelmingly white Iowa, Minnesota, and Wisconsin.[38] Lynchings of African Americans have furthermore been documented in all Midwestern states besides South Dakota.[39] In regard to the death penalty, historic research can point to additional patterns of racial bias. For example, even in the pioneering abolitionist state of Michigan, the overwhelming majority of executions involved Native American men.[40] In Iowa, seven out of the forty-six men executed there were African American; their treatment was marked by racism in press coverage as well as in the tactics used by prosecutors.[41]

Nevertheless, racial violence in the five states was not as prevalent as in the South. Importantly, this comparison is relevant also to the neighboring Lower Midwestern states, where the death penalty is still administered today.[42] The Lower Midwest forms a sort of cultural borderland of the South, arguably shaped in its early history by this proximity.[43] This chapter now turns to very recent history among the Midwestern states that had active death penalty laws in the 2000s: Illinois, Indiana, Kansas, Missouri, Nebraska, Ohio, and South Dakota.

Toward the end of the 1990s, the death penalty in the United States stood at its peak. In terms of executions, the seven active death penalty states in the Midwest had been contributing to the upswing in the 1990s, yet were not comparable to the dominance of states in the South. In 1999 there were seventy-four executions in the South, twelve in the Midwest, eleven in the West, and one in the Northeast.[44] This is not to say that the Midwestern death penalty states were inactive. Table 17.1 displays the number of death sentences and executions in the seven states starting in 1999, divided into two ten-year periods, with the years 2019 to 2022 reported separately. The overall decline of the death penalty is visible, with Illinois

Table 17.1. Death Sentences and Executions in Midwestern States, 1999–2022

State	1999–2008 Death Sentences	1999–2008 Executions	2009–2018 Death Sentences	2009–2018 Executions	2019–2022 Death Sentences	2019–2022 Executions
Illinois	40	1	2	—	—	—
Indiana	10	13	5	1	0	0
Kansas	9	0	4	0	0	0
Missouri	37	34	8	22	1	8
Nebraska	7	0	5	1	1	0
Ohio	53	28	34	28	7	0
South Dakota	3	1	5	3	0	1

Note: Illinois abolished the death penalty in 2011.

Sources: Data from Death Penalty Information Center (DPIC) Execution Database (https://death penaltyinfo.org/executions/execution-database) and Sentencing Data (https://deathpenalty info.org/facts-and-research/sentencing-data/death-sentences-in-the-united-states-from-1977-by -state-and-by-year).

being the most obvious example as the state abolished in 2011; and Kansas, Nebraska, and North Dakota carrying out executions very sparingly, if at all. By the end of the period, it can also be noted that the number of prisoners under sentence of death in the remaining death penalty states varied greatly. During 2022, Ohio's death row was the fifth largest of all thirty-one then active death-penalty states (134 prisoners), while other Midwestern states had comparatively much smaller death rows.[45]

A review of Midwestern legislative activity also reveals insights into the handling of the death penalty among the states under consideration. Death penalty laws are shaped in the state legislatures; however, a limited number of the thousands of bills presented in state legislatures every session become law.[46] In order to consider overall activity beyond implemented laws, Table 17.2 presents bill sponsorship of all pro– or anti–death penalty bills introduced in Midwestern death penalty states 1999 to 2021, divided into sponsorship categories *Democratic*, *Republican*, and *bipartisan*.[47] The table shows that when it comes to bills that aim to restrict or even remove the death penalty, bill sponsors are overwhelmingly Democratic in most states. In Kansas and South Dakota, such bills tend to have bipartisan support. In contrast, pro–death penalty bills are primarily sponsored by Republican legislators in Missouri, Nebraska, and Ohio, while sponsorship in Illinois and Indiana is relatively evenly split between the three categories. Both Kansas and South Dakota show a pattern of bipartisan sponsorship also for bills supportive of the death penalty. In terms of pure numbers, Table 17.2 also shows how bills aiming to

Table 17.2. Partisan Sponsorship by Bill Category, 1999–2021 (Death Penalty States)

	Anti–Death Penalty Bills			Pro–Death Penalty Bills		
	Democratic	Republican	Bipartisan	Democratic	Republican	Bipartisan
Illinois	77 (69)	9 (8)	25 (23)	8 (33)	10 (42)	6 (25)
Indiana	35 (69)	2 (4)	14 (27)	22 (30)	29 (40)	22 (30)
Kansas	2 (6)	2 (6)	29 (88)	0 (0)	1 (8)	12 (92)
Missouri	93 (62)	35 (23)	23 (15)	6 (15)	32 (78)	3 (7)
Nebraska	40 (82)	2 (4)	7 (14)	0 (0)	9 (100)	0 (0)
Ohio	20 (43)	7 (15)	20 (43)	1 (5)	13 (62)	7 (33)
South Dakota	8 (29)	0 (0)	20 (71)	0 (0)	2 (40)	3 (60)
Total	275 (59)	57 (12)	138 (29)	37 (20)	96 (52)	53 (28)

Notes: The percentage of each state's total number of bills by category is included in parenthesis. Percentages may not total 100 due to rounding. Bipartisan sponsorship is defined as 20 percent or more representation by the minority party. Bill content categorization is based on a division of bills between those that aim to restrict the use of the death penalty, or support the defendant during trial or appeal, and those that support its continued use or even aim to expand it. Data collected via each state legislature's official website.

in some way limit the death penalty, or get rid of it altogether, are far more commonly introduced.

When adding together the number of death sentences and executions, as well as legislative activity in the Midwestern death penalty states, an overall picture of a death penalty in decline appears, where the main push toward legal reform following such a path is driven by Democrats, or via bipartisan cooperation. Nevertheless, individual differences remain among the states. First and foremost, Illinois no longer retains the death penalty, being the only state to abolish in the region since North Dakota in 1973. Abolition occurred after a series of miscarriages of justice were uncovered, including wrongful convictions, prosecutorial misconduct, and race discrimination, and involved bipartisan leadership all the way up to the governor's office. The abolition efforts, which were in fact ongoing for decades prior to 2011, represent a major event in the history of the abolition movement, and again put the Midwest at its forefront.[48]

Two states, Kansas and South Dakota, could arguably have followed the same path as Minnesota and North Dakota, yet both reinstated the death penalty in the 1930s. In the case of South Dakota, it is likely that triggering events in the form of heinous and heavily publicized murders resulted in the reinstatement; also, despite being similar to its northern neighbor North Dakota in many ways, South Dakota is generally less liberal.[49] Considering both states' limited record when it comes to the actual use of the death penalty over time, coupled with comparatively less partisan legislative activity in recent years, the current situation seems to provide an opening for continuing the Midwestern tradition of death penalty abolition via local, bipartisan political leadership.

Nebraska's response to the death penalty is similarly ambivalent, and not only when it comes to its sparing use of executions. After the *Furman* decision in 1972, Nebraska's legislature in 1979 passed an abolition bill only to have it vetoed by the governor, in 1999 imposed a moratorium on executions, and again in 2015 passed an abolition bill, then overrode the governor's veto, only to have the death penalty reinstated after a state referendum.[50] A notable legislator in the context, Ernie Chambers—Nebraska's first African American state senator—who led the effort to abolish in 2015, had presented an abolition bill that year, just as he had done every year for decades prior. He was joined by a coalition of liberals and libertarian-minded conservatives, as well as religious groups.[51] Senator Chambers has expressed that the death penalty in Nebraska is racist in character, though research has not confirmed that there is compelling evidence for discriminatory practices in the system.[52]

Remaining Midwestern death penalty states Indiana, Missouri, and Ohio represent the most active. Activity is, however, waning, and just like in other states the primary push to introduce restrictive legislation comes from Democrats or via bipartisan efforts. As Table 17.1 indicates, if nothing dramatically changes the current trajectory, these three states could join other more or less inactive death penalty states. Out of the three, Missouri stands out in terms of death penalty use. It likewise stands out as having been a slave state, with comparatively higher levels of racist violence, including lynchings, but also nonlethal violence such as whippings, documented well into the 1900s. As recently as 2012, the American Bar Association concluded that Missouri's capital punishment system could despite various reforms not be declared as free from the influence of race.[53]

Yet even Missouri is, in the context of the death penalty in the Midwest, not void of contradictions. As mentioned previously, Missouri abolished the death penalty in 1917, only to bring it back again two years later after high-profile murders affected public sentiments.[54] In terms of the state's current status as an active death penalty state, as Table 17.2 shows, legislators still seem open to a restrictive administration of the death penalty, considering their prolific introductions of anti–death penalty legislation.

The Midwestern experience of the death penalty highlights important variety among individual states, potentially blurring straightforward conclusions regarding what lessons can be learned in the process toward national abolition. It does, however, offer clarity on three fundamental points. First, the Midwest provides an example of a unique and incredibly long-lasting legacy in the context of the death penalty abolition movement. As a region, it has made an impact within the context of a historic, global movement toward death penalty abolition. Second, efforts taken to restrict or abolish the death penalty altogether were historically primarily driven by liberal reformers and a variety of local organizations, many of them religious, in the region's northern states. This tradition of forming coalitions to push for abolition is visible in today's state legislatures, where bipartisan efforts to restrict or remove the death penalty in the remaining death penalty states are ongoing. Cory Haala argues that since the 1980s, a regional form of liberalism has developed in the Midwest—a form of "progressive center" that can attract both liberal and more conservative Midwesterners.[55] This could possibly provide fertile ground for abolition in the Lower Midwest, considering the importance of political leadership. Third, the pattern of states in the Upper Midwest being more restrictive in their use of the death penalty compared to the Lower Midwest can be related to a general pattern of less racialized violence in the north. The prevalence of discriminatory practices and racial violence in the criminal justice system, particularly in a former slave state such as Missouri, inevitably puts states in the Lower Midwest on a different path toward abolition. "Less" racialized violence is, however, not the same as "none," meaning the legacy of a violent past *and* one of pioneering, liberal leadership is contained within one and the same region, the Midwest.

NOTES

1. Michigan Catholic Conference, "Catholic Conference Vows Vigorous Opposition to Death Penalty Resolution," press release, February 4, 2015, accessed October 12, 2023, https://www.micatholic.org/advocacy/news-room/news-releases/2015/mcc-opposes-death-penalty-resolution/.

2. Michigan Legislature, "Majority Report of the Select Committee on the Abolishment of Capital Punishment" (Detroit: State of Michigan, 1844).

3. Death Penalty Information Center, "The Death Penalty in 2022: Year End Report" (2022), accessed December 20, 2022, https://deathpenaltyinfo.org/facts-and-research/dpic-reports/dpic-year-end-reports/the-death-penalty-in-2022-year-end-report.

4. Keith Harries and Derral Cheatwood, *The Geography of Executions: The Capital Punishment Quagmire in America* (Lanham, MD: Rowman & Littlefield, 1997), 13.

5. See Carol. S. Steiker and Jordan M. Steiker, "A Tale of Two Nations: Implementation of the Death Penalty in 'Executing' Versus 'Symbolic' States in the United States," *Texas Law Review* 84, no. 7 (2006): 1869–1929.

6. David Garland, *Peculiar Institution: America's Death Penalty in an Age of Abolition* (Cambridge, MA: Belknap Press of Harvard University Press, 2010), 136.

7. *Furman v. Georgia*, 408 U.S. 238 (1972).

8. The *Furman* decision allowed states to rewrite their death penalty statutes, which is precisely what thirty-five states did within a few years, thus enabling the continued practice of capital punishment. See Garland, *Peculiar Institution*, 233.

9. Garland, *Peculiar Institution*, 231–233.

10. Garland, *Peculiar Institution*, 234–235.

11. Garland, *Peculiar Institution*, 247.

12. Death Penalty Information Center, "The Death Penalty in 2022."

13. Caitlin Oprysko, "Capital Punishment/Death Penalty," *Politico*, March 5, 2020, https://www.politico.com/2020-election/candidates-views-on-the-issues/criminal-justice-reform/capital-punishment-death-penalty.

14. Carol S. Steiker and Jordan M. Steiker, "The Rise, Fall, and Afterlife of the Death Penalty in the United States," *Annual Review of Criminology* 3, no. 1 (2020): 299–315.

15. Steiker and Steiker, "The Rise, Fall, and Afterlife."

16. Frank R. Baumgartner, Christian Caron, and Scott Duxbury, "Racial Resentment and the Death Penalty," *Journal of Race, Ethnicity, and Politics* (2022): 16.

17. Garland, *Peculiar Institution*, 37, 120.

18. Garland, *Peculiar Institution*, 38.

19. James H. Lincoln, "The Everlasting Controversy: Michigan and the Death Penalty," *Wayne Law Review* 33, no. 5 (1987): 1765–1790, 1781.

20. John F. Galliher et al., *America without the Death Penalty: States Leading the Way* (Boston, MA: Northeastern University Press, 2002), 28.

21. Lincoln, "The Everlasting Controversy," 1787.

22. Eugene G. Wanger, *Fighting the Death Penalty: A Fifty-Year Journey of Argument and Persuasion* (East Lansing: Michigan State University Press), 110.

23. Stuart Banner, *The Death Penalty: An American History* (Cambridge, MA: Harvard University Press, 2002), 134.

24. Galliher et al., *America without the Death Penalty*, 32.

25. Daniel Belczak, "'Blood for Blood Must Fall': Capital Punishment, Imprisonment, and Criminal Law Reform in Antebellum Wisconsin" (PhD diss., Case Western Reserve University, 2021), 351.

26. Belczak, "Blood for Blood Must Fall," 288.

27. Malik C. Sheherezade and D. Paul Holdsworth, "A Survey of the History of the Death Penalty in the United States," *University of Richmond Law Review* 49, no. 3 (2015): 693–710, 698.

28. Galliher et al., *America without the Death Penalty*, 82.

29. John D. Bessler, *Legacy of Violence: Lynch Mobs and Executions in Minnesota* (Minneapolis: University of Minnesota Press, 2003), 168.

30. Galliher et al., *America without the Death Penalty*, 82.

31. Klas Bergman, *Scandinavians in the State House: How Nordic Immigrants Shaped Minnesota Politics* (St. Paul: Minnesota Historical Society Press, 2017).

32. Galliher et al., *America without the Death Penalty*, 170–171.

33. Galliher et al., *America without the Death Penalty*, 188.

34. John Gregory Jacobsen, "The Death Penalty in the Great Plains," in Gordon

Morris Bakken, ed., *Invitation to an Execution: A History of the Death Penalty in the United States* (Albuquerque: University of New Mexico Press, 2010), 250.

35. Galliher et al., *America without the Death Penalty*, 114.

36. Eliza Husband, "A Geographical Perspective on US Capital Punishment, 1801–1960" (PhD diss., Louisiana State University, 1990), x.

37. Galliher et al., *America without the Death Penalty*, 97.

38. Leslie Schwalm, *Emancipation's Diaspora: Race and Reconstruction in the Upper Midwest* (Chapel Hill: University of North Carolina Press, 2009); Michael Pfeifer, *The Roots of Rough Justice: Origins of American Lynching* (Urbana: University of Illinois Press, 2011).

39. Brent Campney, *Hostile Heartland: Racism, Repression, and Resistance in the Midwest* (Urbana: University of Illinois Press, 2019).

40. Galliher et al., *America without the Death Penalty*, 12.

41. Dick Haws, *Iowa and the Death Penalty: A Troubled Relationship, 1834–1965* (Raleigh, NC: Lulu Press, 2010).

42. Michael Pfeifer, review of *Hostile Heartland: Racism, Repression, and Resistance in the Midwest*, by Brent Campney, *The Historian* 82, no. 4 (2020): 507–508; see also Jack Blocker, *A Little More Freedom: African Americans Enter the Urban Midwest, 1860–1930* (Columbus: Ohio State University Press, 2008), 215.

43. Pfeifer, review of *Hostile Heartland*, 507.

44. Death Penalty Information Center (DPIC) Execution Database, available at https://deathpenaltyinfo.org/executions/execution-database.

45. Death row size in remaining states: Missouri (20), Nebraska (12), Kansas (9), Indiana (8), and South Dakota (1). Data from Death Penalty Information Center, "The Death Penalty in 2022."

46. Peverill Squire and Gary Moncrief, *State Legislatures Today: Politics under the Domes*, 3rd ed. (Lanham, MD: Rowman & Littlefield, 2019).

47. Nebraska's unicameral legislature is nonpartisan, however, legislators are affiliated with one of the two major parties. The Nebraska Blue Books furthermore list party affiliation of each senator; this information has been used to determine partisan bill sponsorship in the data presented in Table 17.2. Party affiliation of legislators in the remaining states was documented via official state legislature websites.

48. Rob Warden, "How and Why Illinois Abolished the Death Penalty," *Minnesota Journal of Law and Inequality* 30, no. 2 (December 2012): 245–286.

49. Galliher et al., *America without the Death Penalty*, 108, 114; James M. Galliher and John F. Galliher, "'Déjà Vu All Over Again': The Recurring Life and Death of Capital Punishment Legislation in Kansas," *Social Problems* 44, no. 3 (1997): 369–385, 377.

50. Austin Sarat et al., "When the Death Penalty Goes Public: Referendum, Initiative, and the Fate of Capital Punishment," *Law and Social Inquiry* 44, no. 2 (May 2019): 391–419, 403.

51. Russell Berman, "How Nebraska Abolished the Death Penalty," *Atlantic*, May 27, 2015, https://www.theatlantic.com/politics/archive/2015/05/how-nebraska-banned-the-death-penalty/394271.

52. David C. Baldus et al., "Arbitrariness and Discrimination in the Administration of the Death Penalty: A Legal and Empirical Analysis of the Nebraska Experience (1973–1999)," *Nebraska Law Review* 81, no. 2 (2002): 486–756.

53. American Bar Association, *Evaluating Fairness and Accuracy in State Death Penalty*

Systems: The Missouri Death Penalty Assessment Report, 2012, accessed October 1, 2023, https://www.americanbar.org/content/dam/aba/administrative/death_penalty_moratorium/final_missouri_assessment_report.pdf.

54. Banner, *The Death Penalty*, 222.

55. Corey Haala, "The Progressive Center: Midwestern Liberalism in the Age of Reagan, 1978–1992" (PhD diss., Marquette University, 2020), 687–688.

18

"Alone in the Fight"

Senator Louis Mahern and the Fight for Gay Rights in Indiana

TIFFANY COSTLEY

❖ ❖ ❖ ❖ ❖ ❖ ❖ ❖ ❖ ❖ ❖ ❖ ❖ ❖ ❖

It started at the opening of the Indiana General Assembly in January 1983, when Democratic assistant minority leader Louis Mahern introduced a new bill. The bill was written as an amendment to the Indiana Civil Rights Act to add "sexual preference" to the list of enumerated protected classes banning discrimination in employment and housing.[1] Much like the federal protections under the Civil Rights Act of 1964, Indiana passed a series of laws starting in 1961 that prohibited employment and accommodation discrimination based on "race, religion, color, sex, handicap, national origin, or ancestry."[2] With Mahern's suggested amendment, Indiana would have the opportunity to be the second state after Wisconsin to protect LGBTQ citizens from all employment and housing discrimination.[3]

In the decade since the Stonewall riot in 1969 New York, the importance of implementing basic civil rights protections based on "sexual preference" in state legislatures became a focus for the LGBTQ community.[4] While the official Democratic Party platform for the 1980 presidential race did not mention "gay discrimination," bills calling for employment and accommodation protections for LGBTQ persons were not unknown in 1983.[5] A similar bill was introduced, but not made law, in Congress in 1982 with Senator Edward Kennedy as one of the sponsors.[6] The District of Columbia banned sexual orientation discrimination in public schools and had statutorily protected employment discrimination in all employment ten years earlier with its "human rights ordinance" in 1973.[7] Rochester, New York, enacted an antidiscrimination policy for city employees that included sexual orientation in 1983, and Buffalo, New York, followed with the same in 1984.[8] In 1979 the California Supreme Court found LGBTQ employment protections within the California State Constitution in the *Gay Law Students Assn. v. Pacific Tel. & Tel. Co.* case.[9] Finally, in 1982 Wisconsin became the first state in the nation to pass a bill for statewide protections for sexual orientation in *all* employment.[10]

The issue of "gay rights," however, had not yet become a "big city" Indianapolis issue, let alone a statewide movement. Further, even in a liberal state like New York, the passage of sexual-orientation employment protections did not come without opposition. In Buffalo, for example, the measure was passed with help from closeted members of the city council, but the city's mayor refused to assign an agency to enforce it, leaving violations unchecked.[11] In Rochester, the bill was met with large protests initiated by local religious groups.[12] On the opposite end in Midwestern Wisconsin, which was the *only* statewide example in 1983, the LGBTQ employment protections bill enjoyed bipartisan backing. The Wisconsin measure also heavily relied on support from the local Catholic diocese.[13] Back in the Indiana General Assembly, Mahern did not even have Democratic Party support from within his own caucus despite being a party leader and member since 1976. Any action on Mahern's bill, other than dying in committee, was unlikely from the start.

By the 1980s, Indiana was considered a Republican-dominated state (it remains so today). In 1983 the state's capital, Indianapolis was also dominated by Republicans, having held a Republican mayor continuously since electing Richard Lugar in 1968. President Ronald Reagan carried Indianapolis in both the 1980 and 1984 presidential elections, by a 10 percent margin.[14] The Reagan Republican wave of the 1980s had brought with it a rise of the new "moral majority" that conflated religious beliefs with political agenda. The religious undertones from Republican political candidates particularly resonated with Hoosiers, where almost 45 percent of the state's population belonged to an organized religion.[15] By 1983, Jerry Falwell and other religious leaders were moving Republicans toward accepting what were previously religious undertones as official party platform.[16] According to historian George H. Nash, public opinion shifted from government solutions of social problems to placing blame on the collapse of societal values.[17] The totality of circumstances meant that religious views on "homosexuals" and the contemporaneously unfolding AIDS crisis increasingly became talking points for conservatives in Indiana pushing single-issue voting. A call by any politician as well-known as

Mahern for employment and housing protections for sexual orientation was certain to raise a few eyebrows in a Republican-run state legislature.

Complicating the issue of discrimination was the AIDS epidemic. The day after Mahern introduced his proposed legislation, the *Indianapolis Star* published an in-depth article discussing the mysterious new "gay plague" that had only been named the "AIDS" virus six months prior.[18] The newness of the virus, and the fact that gay men were mostly affected, allowed religious fanaticism to flourish.[19] Local editorials even wondered aloud if the prevalence of AIDS within the gay community was a natural consequence of morally bad decisions.[20] The result was that AIDS forced the issue of LGBTQ discrimination to the forefront as a literal matter of life and death in 1983. Still, AIDS was a problem for cities with visible gay communities, not Indianapolis, where the movement was not yet as organized. Why did Mahen believe it had a chance in Indiana?

The backdrop of these early 1980s conditions makes Mahern's decision to introduce an antidiscrimination bill seem politically ill-conceived. For Mahern, however, the issue was personal. Mahern's brother Michael, with whom he was extremely close, happened to be gay. Michael was also recently diagnosed with AIDS and would spend his life raising money for AIDS patients.[21] Louis Mahern could often be found out and about in Indianapolis spending time with his brother as a regular at gay bars and other events. For the people attending these events, the fear of being discovered came with real consequences. Mahern often witnessed the fear in real time. He recalled attending events where acquaintances would spot each other but avoid eye contact for fear of being "outed" at their place of employment.[22]

Louis Mahern also happened to be Catholic and was the oldest of ten siblings. Despite his own personal religious beliefs, however, he once told the *Muncie Star Press* that "one person's religion should not limit another person's behavior."[23] Growing up in the Kennedy era in the Southside of Indianapolis, Mahern was surrounded by Catholic Democrats. The South Deanery of Indianapolis, of which Mahern was a member, held a Catholic population of around 200,000 that made up the Indianapolis Archdiocese.[24] "You have to understand. I was 16 years old before I met my first Catholic Republican. I was horrified. It was like a contradiction in terms."[25]

Having a gay brother might be an issue for another Catholic family, but the Maherns were known for speaking out on social injustice. Louis Mahern's parents, Louis Mahern Sr. and Elsye Mahern, were members of "The Concerned Christians" of Indianapolis, which criticized the Archdiocese for not doing enough to address racism and local inequalities during the civil rights movement.[26] Louis Sr. was also a founding member of the Indianapolis Catholic Interracial Counsel. The Indianapolis chapter, formed in 1952, was part of the larger national movement that started in New York and focused on the church's role in race relations in major cities.[27] One Sunday in 1968, Mahern's group placed leaflets on cars in Catholic church parking lots throughout Indianapolis criticizing the Archdiocese's priorities of spending money on church buildings instead of the needs of the local community in which they served.[28] The group's influence on Indianapolis Catholics, and Mahern's parents' involvement, was well known locally. Louis Mahern's brother told the *Indianapolis Star* that his parents were once called "n—lovers" because of their work.[29]

Elsye Mahern (Cantwell) also came from a politically active family. Her brother, Paul Cantwell, then known in Indianapolis as "Mr. Democrat," served as a Marion County commissioner, served on the Indianapolis city council, ran for Indianapolis mayor, and eventually served in the Indiana House of Representatives.[30] Elyse once wrote a heated letter to the editor of the *Indianapolis Star* for criticizing her brother's political resume.[31] Elyse's niece, Paul's daughter Maria, now serves as a Democratic US senator for Washington State, a position she has held since 2001.[32] Elyse herself earned a master's degree and was an outspoken leader of the Indianapolis chapter of the women's liberation movement. Solidifying her belief in women's rights, when being interviewed in 1970 she refused to be referred to as only "someone's wife" and classified herself not as a "feminist" but a "humanist."[33] For Mahern, his parents' strong stance on right and wrong was formed from their Catholic faith, and speaking out about injustice was an everyday part of his homelife: "They took the church's teachings about social justice seriously."[34] It would be impossible for Mahern to ignore his upbringing when advocating in the Indiana General Assembly. The issues Mahern's brother faced as a gay man in Indianapolis were thus front and center for Mahern. More liberal cities like San Francisco were then dealing with the crippling reality of AIDS and the discrimination that resulted from the spread of misinformation.[35] What would happen in a Republican city like Indianapolis without some sort of protection?

Mahern's concern was solidified when he attended the second annual Pride Brunch in Indianapolis in 1982.[36] As Mahern recalled it, he was talking to a group of people about their fear of coworkers finding out they were gay, when a lesbian couple approached him. One of the women stated: "How would you feel if you had to hide the one you loved?"[37] The question stopped him. "I felt a cold feeling in the pit of my stomach."[38] He understood in that moment how being gay meant always hiding a part of yourself at work and in securing housing. This community was simply asking for basic protections against getting fired or evicted the moment their employer or landlord found out they were gay. These were protections he took for granted. Mahern had the platform; he had to use it.[39]

Louis Mahern may have been alone in the General Assembly, but Indianapolis was full of leaders trying to reach state legislators. Mahern was initially approached by Kathy Sarris, president of Justice, Inc., a statewide gay and lesbian rights organization that sponsored the Pride events. Sarris was a well-known local activist who in 1982 was already successful in petitioning local private companies to adopt their own nondiscrimination policies in hiring.[40] She would eventually testify in Congress in support of a federal hate-crimes bill, work to get federal aid in Indiana to support AIDS patients, and be an intricate part of legalizing gay marriage in Indiana prior to the ruling in *Obergefell* that legalized it nationally.[41] Nondiscrimination policies for local companies were a good first step, but Sarris knew Indiana needed statutory protections to ensure sustainability. Sarris asked Mahern what she could do to get a bill before the Indiana state legislature. Mahern gave the standard but sincere politician answer, saying to "talk to legislators," make them aware of specific issues and what "needs to be done" to help the gay and lesbian community, and "invite legislators" to her events in support of their cause. What Sarris was asking for, however, was not help with run-of-the-mill city issues like pot-hole fixes or property tax complaints. Sarris was asking for a legislator to be present at a "gay" event and all the unspoken implications that in the early 1980s came with being seen at such an event. Mahern recalls Sarris's reply to him that of course she had done all those things, but for what seemed to be obvious reasons, she stated that "no one will talk to us."[42] Mahern, flabbergasted at the thought, finally said, "Invite me; I'll come!"[43]

Even with his resolve, the obstacles were high for Mahern's bill. Although Mahern's own district, Indiana Senate District 33, was more than 2 to 1 Democratic, in 1985 there were thirty Republicans and twenty Democrats in the entire state senate.[44] The numbers, mathematically speaking, gave the mandate to Republicans. State Republicans were also known for holding the party line. For every vote taken, there was a solid Republican majority available to pass whatever was before the senate that day. Mahern told the *Indianapolis Star* in 1985 that "Being a member of the minority party is like being a spectator with a really good seat."[45]

Still, if anyone in the legislature could get the Republicans to move, it was Mahern. He was described by a local paper as a "quick witted-liberal" also known as "Louis the Lip."[46] Mahern had a reputation for being bipartisan, and in turn getting bipartisan cooperation. He was touted as one of the few orators who could get Republicans to vote with him.[47]

"Senator Mahern is considered the best extemporaneous speaker in the whole legislature" and an all-around "likable guy."[48] When not in session, he worked in banking and real estate and was known to be friendly on business issues when casting votes. He was a crucial member of the city planning committee that planned downtown Indianapolis development.[49] Much to the dislike of his own caucus, Mahern was even often in agreement with and supportive of the Indianapolis Republican mayor.[50]

Even with all his clout, Mahern could not get his bill to move out of committee in 1983. Undiscouraged, he again introduced the bill at the start of the 1984 General Assembly. Again, it went nowhere. By the 1985 legislative session, Mahern was considering a political career beyond being the assistant minority leader. The upcoming 1986 US senator election would call for a Democratic nominee to run against incumbent Dan Quayle. Mahern felt this was his chance to move to a national stage. When Mahern announced his interest in the position, his reputation in the Indiana General Assembly came under scrutiny. His support of the "gay rights bill," as it was often referred to in the local media, was an obvious target for his opponents. Although he still felt strongly about the need for the added language to the Indiana Civil Rights Act, Mahern told his relieved caucus that he would not again introduce the bill in the 1985 legislative session.

The gay-lesbian task force of the then Indiana Civil Liberties Union (ICLU), held a press conference on Friday, January 4, 1985, to announce Mahern's decision not to introduce the antidiscrimination bill.[51] A spokesperson for the ICLU alleged that Indiana legislators knew that adding employment and housing antidiscrimination protections to the Indiana Civil Rights Act was the right thing to do, but they were "too afraid" to support the addition.[52] Perhaps unfairly, a prominent local gay magazine, *The Works*, proclaimed in all caps: "MAHERN SELLS OUT."[53] The magazine editorial openly wondered if Mahern was forced to withdraw his support because of his aspirations to run against Dan Quayle the following year. To be clear, Mahern stated only that he would not continue to introduce the bill, not that he would no longer support the LGBTQ community. In fact, he would continue to speak at LGBTQ events throughout the year.[54] He recalled later, "I spoke on the steps of the goddamn monument circle, you know?"[55] The fact of the matter was that after two years the bill still did not have caucus support, and Mahern was being pressed not to bring further attention to the issue.[56] Mahern was in a leadership position, and other senators stated, both publicly and privately, that they believed his continued push for "gay rights" reflected badly on their caucus.[57] The assumption that his views reflected the Indiana Democrats as a whole was one they were not willing accept in the early 1980s.

Figure 18.1. Photo of Indiana State Senator Louis Mahern on the steps of the Indiana Statehouse at the end of the 1985 session of the Indiana General Assembly. Credit: ©Chris Minnick, 1985.

From Mahern's perspective, his support was unwavering; no bill would change that. "I certainly never meant to hurt anyone's feelings by not introducing the bill," he explained.[58] The continued time and effort spent in getting the bill heard in committee and onto the floor, however, jeopardized his ability to remain a party leader or state senator in general. In 1985, Mahern was alone in the legislature with this fight. If he did not have the support of his own caucus, it did not make political sense to continue to reintroduce the bill. Even *The Works* editorial in January acknowledged Mahern's frustration in carrying the bill alone with no support. *The Works* maintained, however, that because the national Democratic platform in 1984 took a position in support of gay rights, Mahern should hold the line.[59] Mahern would agree that he wanted to hold the line, but perhaps there were other lines he could hold, such as a US Senate seat, that could more effectively accomplish the same goal.

Mahern announced his candidacy for the US Senate against Dan Quayle in March 1985. The local media surmised that his newly shaved-off mustache, side part, and recent departure from the "gay-rights" bill served as proof that he was attempting to adopt a more "mainstream" political look.[60] Then Indiana Republican chairman Gordon Durnil told the local press that notwithstanding his new look, Mahern's "undoing" would be his support of liberal issues, specifically, the "gay-rights bill."[61] Despite ten years in the state legislature, and his bipartisan reputation, once Mahern sought higher political positions, his support of the LGBTQ community was presented as a liability. It was a take on his reputation that he resented: "I spent four years as a Marine infantry battalion. I am an officer in the third largest bank in the state of Indiana. I am being supported by the president of the Indiana State Chamber of Commerce. I have the lowest AFL-CIO rating of any Democrat in the state Senate. Those do not sound like credentials of a radical liberal."[62] Still, even Democrats in the General Assembly knew his stance on "gay rights" would not be well received by working-class Democrats in rural areas throughout the state. Mahern was popular in the large capital city but was mostly unknown statewide. His inner-city multiracial district was comprised of mostly Democrats, but when it came to LGBTQ protections, "those types of causes might be OK in his district, but they won't wear well stateside."[63] According to Durnil, you could socialize with Mahern, but not vote for him.[64]

Political analysts voiced the opinion that Mahern's "biggest liability" in beating Quayle was his continued introduction of the "gay rights" legislation.[65] Not mentioned was the incredible fundraising disparity between the two candidates; Quayle had the backing of multiple super PACs that would end up raising over $2 million before they stopped needing new donations.[66] Mahern faced a statewide grassroots-style campaign targeted with a single task of raising just enough money to simply remain in the race.[67] Quayle also had statewide name recognition, having first been elected to national office in 1976, on top of being the incumbent to the role.[68] National party leaders were so unbothered by Mahern's run that the Indiana seat was not even considered to be "up for grabs" according to the leaders of both the Democratic and Republican National Conventions.[69] Thus, attacking him for his stance on gay rights was nothing more than a cheap shot aimed at stoking the fears of a mostly conservative statewide constituency. Mahern responded to the criticism by surmising that Hoosiers in general were more tolerant than "cynical politicians" would believe.[70]

In the end, none of the criticism would matter, as it would unfairly be a heart attack that did Mahern in just nine months from his unofficial start to the US Senate race.[71] Jill Long Thompson, a Valparaiso University business professor, would be the one who would step in to challenge Quayle, becoming the first woman in either party to win a US Senate nomination for the state.[72] Quayle won 60 percent of the vote, and went on to become the vice president under George H. W. Bush's presidency. After his long recovery from the heart attack, Mahern returned to the state senate after narrowly winning the Democratic Party primary without a party endorsement and going on to win his last bid for state senator in 1988.[73] The narrow win was a wakeup call to the senator, who was now called "out of touch" with his beliefs by his local precinct.[74]

Mahern sought a new opportunity when in 1990, Indianapolis's own "Minister Mayor," William Hudnut III, announced he would not be seeking reelection after holding the position since 1976.[75] Mahern took the opportunity to run as the Democratic nominee, announcing his candidacy on June 26, 1990.[76] By then, Mahern's early support for "gay rights" had a different meaning. The AIDS epidemic was no longer reduced to the "gay plague" only affecting the gay community. The Ryan White story of a local Indiana teenager stricken with AIDS had brought the issue home to the Midwest, and his story gained worldwide attention.[77] With White's tragic death in April of that year, Hoosiers were no longer willfully ignorant of the life-and-death issues of discrimination facing the gay community. What remained unclear is if that knowledge would transfer to political support.

Mayor Hudnut had a back-and-forth history with the LGBTQ community. In 1982 he wrote a letter to the chief of the Indianapolis Police Department (IPD) in which he expressed concern at the number of young men "trolling" downtown Monument Circle "looking for a homosexual pickup" and urged the chief to use the Vice Squad to "eliminate" the activity.[78] The IPD were rumored to target gay men "loitering" around Monument Circle, an area known within the community to be a safe space to meet other gay men.[79] The continued targeting by police under Hudnut's reign led to protests at the circle for seven straight weeks in 1984.[80] Although he would later announce it was not city policy to discriminate against LGBTQ persons, Hudnut was criticized for not doing more to prevent the outright harassment from the department. In 1984 with the help of Republican leaders in Minneapolis, Hudnut created an ordinance prohibiting operation of adult book and video shops within Indianapolis, mostly known as safe places to be "out." [81] Later that year, Hudnut's administration decided against enacting a city-wide ordinance preventing discrimination based on sexual preference among city employees.[82] Hudnut would, however, eventually sign an executive order in 1988 preventing discrimination against AIDS-positive city employees.[83] Still, Hudnut's departure gave Mahern a chance to be the steady ally the city needed.

The LGBTQ community in Indianapolis was more politically organized by 1990. In addition to its annual brunch, the local Pride organization was slated to hold a "Celebration on the Circle" event in downtown

Indianapolis. The event drew more than three thousand people.[84] Mahern, who had announced his mayoral bid just prior to the event, was a featured speaker, proudly proclaiming that: "what we must try to have is a government that will stop people from hating each other, not stop them from loving each other."[85] The event was a culmination of the efforts of advocates working tirelessly for a decade to be able to hold such an event in public. On his way out as mayor, Hudnut proclaimed June 30, 1990, "Celebration on the Circle Day." The proclamation called on citizens to welcome the gay and lesbian community in town for the Pride event.[86] Hudnut also penned several letters to the various organizers, wishing them a successful event.[87] Hudnut's new stance was not necessarily a change of heart, but rather represented a new understanding of the political power the LGBTQ community had worked for a decade to achieve. In a memo from the special assistant of public affairs, Mark Goff, regarding Hudnut's handling of the proclamation, Goff warned Hudnut that following through with his support of the event was necessary to avoid bad press. Goff even went so far as to remind Hudnut that he was facing an upcoming election for secretary of state and that a possible reason his Republican colleague, John Mutz, lost the recent 1988 election for governor was his lack of support from the roughly fifty thousand politically active nontraditional voters within the gay and lesbian community.[88] The sentiment was a massive departure from the Republican tone just five years earlier.

In his mayoral campaign, Mahern actively sought the support of the LGBTQ community, who were now able to effectively execute their political power. Mahern openly stated that if elected mayor, he would issue an executive order for city employees barring discrimination based on sexual preference.[89] Although he had taken heat for his dropped introduction of the "gay rights" bill in 1985, by 1991 it was water under the bridge. The *Indianapolis Star* took notice, explaining how LGBTQ business owners offered their spaces to Mahern for fundraising events and multiple gay publications endorsed the candidate.[90] Marla Stevens, well-known activist and gay and lesbian coordinator for the Indiana Civil Liberties Union, expressed her excitement that the community was more politically active and now they had a mayoral candidate in Mahern that had supported them for years.[91] Stevens also founded Lesbian, Gay, Bisexual, Transgender Fairness Indiana, an activist group that gained national attention in 1998 after derailing a proposed Indiana bill to prevent LGBTQ persons from adopting children.[92] In a close election for mayor, it became clear that Steven's endorsement, and community support, could have the possibility of tipping the election in Mahern's favor. Estimates of community size in 1991 were somewhere around seventy thousand possible LGBTQ persons throughout Marion County, Indiana.[93] In a city of around 700,000, a mayoral candidate might not do well in ignoring them.

Mahern was running against longtime Republican prosecutor Stephen Goldsmith.[94] Goldsmith had a reputation for what was perceived as by proxy attacks on the gay community. Similar to Hudnut's previous efforts, Goldsmith used an Indiana racketeering statute in 1990 to go after local adult video and bookstores known to cater to the gay community by temporarily freezing their assets in an effort to permanently shut them down for "lewd, obscene, and indecent" content.[95] During the heated campaign, Goldsmith did not hide his position and pointedly stated that he would not "cater" to the concerns of the gay and lesbian community.[96] Mahern did not have to "cater" to anyone in the community. Rather, he was finally able to cash in and receive credit for the efforts he had spearheaded almost ten years prior.

Unlike in the US Senate race in 1986, Mahern's advocacy efforts were not seen as a political deal breaker in 1991. The Goldsmith campaign for its part made a pledge *not* to use Mahern's LGBTQ stance as an attack on his credibility as a mayoral candidate, as was done in the 1986 US Senate race.[97] Even if the Goldsmith camp promised not to use Mahern's support as a liability, plenty of conservative mouthpieces did it for them. Eric Miller, then executive director for Citizens Concerned for the Constitution, called Mahern an "extremist" for his open and long-standing support of the LGBTQ community, stating openly that "most people are not in favor of adopting the homosexual agenda."[98]

Despite his support, and raising more money than any previous Democrat, Mahern's bid for mayor ultimately fell short. He won a little over 40 percent of the votes, in what would turn out to be his last election in the state.[99] After the loss, which fell on his fiftieth birthday, Mahern retired from political office to focus on private business ventures. Overall, the loss was blamed on Mahern's call to raise taxes.[100] Still, local editorials wondered if Mahern was hurt based on his active courting of the "gay vote" in Indianapolis. When the Marion County Republican chairman, John W. Sweezy, was asked about why he thought such a popular local politician lost, he was quick to point to "gay rights and abortion issues" being Mahern's ultimate downfall. "I think it's fine that a man has convictions and states them, but I think the public repudiated them."[101]

It would ultimately be Governor Frank O'Bannon, a longtime friend and colleague of Mahern's, who signed an executive order in 2001 banning discrimination on sexual orientation in all state employment.[102] Bart Peterson, Goldsmith's successor elected in 2000, and the first Democratic mayor of Indianapolis since 1963, enacted employment protections based on sexual preference to city employees in 2004 through an executive order.[103] Still, these protections were limited to government employment. Even in 2004, the state senate refused to even *hear* a bill, like Mahern's, that considered a statewide protection for all employees public or private. The Senate Judiciary chairman, Republican Richard Bray, said about the proposed bill, "It's a bad time for it—if there ever is a good time."[104] More than twenty years after Louis Mahern first introduced the same bill, it was *still* not time in Indiana to protect LGBTQ Hoosiers against employment and housing discrimination. Increasingly, it seemed that the state legislature was representing a minority view. This sentiment was echoed by the Indy Rainbow Chamber of Commerce, which in 2005 told the *Indianapolis Star* that Indianapolis is a "tremendously tolerant" place, but it was the lawmakers themselves that were intolerant.[105]

The current statute for civil rights protection is located under Indiana Code section 22-9-1-2 and still does not contain "sexual orientation" as a protected class. The Seventh Circuit Court of Appeals governing Indiana, however, extended the Title VII employment and accommodation protections to sexual orientation in 2017 with the *Hively v. Ivy Tech Community College of Indiana* decision.[106] The landmark decision was the first federal appellate court decision that recognized sexual orientation as a Title VII employment protection. The decision furthered a federal circuit split, which signaled the Supreme Court to take up the issue in 2020 with the *Bostock v. Clayton County, Georgia* case. In *Bostock*, the Supreme Court upheld the Seventh Circuit decision.[107] Almost forty years after Mahern's effort, the protections he championed were finally solidified by the judiciary.

Reflecting on why he fought so hard and introduced the bill in the first place, Mahern said he did it so that "my brother would know that I loved him."[108] Writing for the *Indianapolis Business Journal*, Mahern said he was "heartened" seeing full rights to the LGBTQ community being extended "state by state," noting that societal change comes as a result of "the softening of our hearts and actually getting to know those who were so recently considered the other."[109] With the ever-changing judiciary, codified state protections remain a need for LGBTQ Hoosiers, who still wait for the Indiana General Assembly to officially soften their hearts.

NOTES

1. "Mahern Withdraws as Gay Rights Sponsor," *Indianapolis Star*, January 5, 1985, 7.
2. See more information on the Indiana Civil Rights Commission official site,

https://www.in.gov/icrc/about-icrc/indiana-civil-rights-laws-and-regulations/indiana-civil-rights-legislative-history/.

3. Raymond A. Smith and Donald P. Haider-Marlke, *Gay and Lesbian Americans and Political Participation* (Santa Barbara, CA: ABC Clio, 2002), 101–102. For a detailed look at Wisconsin's passage of LGBTQ employment projections in 1982, see Stephen Colbrook's chapter in this volume.

4. Smith and Haider-Marlke, *Gay and Lesbian Americans and Political Participation*, 42–47.

5. Gerhard Peters and John T. Woolley, "1980 Democratic Party Platform," Online Democratic Party Platforms, American Presidency Project, https://www.presidency.ucsb.edu/node/273253, accessed May 12, 2022. See also "Gay Civil Rights: Next Item on the Agenda," *Empty Closet* 125 (March 1982), https://www.lib.rochester.edu/IN/RBSCP/Databases/Attachments/Closet/1982/1982_MARCH.pdf; Randy Shilts, *And the Band Played On: Politics, People, and the AIDS Epidemic* (New York: St. Martin's Griffin, 1987), 205.

6. Smith and Haider-Marlke, *Gay and Lesbian Americans and Political Participation*, 295–296. See also "Gay Civil Rights: Next Item on the Agenda," *Empty Closet*.

7. Smith and Haider-Marlke, *Gay and Lesbian Americans and Political Participation*, 89.

8. Smith and Haider-Marlke, *Gay and Lesbian Americans and Political Participation*, 91–93.

9. *Gay Law Students Assn. v. Pacific Tel. & Tel. Co.*, 595 P.2d 592, 156 Cal. Rptr. 14, 24 Cal. 3d 458 (1979). See also Lee Ann Johnson, "Gay Law Students Association v. Pacific Telephone & Telegraph Co.: Constitutional and Statutory Restraints on Employment Discrimination against Homosexuals by Public Utilities," *California Law Review* 68, no. 4 (1980): 680–715.

10. For a detailed look at Wisconsin's passage of LGBTQ employment projections in 1982, see Colbrook's chapter in this volume.

11. Smith and Haider-Marlke, *Gay and Lesbian Americans and Political Participation*, 91.

12. Smith and Haider-Marlke, *Gay and Lesbian Americans and Political Participation*, 93.

13. See Colbrook's chapter.

14. Drew DeSilver, "The Growing Democratic Domination of Nation's Largest Counties," Pew Research Center, July 21, 2016, http://www.pewresearch.org/fact-tank/2016/07/21/the-growing-democratic-domination-of-nations-largest-counties.

15. *Churches and Church Membership in the United States, 1980*, collected by the Glenmary Research Center and distributed by the Association of Religion Data Archives, https://www.thearda.com/us-religion/census/congregational-membership?y=1980&y2=0&t=1&c=18, accessed August 2023.

16. Further explanation of the different divisions that united to make up the larger conservative movement can be found in George Nash, *The Conservative Intellectual Movement in America since 1945* (Wilmington, DE: ISI Books, 2006).

17. Nash, *The Conservative Intellectual Movement in America since 1945*, 360–361.

18. Donald C. Drake, "'Detectives' on Trail of 'Sinister Epidemic," *Indianapolis Star*, January 16, 1983, F1.

19. Shilts, *And the Band Played On*, 126.

20. M. Stanton Evans, "The 'Gay Plague," *Indianapolis News*, July 29, 1983, 9.

21. Author's interview with Louis Mahern.

22. Author's interview with Louis Mahern.

23. Ed Stattmann, "Lottery Bill Clears Senate," *Star Press*, January 21, 1984, 6.

24. For more detailed information on the Archdiocese of Indianapolis, its history, and the location of churches throughout Indianapolis, visit the Archdiocese's website, https://www.archindy.org/index.html. See also Carol Elrod and R. Joseph Gelarden, "Archbishop O'Meara, 70, Leader of Indianapolis Archdiocese, Dies," *Indianapolis Star*, January 11, 1992, 1.

25. John R. O'Neill, "Mahern: A Politician by Choice, a Democrat by Birth," *Indianapolis Star*, April 7, 1991, F5.

26. The Concerned Christians, "Is the Catholic Archdiocese of Indianapolis More Concerned with Brick and Mortar than with Bread and Justice?," *Indianapolis Star*, August 5, 1969, 5.

27. For an in-depth history on the formation of the Catholic Interracial Council in New York, see Martin A. Zielinski, "Working for Interracial Justice: The Catholic Interracial Council of New York, 1934–1964," *U.S. Catholic Historian* 7, no. 2/3 (1988): 233–262, http://www.jstor.org/stable/25153831.

28. "Catholics to Meet over Money Use," *Indianapolis News*, September 2, 1968, 31.

29. Will Higgins, "Still Riding the Crest of History: Mahern's Journey Mirrors that of a Generation," *Indianapolis Star*, January 1, 2011, A8.

30. Tiffany Costley, "Paul F. Cantwell," Encyclopedia of Indianapolis, revised March 2021, https://indyencyclopedia.org/paul-f-cantwell/.

31. Elsye Mahern, "Sister Stands Up for Cantwell," *Indianapolis Star*, April 26, 1968, 11.

32. Alicia Mundy, "Father Introduced Cantwell to Excitement, Pitfalls of Politics," *Seattle Times*, July 28, 2006, https://archive.seattletimes.com/archive/?date=20060728&slug=cantwellyouth28m.

33. Mary Anne Butters, "Women's Lib Goes Public," *Indianapolis Star*, May 10, 1970, 1–2.

34. Author's interview with Mahern.

35. Shilts, *And the Band Played On*, 254–256.

36. Karen Presley, "Straightforward View: Gay Pride," *Indianapolis News*, June 25, 1983, 13. More information on the history of Indiana Pride can be found at https://indypride.org/about/history/& https://indyencyclopedia.org/indy-pride/.

37. Author's interview with Louis Mahern. Mahern expands on the story in Jim Mellowitz, "Can Louis Mahern Make Politics Fun Again?," *Indianapolis Monthly*, June 1985, 45.

38. Mellowitz, "Can Louis Mahern Make Politics Fun Again?"

39. For additional information, see Louis Maherns' oral history interview from January 2015, available at the Indiana Historical Society, https://indianahistory.org/wp-content/uploads/louis-mahern-oral-history-interview.pdf.

40. "Homosexuals Ask End to Job Bias," *Indianapolis News*, November 27, 1982, 16.

41. Ruth Mullen, "Gays Struggle for Acceptance from Uncomprehending Society," *Indianapolis Star*, April 11, 1999, J6. See also Kathy Sarris's oral history interview from January 2015, available at the Indiana Historical Society, https://indianahistorylibrary.on.worldcat.org/oclc/1003854401.

42. Author's interview with Mahern.

43. Author's interview with Mahern.

44. Richard D. Walton, "For Senate Democrats, It's a Lesson in Humility," *Indianapolis Star*, March 11, 1985, 25. See also Gerry C. Lafollette, "Mahern Might Find Himself in a Tough Fight to Keep Job," *Indianapolis News*, December 25, 1987, 37.

45. Walton, "For Senate Democrats, It's a Lesson in Humility," 25.

46. Kit Wager and David Hulen, "Democrat Leaders like Sound of Vandeveer the U.S. Senator," *Evansville Courier and Press*, January 18, 1985, 3.

47. Mellowitz, "Can Louis Mahern Make Politics Fun Again?"

48. Andrea Neal, "12 Legislators Deemed Most Likely to Gain Higher Posts," *Star Press*, January 2, 1983. 1.

49. Wager and Hulen, "Democrat Leaders like Sound of Vandeveer the U.S. Senator."

50. Mellowitz, "Can Louis Mahern Make Politics Fun Again?," 44, 46.

51. "Legislature Drops Gay Sponsorship," *Star Press*, January 6, 1985, 13.

52. "Legislature Drops Gay Sponsorship," *Star Press*, 13.

53. "Mahern Sells Out," *The Works*, January 1985, 7.

54. "BSU Prof to Address Gay Rights Workshop in Indy," *Muncie Evening Press*, August 7, 1985, 6.

55. Author's interview with Mahern.

56. Mellowitz, "Can Louis Mahern Make Politics Fun Again?," 45.

57. Author's interview with Mahern.

58. Author's interview with Mahern.

59. "Mahern Sells Out," *The Works*, 7.

60. Meg Feltton Kopec, "The Good, the Bad, and the Louis Mahern," *Evansville Press and Press*, January 26, 1985, 10.

61. Wager and Hulen, "Democrat Leaders like Sound of Vandeveer the U.S. Senator."

62. Kopee, "The Good, the Bad, and Louis Mahern."

63. Wager and Hulen, "Democrat Leaders like Sound of Vandeveer the U.S. Senator."

64. Wager and Hulen, "Democrat Leaders like Sound of Vandeveer the U.S. Senator."

65. Edward Ziegner, "Mahern: Quayle Beatable," *Indianapolis News*, September 28, 1985, 17.

66. Doug Richardson, "Demos' Campaign Not Long Enough," *Star Press*, November 2, 1986, 50.

67. Louis Mahern for US Senate Committee, Federal Election Commission, Campaign Finance Data, https://www.fec.gov/data/committee/C00195172/.

68. Edward Ziegner, "Lugar, Bowen, Ford, Win in Record Vote," *Indianapolis News*, November 3, 1976, 3.

69. "Mahern Looks Like a Longshot to Experts," *Indianapolis Star*, October 7, 1985, 7.

70. Ziegner, "Mahern: Quayle Beatable."

71. Mark Nichols, "Heart Surgery Ends Mahern Campaign," *Indianapolis Star*, October 27, 1985, 1.

72. John Krull, "Jill Long, on the D.C. Trail," *Indianapolis News*, March 20, 1986, 7.

73. Peter Blum, "Mahern-Murphy Battle Sizzles," *Indianapolis News*, April 26, 1988, 4.

74. O'Neill, "Mahern: A Politician by Choice, a Democrat by Birth."

75. William Hudnut III was a minister of the Indianapolis Second Presbyterian Church for over ten years prior to serving as mayor. Further reading on his tenure can be found at William Hudnut III & Judy Keene, *Minister Mayor* (Philadelphia: Westminster Press, 1987).

76. Patrick J. Traub, "Democrat Mahern, to Run for Mayor," *Indianapolis Star*, June 27, 1990, 1.

77. Dirk Johnson, "Ryan White Dies of AIDS at 18; His Struggle Helped Pierce Myths," *New York Times*, April 9, 1990, 60.

78. "Mayor Hudnut to Richard Blankenbaker and Joseph G. McAtee," June 10, 1982, Box 178, UIndy Institute for Civic Leadership and Digital Mayoral Archives, Hudnut Collection, University of Indiana, https://uindy.historyit.com/item.php?id=434952.

79. "Gays-Police Meeting 'Positive,'" *Indianapolis News*, January 11, 1983, 7. See also Will Higgins, "The Strange but True History of Indianapolis' Gay Bars," *Indianapolis Star*, December 12, 2013, https://www.indystar.com/story/life/2013/12/12/indianapolis-gay-bars/3997591/.

80. "Gay Knights-Update," *The Works*, January 1985, 9.

81. "Pornography Statement," September 7, 1984, Box 142, UIndy Institute for Civic Leadership and Mayoral Archives, Hudnut Collection, http://uindy.historyit.com/item/?itemid=817200. See also "Minneapolis Gets Rights Law to Ban Pornography," *New York Times*, December 31, 1983, https://www.nytimes.com/1983/12/31/us/minneapolis-gets-rights-law-to-ban-pornography.html; Kevin Ehrman-Solberg, "The Battle of the Bookstores and Gay Sexual Liberation in Minneapolis," *Middle West Review* 3, no. 1 (2016): 1–24.

82. "John P. Ryan to Mayor Hudnut," August 29, 1984, Box 68, UIndy Institute for Civic Leadership and Digital Mayoral Archives, Hudnut Collection, https://uindy.historyit.com/item.php?id=410595.

83. "Executive Order No. 1, 1988: Establishing an Aids Policy Regarding City Employees," May 10, 1988, Box 20, UIndy Institute for Civic Leadership and Digital Mayoral Archives, Hudnut Collection, https://uindy.historyit.com/item.php?id=380579.

84. "3000 Attend 'Circle Celebration,'" *The Works*, August 1990, 14.

85. "3000 Attend 'Circle Celebration,'" *The Works*.

86. "Celebration on the Circle Day," June 30, 1990, Box 135, UIndy Institute for Civic Leadership and Digital Mayoral Archives, Hudnut Collection, https://uindy.historyit.com/item.php?id=418890.

87. "Mayor Hudnut to Eric S. Evans," June 26, 1990, and "Mayor Hudnut to Stephanie Turner," June 30, 1990, Box 135, UIndy Institute for Civic Leadership and Digital Mayoral Archives, Hudnut Collection, https://uindy.historyit.com/item.php?id=418867; https://uindy.historyit.com/item.php?id=418152.

88. "Mark J. Goff to Mayor Hudnut," June 13, 1990, Box 135, UIndy Institute for Civic Leadership and Digital Mayoral Archives, Hudnut Collection, https://uindy.historyit.com/item.php?id=418893.

89. Gerry Lanosga, "Touchy Issues Spice Mayoral Race," *Indianapolis News*, November 1, 1991, 2.

90. Patrick Traub, "City's Homosexual Community Vocal in Support of Mahern," *Indianapolis Star*, September 21, 1991, 11.

91. Traub, "City's Homosexual Community Vocal in Support of Mahern," 9.

92. "Gay activist to Be Arraigned Monday for Charges Stemming from Protest," *Indianapolis Star*, September 20, 1988, 31. See also Diane Frederick, "Gay Activist Pleads Not Guilty to Charges Related to Outburst," *Indianapolis News*, September 22, 1998, 3.

93. "Gay Activist to Be Arraigned Monday for Charges Stemming from Protest," *Indianapolis Star*.

94. More information on this election can be found at https://indyencyclopedia.org/municipal-election-of-1991/.

95. "Goldsmith Seeks to Close 5 Video, Book Stores," *The Works*, August 1990, 8.

96. Traub, "City's Homosexual Community Vocal in Support of Mahern," 9.

97. Traub, "City's Homosexual Community Vocal in Support of Mahern," 11.

98. Lanosga, "Touchy Issues Spice Mayoral Race," *Indianapolis News*.

99. Kathleen Schuckel, "Winning Humor Marks Defeat," *Indianapolis News*, November 6, 1991, 1, 7.

100. Doug Richardson, "Politicians Find Tax Increases Can Mean Downfall," *Star Press*, November 12, 1991, 2.

101. James G. Newland Jr., "Big Win Makes Goldsmith a Major Force," *Indianapolis Star*, November 6, 1991, A13.

102. Associated Press, "Sexual Orientation Now Part of State Policy against Discrimination," *Daily Reporter*, August 7, 2001, 3.

103. Tim Evans and John Fritze, "Mayor Adds Policy to Protect Gays," *Indianapolis Star*, March 10, 2004, 21.

104. Tim Evans, "Bill to Protect Rights of Gays Dies in Senate," *Indianapolis Star*, January 28, 2004, 13.

105. Abe Aamidor, "Aiming for Acceptance, Not Just Tolerance," *Indianapolis Star*, June 12, 2005, 14.

106. *Hively v. Ivy Tech Community College of Indiana*, 853 F.3d 339 (2017).

107. *Bostock v. Clayton County, Georgia*, 140 S. Ct. 1731 (2020).

108. Author's interview with Mahern.

109. Louis Mahern, "MAHERN: Look How Far Our Society Has Progressed," *Indianapolis Business Journal*, August 19, 2011, https://www.ibj.com/articles/29040-mahern-look-how-far-our-society-has-progressed.

19

Lambs That Strayed from the Democratic Flock

Catholic Voters in the Midwest

CHAD KINSELLA

❖ ❖ ❖ ❖ ❖ ❖ ❖ ❖ ❖ ❖ ❖ ❖ ❖ ❖ ❖ ❖

The Midwest has long been considered a critical political region for presidential, congressional, and even state and local elections. Within it are key states that are the most apt to be competitive and swing their support to either party. Given the Midwest's key role in national politics and its bellwether status, different groups of voters in this region play an outsized role in determining the national political fortunes of the country. One of these key demographic groups is Catholic voters. Catholic voters have their roots in Democratic politics. A quote from a Democratic county board member captures this relationship: "Whenever I would move to a new place, the first thing I'd look for would be the Catholic Church, and then the Democratic Headquarters."[1] As this quote points out, for a long period of time being Catholic and being a Democrat were considered synonymous. For many Catholics across the Midwest, based on the culture, the unique history of several Catholic immigrant groups, the clustering of these groups in several areas—many of them urban—the use of Catholic schools as opposed to public ones, and the reliance on union membership all meant that the Catholic experience was intertwined with the Democratic Party.[2]

However, Catholics nationally and in the Midwest have drifted away from their traditional Democratic base and become a competitive swing group. This chapter, using data from the American National Election Studies (ANES) and US Religion Census, will analyze where Catholics are in the Midwest and Catholic voting trends from the 1950s to today. It also will establish that Catholics were a key constituency of the Democratic Party through the Kennedy election but slowly strayed from the Democratic Party to the Republican Party in recent decades. Using that same data, an analysis of how Midwestern Catholics have changed politically, socioeconomically, and in their opinions on key issues will be provided. Finally, the analysis will examine those who identify as Catholics in the Midwest in this polarized era (2000 to 2020) to determine which Catholics are more likely to remain loyal to the Democratic Party and those more likely to vote Republican.

In many cases, Catholic identity in the United States, especially for recent immigrants, was tied to being a Democrat. New immigrants, mostly from Europe, streamed into the United States, often settling urban areas where political machines recruited them.[3] Although both Republicans and Democrats established political machines, Democrats were typically more appealing to urban immigrants given that Republicans were viewed as anti-immigrant.[4] Through the Civil War, Catholics in the Midwest remained a key constituency for Democrats. Draft riots in several Midwestern states were led by Catholics and new arrivals from Europe, who were uninterested and uninspired to take part in their new nation's Civil War. Nor were Catholics interested in supporting a Republican Party filled with former anti-Catholic, No Nothing Party members (an anti-immigrant party) and Protestants[5]. Catholic loyalty to the Democratic Party persisted into the next century with the advent of the Prohibition movement and was a focal piece of the New Deal coalition.

CATHOLICS IN THE MIDWEST

Using data from the 2010 US Religion Census: Religious Congregations and Membership Study, a map of Midwestern counties was produced showing the percentage of Catholic adherents compared to the total number of religious adherents (see Figure 19.1). The map highlights where there are large proportions of Catholics in each county. Overall, it is clear that large numbers of Catholics still live near the urban centers, where many of the original Catholic immigrants first arrived; including the Cleveland, Cincinnati, Chicago, and St. Louis metropolitan areas. In many instances, there are large numbers of Catholic adherents in many Rust Belt areas. Catholics tend to cluster in several areas of each state known to be

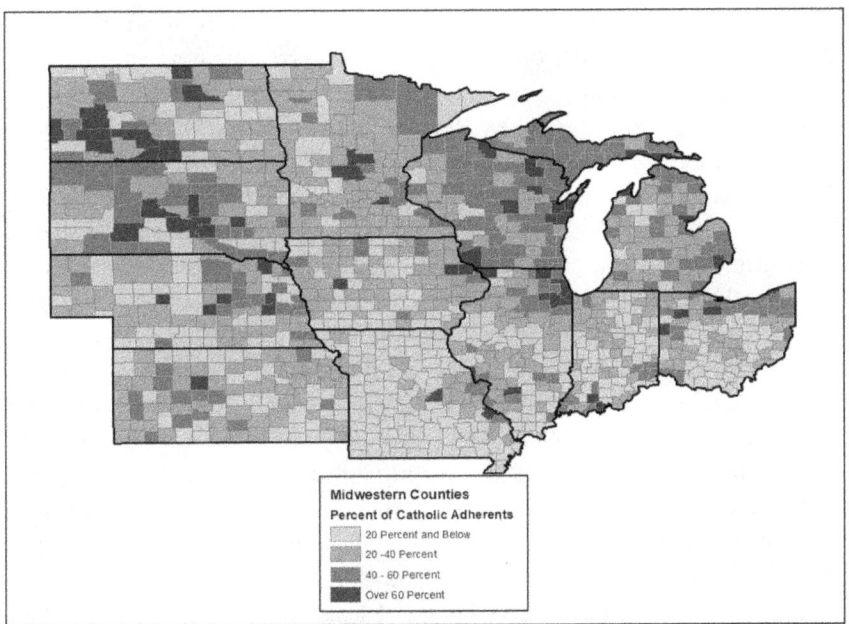

Figure 19.1. Catholic Adherents in the Midwest, per County

Source: Association of Religion Data Archives, 2010 US Religion Census: Religious Congregations and Membership Study.

Democratic bastions such as northern Ohio, northwestern Indiana, the St. Louis area, and Chicago.

Another striking pattern to consider is the density of Catholics across the Midwestern states and those states that have been most and least competitive in recent presidential elections. Overall, the western Midwestern states—the Dakotas, Nebraska, and Kansas—have and remain Republican stalwarts in the region. Indiana, Ohio, Missouri, and Iowa, all in the lower Midwest, typically have larger Catholic populations near some of their urban centers but have large areas of the state that have few Catholics. Indiana is often seen as the least Democratic-friendly state in the Midwest, and Missouri, Iowa, and Ohio were all once major battleground states but have since 2010 or so slowly become less competitive for Democrats. The upper Midwest—Minnesota, Michigan, and Wisconsin—have more counties with larger numbers of Catholic adherents and in recent years have become the new Midwestern battleground states. Finally, Illinois has a large cluster of Catholic adherents around Chicago, but few in the rest of the state. However, the Chicago metropolitan area is the population center of Illinois while central and southern Illinois have been losing population for decades. The Chicago area continues to be a Democratic stronghold and the least competitive Midwestern state for Republicans.

The map clearly shows that Catholics live in several critical areas of several different competitive Midwestern states and in areas that have gradually moved from Democratic support to more Republican. Perhaps one of the best illustrations of this is Mahoning County, Ohio, which is home to Youngstown. Considered part of the Rust Belt, Youngtown is home to a large number of Catholics who for decades supported Democratic Party presidential candidates and in 2020 voted Republican. Similarly, in northern Indiana, St. Joseph County, home to the University of Notre Dame, went from solidly Democratic to one of the most contested in the country in 2016 and 2020—and in the 2022 midterms, federal, state, and most local offices went to the Republican Party for the first time in recent memory. As more Catholic voters have become swing voters over the years, it becomes clear why some states have moved from either battleground status to near-safe Republican, such as Ohio and Missouri; or from almost always safely Democratic to a battleground state, such as Iowa, Wisconsin, and Michigan. Ultimately, the geography of Catholic voters speaks to their importance to both parties in past and future elections.

MIDWESTERN CATHOLIC PRESIDENTIAL VOTE, 1952–2020

Using the ANES[6] datasets, one of the largest continuous public opinion repositories of political information, an analysis was done to examine the presidential voting habits of national and Midwestern Catholics. Table 19.1 displays the presidential vote of Catholics from 1952 to 2020. The presidential vote provides critical evidence for understanding the political behavior of Catholic voters both nationally and in the Midwest. In the Eisenhower elections in the 1950s, it is clear that the Catholic vote was split both nationally and in the Midwest, although a little less so with Midwestern Catholics in his reelection in 1956. This is likely because Dwight D. Eisenhower was a well-known name at this point, having served as the Supreme Allied Commander in World War II and being a national hero credited with the successful defeat of the fascist threat in Europe. One of the most critical elections for Catholics was the 1960 election that pitted Senator John F. Kennedy against Vice President Richard Nixon. Kennedy was from a prominent Irish Catholic family in Massachusetts. Although Kennedy was not the first Catholic to run for president (Al Smith ran in 1928), his campaign galvanized Catholic voters into one large, cohesive voting bloc that overwhelmingly supported his candidacy. Nationally, over 80 percent of Catholics supported Kennedy; the support was even more robust in the Midwest, where Kennedy garnered over 90 percent of the vote—which possibly made the difference in critical Midwestern states such as Illinois, Minnesota, and Michigan. In fact, studies of the 1960 presidential election have shown that, nationally, only 118,000 votes separated Kennedy from Nixon. Given the closeness of that election, anything less than the monolithic Catholic support that he received may have cost Kennedy the race; and it is estimated that he received 17 percent more support from Catholic voters than what a non-Catholic candidate would have expected.[7] Overall, the election of Kennedy was seen by many Catholics as an extraordinary and liberating event[8] that shattered an invisible barrier, allowing them to be finally considered first-class, loyal citizens.[9] The monolithic Catholic vote continued into Lyndon B. Johnson's landslide victory in 1964, where he received 80 percent of the Midwestern Catholic vote.

In the 1968 presidential election, the Catholic vote nationally began to fragment, although Midwest Catholics provided Hubert Humphrey with over 60 percent of their support. The 1968 election, particularly for Democrats, was a major turning point. The Democratic National Convention in Chicago was marred by protest, violence, and a schism in the party between the more liberal, antiwar wing and the old guard of the party. Interestingly enough, the separate wings of the party were represented by two Catholics: Senator Eugene McCarthy as the liberal, antiwar stalwart versus the traditional more machine politics of Mayor Richard Daley of Chicago, who was known to attend Mass every day.

Starting in the 1972 landslide election by Nixon, the Catholic vote splintered, and support for Democratic presidential candidates would thereafter ebb and flow based on the election. Overall, the national Catholic vote and Midwestern Catholic vote mirror each other outside of the 1976 Carter election, where Midwestern Catholics were much less likely to support the former Georgia governor, and the 1992 vote, where Midwestern Catholics were 10 percent less likely to vote for Bill Clinton in an unusual presidential election that had a viable third-party candidate in Ross Perot.

One of the more interesting and telling recent elections was the 2004 presidential election between John Kerry and President George W. Bush. Kerry was the first Catholic to run for president since Kennedy in 1960. Despite this, Catholics nationally and in the Midwest did not coalesce around his candidacy as they did for Kennedy. In fact, the vote split almost evenly between the candidates, highlighting the idea that partisanship

Table 19.1 Presidential Vote of Catholics from 1952 to 2020

	1952	1956	1960	1964	1968	1972	1976	1980	1984
Presidential Vote									
Percent Voting Democratic Nationally	51.6	40.4	82	78.7	55.5	39.5	58.1	41.3	46
Percent Voting Democratic in the Midwest	52.9	56.6	92.3	78	60.6	35	47.6	44.6	51.7
Partisanship									
Democrat	70.5	67	75.9	66.7	77.1	58.3	54.1	58.3	56.5
Republican	24.2	21.1	12.1	25.3	15.6	31	33.6	26	29.9
Independent	5.3	11.9	12.1	8.1	7.3	10.7	12.3	15.6	13.6
Ideology									
Conservative						31.4	31.8	16.7	22.1
Moderate						29.3	29.1	19.8	34.2
Liberal						21.4	14.2	20.8	20.8
Socioeconomic									
At Least Some College Education	10.4	18.5	11.5	30.3	28.9	27.4	32.9	29.1	38.3
Union Household	44	37.5	37.9	32.3	27.1	36.6	39.2	50	35.3
Middle Class (self-identified)		29.5	28.6	56.3	55.9	47.3	49	45.7	50.4
Religion									
Attend Mass Every Week or Almost Every Week						55.9	51	51.1	53
Is Religion Important to You								86	90
Issue Attitudes									
By Law, Abortion Should Never Be Permitted								10.5	16.9
Favor Laws to Protect Homosexuals against Discrimination									
Guaranteed Jobs and Income (1–3 on 7-pt. scale)						14.8	21	23.6	32.4
Government Should Provide Fewer Services, Reduce Spending (1–3 on 7-pt. scale)									24.3

	1988	1992	1996	2000	2004	2008	2012	2016	2020
Presidential Vote									
Percent Voting Democratic Nationally	52.9	49.6	55.2	50.3	50.8	66.6	58.6	52.1	54.3
Percent Voting Democratic in the Midwest	56.8	39.7	50	52.8	52.9	68.3	47.6	46.5	49.9
Partisanship									
Democrat	50.4	48	56.8	51.8	46.7	52.9	46	40.2	40
Republican	39.7	36	34.1	36.5	37	35.3	40.9	47.9	51.1
Independent	9.9	16	9.1	11.7	16.3	11.8	13	12	8.9
Ideology									
Conservative	36.4	31.3	40.6	31.7	29	25.5	41.9	41.1	44.6
Moderate	22	26.7	27.8	31.7	28	17.6	31.4	36.6	28.7
Liberal	13.6	21	18.8	11.7	11.8	19.6	21.3	22.3	26.7
Socioeconomic									
At Least Some College Education	48.8	53.2	63.9	57.6	62.4	56.9	56.3	69.3	68.7
Union Household	34.8	22.3	30.3	21.9	26.9	14	20.3	18.4	17.6
Middle Class (self-identified)	58	51.2		66.2	58.9	36.7	62.7	57.1	
Religion									
Attend Mass Every Week or Almost Every Week	59.1	56.8	55.6	50.4	49.5	50	44.2	33.7	33.9
Is Religion Important to You	84.7	87.9	93.2	87.6	88.2	78.4	81.9	76.1	
Issue Attitudes									
By Law, Abortion Should Never Be Permitted	13.1	13.1	15.8	11.8	17.4	20.7	13.8	12.4	14.6
Favor Laws to Protect Homosexuals against Discrimination	50	65	56.8	75.6	70.9	76.5	77.6	86.3	86.8
Guaranteed Jobs and Income (1–3 on 7-pt. scale)	26.8	22.7	21	22.1	22.6	26.7	23.8	25.2	24.8
Government Should Provide Fewer Services, Reduce Spending (1–3 on 7-pt. scale)	26	29.1	34.6	22.1	20.4	50.1	40.5	42.3	26.2

and partisan loyalties were becoming a more driving force for Catholic voters as opposed to faith.[10] Although President Barack Obama was able to gain a large percentage of the Catholic vote in his near landslide victory in 2008 (where he was able to slightly outperform his national Catholic vote in the Midwest), the Catholic vote again began to split almost evenly again by 2012. More interesting is that Midwest Catholic voters ceased providing a majority of their votes to the Democratic candidate from 2012 forward. Ultimately, Catholic voters were long considered to be a pillar of the Democratic presidential vote, providing nearly a third of the Democratic coalition despite being about a quarter of the population.[11] However, support for Democratic presidential candidates began to wane by 1972 and, after a brief increase in support in 2008 for Obama, decreased again, especially in the Midwest.

THE CHANGING CATHOLIC VOTER

Using the ANES national data, an analysis was done on Midwestern Catholics between 1952 and 2020 to examine how Midwestern Catholics have changed and, in some cases, remained the same. Table 19.1 shows how Catholic voters have changed over the years in their political beliefs and opinions, their sociodemographic characteristics, and their partisanship. First, looking at the sociodemographic trends of Midwestern Catholics, it is clear that there have been huge shifts among a population that was largely urban, uneducated, and working class. In 1952, just over 10 percent of Catholic voters attended any college. Each decade, the number of Midwestern Catholics attending at least some college increased, with large jumps in the 1960s and late 1980s. In 2020 the ANES data shows that nearly 70 percent of Midwestern Catholics attended at least some college, a massive shift in educational attainment in seventy years. The educational attainment clearly affected the economic outlook of Midwestern Catholics. Starting in the 1960s, 50 to 60 percent of Midwestern Catholics self-reported as being middle class. Also, despite the blue-collar union traditions of many Catholic families, union membership dropped substantially during the seventy-year period of ANES data. In the 1980s, 40 to 50 percent of Midwestern Catholics were in union households; by the early 2000s this number was typically below 20 percent. These socioeconomic changes have political consequences as the difference between Catholics and non-Catholics becomes less prevalent, and so too do the voting habits of these two groups.[12]

One area not examined through the ANES data is race and Midwestern

Catholics. Overall, as one would expect based on the history of immigrants from Europe, a large majority of Midwestern Catholics come from ethnic backgrounds that are considered "white." Even as the rest of the country has become more diverse ethnically, Midwestern Catholics ranged from being 84 percent white in 2007 to 82 percent white in 2014. A growing number of Catholics in the Midwest have a Hispanic ethnic background and make up the bulk of non-white Midwestern Catholics, ranging from 11 to 14 percent in the same years.[13] Hispanic Catholics in the Midwest have their own unique experience that includes relying on more liberal, social justice–oriented teachings, particularly when considering labor relations and reliance on unions.[14]

Catholics in the Midwest have changed their patterns of how often they attend Mass. Since the question was first asked in 1972, nearly 60 percent of Midwestern Catholics said they attend Mass once a week or almost weekly. That number dropped significantly, to 34 percent, by 2020. Interestingly, at the same time, the importance of religion to respondents dropped, but by a more modest amount—10 percent. Although the number of Catholics who regularly attend Mass has dropped, identifying as a Catholic and adhering to the beliefs of the Catholic Church remain relatively strong. Like the socioeconomic changes, the changes in church attendance have voting implications. Research has found that, overall, church attendance is associated with partisan voting[15] and, in particular, that Catholics who attend Mass regularly have been a core Republican voting bloc since the 1980s.[16]

Arguably, some of the most critical findings from the ANES data are the ideological, partisan, and issue attitudes. Both the partisan and ideological statistics for Midwestern Catholics offer much of the explanation for presidential and partisan voting behavior in general. Looking at the partisan data, it is clear the highwater mark for Democrats with Midwestern Catholics was in the 1950s and 1960s, when nearly 70 percent of Midwestern Democrats regularly identified with the Democratic Party. In some years, a in 1960, the percent of Midwestern Catholics identifying as Independent and Republican reached near parity. In the 1970s Democratic identification with Midwestern Democrats declined steadily, and, by 1992, for the first time, a majority no longer identified with the Democratic Party. However, in 1996 there was a resurgence of Democratic identification; this continued in 2000. It is interesting to note that the same time a Catholic ran for president in 2004 also coincides with a low point of Catholic identification with the Democratic Party. After a brief resurgence in 2008 for Obama's first-term election as president, the slide of Democratic affiliation continued. In 2016, when Donald Trump won the presidency, was the first time a plurality of Midwestern Catholics identified as Republican; by 2020 a majority of Midwestern Catholics identified as Republicans, completing almost a seventy-year move from the Democratic to Republican affiliation again, during a year when Democrats fielded a Catholic candidate in Joe Biden.

Like other variables in this analysis, partisan affiliation has major implications on how Midwestern Catholic votes. First, it is clear that there is a strong relationship between partisan affiliation and voting for president. Research has shown that partisan identification of Catholics is cited as the major reason that Kerry lost in 2004 and likely explains why, after 2008, Midwestern Catholics voted for President Trump in 2016 and 2020.[17] The relationship between partisanship and voting has only increased over time and currently explains down-ballot voting for federal, state, and local offices as split-ticket voting has decreased significantly because voters support a straight-party ballot, regardless if they live in a state with straight-ticket voting.[18] Second, over time there has been an increased relationship between ideology and partisanship, frequently referred to as sorting, in which conservatives have become Republicans and liberals have become Democrats.[19] Since measuring ideology, the percentage of Midwestern Catholics considering themselves liberals or conservatives has ebbed and flowed, but by 1996, the importance of that relationship between ideology and partisanship began to become more important as the political parties become more sorted and polarized.

Using the ANES data, the attitudes of Midwestern Catholics on several "culture war" issues were examined. The "culture wars" are marked by competing ideas over what the proper vision for American culture should be.[20] As noted by Richard Morrill, Larry Knopp, and Michael Brown, "American society [is] fundamentally shaken by social upheaval around a diverse range of cultural issues from race to gender, sexuality, immigration, religion, and, more broadly, what is often referred to as 'values'—the fundamental moral and ethical belief systems and world views that structure people's lives. . . . These have become increasingly contested in the so-called 'public sphere.'"[21] The public sphere includes political battles at levels and institutions of government. Therefore, it is clear these issues have political overtones to them, and many of them may have direct applications to Catholic voters in general. Midwestern Catholics were asked about abortion on a four-point scale: it should (1) legally never be permitted, (2) be permitted only under certain circumstances, (3) be legal under most circumstances, or (4) be totally legal. Only 10 percent of Midwestern Catholics agreed with the first, most pro-life, option in 1980; this percentage increased slightly over the next several years, reaching its highest support in 2004 and 2008, and then decreased back to around 15 percent. It should be noted that currently six of the nine Supreme Court Justices are Catholic, and the recent *Dobbs v. Jackson* decision that struck down abortion rights guarantees and left abortion policy up to individual states was supported by five of those Catholic justices, including recent appointees Brett Kavanaugh and Amy Coney Barrett.

Another culture war issue is about laws protecting those who identify as LGBTQ. When this question was first asked, 50 percent of Midwestern Catholics agreed that there should be laws protecting gays from discrimination, and this number increased steadily, reaching over 85 percent support by 2016. Although this seems to be counter to what we would expect, a story from the 2004 presidential election may highlight how this question may be interpreted. During the 2004 election, the critical battleground state of Ohio had a statewide same-sex marriage ban that was to be voted on. In Cincinnati, Issue 3 was on the ballot to amend the city charter to provide anyone who identified as being LGBTQ as having legal protections against discrimination. The Catholic Archbishop of Cincinnati urged Catholic voters to ban same-sex marriage but vote to repeal Issue 3, arguing that the ordinance was, in fact, discriminatory.[22] Therefore, Midwestern Catholics may draw a distinction between discrimination and other gay rights. Although there is no ANES data on transgender rights, recent surveys have found that large numbers of Catholics, around 62 percent, do not favor defining gender as something that is fluid and is defined at birth.[23] Overall, there is evidence to suggest that the "culture wars," particularly questions about abortion, are one of the driving forces to move Catholics, as a whole, away from the Democratic Party due to its more liberal stance on several of these issues, particularly within the most recent elections.[24]

The last two issue attitude questions seek to identify if a divide on the role of government explains the divide between Midwestern Catholics. Overall, attitudes on whether the government should be ensuring that all Americans have a job and income has remained static. On a scale of one to seven, respondents could rate how much they felt the government should provide jobs and income. Those that answered a scale of one to three (or closest to agreeing government should do this) remained around 20 percent. Midwestern Catholics split on their attitudes over whether the government should provide fewer services and less spending. Again a seven-point scale was used, and the percentage of respondents who were less inclined to have the government provide more services and spend less increased during the 1990s, dropped, and increased again in 2008. Overall, for many of the culture war questions, it will be important to see who was inclined to answer in the extremes, which is analyzed statistically below.

Finally, although not a part of this analysis, it is important to discuss what Catholic priests believe politically. Clergy, regardless of what religion or Christian denomination, are able to influence their congregations and shape their attitudes by deciding what issues to discuss and how certain political issues fit into church teachings.[25] Studies on priests suggest that they are similar to Catholics overall. A study of priests' political activities in the late 1990s and early 2000s found that a slight majority identified as liberal and that priests as a whole voted for Clinton in 1996 and for Bush in 2000, many citing social issues for their respective vote.[26] Another study completed more recently of a broad range of religious leaders found that Catholic priests reported splitting almost exactly fifty-fifty in their partisanship,[27] in many ways matching the Catholic vote overall in recent years.

MIDWESTERN CATHOLICS IN A PARTISAN ERA

A final analysis of the ANES data seeks to explain the effect of sociodemographic, partisan, and attitudinal factors on Midwestern Catholic partisanship. Using Midwestern Catholics' responses between 2000 and 2020, frequently seen as a heightened polarized era, a regression analysis was completed in Table 19.2. A seven-point partisan scale of partisan affiliation was used as the dependent variable while several sociodemographic and ideological identifiers from Table 19.1 were used as the independent variables.

The results bolster the idea that Midwestern Catholics' partisanship split along familiar demographic and ideological lines. Union households are still a major partisan predictor of Midwestern Catholics. Age, although not strongly significant, was still a significant predictor of partisanship. Gender is a significant predictor of Midwestern Catholic partisanship. This is not surprising since the time period examined is during the height of the "gender gap" seen in partisan affiliation and voting, and was further exacerbated during the Trump elections. Age is another major dividing line among Catholics, particularly pre–Vatican II, Vatican II, and post–Vatican II generations of Catholics.[28] Ideology and attitudes toward both economic and culture war issues are all significant predictors of partisanship. The ideological scale and each of the questions from Table 19.1, including attitudes about abortion, gay rights, government guarantees of jobs and income, and government services and spending, were all significant predictors of partisanship in the model as well. The only variable

Table 19.2 Catholic Voters in a Partisan Era, Predictors of Partisanship, 2000–2020

Variable	Coefficient	Standard Error	Beta
Over 40	–.225	.127*	–.047
Female	–.260	.115**	–.060
At Least Some College	.418	.122**	.092
Attend Mass Regularly	–.113	.120	–.025
Union Household	.428	.143**	.078
Ideology	.122	.029**	.114
Guaranteed Job and Income	–.980	.142**	–.183
Abortion Not Permitted	.927	.179**	.139
Fewer Service, Lower Spending	1.480	.128**	.307
Protect Gays	–.464	.116**	–.106
Constant	2.870	.322**	

Notes: *p < .10, **p < .05. The model was estimated with ordinary least square regression. The dependent variable is party identification.

not significant in the analysis was church attendance, which past studies cited here found to be a predictor of partisanship but did not end up being so here.

THE FUTURE OF THE MIDWESTERN CATHOLIC VOTE

The Midwestern Catholic vote and the Catholic vote, overall, seem to be elusive in the modern political era. According to the analysis here, if there was ever a Catholic vote in which all members of the group acted in near unison to support a candidate and party, it was during the Kennedy election in 1960 and in Johnson's landslide victory in 1964 in support of the Democrats. Since that time, it has slowly splintered and become much more Republican, particularly among Midwestern Catholics. Much of this coincides with the movement of "whites," who make up the vast majority of Midwestern Catholics, from urban areas and blue-collar union jobs to suburban and rural areas and into professional white-collar jobs.[29] Many of these urban industrial areas became part of the Midwestern Rust Belt that has undergone socioeconomic, demographic, and political changes.

It is important to note that since Kennedy's run in 1960, two other Catholics have run for the presidency: John Kerry and Joe Biden. Midwestern Catholics split their vote nearly evenly between the Democratic Catholic candidate and the non-Catholic Republican candidate. In fact, Joe Biden is the first president in the modern era, according to the ANES data, to not have majority support from Midwestern Catholics.

The results of this analysis suggest that ideology and partisanship rule the day. Although Midwestern Catholics go to the same church and have the same religious traditions, it is clear that some put a different emphasis on the different parts of the Catholic faith. It seems clear that the Midwestern Catholic vote will continue to splinter along partisan lines and likely continue the near fifty-fifty split that has become the norm during this partisan era. Although there has not been a Catholic vote in the sense that it is unified and has voted for the same party for some time now, it is not a reason for the two major parties to ignore them. In fact, given that the Midwestern Catholic vote ebbs and flows based on elections and because they live in critical areas of battleground states throughout the Midwest, the need to attract Midwestern Catholics has never been greater. As the battleground status moves from the lower Midwest to the upper Midwest, to states like Michigan, Minnesota, and Wisconsin, winning the Midwestern Catholic vote could be the deciding factor in future elections.

NOTES

1. David Doherty, Conor M. Dowling, and Michael G. Miller, *Small Power: How Local Parties Shape Elections* (New York: Oxford University Press, 2022), 3.

2. Michael J. Pfeifer, *The Making of American Catholicism* (New York: New York University Press, 2021).

3. Matthew J. Burbank, Ronald D. Hrebenar, and Robert C. Benedict, *Parties, Interest Groups, and Political Campaigns* (New York: Oxford University Press, 2008).

4. James A. Reichley. *The Life of the Parties* (New York: Free Press, 1992).

5. Kevin P. Phillips, *The Emerging Republican Majority* (New Rochelle, NY: Arlington House, 1969).

6. American National Election Studies, 2021, ANES Time Series Cumulative Data File , November 18, 2021, version. https://www.electionstudies.org.

7. Philip E. Converse, Angus Campbell, Warren E. Miller, and Donald E. Stokes, "Stability and Change in 1960: A Reinstating Election," *American Political Science Review* 45 (1961): 269–280.

8. Jay P. Dolan, *The American Catholics Experience: A History from Colonial Times to Present*. (Notre Dame, IN: University of Notre Dame Press, 1992).

9. Clyde F. Crews. *American and Catholic: A Popular History of Catholicism in the United States* (Cincinnati, OH: Anthony Messenger Press, 1993).

10. Mark M. Gray, Paul M. Perl, and Mary E. Bendyna, "Camelot Only Come but Once? John F. Kerry and the Catholic Vote," *Presidential Elections Quarterly* 36, no. 2 (2006): 203–222.

11. Robert Axelrod, "Presidential Election Coalitions in 1984," *American Political Science Review* 80, no. 1 (1986): 281–284.

12. Kenneth D. Wald, *Religion and Politics in the United States*, 4th ed. (Lanham, MD: Rowman & Littlefield, 2003); Stephen T. Mockabee. "Catholics: Change and

Continuity," in Matthew J. Wilson, ed., *From Pews to Polling Places: Faith and Politics in the American Religious Mosaic* (Washington, DC: Georgetown University Press, 2007).

13. Pew Research Center, Adults in the Midwest Who Are Catholic, May 2014, https://www.pewresearch.org/religion/religious-landscape-study/religious-tradition/catholic/region/midwest/.

14. Jay P. Dolan and Gilberto M. Hinojosa, *Mexican Americans and the Catholic Church, 1900–1965* (Notre Dame, IN: University of Notre Dame Press, 1994).

15. Robert D. Putnam and David E Campbell, *American Grace: How Religion Divides and Unites Us* (New York: Simon & Schuster, 2012).

16. Gray, Perl, and Bendyna, "Camelot Only Come but Once?"

17. Gray, Perl, and Bendyna, "Camelot Only Come but Once?"; Mockabee, "Catholics: Change and Continuity."

18. Steven Rogers, "National Forces in State Legislative Elections," *ANNALS of the American Academy of Political and Social Sciences* 667, no. 1 (2016): 207–225.

Chad Kinsella, Colleen McTague, and Kevin Raleigh, "Closely and Deeply Divided: Purple Counties in the 2016 Presidential Election," *Applied Geography* 127 (2021): 102386.

19. Matthew Levendusky, *The Partisan Sort: How Liberals Became Democrats and Conservatives Became Republicans* (Chicago: University of Chicago Press, 2009).

20. James Davison Hunter, *Culture Wars: The Struggle to Control the Family, Art, Education, Law, and Politics in America* (New York: Basic Books, 1992); "The Enduring Culture War," in James Davison Hunter and Alan Wolfe, eds., *Is There a Culture War?: A Dialogue on Values and American Public Life* (Washington, DC: Brookings Institution Press, 2007).

21. Richard Morrill, Larry Knopp, and Michael Brown, "Anomalies in Red and Blue: Exceptionalism in American Electoral Geography," *Political Geography* 26, no. 5 (2007): 531.

22. Gregory Korte, "Gay Issue May Energize GOP," *Cincinnati Enquirer*, September 14, 2004, C1.

23. Michael Lipka and Patricia Tevington, "Attitudes about Transgender Issues Vary Widely among Christians, Religious 'Nones' in U.S.," July 7, 2022, https://www.pewresearch.org/short-reads/2022/07/07/attitudes-about-transgender-issues-vary-widely-among-christians-religious-nones-in-u-s/.

24. Steven P. Millies, *Good Intentions: A History of Catholic Voters' Road from Roe to Trump* (Collegeville, MN: Liturgical Press, 2018).

25. Sue E. S. Crawford and Laura R. Olson, *Christian Clergy in American Politics* (Baltimore: Johns Hopkins University Press, 2001); Gregory A. Smith, "The Influence of Priests on the Political Attitudes of Roman Catholics," *Journal for the Scientific Study of Religion* 44, no. 3 (2005): 291–306.

26. Ted G. Jelen, "Catholic Priests and the Political Order: The Political Behavior of Catholic Pastors," *Journal for the Scientific Study of Religion* 42, no. 4 (2003): 591–604.

27. Eitan Hersh and Gabrielle Malina, "Partisan Pastor: The Politics of 130,000 American Religious Leaders." working paper, 2017. Unpublished manuscript.

28. William V. D'Antonio, James D. Davidson, Dean R. Hoge, Katherine Meyer, and William B. Friend, *American Catholics: Gender, Generation, and Commitment*. (Walnut Creek, CA: Altamira, 2001).

29. Thomas J. Sugrue, *The Origins of the Urban Crisis* (Princeton, NJ: Princeton University Press, 2014).

20

The Great Blue Hope

How Senator Sherrod Brown Won Reelection in Donald Trump's Ohio

CHRISTOPHER J. DEVINE

❖ ❖ ❖ ❖ ❖ ❖ ❖ ❖ ❖ ❖ ❖ ❖ ❖ ❖ ❖

Barely one hour after polls closed on November 6, 2018, Sherrod Brown took the stage in Columbus, Ohio, to celebrate his election to a third term in the United States Senate. In the gravelly voice that—along with rumpled suits and disheveled hair—had become part of his everyman brand, Brown called out: "Let our country, let our nation's citizens, our Democratic Party, my fellow elected officials all over the country—let them cast their eyes . . . toward the heartland, to the industrial Midwest." This was not just some desperate bid for attention being broadcast from "fly-over country." Speaking to a national audience that would hear or read these comments—alongside speculation about his presidential ambitions—live or in the coming days, Brown was proclaiming hope for the revival of the Democratic Party. "We will show America . . . how we celebrate the dignity of work. That is the message coming out of Ohio in 2018, and that is the blueprint for America in 2020."[1]

More precisely, his message was this: Democrats *can* win in red states. Democrats *can* take back the Midwest from Donald Trump's Republican Party. And they not only can, but *must*, do so as progressives. This is what Sherrod Brown represented: amid the rubble of a fallen Midwestern "blue wall," here stood the Great Blue Hope.

Indeed, Brown and his supporters encouraged interpretations of his victory in 2018 as a case study for the recovery of Midwestern liberalism and the Democratic Party. This chapter interrogates such interpretations, asking whether Brown's reelection constitutes a replicable model for other Midwestern Democrats. I conclude that while Brown failed to win over many Republicans, he secured reelection by presenting himself—not just in 2018, but throughout his career—as a "progressive populist," in particular by opposing free trade. Whether other Midwestern Democrats can replicate his success—particularly after Brown himself lost his Senate seat in the 2024 election—may depend on factors such as incumbency, the credibility of their Republican opponents, and candidate as well as state demographics.

A MODEL FOR MIDWESTERN DEMOCRATS?

In 2018, Sherrod Brown defeated his Republican opponent, US Representative Jim Renacci, by nearly seven percentage points (53.4 percent to 46.6 percent). For an incumbent to win reelection, and by such a modest margin, hardly seems remarkable. To appreciate the significance of this victory, however, one must consider the state, regional, and national context in which it took place.

First, in terms of state politics, while Brown won reelection in 2018, Republicans swept every other partisan statewide race in Ohio, including the governorship, for the third consecutive election, preserved their overwhelming majority in the state legislature (61 to 38 in the house, 24 to 9 in the senate), and retained twelve of sixteen seats in the US House. Furthermore, Donald Trump won the 2016 presidential election in Ohio—heretofore, the quintessential battleground state—by eight percentage points, representing an eleven percentage-point gain (the seventh-largest in the nation) over 2012.[2]

Second, in terms of regional politics, three of the four Democratic senators who were defeated for reelection in 2018 came from the Midwest: Joe Donnelly (Indiana), Heidi Heitkamp (North Dakota), and Claire McCaskill (Missouri). Trump won each of their states by at least eighteen percentage points. Three other Midwestern Democratic senators, besides Brown, won reelection: Tammy Baldwin (Wisconsin), Amy Klobuchar (Minnesota), and Debbie Stabenow (Michigan). Trump won Wisconsin and Michigan by less than one percentage point; Minnesota voted narrowly for Democrat Hillary Clinton. Brown won reelection by nearly the same margin as Stabenow (6.8 percent versus 6.5 percent, respectively), but by less than Baldwin (10.8 percent) and much less than Klobuchar (24.1 percent). Nonetheless, he was the only Midwestern Democratic

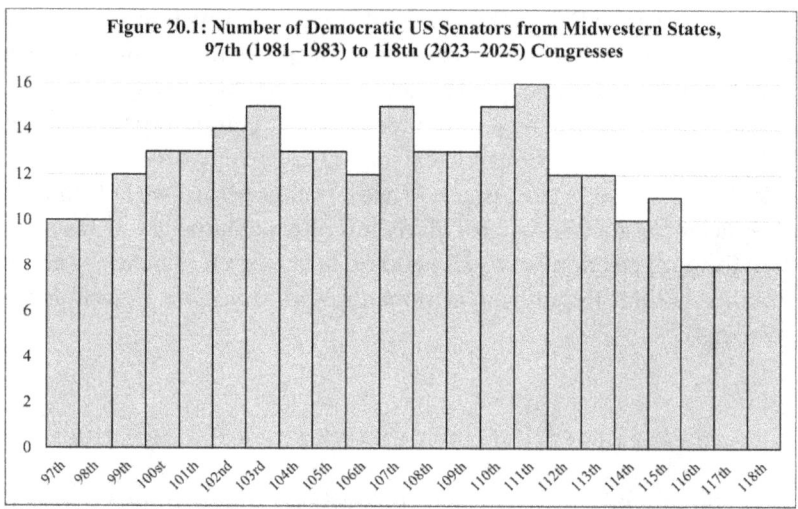

Figure 20.1. Number of Democratic US Senators from Midwestern States, Ninety-Seventh (1981 to 1983) to 118th (2023 to 2025) Congresses

senator to be reelected in a state that Trump won decisively. Trump won all but two Midwestern states (Illinois and Minnesota) in 2016, flipping four (Ohio, Iowa, Michigan, and Wisconsin) that Barack Obama won in 2012 and enabling him to win the election. Michigan and Wisconsin had not voted for a Republican presidential nominee since the 1980s. Trump gained 9.1 percent of the vote in Midwestern states, on average, over 2012. Six of the ten largest Republican gains were in Midwestern states.

Also in Senate elections, Democrats were losing ground in the Midwest. As Figure 20.1 shows, Democrats held only one-third of the Senate seats (8 of 24) from Midwestern states following the 2018 elections—down from two-thirds (16 of 24) a decade earlier. The Midwest was not just central to Donald Trump's election as president in 2016, but also to Democrats' loss of a filibuster-proof majority in the Senate, and then the majority altogether, since 2008. Thus, Sherrod Brown's success in an increasingly "red" state has important implications for understanding how Democrats might compete for control of the US Senate and presidency.

Finally, in terms of national politics, Brown's reelection defied trends toward increasing partisan voting and nationalization of elections. Split-ticket voting has been on the decline for decades. Concomitantly, it has become less common for states to elect senators who belong to different parties, or who belong to a party that did not win that state's vote in the previous presidential election.[3] Brown was one of only three US Senate candidates—along with fellow Democratic incumbents Jon Tester of Montana and Joe Manchin of West Virginia—to win a state in 2018 that voted for another party's presidential candidate by more than 3.5 percentage points in 2016.

What makes Brown's victory extraordinary—and potentially instructive for Democrats—is that he overcame these state, regional, and national disadvantages while running as an unapologetic progressive. Indeed, most of Brown's Democratic Senate colleagues who ran for reelection in Trump states—including the winners (Tester, Manchin, and Bob Casey of Pennsylvania) and losers (Donnelly, Heitkamp, and McCaskill)—voted and campaigned as relative moderates. Brown, in contrast, embraced his ideological cause. On election night, for example, Brown claimed validation for Midwestern liberalism. "You all showed the country that progressives can win, and win decisively, in the heartland," he boasted. "And you showed the country by putting people first and by honoring the dignity of work, we carry a state that Donald Trump won by almost double digits." Political circumstances may have changed, but this was the argument that Sherrod Brown had been making all his life.

WHO IS SHERROD BROWN?

Sherrod Brown was born in Mansfield, Ohio—a small industrial city located about halfway between Columbus and Cleveland—in 1952. Contrary to his working-class image, Brown grew up in a well-to-do family, the son of a doctor and a teacher. Together, they lived in a three-story Colonial and on a 285-acre farm in the summers. Inspired by his mother's passion for civil rights, Brown became politically active at a young age—serving as student council president and organizing an Earth Day march attended by a thousand students while in high school, and volunteering for George McGovern's 1972 presidential campaign while in college. Shortly before graduating from Yale University in 1974 with a degree in Russian Studies, Brown was recruited by a local Democratic Party official from Mansfield—with whom he had made a point of keeping in close contact—to run for a seat in the Ohio House of Representatives. Brown won the race, at just twenty-one years old, making him the youngest person ever elected to the Ohio legislature.[4] He would be reelected three times before winning his first statewide race, for secretary of state, in 1982. In 1990, while seeking a third term in office, Brown suffered the only loss of his career until 2024, to Hamilton County commissioner (and later two-term governor of Ohio) Bob Taft—in what Taft describes as "a somewhat bitter, hotly contested race."[5]

Brown returned to politics by winning an open seat in the US House of Representatives in 1992. His congressional district, which included Mansfield, was largely urban and blue-collar. He narrowly won reelection in 1994, but coasted to victory in subsequent races—even after his district was redrawn to exclude Mansfield and the majority of his former constituents. In the House, Brown distinguished himself as a leading opponent of free trade deals including the North American Free Trade Agreement (NAFTA) and the Central American Free Trade Agreement (CAFTA), which, he said, encouraged the off-shoring of US—particularly Midwestern—manufacturing jobs and facilities. Brown also developed a liberal reputation by advocating for universal health care and voting against the PATRIOT ACT, the Iraq War, and establishing the Department of Homeland Security.

In 2006 Brown ran for the US Senate against two-term incumbent (and future two-term Ohio governor) Mike DeWine. He defeated DeWine decisively (56.2 to 43.8 percent) in a "wave" election year—with Democrats regaining both houses of Congress, and Ohio's governorship, amid an unpopular war in Iraq and a series of high-profile Republican scandals. Indeed, much of Brown's campaign focused on criticizing President George W. Bush's administration and DeWine's support for it. But he also promoted himself as a champion of progressive values, despite Ohio's center-right orientation. In his victory speech, Brown reflected: "A lot of people . . . advised me not to be myself. They advised me to be middle of the road. . . . But, you know, it's a risk worth taking to stand up for what you believe in. And it's a risk worth taking to fight uncompromisingly for progressive values."[6]

As counterintuitive as this approach might seem, in what was then the nation's quintessential swing state, there was some precedent in recent Ohio history for running from the left—and winning. Indeed, Brown took over the US Senate seat occupied for three terms (from 1976 to 1995), by Democrat Howard Metzenbaum—who was described, in terms just as easily applied to Sherrod Brown, as "unabashedly liberal" and "a champion of workers." Much like his successor, it was said that "when other liberals shied away from that label, Metzenbaum embraced it."[7] Sherrod Brown, then, did not write the playbook for winning races in Ohio, or elsewhere in the Midwest, as a proudly progressive Democrat; he inherited it from Metzenbaum and others, and has updated it for the twenty-first century.

In 2012 Brown won reelection by six percentage points (50.7 to 44.7 percent) over Ohio treasurer Josh Mandel. It was one of the most expensive Senate races in the United States, and, to that point, the most expensive race in Ohio history.[8] Ohio also was the main battleground in that year's presidential race, hosting nearly 30 percent of all campaign visits nationwide.[9] Obama won the state, also with 50.7 percent of the vote. Mandel attacked Brown as a "career politician" and a "tax and spend liberal" who supported Obama's Affordable Care Act (ACA), auto bailout, and environmental policies.[10] Brown—while also attacking Mandel's character and record as treasurer—again campaigned on his progressive credentials. As one observer put it: "He's running as a consistent, unapologetic liberal who promotes 'Obamacare' and is as pro-union as they come."[11]

Indeed, Sherrod Brown was one of the most liberal members of the US Senate. According to the leading academic measure of legislative ideology (DW-NOMINATE), in 2018 Brown ranked as more liberal than 87 percent of all US senators, 76 percent of Democratic senators, and all but one Midwestern senator (Tammy Baldwin).[12] From 2007 to 2009, Brown was the fourth most liberal US senator—behind only Bernie Sanders, Barbara Boxer, and Ted Kennedy. While not a particularly effective legislator overall,[13] Brown has taken a leading role in advancing liberal legislative priorities such as banking regulation (e.g., Dodd-Frank) and health care (e.g., ACA, the Healthy Start Reauthorization Act), and opposing free trade deals (e.g., CAFTA, Trans-Pacific Partnership) while also voting to reform NAFTA via the US-Mexico-Canada Agreement (USMCA) and securing an amendment to provide for stronger labor protections.[14]

How does one of the most liberal US senators get reelected in an increasingly red state? In part, because Ohioans do not think Sherrod Brown is *that* liberal. Data from the 2018 Cooperative Congressional Election Study (CCES)—including 64,000 respondents overall, and 1,399 validated voters from Ohio—suggests as much.[15] When asked to place Brown on a seven-point ideological scale, approximately 70 percent of Ohioans correctly identified him as liberal, including 22.5 percent who chose "very liberal," 32.7 percent "liberal," and 16.6 percent "slightly liberal."[16] But, as a Democrat, this is to be expected. Less obvious is whether voters find Brown to be particularly liberal *for a Democrat*. To evaluate this, Figure 20.2 compares the average ideological placements of Sherrod Brown versus "the Democratic Party" among Ohio voters overall and by party.[17] Lower scores indicate greater perceived liberalism.

This evidence indicates that Ohio voters, on average, perceived Brown to be liberal (2.38), but slightly less so than the Democratic Party (2.20). The difference is statistically significant ($p < 0.001$). Independents and Republicans, alike, perceive Brown to be significantly less liberal than his party. Only Democrats perceive Brown to be significantly more liberal than their party, as a whole—which, for many of them, may be a favorable assessment.

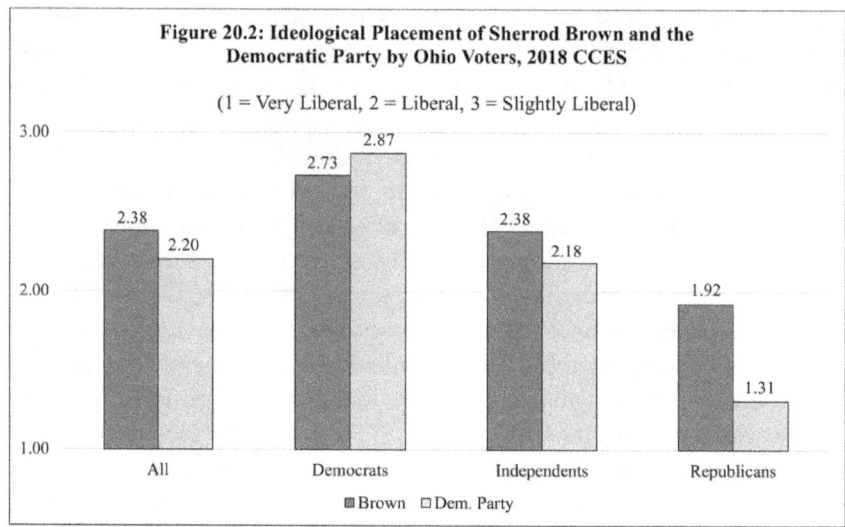

Figure 20.2. Ideological Placement of Sherrod Brown and the Democratic Party by Ohio Voters, 2018 CCES

Perhaps the main reason Ohioans do not view Brown as a relative ideologue is that he presents himself as a progressive *and* a populist—fusing these identities together to create something distinctive, more complex, and thus more difficult to define or attack on familiar political terms. Indeed, political observers trying to make sense of Brown's success often describe him as a "progressive populist."[18] Brown encourages this by embracing both labels. For example, in his 2018 victory speech, Brown rhetorically identified himself with progressives ("We, as progressives, celebrate the dignity of all work. . . . As progressives, we always celebrate hourly wage earners.") and, moments later, with populists ("Populists are not racists, populists are not anti-Semitic. We do not appeal to some by pushing others down. We do not lie.").[19]

Brown's populism comes through in the way he explains policy and himself. Consider, for example, this excerpt from a website promoting his brief flirtation with a presidential run in 2020, which includes some of the greatest hits familiar to anyone who has followed Brown's Senate career:

> Sherrod has always taken on powerful special interests and corruption in Washington. One of his recent bills was called, "just about every policy idea drug lobbyists hate." . . .
>
> And he refused to accept Congressional healthcare until Congress passed the Affordable Care Act. Now he gets his health insurance through the same exchange system available to all Americans under that law. . . .

Sherrod doesn't own individual stocks because he believes Members of Congress should serve the American people, not their stock portfolios. . . .

Sherrod drives a Jeep made by union workers in Toledo, Ohio, and his suits are made by union workers outside of Cleveland.[20]

Brown mentioned the last fact during each of his three Senate debates in 2018, indicating how central it is to his political persona. Indeed, much of Brown's populist appeal owes to his close identification with labor unions and blue-collar workers—one forged not by shared on-the-job experience, but sustained personal contact and political partnership since first taking office in the 1970s.[21] As Ohio steelworker and union representative Jose Arroyo put it: "When he talks to you, he knows the language. He sounds like a working man."[22]

When asked to explain his ideological appeal, Brown reframes the question in populist terms. "Fundamentally, the voters don't see left to right, liberal or conservative, but they want to know if you are on their side," he said in 2012. "Voters look for authenticity. . . . You stand for something, and you stay with it. I think voters will reward that. I don't think of it as a strategy; I think this is who I am."[23] Six years later, nothing had changed. "I don't buy the left and right," Brown said in 2018. To win as a progressive in Ohio, "you have to be authentic about whom you fight for and what you fight against. That's just who I am."[24]

QUALITATIVE ANALYSIS OF THE 2018 CAMPAIGN

"People keep asking me how I'm going to win back the Trump voters," Sherrod Brown said in 2017. "Well, I don't think I've ever lost them."[25] Nonetheless, appealing to Trump voters was central to his 2018 reelection strategy. "We knew in my race we had to get one out of seven Trump voters," he recalled later. "We knew it was mostly female Trump voters, and we did. And we did it with progressive populism, not the phony divide populism of Trump. Real populism . . . brings people together. You campaign through the eyes of workers, and you govern through the eyes of workers."[26]

This strategy was evident in an early campaign advertisement called "For Ohio."[27] It features Brown at an Ohio steel plant, wearing a hardhat and talking with workers. "I'm Sherrod Brown," he says, speaking straight-to-camera with a backhoe operating in the distance. "I've made protecting Ohio workers *my top priority*." While touting his opposition to various free trade agreements, newspaper headlines appear on screen.

"Brown pushes for better trade deals for Ohio," reads one. Another: "Brown hasn't wavered in his position on free-trade deals." Completing the aforementioned formula, the candidate closes by stating for whom and against what he is fighting: "Plenty of senators stand up for Wall Street. But I work for Ohio." Brown's other positive ads built on the same working-class theme—including his efforts to protect jobs at a Whirlpool plant and to secure better wages and benefits for workers across numerous industries—and even the negative ads featured images of him at the steel plant, hardhat fastened.

Brown relentlessly focused on populist themes throughout the campaign, including in the October debates. From the economy to health care to student loan debt, he consistently framed issues in terms of the interests of working people, in opposition to corporate interests. For example, in the second debate, he lamented: "I see a Congress that continues to weigh in on the side of corporations over workers, and Wall Street over consumers. . . . Whether it's prescription drug consumers or financial services consumers, this government has sold them out."[28] In the third debate, he decried "tax cuts for the rich" designed to help "the billionaires and the millionaires." In true populist fashion, Brown positioned himself on the side of "the people"—not the elites. "I measure the economy on how workers are doing in our state, how middle-class workers—is our economy growing that way," he explained. On trade policy, for instance: "I look at every trade agreement as: How does this affect jobs in my state? How does it affect working-class families? How does it affect small businesses in Mansfield, where I grew up?"

"Dignity of work" is the phrase that Brown used to summarize his campaign and his approach to governance. He communicated this message—with remarkable discipline—at nearly every campaign appearance and in each debate, with some version of the following:

> When you love your country, you fight for the people who make it work. When I get up every day, I'm ready for that fight for Ohio workers—whether you punch a clock, whether you swipe a badge, whether you work for tips or for a salary, whether you're raising children or taking care of an aging parent. . . . I believe in the dignity of work, which means if you play by the rules and you work hard, you should be able to get ahead.[29]

It was a plea for progressivism, packaged as populism.

Republican challenger Jim Renacci tried to counter this populist message by casting Brown as a "far-left, career politician" beholden to Washington lobbyists, whereas he—in reality, a four-term congressman and before that a mayor—was "a businessman, not a career politician."[30]

Speaking at a campaign rally for then president Donald Trump—who had recruited Renacci to run for Senate earlier that year, and tweeted his "full endorsement!" during the Republican primary—Renacci summarized the case against his opponent: "Sherrod Brown is the fourth-most-liberal senator in the country. That's not Ohio. . . . He votes like a Hollywood liberal, and he has received the most lobbyist money in the Senate, more than any other senator."[31] In debates, Renacci tried to establish a connection between Brown's ideology and his allegiance to the people of Ohio. "I'm here. I'm out here. I come back, and I get involved with the community," Renacci insisted. "The difference between me and my opponent, Sherrod Brown, is he loves Washington so much—and [Democratic Senate leader] Chuck Schumer—he's forgotten about Ohio."[32] And, in the final debate: "I'm going to continue to work to make Ohio first. He's going to work to make Washington first."[33]

Renacci's attempt to redefine Brown didn't stick, for three reasons. First, Brown maintained a strong presence in Ohio throughout his Senate tenure. As Bob Taft explained in 2022, "Brown stays visible throughout the state, spending a lot of time traveling around and having press conferences. His office also gives very good constituent services and has for a number of years. I think he has established a clear identity in the state which is hard for an opponent to attack or undermine."[34] Indeed, as Brown stressed in debates, he returned to Ohio most weekends during Senate sessions.

Second, Renacci buried his populist counter-message by focusing public attention and media coverage on personal attacks against Brown. Specifically, he said that—according to Democrats' standards for opposing Brett Kavanaugh's recent Supreme Court nomination—Brown was disqualified from office by the fact that his first wife, Larke Recchie, had charged him with "gross neglect of duty" and "extreme cruelty" in divorce filings, and secured a restraining order against him. Brown and Recchie had since reconciled, and she recorded an ad defending Brown. At each debate, when Renacci raised this issue, Brown responded: "Congressman Renacci, my former wife asked you to stop attacking our family. She called these charges and your attacks despicable. She is supporting me, and you should be ashamed of yourself."[35]

Third, Renacci failed to attract or invest the resources necessary to reach voters with his message. His campaign raised only $4.5 million (to Brown's $28.7 million),[36] and spent less than $1 million in total on just two television ads (to Brown's $12.5 million)—the first, in June, accusing Brown of lying about Renacci's lobbying activity, and the second, in October, focusing on Brown's divorce.[37] Renacci later claimed to have lost because of his disadvantages in terms of fundraising and statewide name recognition.[38] But Renacci—who, as one of the wealthiest members of Congress, loaned his campaign $4 million but did not spent most of it—only had himself to blame. His lethargic campaign alienated the outside groups that had spent so heavily on Josh Mandel in 2012. As one Ohio Republican put it, many would-be contributors found themselves wondering not just whether Renacci "has thrown in the towel," but "whether Jim's campaign ever even picked up the towel in the first place."[39]

QUANTITATIVE ANALYSIS OF VOTE CHOICE IN 2018

How did Sherrod Brown win reelection in 2018? Exit polling[40]—as shown in Table 20.1—suggests that, in addition to typically pro-Democratic constituencies such as Black voters and women voters, Brown's populism helped him win over union-affiliated voters and, defying the recently emergent "diploma divide," most voters with *or* without college degrees. Brown nearly met his modest goal of winning over one out of seven Trump voters and did, in fact, win that share of split-ticket voters who supported Mike DeWine for governor.

To better estimate these factors' causal effects, Table 20.2 presents the results of a logistic regression analysis based on data from the 2018 CCES.[41] Again, this analysis only includes validated voters from Ohio. The dependent variable is coded one if the respondent voted for Brown, zero for Renacci, and missing otherwise. The independent variables corresponding to those featured in Table 20.1—party, ideology, gender, race, education, union household—are coded into identical categories. Also, I include variables measuring perceptions of economic conditions over the past year (much worse to much better) and opinions of the Trump tax cuts, repeal of the Affordable Care Act, legalized abortion, and imposing tariffs on imported goods from China (coded from liberal to conservative positions). Finally, I include a variable measuring perceptions of Brown's ideology (very liberal to very conservative).

Table 20.2 indicates that some factors—most notably, living in a union household—did not have an independent, statistically significant effect on vote choice in the 2018 Ohio Senate race. Among demographic factors, the only significant finding is that Sherrod Brown won strong support from Black voters. Policy more clearly influenced vote choice, with Brown gaining support from respondents who shared his critical view of the national economy and his liberal positions on health care, abortion,

Table 20.1. Exit Polling Data, 2018 US Senate Election in Ohio

Demographic	Sample (%)	Brown	Renacci	Difference
Gender				
Men	49	46	53	–7
Women	51	60	40	+20
Race				
Black	12	89	11	+78
White	83	47	53	–6
Education				
High School	26	52	48	+4
Some College	28	54	46	+8
Associate's Degree	13	46	53	–7
Bachelor's Degree	20	55	45	+10
Advanced Degree	13	59	41	+18
Union Household				
Yes	25	62	38	+24
No	75	55	45	+10
Party				
Democrat	33	98	2	+96
Independent	29	56	44	+12
Republican	38	11	89	–78
Ideology				
Liberal	21	94	6	+88
Moderate	41	67	33	+34
Conservative	38	15	85	–70
Vote for President, 2016				
Clinton	36	99	1	+98
Trump	50	12	88	–76
Vote for Governor, 2018				
Corday (Democrat)	48	94	5	+89
DeWine (Republican)	50	14	86	–72

Source: CNN, https://www.cnn.com/election/2018/exit-polls/ohio/senate, accessed January 6, 2022.

and tariffs. Brown's ideology also had a significant and *positive* effect on vote choice—meaning that respondents, in general, were more likely to vote for Brown if they perceived him to be more moderate, or less liberal. If it is the case, as I argue, that Brown's populist messaging keeps most voters from seeing him as ideologically extreme, despite his policy positions and voting record, then this, in fact, may help to explain how a progressive can win in Ohio, and possibly elsewhere in the Midwest. The tariff variable's effect also suggests that Brown's messaging got through

Table 20.2. Vote Choice in Ohio's US Senate Election, 2018 CCES

Variables	Coefficients
Party Identification	−1.442***
	(0.244)
Ideology	−1.379***
	(0.303)
Gender	−0.086
	(0.313)
Race/Ethnicity	1.450**
	(0.500)
Education	−0.101
	(0.107)
Union Household	−0.221
	(0.373)
National Economy	−0.875***
	(0.188)
Trump Tax Cuts	−0.568
	(0.395)
Repeal ACA	−1.491***
	(0.362)
Legal Abortion	−0.831*
	(0.328)
Tariffs on China	0.860*
	(0.341)
Brown's Ideology	0.401***
	(0.109)
Constant	9.795***
	(1.138)
N	1331
Log Pseudolikelihood	−235.084
Proportional Reduction in Error	83.36%

Notes: Dependent variable: 1 = vote for Sherrod Brown; 0 = vote for Jim Renacci; missing, otherwise. Entries are logistic regression coefficients. Standard errors are in parentheses.

***$p < 0.001$; **$p < 0.01$; *$p < 0.05$; ^$p < 0.10$.

to voters, and established common ground from which he could appeal to Trump supporters.

CONCLUSION

Sherrod Brown's reelection to the US Senate in 2018 showed that Democrats—progressives, no less—*can* win in the Midwest, despite steady declines in their ranks over the previous decade and the election of Donald Trump. Qualitative and quantitative analyses of Brown's victory suggest that his "progressive populist" record and campaign messaging—grounded in his vehement opposition to free trade and consistent framing of policy in terms of the interests of working people—have restrained voters' perceptions of his ideological extremity and allowed him to maintain broad appeal in an increasingly red state.

Yet there was good reason to wonder whether Brown represented a replicable model or a dying breed. For one thing, in 2018 Brown was an incumbent senator—one of thirty-one seeking reelection, all but four of whom won—running in a midterm election that favored his party. It is unclear whether Brown could have won without this incumbency advantage, or the "blue wave." The true test of Brown's model for Democratic resurgence in the Midwest will be when a candidate with similar policies and messaging wins a Senate seat that he or she does not already hold. Tim Ryan—a long-time congressman from the blue-collar Youngstown area—tried to do so in 2022, while running for an open US Senate seat against Republican J. D. Vance. Ryan's campaign drew national media attention, largely focusing on its implications for Democrats' immediate and long-term viability in the Midwest—much like Sherrod Brown's campaigns, by "offering his party a potential model for appealing to working-class voters in the Rust Belt."[42] But, at a time when Democrats exceeded expectations nationwide, even gaining a seat in the US Senate, Ryan nonetheless lost to Vance by nearly seven percentage points (53.3 to 46.7 percent).[43]

There were other reasons to question whether Brown's win in 2018 offered hope to Midwestern Democrats. First, Brown benefited from running against a weak candidate who failed to attract much financial support. Particularly given Republicans' recent gains in Midwestern states, Democrats seeking to replicate Brown's performance should expect to face more formidable opponents. Second, Ohio is more diverse, in terms of race or ethnicity, than several other Midwestern states, such as Iowa or even Wisconsin.[44] Given Black voters' strong support for the Democratic Party, progressives elsewhere in the Midwest may find themselves at a relative disadvantage. Third, as a white man, Brown was less likely than women or people of color to be viewed as ideologically extreme—which, according to the evidence from Table 20.2, helped him to win votes.[45] The question, then, is not just whether Brown's model is replicable, but by whom, and under what circumstances, it can be replicated.

Indeed, Sherrod Brown himself was unable to replicate his previous successes in 2024. Despite running once more as an incumbent, and following the same playbook as in prior campaigns, Brown lost to Republican Bernie Moreno by just 3.6 percentage points (50.1 to 46.5 percent). Brown ran 2.6 percentage points ahead of the Democratic presidential candidate, Vice President Kamala Harris, in Ohio, and Moreno five percentage points behind Trump.

Democrats across the Midwest, and throughout much of the United States, ran against the headwinds of an unpopular Biden administration, blamed for high inflation, in 2024. Trump won a second term while reclaiming the Blue Wall states of Pennsylvania, Wisconsin, and Michigan that he had won in 2016. But, despite losing their overall majority and in Ohio, Democrats successfully defended key Midwestern Senate seats in Wisconsin and Michigan, as well as Minnesota.

The Democratic Party should be under no illusions about its standing in the Midwest; generally speaking, it is in a weaker position than it used to be, and a weaker position than the Republican Party today. But Democrats still have a fighting chance, with the right candidate and under the right circumstances. To meet that moment will also require the right message. If Sherrod Brown has anything to say about it—and with Ohio holding another Senate election in 2026, he just might—that message should be one of progressive populism.

NOTES

1. "Election Night Victory Speech," Sherrod Brown, https://www.sherrodbrown.com/news/2018/sherrod-browns-2018-victory-speech, accessed January 6, 2022.

2. The 2016 and 2018 election results come from Dave Leip's Atlas of US Presidential Elections, https://uselectionatlas.org/RESULTS, accessed January 6, 2022.

3. See, for example, Joel Sievert and Seth C. McKee, "Nationalization in U.S. Senate and Gubernatorial Elections," *American Politics Research* 47, no. 5 (2019): 1055–1080.

4. Christopher Hayes, "Who Is Sherrod Brown?," *In These Times*, November 21, 2005; John B. Judis, "Sherrod Brown's Blueprint for Victory," *Washington Post Magazine*, March 19, 2019.

5. Bob Taft, interview with author, January 2, 2022.

6. "Brown Victory Speech," C-SPAN, https://www.c-span.org/video/?195296-7/brown-victory-speech, accessed January 6, 2022.

7. The Associated Press, "Ohio Senator Was a Champion of Labor and Master of Rules," *Los Angeles Times*, March 13, 2008.

8. Karen Kasler, "Ohio Senate Race Gets Nasty Amid Flood of Ads and Cash," NPR, September 20, 2012.

9. Daniel R. Birdsong and Christopher J. Devine, "Fly-*To* Country: The Midwest as Presidential Battleground, 1946–2016," in Jon K. Lauck and Catherine McNicol Stock, eds., *The Conservative Heartland: A Political History of the Postwar American Midwest* (Lawrence: University Press of Kansas, 2020), 72–94.

10. Nick Castele, "Brown Defeats Mandel, Keeps Senate Seat," Ideastream Public Media, November 7, 2012.

11. Kate Nocera, "Ohio's Brown an Unabashed Liberal," *Politico*, September 30, 2012.

12. "Sherrod Brown," VoteView.com, https://voteview.com/person/29389/sherrod-brown, accessed January 6, 2022.

13. Center for Effective Lawmaking, "Find Legislators," https://thelawmakers.org/find-representatives, accessed January 6, 2022.

14. "Senate Passes Trade Agreement with Brown Labor Enforcement and Protection Provisions," Sherrod Brown, https://www.brown.senate.gov/newsroom/press/release/senate-passes-trade-agreement-with-brown-labor-enforcement-and-protection-provisions, accessed January 6, 2022.

15. Brian F. Schaffner, Stephen Ansolabehere, and Sam Luks, "CCES Common Content, 2018," Harvard Dataverse, https://dataverse.harvard.edu/dataset.xhtml?persistentId=doi:10.7910/DVN/ZSBZ7K, accessed February 1, 2021.

16. Nine percent of these respondents classified Brown as moderate, 6.2 percent as conservative, and 12.9 percent could not place him ideologically.

17. Respondents who could not place Brown or the Democratic Party ideologically are excluded from this analysis.

18. Andy Kroll, "Senator Sherrod Brown Knows How to Save the Soul of the Democratic Party," *Rolling Stone*, April 9, 2020.

19. "Election Night Victory Speech."

20. "About," Dignity of Work, https://dignityofwork.com/about, accessed January 6, 2022.

21. Kroll, "Senator Sherrod Brown."

22. Ben Terris, "Sherrod Brown Thinks He Could Have Helped Democrats Win in 2016. But What About 2020?," *Washington Post*, July 24, 2017.

23. Nocera, "Ohio's Brown."

24. Sydney Ember, "Sherrod Brown: Rumpled, Unvarnished and Just Maybe a Candidate for President," *New York Times*, November 15, 2018.

25. Terris, "Sherrod Brown."

26. Kroll, "Senator Sherrod Brown."

27. "For Ohio," Sherrod Brown, https://www.youtube.com/watch?v=GD3qX1eEquU, accessed January 6, 2022.

28. "Ohio Senate Debate (2)," C-SPAN, https://www.c-span.org/video/?453293-1/ohio-senate-debate, accessed January 6, 2022.

29. "Ohio Senate Debate (1)," C-SPAN, https://www.c-span.org/video/?452628-1/ohio-senate-debate, accessed January 6, 2022.

30. Jessie Balmert, "GOP U.S. Rep Jim Renacci Switches to U.S. Senate Race. Goal Is to 'Protect . . . Trump's Agenda,'" *Cincinnati Enquirer*, January 11, 2018.

31. "Remarks at a 'Make America Great Again,' Rally in Lebanon, Ohio," American Presidency Project, https://www.presidency.ucsb.edu/documents/remarks-make-america-great-again-rally-lebanon-ohio, accessed January 6, 2022.

32. "Ohio Senate Debate (1)."

33. "Ohio Senate Debate (3)," C-SPAN, https://www.c-span.org/video/?453316-1/ohio-senate-debate, accessed January 6, 2022.

34. Taft, interview.

35. "Ohio Senate Debate (1)."

36. Renacci—who complained about Brown's fundraising advantage during debates, attributing it to contributions from special interests—raised less money, overall, than Brown did from small donors, alone ("Ohio Senate 2018 Race," Center for Responsive Politics, 2022, https://www.opensecrets.org/races/candidates?cycle=2018&id=OHS1&spec=N, accessed January 6, 2022.

37. Andrew J. Tobias, "Sherrod Brown vs. Jim Renacci: What You Need to Know about the Ohio Senate Race," Cleveland.com, October 11, 2018.

38. Andrew J. Tobias, "Sherrod Brown Cruises to Re-election over Jim Renacci in Ohio's U.S. Senate Race," Cleveland.com, November 7, 2018.

39. Andrew J. Tobias, "Jim Renacci's Lack of Advertising in Senate Races Increasingly Alarms Ohio Republicans," Cleveland.com, October 4, 2018.

40. "Exit Polls," CNN, https://www.cnn.com/election/2018/exit-polls/ohio/senate, accessed January 6, 2022.

41. Schaffner, Ansolabehere, and Luks, "CCES Common Content."

42. Douglas Belkin and John McCormick, "Ohio's Ryan Offers Potential Road Map for Democrats Struggling in Rust Belt," *Wall Street Journal*, October 1, 2022.

43. Democrats did not gain—or lose—any other seats in the Midwest in 2022; the only Democrat to win a Senate race was Illinois incumbent Tammy Duckworth.

44. Asma Khalid, "The Perfect State Index: If Iowa, N.H. Are Too White to Go First, Then Who?," NPR, January 29, 2016.

45. For example, see Sarah A. Fulton and Sarah Allen Gershon, "Too Liberal to Win? Race and Voter Perceptions of Candidate Ideology," *American Politics Research* 46, no. 5 (2018): 909–939; Jeffrey W. Koch, "Do Citizens Apply Gender Stereotypes to Infer Candidates' Ideological Orientations?," *Journal of Politics* 62, no. 2 (2000): 414–429.

About the Contributors

❖ ❖ ❖ ❖ ❖ ❖ ❖

Emiliano Aguilar is an assistant professor of history at the University of Notre Dame, where he teaches courses rooted in political, urban, and labor history, specifically regarding Latinas and Latinos. His manuscript in progress, *Building a Latino Machine: Caught between Corrupt Political Machines and Good Government Reform*, explores how the ethnic Mexican and Puerto Rican community of East Chicago, Indiana, navigated machine politics in the twentieth and twenty-first centuries to further their inclusion in municipal and union politics. His work has appeared in *The Metropole*, *Belt Magazine*, the Immigration and Ethnic History Society's blog, the *Oxford Research Encyclopedia of American History*, and the Indiana Historical Society blog. A chapter of his research was recently published in *Building Sustainable Worlds: Latinx Placemaking in the Midwest* (2022).

Charles McElwain Barber, professor emeritus, Northeastern Illinois University (Chicago), is author of *Judge Aaron Jaffe: Reforming Illinois; A Progressive Tackles State Government, 1970–2015* (2016). His work on German Americans protecting their heritage against nativism from World War I through World War II appears in *Yearbook of German-American Studies* (1995). His work on Senator William Langer of North Dakota and Cardinal Aloisius Muench, Bishop of Fargo, 1935 to 1959, and Papal Visitator Apostolicus in post–World War II Germany, won the 1999 Editors Award of the State Historical Society of North Dakota. A chapter on Senator Langer's advocacy ("The Isolationist as Interventionist: Senator William Langer on the Subject of Ethnic Cleansing, March 29, 1946") also is included in *Ethnic Cleansing in 20th Century Europe* (2004).

Jeff Bloodworth is a professor of history and co-director of the School of Public Service and Global Affairs at Gannon University (Erie, PA). A political historian who works on the history of contemporary American liberalism and genocide studies, he has published widely on the travails of the liberal project, the history of humanitarian intervention, and the American foreign policy impulse abroad. He is currently midway through writing a biography of Speaker Carl Albert, who presided as majority leader during the Great Society and civil rights eras and as Speaker during Watergate. Bloodworth holds a PhD in modern US history from Ohio University's Contemporary History Institute and a certificate in contemporary history from the University of Copenhagen.

Ray E. Boomhower is senior editor of the Indiana Historical Society Press, where he is also responsible for the quarterly popular history magazine *Traces of Indiana and Midwestern History*. His most recent books are *John Bartlow Martin: A Voice for the Underdog*; *Dispatches from the Pacific: The World War II Reporting of Robert L. Sherrod*; and *Richard Tregaskis: Reporting under Fire from Guadalcanal to Vietnam*. Boomhower's work has appeared in the *Indiana Magazine of History*, *Middle West Review*, *Cleveland Review of Books*, *The New Territory*, *Publishers Weekly*, and *Wall Street Journal*.

Camden Burd is an assistant professor of history at Clemson University, where he teaches on topics including American, environmental, and digital history. His scholarship has appeared in a variety of venues including the *Michigan Historical Review*, *IA: The Journal for the Society of Industrial Archaeology*, and *Agricultural History*. For those interested to learn more of his work on the intersections of environmental and political history, see his chapter in *The Conservative Heartland: A Political History of the Postwar American Midwest*, a related edited collection published by the University Press of Kansas.

Stephen Colbrook recently completed his PhD in policy history at University College London. His thesis chartered the history of American federalism's influence on pandemic disease, with a particular focus on the AIDS crisis. His work has appeared in a range of popular and scholarly venues, including *Twentieth Century British History*, *Modern American History*, *Journal of Policy History*, *Journal of American Studies*, and the *Washington Post*.

Tiffany Costley is a local government attorney representing elected officials in Johnson County, Indiana. She received her juris doctorate from Indiana University Robert H. McKinney School of Law in Indianapolis, where she graduated with a certificate in criminal law and civil and human rights law. Prior to attending law school, she earned both her bachelor's and master's degrees in American history at the University of Indianapolis, where she now serves as an adjunct professor for legal studies. She has continued her historical work as a contributor to the *Digital Encyclopedia of Indianapolis* and *Traces* magazine. She is active in legal pro bono work, serving on the Public Outreach Committee for the Indianapolis Bar Association in addition to the Indiana State Bar Membership Committee.

Christopher J. Devine is an associate professor of political science at the University of Dayton. His books on presidential campaigns and elections include *Do Running Mates Matter? The Influence of Vice-Presidential Candidates in Presidential Elections* (with Kyle C. Kopko), *News Media Coverage of the Vice-Presidential Selection Process: What's Wrong with the "Veepstakes"?*, and *I'm Here to Ask for Your Vote: How Presidential Campaign Visits Influence Voters*.

Sean J. Flynn is professor and chair of history at Dakota Wesleyan University, Mitchell, South Dakota. He earned his BA at South Dakota State University and his MA and PhD at Texas Tech University. He is the author of *Without Reservation: Benjamin Reifel and American Indian Acculturation* (2018). He is presently at work on a book about US Senator Karl E. Mundt and the Cold War.

Cory Haala is an assistant professor of history at the University of Wisconsin–Stevens Point. His research focuses on liberalism and grassroots activism in the 1980s Midwest, which is the subject of his forthcoming manuscript, *How Democrats Won the Heartland: Progressive Populism in the Age of Reagan*. The social media chair of the Midwestern History Association, he has written chapters on party politics in Iowa and South Dakota, taught classes on American conservatism and populism, and is working on studies of progressive voter registration initiatives and anti–free trade activism in the Upper Midwest. His work on politics has also appeared in *Time*'s "Made by History" series and on a podcast called "Don't Fight Your Political Enemies. Out-Organize Them." with Indiana Public Media's "Inner States" podcast.

Marc C. Johnson is the author of three books on US Senate history, including most recently *Mansfield and Dirksen: Bipartisan Giants of the Senate*. He is a senior fellow at the Mansfield Center at the University of Montana, and his writing on politics has appeared in the *New York Times*, the *Washington Post*, *The Bulwark*, and many regional newspapers, as well as history journals in Montana and Indiana. A former journalist who hosted news, public affairs, and documentary programming and moderated political debates, he also served as press secretary and chief of staff to Idaho's only four-term governor, Cecil D. Andrus. Johnson chaired both the Federation of State Humanities Councils and Idaho Humanities Council.

About the Contributors

Chad Kinsella is an associate professor of political science and co-director of the Voting System Technical Oversight Program (VSTOP) at Ball State University. His primary research areas are electoral geography, public administration, and state and local politics, and he has published multiple articles and book chapters in these areas. He is also a lifelong Midwestern Catholic; he and his family attend Mass at St. Mary's in Muncie, Indiana.

Dean J. Kotlowski is professor of history at Salisbury University. He is the author of *Nixon's Civil Rights: Politics, Principle, and Policy* (2001) and *Paul V. McNutt and the Age of FDR* (2015) and the editor of *The European Union: From Jean Monnet to the Euro* (2000). He has published over forty articles and book chapters on US political and policy history, including in journals such as *Diplomatic History*, *Pacific Historical Review*, *The Historian*, and *Business History Review*. He has been a historical adviser to the National Archives, Richard Nixon Library, and US Mint. He has served four times as a Fulbright scholar, in the Philippines (2008), Austria (2016), and Australia (2020, 2022), the last of which was a distinguished chair. His book *Toward Self-Determination: Federal Indian Policy from Truman to Clinton* is forthcoming.

Jon K. Lauck is the author of *The Lost Region: Toward a Revival of Midwestern History* (2013), *From Warm Center to Ragged Edge: The Erosion of Midwestern Regionalism, 1920–1965* (2017), and *The Good Country: A History of the American Midwest* (2022). A past president of the Midwestern History Association, he currently serves as an adjunct professor of history and political science at the University of South Dakota and as editor in chief of *Middle West Review*. He earned his PhD in history from the University of Iowa and his law degree from the University of Minnesota. He is currently the president of the Society for the Study of Midwestern Literature.

James (Jamie) McQuaid earned their PhD from Wayne State University. Their dissertation, titled *This Union Cause: The Queer History of the United Auto Workers, 1935–2000*, explores the historical intersection of queer life, identity, and activism with the labor politics of industrial unionism throughout the UAW's history of solidarity. In addition to their work as a union activist and queer historian, McQuaid is also a program coordinator and instructor of record with Labor@Wayne, Wayne State University's employment and labor relations program.

Nicole Poletika specializes in social justice and minority history. She earned an MA in public history from Indiana University–Indianapolis and was an inaugural recipient of Indiana Humanities' Wilma Gibbs Moore Fellowship, for which she examined the 1972 National Black Political

Convention. Poletika helps coordinate women's history programming, such as the Hoosier Women at Work History Conference and the National Women's Suffrage Marker Grant Program. She has authored pieces for the *Digital Encyclopedia of Indianapolis*, serves as editor of the Indiana History blog, and has been published in *Traces of Indiana and Midwestern History* and *Belt Magazine*. She works to advance the burgeoning field of LGBTQ history, assembling and presenting on a panel entitled "On the Margins of the Margins of the Circle City" at the 2022 Queer History Conference.

Emma Ricknell is a senior lecturer in political science at Linnaeus University in Växjö, Sweden. Her research interests include the US death penalty at the state level, which is the focus of her dissertation. Prior to pursuing a PhD, she worked as a paralegal on death penalty appeals in California.

Michael C. Steiner is professor emeritus of American studies at California State University, Fullerton. He has authored or co-authored five books treating the history of Western and Midwestern regionalism, most recently *Regionalists on the Left: Radical Voices from the American West* (2013) and *Horace M. Kallen in the Heartland: The Midwestern Roots of American Pluralism* (University Press of Kansas, 2020). The author of thirty articles on American intellectual and environmental history, including prize-winning essays on Frederick Jackson Turner's sectional thesis and on Walt Disney's architectural packaging of the mythic West, Steiner has recently published essays on Midwestern intellectual history that complement his work on Paul and Sheila Wellstone's contributions to liberal and left-leaning politics in the Midwest.

Catherine McNicol Stock is the Barbara Zaccheo Kohn '72 Professor of History at Connecticut College. She is the author of three books and co-editor of three anthologies that explore politics in rural America in the twentieth century. Her most recent book, *Nuclear Country: The Origins of the Rural New Right* (2020), explores the relationship between militarization and nuclearization on the northern plains and the region's turn to modern conservatism. She is currently working on a project examining the experiences of women leaders on the left who became targets of new conservatives in the 1990s and 2000s.

Jon E. Taylor is professor of history at the University of Central Missouri, where he teaches classes on US history and public history. He is the author of four books on the life, political career, and legacy of Harry S. Truman, including *A President, A Church, and Trails West: Competing Histories in Independence Missouri* (2008) and *Freedom to Serve: Truman, Civil Rights, and Executive Order 9981* (2013). He is currently working on a book about

Truman's Senate career and serves as project director forhistoricmissouri.org, a free mobile app and website that provides users with interpretive and curated narrative tours about the important places, people, and stories unique to Missouri.

Katherine Turk is professor of history and adjunct professor of women's and gender studies at the University of North Carolina at Chapel Hill. Her work has received support from the Harvard Radcliffe Institute, the Andrew W. Mellon Foundation, and the National Endowment for the Humanities. In addition to many scholarly articles and book chapters, her writing has appeared in the *Washington Post*, *Slate*, *Public Seminar*, and elsewhere. She is the author of *Equality on Trial: Gender and Rights in the Modern American Workplace* (2016), which won the Mary Jurich Nickliss and Lerner-Scott Prizes from the Organization of American Historians, and *The Women of NOW: How Feminists Built an Organization That Transformed America* (2023).

Leticia Rose Wiggins is an ethnic studies librarian at Ohio State University. Since earning her PhD in US history from The Ohio State University, she has sought innovative ways to engage the public in conversations surrounding connections between race, gender, and class. She is excited for the potential to explore these connections through accessible and innovative platforms and also loves the process of telling, recording, and sharing audio stories. Wiggins is also passionate about continuing her PhD research through sharing Latina/o/x stories from the Midwest.

Index

❖ ❖ ❖ ❖ ❖ ❖ ❖

1619 Project, 8
1936 election, 232
1948 election, 251, 252, 253
1952 election, 37, 42, 233, 234–235, 320
1956 election, 39, 42, 237, 320
1960 election, 39, 42, 319, 320
1962 election, 238–239
1964 election, 42, 319, 320
1968 election, 240, 319, 320
1970 election, 241
1972 election, 240, 247n51, 247n55, 319, 320
1974 election, 136–137, 240–241
1976 election, 319
1978 election, 241
1980 election, 242, 254, 299, 320
1984 election, 155, 253, 254, 258, 265, 299, 320
1986 election, 242, 265, 303, 304–305
1988 election, 269–270, 306, 321
1990 election, 265
1992 election, 265, 273, 319, 321
1996 election, 241, 265, 321
2000 election, 321
2002 election, 43, 241
2004 election, 43, 242, 277, 319–320, 321, 324, 325
2008 election, 242–243, 321, 324
2010 election, 11n11, 277
2012 election, 43–44, 48, 321, 334–335
2016 election, 321, 324, 331–332
2018 election, 331, 332, 337–342
2020 election, 35, 247n57, 321, 324

Abdnor, Jim, 242, 266, 268
abortion, 3, 154, 155, 176, 324–325
Abourezk, James G., 121, 240, 247n51
Abramowitz, Alan, 231
Acme Steel, 95

African Americans. *See* Black Americans
Agricultural Credit Act, 268–269
agriculture
   1984 election and, 258
   activism in, 133, 135
   Big Pine Creek dam and, 135
   budget cuts regarding, 274
   concerns of, 263
   Democratic Party and, 263, 268
   economic challenges of, 275–276
   emergency aid in, 277
   farm bills of 1985 for, 266–268
   Farm Crisis and, 54, 263–264
   farmer opinions in, 233–234
   Farmers Home Administration (FmHA) and, 55
   farm movement in, 265
   Food, Agriculture, Conservation, and Trade (FACT) Act for, 270–272
   foreclosures in, 51, 221–222, 257
   free trade and, 272–273
   meatpacking in, 276
   morale in, 234
   newsletter regarding, 236
   recession and, 254–255
   Ronald Reagan and, 250–251
   transformation of, 7
   women in, 49–50, 56, 58n11
   See also farm bills/policy
Aguilera, John, 102
Aguirre, Colleen, 100, 102, 103–104, 105, 106
Ahmad, Ahrar, 240
AIDS crisis, 299–300, 306
Ailes, Roger, 256
air power, lack of funding for, 25–26
Alinsky, Saul, 98, 147, 220
Allen, Dozier, 168, 169, 171

❖ 353 ❖

Index

Allen, Zach, 2
Allison, L. T., 171, 173–174
Allott, Gordon, 121
Altman, Jerry, 134
Altman, Kathy, 134
Alverno College, 143
Amalgamated Meat Cutters, 148
American Agriculture Movement, 266
American Farm Bureau, 266
American Federation of State, County, and Municipal Employees (AFSCME), 78
American Indian Movement (AIM), 117
American Indian Policy Review Commission, 121
American Indians
   1952 election and, 37
   1956 election and, 39
   1960 election and, 39
   on culture, 8
   culture of, 118
   in Democratic Party, 35–36, 39, 41–42, 43
   Eisenhowerism and, 36–37, 39, 40
   Food for Peace program for, 120
   House Bill (HB) 892 and, 41
   Indian Child Welfare Act for, 121
   Indian New Deal and, 115
   Indian Self-Determination Act for, 121, 122–123
   Indian Self-Determination and Education Assistance Act for, 117
   isolation of, 118
   liberal ideology and, 113
   poverty of, 119
   prejudice to, 118
   programs benefiting, 42
   Red Power movement and, 43
   red power of, 114
   self-determination of, 113–114, 115, 119, 120, 122–123
   termination policy and, 36, 37–38, 40, 116–117, 118, 121
   treaty rights of, 11n13
   Turtle Mountain Chippewa as, 37–38
   War on Poverty and, 114
American National Election Studies (ANES), 316, 322–323
American Peace Crusade, 236

Americans for Democratic Action (ADA), 29, 80, 81, 82–83
Ancient Forest Protection Act, 139
Anderson, Clinton P., 121
Andrews, Mark, 268
Andrews, Max, 205
Anhut, Charles, 192
Ann Arbor, Michigan, 78–79
Anson, Robert Sam, 237
anticommunism, 19
Area Redevelopment Administration, 42
Arizona, 4
Armed Forces Committee, 27
Armed Services Committee, 24–25, 26
Arnold, Laura Ann, 131
Arroyo, Jose, 337
Assembly Bill (AB) 70 (Wisconsin), 198–200, 202–205
auto industry, 80, 82. *See also* United Auto Workers (UAW)
Axtell, Enos, 18

Bachrach, Peter, 222
Bailly, Ophelia, 156
Baker, Ella, 220
Baker, James, 256
Baldwin, James, 218
Baldwin, Tammy, 331, 335
Banfield, Edward C., 98
Bangstad, Kirk, 1, 2–3
Baraka, Amiri, 173
Barrett, Amy Coney, 325
Bates, Emma, 58n9
Baucus, Max, 271
Bayh, Birch, 2, 130, 235
Belafonte, Harry, 176
Belczak, Daniel, 288
Bellecourt, Clyde, 119–120, 123
Benavente, Dr. Jorge, 101
Benson, Ezra Taft, 26, 233
Berg, Rick, 43, 56–57
Berman, Hy, 212
Berry, E. Y., 40, 42
Biden, Joe, 1, 35, 217, 327
Big John, Brooks, 11n13
Big Pine Creek (Indiana), 128–139
Big Pine Golf Course (Indiana), 135
Binaggio, Charles, 20

Index

Birdsong, Daniel, 4
Bittner and Detella, Inc., 101
Black Americans
   1984 election and, 258
   in auto industry, 91n34
   death penalty and, 287, 290
   in East Chicago, Indiana, 98
   in Gary, Indiana, 166, 167–168
   in Great Depression, 166
   in Minneapolis, 8
   in Missouri, 18, 20
   political power strategies of, 165–166, 172–173
   prejudice to, 118
   as queer, 91n34
   See also racism
Blackfeet Nation (Montana), 116
Black liberalism, 165
Black Magna Carta, 175
Black Nationalists, 168
Black Political Agenda, 166, 175, 176–177
Black Power movement, 173, 175–176
Blackwell, Dr. S. R., 166
Blair, James, 22
Block, John, 266
Blodgett, Jeff, 214, 223
Bloodworth, Jeffrey, 232, 269
Blue Lake, New Mexico, 121
Bond, Kit, 30
bonds, 103–104
Bonior, David, 273
Booth, Heather, 148, 149
Boschwitz, Rudy, 211
Bostock v. Clayton County, Georgia, 309
Bottum, Joseph, 239
Bowen, Otis R., 129
Boxer, Barbara, 335
boycott, at University of Notre Dame, 190
Boyer, Gene, 146
Branstad, Terry, 267
Bray, Richard, 309
Bray, William, 136
Briggs, Frank P., 18, 20
Briggs, Gordon F., 95
Brown, Charlie, 174
Brown, Michael, 324
Brown, Sherrod
   2018 campaign of, 337–340
   2024 campaign of, 343–344
   anti-NAFTA caucus and, 273
   election of, 7, 330–331
   ideological placement of, 336
   as liberal, 335
   as model for Midwestern Democrats, 224, 331–333
   overview of, 333–337, 342–344
   populism of, 336–337
   as progressive populist, 331
   reelection elements of, 332–333
   vote choice analysis regarding, 340–342
Buber, Martin, 216
Buffalo, New York, 299
Burdick, Jocelyn, 60n35
Burdick, Quentin, 56, 235
Burdick, Usher, 51–52
Bureau of Indian Affairs (BIA), 36, 38
Burnette, Robert, 42
Burrus, Bill, 166
Busch Valentine, Trudy, 31
Bush, George H. W., 269–270, 272–273
Bush, George W., 319, 322
Buttigieg, Pete, 224

Cagles Mill reservoir, 129
Calauti, Luci, 55
Caldwell, Lynton, 129, 130–131, 138
California, 299
Cannon, Lou, 252
Cantwell, Paul, 301
capital punishment. *See* death penalty
Cardenas, Gilberto, 190
Cargill, 272
Carleton College (Minnesota), 218–223
Carnahan, Jean, 30
Carnahan, Mel, 30
Carson, Julia, 177–178
Carson, Rachel, 64
Carter, Jimmy, 319
Carter, Steve, 104
Case, Francis, 239
Casey, Bob, 333
Casper, Barry "Mike," 218–219, 222
Catholic Church/Catholicism
   abortion and, 155, 324–325
   Assembly Bill (AB) 70 (Wisconsin) and, 198–200, 202–205

Catholic Church/Catholicism (*cont.*)
  attitudes of, 323, 325–326
  changing vote of, 322–326
  clergy beliefs in, 326
  culture of, 7
  culture war and, 324–325
  Democratic Party and, 7, 315–316, 323–324
  Dignitatis Humanae of, 188
  discrimination and, 325
  education of, 322
  expansion of, 186
  future of vote in, 327–328
  gay movement and, 199–200, 202, 205–206, 325
  gender gap and, 326
  government provisions and, 325–326
  ideology and, 324
  immigration in, 316–317, 323
  Latinos and, 186–187
  Liberal, 201–202
  liberalism in, 185–186
  map regarding, 317
  Mass attendance in, 323
  in the Midwest, 316–318
  partisanship and, 324, 326–327
  presidential vote overview of, 318–322, 324
  public sphere and, 324
  Republican Party and, 316, 324
  sociodemographic trends of, 322
  statistics of, 322–323
  Vatican II and, 186, 188, 200–201
  women's studies in, 143
  See also specific states
Catholic Herald (newspaper), 202
Catholics for a Free Choice (CFFC), 155
Cecil M. Harden reservoir, 129
"Celebration on the Circle Day" (Indianapolis), 306–307
Center for Rural Affairs, 274
Central American Free Trade Agreement (CAFTA), 334
Centro de Estudios Chicanos Investigaciones (Center for Chicano Studies and Research), 190
Cermak, Anton, 99
Chambers, Ernie, 293
Champagne, Duane, 40

Chavez, Bishop Gilbert, 190, 191
Chavis, Benjamin, 172, 174, 175–176
Chicago, Illinois, 141, 147, 148–149, 152–153, 317–318, 319
Chicago NOW, 147–148, 153
Chicago Women's Liberation Union (CWLU), 148–149
Chicano movement, 187, 196n63
Chicano Youth Liberation Conference, 187
Chippewa Indians (Minnesota), 117
Christian Right, 206
Cincinnati, Ohio, 317, 325
CIO-PAC, 81
Citizen Action, 267
Citizens Good Neighborhood Patrol, 175
Citizens in Action, 94–96, 97–98, 99–100, 101–104, 106
Citizens Organized Acting Together (COACT), 267, 270, 272
Civilian Conservation Corps, 65
Civil Rights Act of 1957, 22, 26, 29, 116
Civil Rights Act of 1960, 22, 26, 29
Civil Rights Act of 1964, 22, 26, 29, 118, 145, 298
Civil Rights Act of 1968, 22, 26, 29
Civil Rights Caucus, 22
Civil Rights Division (Department of Justice), 21
civil rights movements, 97
Clarenbach, David, 198, 202–203, 204
Clarenbach, Kathryn "Kay," 145, 146
Clark, Dick, 235
Clark, Hartley, 222
Clean Air Act, 71, 72
Cleaver, Eldridge, 218
Clere, Amy, 174
Cleveland, Ohio, 317
climate change, 72–73
Clinton, Bill, 43, 273–275, 277, 286, 319
Clinton, Hillary, 1, 2, 43, 217, 331
Cloud, Joseph, 136
Coalition of Labor Union Women, 148
Cohen, Lizabeth, 49
Cold War, 18–19, 30
Coleman, Henry, 167, 168, 174
Coleman v. Block, 55
Collins, Mary Jean
  on abortion, 154–155

background of, 141–143
in Chicago, 147
in Chicago NOW, 147–149, 150–156
in civil rights movement, 143–144
in Illinois Nurses Association (INA), 149–150
leadership campaigns of, 149, 154
marriage of, 147
in National Organization for Women (NOW), 145–147
on NOW lunchtime program, 142
at People for the American Way (PFAW), 155–156
photo of, 144, 146, 150
retirement of, 156
on Women's Strike for Equality, 141
Collins, Susan, 247n57
Comitatus, Posse, 265
Committee for Fundamental Judeo-Christian Human Rights (CFJCHR), 202
Committee on Big Pine Creek, 129
Committee on Civil Rights, 18
Committee on Governmental Operations, 24
communism, 24, 253
Community Action Program (OEO), 119
ConAgra, 272
Conason, Joe, 214
"The Concerned Christians" of Indianapolis, 300–301
Concerned Latins Organization, 98
Confederated Salish Tribe, 116
Congressional Black Caucus (CBC), 173
Congressional Populist Caucus (CPC), 265
Congressional Quarterly (newspaper), 271
Conrad, Kent, 55, 56, 265, 268, 270–271, 273, 274, 275
Conroy, Catherine, 145, 146–147
Conservative Christians, 199
conservativism, 72, 253. *See also* Republican Party
Co-Operative Credit Union, 166–167
Copeland, Anthony, 94, 99–100, 106
Cornell, Stephen, 43
corporate agribusiness, 272
Cowie, Jefferson, 185
Craig, Edward, 53
Craig, Minnie, 49, 53, 56, 60n35
Cramer, Kevin, 56–57

Cramer, Kris, 57
Crawford, Bill, 177–178
Cripe, Henry, 132
Cross, Martin, 38, 39
Cruz, Joe De La, 105
Cryts, Wayne, 250, 258
culture war, 324–325
Culver, John, 2
Curtis, Thomas, 29

Dairymen Inc., 271
Dakota Rural Action, 270
Dakota Survival League, 267
Daley, Richard J., 97, 98, 147, 319
dams, 128–139
Danforth, Jack, 27, 30
Daniel, Margaret Truman, 29
Daschle, Tom, 2, 43, 241, 242, 265, 266, 268, 270, 271, 277
Day, Yvonne, 176
Dearborn, Michigan, 8
death penalty
abolition efforts regarding, 292
Democratic Party and, 286
divisions regarding, 285–286, 287, 291, 293–294
Furman v. Georgia and, 286, 293
law promotion for, 286
miscarriages of justice regarding, 292
racial bias and, 290
racial hostility and, 287
state variances regarding, 287–290
statistics regarding, 286, 290–291, 292
support for, 286
See also specific states
decapitalization, 274–275
Deer, Ada, 120
Deggans, Chuck, 171
DeGrieck, Jerry, 78
deindustrialization, 106
Deloria, Reverend Vine Sr., 41
Deloria, Vine Jr., 113, 119, 122
DeLorme, David P., 39
Democratic-Farmer-Labor Party (DFL), 118, 211, 212–213, 219, 223, 251
Democratic Leadership Council, 274
Democratic Leadership Council (DLC), 265–266

Index

Democratic-Nonpartisan League (D-NPL), 49, 50, 54, 56, 58n9
Democratic Party
  from 1946 to 1982, 255
  1988 Democratic National Convention of, 269
  American Indians in, 35–36, 39, 41–42, 43
  challenges to, 72
  characteristics of, 235–236
  Citizens in Action for, 96
  conversion experiences of, 269
  criticism of, 7
  decline of, following farm policy, 277
  demographics of, 2
  detractors in, 96
  disappearance of moderates in, 231
  on division, 6–7
  environmentalism and, 63, 64–65, 66
  Great Depression and, 250
  Green New Deal and, 72–73
  in Harry Truman's term, 18–19
  history of, in the Midwest, 4
  hope for, 342–344
  Latina/o residents in, 96–97
  New Democrats in, 96
  political changes in, 2
  Republican Party as compared to, 71
  support for, 7
  tension in, 96
  union solidarity with, 78
  See also specific states
Denholm, Frank, 241
Dennis, David, 136
Denzer, Susan, 272
Department of Conservation and Resource Development (United Auto Workers), 69
Department of Defense, 26
Department of Justice, 21
Des Moines Register (newspaper), 269, 289
Detroit Police Department, 91n35
Devine, Christopher, 4
Devine, Jenny Barker, 58n11
DeWine, Mike, 334, 340
dichlorodiphenyltrichloroethane (DDT), 64
Diedrich, Larry, 43
Diggs, Charles, 173

Dignitatis Humanae, 188
dignity of work, 338
Dignity/USA, 201, 202
Dirksen, Everett, 236
District of Columbia, 298–299
Dixon, George H., 211
Dobbs v. Jackson, 325
Dodd, Christopher, 217
Dole, Bob, 275
Dole, Robert, 235
Donnell, Forrest, 17, 19
Donnelly, Joe, 331, 333
Dorgan, Byron, 265
Downs, Tom, 288
Dreyer, David, 131–132, 135
Dreyfus, Lee Sherman, 203, 205
Dukakis, Michael, 269–270
Dunlop, Orin L., 39
Durnil, Gordon, 304–305
Dustin, Thomas E., 129

Eagle Forum, 6, 139
Eagleton, Thomas F., 23, 28–29, 30, 247n55
Earth Day, 69
Easley, Harry, 20
East Chicago, Indiana
  1999 election in, 94–95, 104–106
  bonds in, 103–104
  building project in, 101–104
  Citizens in Action in, 94–96, 97–98, 99–100, 101–104, 106
  communication in, 100
  corruption in, 104–106
  demographics of, 95, 99
  division in, 100
  economic conditions of, 95, 101
  immigration in, 99, 186
  infrastructure work in, 104–106
  as last political machine, 97
  lawsuit regarding, 100, 104–106
  liberalism in, 97
  petition in, 102–103
  political machine in, 99
  protesting in, 98
Eberhart, Adolph O., 288–289
E. B. Phillips Day Care Center, 144
Economic Development Administration, 119

Index

economic populism, 263, 266, 268, 276, 277
Eddy, Patricia, 276
education, sexual orientation discrimination in, 298–299
Egipciaco, Edward, 101
Eisenhower, Dwight D./Eisenhower administration
  in 1956 election, 39
  American Indians and, 36–37
  Catholic vote and, 318
  criticism of, 24–26
  election of, 235
  loyalty program and, 21
  political base of, 259n3
  popularity of, 233
  Public Law (PL) 280 and, 37–38, 40
  Stuart Symington and, 24
  termination policy of, 36, 116–117
Eisenhowerism, 36–37, 39, 40
Eisenhuth, Laura, 49
elections
  1936 election, 232
  1948 election, 251, 252, 253
  1952 election, 37, 42, 233, 234–235, 320
  1956 election, 39, 42, 237, 320
  1960 election, 39, 42, 319, 320
  1962 election, 238–239
  1964 election, 42, 319, 320
  1968 election, 240, 319, 320
  1970 election, 241
  1972 election, 240, 247n51, 247n55, 319, 320
  1974 election, 136–137, 240–241
  1976 election, 319
  1978 election, 241
  1980 election, 242, 254, 299, 320
  1984 election, 155, 253, 254, 258, 265, 299, 320
  1986 election, 242, 265, 303, 304–305
  1988 election, 269–270, 306, 321
  1990 election, 265
  1992 election, 265, 273, 319, 321
  1996 election, 241, 265, 321
  2000 election, 321
  2002 election, 43, 241
  2004 election, 43, 242, 277, 319–320, 321, 324, 325
  2008 election, 242–243, 321, 324
  2010 election, 11n11, 277
  2012 election, 43–44, 48, 321, 334–335
  2016 election, 321, 324, 331–332
  2018 election, 331, 332, 337–342
  2020 election, 35, 247n57, 321, 324
electroshock therapy, 93n57
Ellis, James N., 138
Ellison, Emery, 20
Ellison, Ralph, 218
Ellsberg, Daniel, 27
El Plan Espiritual de Aztlán, 187
Emerson Electric Company, 23
employment, 70, 145, 148, 198–200, 202–205, 298–299
Employment Service Office, 38
environmentalism
  as bipartisan, 71
  as burden, 72
  development of, 63–64
  economic threats of, 72
  grassroots movement around, 68–69
  in Michigan, 67–68
  in the New Deal, 65–66
  resource management in, 66–67
  United Auto Workers (UAW) and, 69
  in the Upper Midwest, 63–64
  in Wisconsin, 68–69
  writings regarding, 65
Environmental Protection Agency (EPA), 71
Environmental Working Group, 275
Equal Rights Amendment (ERA), 6, 151–153
Erickson, O. E., 51
Erpenbach, Steve, 243
Espinosa, Lydia, 191–192
Evans, Brock, 139
Executive Order 9835, 18–19, 20
Executive Order 9980, 18
Exon, James, 235, 270

FAIR Act, 273–275
Fair Deal, 25
Fair Employment Practices Commission, 149–150
Fall Creek Gorge, 128, 130
Falwell, Jerry, 299

Index

family politics, 252
farm bills/policy
  1985, 266–268
  1990, 270–272
  Democratic Party and, 263
  importance of, 233
  lack of funding for, 26
  neoliberal turn in, 274
  rejection of, 18
  See also agriculture
Farm Credit System, 269
Farm Crisis, 54–55, 263–264, 268
Farm Emergency Credit Bill, 266
Farmers Home Administration (FmHA), 55
farm-labor protectionism, 269
Farm Policy Reform Act, 267, 268–270
Federal Water Pollution Control Act Amendments of 1961, 67
Feingold, Russ, 265, 273, 277
feminism, 6, 141, 142, 154, 156–157, 157n6
Ferraro, Geraldine, 155, 254
Finlayson, Edith, 144–145
Fishman, Karen, 147
Fixico, Donald L., 37
Flathead Reservation (Montana), 116
Flint, Michigan, 91n34
Flood Control Act, 128
Flores, Augusto, 103
Flores, Bishop Patricio, 190, 191, 196n56
Flosi, Marie, 150
Floyd, George, 8
Food, Agriculture, Conservation, and Trade (FACT) Act, 270–272
Food for Peace program, 119, 120
Ford, Gerald R./Ford administration, 71, 117, 122, 136, 259n3
Foss, Joe, 40–41, 236–237
Frank, Gillian, 199
Franken, Al, 213
Frankfurter, Felix, 215
freedom movements, 5
Freedom to Farm Act, 266, 273–276, 277
Freeman, Walter Jackson, 85, 92n51
Freeman-Wilson, Karen, 178
free trade, 272–273
Friends of the Big Pine Creek, 129
front-porch politics, 1

Fulbright, J. William, 26
Furman v. Georgia, 286, 293

Garcia, Rick, 206
Gardner, Bruce, 276
Garland, David, 286
Gary, Indiana
  Black political power in, 165–166, 170, 171–172
  Black resident control in, 167–168
  cleanup campaign in, 174
  Congressional Black Caucus (CBC) and, 173
  Co-Operative Credit Union in, 166–167
  demographics of, 166, 167–168
  elections in, 167, 169–170, 171, 177–178
  Great Depression in, 166
  housing conditions in, 166
  leadership of, 166
  Muigwithania in, 165, 168–169, 170–171, 178
  National Black Political Convention (NBPC) in, 173–178
  Shock Troops in, 171
  steel industry in, 166
Gary Crusader (newspaper), 166, 167, 177
Gary Land Company, 166
Gary Post-Tribune (newspaper), 174
gay employment rights, 198–200, 202–205, 206, 207. *See also* employment; *specific states*
Gay Law Students Assn. v. Pacific Tel. & Tel. Co, 299
gay movement, 78, 199–200, 202, 205–206, 298–309. *See also* queer/LGBTQ people
Gebhardt, Richard, 268–270
Geelan, Agnes, 52, 55
Geismer, Lily, 96
gender politics, 78
General Agreements on Trade and Tariffs (GATT), 272–273
General Motors (GM), 82
Gingrich, Newt, 273–274
Glasser, Melvin A., 83–84
Glickman, Dan, 274, 276
Goff, Mark, 307
Gokey, Mimi Langer, 52

Index

Goldberg, Carole, 40
Goldsmith, Judy, 153–154
Goldsmith, Stephen, 308
Goldwater, Barry, 42
Gonzalez, Jose G., 189
Gorneau, Patrick, 38
Grassley, Chuck, 266
Great Depression, 128, 166, 250, 266
Great Society, 26, 42, 69–70
Greaves, William, 178n1
Green New Deal, 72–73
Groppi, Father James, 144
Groundswell, 267, 271–272
Gubbrud, Archie, 41, 239
Gulf of Tonkin Resolution, 26
Gulf War, 214
Gunderson, Steve, 271
Gutiérrez, Gustavo, 186, 187–188
Guy, Jack, 132–133, 134, 137

Haala, Cory, 3, 243, 294
Haase, Larry J., 40
Hall, Tammany, 98
Halverson, Mark, 271
Handy-Marchello, Barbara, 49
Hansen, Merle, 269
Harkin, Tom, 6, 264, 265, 266–271, 273, 275
Harpers (magazine), 83
Harriman, Averell, 25
Harris, Fred R., 113
Harris, James T. Jr., 167
Hart, Gary, 254
Hart, John B., 39
Hart, Philip, 66–68
Hartke, Vance, 130
Harvey, Kay, 217
Hatcher, Richard, 167, 168, 169–170, 171–172, 173–174, 175
Haugland, Brynhild, 49
Hawaii, 206
Hawkins, Augustus, 70
Hayes, Charles, 265
Hayes, Isaac, 176
Hazirjian, Lisa Gayle, 95
Hearnes, Warren, 27
Heartland Special, 256–257
Heinz, John, 273
Heitkamp, Doreen, 57

Heitkamp, Heidi, 6, 43, 48–49, 56–57, 264, 273, 331, 333
Heitkamp, Ray, 57
Hennings, Thomas Jr., 19–22, 29–30
Herrington, Paul Lester, 65
Herseth, Ralph, 237
Herseth, Stephanie, 43
Hesburgh, Father Theodore, 185, 191–192, 193
Heschel, Abraham, 216
Hightower, Jim, 277
Hill 57 (Montana), 117
Hillenbrand, John, II, 136
Hirsch, Robert W., 247n51
Hively v. Ivy Tech Community College of Indiana, 309
Hodne, Carol, 264
Hoffa, Jimmy, 22, 238
Holland-Neal, Rev. Dena, 174, 178
Hollings, Ernest, 273
homophile movement, 83
homosexuality, 201, 204. *See also* gay movement; queer/LGBTQ people
Hoover, J. Edgar, 238
Horton, Myles, 220, 222
House Bill (HB) 791 (South Dakota), 41
House Bill (HB) 892 (South Dakota), 41
House Bill 1478 (Indiana), 138
House Concurrent Resolution (HCR) 108, 36, 37–38, 116, 117
House investigative committee, 19
How the Rural Poor Got Power (Wellstone), 221
Hruska, Roman, 236
Hudnut, William, 137
Hudnut, William, III, 306–307
Hughes, Harold E., 289
Human Relations Commission, 172
Human Rights Commission, 118
Human Rights Party, 78
Humphrey, Hubert
    1948 election and, 252
    1968 election and, 319
    American Indians and, 114, 117–120, 122–123
    campaign of, 251–252
    Democratic-Farmer-Labor Party (DFL) and, 212–213

Humphrey, Hubert (*cont.*)
    on environmentalism, 69–70
    on human rights, 8
    influence of, 220, 251
    leadership of, 5, 114
    legacy of, 219
    on Mike Mansfield, 116
    national constituency of, 118–119
    photo of, 27
    on poverty, 119
Humphrey-Hawkins Act, 70
Huntington reservoir, 129

Idaho, 83
ideology, 324
Illinois
    1960 election in, 319
    1984 election in, 265
    2016 election in, 332
    Catholics in, 317–318
    death penalty in, 290–291, 292
    gay employment bill in, 206–207
    as Midwestern state, 11n9
    Ronald Reagan and, 254
    same-sex behavior legislation in, 83
    unemployment in, 255
    See also specific locations
Illinois Federation for Right to Life, 152
Illinois Nurses Association (INA), 149
independent voters, 4
Indiana
    1974 election in, 136–137
    1986 election in, 303, 304–305
    1988 election in, 306
    Catholics in, 317, 318
    death penalty in, 290, 291, 292, 293
    Democratic Party in, 302
    gay rights fight in, 298–309
    House Bill 1478 in, 138
    as Midwestern state, 11n9
    religion in, 299
    Republican Party in, 302
    Senate District 33 in, 302
    unemployment in, 255
    See also specific locations
Indiana Business Magazine (magazine), 97
Indiana Civil Liberties Union (ICLU), 303, 307

Indiana Civil Rights Act, 298, 303
Indiana Conservation Council (ICC), 130
Indian Affairs Commission, 38
Indiana General Assembly, 303
Indiana Open Door Law, 100
Indianapolis, Indiana, 301–302, 306–307
Indianapolis Business Journal (newspaper), 309
Indianapolis Catholic Interracial Counsel, 301
Indianapolis Police Department (IPD), 306
Indianapolis Recorder (newspaper), 170
Indianapolis Star (newspaper), 300, 301, 302, 309
Indian Child Welfare Act, 121
Indian New Deal, 36, 115, 124n8
Indian Self-Determination Act, 121, 122–123
Indian Self-Determination and Education Assistance Act, 117
Industrial Areas Foundation, 98, 147
Industrial Commission, 145
Indy Rainbow Chamber of Commerce, 309
Inland Steel, 95, 102
Institute for Agriculture and Trade Policy (IATP), 272
integrationists, 173
internationalism, 19
The Intruders (Long), 22
Iowa
    1984 election in, 258, 265
    1988 election in, 270
    2016 election in, 332
    Catholics in, 317
    death penalty in, 289, 290
    Farm Crisis in, 264
    as Midwestern state, 11n9
    National Crisis Action Rally in, 266
    recession in, 257
    Ronald Reagan and, 254
Iowa Beef Packers, 272
Iowa Farm Unity Coalition, 266
Iowa Farm Unity Coalition (IFUC), 267
Iowa PrairieFire, 265
Izaak Walton League, 131

Jackson, Jesse, 96, 165, 175–176, 177, 263, 268–270

Index

James, Rich, 100
Jane (abortion counseling service), 148
Jepsen, Roger, 266
Johnson, Lady Bird, 27
Johnson, Lyndon B./Johnson
    administration, 24, 26, 27, 36, 42, 119,
    240, 319
Johnson, Ron, 2
Johnson, Tim, 43, 241, 242–243, 265, 270
Joint Subcommittee on Indian Affairs, 39
joint union-ADA Citizens Advisory
    Committee, 81–82
Jontz, Elaine, 130–139
Jontz, Jim, 130–139
Jorgenson, Christine, 85
Joseph, Peniel, 172
Jourdain, Roger, 118, 124n9
Justice, Inc., 302

Kahn, Si, 220
Kansas, 3, 11n9, 258, 288, 290, 291, 292
Kanten, Anne, 264
Kaptur, Marcy, 273
Kasten, Bob, 266, 273
Katznelson, Ira, 222
Kavanaugh, Brett, 48, 325
Kazin, Michael, 4, 49, 50, 277
Keillor, Garrison, 214, 216
Kem, James P., 18, 19, 24
Kemper, Donald J., 22
Kennedy, Edward, 298, 335
Kennedy, John F./Kennedy
    administration, 26, 36, 39, 42, 63, 238,
    318–319
Kennedy, Robert, 218
Kerrey, Bob, 270
Kerry, John, 43, 319, 322, 324, 327
Kiesling, Mark, 105–106
King, Coretta Scott, 175, 177
King, Martin Luther Jr., 172–173, 218
The King of Steeltown (documentary), 100
Kinsey, Alfred C., 79–80
kitchen table issues, 214
Klobuchar, Amy, 224, 331
Kneip, Richard, 241
Knock, Thomas, 233, 237
Knopp, Larry, 324
Kohnke, Helmut, 130

Kootenai Tribe, 116
Kozachenko, Kathy, 78–79
Krebs, Al, 272
Ku Klux Klan, 217–218

labor movement, 77–78. *See also*
    employment; unions
Lac Du Flambeau (LDF), 2
La Farge, Oliver, 40
La Follette, Robert, 288
Landgrebe, Earl, 136
Lane, James B., 166
Langer, Lydia Cady, 50–53, 59–60n32
Langer, William "Wild Bill," 50–51, 52,
    54, 56
Lanier, Powless "Peter," 51
Lansing, Michael, 50, 245n14
La Raza, 185–186, 187
La Raza Art Festival, 189
Larsen, Carole Jean, 55
Latina/o residents, 96–97, 98, 185, 186–187
Lauck, Jon, 237, 242
Laxalt, Paul, 251
League of Rural Voters (LRV), 263, 265, 269
leaguer-ism, 50
Leahy, Patrick, 216–217, 271, 274, 275
Leary, D. J., 212
Lend-Lease Act, 60n32
Leopold, Aldo, 65
Lesbian, Gay, Bisexual, Transgender
    Fairness Indiana, 307
Le Sueur, Meridel, 212, 220
Levine, Myron, 99
Levitas, Dan, 264
Lewis, Byron, 175–176
Lewis, Fulton Jr., 239
liberal ideology, defined, 113
liberalism, 10–11n9, 96, 185–186, 232, 253,
    263–264, 294
liberation, aspects of, 187–188
liberation theology, 186, 187, 188
Life (magazine), 22
lobotomization, 85, 92n51, 93n57
Lofy, Bill, 214
Long, Edward V., 22–23, 27, 29–30
Long, Paul, 285
Long, William L., 138
The Lorax (Seuss), 139

Lovre, Harold, 234
loyalty program, 18–19, 20–21
Lugar, Richard, 274, 299
Lumbreras, Frank, 104
Lupa, Mary-Ann, 147
Lusk, Bob, 236
lynchings, 290

Madar, Olga, 69
Madison, Wisconsin, 156–157
Mahern, Elsye, 300, 301
Mahern, Louis, 298–309
Mahern, Louis Sr., 300–301
Mahern, Michael, 300
Malcolm X, 172, 177
Maldonado, Myrna, 101
Manchin, Joe, 333
Mandel, Josh, 334
Mansfield, Mike, 27, 114, 115–117, 122–123
manufacturing, transformation of, 7
Marshall Plan, 24
Martin, Louis, 177
Marttila, John, 268
Martz, Glenn, 236
Massachusetts Catholic Conference, 206
Mayor's Actions Program, 172
McCarran Act of 1950, 19
McCarthy, Eugene, 220, 319
McCarthy, Joseph, 22, 24, 236
McCaskill, Claire, 2, 30, 331, 333
McDaniel, Lawrence, 17
McGee, Kenneth "Sunny," 172
McGhee, Heather, 6–7
McGovern, George
　1952 election and, 234–235
　1956 election and, 237
　1960 election and, 237–238
　1962 election and, 238–239
　1968 election and, 240
　1972 election and, 240, 247n51, 247n55
　1974 election and, 240–241
　American Indians and, 115, 120–123
　attacks on, 2
　background of, 120–121
　campaign of, 28, 78, 242
　characteristics of, 233
　criticism of, 234, 236–237, 242
　Democratic Party and, 231, 233, 234
　election of, 234–235
　as face of American liberalism, 240
　faith of, 238
　as head of Food for Peace program, 238
　leadership of, 114
　legacy of, 241–242
　political aspirations of, 239–240
　popularity of, 237
　on Vietnam War, 240
　Wounded Knee takeover and, 121–122
McKee, Guian, 98
McNary, Gene, 29
Meals on Wheels program, 29
meatpacking, 276
Medicaid, 3, 26
Medicare, 26
Medicare Act, 27
Meiers, Ruth, 49, 50, 53–54
Menominee Indians (Wisconsin), 120
Menominee Restoration Act, 120
mental health
　electroshock therapy in, 93n57
　lobotomization for, 85, 92n51, 93n57
　United Auto Workers (UAW) and, 76, 83–84, 85–86, 92n45, 93n57
　William Alanson White Institute (WAWI) and, 85–86
Meranto, Philip J., 168, 170
Merrigan, Kathleen, 274
Metcalf, Lee, 116
Metzenbaum, Howard, 334
Meyers, Sam, 85
Michigan
　1960 election in, 319
　1984 election in, 258
　2016 election in, 331, 332
　capital punishment in, 285
　Catholics in, 317
　death penalty in, 285, 287–288
　environmentalism in, 67–68, 72
　as Midwestern state, 11n9
　National Recreation Areas in, 67–68
　Ronald Reagan and, 254
　unemployment in, 255
　See also specific locations
Michigan Committee Against Capital Punishment, 288

Index

Midwest
  culture of, 7
  demographics of, 4
  economy in, 276
  expansion of, 9
  as "heartland" of America, 7–8
  as progressive center, 294
  recession in, 254–255
  regional depression in, 251
  regional liberalism in, 294
  relationships in, 31
  states in, 11n9
  study of, 3–4
  unemployment in, 251
  uniqueness of, 4
  values of, 258–259
  See also specific locations
Midwest Academy, 148
Midwest Council of La Raza (MWCLR), 185–186, 192, 193–194
Midwestern Populism, 218–223
military, desegregation of, 18
Miller, Chelsea, 156–157
Milwaukee, Wisconsin, 143–144, 145–146, 201–202
Minneapolis, Minnesota, 8, 118, 221–222
Minnesota
  1960 election in, 319
  1984 election in, 258
  1988 election in, 270
  1990 election in, 265
  2016 election in, 331, 332, 344
  American Indians in, 117–118
  Catholics in, 317
  characteristics of, 219
  Citizens Organized Acting Together (COACT) in, 267
  death penalty in, 287, 288–289
  Democratic-Farmer-Labor Party, 118
  Democratic-Farmer-Labor Party (DFL) in, 211
  farm activism in, 267
  as Midwestern state, 11n9
  political climate of, 211–212, 219
  poverty tour in, 214
  protesting in, 221–222
  Ronald Reagan and, 254
  social capital in, 251
  strike in, 222
  unemployment in, 255
  See also specific locations
Minocqua, Wisconsin, 1
Minocqua Brewing Company (MBC), 1, 2–3
Minot Daily News (newspaper), 38
Mississinewa reservoir, 129
Missouri
  Black Americans in, 18, 20
  Catholics in, 317
  death penalty in, 288, 290, 291, 292, 293
  Democratic Party in, 30
  election results of, 17, 18, 29, 31
  local politics in, 30
  as Midwestern state, 11n9
  New Deal coalition and, 17
  Republican Party in, 18, 30
  Ronald Reagan and, 254
  senatorial political revolving in, 30
  unemployment in, 255
moderates, disappearance of, 231
Mondale, Ted, 270
Mondale, Walter
  1948 election and, 251
  1984 election and, 254, 258
  attacks on, 2
  background of, 251–252
  bus tour of, 257–258
  campaign of, 249, 257–258
  criticism of, 257
  at debate, 254, 255–256
  election of, 155
  family politics of, 252
  potential of, 251
Monroe reservoir, 129
Montana, 116
Moore, Leonard, 173
Moral Majority, 205
Moreton, Bethany, 199
Morrill, Richard, 324
Movimiento Estudiantil Chicana/o de Aztlán (MEchA), 189–190
Muigwithania, 165, 168–169, 170–171, 178
Muncie Star Press (newspaper), 300
Mundt, Karl, 233, 236, 237–238, 240
Munis, B. Kal, 232
Murray, James E., 115, 116

Index

Murrow, Edward R., 215
Murtagh, Father Jack, 202
Muskie, Edmund S., 113
Muslims, 8
Mutz, John, 307
Myer, Dillon S., 36
Myers, John T., 129

NAACP, 177
Nader, Ralph, 72, 214
Nash, George H., 299
National Black Political Assembly, 177
National Black Political Convention
    (NBPC), 165, 173–178
National Congress of American Indians
    (NCAI), 113–114, 116
National Council of Catholic Workers, 152
National Council on Indian Opportunity
    (NCIO), 119
National Crisis Action Rally, 266
National Family Farm Coalition (NFFC),
    272
National Farmers Organization (NFO), 267
National Farmers Union (NFU), 265, 267
Nationalists, 173
National Labor Relations Board, 192
National Organization for Women
    (NOW), 6, 141, 142, 144–145, 147–148,
    154–155
National Recreation Areas, 67–68
National Save the Family Farm Coalition
    (NSFFC), 269
National Wilderness Preservation
    System, 72
"Nationtime," 175–176
Native American Rights Fund, 120
Nature Conservancy, 130
Nebraska, 11n9, 258, 264, 290, 291, 292, 293
negative partisanship, 231
Nelson, Dr. William E. Jr., 168, 170
Nelson, Gaylord, 63, 68–69
Netsch, Dawn Clark, 152
Nevada, 4
New Deal, 13n31, 17, 25, 65–66, 97,
    142–143
New Democrats, 96
New Federalism, 71
New Mexico, 4

New Right, 154, 241
New York Times (newspaper), 83
Nichols, John, 217
Nielsen, Kim, 50
Nixon, Richard/Nixon administration
    1960 election and, 39, 42, 319
    American Indians and, 36, 115, 122,
        124n8
    Catholic vote and, 318
    containment policy of, 122
    election results of, 238
    environmentalism programs of, 71
    Indian Self-Determination and
        Education Assistance Act of, 117
    military assets direction by, 27
    resignation of, 136, 259n3
    on termination policy, 42
    termination policy of, 120, 121
Nonpartisan League (NPL), 49, 50, 52–53,
    234, 244–245n14
Norbeck, Peter, 233–234
North American Farm Alliance (NAFA),
    264, 265, 272
North American Free Trade Agreement
    (NAFTA), 266, 273, 334
North Dakota
    1952 election in, 37
    1956 election in, 39
    1960 election in, 39
    1986 election in, 265
    1992 election in, 265
    2012 election in, 43–44, 48
    2020 election in, 35
    death penalty in, 287, 288, 289, 292–293
    as Midwestern state, 11n9
    Turtle Mountain Chippewa in, 37–39
    women elected in, 48–49, 58n9
North Dakota Council of Indians, 38
Northeast Interstate Dairy Compact, 275
Novak, Robert, 247n55
nuclear missile development, 25, 26
nursing, 149–150

Obama, Barack, 43, 178, 322, 332, 335
Obama, Michelle, 224
O'Bannon, Frank, 308–309
O'Brien, Denise, 264
The Observer (newspaper), 185, 192

O'Connor, Cardinal John, 205–206
Office of Economic Opportunity (OEO), 42, 119
Of Men and Marshes (Herrington), 65
Oglala Sioux Tribe (South Dakota), 117
Ohio
   1984 election in, 258
   2004 election in, 325
   2012 election in, 334–335
   2016 election in, 331, 332
   2018 election in, 331, 337–342
   as battleground, 334–335
   Catholics in, 317, 318
   death penalty in, 290, 291, 292, 293
   as Midwestern state, 11n9
   redistricting in, 11n11
   Ronald Reagan and, 254
   as swing state, 334
   unemployment in, 255
Ojibwe (Lake Superior Chippewa), 2, 11n13, 117
Old Boys Network of Minocqua (OBNOM), 2
Older Americans Act, 29
Olson, Floyd B., 219, 220
Olson, James, 23, 25
Oneida County, Wisconsin, 1
O'Neill, Tip, 252
Operation Showcase, 172
Orange, Gilda, 101, 103–104
Organization for a Better Rice County (OBRC), 221
Orleck, Annelise, 95
Ostendorf, David, 272

Pabey, George, 101, 106
El Plan Espiritual de Aztlán, 187
Parmenter, Bill, 129–130, 131
Parra, Ricardo, 185, 187, 188–189, 193
partisanship, 324, 326–327
Pastrick, Robert, 94–95, 97, 99, 100, 101, 104, 105–106
Payne, Ethel L., 177
Peña, Father Robert, 191
Pendergast, James M., 20
Pendergast, Tom, 20
people, environmental and peace (PEP), 70

People for the American Way (PFAW), 155–156
Perot, Ross, 319
Perpich, Rudy, 267
Peterson, Bart, 308–309
Peterson, Collin, 273
Peterson, Helen L., 41
Phillips, Wendell, 224
Pictured Rocks National Lakeshore (Michigan), 67
Pine Ridge Indian Reservation (South Dakota), 41, 43, 117
Piven, Francis Fox, 220
plain people liberalism, 253, 258
Poinsett, Alex, 168, 171, 172
political action committee (PAC), 2–3
political machines, 98–99
pollution, 64, 67
polybrominated biphenyls (PBB), 64
populism, 224, 254, 263, 265, 266, 268, 276, 277, 337
Porras, Pedro, 105–106
Powerline (Wellstone), 222
PrairieFire, 264–265, 267, 272
prairie populism, 254, 265
Pratt, William, 276
Pride Brunch (Indianapolis), 301–302
Pritchard, Richard E., 198
programmatics, 251
Progressive Era, 288
Progressive Party, 81
progressive populism, 265
protesting, 98, 156–157, 184, 189, 221–222
Proxmine, William, 235
Prucha, Francis Paul, 42
Public Housing Administration, 42
Public Law (PL) 280, 36, 37–38, 40
public sphere, 324
public use land, 67–68
Public Welfare Board, 38
Puerto Ricans, 186
Purdue Environmental Action, 131

Quayle, Dan, 303, 304
queer-baiting, 87
queer/LGBTQ people
   Assembly Bill (AB) 70 (Wisconsin) in, 198–200, 202–203

queer/LGBTQ people (*cont.*)
  Black Americans as, 91n34
  Catholicism and, 325
  curing tactics for, 84–85
  discrimination to, 298
  as elected officials, 78–79
  hostility toward, 80
  in industrial work, 79–80
  legislation regarding, 83
  lobotomization of, 85, 92n51, 93n57
  mental health and, 84–86
  rights of, in Indiana, 298–309
  spaces of belonging for, 77–78
  study of, 3–4, 200
  United Auto Workers (UAW) and, 77, 79–80, 82, 87
  See also gay movement

Raasch, Chuck, 240
racial innocence, 8
racism, 217–218, 287, 290
Rackets Committee (Senate), 238
Radigan, Joseph, 171
Randolph, Lonnie, 100
Read, Sister Joel, 143, 145–146
Reagan, Jack, 252
Reagan, Nancy, 256
Reagan, Nelle, 252
Reagan, Ronald
  1980 election and, 250, 254, 299
  1984 election and, 249, 253, 258, 299
  as actor, 252
  anti-abortion stance of, 155
  campaign platform of, 255, 256
  characteristics of, 256–257
  conservatism of, 154
  criticism of, 249
  at debate, 254, 255–256
  election of, 155
  Harry Truman and, 249, 256, 257
  Heartland Special of, 256–257
  on liberalism, 253
  overview of, 252–259
  political philosophy of, 253
  popularity of, 250, 254, 255, 257, 258
  promises of, 266
  recession and, 254–255
  supply-side theory of economics of, 29

  television and, 254
  vetoes of, 266
  work of, 252–253
Recchie, Larke, 339
recession, 254–255
reconversion, 18
red-baiting, 80, 82, 87
Red Map project, 11n11
red power, 114
Red Power movement, 43, 122
Reeves, Albert Jr., 18
Reeves, Albert Sr., 18
regional liberalism, 294
Reid, Harry, 271
Religious Right, 199, 205, 207
Renacci, Jim, 331, 338–340
Republican Party
  from 1946–1982, 255
  American Indians and, 37–38
  challenges to, 72
  Democratic Party as compared to, 71
  environmentalism and, 71
  Environmental Protection Agency (EPA) and, 71
  opposition to, 41, 263
  popularity of, 249–250
  Red Map project of, 11n11
  termination policy and, 36
  See also specific elections; specific members; specific states
Restrepo, Camilo Torres, 193
Riddiough, Chris, 149, 151
Ristau, Kevin, 263
Ritchie, Mark, 263, 272
Roberts, Pat, 274
Robson, Jim, 147, 148
Rochester, New York, 299
Roe, Jeff, 30
Roe v. Wade, 154, 155
Rogers, Earline, 105
Rollins, Ed, 250
Roosevelt, Eleanor, 142–143
Roosevelt, Franklin, 4–5, 17, 20, 25, 97, 142–143
Rose, Tara, 8
Ross, Bernard, 99
Roundtree, Richard, 176
Rouse, Leon, 202, 203, 204

Roxana Crime Watch, 102
Rule 22, 22
Rural Women's Leadership Development Program, 264
Ryan, George, 153
Ryan, Tim, 343

Salamonie reservoir, 129
Saldin, Robert, 232
Samora, Julian, 189–190
Sanchez, Archbishop Robert, 190, 191
Sand County Almanac (Leopold), 65
Sanders, Bernie, 213, 335
Santiago, Luis, 104
Sarris, Kathy, 302
Sautter, Chris, 94
Save the Family Farm Act, 270
Scheir, Nancy, 152
Schlafly, Phyllis, 6, 151–152, 154
Schmitt, Eric, 31
Schulte, Steven C., 40
Schumer, Chuck, 339
Schuster, Sy, 219, 220–221, 223
Seale, Bobby, 176
second-wave feminism, 142, 156, 157n6
Seibert, Marna, 150
self-determination, 113–114, 115, 119, 120, 122–123
Senate Foreign Relations Committee, 117
Senate Rackets Committee, 238
Senate Select Committee on National Water Resources, 66–67
Sexual Behavior in the Human Male (Kinsey), 79–80
sexual politics, 78
sexual preference, 298–309. *See also* gay movement; queer/LGBTQ people
sexual psychopathy, 91n34
Shabaz, John, 204
Shabazz, Betty, 175, 177
Shelton, Robert, 217–218
Shivers, Ayanna, 30–31
Shock Troops, 171
Shrade, Paul, 82
Shropshire, Jackie, 168
Sidewalk Six, 104–106
Silent Spring (Carson), 64
Simon, Paul, 265

Sinner, George, 49
Sioux Indians (Minnesota), 117
1619 Project, 8
Sleeping Bear Dunes National Lakeshore (Michigan), 67
Smeal, Eleanor, 151
Smith, Al, 97, 318–319
Soapes, Thomas F., 18
social capital, 251
social justice, 188
social movements, 97
Soil Conservation Service, 65
Solidarity (magazine), 76
Soma, Tom, 192
Soul, Inc., 172
South Bend Tribune (newspaper), 190
South Dakota
    1952 election in, 37, 42, 234–235
    1956 election in, 42, 237
    1960 election in, 42, 237–238
    1962 election in, 238–239
    1964 election in, 42
    1968 election in, 240
    1970 election in, 241
    1972 election in, 240, 247n51, 247n55
    1974 election in, 240–241
    1978 election in, 241
    1980 election in, 242
    1986 election in, 242, 265
    1996 election in, 241, 265
    2002 election in, 43, 241
    2004 election in, 43, 242
    2008 election in, 242–243
    2020 election results in, 35
    approvals in, 14n45
    characteristics of, 232
    conservativism in, 244n3
    death penalty in, 288, 290, 291, 292–293
    Democratic Party in, 231, 232, 241, 243
    election results in, 232, 233
    House Bill (HB) 791 in, 41
    House Bill (HB) 892 in, 41
    Medicaid expansion in, 3
    as Midwestern state, 11n9
    Pine Ridge Reservation in, 41, 43, 117
    political climate of, 231
    Public Law (PL) 280 in, 40
    Republican Party in, 243

South Dakota (*cont.*)
   Republican Party opposition in, 41–42
   voter registration numbers in, 243
   Wounded Knee takeover in, 117, 120, 121–122
South Dakota Farmers Union, 275
South Dakota Works Progress Administration, 232
Soviet Union, 26
special interest liberalism, 263–264
Sputnik, 26
Stabenow, Debbie, 331
Standing Rock Reservation (South Dakota), 39, 40
Stassen, Harold, 212
State Commissions on the Status of Women, 145
State of Indiana v. Pastrick et al., 104–106
steel industry, 166
Steiker, Carol, 287
Steiker, Jordan, 287
Stevens, Marla, 307
Stevenson, Adlai, 25, 39, 65–66
Stiglich, Stephen R., 94–95, 103, 104
St. Joseph County, Indiana, 318
St. Louis, Missouri, 20, 317
St. Louis Globe-Democrat (newspaper), 19
Stockman, David, 266
Stonewall Uprising, 77, 78, 298
STOP ERA, 152
Strub, Whitney, 199
Subcommittee on Aging, 29
Subcommittee on Civil Rights, 21
Subcommittee on Constitutional Rights, 21
Subcommittee on US Security Agreements and Commissions Abroad, 26–27
suicide, 76
Sunbelt conservatives, 253, 259
supply-side theory of economics, 29
Surplus Property Administration, 23
Sutton, Billie, 14n45
Swearington, Rob, 1
Sweezy, John W., 308
Symington, Stuart, 23–28, 30

Taft, Bob, 333, 339
Taos Pueblo Indians, 121
Taylor, J. E. "Buck," 24
Teamsters, 267
Teamsters Local 364, 184, 193
television, politics and, 254
Tennessee Valley Authority, 65
termination policy, 36, 37–38, 40, 42, 116–117, 118, 121
Terry, Dixon, 269
Tester, Jon, 332–333
Thomas, Robert K., 120
Thompson, James R., 153
Thompson, Jill Long, 305
Thune, John, 43, 241, 242
Tilsen, Kenneth E., 212
The Times (newspaper), 99–100, 101, 104, 105–106
Tisdale, Robert, 222
Toohey, Rev. William, 190
Truman, Bess, 27
Truman, Harry/Truman administration
   1948 election and, 249–250
   Averell Harriman and, 25
   campaign of, 17–18, 236, 249–250, 251–252
   on Cold War, 19
   death of, 29
   Democratic Party of, 18–19
   election of, 17
   on Fair Deal, 25
   influence of, 249, 256, 257
   influence to, 81
   internationalism and, 19
   leadership of, 5
   liberalism of, 250
   loyalty program of, 18–19, 20–21
   McCarran Act of 1950 and, 19
   in Missouri, 20
   on New Deal, 25
   opposition to, 24
   photo of, 27
   plain people liberalism of, 253, 258
   as running mate, 20
   Stuart Symington and, 23, 26, 30
   termination policy and, 36
   on Thomas Hennings, 20–21, 30
Truman Daniel, Margaret, 29
Trump, Donald, 1, 35, 156–157, 323–324, 331–332
Turtle Mountain Chippewa, 37–39
Tweed, Boss, 98

Index

unemployment, 251, 255
unions, 78, 79, 80, 82
United Auto Workers (UAW)
   Americans for Democratic Action
      (ADA) and, 81
   campaign support by, 78–79, 87
   environmental action of, 69
   Farm Crisis and, 268
   Harkin bill and, 267
   mental health-care program of, 76,
      83–84, 85–86, 92n45, 93n57
   militant activism and, 86–87
   queer-baiting and, 87
   queer workers and, 77, 79–80, 82, 83, 87
   unity efforts of, 81–83
United Farm Workers (UFW), 190
United Nations Board of Environmental
   Control, 70
United Packinghouse Workers of America
   (UPWA), 147
universal health care, 214
University of Notre Dame
   bishop treatment at, 191–192
   boycott at, 190
   Centro de Estudios Chicanos
      Investigaciones (Center for Chicano
      Studies and Research) at, 190
   groundskeepers elimination at, 184, 185,
      192–193
   La Raza Art Festival at, 189
   liberation theology and, 188
   Midwest Council of La Raza (MWCLR)
      at, 185, 192, 193–194
   Movimiento Estudiantil Chicana/o de
      Aztlán (MEchA) at, 189–190
   The Observer (newspaper) at, 185
   protesting at, 184, 189
   scholarship discrimination at, 191
   "Values Seminar" at, 193
University of Wisconsin Extension School,
   145
"Up North" podcast (Bangstad), 2–3
US Army Corps of Engineers, 128, 129, 132
US Department of Agriculture (USDA), 264
US News and World Report (magazine), 8, 97
US Religion Census, 316
US Steel, 166
US Steel South Works, 95

Valdez, Joe, 105
Valentine, Trudy Busch, 31
Vance, J. D., 343
Van Dyk, Ted, 270
Van Sickle, Bruce, 55
Van Zuilen, Phil, 219
Van Zuilen, Terese, 219
Vasquez, Robert, 250, 251, 258
Vatican II, 186, 188, 199–201
Vietnam Veterans' Memorial, 223
Vietnam War, 26, 30, 240
Vig, Norman, 219, 220
Villa, Olga, 190, 193
Village Voice (magazine), 83
Vogel, Frank, 54, 265
Vogel, Sarah, 49, 54–56, 264, 273
Voting Rights Act of 1965, 22, 26, 29

Wabash River, 128
Wabash Valley Association, 129
Walker, Daniel, 149
Wallace, Henry A., 18, 81, 236
Walleye Wars, 2
Walz, Tim, 224
Wanger, Eugene, 288
war on crime, 286
War on Poverty, 42, 98, 114, 117
War Powers Act of 1973, 29
Warren County Republicans (Indiana), 135
Washington Post (newspaper), 241–242
Watergate scandal, 136
water resources, conservation of, 67
Watson, Tracy, 265
Watt, William J., 129, 136
Weakland, Rembert, 200, 201–202,
   203–204, 206
Webster, Steven, 231
Wellstone, Leon, 215–216
Wellstone, Minnie, 215
Wellstone, Paul
   1990 farm bill and, 272
   activism of, 221–222
   background of, 215–218
   in Democratic-Farmer-Labor Party
      (DFL), 211, 223
   election of, 211, 265
   on farm policy, 275
   firing of, 222

Wellstone, Paul (*cont.*)
  as grassroots politician, 212–215
  on helpful courage, 226n19
  How the Rural Poor Got Power, 221
  legacy of, 223–224
  Midwestern Populism and, 218–223
  overview of, 211–212
  photo of, 213, 221
  Powerline, 222
  rise of, 6
  as teacher, 219–223
  as upstart professor, 212–215
Wellstone, Sheila, 213, 214, 216–217, 223–224
Wellstone, Stephen, 216
Weschsler, Nancy, 78
Wesson, Cleo, 174
West Side Community Council, 175
Wheat, Alan, 265
White, Heather, 199
White, Ryan, 306
Whitlock, A. B., 166
Whitmer, Gretchen, 224
Wicker, Tom, 258
Wilkins, Roy, 177
William Alanson White Institute (WAWI), 85–86
Williamsport Review-Republican (newspaper), 129, 132
Willkie, Wendell, 232
Wilson, Brad, 265, 277
Wilson, James Q., 98
Winfrey-Harris, Tamar, 7
Wisconsin
  1984 election in, 258
  1988 election in, 270
  1992 election in, 265
  2016 election in, 331, 332, 344
  as battleground state, 1
  Catholicism in, 200, 317
  death penalty in, 287, 288
  Democratic Party in, 203
  Democratic voters in, 1
  election results in, 1, 202–203
  environmentalism in, 68–69
  LGBTQ employment protections bill in, 299
  Menominee Indians (Wisconsin) in, 120
  as Midwestern state, 11n9
  Old Boys Network of Minocqua (OBNOM) in, 2
  redistricting in, 11n11
  Republican Party in, 203
  Ronald Reagan and, 254
  unemployment in, 255
  Walleye Wars in, 2
  See also specific locations
Wisconsin Farmers Union, 275
Wisconsin Farm Unity Alliance (WFUA), 264, 265, 267, 270
Wisconsin Governor's Commission on the Status of Women, 144–145
women
  1984 election and, 258
  as activists, 6
  in agriculture, 49–50
  in Black Power movement, 173
  in Chicano movement, 196n63
  lobotomization of, 92n51
  paradox of, 50
  as political producers, 50
  workplace sex discrimination of, 145, 148
  See also specific women
Women's Strike for Equality, 141, 147–148
Work, Fred, 171
The Works (magazine), 303, 304
World War II, 76–77, 78
Wounded Knee (South Dakota), 117, 120, 121–122
Wright, Richard, 218
Wyatt, Reverend Addie, 148
Wyman, Patrick, 276

Young, Coleman, 176
Young, Milton, 39
Young, Wayne A., 177
Youngstown, Ohio, 251, 318

Zimmerman, Anne, 149
Zimmerman, Jo Ann, 264
Zion, Roger, 137

www.ingramcontent.com/pod-product-compliance
Lightning Source LLC
Chambersburg PA
CBHW021438091125
35182CB00031B/766